COMPARATIVE ECONOMIC SYSTEMS

MARTIN C. SCHNITZER

Professor of Management
College of Business
Virginia Polytechnic Institute
and State University

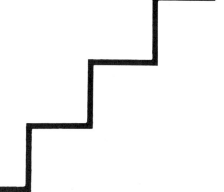

COLLEGE DIVISION South-Western Publishing Co.

CINCINNATI   DALLAS   LIVERMORE

Sponsoring Editor: James M. Keefe
Production Editors: Judith O'Neill and Sharon L. Smith
Production House: Publication Services
Cover and Interior Designer: Jim DeSollar
Marketing Manager: Scott Person

HE78EA
Copyright © 1991
by SOUTH-WESTERN PUBLISHING CO.
Cincinnati, Ohio

Schnitzer, Martin.
    Comparative economic systems/Martin C. Schnitzer. —5th ed.
        p.   cm.
    Includes bibliographical references and index.
    ISBN O-538-80891-8
    1. Comparative economics.   I. Title.
HB90.S35   1991
330.1—dc20   90-33923
                                                         CIP

    3 4 5 6   K i   5 4 3 2 1
Printed in the United States of America

ABOUT THE AUTHOR

Martin C. Schnitzer received his PhD in economics from the University of Florida. He teaches courses in government and business, and international business at Virginia Polytechnic Institute. Dr. Schnitzer is the author of ten books, including one on the Swedish economy and one concerning East and West Germany. He has lectured in Hungary and Poland and served on the U.S. East-West Trade Commission and the Virginia Export Council. He has served as an economic consultant to the U.S. Joint Economic Committee and has published a number of monographs on European economic policy.

PREFACE

Much change has happened in the communist world since the fourth edition of this book was published in 1987. In a relatively short period of time, the Eastern European countries changed from communist to more democratic systems. In East Germany, the Berlin Wall, the symbol of division between East and West, has come down; thousands of East Germans have migrated to West Germany; elections were held in Spring 1990; and reunification with West Germany is probable. A non-Communist was elected President in Poland, and free elections were held in Hungary. In Czechoslavakia hard-line Communist leaders resigned, and the playwright Vaclav Havel, a political prisoner during Communist rule, became acting president. In Romania the dictator Nicolae Ceausescu was overthrown and executed, and in Bulgaria hard-liner Tudor Zhivkov was forced to resign, and the Communist Part lost its constitutionally protected role. In another part of the world, in free elections held in Nicaragua, the Sandinistas were ousted.

Political and economic change has also come to the Soviet Union. Mikhail Gorbachev has introduced sweeping economic and political reforms in an attempt to bolster his country's stagnant economy. These reforms have opened up a virtual Pandora's box of problems. Ethnic unrest throughout the country has increased, and Soviet troops have been used to put down conflict between Christian Armenia and Moslem Azerbaijan. Free elections were held in Lithuania in February 1990, and the opposition party captured more than 70 percent in the Lithuanian Parliament. The opposition favors secession from the Soviet Union. Demands for autonomy or secession are also likely to occur in the other Baltic Republics of Latvia and Estonia. Elections to the People's House of Delegates also occurred in the Soviet Union in March 1990. Despite *perestroika,* the Soviet economy is in deep trouble. Economic growth is low and shortages of consumer goods have increased.

Change has also occurred in the United States and the Western world. Neither the United States nor the Soviet Union has anything like the predominant power it exerted during the period 1945–1985. The Soviet Union has lost political power beyond its borders, raising questions about the future Soviet role in the world. The United States is also losing its position as the predominant world economic power. It has become increasingly dependent on foreign investment for its economic health and has become the world's leading debtor nation, while Japan, now the leading money center of the world, has become the leading creditor nation. Two events in Europe will also have an impact on the American economy. The first will be the reunification of East Germany and West Germany and the second will be the formation of the European Community in 1992.

The purpose of this fifth edition is to discuss the events that have happened to change the world. It is more difficult to compare capitalism and communism today because of what has happened in Eastern Europe; nevertheless, the Soviet Union and China remain communist countries. China has regressed into a totalitarian state after the student demonstrations in 1989 led to a military crackdown. The new world order that will likely exist by the year 2000 is that the United States will be just one of three relatively equal and competing economic superpowers, along with Germany and Japan. The Soviet Union will not be as important as before in international politics because it has lost the ability to maintain aggressive armies outside its borders. It remains to be seen if Gorbachev's *perestroika* can reform the Soviet economy.

ACKNOWLEDGMENTS

I would like to thank the following people who read my manuscript and offered many valuable suggestions:

Mark Lutz
University of Maine

Pat Raines
University of Richmond

Dennis A. O'Connor
Loras College

Richard Spivak
Bryant College

I also wish to thank my wife Joan for her assistance in typing and proofreading the chapters, and my graduate assistant, Nancy Monda, for her work in the library running down endless sources of materials. Finally, I wish to thank the various government agencies, U.S. and foreign, for sending me current economic data, and Chris Pirie for her help in translation. The book was difficult to write because world events constantly dictated revision, but it is as current as can be expected, given the changes that have occurred.

Martin C. Schnitzer
Virginia Polytechnic Institute and State University

CONTENTS

PART 1
Introduction to Economic Systems   1

1   **Market Mechanisms and Capitalism**   3

Capitalism as an Economic System 4
 Private Property · The Profit Motive · The Price System
 · Freedom of Enterprise · Competition · Individualism
 · Consumer Sovereignty · The Protestant Work Ethic ·
 Limited Government

Income Distribution in a Capitalist Economy 11
 Measurements of Income Inequality · Sources of Income ·
 Income Distribution and Marginal Productivity

Saving and Capital Formation under Capitalism 14
The Historical Development of Capitalism 15
 Mercantilism · The Industrial Revolution · Finance
 Capitalism

Modifications of Pure Capitalism 18
 The Decline of the Protestant Work Ethic · The Decline of
 Individualism · Government and the Decline of Laissez-
 Faire · Restrictions on Competition

Summary 20

2   **Market Mechanisms, Economic Problems,**
 and Government Policies   23

Government Regulation of Market Structures 24
 Restraints on Competition · Antitrust Laws

Unemployment 28
 Classical Economic Theory and Unemployment · Keynesian
 Economic Theory

Equity and Income Distribution 34
The Interaction of Wealth and Income • *Tax Policies* •
Transfer Payments

Economic Insecurity 36
Causes of Insecurity • *Government Response* • *Government
Support of Industry and Agriculture*

Social Regulation 39
Inability to Express Negative Wants and Preferences •
Externalities • *Consumer Protection*

Summary 41

3   Nonmarket Mechanisms: Socialism and Communism   **43**

Historical Development of Socialism 44
The Renaissance Utopias • *French Utopian Socialists* •
Socialism and the Industrial Revolution • *Modern Socialism*

Institutions of Socialism 47
Private Property • *The Price System* • *Socialism and
Government*

Communism 49
Karl Marx and Das Kapital • *The Weaknesses of Marxism*
• *The Merits of Marx*

Institutions of Communism 61
Economic Planning • *State Ownership of Property*
• *Concentration of Power in the Communist Party* •
Cooperation

Summary 63

4   Goals of Economic Systems   **65**

Economic Goals 67
Maximum Employment and Economic Security 67
Price Stability 68
Social and Political Consequences of Inflation • *Inflation
and Balance of Payments Problems*

Economic Growth 70
Economic Growth in a Market Economy • *The Role of
Government in Economic Growth* • *Economic Growth in a
Centrally Planned Economy*

Income Distribution 72
Equity in Income Distribution • *Income Distribution Under
Socialism*

Freedom and the Individual 74
   Rationale for Personal Freedom • *Capitalism and
   Democracy* • *Individual Freedom in the Modern
   Democracies* • *Individual Freedom Under Socialism*
Social Goals 77
   The Environment • *Consumer Welfare* • *Education and
   Health*
Summary 81

PART 2
The Modified Economy of the United States   85

5   The Economic System of the United States   87

Large Corporations 88
   Concentration by Firm Size • *The Extent of Concentration
   by Industry* • *Issues Involving Industrial Concentration* •
   Industrial Concentration and Competition
Labor Unions 94
   Development of Labor Unions • *The Decline of Unions*
Government 97
   Public Finance • *Government Regulation and Control* •
   Government as an Employer • *Government Ownership of
   Business*
Summary 104

6   An Appraisal of the United States Economy   107

Reasons for the Decline in Industrial Competitiveness 108
   An Uncompetitive Society • *The United States Has Caught
   the "British Disease"* • *Poor Management* • *Convergence*
Yes, the United States is Losing its Competitive Edge 114
   Saving and Investment • *U.S. Living Standards* • *High
   Technology* • *Lower Manufacturing Productivity* • *Global
   Decline in World Production* • *The United States Is the
   World's Leading Debtor Nation* • *The Budget and Trade
   Deficits*
No, The United States is Not in a Process of Decline 123
   The U.S. Service Sector • *The Rate of Employment* • *U.S.
   Manufacturing Output* • *The Inherent Dynamism of the
   U.S. Economy*

Reaganomics 126
>   *The Results of Reaganomics* · *Trends in Income Distribution*
Summary 130

PART 3
Mixed Economic Systems   **133**

7   Mixed Economic Systems   **135**

Mixed Economic Systems 136
Economic Planning 137
>   *The Soviet Union and Imperative Planning* · *France and*
>   *Indicative Planning* · *Defects in Economic Planning*
Fiscal and Monetary Policies 139
>   *Fiscal Policy* · *Monetary Policy*
State Ownership of Industry 140
>   *State Ownership of Industry in France* · *State Ownership*
>   *of Industry in the United Kingdom*
Income Distribution and Social Welfare 142
>   *Government Distribution Policies* · *The Importance of*
>   *Government* · *Income Distribution and Equality*
Summary 147

8   France   **150**

The Economic System 151
>   *World War II and Nationalization of Industry* ·
>   *Nationalization under Mitterand* · *Public Finance* ·
>   *The Banking System* · *Labor-Management Relations* ·
>   *Government and Business* · *Economic Planning* · *An*
>   *Appraisal of the French Economy* · *Economic Policies*
>   *During the 1980s*
Summary 169

9   Japan   **171**

The Economic System 172
>   *The Meiji Period, 1868–1913* · *Post–World War II*
>   *Development of Japan* · *Public Finance* · *The Banking*
>   *System* · *Labor-Management Relations* · *Government and*
>   *Business Relations* · *The Economic Planning Agency*

An Appraisal of the Japanese Economy 189
    Historical Background • *Japanese Economic Indicators*
The Twenty-First Century: The Asian Century 192
    The Future as Seen by Japan • *Weaknesses of the Japanese*
    Economy
Summary 195

10   The United Kingdom   **197**

The Economic System 198
    Public Finance • *The Banking System* • *Supply-Side*
    Economics and the Thatcher Government • *Labor-*
    Management Relations • *Government and Business*
An Appraisal of the British Economy 209
    Growth Rates • *Inflation and Unemployment* • *Income*
    Redistribution
Summary 215

PART 4
Centrally Planned Economic Systems   217

11   The Communist World in Disarray   **219**

East Germany: The Former Role Model For Communism 221
    The Development of East Germany • *Economic Planning*
    • *Organization of Industry* • *Organization of Agriculture* •
    Other Economic Arrangements
A Comparison of West Germany and East Germany 226
    Income Distribution • *Living Standards* • *Agriculture* •
    Labor Productivity • *The Environment*
German Reunification 236
Economic and Political Reunification 237
East German Elections 238
Other Problems of Reunification 240
Summary 240

12   An Introduction to the Soviet Union   **242**

The Political System 243
    The Communist Party • *Nomenklatura System* • *Organization*
    of the Government • *Gorbachev's Political Reforms*

The Economic System 248
   Economic Planning ▪ *Public Finance* ▪ *Money and Banking*
   ▪ *The Soviet Enterprise*
Agriculture 268
   State Farms ▪ *Collective Farms* ▪ *Private Plots*
Summary 269

13   Reforms and Performance in the Soviet Union   **272**

Economic and Political Reform 273
   Perestroika ▪ *Achievements of Perestroika* ▪ *The Future of*
   Perestroika ▪ *Glasnost* ▪ *Demokratizatsiya*
The Future of Soviet-Style Communism 289
   Will the Communist System Be a Thing of the Past? ▪ *A*
   Post-Communist World
Summary 291

14   Eastern Europe: Hungary and Poland   **294**

Hungary and Poland: Two Countries in Change 295
The Economies of Hungary and Poland 296
   Real Per Capita Growth ▪ *Industrial Production* ▪ *Inflation*
Poland 298
   Religion, History, and Economics ▪ *Religion* ▪ *Problems of*
   the Polish Economy ▪ *Solidarity and Lech Walesa* ▪ *Return*
   of Solidarity
Hungary 307
   Problems of the Hungarian Economy ▪ *Economic Reforms*
   in Hungary ▪ *Political Reforms*
Can Democracy and Free Markets be Achieved? 314
   Bureaucracy ▪ *Changing the Economic System* ▪ *Polish*
   Reforms
Summary 318

15   Yugoslavia   **321**

The Economic System 323
   Economic Planning ▪ *Public Finance* ▪ *The Banking System*
   ▪ *Agriculture* ▪ *The Yugoslav Enterprise*
An Appraisal of the Yugoslav Economy 333
   Economic Problems ▪ *Economic Reforms* ▪ *Comparisons*
   with Socialist Economies
Summary 340

PART 5
Economic Systems of the Less Developed Countries 343

16 Problems of the Less Developed Countries 345

Economic Development 346
Characteristics of the Less Developed Countries 347
*Per Capita Income · Overpopulation · Agriculture · The
Status of Women · Income Distribution · Technological
Dualism*
Theories of Economic Development 355
*Marxist Theory of Economic Development · Rostow's
Theory of Economic Development*
Obstacles to Economic Development 357
*Population · Infrastructure · Low Savings Rate · Limited
Range of Exports · Terms of Trade · Foreign Debt ·
Sociocultural Factors · Physiography*
Solutions For Economic Development 367
Foreign Aid · Internal Policies · Success in East Asia
Summary 371

17 The People's Republic of China 373

Development of The Economic System 374
*The Period of Consolidation, 1949–1952 · The First
Five-Year Plan, 1953–1957 · The Great Leap Forward,
1958–1960 · Proletarian Cultural Revolution, 1966–1969
· The Post–Cultural Revolution Period, 1970–1976 · 1980
to the Present*
The Economic System 380
*Economic Planning · Public Finance · Banking ·
Organization of Industry · Economic Reforms in Industry ·
Organization of Agriculture*
China Enters The 1990s 391
*Economic Growth · Agricultural Production · Industrial
Production · Inflation*
Summary 395

18 Mexico 397

The Economy of Latin America 397
*Per Capita Income · Inflation · Foreign Debt · Foreign
Trade · Population · Unemployment and Poverty*

Mexico: The Economic System 403
*Agriculture • Government Ownership of Enterprise • Public
Finance • Economic Development • Economic Planning*
An Appraisal of the Mexican Economy 409
*The 1988 Presidential Election • Population • Income
Inequality • Foreign Debt • Corruption • Mexico in the
1990s*
Summary 418

19   Nigeria   **420**

Characteristics of Africa 420
*Colonialism • Poverty • Population Growth • Political and
Social Instability • Foreign Trade*
The Development of Nigeria 426
*The Nigerian Economy • Oil • The Role of the Government •
Private Enterprise • Performance of the Nigerian Economy
• Foreign Debt • Population Growth • Corruption •
Political Instability • Agriculture • Poverty • The Structural
Adjustment Program*
Summary 438

PART 6
Conclusion and Evaluation   **441**

20   Economic Systems: Where to Go from Here?   **443**

"Seventy-Two Years on the Road to Nowhere" 443
Problems Facing Communism 445
*Economic Change • Decline of Communism as a
Development Model*
Economic Reform in Eastern Europe 448
Problems of Reform • The Sinatra Doctrine
Comparisons with the West 452
One World or Several? 454
A Multipolar World Economy 454
The European Community 455
*Organization of the European Community 1992 • European
Community–U.S. Relations*
East Asia 457
Japan • "The Little Dragons"

The United States and the New Realities 460
  The New Realities ▪ *The United States and the Year 2000*
The Third World Countries: Orphans at the Feast 462
  Foreign Debt ▪ *Inflation* ▪ *Economic Growth*
The Future World Economy 467
  Why Nations Triumph ▪ *Germany, Japan, and the United
  States Compared*
Summary 470

Appendix   **473**

Index   **475**

INTRODUCTION TO ECONOMIC SYSTEMS

1
MARKET MECHANISMS AND CAPITALISM

2
MARKET MECHANISMS, ECONOMIC PROBLEMS, AND GOVERNMENT POLICIES

3
NONMARKET MECHANISMS: SOCIALISM AND COMMUNISM

4
GOALS OF ECONOMIC SYSTEMS

PART ONE

CHAPTER ONE

MARKET MECHANISMS AND CAPITALISM

A fundamental dilemma of any economic system is a scarcity of resources relative to wants. Decisions are necessary to determine how a given volume of resources is to be allocated to production and how the income derived from production is to be distributed to the various factors—capital, labor, and land—that are responsible for it. Human wants, if not unlimited, are at least indefinitely expansible. But the commodities and services that can satisfy these wants are not, and neither are the factors of production that can produce the desired goods and services. These productive factors usually have alternative uses; that is, they can be used in the production of a number of different goods and services. The system must allocate limited productive resources, which have alternative uses, to the satisfaction of great and growing human wants.

Large amounts of capital will not be available for use in production unless there is a process of saving and capital formation. This process is fundamentally the same in all types of economic systems. It cannot operate unless the available productive resources are more than adequate to provide a bare living for the people of the system. When it *is* able to operate, the process involves spending part of the money income of an economy, directly or indirectly, for capital goods rather than for consumer goods. In a nonmonetary sense, saving and capital formation require the allocation of a part of the productive resources of a country to producing capital goods rather than consumer goods. The cost of obtaining capital goods is the same in all economic systems: It is going without, at present, the qualities of consumer goods and services that could have been produced by the factors of production.

In general, societies have endless ways of organizing and performing their production and distributing functions. In economic and political terms, the possible range is from laissez-faire capitalism through totalitarian communism. The economy of the United States today by no means represents a pure laissez-faire capitalist system. It is, rather, a mixed economic system. There are public enterprises, considerable government regulation and control, and various other elements that hinder the unrestrained functioning of market forces. However, to understand how a capitalist system works, it is necessary to know something about its institutional arrangements. For practical purposes, an *institutional arrangement* is a practice, convention, or custom that is a material and persistent element in the life or culture of an organized group. *Economic institutions* are ways of reacting to certain economic and social phenomena in certain economic situations. Some economic institutions rest on custom, while others are formally recognized through legislative enactment.

CAPITALISM AS AN ECONOMIC SYSTEM

A number of institutional arrangements characterize a capitalist economic system. These arrangements reflect a set of basic beliefs that define how a society should be organized, how goods and services should be produced, and how income should be distributed. In the United States these beliefs are incorporated into the institutional arrangements that typify a capitalist system – private property, the profit motive, the price system, freedom of enterprise, competition, individualism, consumer sovereignty, the work ethic, and limited government. Each of these institutions will be discussed in some detail.

Private Property

Under capitalism there is private ownership of the factors of production—land, labor, and capital. There are also certain rights concerning property. An individual has the right to acquire property, to consume or control it, to buy or sell it, to give it away as a gift, and to bequeath it at death. Private property ownership is supposed to encourage thrift and wealth accumulation and to serve as a stimulus to individual initiative and industry, both of which are considered essential to economic progress.

However, private ownership of property is subject to certain limitations. In practice, even under capitalism, property rights are often restricted by the actions of social groups or government units. Also, a good deal of the private wealth of capitalist systems, such as that of the United States, is owned not by individuals, but rather by business firms. There is actually a good deal of publicly owned property within a capitalistic system. Where public property exists, the exclusive control of wealth is exercised by a group of individuals through some political process.

The Profit Motive

The kinds of goods produced in an economy that relies on market arrangements are determined in the first instance by managers of business firms or by individual entrepreneurs. They are directly responsible for converting resources into products and determining what these products will be, guided by the actions of consumers in the marketplace. The profit motive is the lodestar that draws managers to produce goods that can be sold at prices that are higher than the costs of production. In private enterprise, profit is necessary for survival; it is the payment to owners of capital. Anybody who produces things that do not, directly or indirectly, yield a profit will sooner or later go bankrupt, lose the ownership of the means of production, and so cease to be an independent producer. There can be no other way. Capitalism, in other words, uses profitability as the test of whether any given item should or should not be produced, and if it should, how much of it should be produced.

The Price System

The Price Mechanism. Individuals and businesses under capitalism are supposed to make most types of economic decisions on the basis of prices, price relationships, and price changes. The function of prices is to provide a coordinating mechanism for millions of decentralized private production and distribution units. The prices that prevail in the marketplace determine the kinds and quantities of goods and services that will be produced and how they will be distributed. Price changes are supposed to adjust the quantities of these goods and services available for the market.

It is through the mechanism of prices that scarce resources are allocated to various uses. The interaction between the price system and the pursuit of profits is supposed to keep economic mistakes down to a reasonable level. Profit, which depends on the selling price of goods and the cost of making them, indicates to businesses what people are buying. An industry with a product that commands high prices relative to costs draws businesses, whereas low prices relative to costs check production by causing businesses to drop out.

Price Determination. In a free market economy, demand and supply determine the price at which a purchase or sale of a good is made. Demand originates with the consumer. It involves a desire for a good or service expressed through a willingness to pay money for it in the marketplace. Market demand is the sum of all individual consumers' demands for a particular good or service. There is an inverse relationship between market demand and the price of a good or a service. The higher the price, the lower the quantity of the good or service demanded; the lower the price, the greater the quantity of the good or service in demand.

Supply originates with the producer. It is the quantity of a good or service that a producer is willing to offer at any given price. Market supply is the sum of all the supplies that individual producers will offer in the marketplace at all possible prices over a given period. There is a direct relationship between market supply and price—the higher the price, the greater the supply of goods or services that will be provided.

The interaction of demand and supply determines the price for a good or service in the marketplace. The equilibrium price is the price that equates the quantity demanded with the quantity supplied in a market. It is the one price that will clear the market. At any price above the equilibrium price, supply is greater than demand, and the price must fall. At a price below the equilibrium price, demand is greater than supply, and the price must rise. In the example, the equilibrium price is $3 per pound.

Market Demand	*Price Per Pound*	*Market Supply*
180 pounds	$0.50	40 pounds
140	1.00	50
100	2.00	65
80	3.00	80
60	4.00	100
40	5.00	120

The forces of supply and demand acting through the price mechanism can send effective signals to the marketplace. For example, an increase in demand means that buyers will be willing to purchase more at any price than they were formerly. An increase in demand, with supply remaining constant, would result in an increase in price. The increased price would cause producers to supply more, so quantity would increase also. A decrease in demand would have the opposite effect.

Conversely, an increase in supply with demand remaining constant would result in a decrease in price. The lower price would lead to an increase in the quantity purchased. A decrease in supply would have the opposite effect. Consumers have to pay more for a smaller amount of a good or service.

Figure 1-1 illustrates the determination of prices and output in a free market. Both are determined at the intersection of the demand and supply curves. The equilibrium price is p_0, and q_0 is the quantity supplied. At any price above p_0, the quantity supplied is greater than the quantity demanded, and the price will fall. At any price below p_0, demand is greater than the quantity supplied, and prices will rise.

An increase in demand to D_1 with supply remaining constant will result in an increase in both price and quantity. The new equilibrium price will be p_1 and the quantity will increase to q_1. The increase in demand to D_1 will eventually result in an increase in supply (the supply curve shifts to the right) as producers react to the potential for higher profits. New producers will enter the market, and resources will be shifted from other areas into the market in anticipation of a greater rate of return.[1]

---

[1] For example, as student enrollment in a college town increases, the demand for housing will increase. Townspeople will be willing to rent more rooms, and existing housing will be fully used. Rents will increase and someone will decide to build apartments for students. The supply of housing will increase as available resources are shifted into housing construction.

FIGURE 1-1
Determination
of equilib-
rium price and
output

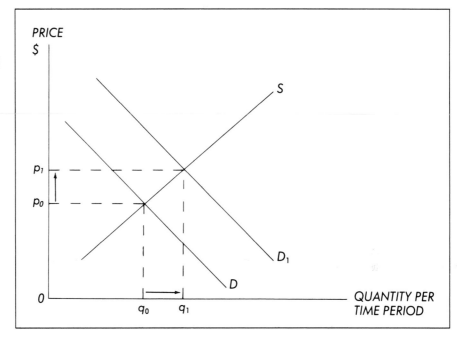

Freedom of Enterprise

Freedom of enterprise is another basic institution of capitalism. It refers to the general right of each individual to engage in any appealing line of economic activity. However, there are limits placed on the choice of an activity. People cannot engage in activities that are deemed socially immoral (e.g., child pornography) or that may harm others (e.g., driving while intoxicated). As far as the government is concerned, the individual is free to move to any part of the country, work in any chosen occupation, and find and operate a business unit in virtually any field of lawful economic activity. By comparing market indicators—prices and costs—the individual is supposed to be able to select a field of activity that promises to be remunerative. The institution of private property furnishes the social sanctions necessary for the use and control of the factors of production vital to the chosen field of activity.

The theory used to justify the existence of freedom of enterprise is quite simply one of social welfare. That is, in choosing fields of economic activity in which they will be the most successful from the point of view of private gain, individuals will also be selecting fields in which they presumably will be most productive to society.

Competition

Given the institutions of private property and freedom of enterprise and given the scarcity of resources and the reliance on a market to allocate them, the attempts of individuals to further their economic self-interest result in competition. Competition is an indispensable part of a free enterprise system. In economic life, self-reliant individuals must struggle and compete for economic rewards—good jobs, high pay, promotions, desirable goods and services, and security in old age. There is the element of social Darwinism in competition: Life is a competitive struggle in which only the fittest, in terms of resources, get to the top.

Certainly, *competition* is one of the "good" words in the American vocabulary. From a very early age, school children are told that the distinguishing characteristic of the historically successful U.S. economic system is competition and that other economic systems have inefficiencies because, in some degree, they lack that magic ingredient in the particular and unique context in which it exists in our economy. It is, therefore, not surprising that by statute and common law our legal system has been actively concerned with the maintenance of a competitive system.

Certain benefits are thought to be derived from competition in the marketplace. A competitive market will:

1. Allow the price mechanism to reflect actual demand and cost and thus maximize efficiency in the use of capital and other resources
2. Encourage product innovation and long-run cost reduction
3. Result in the equitable diffusion of real income
4. Provide consumers with a wide variety of alternative sources of supply

Individualism

Individualism is linked to a set of related institutional values of capitalism. Again there is social Darwinism—life is a competitive struggle where the fit survive and those who are unfit do not. Individualism also involves competition which, when combined with social Darwinism, is supposed to provide some guarantee of progress through the inexorable process of evolution. Individualism is also related to equality of opportunity—the right of each person to succeed or fail on his or her own merit.

The institutions of private property ownership and individualism are related from two standpoints. First, private property ownership provides the spur for individual initiative, a reward to be gained through competition and hard work. Second, it provides some guarantee of individual rights against the encroachments of the state. It follows that a necessary requisite for individualism is a limited state role. The individual would have preference over the state, for the latter is a fictitious body composed of individual people who are considered to represent its members. The idea of individualism can therefore be a safeguard against the tyranny of the state.

To some extent, individualism is linked to the philosophical roots of capitalism.[2] Individualism itself is a distinctive achievement of human consciousness—a

---

[2] George Lodge, *The New American Ideology* (New York: Alfred A. Knopf, 1975), Chapter 1.

mark of high civilization. It is consistent with the principles of a libertarian society in that it carries with it the concept of freedom to live and work as one prefers. There is a sense of privacy in individualism, privacy as something sacred in its own right. Under classical liberalism, the individual is the center of society and the fulcrum that makes a free enterprise system work. Through energy applied to the fulfillment of personal needs, the individual pushes society forward. This does not result from charitable motives, but from the inexorable logic of the system—Adam Smith's "invisible hand." Stated simply, if all people are motivated to work at full capacity, whether they work as laborers, artisans, or executives, the net supply of goods and services available for consumption by all will be increased.

Consumer Sovereignty

In a capitalistic market economy, consumer sovereignty is an important institution because consumption is supposed to be the basic rationale of economic activity. As Adam Smith said, "Consumption is the sole end and purpose of all production; and the interest of the producer ought to be attended to only as far as it is necessary for promoting that of the consumer."[3] Consumer sovereignty assumes, of course, that there is a competitive market economy. Consumers are able to vote with their money by offering more of it for products that are in greater demand and less of it for products that are not in demand. Shifts in supply and demand will occur in response to the way in which consumers spend their money.

In competing for consumers' dollars, producers will produce more of those products that are in demand, for the prices will be higher, and less of those products that are not in demand, for the prices will be lower. Production is the means; consumption is the end. Producers that effectively satisfy the wants of consumers are encouraged by large monetary returns, which enable them in turn to purchase the goods and services required for their operations. On the other hand, producers who do not respond to the wants of consumers will not remain in business very long.

Freedom of choice is linked to consumer sovereignty. In fact, one defense of the market mechanism is the freedom of choice it provides consumers in a capitalistic economy. Consumers are free to accept or reject whatever is produced in the marketplace. The consumer is king because production ultimately is oriented toward meeting the wants of consumers. Freedom of choice is consistent with a laissez-faire economy. It is assumed that consumers are capable of making rational decisions, and in an economy dominated by a large number of buyers and sellers this assumption has some merit. Since the role of the government is minimal, the principle of *caveat emptor*, "let the buyer beware," governs consumer decisions to buy.

---

[3] Adam Smith, *An Inquiry Into the Nature and Causes of The Wealth of Nations* (Indianapolis: Liberty Classics, 1981), p. 660.

The Protestant Work Ethic

The Protestant work ethic is an ideological principle stemming from the Protestant Reformation of the sixteenth century and is associated with the religious reformer John Calvin. Calvin preached a doctrine of salvation that later proved to be consistent with the principles of a capitalist system.[4] According to Calvin and the Puritan ministers in early New England, hard work, diligence, and thrift are earthly signs that individuals are using fully the talents given to them by God for His overall purposes. Salvation is associated with achievement on this earth. Thus, work and economic gain have come to have a moral value. According to this view, it is good for the soul to work; rewards on this earth go to those who achieve the most. Moreover, salvation in the world to come is a reward that is in direct proportion to a deceased person's contribution during life.

The Calvinist doctrine of work and salvation became an integral part of the ideology of capitalism. The hard work of merchants and traders often produced profits, and their thrift led to saving and investment. Saving is the heart of the Protestant work ethic. With Adam Smith's idea of parsimony (or frugality) and Nassau Senior's idea of abstinence, it was established that saving multiplied future production and earned its own reward through interest.

Carried into American society in the nineteenth century, the Protestant work ethic came to mean rewards for those who were economically competent and punishment for those who were incompetent or unambitious. Work was put at the center of American life. Most of the industrial capitalists of the last century belonged to fundamentalist Protestant churches. John D. Rockefeller, who became the richest man of his day, attributed his success to the "glory of God." (Skeptics, however, attributed his success to much more mundane factors than God's beneficence.)[5]

Limited Government

For many years, the idea prevailed that the government in a capitalist system, however it might be organized, should follow a policy of *laissez-faire* with respect to economic activity. That is, activities of the government should be limited to the performance of a few general functions for the good of all citizens, and government should not attempt to control or interfere with the economic activities of private individuals. Laissez-faire assumes that individuals are rational and better

---

[4] Richard H. Tawney, *Religion and the Rise of Capitalism: A Historical Study* (New York: Harcourt, Brace, and World, 1926); and Max Weber, *The Protestant Ethic and the Spirit of Capitalism* (New York: Charles Scribner's Sons, 1930).

[5] See, for example, Matthew Josephson, *The Robber Barons* (New York: Harcourt, Brace, and World, 1934); and Ida M. Tarbell, *The History of the Standard Oil Company* (New York: McClure, Phillips, 1904).

judges of their own interests than any government could possibly be.[6] The interests of individuals are closely identified with those of society as a whole. It is only necessary for government to provide a setting or environment in which individuals can operate freely. This the government was supposed to do by performing only those functions that individuals could not do for themselves: provide for national defense, maintain law and order, carry on diplomatic relations with other countries, and construct roads, schools, and public works.

In a free enterprise market economy, competition is regarded as a virtue rather than a vice. The proper use of resources in a free enterprise system is ensured by the fact that if a firm does not use resources efficiently, it goes broke. If the market is to function effectively, it must operate freely. If there is intervention in any form, then there is no effective mechanism for weeding out inefficient enterprises. Nevertheless, government has always participated to some extent in business activity of capitalist countries. From the very beginning, the government of the United States was interested in the promotion of manufacturing, and it passed tariff laws very early to protect American business interests. Subsidies were used to promote the development of canals, roads, and railroads. Business was a direct beneficiary of those subsidies.

INCOME DISTRIBUTION IN A CAPITALIST ECONOMY

Once goods and services have been produced, the next important question in any economic system is the manner in which these goods and services are to be divided or apportioned among the individual consumers of the economy. The distribution of income does not refer to the processes by which physical goods are brought from producers to consumers, but rather to the distribution of the national income, first in money and then in goods and services, among the owners of the factors of production—land, labor, and capital.

Income distribution in a market economy is based on institutional arrangements, such as the pricing mechanism, associated with this type of system. The demand for a factor of production is derived from the demand for the good the factor helps to produce. High prices are set on scarce factors of production and low prices on plentiful factors. In terms of rewards to labor, workers whose skills are scarce relative to demand enjoy high income, while those whose skills are not

---

[6] The term *laissez-faire* originated in France, possibly as early as the first half of the eighteenth century and was later developed by Adam Smith as a rule of practical economic conduct. In particular, see Adam Smith, *The Wealth of Nations*, Book IV, especially p. 630. Laissez-faire was a reaction to the stringent government restrictions imposed on all phases of economic activity by mercantilism. Under mercantilism, the state controlled all businesses, and one could engage in a particular activity only be receiving a monopoly from the state.

scarce relative to demand do not. Professional football and baseball players receive high salaries because they possess a scarce talent and people are willing to pay to see them perform.

Measurements of Income Inequality

There are various measures of income inequality, including the Lorenz curve and the Pareto and Gini coefficients. Of these measures, the Lorenz curve is most commonly used. The Lorenz curve involves the use of an arithmetic scale that begins with an assumption of income equality as a starting point. Equality in the distribution of income is found when every income-receiving unit receives its proportional share of the total income. If incomes were absolutely uniformly distributed, the lowest 20 percent of income earners would receive exactly 20 percent of the total income; the lowest 80 percent would get exactly 80 percent of the total income; and the highest 20 percent would get only 20 percent of the income. In using a Lorenz curve, the curve of absolute equality would actually be a straight line extending upwards at a 45° angle from left to right, showing that 20 percent of income earners on the horizontal axis receive 20 percent of the income on the vertical axis, 40 percent of income earners receive 40 percent of the income, and so on. Any departure from this line is a departure from complete income equality.

Figure 1-2 illustrates the Lorenz curve. The straight line *OAF* is the line of perfect equality. The line *OBF*—the Lorenz curve—shows a departure from equality. The further *OBF* is from *OAF*, the greater the inequality. There are certain weaknesses in the use of the Lorenz curve as a measure of income distribution. First, one cannot tell by inspecting a curve how unequal the distribution of income is. The use of percentages conceals the number of income-receiving units in the different income brackets. It is also true that the slope of a curve at various points gives no more information than the curve itself. On the other hand, the Lorenz curve is an excellent device for visual presentation of inequalities in the distribution of income. It can also illustrate the effects of changes in taxes and government spending on the distribution of income.

It is possible to avoid relying solely on visual comparisons of Lorenz curves to draw inferences about various income distributions. In a Lorenz diagram the Gini concentration coefficient is the ratio of the area between the diagonal and the Lorenz curve to the total area below the diagonal. For a perfectly equal distribution, the Gini coefficient is zero. The size of the Gini coefficient is tied to the concavity of the Lorenz curve—the greater the concavity, the greater the coefficient. The coefficient, however, is basically an average and does not tell anything about the extent to which inequality of distribution may be marked in various segments of the income distribution.

Table 1-1 presents the distribution of household income by quintiles for several market economies. Perfect equality in the distribution of income would mean that each quintile would contain 20 percent of income. None of the countries comes close to perfect equality in income distribution.

FIGURE 1-2
The Lorenz
Curve

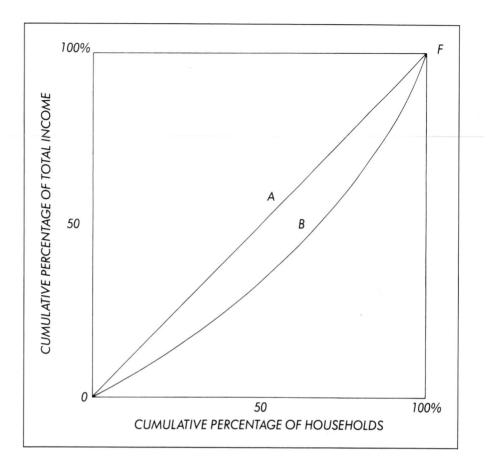

TABLE 1-1
Percentage Shares of Household Income by Quintiles for Selected Market
Economies

Country	Year	Lowest Quintile	Second Quintile	Third Quintile	Fourth Quintile	Highest Quintile
United Kingdom	1979	7.0%	11.5%	17.0%	24.8%	39.7%
Japan	1979	8.7	13.2	17.5	23.1	37.5
Canada	1981	5.3	11.8	18.0	24.9	40.0
West Germany	1979	7.9	12.5	17.0	23.1	39.5
France	1979	7.5	11.5	17.1	23.7	42.2
United States	1981	5.3	11.9	17.9	25.0	39.9
Sweden	1981	7.4	13.1	16.8	21.0	41.7
Italy	1979	6.2	11.3	15.9	22.7	43.9
Australia	1979	5.4	10.0	15.0	22.5	47.1

Source: The World Bank, World Development Report 1989, *p. 223.*

The major socialist countries are not included in Table 1-1. If they were, it would appear that their distribution of income is more equal. However, there is a gap between rhetoric and reality in the socialist countries; it separates claims of egalitarianism from the facts of special privileges for a small elite. These privileges include, among other things, automobiles, country homes, and special shops in which party officials, scientists, technicians, and other members of the elite can buy products not available to the average worker.

Sources of Income

Income in a market economy emanates from two sources: (1) earned income from wages and salaries or self-employment and (2) property income. Property may be regarded as a stock of claims on the value of wealth, including natural resources, capital, and consumer durable goods. The structure of property claims in a capitalist economy is complex. The claims on wealth owned by corporations, for example, may be represented by common or preferred stock, by corporate bonds, and by notes and mortgages. In national income accounting, labor income consists of wages, salaries, and entrepreneurial income, while property income takes the form of rent, interest, and profit. Thus there is a fundamental dichotomy in a capitalist system between labor and nonlabor income.

Income Distribution
and Marginal Productivity

The most basic theory underlying income distribution in a market economy involves the concept of marginal productivity. This concept can be applied to the distribution of both labor and property income. Under competitive conditions, individuals' incomes are determined by (1) the amount of resources they can command and (2) the market evaluation of these resources. Thus the income received by a worker tends to be determined by supply and demand, so that the income received equals the contribution the worker is able to make to the value of goods and services. The contribution to total product made by the worker is known as the *marginal physical product (MPP)* of labor. The dollar value of the contribution is the *marginal revenue product (MRP)* of labor. It is found by multiplying the *MPP* by the selling price of the product. The same reasoning is also applied to the distribution of property income. Resource owners tend to be remunerated according to the marginal revenue products of the resources they own.

SAVING AND CAPITAL FORMATION
UNDER CAPITALISM

In a capitalistic system, large amounts of savings are made by individuals on the basis of the relationship between interest rates and other prices. The necessary condition for such savings is that the interest rate be sufficient to overcome the time preference of the savers. Time preference is the desire to consume income in the present as opposed to some time in the future. A certain amount of savings, however, is independent of the interest rate. Some savings are made to provide for certain financial emergencies or to obtain the power an accumulation of income can bring. People with very large incomes may save almost automatically because of the difficulties involved in finding enough consumption uses for their incomes.[7] Other savings, such as those that result when corporations retain their earnings instead of paying dividends to stockholders, do not depend on the voluntary decisions of the individuals (stockholders) whose earnings are being saved. Finally, there may be forced savings in the form of taxes that government may use directly or indirectly for capital purposes.

The use of capital goods in production clearly involves the existence of savings. Savings are translated into investment in a capitalist system through the market mechanism of supply and demand, with interest rates performing an allocative function. To be able to afford to pay interest on a loan and ultimately to repay the principal, the borrower must be able to put the funds to good use. This tends to exclude less productive uses and thus rations savings to more productive uses.

Under capitalism, saving and investment are carried out in large part by different sets of people for different reasons. Investment is the purchase of capital goods and as such is undertaken largely by businesses. The act of saving is undertaken by both individuals and businesses. With large numbers of scattered savers and borrowers who want to obtain funds for investment purposes, there is clearly a need for some type of intermediary or go-between to bring the savers and borrowers together. This function is performed to a large extent by commercial and investment banks that are privately owned and operated for a profit. They underwrite securities issues for governmental units as well as businesses. The investment bankers bring together the business and government units that desire short- and long-term funds and the individuals and institutions that have these funds to invest.

THE HISTORICAL DEVELOPMENT OF CAPITALISM

The roots of capitalism go back to the Middle Ages, where the search for profit was the dominant motive in the lives of many, especially the merchants of the Italian city-states of Genoa and Venice.[8] In fact, the discovery of America in 1492 can be

---

[7] However, human psychology, as pictured by Hobbes, is an appetitive drive that drives people ferociously to achieve their desires. In a modern society, the engine of appetite is an increased standard of living, with emphasis on display. Thorsten Veblen made a similar point when he contended that people are driven by an impulse for status. See Thomas Hobbes, *Leviathan* (Oxford: Blackwell, 1946); also Thorsten Veblen, *The Theory of the Leisure Class* (Boston: Houghton Mifflin, 1973).

[8] The merchants of the Italian city-states invented almost all of the commercial devices that made a profit-seeking society possible. One such device was double-entry bookkeeping, which showed merchants that they were supposed to show a balance on the right side of the ledger.

attributed to the search for new markets. The Catholic church and other molders of public opinion came to accept the concept of profit in part because they, too, found good use for money. Earlier Catholic church thought had held that money was sterile in that it did not reproduce itself and that it was morally wrong to lend money to earn interest. However, there was nothing wrong in using money to buy something. But when it was seen that, if invested in productive enterprises, money could indeed make more money for the benefit of all, and that payment for the use of money (interest) would alone persuade the owners of money to invest it, the earlier concept was abandoned.

No pronounced break can be discerned between the growing capitalistic practices of the later Middle Ages and those of modern times. The influx of gold and silver from the New World had major political and economic consequences in Europe, contributing to the rise of the nation-states. The new wealthy classes, who engaged in trade everywhere, needed a stable national government to guarantee commerce, protect sea routes, and ensure the arrival of merchant ships. Monarchs, who needed the financial support of wealthy merchants to pay for their wars, were expected to support home commerce. One method of supporting home commerce was by ensuring that only ships of the home country could be used in transporting goods from, and sometimes even to, home ports.

Mercantilism

From the sixteenth to eighteenth centuries, it became accepted theory that a country was wealthy when it had a large reserve of gold and silver bullion. To obtain bullion, the country had to have what was known as a favorable balance of trade, gained by exporting more than was imported. Thus it was in the country's own interest to support home industry to enable it to export as many products as possible. This policy of supporting home industry came to be called *mercantilism*. It meant government intervention everywhere, but particularly in foreign trade. It also meant regulation of commercial relations between the mother country and her colonies; the colonies existed to furnish the mother country with raw materials and goods that could not be produced at home. The colonies were also expected to furnish the mother country with a favorable balance of trade, as represented by an inflow of precious metals into the country. It was against the policy of mercantilism that the thirteen colonies of North America arose and fought for their independence.

The Industrial Revolution

The Industrial Revolution changed national attitudes from the policy of mercantilism to a policy of laissez-faire. Scientific breakthroughs, inventions, and the factory system encouraged specialization and the concentration of production. These, in turn, encouraged a movement from national self-sufficiency to a doctrine of free trade, which was supported by classical economists Adam Smith and David Ricardo and the philosopher John Locke. During the nineteenth century, the amount of world trade increased rapidly while the pattern of world trade changed.

The Industrial Revolution consisted mainly of the application of machinery to manufacturing, mining, transportation, communication, and agriculture, and of the changes in economic organization that attended these applications.[9] Fundamental in the new industrial order was the development of a cheap, portable source of power. James Watt's invention of the condenser and of a practical method for converting the reciprocating motion of the piston into rotary motion made the steam engine a practical prime mover for all kinds of machinery.

The Industrial Revolution probably represented the hallmark of capitalism. The old method of small-scale production in the home with one's own tools could not meet the competition of machine production. The cost of machinery was prohibitive to individual workers. Hence, the factory system arose, with large-scale production in factories using machinery owned by the employer. The factory system stimulated the growth of division of labor and mass production through the standardization of processes and parts. Old industries began to produce on a much larger scale than previously, and new industries developed, offering new goods to satisfy new demands.

Industrial capitalists were created, and it was they who shaped the course of future industrialization by reinvesting their gains in new enterprises. The Industrial Revolution also enormously accentuated the movement toward international economic interdependence. As the people of Europe became more and more engaged in urban industry, they raised less food and became heavy importers of wheat, meat, and other food products. In exchange for food, Europe exported manufactured goods, and the entire world became a marketplace.

The doctrine of laissez-faire fit in with the development of capitalism. It carried with it a sense of independence, personal initiative, and self-responsibility. If individual initiative is respected, it gives free play to entrepreneurs to create products for those who want and will pay for them. A necessary requisite for individualism is a limited state role. The individual should have preference over the state, for the latter is, again, only a fictitious body composed of individual people who are considered to be its members. The ideas of individualism and laissez-faire were therefore regarded by Adam Smith and others as a safeguard against the tyranny of the state.

Finance Capitalism

Constant growth in the use of machinery, and especially mass production, made it increasingly necessary for individual entrepreneurs to raise large amounts of capital. As raising capital became more difficult, the control of industry passed more and more into the hands of a few large investment banking houses. This system became

---

[9] The Industrial Revolution began in England between 1770 and 1825 and in continental Europe after 1815. Some scholars contend that we are in a new period of postindustrial development. See, for example, Daniel Bell, *The Coming of Post-Industrial Society* (New York: Basic Books, Publishers, 1976).

known as *finance capitalism*. Banks became professional accumulators of capital. Corporations, which by the latter part of the nineteenth century had become the dominant form of business unit, were able to obtain large quantities of long-term capital funds by selling their securities with the assistance of investment banks. The banks underwrote and distributed the securities, eventually getting them in the hands of insurance companies, banks, investment trusts, and individual investors. These banking houses were able to acquire an inordinate amount of economic power through the ownership of securities and through the device of the interlocking directorate.

MODIFICATIONS OF PURE CAPITALISM

Various elements have combined over time to transform pure market capitalism to what might be called "state-guided" capitalism. In fact, the term *mixed economic system* is used in later chapters to describe countries that were at one time purely capitalistic. Part of this transformation has been the development of the welfare state, which resulted from the extremely unequal distribution of income that developed during the Industrial Revolution. A growing concentration of economic power in the hands of a few people created extremes of wealth and poverty. In the United States during the 1890s, for example, the department store magnate Marshall Field had an income calculated at $600 per hour; his shopgirls, earning salaries of $3 to $5 a week, had to work three to five years to earn that amount.[10] Working conditions for most workers in the Western industrial world were deplorable: The twelve-hour work day and seven-day work week were not uncommon. There were no child labor laws; children of eight and even younger worked in the coal mines and textile mills in the United States and England.

The Decline of the Protestant Work Ethic

Other factors influenced the transformation of capitalism as well. Thrift, which at one time was a linchpin of the Protestant work ethic, began to decline. Traditional morality, as represented by Puritanism, was challenged by the automobile, movies, and credit cards. A mass production society could not tolerate thrift. Why save when you could buy an automobile on credit? Since the 1920s credit has become the passport to instant gratification. American culture is no longer concerned with how to work and achieve, but with how to spend and enjoy.

The Decline of Individualism

The idea of rugged individualism has always been a greatly romanticized part of the American frontier spirit. This individualism, as epitomized by John Wayne in

---

[10] Cited in Otto Bettman, *The Good Old Days—They Were Terrible* (New York: Random House, 1974), p. 67.

the movie *True Grit*, carried with it a sense of independence, personal initiative, and self-responsibility.[11] Life was a series of challenges to be met head on, as John Wayne did at the end of *True Grit* when he went charging into the four bad men, reins in teeth and guns blazing. It was the individual rather than the state who did the punishing, and moralizing was left to the preachers. There was in individualism the idea of a "just meritocracy."[12] Individuals should be left free to achieve what they can through their own abilities and efforts. Naturally, there will be winners and losers, but this is inevitable in a libertarian society.

To some extent, individualism in the Western world has been superceded by egalitarianism. The decline of individualism is largely a result of urban industrialized life. Individual desires often clash with the wishes of groups. There is frequent disharmony as the individual pulls in one direction while the group wants to go in the other direction. Claims on a community have come to be decided on the basis of group membership rather than individual attributes.[13] Social life has increasingly become organized on a group basis.

Egalitarianism has meant different things during different periods. In the United States, the Jeffersonian concept of equality was an equality of the elect (those eligible to vote).[14] The Jacksonian idea of equality was somewhat simpler. In essence, Jackson felt that any man was just as good as the next one. Equality has come to be defined in terms of equity; hence the emphasis on equality of result, which is defined as a group right rather than an individual right. This equality is not to be achieved through upward mobility or merit, but through government action. The rules of the game must be changed so as to reduce the rewards of competition and the cost of failure. Or, as the Dodo said to Alice in Wonderland when explaining the results of the Caucus race, "Everybody has won and all must have prizes."[15]

Government and the Decline of Laissez-Faire

Government has always played some role in Western society, even during the zenith of capitalism. In the historical development of the United States, government policy was primarily a mixture of measures that provided equality of opportunity for the common man, such as public education, and generous favors for those who knew how to help themselves, such as railroad and canal builders. Tariffs were enacted

---

[11] Henry Hathaway, director, *True Grit*, Paramount Pictures, 1969.

[12] Daniel Bell, "On Meritocracy and Equality," *The Public Interest* (Fall 1972), pp. 18–32.

[13] Daniel Bell, *The Cultural Contradictions of Capitalism* (New York: Basic Books, 1976), pp. 141–145.

[14] To Jefferson, equality meant giving each person an equal opportunity, before the law and under God. He said, "There is a natural aristocracy among men. The grounds of this are virtue and talents. . . . The natural aristocracy I consider as the most precious gift of nature." See Thomas Jefferson, *Notes on the State of Virginia*, ed. Thomas Abernethy (New York: Harper & Row, 1964), pp. 1–10.

[15] Lewis Carroll, *Alice's Adventures in Wonderland* and *Through the Looking Glass* (New York: Airmont Publishing Co., 1965), p. 27.

to protect American business firms from foreign competition. In France, where state participation in the economy had always been important, much of the railroad system was state owned by the 1850s, and the state also had a monopoly over the sale of such products as alcohol, tobacco, and tea. State ownership of certain industries also existed in Prussia.

The Depression of the 1930s was probably the catalyst for increasing the role of government. On the basis of experience during the Depression, organized labor, farmers, business firms, and consumer groups turned to government for assistance in improving their incomes and ensuring economic security. The satisfaction of these demands made for a new concept of government. An increase in the power of the state has become the central fact of modern Western society. Crucial decisions about production and distribution have come to be made through the political process rather than through the marketplace.

Restrictions on Competition

Competition is one of the basic institutions of capitalism. Its justification, like that of other institutions, is found in the notion that it contributes to the social welfare. It is a regulator of economic activity and is thought to maximize productivity, prevent excessive concentration of economic power, and protect consumer interests. *Competition* may be used to describe the economic structure of a nation, applicable to all economic units—individuals, farmers, and business firms. Economic success goes to efficiently operated firms, and failure eliminates inefficiently and wastefully operated firms. The impersonal market system does not lock in products or skills that have become obsolete and therefore nonproductive.

But competition is a hard taskmaster, for there are losers as well as winners. Since losers don't think they should lose, they take action to prevent losing and thus the rules of the game are altered. The market system has been changed in many ways by government action to prevent or cushion the effects of losing. Through subsidies and restraints on foreign competition, uneconomic production and job skills have been maintained by governmental intervention.

Business firms have formed various combinations, cartels, trusts, and holding companies to prevent competition. Workers have joined labor unions to avoid individual competition, and obsolete job skills have been preserved. In the United States, obsolete jobs have been preserved in the construction industry and elsewhere through federal building codes, and inefficient firms, such as Chrysler, have received financial support from the government when otherwise they would have been eliminated by the forces of competition.

SUMMARY

Capitalism is an economic system characterized by a set of institutional arrangements. The centerpiece of capitalism is a freely competitive market where buyers satisfy their wants and sellers supply those wants in order to make a profit. The price mechanism determines resource allocation, and freedom of enterprise and private property ownership provide incentives to save and produce. Individualism is also at the core of the capitalist or free market ideology. It was assumed by Adam Smith and others that people were rational and would try at all times to promote their own personal welfare. The individual, in promoting his or her self-interest, works in the interest of society.

Competition is an indispensable part of a free enterprise system. In economic life, self-reliant individuals must compete for economic rewards (good jobs, high pay, and promotions), and business must compete for consumer incomes. The Protestant work ethic stressed rewards in this life, not in the hereafter. Hard work included thrift, which could provide the savings necessary for investment. The role of government is minimal in a capitalist economy.

The advanced capitalist countries of today have modified the institutions of capitalism. In the operation of capitalist economies, problems arose that seemed impossible for private individuals to solve. Their impact brought a demand for government intervention. As a result, government intervention and regulation is a very common feature of life under capitalism. Consumers are not left to depend solely on competition to furnish them with foods and drugs of acceptable quality and purity; there are laws that provide certain standards in these matters. Capitalistic societies have never been willing to extend complete freedom of enterprise to any individual. That is, it has always been recognized that an individual, in selecting the most profitable field of activity, might well choose something that would be clearly antisocial. In such cases, government has not hesitated to step in with restrictions. But government has also altered the economic institutions of capitalism through, for example, subsidies to farmers and protection of inefficient business firms from competition.

REVIEW QUESTIONS

1. What is meant by the term *institutions* as applied to an economic system?
2. Explain the concept of economic scarcity. Are there things that are not scarce?
3. Apply the concept of scarcity to life in the United States today. Is scarcity still present in the United States? How does scarcity affect an American's life?
4. What are the three factors of production? Why do economists classify resources in this way?
5. What is the function of profit in a market economy?
6. What is the function of the price mechanism in a market system?
7. How are incomes distributed in a market economy?
8. What are some of the factors responsible for the breakdown of a true market economy?
9. The United States economy has diverged from pure market capitalism. Why?

RECOMMENDED READINGS

Bell, Daniel. *The Coming of the Post-Industrial Society*. New York: Basic Books, 1976.

Bell, Daniel. *The Cultural Contradictions of Capitalism*. New York: Basic Books, 1976.

Hacker, Louis M. *The Triumph of American Capitalism*. New York: Simon & Schuster, Inc., 1940.

Heilbroner, Robert L. *The Making of Economic Society*. 4th ed. Englewood Cliffs, NJ: Prentice Hall, 1962.

Hofstadtler, Richard. *Social Darwinism in American Thought*. Rev. ed. Boston: Beacon Press, 1955.

Polanyi, Karl. *The Great Transformation*. New York: Rinehart, 1944.

Smith, Adam. *The Wealth of Nations*. Indianapolis: Liberty Classics, 1981.

Tawney, R. H. *Religion and the Rise of Capitalism*. New York: Harcourt, Brace, and World, 1926.

Toynbee, Arnold. *The Industrial Revolution*. Boston: Beacon Press, 1956.

Weber, Max. *The Protestant Ethic and the Spirit of Capitalism*. New York: Charles Scribner's Sons, 1930.

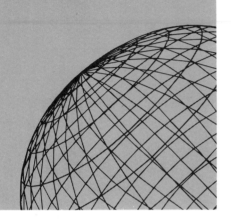

CHAPTER TWO

MARKET MECHANISMS, ECONOMIC PROBLEMS, AND GOVERNMENT POLICIES

The United States, Great Britain, and other countries of European culture have had decades of experience with free market economies. One important principle of free enterprise economies is that if individuals are permitted to pursue their own interests without interference from public authority, they will, in pursuit of their own selfish interests, promote the well-being of all. This will not result from charitable motives, but from the inexorable logic of the system—Adam Smith's "invisible hand." Stated simply, if all people are motivated to work at full capacity—whether as laborers or executives—the net supply of goods and services available for consumption by all will be maximized.

However, there is no ubiquitous human nature that guarantees that, if just allowed to do so, all persons will always pursue profits, income, and satisfaction, and will always benefit each other in the process. The pursuit of profits, income, and satisfaction does not occur innately; it is learned behavior. It is learned by some people from their environments and it is not learned by others at all. The pursuit of individual self-interest is socially beneficial only when the environment is appropriate. But the environment is not always appropriate; the cultural heritages of many societies do not contain the necessary requisites for the development of a successful market system.

Some government intervention is necessary to establish a free economic system. The very atmosphere for the conduct of a free market economy is created by the ability of government to establish and maintain private property, freedom of enterprise, money and credit, and a system of civil laws for adjudicating the private disputes of individuals. However, the role of government in market economies has increased enormously over the last 50 years. One reason is the failure of the market mechanism to allocate resources properly. A breakdown in competitive market forces allows monopoly, oligopoly, and otherwise imperfectly competitive market structures to cause inefficient resource allocation. A second reason is unemployment. The Great Depression of the 1930s created a fundamental shift in government policy away from laissez-faire toward direct government intervention. Third, an unequal distribution of income and wealth created social frictions that threatened to undermine the social and political structure of many capitalist countries. A final reason for government intervention is economic insecurity that results from the operation of a market system. Each of these reasons will be discussed in some detail.

GOVERNMENT REGULATION OF MARKET STRUCTURES

For a market system to work well and to adjust to changing conditions, the prices of goods, services, and resources must be allowed to rise and fall. Changes in prices are the means by which consumers, producers, and resource owners are induced to make adjustments beneficial to others. Thus, if consumer preferences change in favor of some good and its price rises as a result, the higher price induces producers to supply more of the good. If a technological innovation reduces the demand for a particular type of labor, a fall in the relevant wage rate is called for. That fall would encourage employers to reemploy their labor elsewhere.

Restraints on Competition

The United States and many other industrial countries have long depended on competition to provide the discipline that is necessary for efficient allocation of scarce resources. A competitive market will allow prices to reflect actual demand and costs and thus maximize efficiency in the use of capital and other resources. There is also a relationship between a competitive market economy and a democratic political structure: Competition is expected to prevent the development of excessively powerful economic units. When firms find ways to limit competition, the public welfare is adversely affected. Companies have found many ways to restrict competition within their industries. Collusion among companies to limit output results in higher prices.[1] Large enterprises can dominate an industry and provide barriers to entry by other firms.

Monopoly. A monopoly exists when there is only one seller of a commodity that has no close substitutes. A monopoly market is the direct antithesis of a competitive market in that a monopolist can fix prices through control of the supply of the

---

[1] An example is a cartel such as OPEC, the oil cartel, which attempts to limit the output of producers for the purpose of raising the price of the product and the profits of the producers.

commodity. The individual firm and the industry are, in effect, identical, and the market demand curve for the industry is the same as the average revenue or demand curve for the monopolist. Monopoly prices are also frequently higher than prices that would prevail under competition because a monopolist can charge different prices to different consumers. There are no competing sellers to whom buyers may go to avoid price discrimination.

Resource allocation is also less efficient under monopoly. There is no incentive for a monopoly to organize its plant in the most efficient manner because a successful monopolist is able to make a profit by merely restricting supply. Modernization of facilities, experimentation with lower prices and larger output, and managerial incentives may be retarded by the lack of competition.

A monopolist's price and output determination are shown in the accompanying example.[2] Remember that, unlike pure competition, in a monopoly the average revenue is not constant because the price declines as the output increases. The average revenue (AR) column shows the prices at which various quantities of output can be sold, and the marginal revenue (MR) column shows the increments to total revenue (TR) that result from selling additional units of output. In the short run, some costs are fixed and others are variable. In the example, total fixed costs (FC) are assumed to be $500 regardless of the volume of output, and total variable costs (VC) have been given assigned values.

The same analysis is presented graphically in Figure 2-1, which shows the monopolist's average revenue or demand curve (D), marginal revenue curve (MR),

Quantity of Output	AR Price	TR	MR	FC	VC	TC	MC	Profit
10	$ 100	$ 1,000	—	$ 500	$ 483	$ 983	—	$ 17
11	99	1,089	89	500	544	1,044	61	45
12	98	1,176	87	500	598	1,098	54	78
13	96	1,248	72	500	659	1,159	61	89
14	94	1,316	68	500	725	1,225	66	91
15	90	1,350	34	500	802	1,302	77	48
16	85	1,360	10	500	890	1,390	88	−30

short-run marginal cost curve (MC), and average total cost curve (ATC). ATC equals TC divided by output. The marginal revenue curve shows the increment to total revenue that results from selling an additional unit of output while the marginal cost curve shows the cost to produce the additional unit. MR equals MC at an output of

---

[2] The example is for the short run. In the long run, a monopolist is able to adjust its scale of operations because all costs are variable, whereas in the short run it can determine the most profitable rate of operation limited by its existing fixed factors of production.

FIGURE 2-1
Cost and Revenue Curves for a Monopolist

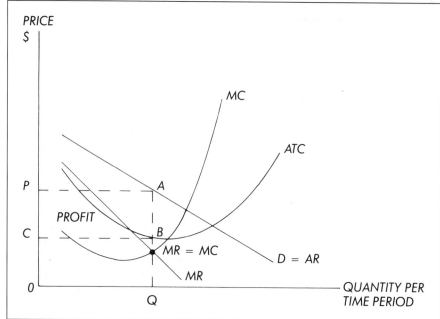

0Q. It would be profitable for the monopolist to expand up to this point, because at all smaller volumes *MC* lies below *MR*. Beyond this point, however, *MC* rises above *MR*. The price at which this quantity can be sold can be determined from the *AR* curve, which is also the monopolist's demand curve.

- 0Q equals output that will be produced to maximize profits. It is 14 units of output in the example.
- 0P equals price that will maximize profits. It is $94 in the example.
- 0PAQ equals total revenue, which is $1,316 in the example.
- 0CBQ equals total cost, which is $1,225 ($500 + $725) in the example.
- PABC equals total profit, which is $91 ($1,316 − $1,225) in the example.

Oligopoly. Oligopoly refers to a market situation in which there are a few sellers of a basically similar product. Many industries in the Western capitalistic countries have oligopolistic qualities: for example, the steel, automobile, and cigarette industries. In fact, oligopoly seems to be a characteristic of industries to which modern methods of production apply. The pattern of oligopolistic industries is for a few giant firms to account for one-half or more of the total industry output, followed by smaller firms that produce the rest. For example, General Motors and Ford account for at least two-thirds of the domestic output of automobiles by American car manufacturers. In West Germany, three chemical companies produce more than 90 percent of domestic chemical products. Typical of most oligopolistic industries is differentiation, which means distinguishing a firm's products from those of its competitors by means of brands and trademarks and creating a preference for the brand through advertising.

Oligopoly markets have several important characteristics:

1. No one firm can increase its revenue through price competition. For example, if one firm raises its prices and other firms do not follow suit, its sales will usually suffer. If one firm lowers its prices, all the others will follow and all the firms will have lower revenue.
2. Prices are identical or almost identical in oligopoly markets.
3. Without price competition, firms are often able to reach some sort of agreement, tacitly or otherwise, as to what the set price will be.

The economic and social losses under oligopoly are similar to those under monopoly. Output in such industries is restricted, prices can be maintained at levels above marginal cost, and too few resources are employed when compared with competitive sectors of the economy.

Nonetheless, oligopoly itself does not always contradict the social interest, since it may be based on economies of scale that can be maintained only by large-sized firms. These economies may be so great in relation to the size of the market served that there is room for only a few firms in the industry. An industry of many small firms with higher costs would not be any more efficient. When, however, oligopoly results from the exclusion of new, potentially efficient firms by such means as collusion, the situation is clearly contrary to the public interest.

Antitrust Laws

In a market economy, competition is necessary to provide the discipline needed for efficient allocation of resources. Any departure from competition can work against the public welfare. A prime example was the development of trusts and other forms of business combinations in the United States in the last century. The trusts were aimed at eliminating competitors and many industries fell under the control of a single trust. Discriminatory pricing practices were numerous, and companies colluded to restrain competition.[3] Some competition took the form of social Darwinism—the "survival of the fittest" principle applied to the business world. However, one outcome of this social Darwinism was cutthroat competition

---

[3] One example was the basing point system. To avoid giving mills located near a consuming center a price advantage in getting business because of lower transportation costs, steel companies adopted a policy of selling all steel and iron products from a base point, which was Pittsburgh, regardless of the origin of the shipment.

where the field of industry became a battleground between rival firms, each intent upon destroying the other.

For these reasons, governments in the United States and other countries passed antitrust laws to protect the public against anticompetitive business practices. These laws are designed to maintain competition by limiting monopoly power, whether achieved through internal growth or by mergers. They also are directed at specific anticompetitive business practices: price fixing, price discrimination against buyers or sellers, tying agreements, interlocking directorates, and other coercive practices. Each device can be used to restrain competition. For example, the aim of a price-fixing agreement, if effective, is the elimination of price competition. The power to fix prices, whether reasonably exercised or not, involves power to control the market.

UNEMPLOYMENT

Probably the most important basis for the increased role of governments in market economies has been their explicit assumption of responsibility for the general economic health of their countries. The Depression of the 1930s was the catalyst for the transformation of the role of the government from passive to active in its use of economic policy measures to achieve the goal of prosperity. The Depression was unprecedented in both size and duration, and its impact on the Western industrial countries was enormous. It did more to reshape the American economy than any other event; there was massive government intervention in many areas of the economy. In Germany, the Depression was a prime contributing factor to the rise to power of Adolf Hitler. The Depression contributed to the rise of militarism in Japan, which resulted in the eventual confrontation with the United States. To many it appeared that the capitalistic system was in a state of collapse and that the demise of capitalism predicted by Marx was about to begin.

Classical Economic Theory and Unemployment

Until the 1930s, no market economy had experienced a deep and prolonged depression. Everything about the past supported the classical economic theory that full employment of labor and other resources could be the norm.[4] There could be lapses from full employment, but self-correcting market forces would pull the economy back to the normal state. Classical economic theory was based on two important assumptions.

---

[4] The term *classical economics* was used by Karl Marx to refer to the writings of David Ricardo and his predecessors, including Adam Smith. Later the term was applied to the writings of John Stuart Mill, A. C. Pigou, and Alfred Marshall.

1. There was a competitive market system in which resources were mobile. There were many buyers and sellers in both the product and resource markets, and prices were free to move either upward or downward.

2. Income was spent automatically at a rate always consistent with full employment. There could not be too much saving, for saving was channeled into investment through the mechanism of the interest rate. If there was excessive saving, the interest rate would fall and investment would increase. Conversely, if there was too little saving, the interest rate would rise and investment would decline. An equilibrium point would always be reached at full employment. Both saving and investment were functions of the interest rate. Since saving was first of all another form of spending, according to classical theory, all income was either spent on consumption or investment.

The basis for classical economic theory was Say's Law of Markets.[5] This law states, in effect, that supply creates its own demand. Supply is the catalyst: Whatever is produced represents the demand for another product. Additional supply creates additional demand; hence, any increase in production is an increase in demand, and therefore overproduction is impossible. This assertion is supported by the argument that goods really exchange for goods, money being merely a medium of exchange. Say reasoned that whenever workers and other resources are used to create goods and services, a demand equal in value to the incomes paid to the factors of production is created automatically. Because the purpose of earning income is to spend it on goods and services, income will automatically equal that output. In an exchange economy, Say's Law means that there will always be a rate of spending sufficient to maintain full employment.

Keynesian Economic Theory

An economic theory is valid until events prove otherwise, and economic life simply did not correspond to the way market economies were supposed to act in the classical system. The automatic adjustment toward a level of full employment did not occur; to the contrary, as the Great Depression continued, serious and prolonged unemployment became the normal condition of the market economies. Under these conditions, not even the staunchest defenders of classical theory could seriously maintain that there were forces in the economy that automatically generated full employment. The classical theory offered little help to policymakers who were responsible for devising measures to combat unemployment. Also, it was no consolation to those who were unemployed to be told that unemployment was temporary and that eventually market forces would lead to the conditions necessary for full employment. What was needed was a new theory that would explain the causes

---

[5] Jean Baptiste Say was a French economist who lived during the time of Adam Smith. His major work, *Treatise on Political Economy*, was the first popular book on economics produced in Europe.

of unemployment and offer solutions for policymakers to follow. This theory was provided by the British economist John Maynard Keynes in his book *The General Theory of Employment, Interest, and Money.*[6]

In Keynesian theory, the level of employment is linked to the total production of goods and services. The volume of production, in turn, depends on the level of spending or aggregate demand. The catalyst in the Keynesian economic framework is aggregate demand, for it determines, at least in the short run, the extent to which an economy's productive capacity will be used. It is at one time both the source of total national income and the basis on which the level of employment is determined. If aggregate demand is not sufficient to employ all available resources, national income will be lower than it need be. If aggregate demand falls, so will income; as national income falls, so will output and employment. When aggregate demand increases, so will national incomes, and output and employment will follow. The key to economic stability is to maintain aggregate demand and national income at levels consistent with high employment of labor and other resources.

Components of Demand.   The two major components of aggregate demand in the Keynesian system are consumer demand for goods and services and investment demand by private business firms for capital goods. Both consumer and investment demand are based on certain determinants. Disposable income, or income after taxes, is the prime determinant of consumption expenditures. As disposable income increases, so will consumption, but not at the same rate. The marginal propensity to consume is the fraction of any change in income that is consumed. The functional relationship is called the *consumption function.*

Investment in the Keynesian framework is determined by the marginal efficiency of capital in conjunction with the interest rate. The former is the expected rate of yield on a capital good, and the latter is the cost of borrowing money. A functional relationship can be expressed as follows: $I = f(n, i)$ where n = marginal efficiency of capital and i = rate of interest.

An Example of the Keynesian Model.   The Keynesian framework can be presented in a basic model. Both national income and employment are determined by aggregate demand, which in turn depends on the marginal propensity to consume and the level of investment. This relationship can be expressed by the equation $Y = C + I$, where Y = total output, C = consumption expenditures, and I = investment expenditures. Y is referred to as aggregate supply and is determined mainly by aggregate demand, $C + I$. Aggregate supply and aggregate demand interact to determine an equilibrium level of national income and output. At any level below the equilibrium point $Y = C + I$, aggregate demand is greater than

---

[6] John Maynard Keynes, *The General Theory of Employment, Interest, and Money* (New York: Harcourt, Brace & Co., 1936).

aggregate supply; at any level above the point of equilibrium, aggregate supply is greater than aggregate demand. The equilibrium level is at 400, for aggregate supply and aggregate demand are equal, and savings of 40 equals investment of 40. Savings represents a withdrawal from income and investment represents an injection into it. Total goods and services produced, Y, is equal to total demand, $C + I$.

Y	C	S	I	$C + I$
0	120	−120	40	160
100	180	− 80	40	220
200	240	− 40	40	280
300	300	0	40	340
400	360	40	40	400
500	420	80	40	460
600	480	120	40	520
700	540	160	40	580

The determination of income and output can also be shown through the use of algebraic equations. In the example, as income increases by 100, consumption increases by 60. The marginal propensity to consume, which is $\Delta C \div \Delta Y$, or 60 $\div$ 100, is 0.6. Since saving is $Y - C$, each increase in Y of 100 results in an increase in S of 40. The marginal propensity to save is $\Delta S \div \Delta Y$, or 40 $\div$ 100, or 0.4. The formulas can be written as follows:

$$Y = C + I$$
$$S = Y - C$$
$$C = C_0 + aY$$
$$I = I$$
$$S = -C_0 + (1 - a)Y$$

Y = income
C = consumer expenditures
I = investment expenditures
C_0 = consumption when Y is zero
a = marginal propensity to consume
$1 - a$ = marginal propensity to save

Solving for Y:

$$Y = C + I$$
$$= C_0 + aY + I$$
$$= 120 + .6Y + 40$$
$$Y - .6Y = 160$$
$$.4Y = 160$$
$$Y = 400$$

Solving for S:

$$S = Y - C$$
$$= Y - (C_0 + aY)$$
$$= -C_0 + (1 - a)Y$$
$$= -120 + (1 - .6)Y$$
$$= -120 + .4(400)$$
$$S = 40$$

This basic macroeconomic model is illustrated in Figure 2-2. The vertical axis measures aggregate demand, or $C + I$, and the horizontal axis measures output, or real gross national product. The 45° line is the aggregate supply schedule that shows, in effect, that total cost of national output must be matched by an equivalent amount of sales proceeds if producers as a whole are to justify total output. The line implies that there must always be an equal vertical amount of

FIGURE 2-2
The Keynesian
Model

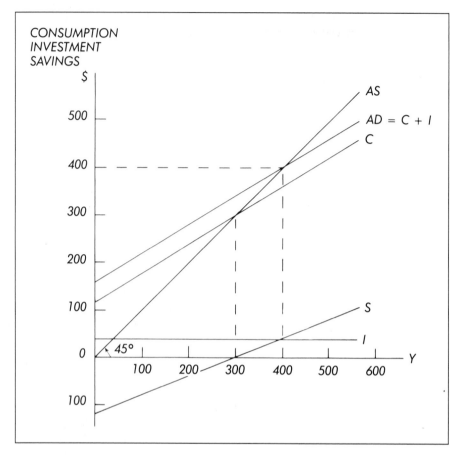

expenditure for each horizontal cost of national output. The aggregate demand line is a schedule associating spending decisions with different levels of real income. Given the aggregate supply and aggregate demand schedules for the economy, the equilibrium level of income and employment will be determined by the intersection of the two schedules. Saving and investment are also equal at this point. There are two fundamental identity equations: $Y = C + I$ and $S = I$.

Implication for Government Policy.   Keynesian economic theory rejects laissez-faire and accepts government intervention as the prime requisite for economic stability. The policy implications are clear: There has to be more government intervention in economic life. Keynes held that classical economic theory was wrong in its assumption that full employment is the norm in a market economy. To the contrary, unemployment could exist for a long period of time, as it did during the 1930s.

The goal of Keynesian economic theory is to create a better economic and social milieu in which industrial capitalism can survive. The first step toward that better environment is the elimination of mass unemployment. High unemployment would be eliminated through use of government fiscal and monetary policies to stimulate consumption and investment expenditures. Government policies are necessary to increase aggregate demand. Assume that in the example above, mass unemployment exists at the level of output of 400. Government spending is introduced to increase total output. Assume that the amount of spending is 80.

Y	C	S	I	G	C + I + G
0	120	−120	40	80	240
100	180	− 80	40	80	320
200	240	− 40	40	80	360
300	300	0	40	80	420
400	360	40	40	80	480
500	420	80	40	80	540
600	480	120	40	80	600
700	540	160	40	80	660

The equilibrium level is now 600. Aggregate demand is 600 and aggregate supply is 600. Total saving of 120 is equal to the sum of private investment and government spending. The equations may now be written as follows:

$$Y = C + I + G \qquad\qquad S = I + G$$
$$C = C_o + aY \qquad\qquad S = -C_0 + (1 - a)Y$$
$$Y = C_0 + aY + I + G \qquad\qquad = -120 + .4(600)$$
$$= 120 + .6Y + 40 + 80 \qquad\qquad = -120 + 240$$
$$Y - .6Y = 240 \qquad\qquad\qquad = 120$$
$$.4Y = 240 \qquad\qquad\qquad 120 = 40 + 80$$
$$Y = 600 \qquad\qquad\qquad 120 = 120$$

Stabilization Policies. Keynesian economics provided the basis for economic policy in most Western capitalistic countries after World War II.[7] The role that governments played in the economies of the capitalist countries increased. They came to act as the main stabilizing force by using policies that influenced an economy's overall expenditure level. Fiscal policy and monetary policy became the two chief instruments used by central governments to attain expenditure levels consistent with economic growth, stable prices, and high employment.

Fiscal Policy. Fiscal policy refers to the tax and expenditure policies of a government. The objective of fiscal policy is to increase or decrease the level of aggregate demand through changes in the level of government expenditures and

---

[7] It is a common misconception that Keynesian economics, or the "new economics" as it came to be called by many, was introduced to the United States during the Kennedy administration.

taxation. An expansionary fiscal policy would stimulate employment and economic growth through an increase in government spending, decrease in taxes, or both. Conversely, fiscal policy can be used to contract the level of aggregate demand. Taxes can be raised, government expenditures can be reduced, or a combination can be used. A government can also run a surplus in its budget.

Monetary Policy. Monetary policy is used by government central banks to control the level of national output and the price level through variations in the money supply.[8] An increase in the money supply will lower interest rates and stimulate private and public spending; a decrease in the money supply will raise interest rates and reduce private and public spending. Central banks cannot fix the amount of credit and its cost independently. If they want to restrain the rate of growth in the money supply, they must allow interest rates to rise as high as possible; if they want to keep interest rates low, they have to accept the consequences in terms of an increase in the money supply. Monetary policy has become an increasingly important economic tool used by governments to achieve given economic objectives. It differs from fiscal policy in that *total* control over it is not always in the hands of government.[9]

EQUITY AND INCOME DISTRIBUTION

It is difficult to reach agreement on the optimum distribution of income. Each individual and group views an economic system from its own position in society. Unanimity of opinion is therefore impossible, and it is highly doubtful if an agreed-upon concept of optimum distribution can be achieved. If so, the actual effect of taxes and government expenditures on the distribution of income will not be determined on the basis of a particular theory of optimum distribution, but rather as a result of a struggle between the dominant political forces at a particular moment. The results will be strongly modified, of course, by political decisions made in the past. This does not mean that theories will play no role whatever, for each group must have a rationale for its position.

The question of what constitutes an equitable distribution of income is hard to answer. It is difficult to justify on purely ethical grounds the position that those

---

[8] The money supply is the total quantity of money existing in an economy at a particular time. It consists of coins and currency, demand deposits, and other checkable account balances. It includes $M1$, which represents the more liquid types of money. Then there is $M2$, which includes assets that are less liquid. Savings accounts and certificates of deposit are examples. $M2$ equals the more broadly defined money supply.

[9] The Federal Reserve System of the United States is an example. The 12 Federal Reserve Banks are under the direction of policies set by its Board of Governors, which operates independently from government influence.

persons who contribute the most to output should receive the most income, which would happen in a market economy. (This is the basis of marginal productivity analysis, as mentioned in Chapter 1.) Problems arise because individuals and families differ with respect to age, health problems, and in many other ways, and therefore have different needs in an objective sense. There are no accepted ethical standards for determining the degree to which contributions to output should be rewarded, nor are there any accepted economic standards for determining how much effort any individual is making. The result is that the Western market-oriented countries have accepted the idea that income distribution is much too important to be left solely to market forces. Many governments have accepted the idea that income ought to be redistributed in favor of those with lower incomes at the expense of those with higher incomes.

The Interaction of Wealth and Income

Inequality of income interacts with and mutually reinforces inequality of wealth. Those with large incomes have a greater ability to save part of their income and accumulate it in the form of wealth or property than do those with small incomes. A family that possesses property or wealth derives more income than just its labor income in wages and salaries. It receives, in addition, rent, dividends, interest, or profits. It can afford to take risks in choosing its occupations and in using its wealth. If these choices are successful, they will augment the wealth and income further.[10] A poor family is usually without a cushion of wealth or discretionary income on which to rely in case a risky venture fails. That family cannot undertake the risky venture for fear of jeopardizing essential income. So it is that in a market system inequality of income and wealth may be cumulatively self-enforcing.

In general, the development of the modern welfare state stems from a dissatisfaction with the distribution of income. One result of market capitalism, as mentioned above, has been an extreme inequality in the distribution of income. This inequality can be attributed primarily to receipts of income from property. The methods that governments have used most widely to distribute income more equitably are progressive income and inheritance taxes, and transfer payments. Policies directed toward a high level of employment also have an effect on the distribution of income.

Tax Policies

The progressive income tax affects the distribution of income in two ways. First, the tax directly reduces the disposable income of individuals. The progressive income tax redistributes income in the direction of greater equality because the share of the

---

[10] The wealthy also do the bulk of saving in a capitalist country. Saving provides the basis for capital formation.

total disposable income received by upper-income groups is reduced and the share received by lower-income groups is raised. The progressive income tax structure brings about this result because the effective rate of taxation—the ratio of total taxes paid to incomes received—increases with the size of the income. Second, there is an indirect effect on incentives. It may be presumed that highly progressive income taxation has a restraining influence on the creation of income. Not only would high marginal rates cause people to think twice before adding to their work output, but they might well have an injurious effect on savings and investment.

Transfer Payments

Transfer payments are different from other government expenditures in that no equivalent value in goods or services is received in exchange. Their chief effect is to redistribute income between individuals, economic and social groups, or geographic regions. Transfer payments normally can be classified in one of two categories. First are transfers of money that go to individuals. Most transfer payments of this type are linked to welfare programs. This kind of transfers has the most direct effect upon the distribution of income in a society. Second, there are transfer payments in the form of subsidies to certain economic sectors, such as agriculture or business, designed to bring about a greater production of a particular commodity than would be forthcoming if the regulation of production was left to market forces. Sometimes, too, subsidies are designed to supply goods or services to particular groups at a cost below the market prices, for example, low-cost lunch programs for poor children.

ECONOMIC INSECURITY

The very nature of a market system provides for a certain amount of economic insecurity. A free enterprise system means the freedom to fail as well as the freedom to gain. Competition in the market place carries with it an element of social Darwinism—the efficient survive and the inefficient do not. The concept of individualism carried with it self-responsibility. A person was responsible for his or her own actions.[11] The Protestant work ethic stressed thrift and hard work. Life's vicissitudes, such as unemployment and old age, were the responsibility of the individual, not the state; and savings were to be set aside to cover them. Life was for the venturesome—people who enjoyed the excitement of not knowing what the future had in store for them and who welcomed the challenge of adjustment. It can be said the United States was settled by venturesome souls who were not interested in economic security, but in the challenge of opening up new frontiers.

---

[11] This attitude was epitomized by W. E. Henley's poem "Invictus," one verse of which is as follows:
It matters not how strait the gate,
Nor charged with punishment the scroll.
I am the master of my fate;
I am the captain of my soul.

Causes of Insecurity

The virtues of the free market are many. It is an affair of many buyers and many sellers, each insistent on getting his or her terms. And if either is not satisfied, that person can go elsewhere and seek to do better. From a societal point of view, one virtue of the market is that it disperses responsibility. If a company introduces a product and finds that the public won't buy it, the loss is its own. If there is a change in buying habits so that a particular industry loses jobs (the U.S. textile industry is an excellent example), the problem is the industry's. If there is a change in demand for the skills of a particular worker, the problem is the worker's. All of this introduces an element of insecurity into a market system.

As the United States and other Western societies developed as industrial nations, new risks developed. Paramount among those risks was unemployment. Industrial accidents were a second risk, and then came other risks, such as the loss of income when one became too old to work. Market capitalism carried with it the idea that incomes were determined by impersonal forces outside of human control. Life was a competitive struggle in which victory went to the swift and resourceful. However, in life's competitive struggle, most people did not fare well. Toward the end of the nineteenth century, working conditions for most workers were deplorable; twelve-hour days and seven-day weeks were not uncommon.

Government Response

In a very short period of time—just a little more than 100 years—changes have taken place in Western society that mandate some type of institutional protection for the individual who in many cases can no longer provide adequate self-protection. Technological change is rapid, posing a constant threat that workers may lose their old jobs and need to undergo expensive and psychologically distressing retraining and education. Consumer preferences may shift away from some product or production may be moved to other countries, causing a loss of jobs and a shutdown of plant facilities.[12] In addition, improved health care means that more people are living longer, and many are not able to accumulate the resources needed to support themselves during retirement. Finally, the modern industrial economy brought with it the business cycle, which introduced an element of insecurity into the market system. Not only did workers lose their jobs, but business firms and banks failed.

All Western governments have now become heavily involved in altering the distribution of market resources directly or indirectly. With this commitment came the responsibility to provide a minimum income if a family is—for whatever reason, including unemployment—unable to take care of itself. There has been in Western societies what sociologist Daniel Bell calls a "revolution of rising expectations,"

---

[12] The decline of the U.S. steel industry is a good example.

which can be translated into entitlement. It means that anyone who is old should have a pension, anyone who is sick should have medical care, and anyone who wants an education should have it. In addition, minimum wage laws set a floor under workers' wages and labor laws limit the number of hours that workers can work each day. Safety laws protect workers from hazardous working conditions and child-labor laws prohibit the employment of children until they reach a certain age.

Government Support of Industry and Agriculture

Competition is the cornerstone of a free market economy. The whole rationale for a competitive market economy is to maximize productivity by channeling resources into the most efficient uses. In a free market economy, government intervention is inappropriate because it tends to lessen the efficiency of the market in fulfilling its objectives. Also, central to the operation of a free market economy is a flexible system of prices determined by supply and demand. Above all else, government should not intervene in market pricing, for that action would strike a mortal blow to the heart of the market system.

However, governments have come to intervene in the marketplace when the results of competition appear undesirable to society. An excellent example is the Chrysler bailout by the U.S. government. On the verge of bankruptcy in 1979, Chrysler asked the U.S. Congress for financial assistance, which was eventually provided in the form of a loan guarantee.[13] If the rules of a competitive market economy had prevailed, Chrysler would have gone broke.[14] It can be argued that if government bails out businesses that fail in the competitive race, it compromises the discipline of the marketplace. Yet it also can be argued that if Chrysler had failed, there would have been an immediate loss of several hundred thousand jobs, which would have created a ripple effect throughout the American economy, creating more unemployment and the loss of tax revenues. Chrysler is only one example of how Western governments have intervened to protect firms and industries that are adversely affected by competition.

Aid to Industry.   Governments not only aid businesses with loans and subsidies, they also protect domestic businesses from the competition of firms in other countries through the use of trade restrictions. A basic premise of a market economy

---

[13] See U.S. Congress, House Committee on Banking, Finance, and Urban Affairs. *The Chrysler Corporation Financial Situation: Hearings on the Chrysler Corporation Loan Guarantee Act,* 96th Cong., 1st Sess. 1979, parts 1 and 2.

[14] Chrysler has become profitable and has repaid all its loans. Nevertheless, it is necessary to point out that import quotas were imposed on Japanese cars. Restricting imports of Japanese cars had the effect of increasing market shares of auto sales for the U.S. auto companies. They were able to increase prices, and profits increased.

is that free trade between countries is desirable. By specializing in the commodities for which it has the greatest comparative advantage and trading a part of its total output with other countries, a nation can produce a greater volume of goods and services than if it tried to be self-sufficient. Conversely, other countries do the same. In a free world market each country would specialize in what it does best and trade would take place on the basis of specialization. Japanese cars would be exchanged for American farm products, and consumer well-being would be maximized in both countries. However, the Japanese government protects its agriculture from the competition of American farm products, and the United States protects its automobile industry from the competition of Japanese cars.

Aid to Agriculture. Agriculture, probably more than any other area of economic activity, fits the economist's concept of pure competition, which is the ideal market situation.[15] There are a large number of buyers and sellers of farm products, and price and output are determined by supply and demand operating in the markets for those products. However, prices for farm products can fluctuate widely, and prices are subject to factors over which farmers have no control. Economic insecurity is the result. One type of government action to protect farmers from the vagaries of the market is through the use of price supports, which assure farmers of a price for their product no matter what the actual market price is. The purpose of price supports is the same as minimum wage laws: to provide a floor below which incomes cannot fall.

Price supports have been used in the United States for 50 years. They circumvent the market determination of both price and output of a product by supply and demand. An example will suffice. Assume that the market-determined price of wheat is $4.50 a bushel. However, farmers contend that the price is too low and want the government to guarantee a higher price. The government sets a support price of $5.25 a bushel for wheat. Figure 2-3 shows the market-determined price and the support price. There is a market-determined output and a support price output. Assume that output under the market price is 1 million bushels and under the support price, 1.2 million bushels. The difference between the two adds to the surplus the government buys to maintain the support price.

SOCIAL REGULATION

Social regulation is broad based in its objectives and enforcement. It encompasses such areas as occupational health and safety, employment opportunities for women

---

[15] Pure competition has the following characteristics: (1) The products of all the sellers are exact substitutes for each other; (2) no seller produces more than a negligible share of market supply; (3) new firms can enter the industry with the same costs as existing firms; (4) there is the absence of collusion; and (5) there is no outside interference in the marketplace.

FIGURE 2-3
Effect of a Support Price Set Higher than the Market-Determined Price

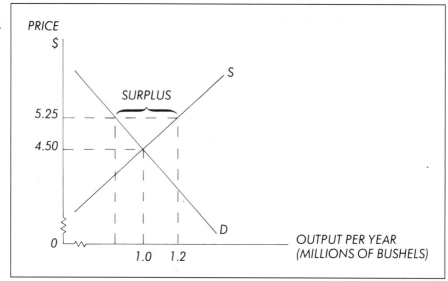

and minorities, consumer product safety, and environmental protection. The government's role in social regulation has increased in the United States and other market economies. Pollution, which is a prime external effect of industrial progress, has become a problem in the market economies.[16] Government regulation requiring air and water standards have been imposed on society.

Inability to Express
Negative Wants and Preferences

In a market economy, the price mechanism gives individuals no opportunity to bid against the production and sale of commodities and services that they regard as undesirable. To the contrary, the price mechanism will provide goods and services that people are willing to pay for, no matter how frivolous or undesirable they are. There may be many people who would be happier if they could prevent the production of, for instance, alcoholic beverages or the emission of noxious fumes from a chemical plant, and would gladly pay the price if given the opportunity to do so. But there seems to be no way that the market price mechanism can take these negative wants or preferences into consideration. The only way this can be done

---

[16] Pollution transends ideology—the Soviet Union has pollution; the Danube river at Budapest, Hungary, is polluted.

is through government action that controls the output of both public and private goods deemed undesirable.

Externalities

Externalities are costs society must bear. Pollution is an externality because one individual can impose its cost on others without having to compensate them. The other individuals then demand government protection in the form of regulation that prohibits or limits the actions of the first individual. As society has become more technologically advanced and congested, one group's meat has become another group's poison. Airports are necessary to facilitate rapid transportation, but their creation brings attendant noise that damages the environment of people who live near them. Thus these persons will coalesce into a group demanding noise abatement measures. Coal is an important source of fuel, but there are externalities in its mining—black lung disease for the miners plus the despoliation of the environment. Competitive markets provide no solution to these externalities; a competitive firm will generate as much, or more, smoke than a noncompetitive one does.

Consumer Protection

A pure market economy assumes that consumers are knowledgeable about products and can make rational choices. However, the average person (in fact even the most intelligent) has neither the ability, time, nor the inclination to become an expert in the intricacies of the many products that industry produces today. Consumer protection regulation has evolved because buying decisions have become more complex as technology has become more sophisticated.

SUMMARY

Government intervention in market economies has increased over time for a number of reasons. In the market system, the distribution of income and wealth can become quite uneven. Governments have redistributed both income and wealth through the use of progressive income and inheritance taxes and through transfer payments. Business fluctuations have created mass unemployment, and governments have used fiscal and monetary policies to stimulate aggregate demand. Concentration of business activities in the hands of a few firms and anticompetitive business practices have resulted in the creation of antitrust laws to regulate business. Economic insecurity in a market economy has been reduced by government action designed to help both individuals and groups. Governments have introduced social security measures to protect individuals from the loss of income resulting from unemployment or old age. Groups such as farmers are protected against fluctuations in market prices through price supports and subsidies. Finally, governments have intervened to provide regulation when the negative wants of consumers cannot be expressed in the market.

REVIEW QUESTIONS

1. What are negative wants? Why are they difficult to express in the market-place?
2. Compare the classical and Keynesian views of unemployment.
3. Monopolies are generally considered undesirable in a free market economy. Discuss.
4. What are the objectives of antitrust laws?
5. Keynesian economics increased the importance of government in the Western market economies. Discuss.
6. What are transfer payments?
7. Distinguish between fiscal and monetary policy.
8. In what ways have governments altered the allocation of resources by the price mechanism?
9. What was Say's Law of Markets? What relevance did it have to classical economic theory?
10. In what ways have governments protected business firms from competition?

RECOMMENDED READINGS

Baumol, William J., John C. Panzar, and Robert D. Willig. *Contestable Markets and the Theory of Industry Structure*. San Diego, CA: Harcourt Brace Jovanovich Inc., 1982.

Bronfenbrenner, Martin, Werner Sechel, and Wayland Gardner. *Economics.* Boston: Houghton Mifflin Co., 1984. Chapters 11 and 12.

Gilder, George. *Wealth and Poverty*. New York: Basic Books Inc., Publishers, 1981.

Heilbroner, Robert J. *The Worldly Philosophers: The Lives, Times and Ideas of the Great Economic Thinkers*, 6th ed. New York: Simon & Schuster Inc., 1984.

Keynes, John Maynard. *The General Theory of Employment, Interest, and Money*. New York: Harcourt, Brace & Co., 1936.

Schnitzer, Martin C. *Contemporary Government and Business Relations*, 3d ed. Boston: Houghton Mifflin Co., 1987. Chapters 2 and 18.

Steiner, George A., and John P. Steiner. *Business, Government & Society: A Managerial Perspective*, 5th ed. New York: Random House Inc., 1988.

Thurow, Lester. *The Zero-Sum Society*. New York: Penguin Books, 1981.

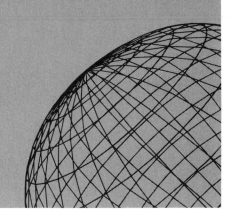

CHAPTER THREE

NONMARKET MECHANISMS: SOCIALISM AND COMMUNISM

Differences in economic and political institutions are one way to compare economic systems. Capitalism is an economic-cultural system, organized economically around the institutions of private property and the production of goods for profit and based culturally on the idea that the individual is the center of society. Other economic systems can be defined in terms of the modifications they would make in these institutions. For example, in a capitalist economy the agents of production—land, labor, and capital—are privately owned. In a socialist system, the agents of production are owned by a public authority and are operated not with a view of profit by sale to other people, but for direct service of those whom the authority represents.

However, one caveat is in order. There are many definitions of socialism, and it is necessary to differentiate between socialism as the concept is applied to the government of France and socialism used as a self-description of the countries controlled by communist parties—the Soviet Union, China, Cuba, North Korea, and Vietnam. To the West these countries are communist.

To avoid confusion, in Marxist terminology there are two stages of communism. The first stage, or *socialism*, is a transitional stage during which some elements of capitalism are retained. The second stage, or *communism*, is a higher stage to be marked by an age of plenty, distribution according to needs, the absence of money and the market mechanism, the disappearance of the last vestiges of capitalism, and the withering away of the state. The Soviet Union calls itself a socialist country (Union of Soviet Socialist Republics—USSR). It is a state-directed society that has sought to fuse all realms into a single monolith and to impose a common direction, from economics to politics to culture, through a single institution, the Communist Party. Bureaucratic collectivism characterizes the Soviet economy.

In a non-Marxist form, socialism is an economic system that would modify, but not eliminate, many of the institutions of capitalism. The extent of modification is something that has never been completely delineated by socialists because there are many variations of socialism. Some socialists favor the complete elimination of private property with replacement by public property ownership. Other socialists favor placing maximum reliance on the market mechanism while supplementing it with government direction and planning in order to achieve the desired economic and social objectives.

Socialism today has also come to be associated with the concept of a welfare state, where the state, through a wide variety of transfer payments, assumes responsibility for protecting its citizens against all of the vicissitudes of life. Private ownership of the agents of production is permitted, with state ownership of those facets of production and distribution considered vital to the interests of society. In reality Western society has incorporated many of the principles of both capitalism and socialism.

HISTORICAL DEVELOPMENT OF SOCIALISM

The words *socialist* and *socialism* are relatively new concepts. They first came into use in England and France in the early part of the last century and were applied to the doctrines of certain writers who were seeking a transformation of the economic and moral basis of society by the substitution of social for individual control of life and work.[1] The word *socialism* was popularized as the antithesis of *individualism*. However, precursors of socialism can be found among the medieval writers and even going back as far as Plato. For example, Thomas Aquinas believed that property ownership should be private, but that the use of goods should be in common. Whatever goods a man possessed should be shared with the poor. He considered poverty undesirable because it led to sin, and he proposed that both church and state should help poor people bring healthy children into the world.

The Renaissance Utopias

During the Renaissance a number of scholars turned their attention to the construction of imaginary communities, or utopias, in which society was organized so as to remove all of the evils of the day. These utopias were primarily economic and social rather than religious. For the most part, they formed a definite pattern, the

---

[1] *Socialist* seems to have been used first in England to describe the followers of Robert Owen. The word *socialism* was used in France to describe the writings of Saint-Simon and Fourier.

authors placing a group of regenerated people on an isolated land area where they could be free from contamination by the rest of the world. Rigid conditions would then be set up by means of which an ideal state would be attained. For example, in Sir Thomas More's *Utopia*, everything is owned in common and there is no money.[2] In the middle of each city is a marketplace to which each family takes the things it produces; from these central marketplaces products are distributed to central warehouses from which each family draws what it needs. Women and men have equal rights, and the households are arranged so that the women are relieved of some of their most time-consuming domestic duties.

French Utopian Socialists

French utopian socialism was associated with the French Revolution and later with the Industrial Revolution. The French Revolution created a great economic and political upheaval, the impact of which was felt all over Europe. In France every political and social division became rooted in the alignment of the revolution. Commercial business interests, as represented by a merchant class, replaced the aristocracy, who had gone to the guillotine. A large class of urban workers who had helped make a revolution found that their living conditions were largely unchanged. The fact that a great political revolution had taken place in France and that socially the results of this revolution were largely unsatisfactory set the stage for a new group of reformers, the French utopian socialists.

In general, the ideas of the utopian socialists were based on the theory that nature had ordained all things to serve the happiness of humankind and that every person had natural rights due at birth.[3] Furthermore, it was believed that human beings were perfect in the original state. However, at various times in the past, people had tampered with the natural order of things by establishing customs and institutions that ran contrary to it. As a result, people in the existing state were not happy, enjoyed few if any rights, and certainly were far from being perfect. Having discovered the cause of human difficulties, the utopian socialists proceeded to the obvious solution of the problem of social regeneration. If people had been rendered bad by unnatural customs and institutions, the thing to do was to discover the nature of the original state of goodness and then reorganize society so as to give nature's forces full play, unhampered by the conventions and institutions of the existing social environment.

However, the French utopian socialists could not agree on how to reorganize society. Some advocated the elimination of private property, considering it the main reason for human degeneracy. Others favored complete income equality. Babeuf proposed that production be carried out in common, distribution be shared

---

[2] Lewis Mumford, *The Stories of Utopias* (New York: Boni and Liveright, 1922), pp. 23–37.
[3] Richard T. Fly, *French and German Socialists in Modern Times* (New York: Harper, 1883), pp. 37–51.

in common, and children be brought up in such a way as to prevent the growth of individual differences. Saint-Simon, one of the better known early French utopian socialists, rejected the whole idea of equality, arguing instead that people were naturally unequal and that any attempt to make them equal would involve greater injustices than actually existed at the time. However, differences were to be based on talent, rather than the inheritance of wealth. Saint-Simon favored an economic mechanism that would require each person to labor according to his or her capacity and would provide rewards on the basis of service. Charles Fourier worked out a plan for cooperative living in small communities that he hoped would lead to a transformation of society. These communities were called *phalanxes*, and each phalanx was to be self-sufficient. The highest pay would go to those performing the most necessary work, as determined by the members of the phalanx.

Socialism and the Industrial Revolution

The Industrial Revolution was in due course to revolutionize the economic life of the whole Western world. The availability of new technology encouraged the formation of real capital with which the technology might be put into widespread use. The availability of resources for use in capital formation encouraged the search for new technology that, once discovered, could be embodied in the real capital. The new technology enabled gross national product to be large enough to provide sufficient consumer goods to satisfy the minimum subsistence needs of the population and still have some resources left over. Population growth provided labor to use the enlarged amounts of real capital to increase total national output.

However, there was a darker side to the Industrial Revolution. Working conditions in factories were unpleasant. Equipment was sometimes dangerous and caused workers to have serious accidents. Average wages of industrial workers were low, largely because the rapid expansion of population provided a large number of workers for the labor force. These workers concentrated in the industrial cities and competed with each other for jobs.

The cities that grew up or expanded to house the workers were unattractive and unpleasant. Many of them consisted of slums with houses of poor quality when constructed and in a constant state of disrepair thereafter. Charles Dickens, that great chronicler of English society in the nineteenth century, has a rather graphic description of the squalor of the London slums in his book *Bleak House.*

> *Jo lives—that is to say that Jo has not yet died—in a ruinous place known to the like of him by the name of Tom-all-Alone's. It is a black, dilapidated street, avoided by all decent people, where the crazy houses were seized upon, when their decay was far advanced, by some bold vagrants who after establishing their own possession took to letting them out in lodgings. Now, these tumbling tenements contain by night, a swarm of misery. As on the ruined human wretch vermin parasites appear, so these ruinous shelters have bred a crowd of foul existence that crawls in and out of gaps in walls and boards; and rocks itself to sleep in maggot numbers,*

*where the rain drips in; and comes and goes, fetching and carrying fever
and sowing more evil in its every footprint.*[4]

Modern Socialism

Modern socialism, as opposed to utopian socialism, had its genesis during the Industrial Revolution. It developed as a social reform movement to protest the seamy
side of the Industrial Revolution. Robert Owen, an early English socialist, was
considered a utopian socialist in that he developed a scheme for social regeneration; change society, you change the person. He believed that true happiness is
found in making others happy.[5] Owen, unlike many other social reformers, had the
money to carry out his plan of social regeneration. He created a textile mill at New
Lanark in Scotland in 1800, reducing the hours of work to 10 1/2 hours per day
and raising wages.[6] He did not employ children under the age of 10. Education
and playgrounds were provided for the children of mill workers. The experiment
made money, and Owen was able to get a factory reform bill introduced in Parliament. However, other mill owners were not willing to adopt similar measures.
Subsequent experiments by Owen were unsuccessful. He came to the United States
and created a community called New Harmony in Indiana. His attempts to create
a perfect community there failed, too.

Socialism coalesced into a political movement in England around the middle of
the last century. A contributing factor in its development was mass unemployment
created by business recessions. One of the basic defects of capitalism was the
constant recurrence of recessions. In England and in other countries, unemployment
and labor unrest began to occur more frequently, and a working class movement
developed in these countries.

The movement found its support in labor unions and in intellectuals who were
not of the working class but who felt that the political and economic structure of
society had to be reformed for the benefit of the workers. A split developed between
Marxist and non-Marxist socialists, with the former preaching class revolution and
the overthrow of the existing political and social order, and the latter believing in
the attainment of economic, political, and social reforms by working within the
existing system. Political parties representing both the Marxist and non-Marxist
points of view had been formed in France and Germany by 1900.

INSTITUTIONS OF SOCIALISM

Socialism developed into a viable political force in Western Europe around the latter part of the last century and has continued to develop during this century. Socialist

---

[4] Charles Dickens, *Bleak House* (New York: Signet Books, 1964), pp. 232–233.

[5] Or, in the words of Paul, "remember the words of the Lord Jesus, how He said, it is more blessed to
give than to receive" (Acts 20:35).

[6] By the standards of those days, these provisions were not harsh.

parties captured control of the governments of France and Greece in elections held in 1981. Socialism is an important political force today, but, like capitalism, it has lost much of its original meaning. There are certain institutional arrangements that set socialism apart from capitalism and communism. These arrangements represent a modification in most of the institutions of capitalism, since socialism developed in opposition to some of the worst abuses of capitalism.

Private Property

Under ideal socialism, the rights of private property would be limited to consumption goods; productive wealth, land, and capital would in general be owned by society as a whole. Socialists today say that the social ownership of the means of production would be limited to the land and capital used in large-scale production. For example, the socialist government of François Mitterand proposed the nationalization of some French banks (the more important ones have already been nationalized) and some key industries, such as aluminum. In France, one car company (Renault) is state-owned, but another car company (Peugeot) is not.

Most socialists would permit private individuals to own and operate small farms, stores, and repair shops. Some even contend that certain industries, operating satisfactorily under private ownership and unsuited to government ownership and operation, be left alone to function in the hands of individuals. Modern socialists thus do not adhere to ideal socialism when it comes to the right of private property ownership.

The Price System

According to many socialists, the ideal socialist system would retain money and the price system, but it would not rely on price movements and price relationships in making important economic decisions to nearly as great an extent as does a capitalist system. Decisions as to the kinds and quantities of goods, particularly public goods, would be made by the government. A major socialist criticism of the price mechanism in a market economy is that prices do not reflect nonmarket wants of the people, such as the desire for economic security. Nor can negative wants be expressed through the price mechanism.[7] Also, individuals with large sums of money can express their wants through prices and thereby channel resources to the production of goods that the mass of consumers cannot afford. Socialism would divert productive resources to satisfy basic wants of all of the people before the relatively less important wants of the few with large incomes are satisfied.

---

[7] For example, there may be a number of people whose total satisfaction would be much increased if they could prevent the publication and sale of pornographic books or the production and sale of cigarettes. They might well be glad to pay a price to obtain that satisfaction of their negative preferences if the opportunity could be given them to do so. But there seems to be no way, short of government edict, in which the market mechanism can take these negative preferences into account.

Socialism and Government

Perhaps because various noncapitalistic economic systems have so often operated under dictatorial governments, there is a tendency in popular discussion to link capitalism with democracy and to link socialism and communism with dictatorship. However, this is not the case with socialism. European social democratic parties have operated within the framework of democracy. The 1981 elections of socialist governments in France and Greece illustrate the point.

By the early 1960s, many of the European social democratic parties severed completely whatever remaining ideological ties they had with Marx and communism.[8] They abandoned their traditional opposition to private property and their goal of social ownership and turned their attention to improving the public mix of total goods and services. Thus, what have developed in Western Europe are mixed capitalist-socialist economies. When socialists come into power, the tilt is toward socialism; there is still reliance on a market economy, but also heavy government direction and planning to achieve desired social and economic objectives.

COMMUNISM

Early hints of communism can be found in Plato's *Republic*.[9] Plato's criticisms of the economic and social structure of his time led to his proposal for an ideal state. The state described in the *Republic* is a city-state, a type of political organization quite common in Greece at the time (431–351 B.C.). Among other things, Plato's ideal republic is a communist society in which all things are held in common, at least as far as the upper classes are concerned. The upper classes, or guardians of the state, eat in common dining rooms and live in common quarters, receiving their support from contributions made by the citizens at large.[10] Members of this group never consider their own personal interests but always work for the good of the whole state. To ensure their disinterest, Plato does not have any private interest, not even a private family life. However, Plato's communism was not for the masses, who were excluded from political life in his republic. Instead, it was communism of the select.

---

[8] The staunchest European supporter of President Reagan's attempts to attain military parity with the Soviet Union is the socialist president of France, François Mitterand. Even though there were communists in his government, Mitterand is in opposition to the Soviet Union, regarding it as a threat to the security of Western Europe. It is interesting to note that the massive anti-nuclear missile demonstrations against U.S. policy were held in Holland, the United Kingdom, and other European countries, but not in France. In fact, the French were busy with construction of their own nuclear warheads.

[9] In Irwin Edman, ed., *The Works of Plato* (New York: Modern Library, Inc., 1956), pp. 397–481.

[10] In Plato's republic there are three social classes, the rulers or guardians, the auxiliary guardians, and the artisans. The ruling class is selected from the auxiliary class and is composed of philosophers who have been selected after a long course of study. The artisans comprise the largest group of the republic but have little status.

Karl Marx and Das Kapital

Both modern communism and socialism began in England and were reactions against capitalism. As mentioned previously, unequal incomes, squalor, and poverty were characteristic of industrial life in England. The winds of revolution that had blown in from France had died away, and rank and privilege were firmly entrenched. The upper class was all-powerful over a tenantry for the most part unenfranchised.

Flattered, adulated, deferred to, the English aristocracy reigned supreme, with incomes enormously increased by the Industrial Revolution and as yet untaxed. The aristocracy was subject to no ordinary laws and held the government firmly in its hands. However, an entrepreneurial class had begun to emerge as a result of the Industrial Revolution, and the two classes clashed over government control. This conflict did very little to ameliorate the working conditions of the industrial masses.

This was the general economic and social milieu within which Karl Marx wrote *Das Kapital*. It is necessary to remember that Marx was a product of his time and that the activities of other persons in England, as well as in other countries, had attracted widespread attention to the problem of poverty. Marx is important because in *Das Kapital* he presented a dynamic theory of economics that still serves as the basis of much of communist dogma. The most important elements of the theory are summarized as follows.

The Marxist Theory of Income Distribution.   According to Marx, the way in which people make a living at any given time is conditioned by the nature of the existing productive forces. There are three productive forces: natural resources, capital equipment, and human resources. Since people must use these productive forces in the process of making a living, some sort of relationship between people and the productive forces is necessary. Specifically, the property relation is involved. People may own certain productive forces individually, as in a capitalist society, or they may own them collectively, as in a socialist society. Under capitalism, there were people who owned property or capital and there were people who owned only their own labor. Marx called the former the capitalists or the *bourgeoisie* and the latter the *proletariat* or the workers.

The Labor Theory of Value.   Many economists of the eighteenth and nineteenth centuries, including Adam Smith and David Ricardo, believed that labor supplied the common denominator of value.[11] Marx adopted this idea and made it the basis for his own theory of income distribution. He stated that the one thing common to all commodities is labor and that the value of a commodity is determined by the

---

[11] *Value* may be defined as the worth of a commodity or service as measured by its ability to command other goods and services in return. It is, in short, exchange value, which is the power to command exchange in the market.

amount of socially necessary labor required for its production. *Socially necessary labor*, as defined by Marx, is the amount of time necessary to produce a given product under existing average conditions of production and with the average degree of skill and intensity of labor.[12] The relative prices of two products will be in the same proportion as the amount of socially necessary labor required to produce them. If two hours of labor are required to make a pair of shoes and five hours of labor are required to build a cart, the price of shoes in the market will be two-fifths that of the cart.

The price of labor is the wage rate. The wage rate determines the income of those who own their own labor. Marx asserted that the wage rate itself is determined by the labor theory of value. How much a worker receives in income in return for working for an employer depends on how many labor hours are required to produce the necessities of life for that worker. If the necessities can be produced with five hours of labor per day, a worker can produce and be available to the employer for work if five hours wages are paid to the worker each day. Even if the worker actually works twelve hours each day for an employer, the pay will only be for five hours because that is all it takes to sustain the worker. That is all the pay can be, under a labor theory of value. In effect, Marx believed in a subsistence theory of wages in a system of market capitalism.

Theory of Surplus Value.   Although all value is created by the workers, it is expropriated by employers in the form of *surplus value*, which can be defined as the difference between the value created by the workers and the value of their labor power. When a worker sells labor power to an employer, the worker gives up all title and claim to the products of that labor. Income in the Marxist scheme is divided into two categories—surplus value, which is the source of all profit, and labor income. Value in the Marxist rubric can be expressed in the formula $C + V + S$, where C represents raw materials and capital consumption, V represents various outlays on wages, and S represents surplus value in the form of rent, interest, and profit. The C component, raw materials and capital, although clearly not labor, is explained away by Marx, who regarded it as stored-up labor from past periods. Thus the remainder, $V + S$, represents net output, which consists of the two basic income shares, wages and profit.

How much a worker gets as a wage is based on the amount of labor time socially necessary to produce subsistence or maintenance for the worker and the worker's family. Assume that this subsistence requires only five hours of socially necessary labor time for its production. If the worker worked only five hours for the employer, the worker would be fully paid and there would be no surplus value. However, it is the employer's right to set the length of the working day, and it will normally be set at a number of hours greater than that required to produce

---

[12] Karl Marx, *Das Kapital* (New York: Modern Library, Inc., 1906), pp. 198–331.

the worker's subsistence. The difference between the actual hours worked and the labor time needed for subsistence is surplus value.

The Dynamic Weaknesses of Market Capitalism.   The market distribution of income between workers and property owners was bound, according to Marx, to be a source of increasing difficulty for capitalist economies.

Crisis and Depressions.   For one thing, it would sometimes be difficult to sell the output being produced. The workers received money income enough to buy only part of the total output. This part would necessarily take the form of subsistence or consumer goods. The capitalists received the rest, an amount sufficient to buy the remainder of the output of goods and services. But would they buy it? Of course they would buy some of it to satisfy their own consumption desires. The rest they might purchase in the form of capital goods with which to carry on production and to expand productive capacity if they found such a purchase profitable. However, from time to time there would be periods of months or even years when they would not find it profitable to expand capacity. These would be periods of crisis and depression. During these times there would be sharply increased financial losses for business, unsold output, business bankruptcies, falling prices, and unemployment.

Worsening Trends.   Marx suggested that these crises and depressions would become increasingly severe. In each successive crisis, the weakest firms would disappear, being absorbed or replaced by a smaller number of larger firms. In the long run the number of firms and the number of capitalists would decline both absolutely and relative to the size of the economy and of the population. The proletariat would be absolutely and relatively enlarged.

The capitalist employers would be impelled by competition among themselves to substitute machinery or capital for labor, even though it was labor that provided surplus value and profits. The capitalists would be impelled to discover and introduce into use new technology because it would reduce the cost of subsistence needs for labor and thereby enlarge the amount of surplus value and profit. The increasingly severe crises, the substitution of capital for labor, and the introduction of new technology would create a larger and larger volume of unemployment among the workers. There would be an ever-increasing *industrial reserve army* of the unemployed.

Marx felt that the rate of profit on capital would fall continually lower, primarily because of the replacement of laborers with machines. The laborers were the source of all surplus and hence of all profits. Machines produced no surplus and, therefore, did not contribute to profits. The capitalists, desperately seeking to sustain profits, would seek ways to increase the surplus value by greater exploitation of the workers. They would resort to longer working hours, more intense work, and the employment of children.

There would be more and more severe crises, fewer and fewer capitalists, larger and larger unemployment, lower and lower profit rates, bigger and bigger amounts of unsold goods, and ever more outrageous exploitation of the workers by the capitalists. These trends would ultimately lead, in the Marxist view, to the end of market capitalism. It would be replaced with a new economic system, or rather, with a whole new society. In Marx's view, economic arrangements were causally determinant of all else in society, and capitalism's inevitable demise would mean a complete change of everything else in society.[13] Because Marx felt that the character of a society wholly depended upon its economic system, his philosophy is labeled one of *materialism*.

Economically Determined History. To reiterate, Marx contended that economic conditions were the basic causal forces shaping the nature of society. All other aspects of society—political, religious, and philosophical—depended upon the economic system of the society.

Materialism. For example, in a primitive nomad society where horses might be of particular importance in enabling the people to gather food and to exist in general, the ownership of horses would also be important to the people. Those persons who owned the horses would be able to control the others. That is, those who possessed the principal means of production would also possess the ability to rule. The religion and philosophy of the nomad society would revolve about horses and those who owned them. The patterns of marriage and inheritance would be heavily influenced by considerations regarding the use and ownership of horses.

In a society that had amassed considerable real capital and technology, the capital would be the principal means of production. The society would be organized around the existence, ownership, control, and use of the capital. Political power would reside with the owners and controllers of capital, the capitalists. Religion and philosophy would sanctify the ownership and rationalize the social dominance of the owners.

In some advanced societies with great real capital, all ownership and control might be exercised by the government. It would act on behalf of all the people. Political power would rest with all the people. A philosophy of altruism would develop among them.

In the most advanced society, so much capital and such advanced technology would exist that enough goods and services would be produced to more than com-

---

[13] A clear, entertaining, and brief explanation of Marx's theories appears in Sir Alexander Gray, *The Development of Economic Doctrine: An Introductory Survey* (New York: John Wiley & Sons, Inc., 1931), Chap. 11. A more technically difficult account, which assumes more knowledge of economic analysis, can be found in Mark Blaug, *Economic Theory in Retrospect*, rev. ed. (Homewood, Ill.: Richard D. Irwin, Inc., 1968), Chap. 7.

pletely satisfy the desires of everyone. The ownership of the means of production would cease to matter. Political control over others would cease to have significance. Interpersonal animosity, based on the covetousness of each for the material goods and services of others, would disappear. Government, no longer necessary as the instrument by which some controlled others or by which some were protected from others, would gradually wither away.

The Dialectic.   Marx's view of philosophy and history is called a *dialectic*. From the philosopher Hegel, Marx adopted the notion that everything that happened in the world could be explained by the clash of opposites. In simple terms, Hegel claimed that a proper understanding of the world could be achieved if all change were viewed as the result of clashing ideas. First, there is an idea, such as scarcity. Then there emerges an opposite idea, such as abundance. Finally, the two opposing ideas are combined into a new and superior idea, such as *economy*, which is a means to achieve abundance out of scarcity.

Marx adopted the notion of the clashing of opposites to produce a successor synthesis. However, he rejected the view that this clashing and synthesis took place basically and most significantly in the realm of ideas. Rather, according to Marx, the essentially basic and causal conflict and synthesis took place, as his philosophy of materialism suggests, in the real world of economic events, economic classes, and economic systems.

Dialectical Materialism.   Marx welded together his views of the primacy of economic arrangements and of history as progressive conflict into the doctrine of *dialectical materialism*. According to this doctrine, a society, such as that of Europe during the Middle Ages, is based on an economic system, such as manorial agriculture. A political structure, such as feudalism, and a philosophical and religious structure, such as medieval Catholicism, grow up in harmony with the economic base. There are three socioeconomic classes: landed nobility, clergy, and serfs. The economic system is successful in filling the material needs of the people. In fact, it is too successful for its own permanence.

The increasing productive ability of the manorial system makes it possible for some people to leave agriculture and become traders or craftsmen. Others have sufficient time to make economically useful discoveries and innovations. Gradually the techniques of production and other economic arrangements change. Local economic self-sufficiency decreases as trading increases. First guilds and then factory workers carry on production in place of the manorial serfs or craftsmen. There begins to grow up a new socioeconomic class made up of the shopkeeping proprietors, the factory managers and owners, and the merchant traders.

In the meantime, the political power remains, in an increasingly outmoded way, with the hereditary landed aristocracy. The religious rules grow more and more inappropriate for the economic system. For example, doctrines against usury and in favor of just prices become obsolete. Finally, the economic system and the seat of real power have changed enough that the new class, the bourgeoisie, is able to wrest political power from the landed nobility. They do so either by forceful revolution, by new laws, or by influence with the sovereign. They also reshape the religious code, perhaps by replacing Catholicism with Protestantism.

Capitalism thereby replaces feudalism. Then, because of its inherent nature, capitalism under the bourgeoisie unintentionally promotes its own replacement. Capitalism brings together the working proletariat and infuses in them a unity born of misery and exploitation. The class conflict between the proletariat and the bourgeoisie sharpens with conditions increasingly favorable to a proletarian victory. The political superstructure of government is in the hands of the bourgeoisie, who use it to perpetuate their power. However, it fails to reflect the underlying economic reality of bourgeoisie weakness and proletarian strength. Religion has been used as a device for cowing the workers, for justifying their exploitation, and for drugging them with visions of heaven so that they will accept their earthly misery. However, religion becomes more and more obviously a sham.

Eventually, the workers topple the bourgeoisie government, seize the means of production, abolish private property, and set up a socialist state under the dictatorship of the proletariat. The economic system is thus converted to socialism. Then, because all else follows from economic change, the society becomes ultimately a communist one, without government, scarcity, conflict, or classes.[14]

The Weaknesses of Marxism

What is wrong with Marx's views? Each of Marx's main ideas can be attacked on a number of grounds.

The Labor Theory of Value.   The labor theory of value, as an explanation of what determines relative prices of goods and services, is extremely vulnerable to criticism. Marx anticipated some of these criticisms and tried to deal with them.

Exceptions to the Theory.   A piece of fertile land may exist and command a high price without any human labor at all having been expended on its creation. Such nonreproducible goods, Marx said, fall in a special category. The prices or values of this category are determined without reference to amounts of labor. Then what of a durable good that was produced some time ago and for whose production a technological improvement has been discovered in the meantime? The value of such a good will fall, Marx would say, in the meantime. It is not the amount of original labor expended but the amount necessary to replace a good that is the determining variable.

---

[14] A readable account of world history, including the Industrial Revolution, as seen by a modern Marxist, is Leo Huberman, *Man's Worldly Goods: The Story of the Wealth of Nations* (New York: Monthly Review Press, 1952).

What of a unit of a good much like many other units of the same good except that it embodies a much greater amount of labor because it was turned out by a very slow, inept worker? Will it on that account be much more valuable than the other units? No, it will not, because it is the actual amount of *socially necessary* labor that determines values and prices, Marx would answer. What of a good, like a hideous piece of sculpture, on the production of which a great amount of labor has been expended but which cannot be sold for any price because no one wants it? Can it, all in all, be said to be of great value? No, Marx might answer, because labor expended on a useless product is not socially necessary labor. What of a good produced by a monopolist and sold at a high price? Is its price in proportion to the labor in it? Admittedly it is not, for monopoly may distort prices from true values.

The Problem of Diverse Kinds of Labor.   What of two goods, one of which embodies four hours of unskilled labor and the other, four hours of skilled labor? Will the two goods sell at the same price? Do they have equal value? No, in creating and determining value, one hour of skilled labor counts for more than one hour of unskilled labor. To compute value, one must convert skilled labor into unskilled labor by multiplying the number of hours of skilled labor by an appropriate conversion number. How can the appropriate number be known? It is determined, in part, by the number of hours of labor socially necessary to produce the goods and services needed to sustain the skilled laborers through the period of training. It is also determined, in part, by the number of hours required for every laborer, skilled or unskilled, to produce the goods needed to rear that person from infancy and for subsistence during working years.

Unfortunately, too many qualifications and exceptions spoil the attraction of a generalization. There is little left of the labor theory of value after all the obviously necessary modifications are taken into account. Furthermore, the modifications suggested above are incomplete. In the last case, for example, the number of labor hours necessary to sustain a worker consists itself of some hours of unskilled labor and some of skilled labor. To add the two together, a conversion number must be available. Of course, it is not available, for it is precisely what the whole procedure is set up to find.

Alternative Modern Theory.   Modern economic theory, developed since Marx, explains values or prices in terms of degree of scarcity. According to this theory, the value of a thing in exchange for something else depends on how scarce it is. Its scarcity in turn depends on the state of its supply and the state of demand for it. Behind supply and demand lie a great many interdependent determinants. The scarcity theory is a complicated one, but it provides a more satisfactory explanation than the labor theory of value. The scarcity theory treats not only labor but also capital and natural resources as productive and value-creating.

Marx's labor theory of value is weak. His use of it as a basis for attacking the capitalistic market society's distribution of income makes that attack weak.

One might still condemn market capitalism or market capitalism's distribution of income. However, one would probably do so for some reason other than because one believed that only labor had the power to create value and that all value was in proportion to labor used.

The Subsistence Theory of Wages.   Another element in Marx's theory of market capitalism is the subsistence theory of wages. Marx vacillated between two alternative explanations of this theory. One is that the wage rate will tend to fall until workers receive only enough income to provide a minimum physical existence for themselves. The other is that the wage rate will tend to fall until workers receive only enough to provide a psychologically or culturally determined minimum level of living for themselves.[15] The latter minimum might change as attitudes changed. It might vary from place to place, depending upon the attitudes prevailing in the society of each place. Marx did not give a satisfactory causal explanation of why the wage rate under market capitalism tended toward a subsistence minimum, however defined.

The Malthusian Explanation.   Marx rejected the explanation offered by such people as Thomas Malthus. Malthus had argued that any wage higher than subsistence would reduce the death rate or raise the birth rate. These changes would cause the population and the supply of labor to increase. The increase would depress the market for labor and force the wage rate down. Perhaps Marx rejected the Malthusian explanation because it seemed to place the blame on the workers or to suggest that any economic system, not just market capitalism, would produce the same undesirable result.

Lopsided Bargaining Power.   Marx did contend that the bargaining power of each individual worker would be small relative to that of a capitalist employer in the negotiations on wage rates. A worker sometimes has no real alternative, other than unemployment, to accepting a job from one accessible employer. On the other hand, most employers either can offer work to any one of a number of different workers who are competing with each other for jobs or can withhold work entirely by shutting down operations.

Critics of Marx have pointed out that, at least sometimes, workers have considerable bargaining power. Their power arises because of their unusual skills, because they band together in labor unions, because there is competition among employers for their services, or because without their labor real capital is unprofitable. Even with weak bargaining power, there is no proof that the wage rate will fall to the subsistence level.

---

[15] See Thomas Sowell, *Marxism* (New York: William Morrow & Co., Inc., 1985), pp. 136–137.

The Reserve Army of the Unemployed. Marx also contended that there usually would be substantial numbers of unemployed workers. They would always be ready to compete with those who had jobs. They would also furnish an inexhaustible supply of labor at a minimum subsistence wage rate, no matter how strong the demand for labor.

Critics of this argument emphasize that Marx never really convincingly demonstrated that capitalism creates unemployment. Indeed, if Marx were right that only labor creates surplus value and profits, capitalist employers would seek out and employ every available worker because, by so doing, profits could be maximized. Actually, real wages in countries heavily dependent upon market capitalism have risen substantially in the long run. A Marxist may choose to dismiss this evidence by claiming that it merely reflects a rising psychological minimum subsistence level. But one can reasonably rejoin that capitalism is performing well, not badly, in this respect. It has raised both aspirations and the means to fulfill them.

The Theory of Surplus Value. The theory of surplus value asserts that workers usually produce more goods and services than are needed for their subsistence. This assertion seems acceptable. It is probably equally acceptable, however, to assert that land is capable of producing more crop than that needed to reseed the land adequately in the next growing season. Likewise, a labor-saving machine may spare more labor hours than were required to make it. As the basis for an attack on market capitalism, the theory of surplus value is no attack at all unless supplemented by a labor theory of value and a subsistence theory of wages. If these latter two ideas are not valid, the theory of surplus value loses its sting for market capitalism.

Actually, land, labor, and capital cooperate in most production activities, regardless of the economic system. The complete removal of any one of these three factors would cause production to cease almost entirely. As long as they do cooperate, the productive output is usually more than enough to replace the worn equipment, maintain the natural resources, and provide for the subsistence needs of the workers. The excess may take the form either of suprasubsistence consumer goods or of capital goods that increase the society's stock of real capital.

The Theory of Crises and Trends. Another element in Marx's attack on market capitalism is the crisis or business cycle. These do occur in many forms of capitalistic economic systems. They had been the object of economists' inquiries and theories before Marx and they have continued to be afterward. Marx's explanation of them was incomplete and faulty, and we have not yet achieved a complete understanding of them. However, as a result of economic studies undertaken since the Great Depression, most economists believe that mixed economic systems can avoid severe crises and cycles by accepting rather modest government economic intervention. In any case, crises and cycles have not yet forced the complete collapse of market capitalism and its replacement with Marxist socialism or communism.

Many of the trends Marx predicted would carry capitalism to its doom have not been corroborated by subsequent history. Most striking has been the failure of the capitalist owners to become a smaller and smaller percentage of the population and the proletariat a larger and larger percentage. An increasingly greater portion of the people of Western Europe and North America possess property in the form of savings accounts, shares of corporate stock, government bonds, houses, automobiles, and durable consumer goods. The proletarian proportion of the populace has diminished as skilled white-collar and service workers have come to outnumber unskilled, manual workers.

The percentage of the labor force unemployed has not increased in the long run, as Marx predicted it would. The quality of life of the majority of the population has not become increasingly miserable. Working conditions have improved, not deteriorated, on the average at least. In the long run, the rate of profit on capital has not fallen as much as Marx predicted. Technological and social changes have provided new, profitable opportunities for the use of machinery and other capital goods. The governments of most capitalist countries have not resolutely blocked every attempt by the majority of the people to obtain legislation to improve their lot. It would be laughable to contend that for most noncommunist, developed countries the government is used as the instrument by which an increasingly small number of capitalists keep subjugated an ever more preponderant working class.

The Theory of Economic Determinism and Dialectical Materialism.   Marx's emphasis upon the economic system of a society as determinant of all else about society is also easily criticized.

Economics as Only One of Many Interdependent Forces.   The economic system is as much a result as a cause of the general character of society. Religion and philosophy, for example, help to determine economic organization. A people's religion may emphasize the evil of the accumulation of material goods and the virtue of asceticism. In consequence, the economic system is likely to remain a traditional one, and economic growth will not occur. Alternatively, religion may lay stress upon individual responsibility and upon working hard, saving much, and investing productively. As a result, the economic system is likely to become a market one with rapid change. A people's philosophy may accord great prestige to those who are very successful in military, spiritual, or governmental affairs and little prestige to those who are economically successful. Then the economic system of the people is likely to remain organized around the principle of tradition, and what modern Westerners regard as economic progress will probably be slow.

The political system of a society may place and keep in power those who wish to maintain the status quo. Then economic change will probably occur only slowly. The cultural heritage of a people may include a great accumulated stock of technological knowledge. The economic system of that people will probably be very different from that of a people with little such knowledge. The physical environment of a people is also likely to shape their economic system. The tropics may offer no challenge to traditional economic organization, which remains primitive. The arctic may offer too great a challenge, which prevents economic organization from being anything but traditional and primitive.

Monocausal Theories of History.   It is implausible that human history is simply a sequence of economic changes that bring about other changes. Such a theory of history probably deserves the same derision as every other monocausal explanation of history. For example, one other such theory is the *hero theory*, which claims that the shape of history is the result of the appearance from time to time of extremely influential people such as Plato, Jesus, Caesar, Charlemagne, Columbus, Luther, Marx, and Lenin. Another is the *idea theory*, which stresses the great historical influence of ideas such as monotheism, asceticism, altruism, capitalism, democracy, and communism. Another is the *war theory*, which claims that conflicts of arms provide the key to the understanding of history. There is also the *political theory*, which claims that history is the sequence of governments.[16]

Marx's selection of struggles between economic classes as the vehicle of historical progress is also not convincing. People generally have not thought of themselves primarily as members of an economic class, but as members of a family, an occupation, a tribe, a race, a district, or a nation, or simply as individuals. A theory of history that explains behavior as arising out of a loyalty that people do not have does not explain much.

The Merits of Marx

Marx's theory was not totally without merit. He did indicate some of the weaknesses of the market capitalism of his time and place. The inequality of income, wealth, and power of nineteenth-century European capitalism was too great to be permanently tolerated by the populace and too great by twentieth-century Western standards. Marx correctly predicted some of the trends in market capitalism. Recurrent and sometimes severe business fluctuations have taken place. Unemployment has been a persistent problem. Inordinate political and social power has accrued to the economically most successful. Control, if not ownership, has been concentrated in the hands of those who guide the great private corporations.

Marx was perhaps the first to try to explain why history had occurred as it had rather than merely to describe what had occurred. He attempted to integrate economic theory with history. He was undoubtedly one of the few of his time to do so.

---

[16] A brief elaboration of this kind of criticism of Marx can be found in William Ebenstein, *Today's Isms: Communism, Fascism, Capitalism, and Socialism*, 7th ed. (Englewood Cliffs, N.J.: Prentice-Hall Inc., 1973), Chap. 1.

Perhaps Marx's greatest achievement was as a propagandist or as an inspiration for revolution and reform. It is ironic that Marx denied the influence of ideas on history and claimed instead the ascendancy of events, because his own ideas have inspired and provoked people ever since he propounded them. Perhaps half the earth's people are either led by or want to be led by those who proclaim their allegiance to Marxism. This is not to say, of course, that the world today is markedly different than it would be had Marx never lived. It is entirely possible that events subsequent to Marx's time, such as the Russian and Chinese communist revolutions, would have taken place whether or not Marx had ever existed. People like Lenin and Mao, bent on seizing power and on changing society, are likely to pluck from the pages of previous history one name if not another to sanctify their actions and increase the probability of their success. Historical speculation aside, however, it is easy to claim for Marx that no other person did as much as he to besmirch the reputation of market capitalism.

INSTITUTIONS OF COMMUNISM

Communism, in Marxist ideology, is supposed to be the final stage of historical development. It is the end result of a classless society with the withering away of the state, and production from each according to ability and distribution to each according to need. However, modern communism is far removed from ideal or pure communism, nor can it be considered a transitory stage through which a country passes on its way to pure communism. There are variations in communism as practiced today, ranging from the bureaucratic collectivism of the Soviet Union to a supplementary market economy in Yugoslavia. All communist countries subscribe, or at least pay lip service, to Marxism-Leninism, which provides an ideological guideline for various institutional arrangements that distinguish modern communism from other economic systems.

Economic Planning

The role of economic planning in the communist countries is to allocate resources through the setting of economic targets by a central planning agency. As represented by the planning agency, the state, rather than the market mechanism, determines both output and its distribution. A rationale for central planning is the elimination of the wasteful use of resources that often occurs in a capitalist system. This waste is exemplified by planned product obsolescence, the duplication of goods and services, unnecessary product differentiation, and conspicuous consumption. Since the state has control over resource allocation in a communist system, presumably planning can make better use of resources.

The primacy of social over private preference is ensured by planning. Through the mechanism of the plan, the state is supposed to be in a better position to study social costs and benefits of resource allocation, which the market mechanism in a capitalist system cannot do. However, a weakness of planning is that prices, which are an integral part of the market mechanism under capitalism, have never been integrated into planning and do not perform a rational allocative function. This makes decision making under economic planning highly arbitrary.

State Ownership of Property

Most property is owned by the state under communism. Included under property is land and capital. Labor is in a somewhat different position. It is supposed to be the only factor of production capable of creating value. As the means of production are owned by the state, owners and workers are supposed to be the same people, so there should be no antagonism between the employer (the state) and the employees (the workers).[17]

The purpose of state ownership of property is simple. Of all of the capitalist institutions, private property ownership was regarded as being the one institution most responsible for the evils of capitalism. It was responsible for the division of society into two opposing classes—the bourgeoisie and the proletariat. The bourgeoisie controlled land and capital and exploited the workers by appropriating their surplus value. Property inheritance contributed to a widening income division between rich and poor and provided the former with unearned income. Interest and dividend payments accrued only to those few persons who had a claim on the ownership of capital.

Concentration of Power in the Communist Party

The Communist Party is supposed to represent the interests of the working class. It is the sole proprietor of political power and is involved in all phases of economic activity. For example, the election of trade union officials is usually arranged by the Communist Party, and higher union positions are mostly occupied by party members. In all factories, collective farms, military units, or organizations, the Communist Party maintains local units or cells. Under the supervision of higher party organizations, they attempt to improve the discipline and political education of the workers and spur them on to the fulfillment of planned economic goals.

Cooperation

Individualism, which is one of the basic institutions of capitalism, is replaced by cooperation. Individualism is supposed to foster acquisitive ambitions, which are contrary to the ideal of the "communist person" free of such antisocial instincts. In a communist country, the interests of the individual are subordinate to those of society. Communism has the conception of regenerated people in a regenerated

---

[17] This would make it impossible for workers to strike against the state, because they would be striking against themselves. The strikes by labor in Poland have put an end to this fiction.

society, acting in tandem with their fellow human beings rather than in competition against them. This cooperation is supposed to lead to the development of the perfect society or, as the placards say in May Day parades in communist countries, "We are building for socialism." Competition is directed toward the attainment of political and social goals. In the Olympic games, the communist countries do quite well because success in sports is one way to tout the superiority of the communist system.

SUMMARY

Although the philosophical roots of socialism and communism go back thousands of years, modern socialism and communism are products of the Industrial Revolution. Although it produced many benefits, the Industrial Revolution also had its seamy side: squalor, poor working conditions, low wages, and income insecurity. Both socialism and communism promised a new economic and social order, but they differed in degree as to how the new order would be achieved. The socialists believed in the attainment of a new society through an evolutionary process; the communists believed in class revolution, with the ultimate dictatorship of the proletariat. Socialism in the latter part of the twentieth century has come to be equated with the democratic process as socialist parties have won major elections in France and Greece. Socialists advocate nationalization of certain key industries and increased welfare measures but leave such capitalist institutions as private property and the price mechanism pretty much intact. Communism has come to mean bureaucratic collectivism with the state, as represented by the Communist Party, making the decisions concerning production and distribution of goods and services.

REVIEW QUESTIONS

1. What role did market conditions have in creating the bad conditions for the working classes of Britain in the last century?
2. What was utopian socialism?
3. Marx is said to have had an interpretation of history and explanation of social existence in his "dialectical materialism." What is dialectical materialism?
4. In the Marxist framework, what is the difference between socialism and communism?
5. What was Marx's labor theory of value? How can this theory be criticized?
6. What was Marx's theory of surplus value? Is it a valid theory?
7. What were the causes and consequences, according to Marx, of the distribution of income under market capitalism? What was Marx's theory of income distribution?

8. What are some of the institutions of modern socialism?
9. What was the difference between socialism in France today and socialism in England in the eighteenth and nineteenth centuries?

RECOMMENDED READINGS

Balinsky, Alexander. *Marx's Economics: Origin and Development*. Lexington, Mass.: D.C. Heath & Co., 1970.

Dickens, Charles. *Hard Times*. New York: Signet Books, 1962. [A novel protesting working conditions and education in 19th-century England.]

Gray, Alexander. *The Development of Economic Doctrine: An Introductory Survey*. New York: John Wiley & Sons, Inc., 1931.

Hammond, John L., and Barbara Hammond. *The Rise of Modern Industry*. New York: Harper & Row, Publishers, Inc., 1969.

Harrington, Michael. *Socialism*. New York: Monthly Review Press, 1972.

Hill, Christopher. *Reformation to Industrial Revolution*. Baltimore: Penguin Books, 1969.

Marx, Karl. *Das Kapital*. New York: Modern Library, Inc., 1906.

Taylor, Philip A.M., ed. *The Industrial Revolution in Britain: Triumph or Disaster?* Rev. ed. Lexington, Mass.: D.C. Heath & Co., 1970.

Toynbee, Arnold. *The Industrial Revolution*. Boston: Beacon Press, 1956.

Tucker, Robert C. *The Marxian Revolutionary Idea*. New York: W.W. Norton & Co., Inc., 1969.

CHAPTER FOUR

GOALS OF ECONOMIC SYSTEMS

The countries of the world can be divided into three categories: (1) the developed market economies, including the United States, Japan, Western Europe, Australia, and New Zealand; (2) the socialist economies of the Soviet Union and China; and (3) the developing and less developed countries, which are far more numerous and compose most of the world's population. Included in the last category are countries that rely on the market mechanism to allocate resources and countries that rely on central economic planning to allocate resources. An example of a country that relies on the market mechanism as a resource allocator is Taiwan, while Cuba allocates resources through central economic planning. Most less developed and developing countries have some mixture of a market and a planned economy. China, a less developed communist country, is using both economic planning and the market mechanism to allocate resources.

Figure 4-1 presents a breakdown of world gross national product and population by three categories—developed noncommunist countries, less developed noncommunist countries, and communist countries—for 1988.[1] The United States accounted for 26.1 percent of world GNP; other developed noncommunist countries accounted for 39.2 percent. The less developed noncommunist countries accounted for 12.7 percent of world GNP, and the communist countries for 22.0 percent. The United States and the other developed noncommunist countries have by far the smallest percentage of the world population, accounting for 16.8 percent of the total in 1988. The less

---

[1] The countries are referred to as communist and their economies as centrally planned socialist. Some of the previously communist countries—Hungry, Poland, and East Germany—are no longer communist; 1988 will probably be the last year for which comparisons can be made.

FIGURE 4-1
World Gross
National Prod-
uct and Popula-
tion, 1988

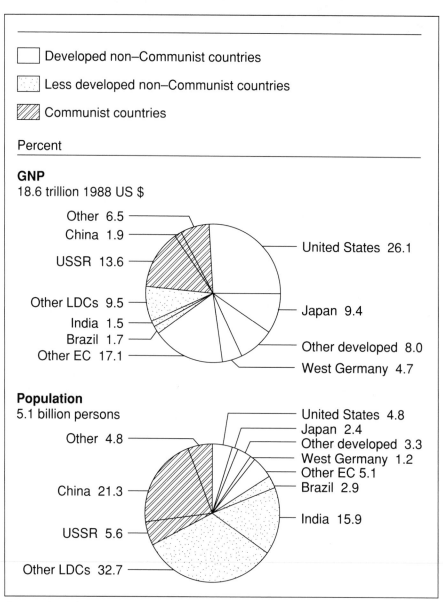

☐ Developed non–Communist countries

▦ Less developed non–Communist countries

▨ Communist countries

Percent

GNP
18.6 trillion 1988 US $

Other 6.5
China 1.9
USSR 13.6
Other LDCs 9.5
India 1.5
Brazil 1.7
Other EC 17.1

United States 26.1
Japan 9.4
Other developed 8.0
West Germany 4.7

Population
5.1 billion persons

Other 4.8
China 21.3
USSR 5.6
Other LDCs 32.7

United States 4.8
Japan 2.4
Other developed 3.3
West Germany 1.2
Other EC 5.1
Brazil 2.9
India 15.9

Source: Central Intelligence Agency, Handbook of Economic Statistics, 1989 *(Washington: USGPO, 1989), p. 12.*

developed noncommunist countries accounted for 51.5 percent, with India alone having a population almost equal to the combined totals for the developed noncommunist countries. The communist countries, including China, the largest less developed country in the world, have 31.4 percent of the world's population. When China is added to the population of the other less developed countries, the combined total is equal to 72.8 percent of the world's population.[2]

ECONOMIC GOALS

All economic systems have economic and social goals and can be evaluated on the basis of their goal attainment. These goals include maximum employment and economic security, price stability, and economic growth. To these three, a fourth goal, equitable distribution of income, may also be added. The results of production must be shared among members of society in a way that is considered just and equitable. However, no absolute standard of income distribution can satisfy everyone. In addition, noneconomic goals, such as the political freedom of the individual in society, are very important. Recent events in Poland and South Africa illustrate that, to many people, individual freedom is as important as full employment and a high rate of economic growth and should be factored into any comparison of economic systems. Social welfare goals, such as a clean environment, can also be included.

Conflicts often arise among accepted economic and social goals, so that choices and tradeoffs are necessary at the most general policy levels. For example, there can be a conflict between the reduction of income inequality and reduction of incentives to work. There can be a conflict between economic growth and protection of the environment. The opportunity cost of production can also be expressed as a tradeoff—how much of one good or service must be given up to gain a certain quantity of another good or service. Resources are limited in any society, and choices must be made as to what can be produced.

MAXIMUM EMPLOYMENT AND ECONOMIC SECURITY

The Depression of the 1930s led most Western countries to assume national responsibility for the human tragedy and economic waste of involuntary unemployment. Unemployment had previously been regarded as almost solely the responsibility of the individual, who was to look out for himself or herself within the market mechanism. Unemployment carried with it economic insecurity because family savings vanished when it was prolonged. Poverty was also an end result of unemployment. Moreover, unemployment was the *bete noire* of capitalism, the situation that Marx predicted would bring down capitalism. Capitalist countries had a vested interest

---

[2] In Chapter 16 a distinction will be made between less developed and developing countries. Brazil is a developing country, but China and India are less developed countries.

in the amelioration of unemployment, for it carried with it the potential for social unrest.

Economic security involves more than just having a job. The Western countries decided that they could not in good conscience permit their citizens to be inadequately nourished, clothed, or housed; their sick to be denied medical care; or their young to be deprived of schooling. Unemployment insurance and public assistance recognize this social obligation. This protection can assume many forms. Old-age pensions benefit those who have retired from work, many of whom have been unable to accumulate sufficient savings during their working lives to support them when they retire. Family allowances benefit families who have children and reduce the cost of their maintenance. Housing allowances and food programs generally benefit low-income families. Workers' compensation provides income for those workers injured on the job. National health insurance, which most countries have, protects workers against the cost of major illnesses.

One way to compare different economic systems is on the basis of how well they protect their citizens from economic insecurity. A supposed strength of socialist countries is that, through central planning, unemployment is eliminated. At first glance, the capitalist countries suffer by comparison. The unemployment rate in the United States in the fourth quarter of 1989 was 5.3 percent; in the United Kingdom, 5.9 percent. Conversely, there is full employment in the Soviet Union and the other socialist countries. However, a *caveat* is in order. There are many ways to disguise unemployment. The military is one way to create employment for many youths. There is also underemployment of labor, with workers in jobs that require little or no skills.

PRICE STABILITY

Price stability is another economic goal. Inflation results in arbitrary and regressive changes in the distribution of wealth and income. It retards economic growth by diverting resources and energy from the production of goods and services to attempts by both businesses and individuals to lessen the impact of inflation on their own economic positions.

Attempts to protect individual positions from the effects of inflation can give rise to social, economic, and political strife just as quickly as mass unemployment can.[3] In fact, inflation is probably a greater evil today than mass unemployment. Countries such as Argentina, Israel, and Mexico have experienced price-level increases greater than 200 percent a year. These price increases are not only bad for

---

[3] The rate of inflation in Argentina increased at an annual rate of 1,010 percent during the 1980s. In 1985, Argentina issued a new national currency called the *austral*. To maintain its value, the government vowed that it would no longer print money to cover expenses. A similar chain of events happened in Germany in 1923. Inflation reached astronomical proportions and contributed to social unrest. The German government issued a new currency with a new value.

domestic economics, but also contributed to balance-of-payments problems because the price increases are greater than those experienced by other countries.

In a modern economy, the government actively tries to regulate the money supply, either through its treasury or its central bank. One frequent cause of inflation, therefore, is government monetary policy itself. For one reason or another, the state may wish to increase the money supply. A government's own fiscal deficit is one common reason. Thus, a period of high government spending, like a war, is almost always a period of inflation. In themselves, of course, government deficits are not always inflationary. When resources are idle, a governmental deficit can stimulate an economy without fostering inflation. If taxes do not cover expenditures, the government may borrow all the funds it needs from the existing pool of savings in the domestic capital market. The borrowed funds are thereby used for government spending rather than private purposes. If the supply of savings is adequate to satisfy the borrowing needs of both government and private borrowers, inflation does not occur.[4] Deficits create inflation when central banks regularly create extra money to cover them.

Social and Political Consequences of Inflation

The impact of inflation is felt unevenly by different groups in an economy. One of the social consequences of inflation is the redistribution of income and wealth among economic groups. Debtors as a group fare well during inflation because they are not only in a better position to repay their debts, but also to pay them in money whose purchasing power is lower than when they borrowed. Creditors, on the other hand, stand to lose since they receive less in real terms than if they had received the repayments during a period of low prices. Those on fixed incomes usually lose during a period of inflation in that their real income declines while the cost of living increases. Wealth in the form of savings accounts, bonds, and cash drops in real value when prices rise, but wealth held in the form of property or common stocks will generally increase when prices rise.

Inflation became a problem during the 1970s in the Western countries for several reasons. One reason was the burgeoning spending policies of Western governments.[5] Keynesian economics has a built-in inflationary bias. An emphasis on full-employment policies led Western governments to stimulate aggregate demand whenever there was an economic downturn. This led to expectations on the part of both business firms and unions that an increase in government spending would always bail out an economy from a recession. Keynesian demand management that smoothes out the business cycle also eliminates many of the incentives for

---

[4] Japan has a larger deficit in its budget than does the United States. However, the pool of saving is much larger in Japan than in the United States and interest rates are lower. Inflation has been lower in Japan than in the United States.

[5] Another was the rise in oil prices during 1973 and 1974.

business and labor to be efficient. An economic policy that mitigates the effect of the business cycle can also reduce its benefits. Providing full employment without inflationary fiscal and monetary policies became a problem that governments found more difficult to resolve.

Inflation and Balance of Payments Problems

Inflation has both an internal and external effect on a country's balance of payments. Internal inflation can cause domestic products to become more expensive than imported products. Exports decrease and imports increase, which creates a deficit in the balance of payments and a loss of foreign exchange reserves. If this continues to happen, it becomes less likely that a country can continue to convert its own currency into foreign currencies. Inflation also encourages capital outflows. The result is the imposition of austerity measures including anti-inflation monetary policy, policies to restrict imports, and price increases or currency devaluation. Devaluation is a downward adjustment of a currency's official par value or exchange rate relative to other currencies. Protection of domestic industries by tariffs and other restrictions on imports can also be used to correct balance of payments problems.

The problem of price stability is different in a centrally planned economy because pricing is not merely a question of economics but also of ideology and politics. Pricing policy is the responsibility of the government through various administrative agencies. Prices are determined within the framework of important economic and social goals. For example, prices for food and other necessities are kept low for consumers through government subsidies. Wages are also regulated by the government, so on an *a priori* basis it would appear that inflation is impossible. In reality, centrally planned economies are not immune to inflation. For one thing, the prices of consumer goods are not indicative of their value. In Poland, for example, almost half of government budget expenditures were committed to subsidizing food prices at a low level. Inflation is suppressed because the price of food is set below its value. The suppressed inflation is demonstrated in the long lines of people waiting to purchase the limited supply.

ECONOMIC GROWTH

Economic growth can be defined most simply and directly as the expansion of a nation's capability to produce the goods and services its people want. It is the measure of the rate of increase in an economy's real output or income over time. Continued increases in the output of goods and services form the basis for an increase in the standard of living for families and individuals in a society. Moreover, it is not difficult to reconcile the goals of maximum employment and economic security with economic growth, for the latter is necessary to absorb new entrants into the labor force and to accommodate workers who become unemployed because of changes in technology. Rising levels of output are also needed to improve the social well-being of society. If a nation does not have economic growth, it will not be able to obtain the resources to expand its schools, medical care, hospitals, and other things it needs. A dynamic, expanding economy eases the social and economic transitions required by a society that is experiencing technological change and that demands social improvements.

The heart of all modern industrial societies, capitalist or socialist, is the ability to set aside a portion of total output for savings and capital formation—fundamental requisites for economic growth. Economic growth has become important to both the developed and developing countries as the source of individual motivation, the basis of political solidarity, and the grounds for the motivation of a society for a common purpose, namely, the promise of a better life for all of its citizens.

Economic Growth in a Market Economy

Recall the process by which economic growth is brought about in a market economy. The basic decisions regarding growth are made by individual households and businesses. Each of these individual units decides such things as how much to save, how much to invest, how much education to purchase, and how much research and exploration to undertake on the basis of a comparison of the benefits and costs of these activities. For example, in a market economy each business firm decides for itself the amount of research it will undertake. It does this on the basis of the marginal cost and benefits of the research. The main cost is the expense of the research. The main benefit is the greater profit from reduced costs for existing production or from new products that provide an advantage over competitors and enable profits to be larger.

Saving is a prime requisite for economic growth, for without it there would be no capital formation. In a market economy, decisions to save are made by households out of their disposable incomes. There is a cost in saving: the sacrifice of the goods and services a household could buy and enjoy now if it did not save. The principal benefit to a household from saving is the goods and services it will be able to enjoy in the future as well as the earnings from savings. In a market economy, savings are transmitted through financial institutions and loaned to business firms. The firms use the borrowed funds to purchase the use of resources to create capital goods. The capital goods so created make possible thereafter a larger real output and real gross national product.

The Role of Government in Economic Growth

In the market economies, government policies have come to play a strong role in the process of economic growth. Fiscal policy measures can be directed toward influencing the level of aggregate demand so as to bring it into line with an economy's changing productive capacity. Government expenditures, transfers, and taxes can also operate on the supply side and thus influence productive capacity.

For example, government tax policy can be used to increase the rate of saving.[6] Government expenditures on improving the health, education, and training of the labor force also have an impact on economic growth, as do expenditures on research and development. In the less developed countries, governments also have to participate directly in the formation of capital because the rate of saving is low; the market system is ineffective and the entrepreneurial class, undeveloped.

Economic Growth in a Centrally Planned Economy

In a centrally planned economy, the state is the prime determinant of economic growth. The economic plan determines the rate of economic growth to be achieved, as well as the allocation of resources to the attainment of that rate. Saving is done by the state by controlling the amount of resources allocated to consumption. This is, in effect, forced saving in that consumers must do with less so that resources can be diverted into capital formation. The planned economy has an advantage over a market economy when it comes to the goal of a high growth rate: The state can allocate resources into areas that contribute to high growth rates. Economic growth is never allowed to be hampered by a lack of money. If there are physical resources available and if the production has priority under the economic plan, the means of financing will be available. Figure 4-2 presents trends in real economic growth in the same three categories presented earlier in this chapter.

INCOME DISTRIBUTION

It was mentioned in Chapter 2 that most governments have become involved in altering the distribution of market resources both directly and indirectly. This represents a departure from the free market idea that an individual's income is determined by the impersonal forces of supply and demand operating in the marketplace. However, this idea had to be modified because it was easy to see that large incomes accrued to some persons not on the basis of their contribution to total output, but through inherited wealth or other accidents of birth or through the exercise of special privileges. Moreover, capricious economic and social changes often worked hardships on even the most productive persons. The result of free market capitalism was extreme inequality in the distribution of income and wealth. This inequality has been reduced over time by government use of progressive income and inheritance taxes and by transfer payments to redistribute income.

Equity in Income Distribution

The issue of equity concerns the disparities in income distribution among people and the role of the government in reducing these disparities or at least containing

---

[6] The Individual Retirement Accounts (IRAs) were a good example. People were allowed to defer the income tax on income of up to $2,000 per year for individuals and $2,250 for married couples ($4,000 if both work) if they put their money in IRA accounts.

FIGURE 4-2
Real Gross
National
Product Trends
1961–1988

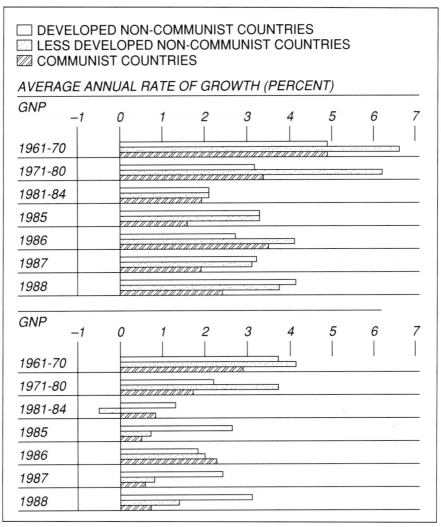

Source: Central Intelligence Agency, Handbook of Economic Statistics, 1989 (Washington: USGPO, 1989), p. 12.

their undue influence. However, we cannot insist that perfect equality in the distribution of income and wealth would be necessary for the existence of an economic optimum. There is no objective way to compare satisfaction or utility between persons.[7] There is also no way to measure aggregate satisfaction for the whole

[7] The theory of utility analysis assumes that a person's additional satisfaction or marginal utility grows less as he or she consumes more and more units of the same product. It also holds that the marginal utility for a rich person is less than that for a poor person. For example, a rich person would assign less additional satisfaction to consuming another steak than would a poor person. However, it is not valid to compare the utility that two different individuals receive from the same good or service.

population of an economy because of differences among individuals in their capacities to experience satisfaction. The assumption that all individuals have equal capacities for satisfaction cannot be proven scientifically. Thus, it is necessary to know more about the psychological basis of human wants before a given condition can be considered an economic optimum. To what extent is it possible for income to measure the magnitude of human needs and wants?

Income Distribution Under Socialism

Income distribution under socialism refers to the allocation of national income by distributive shares, primarily in the form of wages paid to workers. Interest does figure in the national income to some extent, since a part of the income received by individual producers may be considered a return on the relatively small amounts of capital they own. Interest is also used as a device to encourage personal savings, which is regarded as necessary to put a brake on excess consumer demand, and there are interest-rate differentials in favor of long-term deposits. Profits, which are distributed in the form of dividends or retained by corporate shareholders in a capitalist system, occupy a different role under socialism. They are used as a criterion of enterprise performance and, up to a point, of the efficiency of production.

Income distribution is determined by the state within the framework of the economic plan. The total amount of wages to be paid depends on the division of the national income between accumulation and consumption, and further, the division of consumption between the social consumption fund and the wage fund. The total wage fund is partitioned into wage funds for all economic fields. In its economic planning, the state is able to determine the total wages for the economy by multiplying the planned number of workers by the wage rates it has set. Wages are changed as seems necessary to achieve government policy and particular production ends. For example, in order to attract more workers to a given industry, the wages it pays may be raised while other wages remain constant or are allowed to decline. Direct pressure from workers would in general have little or no effect on wage determination.

FREEDOM AND THE INDIVIDUAL

In Western society over the last 200 years, the individual has assumed precedence over the state. Before this time, the king, lord, or any ruler had precedence over the individual. The individual ethic is also the ethic of personal freedom. Individual freedom means minimizing the obligations society imposes on the individual. Beginning with the Industrial Revolution, the private individual's economic interest in accumulation was pursued in the market, and the enhancement of self-interest became the free choice of a personal life-style. This was linked to the concept of freedom—to be free from the ties of community or state; to be responsible for oneself; and to handle one's life in accordance with one's ambition and personal merit.

Rationale for Personal Freedom

The idea of personal liberty as an individual right is a relatively new phenomenon. It was not a part of the legal conceptions of the Romans and Greeks; this seems also to hold true of the Jewish, Chinese, and other ancient civilizations. The dominance of the ideal of personal liberty has been the exception rather than the rule, even in the West. The desire not to be impinged upon, to be left to oneself, has become a mark of high civilization in Western society. The freedom to live and to do as one prefers is supported by a number of economic and philosophical justifications. For Adam Smith, an economic system in which each individual pursued his or her own self-interest was the basis for freedom, self-satisfaction, and mutual advantage. When rationally pursued through the division of labor, it became the basis for the accumulation of wealth. Smith insisted that social well-being is the outcome of individual activity and that individual activity becomes greater the less it is hampered by government interference.

The philosopher John Locke held that individuals have a ready-made body of rights that are the responsibility of government to preserve. The primary assumption of Locke's argument is that the liberty of the individual is at variance with the government. Also central to Locke's philosophy was the doctrine of individual property rights. In Locke's view, property was the extension of an individual's labor and should be protected against exploitation by others. He wrote a defense of the right of persons who own property to enjoy its fruits without constant interference from the arbitrary actions of government. For Locke, freedom from the arbitrary actions of government, above all, was the postulate from which liberty arises.

Capitalism and Democracy

Democracy is a socio-political system in which legitimacy lies in the consent of the governed, where the political arena is available to various contending groups, and where fundamental liberties are safeguarded. The beginnings of the idea of democracy are associated with the city-states of ancient Greece. Greek democracy was direct in that all of the male citizens of a city-state formed the legislature and had the right to vote.[8] After the decline of the Greek city-state, democracy went into a period of eclipse for about 2,000 years, only to be revived by the American and French revolutions. Both gave rise to ideas and institutions that did much to determine the distinctive characteristics of modern democratic governments. The basic organ of government is the representative legislature or parliament. Their underlying ethical basis is the conception that all persons are created equal and

---

[8] Women were disenfranchised and there was a large class of slaves who enjoyed no rights at all. Ancient Greek democracy was not only compatible with slavery, it presupposed slavery, which alone permitted the necessary leisure for the citizens to devote themselves to public affairs. It recognized the equality of all male citizens, but failed to develop a general conception of the equality of all mankind.

that governments exist for the purpose of protecting people in the exercise of certain basic rights.

Although capitalism and modern democracy historically have risen together and have been commonly justified by philosophical liberalism, there is nothing that makes it theoretically or practically necessary for the two to be yoked.[9] Actually, the government of a capitalist system does not have to be democratic in the strict sense of the term, which would presumably involve direct and equal participation in the government by all citizens. In a large and heavily populated capitalistic system, it would be impossible for all citizens to participate directly in the government. In modern society, the political system has become increasingly autonomous, and fiscal management has become increasingly independent of capitalism. However, the government of a capitalist system could scarcely be a dictatorship, for it is difficult to imagine a dictatorial government that would not restrict economic life to an extent that would be inconsistent with the operation of capitalist institutions.

Individual Freedom in the Modern Democracies

The United States, Canada, and the countries of Western Europe are all democracies. Japan, Australia, and New Zealand can be added to them. These countries have free elections and have two or more political parties that compete for elective offices. They guarantee certain rights to their citizens. One is the freedom to live as one prefers. The sense of privacy is regarded as sacred, for it guards against the tyranny of the community. Freedom of speech is a second right. It means that the state, or for that matter individuals, cannot restrict people either in the views they hold or the views they express. A third right is freedom of the press, which is regarded as one of the great bulwarks of liberty.[10] This freedom preserves the people's right to know and to be informed. Freedom of religion is a fourth right. In most modern democracies there is a separation of church and state. Some of the democratic countries have one religion;[11] others, such as the United States, have a variety of religions, all of which are tolerated. There is also the right not to participate.

Individual Freedom Under Socialism

The relationship between the individual and the state is different in the socialist countries. To put it simply, the individual is subservient to the interests of the

---

[9] France is a democracy with a socialist government, with a mixture of public and private enterprise.
[10] The Virginia Bill of Rights states that the freedom of the press is one of the great bulwarks of liberty and can never be restrained but by despotic governments.
[11] Sweden is an example; 99 percent of its citizens are Lutheran. Italy, on the other hand, is a Catholic country.

state. Power is concentrated in the communist party, which is supposed to represent the working classes. The system of government is based on monoparty rule. No opposition parties are allowed unless the party permits some form of opposition. Elections are held to ratify the choices that the party makes. It provides the continuity of economic policy and it makes overall value judgments. For example, any outside influence, particularly something like rock music, is considered decadent.

The fundamental freedoms that individuals take for granted in democracies either do not exist or exist in varying degrees in the socialist countries. Freedom of the press does not exist, for the press is the mouthpiece of the state. The press may criticize or report negatively on some result of party action, but it rarely criticizes the party itself. There is no freedom of speech, at least in public.[12] Freedom of religion varies from country to country. In the Soviet Union, religion is at best tolerated. The freedom to live as one prefers is a rather limited option in the socialist countries. The state, as represented by the party, attempts to impose a common direction, from economics to culture, on everyone.

SOCIAL GOALS

There are certain social costs that result from the operation of any industry or business. The operation of a business may be injurious to the health of its workers. It may discharge wastes that pollute streams and kill fish, or it may emit smoke, soot, and grime that will be costly to its neighbors in a number of ways. Consumption of certain products can also increase social costs. Excessive alcohol consumption results in job absenteeism and a loss of productivity that is a disadvantage to society. If production decisions are based solely on the relationship of prices and costs in the market, many goods may be produced and sold that would not be produced if their prices included the full social costs of production.[13] The production of alcohol and cigarettes is an example.

The Environment

The quality of the environment has emerged as one of the more important economic and social issues of this century. It is common to all advanced industrial countries, regardless of their ideologies. In the Soviet Union, inadequately treated industrial effluents have polluted rivers and lakes. In Poland, the Vistula river is polluted, and Warsaw was recently without water for several days because a chemical plant dumped mercury into it. Unlike the famous waltz of Johann Strauss, "The Blue

---

[12] Private speech is another matter. The author heard much criticism of the Polish economy, its leaders, and the Russians from a number of Poles when he was in Poland.

[13] The costs to society are not created by business alone. Increasing urbanization creates social costs. The desire for higher living standards creates social costs.

Danube," the Danube is not blue, but a dirty brown at Budapest and Vienna. Of all the major industrial countries, given its small land area and crowded cities, Japan has had the worst pollution problem. In West Germany, the famous Black Forest is in danger of being destroyed by cars' exhaust fumes.

The desire for a clean environment represents an extension of human wants, it increases as a country's standard of living increases. Poor countries cannot afford the luxury of being concerned about clean air, clean water, and the preservation of the snail darter. Both money and real incomes are low, and people are interested only in physiological survival. Food and shelter constitute their main demands. As countries become wealthier, the wants of their citizens are upgraded toward more and better goods and services. Physiological survival is no longer a main concern. Meanwhile, pollution increases along with a rising real standard of living. It represents a blockage that causes various needs to remain unsatisfied, such as the need for clean recreational facilities. People cannot achieve a higher real standard of living unless something can be done about the condition of the environment.

Consumer Welfare

In a capitalist economy, consumer sovereignty is an important institution because consumption is the basic rationale for economic activity. As Adam Smith said, "Consumption is the sole end and purpose of all production; and the interest of the producer ought to be attended to only as far as it is necessary for promoting that of the consumer."[14] Production is the means; consumption is the end. Producers that effectively satisfy the wants of the consumers are rewarded by large monetary returns, which in turn enable them to purchase the goods and services they require in their operations. On the other hand, those producers that do not respond to the wants of consumers will not remain in business for very long. Supply and demand will shift in response to the way in which consumers spend their money.

Consumer welfare under capitalism is subject to several criticisms. First, producers take the initiative to increase the volume and variety of consumer goods.[15] Are consumers better off with a proliferation of breakfast cereals or is it a waste of scarce resources?[16] Second, producers use sophisticated marketing methods, including advertising, that influence the consumer's choice of goods. Marketing people argue that the purpose of advertising is to provide product information for the consumer. But it also can be argued that the purpose of advertising is to entice consumers into buying products that, for the most part, they do not

[14] Adam Smith, *The Wealth of Nations* (Indianapolis: Liberty Classics, 1981), p. 660.

[15] Henry Ford revolutionized the automobile industry with the production of the Model T. It came in one style and one color (black), and it was cheap and durable. General Motors came along with planned obsolescence, with new models and style changes every year. The purpose was to make the consumer unhappy with his or her car, even though it was perfectly good.

[16] Do sugar-laden cereals and other breakfast foods with exotic names really contribute to consumer welfare?

need or that could even prove injurious to their health.[17] Third, the market and price mechanism never ask consumers to specify for which commodities and services they would like the scarce resources of society used. Consumers are not totally passive, however; they can exercise a considerable degree of selectivity despite the persistent advertising aimed at them. So there is some freedom of choice, though it is limited to the range of available alternatives.

In a planned socialist economy, consumer sovereignty hardly exists. The state reduces choice to a minimum by presenting only a narrow and biased range of alternatives. There is one major advantage to state control over consumption: Resources are not wasted on the production of a wide variety of frivolous goods that are not necessary to basic survival. However, there are also disadvantages. First, in the absence of the price mechanism to allocate resources in a market economy, the production of goods in a socialist economy is often arbitrary. The result is that often some goods are overproduced and others underproduced. Queueing up to purchase consumer goods is a common phenomenon in many socialist countries. Second, in the absence of competition between producers, there is no incentive to be efficient. Many consumer goods are poorly made, and consumer welfare is not maximized.

Education and Health

Improved education and health are important goals in any society because they both have an impact on the development of human capital. Human capital is the productive power of individuals and is developed through expenditures for education and health care. Society as a whole depends on educated people to carry on the research and development leading to new products and new processes that raise the nation's standard of living. How productive people are and how much they earn affects a society's rate of economic growth and its distribution of income. Health, both physical and mental, is also important in that it affects the quantity and quality of the labor force in a society. Poor health standards will lower labor's capacity to produce; excellent health standards will increase labor productivity.

Table 4-1 presents a comparison of education indicators for three categories of selected countries: less developed countries, developed countries, and communist countries. Many countries, such as Brazil and Mexico, are considered developing countries and are not included in the table. Sudan and Chad are among the poorest countries in the world. The level of human capital is low because few persons have an education above primary school level. China, which is also a less developed country but a communist one, would also have low human capital. The more developed capitalistic and communist countries have higher quality human capital because a large percentage of their population has had a secondary school or

---

[17] A very good example is cigarette smoking. Many young people begin smoking cigarettes because advertising makes it appear sophisticated and grown up.

TABLE 4-1

A Comparison of Education Indicators for Selected Countries[a]

Country	Primary School	Secondary School	Higher School
Less developed			
Haiti	88%	18%	1%
India	92	35	9
Sudan	49	19	2
Parkistan	47	17	5
Chad	38	6	1
Developed			
Italy	100%	75%	26%
United Kingdom	100	89	22
Japan	100	96	30
France	100	90	30
West Germany	100	74	30
United States	100	97	57
Communist			
Hungary[b]	100%	72%	15%
Poland[b]	100	78	17
East Germany[b]	96	79	30
Cuba	100	85	21
China	100	39	2
Soviet Union	100	99	21

[a] Number of students enrolled as a percentage of age group.
[b] Hungary, Poland, and East Germany are no longer communist.
Source: The World Bank, World Development Report 1988, *pp. 280–281.*

higher education. The table does not, however, compare the quality of education, which varies from country to country. Japan is regarded by many experts as having the best educational system in the world.

Table 4-2 presents a comparison of health-related indicators for the same selected less developed countries, developed countries, and communist countries. The number of physicians and nurses relative to the size of the population is very low in the less developed countries, and the daily calorie intake is below the normal requirement. In the developed market countries and communist countries, the health-related indicators indicate that both types of countries are adequately served by physicians and nurses, and the daily calorie supply per capita is above the normal daily requirement. The table does not indicate the quality of medical service or the number of hospitals available for the population. In the great majority of countries, medical care is either provided free as a part of a national health plan, or there is some form of shared payment by the government and the patient.

TABLE 4-2

A Comparison of Health-Related Indicators for Selected Countries

| Country | Population per Healthcare Worker | | Daily per Capita Calorie Intake | |
	Physician	Nurse	Total	Percentage of Daily Requirement
Less developed				
Haiti	9,200	2,490	1,903	84%
India	3,700	4,670	2,047	93
Sudan	9,800	1,440	2,250	96
Pakistan	2,910	5,870	2,277	99
Chad	47,640	3,860	1,620	68
Developed				
Italy	340	250	3,520	140%
United Kingdom	650	120	3,232	128
Japan	780	210	2,891	124
France	580	110	3,572	142
West Germany	450	170	3,382	127
United States	520	180	3,616	137
Communist				
Hungary[a]	400	160	3,520	134%
Poland[a]	570	230	3,288	126
East Germany[a]	520	180	3,787	145
Cuba	720	370	2,997	130
China	1,740	1,670	2,562	110
Soviet Union	270	100	3,400	132

[a] Hungary, Poland, and East Germany are no longer communist countries.

Source: The World Bank, World Development Report 1988, *pp. 278–279.*

SUMMARY

Both capitalist and socialist economies have specific economic and social goals and can be judged on the basis of how those goals are fulfilled. There are three major economic goals: full employment, price stability, and economic growth. These goals cannot be precisely defined and the attainment of one may not necessarily lead to the attainment of the others. Another goal is an equitable distribution of income. This goal, too, does not lend itself to a precise definition. What is the right degree of income inequality? Considerable government intervention is an indispensable requisite for the attainment of all of these goals. In the capitalist countries, the government coordinates the direction of economic policy and participates in the economy through expenditures that affect the allocation of resources and through the use of taxation and transfer payments to redistribute income. In socialist countries, the state is the employer and distributor of income.

There are also other goals that should be considered in comparing economic systems. One is individual rights and freedom. In some countries, democracy has become the prevailing socio-political system. There are certain guarantees of individual rights that democracy carries with it, such as freedom of speech, freedom of religion, and freedom of the press. The relationship between the individual and the state is different in socialist countries—the rights of the individual are subservient to the interests of the state.

Finally, there are social goals that can be used in comparing economic systems. These goals center around what can be referred to as the quality of life. A very important problem that confronts all industrial societies today, regardless of their ideology, is pollution of the environment.

REVIEW QUESTIONS

1. Democracy could exist only in a capitalistic country. Do you agree?
2. Capitalist and socialist countries have similar economic goals. Discuss.
3. Centrally planned economies generally do a better job of creating full employment than market economies. Discuss.
4. Do socialist countries have more equality in the distribution of income than capitalist countries?
5. The concept of individual freedom is relatively new. Discuss.
6. What is the philosophical justification for freedom of the individual in a capitalist society?
7. What is the relationship of the individual to the state in a socialist economy?
8. Compare the role of the consumer in market and centrally planned economies.
9. How is income distributed in a centrally planned economy?
10. Why are environmental problems of importance in comparing capitalism and socialism?

RECOMMENDED READINGS

Bell, Daniel. *The Cultural Contradictions of Capitalism*. New York: Basic Books, Publishers, 1976.

Blinder, Alan S. *Hard Heads, Soft Hearts*. Reading, Mass.: Addison-Wesley Publishing Co., 1987.

Brittain, John H. *The Inheritance of Economic Status*. Washington: Brookings Institution, 1978.

Kennedy, Paul. *The Rise & Fall of the Great Powers*. New York: Random House, 1987.

Locke, John. *The Second Treatise of Government*. Edited by C. B. Macphearson. Indianapolis: Hackett Publishing Co., 1980.

North, Douglas C. *Structure and Change in Economic History*. New York: W. W. Norton & Co., 1982.

Nozeck, Robert. *Anarchy, State, and Utopia*. New York: Basic Books, Publishers, 1974.

Okun, Arthur. *Equality and Efficiency: The Big Tradeoff*. Washington: Brookings Institution, 1976.

Olson, Mancur. *The Rise and Decline of Nations*. New Haven, Conn.: Yale University Press, 1982.

Wiles, Peter J. D. *Distribution of Income: East and West*. Amsterdam: North-Holland Publishing Co., 1974.

Williamson, Jeffrey, and Peter Lindert. *American Inequality*. New York: Academic Press, 1981.

THE MODIFIED MARKET ECONOMY OF THE UNITED STATES

5
THE ECONOMIC SYSTEM OF THE
UNITED STATES

6
AN APPRAISAL OF THE UNITED STATES
ECONOMY

PART TWO

CHAPTER FIVE

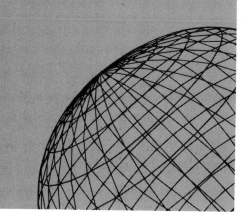

THE ECONOMIC SYSTEM OF THE UNITED STATES

The American economic system is dominated by three major institutions—business, labor, and government. Although upon the market mechanism allocates resources, it cannot be said that the United States conforms to the model of a pure market economy. Instead, the rules of the game have been modified over time as various groups or individuals sought protection against the results of a free market economy. Many changes have occurred over time to supplement and modify the effects of the market mechanism so that the consequences are not what they would be with a free market system. Thus, it is more appropriate to call the United States a modified market economy in which the role of government is of considerable importance.

One part of the institutional arrangement is the large corporation. The original impetus for the emergence of the large corporation was partly technological—economies of scale become available with bigness—and partly monopolistic—bigness provides control over markets and over rivals. These large corporations helped to modify the market system. Moreover, large corporations have also been in part responsible for the development of the two other institutions that have also served to modify the market mechanism—labor unions and big government. Both of these have become major features of the U.S. economic system as well as other countries still relying heavily on the market system. Both have become major means to counteract some of the undesirable results of large business firms and to mitigate some of the undesirable effects of a pure market system.

Of the two, government is by far the more important institution. It has intervened in the U.S. economy in several ways: to redistribute income between groups through taxes and transfer payments, to manage the economy through fiscal and monetary policy, and to protect various special interest groups against such things as discrimination and foreign competition.

LARGE CORPORATIONS

The concentration of industry in the hands of a few firms is a fact of life in the United States and other major industrial countries, regardless of their political ideology. The trend toward industrial concentration in the United States began in the last century, when many industries came to be dominated by a few relatively large firms or even by only one firm. In the 1920s largeness was stimulated by changes occurring in the economy as a whole, in particular the mass production of the automobile and the development of the electrical appliance and broadcasting industries. General Motors became the leader in the automobile industry through a series of mergers with other auto firms. Size became an advantage when using modern marketing and production methods.

World War II contributed to the trend toward largeness. The industrial might of the United States was probably the decisive factor in contributing to the Allied victory over the Axis powers. Large corporations produced the airplanes and tanks used by the United States and its allies in the war.[1] During the 1960s and 1970s the trend toward largeness was facilitated by the development of a new type of merger called the *conglomerate* merger, a union of disparate companies.

Concentration by Firm Size

Table 5-1 presents payrolls, value added by manufacturing, and capital expenditures for a distribution of firms based on number of employees. The data are for 1982. Firms employing 1,000 or more workers accounted for 0.6 percent of all firms, but accounted for 25.2 percent of total employment in manufacturing, 33.1 percent of

TABLE 5-1
Distribution of Industry in the United States by Employment Size for 1982 (establishments and employees in thousands; money in millions of dollars)

	Employment Size					
	Total	**Under 20**	**20–99**	**100–249**	**250–999**	**1,000 and over**
Establishments	348	230	84	21	1	2
Employees	17,818	1,405	3,662	3,287	4,977	4,486
Payroll	341,406	20,404	59,103	55,708	93,125	113,068
Value added by manufacturing	842,117	45,997	135,932	134,379	247,729	260,081
New capital expenditures	74,562	3,639	9,469	12,323	23,331	25,800

Source: U.S. Department of Commerce, Bureau of the Census, 1982 Census of Manufactures: General Summary (Washington: USGPO, 1986), pp. 1–3.

[1] The author saw some old destroyed Sherman tanks rusting on a farm in Poland. They represented part of the thousands of tanks sent by the United States to the Soviet Union in World War II.

total value of payrolls, 31.5 percent of value added by manufacturing, and 34.6 percent of new capital expenditures. However, these percentages show a decline when compared to statistics for 1977. The respective percentages for 1977 were as follows: employment in manufacturing, 28 percent; total value of payrolls, 35.4 percent; value added by manufacturing, 34.2 percent; new capital expenditures, 35.8 percent. However, it can be said that approximately 2 percent of all industrial firms in the United States produced about half of the value added by manufacturing and about half of all new capital expenditures for 1982.

The Extent of Concentration by Industry

The extent of concentration in the United States varies considerably by industry. In some industries, one large firm is clearly dominant in that it contributes 50 percent or more of total output. General Motors, with more than 60 percent of U.S. domestic output of automobiles, is an example. In other industries, a few firms may account for the bulk of sales, with no one firm clearly dominant over the others. The tobacco industry, with Reynolds Industries, Philip Morris, and American Brands, is a case in point. There are some industries that have little or no such concentration, and thus approximate the market situation called *pure competition* in which no seller produces more than a negligible share of market supply. The shoe and clothing industries afford examples. The degree of concentration by industry is shown in Table 5-2, which compares the output of the four largest firms in a number of high- and low-concentration industries. However, a high degree of concentration alone does not necessarily mean there is a monopoly or a general lack of competition.

Issues Involving Industrial Concentration

In a number of industries, a certain amount of industrial concentration is apparently inevitable. Some types of business organizations lend themselves to large-scale production. For example, there are industries in which the product itself is highly complex and can be constructed only by a large and diversified organization. Automobiles and computers are a case in point. There are industries in which the product is large in size, requiring complex equipment for construction and large capital investments—for example, shipbuilding and locomotives. Then there are industries that require a large capital investment, particularly in plant and equipment. For example, there are many good reasons for manufacturing iron and steel on a large scale. One of the most important is the tremendous outlay necessary to secure blast furnaces, steel furnaces, and other equipment. Finally, there are industries requiring a natural resource that is available only in limited amounts and in specific geographic locations. Examples of this are the lead and petroleum industries.

Moreover, industrial concentration may well be an inevitable result of advancing technology in all industrial countries, regardless of their ideologies. Data show that for the same industries, concentration ratios are generally higher in other Western countries than in the United States; foreign industries in which concentration is

TABLE 5-2

The Extent of Concentration by Industry in the United States (output measured by value of shipment)

Concentration	Shipment Percentage of Four Largest Firms
High Concentration	
Motor vehicles	93
Cereal breakfast foods	87
Cigarettes	82
Sewing machines	80
Metal cans	79
Tires	72
Soap	70
Aircraft	75
Low Concentration	
Oil refining	30
Meat packing	24
Machine tools	21
Book publishers	18
Concrete products	10
Women's dresses	9
Fur goods	8

Source: U.S. Bureau of the Census, 1982 Census of Manufacturers: Concentration Ratios in Manufacturing (Washington: USGPO, 1986), pp. 12–65.

high are generally the same as those in which concentration is high in the United States; and industries that are not highly concentrated in foreign countries are generally not concentrated industries in the United States also. In West Germany, three chemical companies produce 80 percent of all chemical products.[2] The French aluminum firm Pechiney Ugine Kuhlmann produces 90 percent of French aluminum products, specialty steels, and nonferrous metals such as titanium and zirconium.[3] In Japan two automobile companies account for 60 percent of all Japanese automobile production.[4] These data strongly suggest that fundamental technological and

[2] Statistiches Bundesant, *Statistisches Jahrbuch für die Bundesrepublik Deutschland*, 1987 (Wiesbaden: Kohlhammer, 1987), p. 235.

[3] Ministerie de l'Economie et des Finances, *Statistiques Francais 1987* (Paris, 1987). The greatest degree of industrial concentration in all Western countries may be in France. This also holds true in banking.

[4] *Japan Statistical Yearbook*, 1987 (Tokyo: Office of the Prime Minister, 1987), p. 33.

economic factors determine to some extent the degree of concentration of industries in all market economies.

The extent of industrial concentration was even higher in the advanced socialist economies than in the United States.[5] To some extent the centralized planning characteristic of socialist economies necessitated the concentration of output into large production units. The organization of industry had to be considered a basic part of the economic and political organization of the state. There was a constant effort to combine industrial and agricultural enterprises into larger units to increase output to supply the population and to export to world markets. In Poland the tractor combine URSUS produced 100 percent of all tractors made in the country, and in Hungary the combine RABA produced all the heavy-duty trucks, tractors, and railroad equipment made there.[6] The high degree of concentration in centrally planned economies may be used as evidence that large-scale operations and the concentration that accompany them do yield economies of scale.

Industrial concentration also can transcend national boundaries. Large American firms acquire foreign firms, and large foreign firms acquire American firms. As competition becomes global, additional economies of scale may be effected. For example, it is conceivable that, by the end of the century, only a handful of automobile companies would be left in the world. Perhaps this is the final extension of an evolutionary process that began with the creation of the automobile industry when there were literally hundreds of firms turning out autos for the populace who could afford them. This world trend may be irreversible, regardless of the product; and laws, antitrust and otherwise, will have to be restructured within a global frame of reference.

Advantages of Concentration.   There are certain advantages to large-scale production. An expansion in output often permits a firm greater specialization in the use of both labor and capital equipment. Overhead costs can be spread over a larger output, which results in a lower unit cost. Economies can result from new combinations of the factors of production (land, labor, and capital), which results in lower minimum costs. Economies of scale result when more of all factors are used and the total output increases at a rate greater than the increase in the production factors. Frequently, highly specialized labor and capital equipment can be added to a production unit only in large, indivisible amounts and cannot be used profitably in small-scale operations. In fact, smaller business units may well result in higher unit costs in many industries, and therefore the best answer to the problems of concentration may not be breaking up large firms. Market power can be based on

---

[5] Frederick L. Pryor, "An International Comparison of Concentration Ratios," *Review of Economics and Statistics* (May 1972), pp. 130–140.

[6] Martin Schnitzer, *U.S. Business Involvement in Eastern Europe* (New York: Praeger Publishers, 1980), pp. 81 and 103.

underlying economies of scale and technological or managerial leadership. In some cases, large firms are the price of efficiency and innovation.[7]

Problems of Concentration.   However, industrial concentration also carries with it certain problems. In a competitive market economy, the interest of producers and consumers coincide because the way to larger profits for producers is through greater efficiency, price reductions, and increased sales volume, all of which naturally benefit consumers, too. In a monopolistic market, or one approaching this state, profits may be maximized at the expense of the consumer by selling a smaller quantity of goods at a higher price than under competitive conditions. The existence of monopoly power also means that the spur to efficiency and technical progress that competition provides is often lacking.

There is evidence that small- or medium-sized firms are often more innovative than large firms. A case in point is Apple Computer Company, which was created in the 1970s by two men in their twenties who started their operations in a garage. The computer data processing industry was and is still dominated by IBM. In 1980, when Apple was just getting started, IBM's total sales amounted to $25.9 billion, in comparison to total industry sales of $52 billion. But IBM had grown somewhat complacent during the 1970s, and Apple came out with a line of personal computers that were inexpensive and easy to use. Apple became the leading exponent of technology for the masses. By 1985, Apple's total sales amounted to around $2 billion.

Small firms are often put in the position of having to innovate in order to survive. From this comes a willingness to take risks. Big firms, like big governments, can be so encrusted with bureaucracy that they have more desire to maintain the status quo than to be experimental. Besides, experimentation usually requires approval from someone in the hierarchy of the organization. This can be disturbing, for often no one in the hierarchy wants to be held responsible in the event of failure. It is often much easier to go out and absorb a smaller company that has already made the innovation and has survived the risk of failure.

Finally, large firms in certain situations can exercise discretionary power over prices and entry into markets. It is the power to engage in restrictive practices that provides one of the bases of American antitrust policy.

Industrial Concentration and Competition

Although few American industries operate under the textbook definition of perfect competition, we should not jump to the conclusion that there is no competition at all. Competition can exist in a number of forms. Firms in an industry can compete

---

[7] In a case involving Alcoa, the U.S. Supreme Court was unwilling to split up the company for fear of losing substantial economies of scale in production and in research and development.

against each other on the basis of quality and product differentiation. Coca-Cola and PepsiCo wage war with each other for the hearts and minds of the soft drinkers of the world.[8] The war is fought through advertising that creates an image for Coca-Cola, Pepsi-Cola and their offspring. Firms in any given industry also compete on the basis of technology. That is, they try to develop improved machines and production methods that will lower their production costs and render obsolete the machines and methods of competitors. Moreover, firms in an industry compete for customers with firms in industries that produce other products intended for the satisfaction of the same general consumer want. They also can compete with firms in completely unrelated industries for the limited incomes of consumers in general.

Global Competition.   Most major corporations do not confine themselves to domestic operations, but participate widely in business outside of the continental limits of their respective countries through the ownership of foreign subsidiaries. These companies are called *multinational* corporations and are limited to no one country or ideology. They transcend natural boundaries and produce more and more of the world's GNP. Some of the current multinational corporations have sales volumes larger than the GNPs of many middle-sized European countries, and considerably larger than the GNPs of typical less developed African and Asian countries. Competition between multinational corporations for international markets is fierce. One battleground is the American automobile market, where Japanese automobile companies have increased their share of the market at the expense of the U.S. auto companies.[9]

Concentration and The Reagan Administration.   There is one thing that can be said about the Reagan administration: It never met a merger or takeover it didn't like. It maintained a laissez-faire attitude toward them, and hundreds were consummated during the eight years it was in office. The period also witnessed the rise of the corporate raiders, such as T. Boone Pickens, Carl Icahn, and Donald Trump, who financed their acquisitions through the sale of high-yield junk bonds to wealthy investors. Some companies were simply in the business of buying out other companies. The classic example was the leveraged buyout of RJR-Nabisco by the Wall Street firm of Kohlberg, Kravis, Roberts (KKR) for $24.8 billion.

---

[8] The decision of Coca-Cola to introduce a new Coke is regarded as a major marketing fiasco. Whether it is or not remains to be seen. Coca-Cola and PepsiCo dominate the U.S. soft drink market. An increase in one percentage point in market shares represents an increase of $100 million in soft drink sales. Coca-Cola and PepsiCo compete through advertising and control over counter space in supermarkets.

[9] In 1981 import quotas were imposed on Japanese cars shipped to the United States. This limitation probably saved Chrysler from going bankrupt. The U.S. automobile industry, which lost $4 billion in 1981, made a $10 billion profit in 1984.

This was the largest corporate takeover in American history. Seldom since the age of the 19th century robber barons has corporate behavior been so open to question as it was during the wave of takeovers that punctuated the last years of the Reagan administration.

Table 5-3 presents the number and value of acquisitions, including takeovers, from 1979 to the middle of 1988. The number of acquisitions increased from a low of 1,526 in 1979, and accelerated rapidly during the Reagan years. The number of takeovers increased from a low of 3 to a high of 34 in 1986. Takeovers constituted more than a third of the reported value of acquisitions during the period 1984–1988.

LABOR UNIONS

The workers in many capitalistic countries, the United States in particular, have not been content to rely entirely on government intervention to improve their economic status. Instead, they have banded together into labor unions to bargain collectively with employers. The individual worker is usually at a disadvantage in bargaining with an employer—lack of financial resources requires an earned income. On the other hand, while an employer must have employees, one worker more or less doesn't mean much. Under collective bargaining, the worker's disadvantage is greatly reduced. The worker's need for a job is not reduced, but the question facing the employer becomes one of having or not having a complete labor force rather than one of having or not having a particular worker. Gathered together in a union and delegating the task of bargaining with the employer to an official or agent of the union, the workers can often obtain much better terms of employment than each could obtain for himself.

TABLE 5-3
Corporate Acquisitions, Including Takeovers, 1979–1988

Year	No. of Acquisitions	Value (billions)	No. of Takeovers	Value of Takeovers (billions)
1979	1526	$ 34.2	3	$ 6.2
1980	1565	33.1	3	6.5
1981	2326	67.0	8	20.6
1982	2295	60.4	9	24.0
1983	2345	52.3	7	10.4
1984	3064	125.2	19	55.2
1985	3165	139.1	26	60.8
1986	4022	190.0	34	68.8
1987	3701	167.5	30	62.2
1988 (Jan.–July)	1656	82.1	14	32.4

Source: Data provided by Peter W. Rodino, Chairman, Committee on the Judiciary, U.S. House of Representatives.

Development of Labor Unions

Labor unions are a product of the last century. Unions that existed before the Civil War were generally temporary bodies established to redress certain grievances and dissolved when either successful or defeated. The labor movement accelerated after the Civil War. The development of large, impersonal business units seemed to many workers to place them at the mercy of employers. In 1869 the first major U.S. labor union, the Knights of Labor, was organized in Philadelphia. The union did not last long, in part because of poor leadership. In 1881 the American Federation of Labor (AFL) was created. As a federation of craft unions, the AFL made no effort for many years to enroll unskilled labor. Under Samuel Gompers, the AFL adopted a policy of political neutrality. Its main thrust was economic—more pay and an eight-hour work day. Other unions, in particular the International Workers of the World (IWW), were more militant. They believed in class conflict and resorted to violent means including general strikes and sabotage, to achieve their goals.

The labor movement declined in importance during the 1920s. The AFL lost more than a million members during the decade, and efforts to unionize new industries proved unsuccessful. There were several factors responsible for the decline of unionism in the 1920s. The "red scare" after the end of World War I was one factor. Some unions, particularly the IWW, had been sympathetic to the Bolshevik Revolution in Russia. There was public concern that somehow communists were infiltrating the United States, and all unions were lumped in with the IWW. The sensational murder trial and execution of Sacco and Vanzetti, both of whom were anarchists, convinced many employers that bomb throwers and communists were lurking behind every lamppost.

Another factor responsible for the decline of unionism was the unsympathetic attitude of the government. Government opposition helped to break up strikes in the coal and steel industries in 1919, and conservative court decisions hampered union activity during the 1920s. Laissez-faire was advocated as public policy; unions were blamed for rising prices. Finally, business firms organized an attack on unionism by popularizing the open shop and organizing company unions.

The halcyon days of organized labor occurred during the New Deal of Franklin D. Roosevelt. In 1935 the National Labor Relations Act was passed. This law required employers to bargain collectively with representatives of their employees and prohibited employers from carrying on unfair labor practices or interfering in the organization of unions. The act was intended to stimulate the growth of organized labor, and it did just that. Union memberships more than tripled during the 1930s, and many plants and industries that had previously escaped unionization were organized.

A split within the ranks of labor itself occurred in 1935, when union leaders within the AFL left it to form the Congress of Industrial Organization (CIO). The CIO was interested in organizing workers in the mass production industries. It was highly successful in securing recognition of unions for employees in the automobile and steel industries. Labor achieved at least a parity with management by the end of the 1930s and also gained in terms of social welfare. The Fair Labor Standards Act of 1938 mandated minimum wages and maximum hours for labor engaged in interstate commerce.

During the latter part of World War II and in the immediate postwar period, a series of labor strikes convinced Congress that new legislation in the field of labor relations was needed. The Labor-Management Relations Act (Taft-Hartley Act) was passed in 1947 to eliminate some specific abuses on the part of labor unions and to equalize bargaining conditions between labor and management. The closed shop was outlawed and the union shop was permitted only under strict regulation. A notice was required 60 days before a strike or a lockout could be called, and the government could obtain an injunction against a union, postponing for 80 days any strike that would affect the national interest. Unions could be sued for breach of contract if they participated in jurisdictional strikes and boycotts. The pendulum, which had swung in favor of labor unions, swung back to a more centrist position.

The Decline of Unions

As reflected in Table 5-4, union membership peaked in the 1950s and has fallen since then. A major reason is the shift from a goods-producing to a service society. The United States has entered a postindustrial age with a change in the type of work people do—from physically intensive to knowledge-intensive labor. In 1945, 43.4 percent of all workers were employed in manufacturing; by 1989 the percentage of workers employed in manufacturing had decreased to 23.3 percent of the labor force. Conversely, the number of persons in the service jobs increased from 56.6 percent of the labor force in 1945 to 77.7 percent in 1989. In 1945, 38.5 percent of all workers employed in manufacturing belonged to unions; by 1989, union workers employed in manufacturing decreased to 19.3 percent of the total manufacturing labor force.

Unionism has never been strong in the service area. White-collar workers tend to identify more with management than blue-collar workers do. There is also a

TABLE 5-4

Union Membership as a Percentage of the U.S. Labor Force, 1945–1989

Year	Union Membership	Year	Union Membership
1945	21.9%	1970	22.6%
1950	22.3	1975	21.7
1955	24.7	1980	21.2
1960	23.6	1984	20.6
1965	22.4	1988	19.9
		1989	19.3

Source: Economic Report of the President *(Washington D.C.: USGPO, 1990), pp. 294–295.*

certain snob appeal about white-collar jobs, which is coupled with a tendency to look down on blue-collar manufacturing workers. By 2000 even more people will be employed in miscellaneous service-type jobs such as data processing, hotels, and restaurants.[10]

GOVERNMENT

Government intervention and participation in the U.S. economy can be divided into four areas. First, there is public finance, where government is a purchaser of goods and services as well as a tax collector. Government economic stabilization policies may also be considered a part of this area. Second, government regulation and control prescribe specific conditions under which private economic activity can or cannot take place. Government may interpose itself as a part of management of certain industries, such as public utilities, and regulate rates and the provision of services. It may also affect the character of private business operations both directly and indirectly through antitrust and other laws. Third, government (at all levels) is the single largest employer in the American economy, and as such it competes directly with private industry for labor. The government also affects the level of wages and salaries. Fourth, government owns and operates certain types of business enterprises and is a major provider of credit. In fact, a shift in emphasis from market to political decisions has taken place in the American economy in recent years, in great measure in response to increased demands from a wide variety of special interest groups.

Public Finance

Public finance is the most straightforward example of the extent of government participation in the "mixed" economy of the United States. Taxes provide the government with control over the nation's resources and also affect the distribution of income and wealth. Government expenditures for goods and services divert resources from the private to the public sector of the economy. Through its own expenditures, the government has literally created whole industries. It has conducted much of the basic research in certain industries, and it has given impetus and direction to technological change. Government transfer payments redistribute income from one economic group to another. The direct subsidies and indirect benefits offered by government to special interest groups, such as farmers and shipbuilders, are too numerous to mention. In addition, preferential tax treatment is accorded to some firms and industries to achieve desired economic goals. Examples of special tax treatment include the investment credit, depletion allowances for mineral extraction companies, and accelerated depreciation.

---

[10] Bureau of Labor Statistics, *Occupational Outlook Handbook*, *1987–88* (Washington: USGPO, 1988).

Government Spending. The economic influence of the public sector has grown steadily throughout this century and has become particularly pervasive during the last 20 years. To some extent, this increase in influence can be attributed to a growing acceptance of the role of government in public welfare. Increased industrial development of the U.S. economy has resulted in changes in the size and complexity of business enterprises, and the regulatory operations of the government have been stepped up. Government spending for national defense is also large; it accounts for around 30 percent of total government purchases of goods and services.

Economic growth has spurred a trend toward urban living. As more of the nation's population has become concentrated in urban areas, the inevitable result has been an increase in demand for a variety of services provided through the public sector. But regardless of the causes, the growth in both absolute and relative importance of the public sector to the U.S. economy is clear, as Table 5-5 indicates. Government spending on goods and services accounted for around 20 percent of the gross national product in 1989. If transfer payments are added to government spending on goods and services, total government expenditures amount to one-third of gross national product.

Taxes. The composition of taxes is also important in analyzing the role of government in the U.S. economy. Government expenditures are, at least in part, covered by taxes on business firms and individuals. Thus, the type of taxes levied determines who ultimately pays for government expenditures. Taxes also have an income redistribution effect. When government extracts taxes, it lowers someone's income; but when that money is spent, it also raises someone's income.

TABLE 5-5

U.S. Government Spending Compared to Gross National Product for Selected Years (billions of dollars)

Year	Gross National Product	Government Spending on Goods and Services		
		Total	Federal	State and Local
1929	$ 103.9	$ 8.9	$ 1.5	$ 7.4
1939	91.3	13.6	5.3	8.3
1945	213.4	83.0	74.8	8.2
1950	288.3	38.8	19.0	19.8
1960	515.3	100.6	54.4	46.2
1970	1,015.5	218.2	98.8	119.4
1980	2,732.0	530.3	208.1	322.2
1985	4.010.3	818.6	353.9	464.7
1987	4,524.3	926.1	381.6	544.5
1989	5,233.2	1,036.7	404.1	632.5

Source: Economic Report of the President *(Washington: USGPO, 1990), pp. 284–295.*

Many public policy theorists believe that variations in the rate of economic growth can be attributed to different tax systems. Many feel that the reason the Japanese growth rate is far superior to that of the United States is that Japanese tax policy favors saving and investment. The economic policies of the Reagan administration center heavily on tax-cutting measures designed to promote capital formation by increasing the rate of saving. Special incentives have been given to certain persons, corporations, or activities to influence shifts in saving behavior.

Economic Stabilization Policies. The acceptance of economic policies designed to promote stability and the use of the tax/transfer-payment mechanism to promote income redistribution tend to characterize the economic role of Western governments, including the United States, in much of the twentieth century. Economic stabilization policies include fiscal and monetary devices. Fiscal policy in the United States is effected through the federal budget, which can be used to change the level of economic activity in the economy. Taxes represent a withdrawal of income from the income stream, while government expenditures represent an injection of income into it. When the government's revenue, as represented by taxes and other revenues, exceeds expenditures, the net effect is to dampen the level of activity in the economy. On the other hand, when government expenditures exceed revenues, the net effect is to stimulate the economy. Budget surpluses or deficits, then, can be used to change the level of economic activity.

Monetary policy is another economic stabilization tool used in the United States and other Western countries. It involves operations by the central banking authorities to change the stock of money, its rate of turnover, and the volume of close money substitutes. The Federal Reserve is technically a privately owned corporation, but it is actually an independent government agency subject to control by Congress and the president. It may be regarded as the central bank of the United States, comparable, for example, to the Bank of England in the United Kingdom and the Deutsche Bundesbank in West Germany.

The Federal Reserve may take action to counteract either inflation or deflation. It effects monetary policy in the United States through open market operations and control over discount rates[11] and legal reserves that commercial banks have to maintain against demand deposits. Raising discount rates and legal reserve requirements are anti-inflation measures; lowering them achieves the opposite result. The Federal Reserve may also either buy or sell U. S. government bonds in the open market. If it buys bonds from commercial banks, demand deposits are increased and banks have more money to lend. Conversely, if it sells bonds to commercial banks, the reverse is true.

---

[11] The discount rate is the interest rate charged when commercial banks borrow from the Federal Reserve. In turn, the discount rate affects the interest rate commercial banks charge their customers.

Transfer Payments. The composition of the federal budget has been altered considerably since 1960. Transfer payments have increased more rapidly than any single component in the budget, as Table 5-6 indicates. Total outlays for transfer payments and for other social welfare programs amounted to around 41 percent of the federal budget in 1989. When state and local government expenditures on social welfare programs are also taken into consideration, total government expenditures on social welfare programs amounted to $447 billion in 1989. In the state of California on any given day, about 40 percent of the people received some form of state transfer payment.

There are a wide variety of transfer programs, ranging from food stamps to Medicare to welfare payments. Money spent on entitlement programs has risen at a rate three times as fast as the U.S. gross national product. These funds are provided from general taxes or government borrowing. For example, unemployment compensation provides aid to unemployed workers and is financed by a payroll tax employers.

There are also regular social security programs, created under the Social Security Act of 1937. The most important of these is the old age, survivors, and disability insurance program, which is financed by a payroll tax on both employer and employee.[12] The tax receipts are placed in a reserve fund, and payments are made to workers who have retired or who are disabled and to the spouses and young children of workers who have died. The program was expanded in the mid-1960s

TABLE 5-6

Major Categories of Federal Government Expenditures (billions of dollars)

Fiscal Year	Transfer Payments	Purchases of Goods and Services
1960	$ 20.6	$ 52.9
1965	28.4	65.6
1970	55.3	99.8
1975	131.9	123.9
1980	235.4	199.9
1985	360.6	340.4
1986	380.5	368.4
1987	398.7	374.9
1988	421.3	375.3
1989	447.4	396.4

Source: Executive Office of the President, Office of Management & Budget, Budget of the United States, Fiscal Year 1989 (Washington, USGPO, 1988), pp. 6g-42–6g-47.

---

[12] The combined rate in 1990 was 15.3 percent on incomes up to $51,300.

when hospital care coverage began to be provided for older persons and voluntary medical insurance had become available to them.

Government Regulation and Control

Government regulation, particularly of business, is a second area in which government has become firmly entrenched in the U.S. economy. This sphere of public sector influence has developed by fits and starts. In the 1880s the trust movement threatened to envelop much of American industry. This brought about a public demand for control over the monopolies, with the result that the Sherman Anti-Trust Act was passed in 1890.

The Depression, which began with the stock market crash of 1929 and continued until the wartime mobilization of the early 1940s, was a severe crisis. In response to that crisis, many new government agencies were created, most of which impinged in some way on business firms. By the end of the Depression, the federal government exercised extensive regulation and control over business. There was little additional government intervention until the late 1960s and early 1970s, when environmental protection, minority employment, and consumer protection became dominant issues.

Antitrust Regulation.   One important area of government regulation is antitrust activity to prevent anticompetitive business practices. This activity generally has sprung from the concept that concentration interferes with the efficient operation of a competitive market economy and that the most effective method of regulation is to prevent concentration from developing in the first place. Antitrust laws are designed to promote and maintain competition in industry. There is a fundamental social interest in the efficacy of the competitive market system. Society wants competition in order to get the maximum output of the goods and services at the lowest possible prices using the most efficient production techniques.

Anticompetitive practices can be divided into several categories. First, there could be an industry in which a few firms are dominant and price competition is therefore minimal. Second, mergers between business firms can create an imperfectly competitive market situation. Third, anticompetitive business practices may involve certain types of market abuses, such as price fixing and market sharing.

Public Utility Regulation.   Certain industries vitally affect the public interest by providing a service that is considered too important to society to be left to the vagaries of the market or to private enterprise to provide as it sees fit. In countries with systems similar to our own, industries directly affecting the public interest are owned and operated by their governments. In the United States, however, when one or both of two conditions exist in an industry, a *natural monopoly* is usually created and regulated by the government. First, economies of scale can occur if output is concentrated in one firm, with the result that one firm can supply the market more efficiently than two or more firms; second, unrestrained competition between firms in the industry is deemed by society to be undesirable. Included under the category of natural monopolies are electricity, gas, local telephone service, and broadcasting.

Social Regulation.   During the 1970s the federal government extended its participation in the market system. More and more effort was directed toward cushioning individual risks and regulating personal and institutional conduct. Social regulation is broad-based in terms of objectives. It encompasses such areas as occupational health and safety, equal employment opportunity, consumer product safety, and environmental protection. These areas have specific social goals—a cleaner environment, safer consumer products, employment of minorities, and so forth. A number of important regulatory commissions, most of which were created during the 1970s, enforce the laws designed to achieve these social goals.

The Consumer Product Safety Commission, the Occupational Safety and Health Administration, the Equal Employment Opportunity Commission, and the Environmental Protection Agency are examples of regulatory agencies. For these relative newcomers to the federal government hierarchy of administrative agencies and commissions, jurisdiction extends to most of the private sector and at times to productive activities in the government itself. However, each of these newer agencies has a rather narrow range of responsibility. For example, the Equal Employment Opportunity Commission is responsible only for employment policies of some firms, whereas the Federal Aviation Administration (FAA) is responsible for all the activities of anyone who flies.

Government as an Employer

One measure of the magnitude of the public sector is the number of persons employed directly by one or another governmental unit. When the armed forces are included, some 16 percent of the total labor force is employed directly in the public sector. This percentage may increase in the future, particularly at the state and local levels, since the demand for social services is expected to increase.[13] In addition, numerous other jobs are related indirectly to government employment. An army base, defense plant, or state university often supports the economy of a whole area. The public sector sets wage standards in many areas and competes against the private sector for labor resources. However, the productivity of the public sector is often low in comparison to productivity in the private sector; as the public sector expands relative to the private sector, productivity in general will decline.[14]

In the private sector, the profit-and-loss system produces an incentive to stimulate efficiency. Competition between business firms also encourages maximum efficiency in the use of capital and other resources, including labor. Both factors

---

[13] Defense expenditures will probably decrease.

[14] U.S. Congress, Joint Economic Committee, *Productivity in the Federal Government* (Washington: USGPO, May 31, 1979), pp. 1–12.

are lacking in government, for it is not in business to make a profit; nor is there a need to be competitive, because there is no competition between government units. There is no stimulus for productivity. No government agency has ever gone broke. In fact, some observers have argued that agency managers have strong incentives not to improve production if such gains lead to budget cuts. The prestige of an agency manager is often measured by the number of employees the agency has; thus, the fewer the employees, the lower the prestige. The disincentive possibility means that Congress or state legislatures must in effect fill the role played by the profit-and-loss system.

Government Ownership of Business

Government ownership of business is quite limited in the United States in comparison to other major Western industrial countries. In France, for example, the railroads, coal mines, and most of the banking system, airlines, electric power facilities, and insurance companies are state owned. The government also has a large interest in the petroleum and natural gas industries and is involved in the production of motor vehicles and airplanes. In the United Kingdom, the coal mines, steel industry, railways, trucking, and electricity and gas industries are state owned. In West Germany, government ownership is limited to the railroads, airlines, public utilities, and coal mines. However, in all three countries, private enterprise is still dominant in that it employs by far the greater percentage of workers and contributes the greater part of the gross national product.

In the United States, all levels of government own and operate productive facilities of many kinds. Airports, but not railway terminals, are usually government owned. Governmental units own and operate the plants that provide water, gas, and electricity to thousands of cities and towns, as well as owning local transportation systems, warehouses, printing companies, and a wide variety of other facilities. Government also produces, either directly or indirectly, atomic power and many other goods. It carries on projects connected with reforestation, soil erosion control, slum clearance, rural electrification, and housing. This does not mean that government ownership and operation is necessarily preferred. In many cases, the resources required are too large and risks too great or the likelihood of profit too small to attract private enterprise, and government is compelled to perform the tasks instead.

One illustration of this point is the Tennessee Valley Authority (TVA), a major public enterprise for the production and distribution of electrical power in the southeastern United States. At one time, the area adjacent to the Tennessee River was one of the most impoverished in the United States. Flooding and soil erosion were common, and most homes in the area were without electricity. The area was also generally unattractive to industry. The TVA was created to erect dams and hydroelectric plants to provide electric power, to improve navigation on the Tennessee River, to promote flood control, to prevent soil erosion, to reforest the area, and to contribute to the nation's defense through the manufacture of artificial nitrates.

It was opposed by private companies, in particular the utility companies, because it was empowered to sell electricity in direct competition with them. However, the utility companies in the Tennessee Valley area had never considered it profitable to provide anything more than minimal service. The TVA was also supposed to serve as a yardstick of efficiency, but government ownership and operation of power facilities does not always mean lower rates or greater efficiency. Opinion on TVA's efficiency is mixed. The TVA is efficient when compared to other government agencies, but when compared to private business it does not look as good.

Government credit programs constitute a gray area in that they do not involve outright state ownership of industry. However, federal credit programs have an impact on private industry that should be mentioned. Direct, insured, and federally sponsored agency loans passed the $500 billion mark in 1980 and have continued to increase. These programs have three main functions: to eliminate gaps in the credit market, to provide subsidies that stimulate socially desirable activity, and to stimulate the economy. The first two of these functions are microeconomic in effect in that they are supposed to affect the types of activity for which credit is made available, the geographical location of those activities, and the types of borrowers who have access to credit. For example, Federal Housing Administration (FHA) and Veterans' Administration (VA) mortgage insurance programs have resulted in an increased demand for housing. The third function is macroeconomic in nature in that federal lending affects the level of economic activity on a large scale—in particular, the gross national product and employment.

SUMMARY

Three important types of economic organizations have developed in the United States—big business, big labor, and big government. The three have developed partly in response to the needs and deficiencies of the market mechanism. Big business, as represented by large corporations, developed first and pervades all areas of economic activity ranging from manufacturing to banking and from communications to retailing. Whether this is good or bad is a matter of opinion. Large-scale production and distribution can effect economies of scale and the result can be lower prices for consumers. However, largeness can result in a lessening of innovation and price competition. In all advanced industrial countries, regardless of their political and economic ideologies, large industrial organizations are a fact of life.

Labor unions in part offset the power of corporations and also reduce the power of market forces in labor markets by creating a monopoly for certain types of workers. Unions gained in popularity and strength during the Great Depression. However, union membership began to peak during the 1950s and has been declining as a percentage of the total labor force. There has been a decline in employment in the manufacturing sector of the economy, where union membership has been the highest, and an increase in employment in the service sector, where union membership has never been strong. The increased education and mobility of American workers has also tended to work against an increase in union membership.

Undoubtedly, the most important modification of the U.S. market system has been achieved through an increase in the role of the public or government sector. Public education has been provided, business monopolies have been curbed, and taxes and transfer payments have been used to redistribute incomes. Fiscal and monetary policies have been used, albeit with limited success, to attain full employment and price stability. A variety of government regulations have been adopted to achieve various social goals, such as a cleaner environment and the employment of minorities. The social security program has been expanded over time to reduce economic insecurity. Government purchase of goods and services now amounts to around 20 percent of the gross national product. It is clear that government intervention in the economy has become large enough to justify the classification of the United States as a mixed rather than a strictly market system. How successful this mixture has been is the subject of the next chapter.

REVIEW QUESTIONS

1. In what ways can the development of large corporations be regarded as a departure from a market system?
2. What is a multinational corporation?
3. In what ways can the development of labor unions be regarded as a departure from a market system?
4. What is meant by the term "entitlements"?
5. What are some of the factors responsible for the increase in the role of government in U.S. society?
6. Discuss the purpose of U.S. antitrust regulation.
7. What are some of the factors responsible for the decline of unionism in the United States?

RECOMMENDED READINGS

Economic Report of the President 1990. Washington, DC: U.S. Government Printing Office, 1990.

Executive Office of the President, Office of Management & Budget. *Budget of the United States Government, Fiscal Year 1990*. Washington, DC: U.S. Government Printing Office, 1989.

Neal, Alfred. *Business Power & Public Policy*. New York: Praeger, 1982.

Rees, Albert. *The Economics of Trade Unions*, 3d ed., Chicago: University of Chicago Press, 1988.

Schnitzer, Martin C. *Contemporary Government & Business Relations*. 4th ed., Boston: Houghton Mifflin Co., 1990.

Steiner, George A., and John F. Steiner. *Business, Government, and Society*. 5th ed., New York: Random House, 1988.

Waldman, Jerome. *The Economics of Antitrust*. Boston: Little, Brown, 1986.

Weston, J. Fred. "Industrial Concentration, Mergers, & Growth." *Mergers & Economic Efficiency*. Vol. 2. Washington, DC: U.S. Government Printing Office, 1982.

CHAPTER SIX

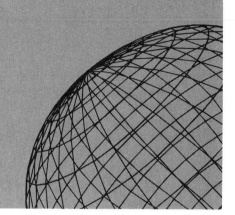

AN APPRAISAL OF THE UNITED STATES ECONOMY

Paul Kennedy, author of the 1988 best seller *The Rise and Fall of the Great Powers,* states: "In the largest sense of all, therefore, the only answer to the question increasingly debated by the public of whether the United States can preserve its existing position is no, because it has simply not been given to any one society to remain permanently ahead of all of the others. That would imply a freezing of the differentiated patterns of growth rates, technological advancements, and military developments which have existed since time immemorial."[1]

Clyde V. Prestowitz, author of *Trading Places,* states: "Monday, October 19, 1987 marked the end of the American century twelve years before its time. This date signaled as clearly as any bugle call the most serious defeat the United States has ever suffered."[2] By trading places, Prestowitz is referring to Japan. In industry after industry, whether it is in semiconductors or machine tools or automobiles, the United States has ceded first place to Japan.

The first writer is one of a group of declinist theorists who contend that the United States in particular and the West in general are in a process of decline. Kennedy traces the rise and fall of Spain, France, and other powers, ending with the United States. In each case, the reason for their decline is imperial overreach. The problem with Spain was that its expenditures on military conquests overreached its capacity to pay for them; the problem with the United States today is the same in that it is playing military policeman for the world but is no longer capable of doing so. Kennedy is joined by another decline theorist, Mancur Olsen, who wrote *The Rise and Fall of*

[1] Paul Kennedy, *The Rise and Fall of the Great Powers* (New York: Random House, 1987), p. 533.

[2] Clyde V. Prestowitz, Jr. *Trading Places* (New York: Basic Books, 1988), pp. 4–5.

Nations (New Haven: Yale University Press, 1983). He contends that mature societies start to decline when layers of powerful special interest groups succeed in impeding the normal "creative destruction" of capitalism.[3] In order to hold on to what they have, they resist change. But society pays for obsolescence and inefficiency, and the result is decline.

Prestowitz belongs to the Japan-will-win school. He and others cite Japanese feats in the area of high technology, once exclusively the preserve of the United States. In a relatively short period of time, Japan has transformed itself into a world superpower through hard work and a social organization so cohesive and well managed that it is the envy of much of the world. With methodical precision, Japan has assumed leadership in industry after industry, moving from heavy industry to high technology. Now, the yen has replaced the dollar as the symbol of financial strength, and Japan is buying up assets in the United States and the rest of the world. Moreover, during the 1980s Japan became the leading creditor nation in the world, and the United States became the leading debtor nation. Japan has now become a financial powerhouse. In *Yen! Japan's New Financial Empire and Its Threat to America* (New York: Simon & Schuster, 1988), Daniel Burstein develops a future scenario of America battered by debts and prolonged economic crisis, electing a president who will get tough with Japan.

Finally, there is the "God is in his heaven and all is right with America" school, which is epitomized by *The Wall Street Journal* in two separate articles entitled "The 1990's and Beyond."[4] The United States is still the economic colossus of the world and will remain so for the foreseeable future. The problems it now faces are just temporary wrinkles that will be ironed out. As for Japan, it has too many problems of its own to seriously challenge the United States for economic leadership. It is a one-dimensional power whose economic might is not bolstered by military, political, and ideological clout. It is not particularly loved, especially in its own backyard, where China and other Asian countries remember past Japanese aggressions. Japan is also vulnerable to what happens in its foreign markets, while the enormous domestic markets of the United States virtually guarantee self sufficiency for its industries.

REASONS FOR THE DECLINE IN INDUSTRIAL COMPETITIVENESS

A well-known quote from Shakespeare can be paraphrased as follows: The fault, dear America, is not in Japan or South Korea, but in ourselves that we are losing

---

[3] The term "creative destruction" is associated with the economist Joseph Schumpeter, who predicted the end of capitalist civilization. To Schumpeter, the entrepreneur was the creator, the one who got things done and who moved society. This creative dynamism was responsible for change, with the new replacing the old. Eventually, however, bureaucracy and other groups replace individual action, and economic progress then begins to decline as society becomes more stratified.

[4] *The Wall Street Journal*, Monday, January 23, 1989, pp. A1 and A5; Monday, January 30, 1989, pp. A1 and A8.

competitively.[5] It is, of course, easy to blame Japan for all of our problems. In part, it goes back to World War II when we were the good guys, and they were the bad guys who never would fight fair and would get their come-uppance at the hands of John Wayne or Errol Flynn. Today, we blame our trade problems on the Japanese, who we say don't play fair and open their export markets to us. We also accuse the Japanese of copying our technology and picking the brains of our best scientists.[6] To some extent this is true, but it is also patronizing because it assumes that the Japanese are incapable of original thinking and that we have a monopoly on the world's "smarts." Both assumptions are false.

Four reasons can be advanced to explain the decline in U.S. competitiveness. To some extent, they are interrelated. The first comes under the generic nomenclature of self-indulgence and includes crime and drugs. The second is euphemistically referred to as the "the British disease," which allegedly means that Americans have lost the Protestant work ethic, which carries with it a concomitant decline in productivity. The third holds American management responsible for America's competitive decline, because they are too interested in short-term objectives and are not conditioned to compete in global markets. The fourth reason is that it was only a matter of time that other countries, whose economies were destroyed by World War II, would catch up to the United States.

An Uncompetitive Society

Richard Lamm, the former governor of Colorado, offers a rather interesting explanation for why the United States is losing its competitive edge.[7] Better education and better management are not enough to restore America's competitive position because there are a number of internal handicaps which are as follows:

1. No modern industrial society has the rate of drug addiction, teenage pregnancy, and functional illiteracy that we do. Drug abuse provides a consummate example of what is wrong with American society today. The cost of drug abuse to the American economy is $200 billion a year, and is steadily climbing.[8] Drugs are the prime cause of crime, absenteeism in the workplace, and increasing hospitalization and other health care costs. According to the National Council on Alcoholism, 10 percent of the American population over 15 years old is chemically dependent on alcohol. The economic impact of drug abuse is illustrated by the 1984 figures from the Division of Substance Abuse Services of the State of New York. According to their statistics, the average active drug addict costs the state $32,700

---

[5] The correct quote is: "The fault, dear Brutus, is not in our stars, but in ourselves, that we are underlings" (*The Tragedy of Julius Ceasar; I, ii*).

[6] Joel Dreyfuss, "How Japan Picks America's Brains," *Fortune* (December 21, 1987), pp. 79–89.

[7] Richard Lamm, "The Uncompetitive Society," *U.S. News & World Report* (April 25, 1988), p. 9. He is now director of the University of Denver's Center for Public Policy.

[8] Joint Economic Committee of the U.S. Congress, *The Cost to the U.S. Economy of Drug Abuse* (Hearings before the Subcommittee on Economic Goals & Intergovernmental Policy, 99th Cong., 1st Session, 1986), p. 3.

a year—$26,800 in theft losses, $3,300 in law enforcement costs, and $2,600 in health expenses.[9] Drug abuse has been estimated to cost national business firms between $20 and $35 billion annually due to absenteeism, theft, poor performance, and higher health costs.

2. The cartoon character Pogo once said, "We have met the enemy and he is us." It is rather absurd to be talking about meeting foreign competition until we get our own house in order. Take, for example, education. One-fifth of American adults are functionally illiterate, and 30 percent of American teenagers drop out of high school before they graduate, compared to 2 percent in Japan.[10] In international student achievement comparisons, Americans do poorly in math and sciences.[11] One-third of U.S. secondary schools do not offer their students enough mathematics to qualify them to enter accredited engineering schools. College-bound students in Europe and Japan have usually had two more years of math and science than their American counterparts. The ability of the United States to retain leadership in emerging technologies and the jobs they create depends on a better-educated work force.

Table 6-1 presents an international comparison of the performance of twelfth-grade students in thirteen countries in math and science. It shows the poor performance of U.S. students in comparison with foreign students. American students take fewer science and math courses in high school than students in other industrial countries. Consequently, they score lower on international tests in these areas, and fewer are prepared to pursue higher education in these fields. America's ability to compete in technology development is linked closely to its supply of skilled

TABLE 6-1
U.S. Ranking on International Math and Science Achievement Tests

Type of Achievement Test	United States	Japan	Hungary
Geometry	11	2	12
Biology	13	10	3
Algebra	12	1	11
Physics	9	4	3
Calculus	11	2	12
Chemistry	11	4	5

Source: International Association for Evaluation of Educational Achievement, Changing America, The New Face of Science & Engineering, Washington, DC: Task Force on Women, the Handicapped and Minorities in Science and Technology, 1988, p. 9.

---

[9] Joint Economic Committee (1986), p. 4.

[10] World Bank, 1988 Statistical Yearbook (New York: Oxford University Press), p. 28.

[11] Joint Economic Committee of the U.S. Congress, International Student Achievement Comparisons and Teacher Shortages in Math and Science (98th Cong., 1st Sess., 1983), pp. 3–7.

technical workers. It is evident that the nation faces significant human resource problems. By the year 2000, the number of jobs requiring college degrees will increase. However, the educational system is failing to produce the number of scientists and engineers needed to meet future demand. Also, 40 percent of all college engineering teachers are foreigners who have been educated in the United States.[12]

The results of the comparison are rather revealing. The only communist country included was Hungary, and twelfth grade students in that country generally did better than U.S. students. It can be concluded that Russian students also score better than American students in math and science tests. West Germany and France were not included in the test comparisons, but both countries have excellent educational systems where students on average attend classes for 240 days, compared to 180 days for American students. Students from the East Asian countries are far superior to their American counterparts on math and science tests. Unfortunately for the United States, the competition in the future will come from the highly literate, well-educated labor forces of the East Asian countries.

The National Alliance for Business provides some statistics that create concerns about America's most important asset, its human resources.[13]

1. Twenty-three million adults are functionally illiterate in America today; another 47 million are borderline illiterates.
2. Eighty percent of all new entrants to the labor force will be minorities, women, and immigrants, traditionally the least prepared to work.
3. Over one million youths drop out of high school each year. The dropout rates of many urban schools are close to 50 percent.
4. Each year's dropouts cost America $240 billion in lost earnings and foregone taxes over their lifetimes.
5. By the year 2000, 50 percent of all jobs in America will require education beyond high school and 30 percent will require a college degree.

A character in Shakespeare's play *King Henry VI*, Part II (Act IV, Scene ii) said: "The first thing we do, let's kill all the lawyers." The United States is the most litigious society in the world. Two-thirds of the lawyers on the planet live in the United States. There are more lawyers in Washington, D.C. than there are in Japan. All of the other countries in the world combined do not spend as much time in court as we do. Warren Burger, who was once a Supreme Court Justice, once made the statement that America had too many lawyers and that they and the myriad of lawsuits constituted a drag on U.S. productivity. To put it another way, Japan produces engineers and the United States produces lawyers.

---

[12] Paul Doigan & Mack Gilkeson, "ASEE Survey of Engineering Faculty and Graduate Students, Fall 1985," *Engineering Education* (October 1986), pp. 51–56.
[13] National Alliance for Business, *The Road Ahead* (New York 1988), p. 1.

3. The United States is the most crime-ridden, violent society in the world. There are more homicides in a year in the United States than in all of Western Europe and Japan combined. Many of the major cities in the United States are battle zones in which no one dares to appear at night. Teenage gangs prey on each other and on innocent bystanders. Many crimes are drug related. In Baltimore, for example, 243 drug addicts committed 500,000 crimes over an 11-year period.[14] Then, too, there is the American preoccupation with guns—an inalienable right, according to the National Rifle Association (NRA), which wraps itself in the Constitution and the flag. According to the NRA, it is not guns that kill, but people. Besides, it is necessary for Americans to protect themselves against savage hordes of aliens who may cross the border at any minute intent on rapine and slaughter.

The United States Has Caught the "British Disease"

The Spaniards introduced syphilis into the New World, killing off half the Indian population of North America. However, the "British disease" is not a social disease, but a pejorative term that Americans have applied to the British, and now the Japanese are applying it to us. Basically, it means the lack of desire to work hard and an overdependence on the welfare state. New entrants into the U.S. labor force are less skilled and motivated than their international competitors; they come out of an educational system that deemphasizes merit, excellence, and discipline as it levels down elitist values. Society focuses on short-term consumer values and entitlements and ignores producer values and the requisite of increased productivity. Manufacturers do not insist on product quality and manufacturing excellence, but on quantity and profit margins.

The Harvard sociologist Daniel Bell once made the statement that the Protestant work ethic disappeared with the advent of the credit card. The Protestant work ethic is one of the fundamental institutions of Western capitalist societies.[15] In the United States, it was a driving force in the economic development of the country. It stressed hard work, thrift, and the postponement of the consumption of goods until you could pay for them. God rewarded you in direct proportion to what you contributed in this world, so John D. Rockefeller was able to ascribe his monetary success to the fact that God had rewarded him because he worked hard. Generations of Americans were raised to believe in the Protestant work ethic: that hard work would get you ahead and that, as in the fable of the grasshopper and the ant, indolence would get you nowhere. But times have changed, and it can be argued that the Asian nations, not the United States, have the work ethic.

---

[14] Joint Economic Committee (1986), p. 27.

[15] R. H. Tawney, *Religion and the Rise of Capitalism* (New York: Harcourt, Brace and World, 1926), and Max Weber, *The Protestant Ethic and the Spirit of Capitalism* (New York: Charles Scribner and Sons, 1930).

Poor Management

A third explanation for the decline in U.S. competitiveness lays the blame on American managers. American companies are overstaffed, and managers think only in terms of short-term objectives. This is linked to a characteristically American preoccupation with immediate solutions to every problem. Managers are judged successful if profits continue to rise and dividends are increased every year. Consequently, American management places more emphasis on marketing than on manufacturing and invests too little in the future. In addition, they are outhustled abroad because they have not really had to compete until recently; for 30 years after the end of World War II, they had domestic and world markets to themselves. Now the rest of the world has caught up to the United States and, compounding the problem, most American managers, like most Americans, know little or nothing about foreign cultures.

The criticism of American managers extends into the area of labor-management relations. It is argued that management practices appropriate for assembly line production have become obsolete and that the more flexible management techniques, such as quality circles, used by Japan and other countries are superior.[16] Japanese managers allow more participation in the decision-making process by workers.[17] This participation makes the workers feel as though they are part of the team. However, it is difficult to attribute the high productivity of Japanese industry to that one factor alone. High productivity in Japanese industry is due to a number of cultural factors and the high literacy of Japanese workers. However, some U.S. business firms have been spurred to take corrective action, which has ranged from emphasizing product quality and improving employee relations to sharply reducing white-collar staff.[18]

Convergence

It is important to remember that the economies of Western Europe and Japan were damaged by two major world wars. During World War I, most of the fighting was done in western and central Europe, with the United States a participant at the very end of the war. The industrial base of the Western European countries was damaged; the United States was untouched and came out of the war as the leading creditor nation. Between the wars, the United States did not have a particularly high growth in comparison to other industrial countries,[19] but World War II had a

---

[16] Bruce R. Scott, "National Strategies," *U.S. Competitiveness in the World Economy*, edited by Bruce R. Scott & George C. Lodge, (Boston, Mass.: Harvard University Press, 1985).

[17] William Ouchi, *Theory Z* (Reading, MA: Addison-Wesley, 1981).

[18] Raymond Vernon, "Can U.S. Manufacturing Come Back?" *Harvard Business Review*, vol. 69 (July–August 1984), pp. 98–106.

[19] Edward F. Dennison, *Why Growth Rates Differ: Post-War Experiences in Nine Western Countries* (Washington, DC: The Brookings Institution, 1967).

more devastating impact on other industrial countries. The economies of France, Germany, the Soviet Union, Italy, and Japan were literally destroyed by the war, while the United States remained untouched. Germany was split into three parts, with West Germany created out of one part. It can be said that the major world competitors to the United States had to rebuild their economies from scratch but that it was only a matter of time before they caught up with us.

Table 6-2 presents the average annual rate of growth in per capita GNP for the major industrial countries for the period 1965–1987. As the table indicates, the growth rate of the United States was lower than the other industrial countries.[20]

YES, THE UNITED STATES IS LOSING ITS COMPETITIVE EDGE

There are a number of rather convincing reasons advanced to prove that the United States is losing competitively to other countries. First, the United States lags behind other industrial countries in the rate of saving investment. Second, the U.S. standard of living has not increased as rapidly as other countries'. Third, the United States is getting beat in the high-tech area. Fourth, the United States has a lower rate of productivity growth in manufacturing than other countries have. Finally, the United States has shown a relative decline industrially as measured against world manufacturing production of textiles, iron and steel, shipbuilding, and basic

TABLE 6-2
Comparison of Average Annual Increase in Per Capita GNP For Major Industrial Countries, 1965–1987 (percent)

Country	1965–1987
Italy	2.7
West Germany	2.5
France	2.7
Japan	4.2
Canada	2.7
United Kingdom	1.7
United States	1.5

Source: World Bank, World Development Report 1989 (New York: Oxford University Press, 1989), Table 1, p. 165.

[20] In 1913 the U.S. share of world manufacturing was 31.5 percent. It hit a high of 48.1 percent in 1953, but by 1987 fell to 31.4 percent, approximately the same share it had in 1913.

chemicals, and it is also losing its global share of automobiles, robotics, machine tools, and computers. It is necessary to explore in depth each of these four reasons.

Saving and Investment

The United States has not had a high rate of savings in comparison with other countries. Large federal budget deficits have absorbed more than two-thirds of private savings in recent years, and national saving has averaged less than 3 percent of GNP. A low rate of national saving hurts manufacturing in two ways. First, it reduces the supply of capital and chokes off much-needed investment. This hurts manufacturers in their role as producers of capital equipment, and it discourages them from making productivity-enhancing investments. Second, the low national saving rate forces the United States to borrow from abroad in order to finance investment, which makes trade deficits inevitable. Part of this borrowing comes from Japan, currently the world's leading creditor nation and the major industrial competition to the United States. As Table 6-3 indicates, the Japanese have a much higher rate of saving and investment.

U.S. Living Standards

Although in absolute terms the United States still has the highest standard of living, since 1972 the U.S. standard of living has increased only one-fourth as fast as West Germany's and one-seventh as fast as Japan's. In 1987 America's standard of living continued to grow more slowly than other industrial countries. A rising standard of living is the ultimate goal of any nation. A comparison of changes in living standards for major countries is presented in Table 6-4. It focuses on workers rather than on the overall population. It shows on a per worker basis how much income is generated, plus or minus any change in what is owed to foreigners. By taking into account changes in foreign debt, the measure gives insight into future living standards.

TABLE 6-3
A Comparison of U.S. and Japanese Saving and Investment Rates (percent)

Year	U.S.		Japan	
	Saving	Investment	Saving	Investment
1975	2.8	2.1	19.4	19.9
1980	4.4	4.2	18.3	19.5
1981	5.3	5.2	18.5	18.6
1983	2.0	3.2	17.0	15.5
1985	3.2	6.2	16.7	13.0
1986	2.0	5.5	16.5	13.1

Source: Rudiger Dornbusch, James Poterba, and Lawrence Summers, The Case for Manufacturing in America's Future *(New York: Eastman Kodak Company, 1988), p. 15.*

TABLE 6-4

A Comparison of Standard of Living Indexes for the United States and Other Countries, 1979–1987

	1979	1980	1981	1982	1983	1984	1985	1986	1987
United States relative to Summit countries[a]	84.8	83.6	83.0	80.5	80.8	81.2	80.5	79.8	78.9
U.S. index	101.7	101.0	101.9	100.3	102.7	105.5	106.8	107.7	108.3
Summit index	119.9	120.9	122.7	124.5	127.0	129.9	132.7	134.9	137.4
Germany index	123.4	123.5	124.6	125.4	129.7	131.8	133.8	136.0	137.6
Japan index	124.8	129.0	132.9	135.3	137.3	143.3	149.0	151.3	155.9

[a] The Summit countries are the United States, United Kingdom, France, West Germany, Italy, and Japan.

Source: Council on Competitiveness, Competitiveness Index *(Washington: USGPO, 1988), p. 6.*

High Technology

Probably the most serious challenge to U.S. competitiveness is in the area of high technology, which represents the future. The United States has blown its lead in high technology, and the problem could become a crisis. Foreign competition has ruined Silicon Valley, once considered the Mecca of high technology. In 1987 the U.S. trade deficit with Japan in electronics was almost as large as it was for automobiles. Between 1970 and 1988, the U.S. share of its own consumer electronics market fell from 100 percent to under 5 percent; color TV sales fell from 90 percent to 10 percent; and phones, from 99 percent to 25 percent. Now the Japanese have developed high-definition television, which can transmit about six times more information to the screen and which widens receivers to movie screen proportions, bringing more colorful, detailed pictures into the home. Japan has seized the world lead in an emerging multibillion dollar technology. The new technology could prove decisive in the U.S. attempt to maintain a healthy semiconductor industry, since high-definition TV will consume large quantities of chips.

Semiconductors are the fundamental building blocks of modern electronics. These are small, rectangular chips made of silicon. Each chip is the size of a fingernail and is crammed with microscopic circuits capable of storing and processing enormous amounts of information. They operate products ranging from digital watches and videocassette recorders to supercomputers and the telephone network. In addition, they are essential to advanced weapon systems. The semiconductor industry, invented in the United States and consummate symbol of its dynamism, has come to be a paradigm of the rise of Japan and the decline of the United States in the latter part of the twentieth century. But there is more than just semiconductors. The Japanese have come to dominate virtually all of the high-technology industries, including disk drives, robots, printers, optical fiber electronics, satellite ground stations, and advanced industrial ceramics. Many products associated with U.S. companies, such as personal computers, are made in Japan.

In the two decades following World War II, U.S. firms dominated the commercial application of technology. Over time, however, foreign firms assimilated state-of-the-art technology, often American in origin; improved it; generated their own products and processes; and brought them skillfully to market. Table 6-5 presents the commercial challenge to U.S. technology. In the post–World War II era, technology has been a leading U.S. export strength. However, since 1970, many U.S. industries have lost their domination of foreign and even domestic markets to foreign competitors. Nowhere is that more clear than in the production of color television sets, where U.S. firms now have only 10 percent of a $14 billion domestic market.

During the 1960s and 1970s U.S. companies dominated the world market for the design and manufacture of semiconductors and computers. However, in the 1970s Japan targeted semiconductors as a strategic industry. By 1983 Japan-based firms' share of the world market was equal to that of firms based in the United States. By 1986 the Japanese had taken 65 percent of the world market, while the U.S. share had fallen to 30 percent. As Table 6-6 indicates, these market shifts are even more dramatic for dynamic random access memory products (DRAM), which constitute a core semiconductor technology. Combining their edge in memory technology with aggressive pricing policies, the Japanese have achieved a sweep of the world DRAM market.

Foreign countries have made inroads into a number of industries pioneered and dominated by American firms. Consumer electronics is one area. Since 1970

TABLE 6-5
The Erosion of the U.S. Share of Technology Markets, 1970–1987

Technology	Pioneered by	U.S. Companies' Share of American Markets (percent)			
		1970	1975	1980	1987
Phonographs	U.S.	90	40	30	1
Television					
Black & white	U.S.	65	30	15	2
Color	U.S.	90	80	60	10
Audio tape recorders	U.S.	40	10	10	1
Video cassette recorders	U.S.	10	10	10	1
Machine tools					
Numerically controlled lathes	U.S.	100	92	70	40
Machining centers	U.S.	100	97	79	35
Telephone sets	U.S.	99	95	88	25
Ball-bearing	Germany	88	83	71	71
Semiconductors					
Manufacturing equipment	U.S.	100	90	75	75
Semiconductors	U.S.	89	70	65	64

Source: Council on Competitiveness, Keeping Up The Pace: The Commercial Challenge to U.S. Competitiveness (Washington, DC: USGPO, 1988), p. 15.

TABLE 6-6

World Share of Dynamic Random Access Memory
Products (DRAM) (percent)

	1975	1980	1987
United States	95.8	55.6	17.9
Japan	4.2	39.4	73.0
Europe	—	5.0	2.0
Rest of the world	—	—	2.1

Source: Council on Competitiveness, Keeping Up The
Pace: The Commercial Challenge to U.S. Competitiveness *(Washington, DC: USGPO, 1988), p. 17.*

the United States has lost virtually the entire consumer electronics market to Japan
and other countries. In 1987 it had less than 5 percent of its own domestic market,
estimated at $25 billion.[21] This has repercussions for other parts of the electronics
industry. This connection has been likened to the biological food chain in that
when one link is weakened, other links feel the injury. While the U.S. continues to
enjoy a market presence in related fields, such as home computers, telephones, and
calculators, the erosion of the U.S. position in consumer electronics could have a
deleterious effect on the U.S. lead in other electronic areas.

Lower Manufacturing Productivity

Another measure of U.S. industrial competitiveness is a comparison with other
nations' trends in manufacturing productivity. If productivity is low, it affects a
country's cost competitiveness and the standard of living. It implies that real wages
cannot rise as fast as they can in high-productivity countries. Lower productivity
also has an impact on exports and imports. It has contributed in part to the unfavorable balance in the U.S. merchandise trade account and has resulted in import
penetration, which is defined as the share of imports in apparent consumption (i.e.,
production less exports). Rising imports in the U.S. capital goods sector have been
particularly dramatic in 1987; for example, nearly 40 percent of all manufacturing
equipment was imported. In Japan, which is the United States' number one trade
competitor, productivity growth has been higher than in any industrialized country. Table 6-7 presents a comparison of annual percent changes in manufacturing
productivity for the Summit countries from 1960 to 1986.

Labor productivity is another way to measure manufacturing performance.
This can be done by using gross domestic product per worker, which also includes
services and government activities as well as manufacturing. Table 6-8 presents a
comparison of average annual changes in real gross domestic product per employed

---

[21] Council on Competitiveness, *Keeping Up The Pace* (Washington, DC: 1988), p. 16.

TABLE 6-7
Annual Percent Changes in Manufacturing Productivity For the Summit Countries
(percent)

	United States	Canada	Japan	France	Germany	Italy	United Kingdom
1960–1986	2.8	3.3	7.9	5.2	4.6	5.7	3.6
1960–1973	3.2	4.5	10.3	6.5	5.8	7.5	4.2
1973–1979	1.4	2.1	5.5	4.9	4.3	3.3	1.2
1979–1986	3.5	2.3	5.6	3.1	2.7	4.3	4.5

Source: Congress of the United States, Office of Technology Assessment, Paying the Bill: Manufacturing & America's Trade Deficit *(Washington, DC: USGPO, 1988), p. 45.*

person. The rate of productivity growth in the U.S. economy has only recovered slightly from the low-growth period of the 1970s. Conversely, Japan has put an enormous effort into increasing productivity in industries such as steel, autos, and electronics that have been central to their export-led growth strategy. In many areas, the Japanese have forged ahead of the United States in terms of productivity. For example, the International Motor Vehicle Program found that in the mid-1980s it took, on average, 19.1 hours to build a car in Japanese assembly plants. In American-managed plants, the average time for assembly was 26.5 hours.[22]

Global Decline in World Production

Again, it is necessary to emphasize the fact that America's economic decline is only relative, not absolute. It is not becoming poorer, and its economy, which increased at a growth rate close to 4 percent in 1988, is hardly weak. The gross

TABLE 6-8
Average Annual Changes in Real Gross Domestic Product Per Employed Person
in the Summit Countries, 1960–1986 (percent)

Year	United States	Canada	Japan	France	Germany	Italy	United Kingdom
1960–1986	1.2	1.9	5.5	3.6	3.1	3.7	2.2
1960–1973	1.9	2.6	8.2	4.9	4.1	5.8	2.9
1973–1979	0.0	1.3	2.9	2.7	2.9	1.7	1.3
1979–1986	0.8	1.0	2.8	1.9	1.6	1.6	1.7

Source: Congress of the United States, Office of Technology Assessment, Paying the Bill: Manufacturing & America's Trade Deficit *(Washington, DC: USGPO, 1988), p. 48.*

---

[22] Congress of the United States, Office of Technology Assessment, *Paying the Bill: Manufacturing & America's Trade Deficit* (Washington, DC: U.S. Government Printing Office, 1988), p. 49.

national product of the United States for 1988 is around $4.5 trillion, far surpassing second-place Japan's $2.1 trillion. But the United States has ceased to dominate the world economy the way it did for nearly four decades after World War II. The United States still remains first among a group of increasingly assertive industrial countries. However, Japan has come to dominate some of the growth industries of the future. It produces 70 percent of the world supply of robots. In 31 areas of high technology, it is ahead in 25,[23] and it produces most of the world's supply of memory chips.

The United States Is the World's Leading Debtor Nation

Here is a prelude to a twenty-first century scenario. It is November 2004, and America, battered by astronomical debts and reeling from prolonged economic decline, is gripped by a new and grave economic crisis. Like all such events, the causes are multiple and complex. But the president-elect and the voters who chose him by a landslide see only one single cause and a single culprit for America's problems: the Japanese. The president has campaigned on the slogan of "standing up to the Japanese" and has vowed to bring an end to what he calls "the historic pattern of underestimating the Japanese menace."[24]

Sound unrealistic? It is entirely possible. The United States began the 1980s as the world's leading creditor nation and at the end of the decade, it was the world's leading debtor nation. Japan is now the leading creditor nation. At the end of 1987 foreign individuals, companies, and governments held $368.2 billion more in U.S. assets than the total of all U.S. owned assets abroad.[25] Conversely, Japan had a surplus of $240 billion in foreign assets.[26] In 1989 Japan had 17 of the 25 largest banks in the world; the United States had only one.[27] It had eight of the ten largest banks in the world, and each had assets in excess of $300 billion. Moreover, the United States had a surplus in its merchandise trade account; it ended 1989 with a deficit of $108.5 billion. Its greatest trade deficit was with Japan.[28] The Tokyo Stock Exchange is larger than the New York Stock Exchange in terms of sales volume, and the Nomura Securities Company is the largest in the world, with assets twenty times greater than those of Merrill Lynch.[29]

[23] Council on Competitiveness, *Competitive Index* (Washington, DC: 1988), p. 27.
[24] Daniel Burstein, *Yen! Japan's New Financial Empire and Its Threat To America* (New York: Simon and Schuster, 1988), p. 13.
[25] Linda M. Spencer, *American Assets: An Examination of Foreign Investment in the United States* (Washington, DC: Congressional Economic Leadership Institute, 1988), p. 40.
[26] C. Michael Aho and Marc Levinson, *After Reagan: Confronting the World Economy* (New York: Council on Foreign Relations, 1988), p. 78.
[27] *Fortune*, July 30, 1990, p. 325.
[28] *The Washington Post*, February 1, 1989, p. D1.
[29] Burstein, p. 32.

There are two types of investment: direct and portfolio. Direct investment involves the acquisition of companies, factories, and real estate. It is in contrast to portfolio investment, which involves the acquisition of government securities and the stocks and bonds of private companies. By the end of 1987 total foreign direct and portfolio investment in the United States amounted to $1.54 trillion, and total U.S. direct and portfolio investment in foreign countries amounted to $1.16 trillion.[30] Foreign direct investment in U.S. companies, factories, and real estate amounted to $262 billion at the end of 1987, while U.S. direct investment abroad amounted to $1.27 trillion and U.S. portfolio investment abroad amounted to $859 billion. Moreover, as Table 6-9 indicates, the shift from the world's leading creditor nation to the world's leading debtor nation began during the 1980s.

The Budget and Trade Deficits

The debtor status of the United States can be linked to the U.S. budget and trade deficits. The deficit in the federal budget is the primary catalyst because it is linked to the U.S. trade deficit, the status of the United States as the the world's lead-

TABLE 6-9

U.S. Assets Abroad and Foreign Assets in the United States for 1980 and 1987 (billions of dollars)

Type of Assets	1980	1987
U.S. Assets Abroad		
Portfolio	$ 392	$ 859
Direct	225	309
Total	617	1,168
Foreign Assets in the United States		
Portfolio	418	1,274
Direct	83	262
Total	501	1,536

Source: Linda M. Spencer, American Assets: An Examination of Foreign Investment in the United States (Washington, DC: Congressional Economic Leadership Institute, 1988), p. 49.

---

[30] U.S. Department of Commerce, *Survey of Current Business* (July 1988), p. 3. At the end of 1989 foreign investment in the United States amounted to $2.0 trillion, and U.S. investment abroad amounted to $1.4 trillion.

ing debtor nation, savings and investment, and industrial competitiveness. It also increases the national debt, which has tripled since 1980. The budget deficit has created several problems. First, interest payments on the national debt are a fixed cost that has to be covered as a part of government expenditures. In the fiscal year 1990, interest payments accounted for 15 percent of total federal government expenditures.[31] Second, to finance the deficit and to refinance that part of the national debt that comes due, the U.S. Treasury constantly has to borrow money in competition with private investors. This raises the cost of borrowing. Third, much of the borrowing by the U.S. Treasury has been from overseas investors. This has created the debtor status of the United States.

When it is reported on the nightly news and in the newspapers, the trade deficit refers to the merchandise trade deficit, which is the difference between goods imported into the United States and exports from the United States to the other countries.[32] The U.S. merchandise trade deficit was $118.7 billion in 1988, and in 1989 it was $108.5 billion. Table 6-10 presents the ten leading country markets for U.S. exports and the ten leading country suppliers of imports for 1988. The major part of the total deficit is concentrated in two major trading areas: the East Asian countries and Canada. In fact, half of the merchandise trade deficit for 1988 was with three East Asian countries: Japan, Taiwan, and South Korea. Demand in the United States for protection against imports from these countries has increased.

TABLE 6-10

Top Ten U.S. Merchandise Export and Import Markets for 1989 (billions)

Merchandise Exports		Merchandise Imports	
Canada	$ 78.6	Japan	$ 93.6
Japan	44.6	Canada	88.2
Mexico	25.0	Mexico	27.2
United Kingdom	20.9	West Germany	24.8
West Germany	16.9	Taiwan	24.3
South Korea	13.5	South Korea	19.7
France	11.6	United Kingdom	18.2
Netherlands	11.4	France	13.0
Taiwan	11.3	China	12.0
Belgium-Luxembourg	8.7	Italy	11.9
Total merchandise exports	364.4	Total merchandise imports	472.9

Source: U.S. Department of Commerce, Business America, Vol. 111, No. 8, April 23, 1990, p. 5.

---

[31] Executive Office of the President, Office of Management and Budget, *Budget of the United States Government, Fiscal Year 1990* (Washington, DC: U.S. Government Printing Office, 1990), pp. 1–2.

[32] The merchandise trade account is part of the current account, which also includes service transactions. The current account is one of four accounts in a country's balance of payments. The others are the capital account, unilateral transfers, and the official reserve account.

NO, THE UNITED STATES IS NOT IN A PROCESS OF DECLINE

The "God's in his heaven and all's right with America" school argues that there is nothing inherently wrong with the U.S. economy. Although it is true that Japan is gaining on us or has surpassed us in certain areas of high technology, the American economy is too large and too dynamic for Japan or any other country to overtake us. Although Japan may be rich, it is poor in terms of world leadership and is not popular with other Asian countries within its economic and political sphere of influence.[33] Economic strength ultimately rests on human resources. Here, too, the United States has an advantage. While Japan, despite a rapidly aging population, works hard to maintain its racial purity by closing its doors to outsiders, America's human resources are continually replenished by successive waves of immigrants.[34] The vitality, creativity, and initiative of its people give America its edge over Japan, particularly in the long run.[35]

TABLE 6-11
The Position of the United States in a Global Economy, 1988

	United States	**Japan**	**U.S.S.R.**	**EC**[a]
Population (millions)	246.0	122.6	286.4	324.4
GNP (billions of dollars)	4,864.5	1,758.4	2,535.3	4,059.7
Per capita GNP (dollars)	18,770.0	14,340.0	8,850.0	12,510.0
GNP growth rate (percent)				
1981–85	1.8	3.2	1.0	1.2
1988	2.9	5.1	0.5	3.5
Inflation (percent)	3.7	1.0	3.3	8.4
Unemployment rate	5.4	2.5	NA	9.2
Foreign trade				
Exports (millions)	321.6	264.9	110.7	1,064.2
Imports (millions)	459.6	187.4	107.3	1,080.6
Agriculture				
Grain production[b]	840.0	110.0	620.0	510.0
Life expectancy (years)	75.0	79.0	69.0	76.0

[a] European Community.
[b] Kilograms per capita.
Source: Central Intelligence Agency, Handbook of Economic Statistics 1989 *(Springfield, VA: National Technical Information Service, 1989), Tables 1, 2, 3, 7, 11.*

---

[33] Japanese politicians are not exactly good at public relations. A cabinet member was quoted as saying that Japanese atrocities against China in the 1930s and 1940s did not actually occur. This would be like the Germans claiming that there were no concentration camps. Japan had to apologize to China.

[34] The subject of racial purity also caused a highly placed Japanese politician to say that the reason that Japan would do better than the United States is that it is racially pure. It had no blacks or other minorities to hold it back. Japan had to apologize to the United States.

[35] *The Wall Street Journal,* "The 90s and Beyond: The U.S. Stands to Retain Its Global Leadership," Monday, January 23, 1989, p. A8.

As Table 6-11 indicates, economically the United States remains the world's largest producer of goods and services. The United States is the world's free enterprise model, with incentives to grow and prosper. As for its problems, they too will pass. The federal budget deficit, although troublesome, can be eliminated. The U.S. economy has grown so rapidly during the 1980s that, as a percentage of GNP, the deficit now is roughly equivalent to the 2.8 percent it was in 1980. In fact, the United States is not that much different from other industrial countries when it comes to running budget deficits.[36] The trade deficit appears to be on the way to fixing itself. With the dollar weak against other currencies, American goods are cheaper and thus easier to sell abroad and the trade deficit is gradually shrinking.

The Harvard sociologist, Daniel Bell, wrote a book called *The Coming of Post-Industrial Society* (New York: Basic Books, 1976.) His premise was that the United States was in the process of change from an industrial economy to a service economy. The same held true for other industrial countries. Developing countries, with lower labor costs, would be the emerging industrial societies. According to Bell, this was an inevitable concomitant of economic development. In the United States today, 70 percent of all workers are employed in service jobs. In West Germany, Japan, and other major industrial countries, a majority of workers are employed in service jobs. As the world moves from material-based production to knowledge-based production, the traditional heavy industries, such as steel, will continue to decline, particularly in the employment of blue-collar workers.

The U.S. Service Sector

Because of the boom in the service sector, the United States has been creating more jobs over the past decade than at any other time in its history, and far better than in Western Europe and Japan. The United States creates more jobs in one year than all of Western Europe in a decade. Moreover, many of these are high-paying jobs and are far from the hamburger-flipping jobs that are normally associated with service employment. The service sector comprises a broad array of activities, including health, legal, education, repair, and personal and business services.[37]

The Rate of Employment

One important measure of an economy is its ability to provide jobs for those who seek work. The rate of unemployment in the United States is lower than it is in all the other industrial countries, with the exception of Japan. In fact, other countries look at the United States as the "great job machine," an economy that is constantly able to create jobs. Table 6-12 presents the unemployment rate in July 1989 for the United States and other major industrial countries. The unemployment rate for the year 1988 is also included.

---

[36] However, it must be mentioned that the rate of saving is much higher in Japan and West Germany, meaning that there is a larger supply of loanable funds and a lower interest rate for them.

[37] U.S. Department of Labor, Bureau of Labor Statistics, *Employment by Occupations*, 1972–1987.

TABLE 6-12
Unemployment Rates for 1988 and 1989 for Major Industrial Countries (percent)

Country	1988 Unemployment Rate	July 1989 Unemployment Rate
United States	5.5	5.3
Canada	7.8	7.5
Japan	2.5	2.3
France	10.4	10.1
West Germany	6.3	5.7
Italy	7.9	7.8
United Kingdom	8.3	6.4

Source: Economic Report of the President 1990 *(Washington, DC: USGPO, 1990), Table 3-108, p. 417.*

U.S. Manufacturing Output

Those who argue that the United States is not declining competitively contend that the move from manufacturing to services occurs naturally in all advanced countries and that U.S. manufacturing is increasing in output in absolute terms, even though blue-collar employment is declining. This is a natural trend as the world moves from material-based to knowledge-based production. Table 6-13 can be used to buttress their claim that manufacturing production in the United States has increased in absolute terms and also relative to industrial production in other countries.

The Inherent Dynamism of the U.S. Economy

It can also be argued that the U.S. economy is so large and variegated that some regions and sectors are likely to be growing at the same time that others are declining.

TABLE 6-13
Manufacturing Output in the United States and Other Countries, 1980–1987 (1977 = 100%)

Year	U.S.	Japan	West Germany	France	United Kingdom
1980	108.6	119.2	108.0	106.0	99.8
1981	111.0	120.4	106.2	106.0	96.4
1982	103.1	120.9	103.1	104.0	98.2
1983	109.2	125.1	104.1	104.0	101.7
1984	121.4	138.9	107.6	105.0	103.2
1985	123.7	145.1	112.9	106.0	107.9
1986	125.1	144.5	115.1	106.0	109.5
1987	129.8	148.4	115.4	107.0	111.2
1988	137.1	159.2	117.8	114.0	118.1

Source: Economic Report of the President 1990 *(Washington, DC: USGPO, 1990), Table C-107, p. 416.*

Therefore, to say that the economy is in decline is too sweeping a generalization. For most of the 1980s the steel producing states have been referred to as the "Rust Belt," where companies have shut down and thousands of highly paid steel workers have lost their jobs.[38] However, an article in *Fortune* called "The Resurrection of the Rust Belt" states that manufacturing has made a comeback and that steel and other industries are more competitive than ever.[39] For the first time in a decade, USX (U.S. Steel) can export steel profitably. This was not done easily, because it shut down the seven least efficient of its 12 steel mills, and reduced its workforce from 75,000 to 20,000. Other industries have also developed in the Rust Belt states, and the unemployment rate, which averaged 12 percent in 1982, has been cut in half.

REAGANOMICS

Reaganomics, the term used to describe the economic policies instituted since the election of Ronald Reagan, had five components: a large across-the-board tax cut, a cut in social welfare spending, an increase in defense spending, less government regulation, and restricted growth in the money supply. The tax cut reflected a belief in the efficacy of supply-side economics. The cuts were designed to favor those persons who made fifty thousand dollars or more, for they provide the bulk of savings in the United States. Savings were supposed to increase and to be channeled into investment. This created a tax cut flow from savings to investment to increased productivity. Cuts in social welfare expenditures were designed to limit increases in entitlement programs. Increases in defense spending were not designed for economic reasons but had the effect of increasing the deficit in the federal budget because they were larger than cuts in civilian spending. Antitrust and other forms of government regulation were relaxed because they discouraged investment and were too costly to business. The slow rate of growth in the money supply was designed to reduce inflation.

The Results of Reaganomics

President Reagan will be regarded as one of the most popular and charismatic U.S. presidents of this century, but there is much controversy concerning his performance as president. Those who think that he was an outstanding president point to the economic prosperity of the country and the improved relationship with the Soviet Union. Those who are critical of him point to the massive increase in the size of the federal deficit problem as a direct legacy of Reaganomics. The truth, as it is in most controversies, lies somewhere in the middle. So it is important to examine the impact of Reaganomics on the U.S. economy.

---

[38] The Rust Belt includes the steel producing areas of Pennsylvania and the industrial Midwest.
[39] Myron Magnet, "The Resurrection of the Rust Belt," *Fortune* (August 15, 1988), pp. 40–47.

When Ronald Reagan was first elected president in 1980, the most important problem confronting the U.S. economy was the rate of inflation. The consumer price index increased at a rate of 13.3 percent in 1979 and 12.4 percent in 1980. The U.S. economy had performed poorly during the 1970s, and the average American family was no better off at the end of the decade than it was at the beginning of it. President Carter had said that Americans had to expect that rising living standards could not be automatically taken for granted. Our relations with the Soviet Union were poor, and President Carter refused to let American athletes participate in the Olympic games held in Moscow in 1980. There was also concern that the Carter and previous administrations had neglected defense expenditures to the extent that the Russians had a vast military superiority over us.

Table 6-14 presents the rate of inflation, the rate of unemployment, and the real rate of economic growth for the United States during the eight years that Ronald Reagan was in office. Probably the single most important accomplishment of the Reagan administration was the reduction of the inflation rates. This was achieved at some cost. The tight money policy of the Federal Reserve increased interest rates, and contributed to a major recession in 1982 and 1983. The unemployment rate increased to 9.7 percent in 1982. There was also a decline of 2.5 percent in the real rate of growth in GNP for the same year. The real rate of economic growth, although unspectacular, was higher than the real rate of growth for other countries,

TABLE 6-14
Economic Indicators in Comparison of the 1980s and 1970s (percent)

Years	Unemployment	Economic Growth	Inflation	Profits Related to GNP
1970–1979	6.2	2.8	7.1	7.9
1980	7.1	0.2	13.5	6.5
Reagan Years				
1981	7.6	1.9	10.4	6.2
1982	9.7	2.5	6.1	4.7
1983	9.6	3.6	3.2	6.3
1984	7.5	6.8	4.3	7.1
1985	7.2	3.0	3.6	6.9
1986	7.0	3.0	1.9	6.7
1987	6.2	2.9	3.7	6.6
1988	5.8	3.0	4.1	6.6
Reagan Average				
	7.6	2.7	4.2	6.4

Source: Congress of the United States, Congressional Budget Office, The Changing Distribution of Federal Taxes: A Closer Look at 1980 (Washington, DC: USGPO, 1988), p. 12.

with the exception of Japan. There was a sustained increase in economic growth during the last six years of the Reagan administration, and unemployment showed a decline. Also presented in the table are corporate profits expressed as a percentage of GNP.

However, it can be argued that there is a reverse side to the coin. The six years of uninterrupted prosperity have been financed through increasing the deficit in the federal budget. Although running a deficit in the budget is standard Keynesian economic policy, the idea is that deficits should be run by a government during a recession when there is underutilization of resources and it is necessary to stimulate aggregate demand. Conversely, a government should run a surplus when the economy is healthy. The summation of budget deficits run by the Reagan administration is $1.3 trillion, as indicated in Table 6-15.

A second criticism of Reaganomics is that inequality in the distribution of income has increased. This criticism is buttressed by the Congressional Budget Office (CBO) in a study that showed a slippage in income for certain groups in the American economy.[40] A comparison of median family incomes was made by types of families for a 16-year period from 1970 to 1986. Price changes were adjusted to

TABLE 6-15
Federal Budget Deficit and Gross Federal Debt
1981–1989 (billions of dollars)

Fiscal Year	Deficit	Gross Federal Debt[a]
1981	− 78.9	1,004
1982	− 127.9	1,147
1983	− 207.8	1,382
1984	− 185.3	1,577
1985	− 212.3	1,827
1986	− 221.2	2,130
1987	− 150.4	2,355
1988	− 146.7	2,582
1989	− 130.0	2,825

[a] End of period.
Sources: Economic Report of the President 1989 *(Washington, DC: USGPO, 1989), Table B-76, p. 397; Executive Office of the President, Office of the President,* Budget of the United States Government, Fiscal Year 1989 *(Washington, DC: USGPO, 1988), p. 2b-11.*

[40] Congress of the United States, *Trends in Family Income,* 1970–1986 (Washington, DC: U.S. Government Printing Office, 1988), pp. 4–15.

make a real comparison of incomes during the time period. The CBO study found that median adjusted family income fell sharply for low-income single mothers with children. While median adjusted family income rose at every income level for married couples with children and childless families, for low-income single mothers with children it rose by one-sixth between 1970 and 1977 and then fell one-fourth over the next nine years.

Trends in Income Distribution

Recent decades have witnessed no real movement toward equality in the distribution of income in the United States. There is an apparent conflict between the goals of an egalitarian society and the existence of marked income inequality. However, in a market economy, there is bound to be inequality because income distribution is based on institutional arrangements, such as the pricing process, that are associated with this type of system. High prices are set on scarce agents of production and low prices on plentiful agents. In terms of rewards to labor, those persons whose skills are scarce relative to demand enjoy a high level of income, whereas those whose skills are not scarce do not. In a market economy, people are supposedly rewarded on the basis of their contribution to marketable output which, in turn, reflects consumer preferences and income.

Table 6-16 presents income distribution in the United States for a forty-year period, 1947–1987. The frame of reference is personal income, which includes that part of national income actually received by persons or households and income transfers from government and business. Wages and salaries, income from rental properties, interest, and dividends are part of personal income. The table indicates that some change has occurred in the distribution of family income based on quintiles. The lowest fifth of family income recipients received 5.5 percent of total family income in 1976 and 4.6 percent in 1987. Conversely, the highest one-fifth of family income recipients received 41.4 percent of total family income in

TABLE 6-16
Distribution of Family Income in the United States 1947–1987 (percent)

	1947	1960	1971	1979	1983	1987
Lowest Quintile	5.0	4.9	5.5	5.3	4.7	4.6
Second Quintile	11.9	12.0	11.9	11.7	11.2	10.8
Third Quintile	17.0	17.5	17.3	17.2	17.1	16.9
Fourth Quintile	22.1	23.6	23.7	24.4	24.3	24.1
Highest Quintile	43.0	42.0	41.6	41.4	42.7	43.7

Source: U.S. Department of Commerce, Bureau of the Census, "Current Population Reports," Money, Income, and Poverty Status in the United States 1987 (Washington, DC: USGPO, 1987), Table 4, p. 17.

1979 and 43.7 percent in 1987.[41] The share of family income received by the lowest two quintiles of family recipients declined from 17.0 percent of family income in 1979 to 15.4 percent in 1987, while the share of family income received by the top two quintiles increased from 65.8 percent in 1979 to 67.8 percent in 1987.

SUMMARY

One of the more important subjects debated during the 1980s has been whether or not the United States is in the process of economic decline. In part, this debate centers on the rise of Japan as a world economic power. Times have changed since the Japanese made cheap products that were sold in the five-and-ten-cents stores of America. During the 1960s, the Japanese started making cars, cameras, and calculators that were cheaper and better than those made in the United States. But things began to change rather dramatically during the 1980s. The Japanese began to mount a challenge to the United States in high technology, an area in which we thought our world lead was insurmountable. After all, the Japanese were essentially copycats, while we had our creativity, our ideas, and our Nobel Prize winners. During the 1980s Japan also became the world's leading creditor nation, while the United States became the world's leading debtor nation.

However, the performance of the United States during the 1980s has been quite good in several areas. It has done an excellent job in finding jobs for workers. Some 15 million new jobs were created during the period 1980–1988. Contrary to popular belief, most jobs were not of the hamburger-flipping type. The United States can be legitimately called "the great job machine." The U.S. growth rate during the 1980s was superior to all major industrial countries with the exception of Japan. The United States has achieved a sustained rate of growth and prosperity for the longest time period since the end of World War II, despite constant predictions of a recession. The rate of inflation has been relatively low in comparison to the other countries during the decade, despite major increases in 1980 and 1981.

That is not to say that the United States is free from economic and social problems. The use of drugs has reached epidemic proportions, and the inner cities have become battle zones. The educational system is considered inferior to those of other industrial countries. The deficit in the federal budget has inhibited the rate of savings and capital formation and has contributed to the U.S position as the world's leading debtor nation. The deficit in the U.S. merchandise trade account has created problems, and the decline in the value of the dollar in world markets reflects an international loss of confidence in the ability of the United States to manage its internal affairs. As Paul Kennedy has said, it may simply not be in the cards for any one country to remain number one forever.

---

[41] For perfect equality in income distribution to exist, each quintile would have to receive exactly 20 percent of personal income. Perfect income inequality would exist if the highest quintile got 100 percent of personal income.

REVIEW QUESTIONS

1. What are some of the reasons advanced for the decline in U.S. competitiveness?
2. What is the role of education in world competition between the major industrial countries?
3. How does the United States rate in math and science education compared to other major countries?
4. Do you agree with Richard Lamm's reasons as to why the United States is an uncompetitive society?
5. Explain why a low rate of saving can have an impact on economic development.
6. What are some of the reasons why the United States has become the leading debtor country in the world?
7. Japan is now the leading creditor country in the world. What significance does this have for the United States?
8. What is meant by a trade deficit? With which countries does the United States have a trade deficit?
9. What impact does the deficit in the federal budget have on U.S. competitiveness?
10. How can the competitive position of the United States in the world economy be improved?

RECOMMENDED READINGS

Aho, C. Michael, and Marc Levenson. *After Reagan: Confronting The Changed World Economy*. New York: Council on Foreign Relations, 1988.

Beeman, William J., and Isaiah Frank. *New Dynamics on the Global Economy*. New York: Committee for Economic Development, 1989.

Economic Report of the President 1990. Washington, DC: U.S. Government Printing Office, 1990.

Feldstein, Martin, ed. *The United States in the World Economy*. Chicago: National Bureau of Economic Research, 1988.

Friedman, Benjamin. *Day of Reckoning*. New York: Random House, 1988.

Kennedy, Paul. *The Rise and Fall of the Great Powers*. New York: Random House, 1987.

Lamm, Richard. "The Uncompetitive Society." *U.S. News & World Report*, April 25, 1988, p. 9.

Olsen, Mancur. *The Rise and Fall of Nations*. New Haven: Yale University Press, 1983.

Spencer, Linda M. *American Assets: An Examination of Foreign Investment in the United States*. Washington, DC: U.S. Government Printing Office, 1988.

U.S. Congress, Office of Technology Assessment. *Paying the Bill: Manufacturing and America's Trade Deficit*. Washington, DC: U.S. Government Printing Office, 1988.

U.S. Joint Economic Committee, Congress of the United States. *The 1988 Joint Economic Report*. Washington, DC: U.S. Government Printing Office, 1988.

Wysocki, Bernard, Jr. "The Final Frontier." *The Wall Street Journal*. November 14, 1988, Sec. 4, pp. R1, R3.

MIXED
ECONOMIC
SYSTEMS

7
MIXED ECONOMIC SYSTEMS

8
FRANCE

9
JAPAN

10
THE UNITED KINGDOM

PART THREE

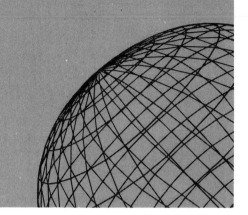

CHAPTER SEVEN

MIXED ECONOMIC SYSTEMS

Many books on comparative economic systems classify countries on the basis of "isms"— capitalism, communism, and socialism. A set of institutions is defined for each system, and various countries are classified as belonging to one system or another. At one time there were certainly clear-cut lines of demarcation between the various systems, but recent developments have tended to obfuscate many differences that once existed. Countries can no longer be dumped into a box neatly labeled capitalism, communism, or socialism. Pure capitalism and pure communism do not exist; institutional arrangements of each do. Current economic reforms in China have incorporated many of the arrangements of a capitalist market economy, but the country still considers itself a socialist country in the Marxist sense. Moreover, some of the goals of such disparate societies as the United States and the Soviet Union are similar, but the methods designed to achieve them are different. One example is high growth rates.

The idea, once prevalent in capitalist societies, that acting in one's self-interest benefits other members of society is no longer accepted as an article of faith. With large corporations, labor unions, and big government in all noncommunist industrialized countries, the capitalist system of the early part of this century no longer exists. There is less willingness to let all economic decisions be resolved by the impersonal forces of the market. One of the most distinctive changes has been a demand for equality in the distribution of income. The issue of equality includes the role of government in reducing or containing income disparities between persons. This has meant an enormous expansion in government transfer payments and services in all Western countries.

MIXED ECONOMIC SYSTEMS

The term *mixed economic system* can be applied to the western European countries, Japan, and also the United States.[1] A mixed economic system combines some of the basic features of capitalism (private enterprise, the price mechanism, and profit) along with considerable government intervention in the economy. Three countries can be used as prototypes of mixed economic systems—France, Japan, and the United Kingdom. Among these three countries, however, there is considerable variation in the extent and type of government intervention in the economy. In France some industries are state owned and there is a well-developed social welfare state. The United Kingdom, under the Thatcher government, has attempted some rollback in state participation in the economy. Conversely, Japan does not have a comprehensive social welfare system; most industries are privately owned; and planning is a cooperative arrangement between business and government. Nevertheless, it is possible to identify certain characteristics that are applicable to the economies of these and other Western industrial countries.

1. The role of government in economic policy is pervasive. A commitment to full employment dominated economic policy in most Western countries until the early 1970s. Memories of mass unemployment during the Depression remained fresh in the minds of Western government policymakers. Fiscal and monetary policies were subverted to the objective of full employment; price stability as an economic goal was secondary in importance. During the 1970s, serious problems occurred to force at least a partial reevaluation of economic policy. Double-digit inflation and faltering growth rates, caused in part by OPEC oil price increases, focused attention on inflation and growth policies.

2. The creation of elaborate social welfare programs has caused the name *welfare state* to be used in describing the economic and social systems of these countries, particularly the United Kingdom. These programs provide a wide variety of social welfare transfer payments and constitute a sizable part of total government expenditures. Western governments have become heavily involved in altering the distribution of income through the use of transfer payments. Advanced industrial countries, with their delicate social and physical interactions, cannot tolerate extreme deprivation. It would be too easy for those with nothing to lose to disrupt the rest of society.

3. There is a basic reliance on free enterprise and the market system in all three countries. Facilities for production and distribution remain primarily in the hands of private enterprise.[2] Nevertheless, the government plays an important role. Control over the budget and credit gives the government enormous lever-

---

[1] Japan is not a Western country, but it is a capitalist country with the government playing a strong role in the economy. The Western European countries would be included as Western countries; for that matter, so would Australia, even though geographically it is not Western.

[2] Even in France, which has gone through recent nationalization of banking and other industries, 82 percent of all industry is still privately owned.

age over the decisions of business firms. Tax policies are used to influence resource allocation and tax incentives are used to stimulate industrial development. In Japan there is a close working relationship between business and government. However, government makes no effort to subsidize or bail out inefficient firms or industries.[3]

4. There is some reliance on economic planning of the indicative type, particularly in France. Planning, as used in France, is a system for centrally guiding the whole economy in the direction the planners would like it to go. Supporters of the French indicative economic planning contend that it is free from the elements of political authoritarianism and economic regimentation associated with Soviet-type command plans and from the defects of the unplanned, free market economies that existed in the United States and Western Europe prior to World War II.

5. There is some state ownership of industry. In France, the private part of the French banking system was nationalized by the Mitterand government in the fall of 1981. However, the major part of the banking system had been state owned since 1945, when de Gaulle nationalized it. Much nationalization that occurred in both France and the United Kingdom took place in the period immediately after World War II for reasons that had little to do with political or economic ideology. For example, the French automotive firm Renault was nationalized by the de Gaulle government because its owners had collaborated with the Nazis.

Before examining the economic systems of France, Japan, and the United Kingdom, it is desirable to explore the characteristics mentioned above in some detail to provide a frame of reference. Perhaps the key point to remember is that, although the free market is recognized as the normal mechanism of resource allocation, government plays a very important role in developing economic policy and redistribution incomes. Few subjects are as emotionally charged as how public policy should be used to influence the distribution of income. At issue is the question of how the total income of society is to be divided among its citizens.

ECONOMIC PLANNING

The objectives of economic planning are certain general aims of economic policy expressed in qualitative terms: achieving a high rate of economic growth with full employment, achieving price stability and balance of payments equilibrium, lessening the relative income difference between rich and poor, industrializing poorer regions, and so on. Economic planning is an attempt to coordinate the economic activities of different sectors of society in the interest of optimal economic growth and structural balance.

---

[3] Yoshi Tsurumi, "How to Handle the Next Chrysler," *Fortune* (June 16, 1980), pp. 87–89.

United States history includes examples of economic plans. In the late eighteenth century, both Alexander Hamilton and Albert Gallatin (secretary of the treasury under President Jefferson) prepared comprehensive plans for the development of the country. In fact, the rapid economic growth of the United States in the early nineteenth century may be ascribed largely to Hamilton's foresight and genius for planning. President Kennedy supplied another example of planning in the early 1960s when he established the goal of landing a man on the moon within that same decade. The government aided businesses in developing new technology, a plan was proposed, and the cost was estimated in advance.

Economic planning can be classified as imperative or indicative, with gradations between these two extremes. *Imperative planning* would apply to a centralized macroeconomic plan in an economy dominated by its public sector. The government assumes control and regulation of output, prices, and wages. There is no reliance on the free market to allocate resources. *Indicative planning* would apply in an economy in which the government indicates a series of goals and either directly or indirectly stimulates certain desired economic activities through the budget, tax and transfer payment policies, and control over the supply of credit and interest rates. The free market, subject to some alterations, is recognized as the normal mechanism of resource allocation.

The Soviet Union and Imperative Planning

The Russian economic plan is an example of imperative economic planning. The planners, as would be true in any country, start with limited resources and must allocate them to each economic sector to maintain some kind of balance for the normal production of goods and services needed for the country. Russian economic planning consists of selected physical targets for output, employment, and consumption by sectors and regions. A plan is built around output goals and capacity growth needed for leading industries and their supportive branches and for other sectors of secondary importance. A system of input-output balances is used to derive the various output and employment targets. Plans are drawn up on the basis of directives from the leadership of the Communist party, which also controls the government. Consumer sovereignty is pretty much disregarded in the Soviet Union, and failure to fulfill the goals defined by the planners redounds to the serious disadvantage of those who are responsible. Needless to say, this leads to state enterprises playing it safe and avoiding innovation.

France and Indicative Planning

French economic planning is an example of indicative planning.[4] It is much less extreme or coercive than Russian planning and is essentially a set of directives or

---

[4] The term *indicative* may be a misnomer. Although French planning is not imperative or mandatory, it does attempt to guide the economy in a certain direction, and it does have the machinery to make its preferences effective. The nationalization of private French banks in 1981 gives the state even more control over credit.

guidelines to help guide the planning of private industry as well as the public sector of the economy. Nevertheless, there is a certain amount of government intervention in the implementation of planning, which has taken the form of indirect control over credit and taxation to encourage desirable objectives. There exists in France a whole range of measures to reward industries that conform to the plan. These include access to bank credit, tax concessions and, within the policy for regional development, subsidies for factories and equipment.

Defects in Economic Planning

Indicative economic planning was once held up by its advocates as a cure-all for economic problems. However, planning has its defects as well as its virtues. Countries with some form of economic planning have not fared any better than the United States in the areas of employment and inflation, particularly in the 1980s.[5] Forecasting, which is supposed to be easier when economic planning is involved, has not been that successful. Even in Japan's carefully monitored economy, it has proven quite difficult to predict variables in the Japanese private sector for a protracted time span, say, more than six months to a year. Random shocks in the world economy can throw off even the best of forecasts.

FISCAL AND MONETARY POLICIES

Government fiscal and monetary policies play important roles in mixed economic systems. The primary purpose of each is economic stabilization, which has the dual goals of controlling tendencies toward inflation or large-scale unemployment. A second objective, which is related, is a desirable rate of economic growth. This refers to real per capita increases in goods and services produced over a time. A high rate of economic growth is reflected in higher living standards. Full employment without economic growth is meaningless. In comparing the efficiency and effectiveness of various economic systems, economic growth is certainly a valid criterion. The process of influencing price level stability and full employment through fiscal and monetary policies can also be used to influence the rate of economic growth.

Fiscal Policy

On the whole, fiscal policy means the government carries the major responsibility for providing the conditions necessary for economic growth in the Western European countries and Japan. This substantial level of government participation in economic activity is regarded in the United States as properly the sphere for private action. The term *public investment* would embrace a much wider range of economic activities in France or the United Kingdom than it would in the United States.

---

[5] The French unemployment rate reached 10.2 percent in the third quarter of 1989 and the rate of inflation was around 5 percent. Both rates were higher than the U.S. rates.

The relatively large government ownership of public utilities, transportation and communication facilities, and many basic industries means expenditure policies in these countries are much more directly involved in the expansion of total productive capacity than is true in the United States. Public investment in these industries has been pursued vigorously to stimulate employment and economic growth.

Monetary Policy

Monetary policy refers to central bank actions designed to lessen fluctuations in investment and consumer spending through the regulation and use of the supply of money. The central banks of France, the United Kingdom, and Japan are state owned and thus have less autonomy than the Federal Reserve of the United States. The Bank of England enjoys autonomy in determining and guiding monetary policy, but its policies are closely coordinated with those of the government. In Japan the central bank serves as the fiscal agent of the government and is a major source of financial capital.

When inflation became the main economic problem in the Western European countries and Japan, central bank monetary policies became more important than government fiscal policies. The latter, which are easier to expedite during a period of unemployment, become a political liability during inflation, as both Ronald Reagan and Margaret Thatcher have found out. It is easier to cut taxes than to raise them, and it is harder to cut government expenditures than to increase them.

STATE OWNERSHIP OF INDUSTRY

State ownership of industry is a distinct manifestation of socialism. The reasons for state ownership are perhaps obvious. It is alleged by the socialists that production for profit under a capitalist system leads to social waste and unemployment. In addition, certain wants, such as public health and education, are difficult to express in the marketplace; as a result, they are not adequately fulfilled under capitalism. Since profit is the basic entrepreneurial motive in a free enterprise system, social costs—polluted streams, polluted air, and wasted natural resources—are not considered. There are also certain industries affecting the public interest that are considered by socialists to be too important to be left in private hands. Banks and railroads are examples. Finally, state ownership of key industries gives the government greater control over the enforcement of fiscal and monetary policies.

For the most part, state ownership of industry in Western Europe had no relationship to political ideology until the 1981 election of Francois Mitterand, a Socialist leader, as president of France. In most countries, certain industries have always been operated by government. In France, for example, there was a mixed system of public and private ownership and control before the Franco-Prussian War. The government of the United Kingdom, wishing to coordinate telegraph services with the post office, had the postmaster general take over all telegraph companies in 1869. In 1896 the post office bought all the long-distance telephone lines from private telephone companies, and in 1911 it bought all privately owned telephone properties. In Japan, government control and operation of certain industries dates back to the Meiji Restoration of 1868.

State Ownership of Industry in France

A wave of nationalization developed in the United Kingdom and France in the period immediately following World War II. However, socialism was only one of several factors responsible for it. France emerged from the German occupation a stripped and debilitated economy, desperately short of raw materials, consumer goods, and food supplies. Transportation was paralyzed, industrial production had fallen to 40 percent of the 1938 level, a generalized black market had replaced the usual channels of trade, and an inflated currency threatened to bring the whole economy down in chaos. In order to achieve economic recovery, the French government had to play an important role. The immediate postwar years were consequently characterized by a policy of economic *dirigisme* (direction), as opposed to a quick return to a market economy, which was the way West Germany chose. The *dirigisme* policy brought with it some important nationalizations affecting the gas and electric power industries, almost the whole of coal mining, the Renault motor works, the Bank of France, the four largest deposit banks, and the larger insurance companies.

Renault: A Case Study of State Ownership. Renault is one of the oldest manufacturers of automobiles. The first Renault car was produced in 1898. In 1914 taxis built by Renault carried French soldiers to the First Battle of the Marne. From 1918 to 1939 the company was the largest producer of automobiles in Western Europe. However, Louis Renault, the company's owner, was accused of collaborating with the Nazis during World War II, and as punishment the company was nationalized by the de Gaulle government in 1945. Since that time the company has been owned by the government and run by government appointees.[6] Renault has been run on strictly commercial lines and is expected to pay its own way. It pays taxes and uses the same accounting system as any private company in France. It is one of France's leading exporters, a factor that has led the government to avoid general interference with managerial decisions.

State Ownership of Industry in the United Kingdom

When the Labour party came into office in the United Kingdom in 1946, a limited number of industries were brought under state ownership. Coal was one industry

---

[6] Representatives of the ministries of industries, economy, defense, and transportation are on the supervisory board.

that was nationalized. It is probable that the Conservative party, had it remained in office, would have also nationalized the coal industry. The Bank of England was already in effect a public institution. Its change to nationalized status was hardly more than a change of title. The railroads, nationalized by the Transportation Act, were pretty much subject to government control from the outset.

The nationalization of the British steel industry by the Labour party, however, was a much more specific socialist measure, and it aroused considerable controversy. The industry was nationalized because it was considered desirable for the government to assume control over an industry upon which the British economy was dependent. Government also believed that there was too much concentration of economic power in the few companies in the industry. Through trade associations, these companies had adopted price fixing and other cartel practices.

British Steel Corporation: A Case Study of State Ownership. The British steel industry was nationalized by the Labour government in 1951 and denationalized by the Conservative government when it came into office in the same year. The industry was renationalized in 1967 by the Labour government, which was once more in office; the 14 largest companies, accounting for 92 percent of total raw steel output, were merged into the state-owned British Steel Corporation. The government saw the nationalization as the only way to inject large amounts of capital into the industry and to eliminate obsolete facilities. Unions regarded nationalization as a means to ensure job security and high pay for their members.

The performance by the British Steel Corporation was generally poor until the latter part of the 1980s. It lost money each year from 1976 to 1984. Losses were covered by the British Treasury. The company could not compete successfully in the international steel market against Japanese and South Korean steel producers. In 1980 British Steel got into the Guinness Book of Records with the biggest annual loss up to that time, some $4 billion. However, improved management turned the company around. The number of steelworkers fell from 250,000 in 1971 to 54,000 workers in 1988. Modern technology was introduced, labor productivity increased, and in 1988 the company made a profit of $698 million on total sales of $7.0 billion.[7]

INCOME DISTRIBUTION AND SOCIAL WELFARE

Despite Marxist predictions of inevitable collapse, capitalism has shown a surprising ability not only to survive but also to expand and adapt to the democratic conditions of modern industrialized society that, it must not be forgotten, it has helped to create. One manifestation of this adaption has been the development

---

[7] *Fortune* (July 31, 1989), p. 294.

of what can be called *welfare statism*. Actually, a precursor of the welfare state was the social welfare program developed in Germany in 1883, when Bismarck's opposition to socialism and his jealousy of the trade union movement led him to sponsor health insurance and old-age insurance. Bismarck, a political pragmatist of the first order, realized that social legislation was necessary to remove the causes around which socialism was developing. Another precursor of the modern welfare state was the social welfare program of the Liberal government in the United Kingdom. Developed in 1908, the program included social insurance for health and unemployment, old age pensions, and assistance to low-income workers through the statutory fixing of minimum wages.

The fundamental premise of the welfare state as it has developed in the capitalistic countries is that governments must intervene to achieve certain economic and social objectives. Two goals are emphasized: an equitable distribution of income and wealth and security of living standards against such vagaries of life as unemployment, ill health, and old age. The development of the welfare state stemmed from dissatisfaction with the distribution of income and wealth. Under a purely competitive market economy, market forces would compensate people on the basis of their contributions to total output. However, this idea was modified when extreme income and wealth disparities between the rich and poor developed. Often these disparities had nothing to do with a person's contribution to total output, but were based on inherited wealth or other special privileges.

Government Distribution Policies

The public sector of an economy is engaged in two major types of activities, each of which can be measured by the expenditures made in carrying it out. One activity involves the provision of a broad array of goods and services—including roads, education, and police protection. These purchases represent a transfer of resources from the private sector of an economy to the public sector, and they also represent the contribution of the government sector to total gross national product. A measure that can be used to indicate the extent to which Western governments contribute to the national output of goods and services is the ratio of government spending on goods and services to gross national product.

The other activity involves the use of transfer payments as an instrument for the redistribution of income, generally with the dual objectives of greater income equality and the provision of some minimum standard of living for everyone. Transfer payments, as distinguished from government purchases of goods and services, involve only the transfer of income from one group to another and provide no equivalent value in terms of goods and services. Transfer payments in most Western countries have come to include family allowances, old age pensions, accident benefits, and unemployment compensation. Some services, such as free medical care, are normally considered direct government purchases of services, purchases that absorb resources the same way as does spending for other goods and services.

The Importance of Government

The economic influence of government is of paramount importance in the analysis of mixed economic systems. This influence can be measured using three criteria.

1. The relationship of government expenditures to gross national product indicates the extent to which resources have been diverted from private to public use.
2. The relationship of transfer payments to total government expenditures indicates the extent to which government expenditures are used to redistribute income.
3. The relationship of taxes to gross national product indicates the extent to which governments have control over economic resources.

Table 7-1 presents government expenditures expressed as percentages of gross national product for selected industrial countries for 1987. Japan and the United States had the lowest ratio of government outlays to gross national product, while Belgium and the Netherlands had the highest. Expenditures include both government spending for goods and services and transfer payments. Government expenditures as percentage of gross national product increased during the 1970s but leveled off during the 1980s and even showed a decline in some countries as an economic recession created a decline in tax revenues.

Table 7-2 presents transfer payments expressed as a percentage of total government expenditures for the same countries. The United States, Japan, the United Kingdom, and Italy ranked at the bottom, while West Germany and Sweden ranked at the top. It is necessary to point out that only central government expenditures are used. Some countries are much more centralized than others. France is an example. Most government expenditures in France are made by the government. The United States and West Germany are federal republics, with state and local government expenditures constituting an important component of total government expenditures.

The allocation of resources from the private sector to the public sector is accomplished through taxation. Thus, the costs of public activities are borne by the

TABLE 7-1

Government Expenditures Expressed
as a Percentage of GNP for Selected Countries

Italy	50.2	Denmark	39.5
Belgium	56.7	Canada	25.4
United Kingdom	40.6	Netherlands	56.6
Japan	17.4	Sweden	44.1
France	44.1	Norway	40.6
West Germany	29.9	United States	24.5

Source: The World Bank, World Development Report
1988, p. 267.

TABLE 7-2

Transfer Payments Expressed as a Percentage of
Central Government Expenditures for Selected
Countries, 1987

Italy	30.0	Denmark	40.0
Belgium	41.5	Canada	33.8
United Kingdom	30.2	Netherlands	39.8
Japan	23.5	Sweden	51.8
France	44.1	Norway	33.8
West Germany	50.5	United States	31.0

Source: The World Bank, World Development Report
1988, *p. 267.*

taxpayers of a nation. Taxation can also result in income redistribution if various
income groups have different proportions of total national income after taxes than
before. Income redistribution will occur particularly if the tax system is progressive. However, there are limits to the extent to which progressive taxation can be
used. In France, for example, the bulk of social welfare expenditures is financed
by indirect taxation, in particular the value-added tax. In countries with mixed
economic systems the growth of social welfare expenditures has brought with it an
increase in the use of indirect taxation.

Table 7-3 presents the relationship of taxes to gross national product and a
comparison of various sources of tax revenues for the 12 countries. Taxes expressed
as a percentage of GNP ranged from a high of 51.6 percent in the Netherlands to a
low of 12.6 percent in Japan. Income taxes represented 67.4 percent of total revenue
for Japan compared to a low of 17.5 percent for West Germany. Social security
contributions expressed as a percentage of total national government revenue ranged
from a high of 53.3 percent for West Germany to a low of 0.0 percent for Japan.
Indirect taxes expressed as a percentage of total national government revenue ranged
from a high of 41.7 percent in Denmark to a low of 3.9 percent in the United States.
It should be remembered that indirect taxes, such as sales taxes, are much more
widely used by state and local governments in the United States than by the national
government.

Income Distribution and Equality

Alexis de Tocqueville argued in the late 1830s that what was distinctive about
modern society was a demand for equality. That thrust has continued today, long
after it first emerged as a powerful political force. Income redistribution in favor of
lower-income groups has long been a cardinal objective of socialism. While very
few socialists would favor complete income equality, recognizing that there are
differences in ability and talent, most would favor the elimination of wide income
disparities between rich and poor. Socialists object to the concentration of wealth

TABLE 7-3

Sources of Tax Revenues Expressed as a Percentage of Total Current Government Revenue; Taxes Expressed as a Percentage of GNP for Selected Countries, 1987

Country	Percentage of Total Government Revenue			Taxes as Percentage of GNP
	Income Taxes	Social Security	Indirect Taxes	
Italy	38.5	28.7	23.5	36.7
Belgium	37.9	34.0	21.4	46.5
United Kingdom	38.9	17.5	30.4	37.9
Netherlands	24.3	37.9	20.6	51.6
Japan	67.4	0.0	18.9	12.6
France	17.5	43.8	29.9	40.9
West Germany	17.5	53.3	21.8	29.7
Denmark	37.2	3.7	41.7	43.8
Canada	48.2	14.5	18.3	19.7
Sweden	16.0	29.8	29.6	41.1
Norway	20.2	21.8	39.7	48.4
United States	50.1	33.9	3.9	18.3

Source: The World Bank, World Development Report 1988, *p. 269.*

in the hands of a few persons, which leads to considerable income inequality. The *rentier* class, or "coupon clippers," are looked upon with disdain. The socialists would attempt to correct this unequal distribution of income through the use of progressive income taxes, gift and inheritance taxes, and a wide variety of transfer payments designed to raise the incomes of the poor. In Western society, much of this has already occurred, but not to the extent that many socialists would like. The state has inevitably become the arena for the fulfillment of both private and group wants, but there comes a point where demands cannot be easily matched by state revenues.[8]

It is difficult to reach agreement on what can be considered an optimum distribution of income. Individuals and groups view an economic system from their

---

[8] Joseph Schumpeter wrote: "The fiscal capacity of the state has its limits not only in the sense in which this is self-evident and which would be valid also for a socialist community, but in a much narrower and, for the tax state, more painful sense. If the will of the people demands higher and higher public expenditures, if more and more means are used for purposes for which private individuals have not produced them, if more and more power stands behind this will, and if finally all parts of the people are gripped by entirely new ideas about public property—then the tax state will have run its course and society will have to depend on other motive forces for its economy than self-interest." "The Crisis of the Tax State," *International Economic Papers*, No. 4 (New York: Macmillan Publishing Co., 1954), pp. 5–38.

own positions in society. Unanimity of opinion is therefore impossible, and it is highly doubtful if a concept of optimum income distribution can be agreed upon.[9] If such is the case, the actual effect of taxes and government expenditures on the distribution of income will not be determined on the basis of a particular theory of optimum distribution, but rather as a result of a struggle between the dominant political forces in a society at a particular moment in time. The results will be strongly modified, of course, by political decisions made in the past. This does not mean that theories will play no role whatever, for each social group must have a rationale for its position.

Some industrial countries display more income inequality than others. Comparisons are made difficult because of all the different aspects of the concept of income distribution. Probably the main bone of contention between capitalism and communism concerns how each system distributes its income. But even among countries considered capitalist and countries considered communist, there are wide variations in patterns of income distribution. It is also apparent that no one country has a lock on what can be considered a "just" society. Discrimination of one form or another is likely to exist, regardless of the country.[10]

Comparisons between countries are also difficult because of differences in statistical observation and classification. Typically, the data used would have to involve the distribution of income before taxes and transfers because government taxes, expenditures on goods and services, and transfer payments alter the distribution of income.

SUMMARY

The three countries that have been discussed in this chapter—France, Japan, and the United Kingdom—have mixed economic systems, meaning that they have elements of both capitalism and socialism. The governments of these countries pursue economic and social policies of participation and intervention to a greater degree than in the United States. Although private enterprise is dominant and a market system prevails in all three countries, government participation in economic activity cannot be minimized as an influence. It covers several specific areas, which can be summarized as follows.

---

[9] Even when arbitrary differences such as class or sexual privileges are eliminated, there will be differences in income, status, and authority between persons—differences arising out of talent, motivation, effort, and achievement. And individuals will want to exercise the reward and powers of those achievements. The question of justice arises, as Daniel Bell wrote in *The Coming of Post-Industrial Society* (New York: Basic Books Inc., Publishers, 1976, pp. 9–12), when those on top can convert their authority positions into large discrepant material and social advantages over others.

[10] During the 1970s various groups in the United States accused the country of various forms of discrimination—racial, sexual, and so forth. It was inferred that somehow these and other forms of discrimination did not exist elsewhere. That is not true; the Soviet Union probably has more sexism than the United States.

1. Economic planning, which involves a certain amount of state intervention, is used in varying degrees, ranging from the formal French indicative plan, which is usually set for a four-year period, to more informal forecasting and general direction plans.
2. Fiscal and monetary policy measures are an important part of economic policy. These measures have generally been used to maintain a high level of aggregate demand during most of the postwar period; in the 1970s, however, inflation became the dominant economic problem.
3. State ownership of key industries that can influence the volume of public expenditures is a fact of life. These industries are indeed very large businesses and are often the largest employers in the country.
4. Transfer payments, through the medium of social welfare expenditures, have served to create what can be considered the welfare state. These payments, which are broad and comprehensive in coverage, have an important impact on income redistribution between and within income groups.

It is assumed that, through government direction and participation, a mixed economic system can ameliorate or eliminate some of the major flaws of a purely capitalistic system—namely, unemployment and economic insecurity—as well as accomplish a high rate of economic growth. Whether this is actually the case is highly problematical. The performance of the British economy over the last three decades has generally been poor, particularly in terms of economic growth. Inflation became a problem in the Western European countries in the late 1970s and early 1980s. Economic policy measures that worked when unemployment was the only problem are no longer relevant for the times.

REVIEW QUESTIONS

1. How are supplies of productive agents allocated or distributed among industries in mixed economic systems?
2. Discuss the effects of great income inequality on the distribution of goods and services in a capitalistic system.
3. Discuss some of the reasons for the nationalization of industry in the United Kingdom and France.
4. The term *mixed economy* is probably more applicable to the economic systems of the Western European countries than the terms *capitalism* and *socialism*. Why?
5. Discuss the role of government with reference to monetary and fiscal policies in a mixed economy.
6. Discuss the importance of economic planning in a mixed economic system.
7. The major flaws of a capitalistic system—unemployment, income inequality, and social waste—have been eliminated in such countries as France and the United Kingdom. Do you agree?

8.   Discuss the importance of social welfare expenditures in a mixed economic system.

RECOMMENDED READINGS

Beveridge, William. *Full Employment in a Free Society* 2d ed., Atlantic Highlands, NJ: Humanities Press Inc., 1960.

Dobb, Maurice H. *On Economic Theory and Socialism.* Boston MA: Routledge & Kegan Paul Inc., 1965.

Friedman, Milton. *Capitalism and Freedom* Chicago: University of Chicago Press, 1962.

Myrdal, Gunnar. *Beyond the Welfare State.* New Haven, CT: Yale University Press, 1960.

Sweezy, Paul W. *Socialism.* New York: McGraw-Hill Book Co., 1949.

Tinbergen, Jan. *Production, Income and Welfare.* Lincoln University of Nebraska Press, 1985.

Wright, David M. *Capitalism.* Chicago: Henry Regnery Co., 1962.

CHAPTER EIGHT

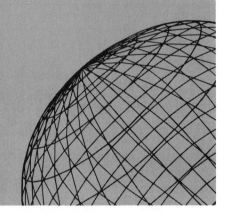

FRANCE

In May 1981, François Mitterand, a socialist, was elected President of France and the Socialist Party gained control of the French National Assembly, thus creating a mandate for more government control of the French economy. The election of Mitterand was a landmark: It was the first major victory for a democratic socialist party in any major country in this century. Although France did have a socialist government in 1936 called the Popular Front, it was a coalition government that lasted only for a year. Other countries, England and Germany for example, have political parties that embrace many of the principles of democratic socialism, but they are not called socialist parties. France is governed by a Socialist Party that believes in specific economic and social principles. Although Mitterand was supported by the French Communist Party, the goals of the two parties are *not* one and the same.

The French economy has had some economic planning since the end of World War II, and some state ownership of industry that dates back to the last century, but the Mitterand government further shifted the public-private resource mix toward the public share. Major changes included nationalization of all but a few of the privately owned banks and creation of a dominant position in practically the whole steel industry, all aluminum production, half of glass production, the whole electronics sector, and an important part of the pharmaceutical and metallurgical sectors, among others. Furthermore, the nationalized sectors became the principal customer and supplier of many other industrial sectors. Thus, even though private enterprise still accounts for around 80 percent of total output of goods and services and the market mechanism is the main allocator of resources, the government directly or indirectly controls many important sectors of the French economy.

THE ECONOMIC SYSTEM

Government participation in business and industry is far greater in France than in the United States or West Germany. In addition to industries nationalized by Mitterand, the French government controls all the railroads, coal mines, and virtually all electrical power production and has controlling interest in the airlines. The Bank of France and the four largest deposit banks were controlled by the government before the Mitterand government came to power. A segment of the insurance industry is nationalized. The government has a large interest in the petroleum and natural gas industries and is involved in the production of motor vehicles and planes. Direct regulation and selective intervention in other industries is also common. Investment plans of major companies are often discussed with government agencies able to help provide financing; the government controls mergers and other changes in the organization of private firms.

State intervention in the French economy is not new; it dates back to the time of Jean Baptiste Colbert (1619–1683), who was finance minister under King Louis XIV. Colbert believed that France could and should be the greatest industrial country of Europe. He developed a state policy of supporting national commercial and industrial interests. To promote foreign trade, industries were created using state funds. He also fostered mercantilism, the theory of national economy that held that commerce should be regulated so as to secure a favorable balance of trade in order to increase the store of precious metals within a country. A canal was dug from the Bay of Biscay to the Mediterranean to improve the flow of trade between the different areas of France, while the highway system was made the best in Europe.

The Industrial Revolution, for the most part, largely bypassed France. Through the end of the last century, France was primarily an agricultural country, with the *petit bourgeoisie* (small business owners) concentrated in the cities. There was an industrial base in northern France, concentrated in the steel, textile, and coal-mining industries, but by no means was France the industrial equal of England or Germany. The state continued to play an important role in the French economy. In industry, the French railway system was developed by the government, and the telephone system was made a government monopoly in 1889.

World War II and Nationalization of Industry

An increase in government ownership of industry resulted from a series of nation-alizations immediately after World War II. The Bank of France, the four largest deposit banks, 34 insurance companies, the electric and gas industries, the coal mines, Air France, and one automobile company were nationalized.[1]

---

[1] The automobile and aircraft companies were nationalized for cooperating with the Germans.

One reason for nationalization was a desire to continue the Popular Front program of 1936, which was an assault on economic institutions that had for decades preserved a hopelessly outmoded capitalism.[2] Manufacturing and agriculture were both protected by high tariffs and import quotas and, in many cases, by subsidies and producers' agreements allocating production and markets. This had led to a static economy with restricted competition and little incentive to improve production methods or to experiment with new products. The Depression had created mass unemployment and social unrest in France. The Popular Front sponsored social programs similar to those developed by Franklin D. Roosevelt during the New Deal.

A second reason for nationalization was the desire to develop a blueprint to rehabilitate the war-torn economy and stimulate economic growth. Discussions in France concerning the way in which economic recovery could most quickly be accomplished led to the view that the French government would need to play an active role. The result was a call for formal and systematic economic planning. France adopted a policy of economic *dirigisme* (direction), as opposed to a quick return to a liberal or market economy, which was the way West Germany chose. The first economic plan, begun in 1946 and often called the *Monnet Plan*, advocated direct government control over economic activity. The Marshall Plan, which funneled U.S. postwar aid through central governments, strengthened acceptance of the government's role in rebuilding the French economy. It was felt that government control over investment in industries damaged by the war could be carried out best through nationalization of a number of basic industries, such as coal.

Nationalization under Mitterand

Socialism represents a departure from the institutions of capitalism. Socialists contend that there are several major flaws in a capitalist system—unemployment, income inequality, and social waste. They would amend these flaws by altering some of the capitalist institutions that presumably are responsible for them. There would be more public ownership of industries considered vital to the national interest. Income distribution would become more of a public function, and income disparities would be reduced through progressive income taxation and transfer payments. Great emphasis would be placed on medical care, family allowances, and retirement benefits. Decisions concerning the kinds and quantities of goods to produce, the allocation of available resources to various uses, and the distribution of resources between consumption and capital goods would be made by the government through some form of planning and greater control over the allocation of credit. There would also be at least a major modification of private profit making.

---

[2] The Popular Front was an amalgam of a number of political groups and was headed by Leon Blum, who became the first socialist president of France.

Industry. With this blueprint, it is easier to follow the objectives of the new socialist government of President Mitterand. On October 26, 1981, the French General Assembly approved measures designed to restructure industry and banking. Five industrial groups came under full state control. They are the Companie Générale d'Electricité, Saint Gobain (glass and chemicals), Pechiney-Ugine-Kuhlmann (aluminum and chemicals), Rhone-Poulenc (pharmaceuticals), and Thomson-Brandt (electronics and arms). Two other companies were partially nationalized; the Dassault aviation firm has 51 percent state ownership, as does the arms division of Matra. The USINOR and SACILOR steel firms were nationalized by a simple conversion of large state credits into shares. The French government took over the holdings of two U.S.-based companies, ITT and Honeywell.

After nationalization, the French government owned 14 of the 20 largest industrial firms in France, including the three largest—Elf Aquitaine, Francais des Petroles, and Renault. The percentage of French industrial sales produced by state-controlled companies increased from 18 to 32 percent after the nationalization. The government's share increased from nothing to 36 percent in computers and office equipment, from 1 percent to 80 percent in steel making, from 1 percent to 44 percent in electronics, and from 50 to 84 percent in plane making.

However, Mitterand proved to be much more pragmatic than doctrinaire in running the French economy. To some extent, this could be attributed to the fact that during the 1980s the governments of Canada, Italy, Japan, the United Kingdom, the United States, and West Germany were run by center-right or conservative political parties. The political and economic trends during the 1980s for these and other countries was away from a welfare state and toward reliance on the free market. In 1986, elections were held in France and Mitterand was forced to share power with a center-right government that privatized large companies, such as Saint Gobain, which makes glass and chemicals. In 1988, the socialists achieved control of the government and discontinued the process of privatization. As of 1989, the French government owns most of the major banks, all of the insurance companies, and the following major companies (see Table 8-1).

Banking. The Mitterand government nationalized most of the privately owned banks, leaving only a small percentage of the nation's bank deposits in the hands of privately owned institutions. The action made France the only noncommunist country in the world to have credit almost totally under government control. The rationale for state control of credit was the desire on the part of the Mitterand government to restimulate an economy beset by low growth, double-digit inflation, and unemployment. The government, then, is in the position of deciding how credit is to be allocated, a decision that, in a pure market system, is made by the forces of supply and demand.[3]

---

[3] The center-right government privatized a number of French banks, including Société Générale, with 1988 assets of $153 billion, Paribas, with assets of $122 billion, and Financière de Suez, with assets of $64 billion.

TABLE 8-1
Major Companies Owned by the French Government in 1989 (millions of dollars)

Company	Sales	Assets
Renault	$27,109	$18,185
CGE[a]	21,487	29,590
Elf Aquitaine[b]	21,175	28,032
Usinor	13,247	13,188
Thomson	12,566	21,816
Phone-Poulenc	10,971	11,169
Pechiny	8,616	13,031
Aerospatiale	6,417	8,596
Bull	5,297	4,461
CEA-Industrie	4,904	15,231

[a] Cie Générale Electricité is a state-owned electronics firm
[b] Elf Aquitaine is the state-owned oil refining company.
Source: Fortune *(July 31, 1989), pp. 291-296.*

Public Finance

French public finance is highly centralized. The national government accounts for about 86 percent of total tax receipts, and local governments for the remaining 14 percent. Both national and local governments rely extensively on indirect taxes as revenue sources; in 1989 approximately 69 percent of all tax receipts came from indirect taxes. The most important national tax, the value-added tax, and the most important local tax, the retail sales tax, are both indirect taxes. The most important direct taxes, the personal and corporate income taxes, are both national taxes and have no counterpart at the local level. The property tax, which is the major source of tax revenue to local governments in the United States, is not an important source of revenue at the local level in France.

The French Tax System. The tax system in France has several characteristics that differ from the tax systems of other countries. Greater emphasis is placed on sales taxation in France than in other advanced industrial countries. Also, tax incentives are widely used to stimulate scientific research and development, to encourage the modernization of plants and equipment, and to facilitate regional economic development. Another characteristic of the French tax system is innovation. In the value-added tax, France developed a tax that has been adopted by many countries and that has been proposed from time to time in the United States.

The Value-Added Tax. The value-added tax is one of the world's most widely used taxes. First introduced in France in 1954, the tax applies to all firms engaged in manufacture, wholesale, and service. Value added is gross receipts during the period less amounts paid for commodities. Thus the tax does not discriminate against particular distribution channels because it is reduced for each transaction. At the same time, it permits the impact of the tax to be spread over a wide range of activities. An example of the value-added tax is presented below. Assume three business firms: a manufacturer selling a product to a wholesaler for $100, who sells it to a retailer for $125, who finally sells it to the ultimate consumer for $200. Assume a tax rate of 10 percent on each transaction.

	Value of Product	Value Added	Value-Added Tax
Manufacturing stage	$100	$100	$10.00
Wholesale stage	125	25	2.50
Retail stage	200	75	7.50
Final value	$200	$200	
Value-added tax			$20.00

The French value-added tax applies to all domestic transactions in goods and services at all levels of the industrial and commercial cycle. It is levied on imports at the time of their entry into the French customs territory. The typical rate of the French value-added tax is 18.6 percent.[4] A reduced rate of 5.5 percent applies to the production and sale of food and other necessities; luxury products, including automobiles, are subject to a higher rate of 33.3 percent. Certain basic raw materials, such as cotton and copper, are exempt from the tax.

The value-added tax is used as an economic policy instrument in France. Export transactions are exempted from the tax. It is also used to encourage expansion and modernization of industry because capital goods are, in general, accorded favorable treatment under the tax.

Income and Wealth Taxes. French taxes also include the personal income tax, which is progressive and is levied on income from wages and salaries, dividends and interest, capital gains, and profits from commercial activities. The personal income tax was made more progressive by the Mitterand government. However, the progressivity of the tax is decreased by the family quotient system, which allows income to be divided into a certain number of shares based on the number of dependents in a family. There is a social security tax of 15 percent on employee income.[5]

The corporate income tax rate is 42 percent on net profit earned in France. Income earned outside of France is generally not taxed, which provides an incentive for exports. Capital gains are taxed at a rate of 15 percent, and interest income is taxed at rates ranging from 15 to 50 percent.

---

[4] Harvard Law School, *Taxation in France*, World Tax Series (Chicago: Commerce Clearing House, Inc., 1988), p. 76.

[5] *Individual Taxes: A Worldwide Summary*. (New York: Price Waterhouse and Co., 1988), pp. 99–102.

Table 8-2 presents revenue sources for the French state budget for 1989. The value-added tax is by far the most important source of revenue. Social Security tax revenues are not in the state budget but are part of the social budget.

Table 8-3 presents a comparison of tax revenue sources for France and other major countries. Included in the table are social security taxes. Social security and sales taxes are important revenue sources in France, but income taxes are not. The French tax system is basically regressive.

Table 8-4 compares tax burdens in France and other major countries for 1987. The French tax burden is high in comparison with the United States and Japan. Indirect taxes account for most of the French tax burden, while in the United States and Japan the burden is more on income tax payers.

Government Expenditures. Total French government expenditures amounted to 44 percent of gross national product in 1988. France has two budgets—the national budget and the social budget. The national budget contains the receipts from basic revenue sources (such as the value-added tax and the personal income tax), and the national expenditures, including spending on goods and services, spending for capital formation, and interest on the public debt.

The social budget covers both social security expenditures—old age and disability insurance, medical care, family allowances, and worker's compensation— and outlays for veterans' pensions and miscellaneous welfare payments. The social budget is used because the bulk of French social welfare expenditures is financed not out of national tax revenues, but by special taxes paid by employers and employees. These taxes are not paid to the national treasury, but to special social security funds from which the benefits are paid.

There are two separate social welfare systems—a family allowance system and a general social security system. Both systems are comprehensive in coverage.

TABLE 8-2

Revenue Sources of the French State Budget, 1989 (percent)

Taxes	Percent
Value-added tax	41.0
Personal income tax	17.7
Corporate income tax	9.8
Other taxes[a]	16.3
Gasoline tax	8.2
Non-fiscal sources	7.0
	100.0

[a] Other taxes include cigarette and alcoholic beverages taxes, transfer taxes, license taxes, and others.

Source: *Ministre de L'Economie,* Le Budget De L'Etat *(Paris: SEVPO, 1989).*

TABLE 8-3

A Comparison of Tax Revenue Sources for France and Other countries, 1987 (percent)

Country	Personal	Corporate	Social Security	Property	Sales	Other
France	13.0	5.0	42.8	4.8	29.4	5.0
United States	35.4	7.0	29.8	10.3	17.5	—
Italy	22.2	15.1	34.8	3.4	24.0	0.5
Japan	25.0	20.7	29.8	10.9	13.4	0.1
United Kingdom	26.8	10.5	18.3	13.1	31.3	—
Sweden	37.0	4.5	23.9	5.8	24.3	4.5
Belgium	33.7	6.7	33.6	1.9	24.0	0.1

Source: Ministre de L'Economie, Le Budget De L'Etat 1989 *(Paris: SEVPO, 1989),p. 4.*

The family allowance system, which is financed by a tax on employers, provides tax-exempt monthly payments for the second, third, and subsequent children in a family; a special allowance for families with only one wage earner; prenatal and maternity allowances; and, in certain circumstances, a housing allowance. The general social security system provides health insurance, maternity benefits, pension benefits, and old-age and survivors' benefits. Health insurance benefits compensate for the loss of earnings, as well as the medical costs of being sick. In addition, there are special systems for farmworkers, coal miners, railroad workers, public utility employees, seamen, and public employees. There is some intermingling of the general and special systems, with workers receiving benefits from both systems. Total transfer payments from the social welfare system—family allowances and social security—accounted for 22.0 percent of French national income in 1987.[6]

TABLE 8-4

A Comparison of Tax Burdens in France and Other Countries, 1987 (percent of GNP)

Country	Percent
France	44.2
United States	29.0
Italy	36.2
Japan	28.8
United Kingdom	39.0
Sweden	53.5
Belgium	45.4

Source: Ministre d L'Economie, Le Budget De L'Etat 1989 *(Paris, SEVPO, 1989), p. 4.*

[6] Organization for Economic Cooperation and Development, *National Accounts 1960–1987* (Paris: Department of Economics and Statistics, 1988), p. 48

Until the election of François Mitterand, redistribution of income was not a major goal of taxation in France. The value-added tax, rather than the personal income tax, was the single most important revenue source. The progressivity of the income tax was reduced through the family quotient system and income splitting; tax evasion among the French of all social classes was a fact of life. A result was that France had the most unequal distribution of income of all the major Western industrial countries.[7] The Mitterand government raised income, wealth, and inheritance taxes, and doubled tax levels on yachts, speedboats, and luxury cars.[8] The "soak the rich" tax policies of the Mitterand government resulted in a flight of French capital to other countries.

The Banking System

France has a comprehensive banking system headed by the Bank of France. The system includes two types of banks—commercial banks and specialized credit institutions. Unlike the banking systems of the United States and United Kingdom, the French banking system is, with few exceptions, publicly owned. This gives the government control over the allocation of credit to all sectors of the French economy. Ownership provides the government with direct leverage for the implementation of credit policies that agree with the French economic plan.

The Central Bank. The Bank of France was organized by Napoleon Bonaparte in 1800 as a privately owned company. In 1803 it was given a monopoly for note issuance in the Paris area, and in 1848 that monopoly was extended to all of France. In 1946 the Bank of France was nationalized; the shareholders received negotiable government securities in exchange for their stock. The French government was then able to assume ultimate control over monetary policy.

A National Credit Council was created and given the power to regulate the operations of all types of banks in France; this power is exercised through the Bank of France. Members of the council represent government departments concerned with economic problems and various economic and financial special interest groups. Within the policy framework set by the council, the Bank of France has the responsibility for implementing monetary policy. It uses many credit control measures—changes in the discount rate, imposition of rediscount ceilings, control of minimum reserves to be held by the banks in the form of Treasury paper, open market operations, and certain measures of qualitative control. However, the power of the Bank of France to implement monetary policy is circumscribed to a certain extent by the existence of specialized credit institutions that have considerable influence on both the demand for money and the character of investments for which financing is sought.

---

[7] Malcolm Sawyer and Frank Wasserman, "Income Distribution in OECD Countries," *OECD Economic Outlook* (July 1976), p. 14.

[8] "Bad Times for the Good Life," *Newsweek* (November 30, 1981), pp. 46–47.

The Commercial Banks. The two largest commercial banks—Banque Nationale de Paris, and Société Générale—were nationalized in 1945. These two banks are among the 25 largest commercial banks in the world.[9] They operate branch banks throughout France and make consumer and business loans, actively competing against each other for the demand and time deposits of the French public. The size of these banks makes it easier to implement the state economic plans and to carry out monetary policy. Nationalization of private banks such as the Crédit Commercial de France by the Mitterand government has increased the extent of state control over commercial banking.[10]

Specialized Credit Institutions. There are in France a number of public and semipublic credit institutions. Through these institutions the French government exercises its considerable financial powers to determine the allocation of savings into particular investment channels. They are diverse in that some are banks while others are not, but as a common feature they tend to specialize in one or a few lines of activity. Their loanable funds come from savings deposits, bond issues, and the French Treasury. The French Treasury plays a central and dominant role in the French capital market, and it accounts for around 50 percent of savings in France. The Treasury controls the capital market to the extent that no important borrower can have access to funds without its consent. Moreover, control over the financial circuits of the country means that the Treasury has a priority claim on resources.

The Caisse National de Crédit Agricole. The Crédit Agricole, with assets of around $240 billion, is larger than any U.S. Bank.[11] It is the umbrella organization for 94 regional agricultural banks, in which capacity it receives all of their long-term deposits and assumes the risk on their long-term loans. It is a public institution controlled by the Ministry of Agriculture. It receives funds from the Treasury and private depositors and through the issue of bonds in the capital market.

The Crédit National. The main function of this government-owned institution is to allocate a part of the funds from the national budget to private industry for investment purposes. (The Treasury retains the right to restrain the borrowing and lending activity of the Crédit National directly.) It makes several types of loans, all of which are made at subsidized rates of interest. These loans go to specially favored economic sectors, particularly exports and energy, at subsidized rates of interest.[12] Loans are also made to small business firms.

---

[9] *Fortune* (1990), p. 324.

[10] French banks in which foreign investors have a joint interest have not yet been nationalized.

[11] *Fortune* (1990), p. 324.

[12] Jacques Melitz, "The French Financial System: Mechanisms and Propositions of Reform" (Paper presented to the Conference on the Political Economy of France, American Enterprise Institute, Washington, D.C., May 29–31, 1980).

The Caisse de Dépots. This state-owned institution manages the funds of the social security and postal savings systems. It is a type of intermediary virtually unique to the French banking system, under which the nationwide network of savings banks do no lending of their own. Instead, the Caisse de Dépots receives most of the savings banks' deposits and is responsible for their distribution. It lends a part to local governments and a part to the Treasury itself to finance the federal deficit. It controls the levers on a wide range of credit policy instruments. With the Bank of France, it controls the marginal cost of money to the banking sector and thus influences interest rates.

Credit Policy. The French financial system is characterized by a small number of very large financial institutions ranging from commercial banks to the French Treasury. Since virtually all credit is channeled through these institutions, monetary and credit policies are relatively easy to expedite. The government influences most aspects of this centralized system. It sets lending priorities for banks, limits their total credit extension, and controls their interest rates. This control is the key enabling influence for the implementation of French industrial policy. The existence of a small number of lending institutions makes it easier to allocate credit to those industries given the highest priority in the French economic plan.[13]

Labor-Management Relations

The French trade union movement is dominated by several large labor confederations that, although ideologically different, are united in a general unwillingness to accept the basic institutions of capitalism. The largest trade union confederation is the Confederation Générale du Travail (CGT), which is Communist led and has a membership of 1.5 million workers. It is militant in philosophy and activity and supports the French Communist Party. The CGT is divided into departmental unions and industrial federations. To be affiliated with the CGT, each union must first join a departmental union, which brings together all unions in a region, regardless of their trade. Other important unions are the Confederation Française Democratique du Travail and the Force Ouvrière, both of which support the Socialist Party.

Employers are also organized into associations. The most important employers' federation is the Conseil National du Patronat Française (National Council of French Employers). It consists of some 170 trade associations and three major federations. The trade associations represent their members in the negotiation of collective bargaining agreements. Another employers' association is the Center des Jeunes Patrons. This association supports government economic planning, maintenance of full-employment policies, and participative labor-management relations.

---

[13] U.S. Congress, Joint Economic Committee, *Monetary Policy, Selective Credit Policy, and Industrial Policy in France, Britain, West Germany, and Sweden*, 97th Cong., 1st sess., 1981, p. 35.

Given the rather diverse political views of labor and management, relations between the two groups have not been harmonious. Labor-management agreements have tended to transcend the normal areas of wage demands and working conditions. Profit sharing and works councils have also entered into the bargaining process. It is in the works council that plant managers and the elected officials of all the employees sit together and express their views. Several unions may represent the workers in a particular plant. This means that management must face different unions, acting through different channels. The situation is much more complex and ambiguous than in other countries, where management usually faces only one union and handles problems with that union through collective bargaining.

Government and Business

State intervention in the economy dates back many centuries and has come to be accepted as permanent. Public policies in France have included both protection and promotion of key industrial sectors through financial subsidies of many types, price controls, encouragement of mergers to increase the size and market power of French-owned corporations, export promotion, and support for new technology in industries such as computers, semiconductors, and aerospace.[14] In addition, there is considerable government ownership in the French economy, which has been increased by the Mitterand government. In fact, the sharp distinction between public and private sectors of countries such as the United States and Japan has never existed in France. The French government is highly centralized with an elite bureaucracy that has considerable autonomy in shaping industrial policy that affects both nationalized and private industries. Although a variety of government agencies influence policy making, much of the power resides in the state-owned financial institutions. Thus, government is very much a part of business.

Some specific government control devices are discussed below. They include public investment both in the nationalized sector of the economy and in officially approved private channels, compulsory profit sharing, taxes and subsidies, and price controls.

The Nationalized Industries. Nationalization of important sectors of the economy has given the government control over the prices and products of key industries. It has also given the government considerable control over the allocation of credit through the public lending institutions that channel savings into favored sectors of the economy. A shortage of capital after World War II gave the government considerable leverage in the manipulation of credit to influence business decisions.

The nationalized industries function for the most part under the nominal control of public boards on which representatives of labor, management, and the customers

[14] Joseph Zysman, *Political Strategies for Industrial Order: State, Market, and Industry in France* (Berkeley: University of California Press, 1977), pp. 59–67.

of the enterprise in question are represented. In practice, however, the government has retained a strong hand through its authority to appoint the general managers, whose powers have increased at the expense of the public boards. More and more basic policy is determined by the ministries under whose jurisdiction the nationalized industries fall. Decisions with respect to prices, costs, and investments have become the responsibility of various government agencies.

The nationalized industries are operated within a framework of objectives. These objectives include increasing production to meet certain economic goals, implementing a large-scale modernization program to expand capacity and raise productivity, lowering industrial costs, subsidizing various economic and social groups, improving working conditions and labor relations, and achieving the breakeven point in production.

Compulsory Profit Sharing. Aside from the nationalized industries, the interference of the French government in business is considerable. For example, in January 1968 the government established an obligatory profit-sharing plan affecting the employees of all private enterprises in France employing more than 100 people. The workers' share of profits is calculated on the percentage contributed by labor to the total value added by the enterprise. Prior to calculating the amount of profits that are to be distributed to the workers, however, enterprises are permitted to deduct from taxable profits the corporate income tax as well as a 5 percent return on invested capital, including legal reserves. Employers and employees are supposed to form company works committees to select the method by which profits are distributed.

Monetary and Fiscal Devices. The French government has been very active in the use of monetary and fiscal devices designed to foster investment and influence regional development. Regional development is a fundamental goal of French economic policy, and many tax incentives are provided to industry to encourage industrial decentralization. Special grants are provided to firms that locate in regions that have below-average incomes. Exemptions from local business taxes and special depreciation provisions are also provided. The government has also used tax incentives to encourage corporate mergers.

Economic Planning

There was a time when French economic planning received considerable attention in Western countries. It was regarded as a middle-ground approach between an unplanned, free market capitalist system and an imperative, or directive, planned economic system.[15] The worst evils of each system were presumably eliminated by

---

[15] Stephen Cohen, *Modern Capitalist Planning: The French Model* (Berkeley: University of California Press, 1977), pp. 7–27.

French planning, which provided a series of blueprints for the economy to follow over a specific period of time. There would be less wasteful use of resources than in an unplanned market economy, but there would be more reliance on the price mechanism to allocate resources than in a centrally planned economy. There was no element of overt coercion, but the government could influence the allocation of resources into areas that conformed with the plan objectives. Priorities set in the plan provided business firms with a frame of reference in terms of investment decisions. Many people believed that economic planning was responsible for the above-average postwar rate of economic growth in France.

However, in decades following the end of World War II, French economic planning became less important. By the 1970s indicative planning as originally conceived had been largely abandoned—in part a victim of the increasing complexity of the expanding French economy and in part because of the impact of world prices, particularly of oil, on the French economy. Planning has survived, however, and has regained influence as the focal point of the decision-making process of the socialist government. For one thing, the institutions that already existed to facilitate economic planning have equipped the government with the tools for regulating the economy and promoting economic growth. The gamut of French industry, ranging from aerospace to steel, has benefitted from state support and a state-created environment of steadily increasing demand.[16] The French planners also established a series of specialized credit institutions to ensure priority industries access to credit and to direct subsidies from the French Treasury. The socialists, who believe in a strong government role in the French economy, inherited a planning mechanism and institutions that expedited state control of the economy.

The instruments through which planning has been expedited since its inception are simple and direct. The state spends money, the state lends money, and the state owns and operates major enterprises in both the infrastructure and the final-goods manufacturing sectors. Let us review the development of French economic planning from its inception after World War II, keeping in mind that planning was a part of the policy of economic *dirigisme* that began with the Monnet Plan.

Development of French Planning. The formation of the Popular Front government in 1936 under Socialist Premier Leon Blum marked the first phase of economic planning in France in that it extended the responsibility of the government more deeply than ever before into the economy. The Popular Front nationalized the armament industry, introduced a graduated income tax, and institutionalized a government-protected system of collective bargaining.

In 1944 the National Council of the Resistance, a coalition group, produced a plan for France's future that called for the nationalization of primary resources

---

[16] U.S. Congress, Office of Technology Assessment, *U.S. Industrial Competitiveness: A Comparison of Steel, Electronics, and Automobiles*, 99th Cong., 1st sess., 1985, p. 195.

and energy, state control of banks and insurance, and the participation of labor in industrial management. Formal planning began with the Monnet Plan, or "First French Plan," which had the objective of restructuring six basic areas of the French economy—coal, electricity, steel, cement, transportation, and agricultural equipment. Its primary objectives were set out in terms of the growth in capacity and output needed in those sectors. The corresponding investments were in large part financed by Treasury funds. Controls were placed over new capital issues and over the distribution of medium- and long-term credit. Priority allocations of raw materials, building permits, and permits to install new equipment were also used to channel production and investment in the desired direction.

Altogether, nine plans have been completed, with a tenth in process. The typical plan has lasted for four years. The plans have varied in their objectives.[17] The First Plan was designed to develop basic sectors of the economy that would exert a motivating force on all economic sectors. The Second French Plan (1954–1957) differed from the First Plan in that it applied to the entire economy rather than to a few basic sectors. Other plans have aimed at developing various social and economic sectors of the country. The Fourth Plan (1962–1965) involved social action in support of the less favored sectors of society—farmers, the aged, low-income workers, and students. This was done through increasing subsidies and welfare benefits. The Sixth Plan (1971–1975) placed emphasis on the development of a computer industry. The plan also gave priority to the aerospace industry.

Planning Under Mitterand. Economic planning has become important under the Mitterand government. The Eighth Plan, which had been initiated by Mitterand's predecessor, Giscard d'Estaing, was discarded, and an interim plan covering the period from 1982 through 1983 was added. The plan had several objectives, one of which was the nationalization of five major industrial groups as well as banks and financial institutions.[18] A second objective was the decentralization of economic and political power to the regions, departments, and communes of France. Another objective was to reduce the work week to 39 hours and to increase social welfare expenditures. An objective that was not achieved was to increase the real economic growth rate of the French economy to 3 percent per year over the interim two-year period.

The Ninth Plan, which lasted from 1984 to 1988, was then developed. Inflation was a major problem, economic growth rates had declined, and there was a need to improve France's industrial competitiveness in world markets. The state of the French economy forced a general retrenchment on social spending, much to the displeasure of doctrinaire socialists and communists. The Ninth Plan had sev-

---

[17] For a more complete discussion of each plan, see the third edition of this text, pages 166 and 167.
[18] "France," *Economic Surveys*, p. 40.

eral major goals, the first of which was an industrial strategy. The objective was to increase investment from 11.1 percent of French gross domestic product in 1982 to 12.3 percent in 1988, and from 3.0 percent to 4.4 percent over the same period for the nationalized industries.[19] Emphasis was placed on internal financing for the nationalized industries to make them more competitive in world markets. A second goal of the plan was to achieve an annual real economic growth rate of 1.5 to 2.5 percent during the plan period. This was not achieved in 1984 or 1985 but was in 1986, 1987, and 1988. Other objectives of the plan included the development of small- and medium-sized firms in the private sector of the economy and the introduction of new technology in the consumer goods industries.

The French Tenth Four-Year Plan 1989–1992. The French Tenth Plan was announced on June 20, 1989. This four-year plan had been under preparation since the summer of 1988. The rationale of the plan is to prepare France for entrance into the European Community of 12 countries, which is to be created in 1992. One of its important objectives is to reduce unemployment, (around 9.5 percent of the French labor force in June 1989) through job training, particularly in the scientific and technical areas. French fiscal and monetary policy is to be used to achieve job-generating growth. The plan also attaches the allocation of public-sector resources to five major areas of priority:[20]

1. Education and training for jobs that will improve productivity when France enters the European Community in 1992.
2. Regional economic development and planning to stimulate various less developed regions of France, particularly in the Verdun area in northeastern France and areas in southwest France. This will be done through increased government spending out of the state budget.
3. Increased government spending to improve productivity in agriculture.
4. Increased government expenditures on research and development in the scientific and high technology industries.
5. Consolidation of the French social welfare system under the state social budget.

The Mechanics of French Planning. French planning is essentially a statement of the direction the economy should take over a period of time. In concert with the representatives of agriculture, business, and labor, the government draws up a plan for the future development of the economy. The Commissariat au Plan (Planning Commission) is the administrative agency responsible for the development of

[19] *Quarterly Economic Review of France*, Second Quarter, 1984 (London: The Economist Intelligence Unit, 1984), p. 4.

[20] *Assemblée Nationale, Projet de Loi. No. 706, Approuvant le 10th Plan (1989–1992)*, Seconde Session Ordinaire de 1988–1989, Juin 20, 1989.

the plan. The commission has no power of its own, but prepares the plan, submits it for approval to government authorities, and sees to its implementation once it is approved. It is responsible to the premier for its actions. It is headed by a commissaire general (director) and has a staff of planning specialists. A large contribution toward the work of preparing the plan comes from other government offices.

Instruments of French Planning. French economic planning relies on allocation of investment funds and on tax incentives to accomplish its implementation, rather than on authoritarian directives or exhortations. Physical restraints are few and are limited to permits required for opening new petroleum refineries or expanding old ones. For environmental reasons, special installation permits are required for new plants and plant extensions of more than a certain size in the Paris area.

Credit Allocation. Allocation of credit is an important instrument of French planning. The Treasury is the major source of funds that finance investment in the public and private sectors of the economy. Most of these funds are channeled through a special Treasury account called the *Fund for Economic and Social Development.* Because interest rates on the loans are below what the borrower would have to pay in the market, there is great demand for them. The Fund can see that there is conformity with the objectives of the Plan, both in the nature and priority of investments.

There are other ways in which investment can be influenced to favor the objectives of the Plan. One is selective control by the Ministry of Finance over all issues of stocks and bonds; another is control by the Planning Commissariat over long-term borrowing from the major semipublic credit institutions—Crédit National, Crédit Foncier, and Crédit Agricole. These public institutions can make long-term loans out of advances from the Fund for Economic and Social Development, from their own resources, and from funds raised in the capital market.

Selectivity in the granting of short-term credit was used for the first time in 1963 to reduce the inflationary pressures prevalent in the economy. However, the commercial banks favored borrowers who intended to follow the objectives of the Fourth Plan, particularly with respect to investment in areas with high unemployment. This favoritism represented an attempt by the government to influence investment decisions through the short- and medium-term lending policies of the commercial banks.[21] Favorable consideration was also to be shown to borrowers who intended to finance investments that would reduce costs and prices of exports.

[21] The commercial banks were asked, not ordered, by the government to pursue a selective lending policy.

Tax Incentives. Tax incentives are selective between one activity that conforms to the aim of the Plan and another that does not.[22] There are several examples of selective tax measures.

1. As mentioned previously, incentives are provided under the value-added tax. Special credits under the value-added tax are also provided for housing construction.
2. Although dividends are not generally deductible from taxable income in computing the corporate income tax, corporations can make this deduction, provided that the proceeds received for the stock were used in connection with regional development or plant and equipment modernization plans. Application for deduction must be filed with the Planning Commissariat, and approval or disapproval is given by the Ministry of Finance.
3. A reduction is also given on the transfer tax on land and buildings if the transfer is connected with the program for regional development and industrial decentralization.
4. There is partial relief or total exemption from the business license tax for firms that help promote the Plan's regional development programs.

The use of tax incentive devices to hasten the modernization and decentralization of French industry is an essential feature of the French tax system. Tax incentives are used by many European countries to accomplish the same objectives, plan or no plan. Since modernization and decentralization of industry are objectives of the French Plans, tax incentives can be considered a legitimate instrument of French planning.

Public Investment. Public investment is also an important instrument of French economic planning. It has increased under the Mitterand government, with much of the increase going to the industries that were nationalized. Part of the increase has gone to industries to finance research and development in order to make them more competitive in world markets, and another part has been used to fund job-creating projects.

In 1988, investment financed by the French government amounted to about $112 billion, or about 51 percent of all industrial investment in France. Public investment is financed from two main sources—general tax revenues and deficits

---

[22] The use of tax incentives is not new in France. Its use dates back to the time of Colbert and French mercantilism. It reflects a view that taxation should not be neutral but should be used to achieve certain economic objectives. However, the neutrality aspects of the French tax system considerably outweigh the incentive aspects. Tax incentives are basically confined to regional development, housing construction, exports, and scientific research, and to a considerable degree are automatic in that no government approval is needed.

in the French national budget. The investments of the nationalized industries, from their retained earnings, also represent a part of total public investment.

An Appraisal of the French Economy

During the period 1970–1980, the French economy performed the best in Western Europe, as measured by average annual increases in real gross national product and industrial production. For example, growth in industrial production increased at an average annual rate of 3.4 percent in France compared to 2.5 percent in West Germany and 1.8 percent in the United Kingdom.[23] However, the performance of the French economy in the 1980s was mediocre in comparison with other western industrial countries. Its growth rate for the period 1980–1987 was at an average annual rate of 1.6 percent compared to 2.3 percent for the OECD (Organization for Economic Cooperation and Development) countries.[24] Its economic performance relative to the United States and the major Western European countries, as Table 8-5 indicates, was below par.

Economic Policies During the 1980s

Following an attempt to inflate the economy in 1981 and 1982, the Mitterand government pursued a policy of slow growth aimed at reducing both inflation and a current-accounts deficit. By 1986, inflation had decreased to around 2.5 percent, but unemployment had increased to around 9 percent. The Mitterand government closed down inefficient steel mills and coal mines. Government subsidies were denied to one of France's most prestigious firms, Creusot Loire, thereby allowing it to go into bankruptcy and subsequent dismantling. Some 200,000 jobs were eliminated in the nationalized industries, and cuts in social welfare spending were made in the French budget.

TABLE 8-5

Growth Rates in Real GNP for France and Other Countries (percent)

	1976–1983	1984	1985	1986	1987	1988	1989
France	2.5	1.3	1.9	2.3	1.9	3.4	3.4
Canada	2.7	6.3	4.8	3.1	4.5	5.0	2.9
United States	2.5	6.8	3.4	2.7	3.7	4.4	4.2
Japan	4.4	5.1	4.9	2.5	4.5	5.7	4.9
Italy	3.3	3.0	2.6	2.5	3.0	3.9	3.3
West Germany	2.4	3.3	1.9	2.3	1.7	3.6	4.3

Source: Economic Report of the President, 1990 *(Washington: USGPO, 1990), p. 419.*

---

[23] *Economic Report of the President 1986* (Washington: U. S. Government Printing Office, 1986), p. 377.

[24] OECD, *National Accounts, 1960–1987*, pp. 18 and 48.

A center-right government was elected in 1986 and shared power with Mitterand.[25] It continued the policy of fiscal and monetary discipline indicated by Mitterand and reduced taxes, introduced more tax incentives, privatized some 65 state-controlled industries, removed most price controls,[26] and relied on a more market-oriented approach to stimulate investment and job opportunities. In 1988, the socialists won a majority of seats in a parliamentary election but pledged not to undo the policies of the previous center-right government, save in one area. Consistent with its belief that the French government has a more important role to play in the economy, it has halted the program of privatization.

SUMMARY

Although France can be considered as having a mixed economic system, the government plays a more dominant role in the national economy than do the governments of the United States, Japan, and the United Kingdom. However, state control is not new in France; it dates back to the times of Louis XIV and his finance minister Jean Baptiste Colbert. Current government intervention in the economy began after World War II, when banks and certain industries were nationalized and the first of a number of plans were initiated by the government. A number of industries were further nationalized by the socialist government when it came to power in 1981. Contrary to expectations, Mitterand has proved to be a pragmatist when it comes to managing the economy and has relied on free market forces to stimulate economic development.

REVIEW QUESTIONS

1. French economic planning is called indicative rather than imperative. Explain.
2. Discuss the reasons for the postwar nationalization of certain of the French industries.
3. The French government plays an important role in the banking system. Explain.
4. The French government influences the investment decisions of business firms in several ways. What are these ways?
5. Discuss the policy instruments used to implement the French Plans.

---

[25] This is analogous to the United States where a Republican president shares power with a Democratic congress.

[26] Price controls have been used extensively since World War II. The trend since that time has been to relax controls, and only tax fares are now subject to regulation.

6.   What is the function of the Bank of France?
7.   What are some of the changes the Mitterand socialist government has made in the French economy?
8.   Discuss the performance of the French Economy in the 1980s.

RECOMMENDED READINGS

Ardagh, John. *France in the 1980s*. New York: Penguin Books, 1983.

Belassa, Bela. *The First Year of Socialist Government in France*. Washington, DC: American Enterprise Institute, 1982.

Bell, Davis S. *The French Socialist Party: Resurgence and Victory*. Oxford: Oxford University Press, 1984.

Cerny, Philip, and Martin Schain, eds. *Socialism, the State, and Public Policy in France*. New York: Methuen Inc., 1985.

Cohen, Stephen, and Peter Gourevetch. *France in the Troubled World Economy*. Boston: Butterworth Publishers, 1982.

Estrin, Saul and Peter Holmes. *French Planning in Theory and Practice*. Boston: Allen and Unwin, 1983.

Kuisel, Richard. *Capitalism and the State in Modern France*. New York: Cambridge University Press, 1982.

Lutz, Vera. *Central Planning for the Market Economy: An Analysis of the French Theory and Experience*. London: Longmans Green, 1969.

Mitterand, François. *The Wheat and the Chaff*. New York: Seaver Books, 1982.

Peyrefitte, Alain. *The Trouble With France*. New York: Alfred A. Knopf Inc., 1982.

CHAPTER NINE

JAPAN

World War II formally ended in August 1945 when Japan capitulated to the United States. Although the United States won that war, it could lose the current one—namely, a fight for supremacy as the world's leading economic power.[1] The evidence is that Japan is gaining and could overtake the United States. The United States started the 1980s as the world's leading creditor nation and will end it as the world's leading debtor nation. The United States has lost whole sectors of industry to Japan. To give an example, the whole video and television area belongs to Japan. The U.S. share of the consumer electronics market has slipped from about 100 percent in 1970 to less than 5 percent today. Between 1970 and 1987, America's share of the U.S. market in phonographs dropped from 90 percent to 1 percent; for color TVs from 90 percent to 10 percent; in machine tools from 100 percent to about 35 percent; and VCRs from 10 percent to 1 percent.[2] From the period 1982 to 1987 Japanese companies have taken the lead in winning U.S. patents.

There has always been a tendency in the United States to underestimate the Japanese. After all, John Wayne and Errol Flynn destroyed whole Japanese armies singlehandedly in World War II war movies, and the Japanese used to make junk goods that were sold in dimestores. A later phase had many people in the United States saying that the Japanese were good at imitating others but that they were not creative enough to be good in the sophisticated area of computers and telecommunications. Myths die hard, but the Japanese are for real.

---

[1] See Clyde V. Prestowitz, Jr. *Trading Places: How We Allowed Japan to Take the Lead* (New York: Basic Books, 1988).

[2] Council on Competitiveness, *Keeping Up The Pace: The Commercial Challenge to U.S. Competitiveness* (Washington, DC: 1988), p. 15.

The phenomenal performance of the Japanese economy is even more remarkable when one considers the economic base from which the country operates. The land area of Japan is small, the natural resources are limited, and the population is large. Japan is vulnerable to world upheavals because it imports such a high percentage of resources. Dependence on exports and imports is a way of life for the Japanese economy. There has been considerable pressure to gain reserves of foreign currency and gold to cover a balance-of-payments deficit incurred to pay for the imports necessary to sustain industrial development. Thus, it is imperative for the Japanese to be successful in world competition so that they can earn the foreign reserves necessary to cover their import needs. Government tax and foreign trade policies encourage industries that can be competitive in international markets.

During the 1970s and 1980s, the Japanese economy has been the most successful in the world. It is important to examine the factors responsible for this success. How could a country come back from the zero point in August 1945, when the war ended and the economy was in ruins? Forty percent of the urban area had been destroyed, and urban population had dropped to less than half of prewar levels. Industry was at a standstill and agriculture, short of equipment and personnel, had declined. The per capita annual income was $20; 50 percent of the working population was unemployed. The economy, with American aid, could go no place but up, and it has gone up at a rate unprecedented in the Western world. Success can be attributed to a combination of factors the Japanese have melded together. Japan stands as a model to the world, especially the Third World, for its success transcends its culture and history.

THE ECONOMIC SYSTEM

Japan has an economic philosophy that embraces the basic concepts of a modern capitalist economy. This philosophy was grafted onto a country that had virtually no outside contact with the Western world before 1853, when Commodore Matthew C. Perry and his American naval squadron forced Japan against its will to open itself to the West.[3] With the shock of exposure to the outside world, it became apparent to the Japanese that they had to make a choice: Either create a modern industrial state or become another market for Western goods. They chose the former, and in a relatively short period, Japan was transformed from an underdeveloped country into a world economic power. It did this by emulating the industrial powers of the West in every possible way; it cast aside behavioral patterns of centuries in favor of anything Western. By the beginning of this century, Japan had achieved sufficient industrial and military might to inflict a military defeat upon the forces of the Russian empire.

---

[3] Actually, Christian missionaries had reached Japan by the middle of the fifteenth century. The Dutch established a trading post at Nagasaki in 1638 and maintained it for several centuries. Dutch became the language of Western learning in Japan, and through books brought in from Holland, Japanese scholars managed to keep at least partially abreast of intellectual and scientific progress in the West.

The economic development of Japan can be divided into two major time periods: the Meiji Period from 1868 to 1913 and the period following the end of World War II from 1948 to 1960. Each period is significant in understanding how Japan has transformed itself into a major world power. A common denominator of each period was the role the Japanese government played in stimulating economic development. Human capital was also important in aiding economic growth, for Japan has had few natural resources and land was far from abundant relative to the size of the population.

The Meiji Period, 1868–1913

The Meiji Restoration of 1868 marks the beginning of the development of Japan as a modern industrial nation.[4] In the first years after the Restoration, the most important development in Japan was the creation of an environment conducive to economic growth. In order to survive the economic encroachments of the Western powers, Japan, by national policy, had to master the secret of industry. To gain the necessary knowledge, Japanese students were sent to study the technology of Western nations. Also, Western engineers and technicians were temporarily employed in Japan to teach the Japanese the techniques of production. The Japanese learned to adapt the technology of the West for their own purposes.

The Role of Government.   The government became a major operator of key industries. The modernization of Japan during the later part of the last century included the nationalization of key sectors of the economy—the postal service, telephone and telegraph communications, and railways. The government also built and operated iron foundries, shipyards, machine shops, and factories. Tobacco, salt, and camphor became government monopolies.[5] The government provided technical and financial assistance to private interests in other industries.

The financial and monetary base for the economy was provided in 1882 when the Bank of Japan was formed. Tax policies were designed to stimulate capital formation. Taxes were levied on agricultural land and the sale of farm products. The proceeds provided for public capital formation, which went into the development of roads and education facilities. Expenditures on arsenals, navy yards, warships, and the like provided a military underpinning to the process of economic development.

The Role of Private Enterprise.   While the government was involved in providing the conditions requisite to economic growth and industrial development, private

---

[4] The Meiji Restoration was called a "restoration" because the powers of the government that the Tokugawa Shogunate had usurped were restored to the emperor of Japan, who came to be known posthumously as the Emperor Meiji.

[5] The government also financed the development of experimental or pilot plants to train Japanese workers and to adopt Western production techniques to Japanese conditions. These plants became models for private industry to follow.

enterprise also flourished and developed during the Meiji Period. An important development during the Meiji Period was the displacement of the *samurai*, or warrior caste, which had dominated Japan for centuries. The samurai were integrated into Japanese society, and some went into business. Therefore, in Japan business people were drawn from the upper classes of society and enjoyed immediate respect and prestige. In this respect, Japan started at an advantage, for in most developing countries, the business class is composed largely of people in lower social classes or racial and religious minorities not respected by the population. By building up export industries based on low-cost labor, Japan was able to increase exports to provide foreign exchange to purchase food and raw materials needed by the economy.

Japanese capitalism was characterized by the development of concentrated economic power in the form of business combines call *zaibatsus*. Each combine consisted of 20 to 30 major firms, all concentrated around a large bank. These major firms represented each of the important industrial sectors in the economy, so that a group would typically include a shipping company, a steel company, an insurance company, and so forth. Zaibatsu combines were larger than any American corporation and were under the control and management of a few family dynasties. The Mitsui combine, for example, employed 1,800,000 workers prior to World War II, and Mitsubishi employed 1,000,000 workers.[6] There was a working relationship between the zaibatsus and the Japanese government in that the latter, through military force or otherwise, provided penetration of new markets.

Post–World War II Development of Japan

With Japan's defeat in World War II and the subsequent occupation by the United States came problems of reform and reorganization for the economy. A new constitution, which incorporated Western principles of democratic parliamentary government, was promulgated in November 1946.[7] The dissolution of the zaibatsu into a number of independent business enterprises was another part of U.S. occupation policy. Antitrust laws molded after the U.S. Sherman and Clayton Acts were imposed on the Japanese. Later, however, the Japanese government enacted various laws to exempt certain industries from antitrust legislation. These exemptions were designed to improve Japan's position as a world exporter by allowing certain types of export cartels.[8] The U.S. occupation of Japan also resulted in the introduction of consumer technology, which the Japanese readily assimilated. The Japanese became wards of the United States and received gifts, low-interest

---

[6] Corwin Edwards, "The Dissolution of Zaibatsu Continues." *Pacific Affairs* (September, 1946), pp. 8–24.

[7] The U.S. military occupation of Japan ended in 1952.

[8] Japanese antimonopoly laws permit the development of cartels and other forms of business combinations to a far greater extent than is permitted by U.S. antitrust laws.

loans, and machinery that restored productive capacity in a number of industries, especially textiles. [9]

However, Japanese economic development policy could not depend on American largesse alone. Local needs had to be satisfied first. The shipbuilding industry was destroyed during the war and, as a small island country, Japan needed ships of every type for survival. With government aid, the shipbuilding industry developed rapidly; by 1956 the Japanese had become the world's largest producer of ships.

Japan also developed an export strategy to achieve industrial development. For exports, the country's leaders recognized that they would have to depend on handicrafts, textiles, and other small-scale industries in which Japan enjoyed the advantage of low-cost labor. Human capital was an important factor in the early post-war period. Veterans were absorbed in the labor-intensive industries. Earnings from exports were used to finance the acquisition of machine tools that would help Japan produce modern machinery. This led to the development of other industries, notably Honda, which developed from a one-man operation in 1951 to the largest motorcycle company in the world.

The Role of the Japanese Government.   The Japanese government has played and continues to play an important role in the development of the Japanese economy. The postwar development of Japanese industry was facilitated through government grants and low-interest loans. There has also been extensive use of fiscal and monetary policies to stimulate economic growth. Tax policy is used to achieve specific policy objectives. Special tax incentives are used to promote a high rate of saving, investment, and capital formation. There are also special tax incentives to promote the introduction of new products and technology. Probably most important of all has been the development of a close working relationship between government and business. This relationship is based to some extent on the realization that Japan has few natural resources and that it is necessary to reach some consensus over resource allocation. Government and business leaders attempt to decide on policy objectives that will promote the national interest rather than that of a special interest group. [10]

The Role of Private Enterprise.   Japan is characterized as having a *dual economy*. Japanese corporations are among the world's largest, and many engage in a wide variety of business activities. Around each major corporation are several satellite companies. These satellite companies, which are often small, family-owned operations employing up to 100 workers, are important to the Japanese economy. They typically manufacture a subassembly or provide a service sold only to their major

---

[9] Jean-Jacques Servan-Schreiber, *The World Challenge* (New York: Simon and Schuster Inc., 1981), pp. 178–184.

[10] Peter F. Drucker, "Behind Japan's Success," *Harvard Business Review* (January–February 1981), pp. 83–90.

customer.[11] The relationship between a satellite company and its major customer constitutes a bilateral monopoly, in which the satellite has only one customer for its product, and the major firm has only one supplier for each of its inputs. This bilateral monopoly relationship makes it difficult for foreign firms to do business in Japan.

The Keiretsu.   The zaibatsu have been reassembled into a group arrangement called the *keiretsu*. There are six keiretsu in Japan—Sumitomo, Mitsui, Mitsubishi, Sanwa, Fuyo, and Dai Ichi Kangyo—and most of the largest corporations in Japan are linked to one group or another. The keiretsu are enormous in size and consist of companies in many fields. The Sumitomo group, for example, includes firms in banking, electronics, glass, insurance, oil, forestry, and metals.[12] The total volume of business each group does runs in hundreds of billions of dollars. The typical keiretsu would have sales of around $300 billion a year, an amount three times as much as General Motors, which is the single largest corporation in the world. There are interlocking directorates in each group, and companies affiliated with a group can own stock in each other. Loans to members of a group can be made at favorable rates of interest by banks that are also group members.

Management of a keiretsu is provided by the heads of each company affiliated with it. These executives conduct business strategy for their group relative to the other groups, and they coordinate the policies of member companies with respect to political, business, and world affairs. Members of a group may support each other financially. For example, if one member of a group is in danger of going bankrupt, banks in the group can make low-cost loans to it, and other members may increase their purchases of its product or hire its workers. Members can buy each other's products, thus creating a built-in stable market that helps to reduce risk. The group arrangement also pertains to international trade.

Table 9-1 and Figure 9-1 present the financial strength and the organization of a keiretsu. In Table 9-1 the value in assets of various members of the Sumitomo keiretsu are presented. These values are limited to only those firms listed in Fortune's International 500 largest industrial firms and Fortune's list of the 100 largest foreign banks. Many of the Sumitomo firms in the keiretsu are not included in the table, because they were not listed in Fortune's 500. A frame of reference are the assets of General Motors, the world's largest industrial company, which were $173,297.1 (million) in 1989.

Figure 9-1 presents the interlocking arrangements of members of a keiretsu. There are construction firms, trading firms, and warehousing firms. Each group develops a trade strategy that pertains to exporting, importing, and investing in other countries. Group loyalty is very important, for when a choice has to be made between a foreign-import and a similar product produced by a group member, other members will buy the local product even though the import is much cheaper.[13]

[11] William Ouchi, *Theory Z* (Reading, MA: Addison-Wesley Publishing Co., Inc., 1981), p. 18.
[12] Prestowitz, *Trading Places*, pp. 157–159.
[13] Prestowitz, *Trading Places*, p. 162.

TABLE 9-1
The Sumitomo Keiretsu Measured by Value of
Assets (millions of dollars)

Members	Assets
Sumitomo Bank	407,227.3
Sumitomo Trust and Banking	207,582.6
Sumitomo Chemical	7,497.6
Sumitomo Electric	5,737.0
Sumitomo Heavy Industries	3,574.9
Sumitomo Metal Industries	14,759.5
Sumitomo Rubber	3,108.2
General Motors	173,297.1

Source: "The International 500," Fortune (July 30, 1990), pp. 269–292.

Needless to say, the keiretsu arrangement would not be tolerated in the United States, for it would violate about every provision of all the U.S. antitrust laws. A comparable American equivalent to a keiretsu would involve Chase Manhattan Bank, Inland Steel, Pittsburgh Plate Glass, Reynolds Aluminum, IBM, and DuPont.[14] There would be an interlocking directorate arrangement, cross-stockownership, and cooperation between each company. They would buy from each other and sell to each other. Chase Manhattan would lend money at favorable interest rates to group members. The chief executives of each firm would hold monthly meetings to discuss business strategy relative to other groups. This is the direct antithesis to the American belief in competition in the marketplace.

The Trading Companies (Sogo Shoshas).   Another important form of business organization is the trading company, or *sogo shosha*.[15] There are a half dozen trading companies and they are the largest enterprises of any type, banks or otherwise, in the world. Most Japanese foreign trade is done through the trading companies, each of which is represented in every country in the world. They are responsible for information gathering. A trading company may be part of a keiretsu. It functions as the umbrella company for the keiretsu, but is a separate entity. Sogo shoshas handle most of Japanese exports and imports and serve as screening mechanisms to filter out any imports that might be damaging to members of a keiretsu. For example, if soda ash can be imported more cheaply than it can be made in Japan, a trading company may limit its importation to protect the Japanese manufacture of it.

---

[14] Prestowitz, *Trading Places*, p. 160.

[15] See Kiyoshi, Kojima. *Japan's General Trading Companies: Merchants of Economic Development* (Paris: Organization for Economic Cooperation and Development, 1984).

FIGURE 9-1 Sumitomo Group

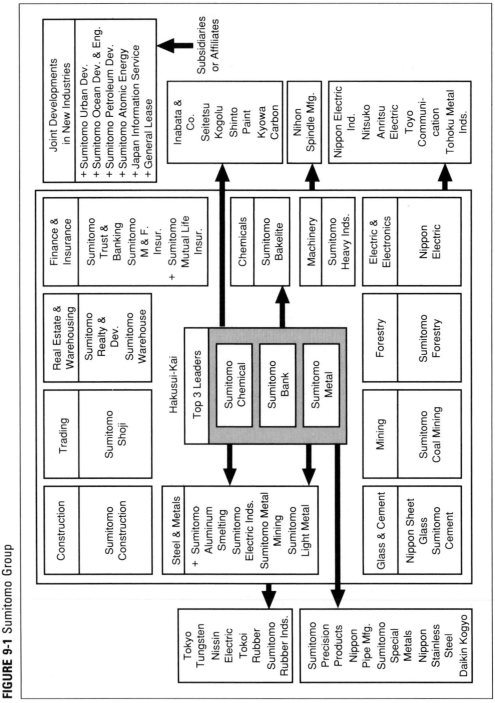

Source: Clyde V. Prestowitz, Jr., Trading Places: How We Allowed Japan to Take the Lead (New York: Basic Books, 1988), p. 158.

178

Table 9-2 presents the six major trading companies in Japan as measured by total revenue in 1988. Toyota, the largest manufacturing company in Japan, is used as a frame of reference. The top four trading companies had higher revenues than General Motors, which is the largest manufacturing company in the world. It should be noted that the Sumitomo trading company is a part of the Sumitomo keiretsu, and the Mitsubishi trading company is part of the Mitsubishi keiretsu.

Public Finance

One factor that complicates the subject of public finance in Japan is the role industrial enterprise plays in the life of the average Japanese worker. It can be said that enterprise has usurped many of the functions of the welfare state. One important characteristic of many Japanese companies is lifetime employment, which is the rubric under which various facets of Japanese life are integrated.[16] Once hired, a new employee is retained until mandatory retirement at age 55.[17] A number of functions that are normally provided at least in part by the government are provided by the Japanese enterprise—such things as medical care, low-cost housing, and subsidized meals, all of which would count in the income redistribution process. Upon retirement, a company pays each retiree a lump sum separation typically amounting to five or six years' salary. This means that social welfare expenditures in Japan are low in comparison with other countries.

Government spending and transfers are handled in the national budget, which consists of general accounts, special accounts, and government agency accounts. General accounts include expenditures for education, science and technology, social security, land conservation and development, allocations to local governments, and national defense. The main revenue sources are taxes, monopoly profits, and bond

TABLE 9-2

The Largest Trading Companies in 1988 (millions)

	Revenues
Mitsui and Co.	$130,667
Sumitomo Corp.	115,570
C. Itoh and Co.	111,237
Mitsubishi Corp.	104,196
Marubeni Corp.	99,475
Nissho Iwai	81,371
Toyota	53,818

Source: Forbes, July 14, 1989, p. 289

---

[16] Not all Japanese workers are guaranteed lifetime employment; about 35 percent of the work force has lifetime employment.

[17] Ouchi, *Theory Z*, pp. 17–18.

revenues. Special accounts are used for purposes where the government either undertakes specific projects or finances a specific expenditure with a specific revenue. The government agency accounts are for those public corporations financed by the government whose budgets are subject to the approval of the Diet.[18] These include three public corporations, the Japan Telephone and Telegraph Company, the Japan National Railways, and the Japan Monopoly Corporation; two banks, the Japan Development Bank and the Japan Export-Import Bank; and several other credit institutions, including the Small Business Finance Corporation and the Housing Loan Corporation.

Taxation in Japan.   The two most imporant taxes in Japan are the personal and corporate income taxes, which accounted for approximately 65 percent of national government revenues in 1988. The tax rates are altered frequently because the national government has the authority to alter the base and rates annually and usually does. For example, the personal income tax rate ranged from 10.5 percent on taxable incomes of around $7,500 or less to 60 percent on taxable income in excess of $250,000.[19] Annual changes in the tax laws constitute an important part of the government's budgetary policy and are called the "tax cut" policy. To stimulate economic growth, the government has changed the rates of the personal and corporate income taxes almost every year since 1950.

Savings.   Japan is a nation of savers. In part, it is a result of the Confucian cultural bent toward savings, but, more important, it is a result of conscious government economic policy to promote growth and industrial development. After World War II, a decision was made to generate internally instead of from foreign sources the capital necessary to encourage an industrial rebirth. To accomplish this objective, the national rate of savings had to be increased. The national government adopted a number of pro-savings policies. A very important way to increase the rate of savings is through a Postal Savings account. Interest on savings on deposits of up to $13,000 is exempt from the personal income tax. In addition, an individual can set up several Postal Savings accounts in the names of family members so that each can get the maximum tax-free interest.[20]

Investment.   In addition to a plenitude of savings, investment is also encouraged by tax policies directed toward corporations. For example, a corporate tax credit of up to 8.4 percent is permitted on the acquisition of machinery and equipment.[21]

---

[18] The Diet is Japan's legislative body to which representatives of the political parties are elected.

[19] *Individual Taxes: A Worldwide Summary, 1988 Edition* (New York: Price Waterhouse and Co., 1988), p. 152.

[20] Tax reform is imminent as a growing emphasis is placed on domestic consumption. Taxes may be placed on savings.

[21] *Corporate Taxes: A Worldwide Summary, 1988 Edition* (New York: Price Waterhouse, 1988), pp. 225–229.

Total credits are limited to 20 percent of corporate income. Industries contributing to exports get special tax breaks. A special tax credit is allowed against the corporate income tax for corporations having increased their research and development expenditures. There are also tax provisions to promote the introduction of new products and technology. These include exemptions from personal or corporate income taxes on revenues from the sale of new products approved by the Ministry of Finance, duty-free importation of certain types of machinery and equipment, and favorable tax treatment of patents and royalties.[22]

Government Expenditures.   In 1987 total government expenditures of all types amounted to 23 percent of Japan's gross national product, a lower percentage than any other major industrial nation.[23] Government spending is broken down into two categories—general government consumption and spending on capital formation. General consumption spending is evenly divided between the national government and local governments. Japan has had a long tradition of local autonomy, and the importance of local finance in relation to national finance is greater in Japan than it is in the United Kingdom or France.

Spending on capital formation is made by the national government and equals about 10 percent of gross national product. This spending is made through the *Financial Loan and Investment Program*, which is a separate budget entity. Included in this program is spending for housing; water and sewage facilities; agriculture and small industries; roads, transportation, and regional development; and key industries and export promotion.

Government expenditures and tax policies place more emphasis on a high rate of economic growth than on income redistribution. Priority within the budget is given to spending that increases capital formation and thus allows the nation to increase its output of goods. A lower priority has been assigned to social welfare expenditures, in part because of the policy of lifetime employment provided by large industrial enterprises. The industrial enterprise is regarded as a family where employees, rather than being hired, are adopted as members of the family. Their participation in the enterprise family is based on more than their actual contribution in terms of skill. The wage system is not simply compensation for work but is rather a kind of "life income" determined by an employee's age and family situation. The basic wage often comprises only 50 percent of annual income; the remainder is paid in the form of various allowances and benefits.[24]

Fiscal Policy.   Fiscal policy plays an important role in the development of the Japanese economy. Changes in the level of taxation, in spending in the govern-

---

[22] *Corporate Taxes*, p. 229.

[23] Organization for Economic Cooperation and Development, "Japan," *Economic Surveys* (Paris: July 1988), p. 19.

[24] Robert Christopher, *The Japanese Mind* (New York: Simon and Schuster, 1983), p. 248.

ment general accounts budget, and in the government financial loan and investment program are the three devices used to affect the level of aggregate demand. Maintenance of a high rate of economic growth, as opposed to income redistribution or the provision of socially desirable goods and services, has been the dominant objective of fiscal policy. However, the emphasis on sustained economic growth works to the advantage of the Japanese people in the form of continued increases in the per capita output of goods and services. Government fiscal policy, by supporting a continuous increase in private and public investment, has been conducive to a high rate of economic growth in Japan.

The Banking System

The banking system of Japan can be divided into a number of institutions, with the Bank of Japan providing the connecting link in the system. Japanese banks are classified as commercial banks, long-term credit banks, and foreign exchange banks. There are private financial institutions that specialize in financing small- and medium-sized enterprises and investment in agricultural equipment. In addition, there are also government-owned financial institutions that supplement the functions of the private financial institutions. Included among the government financial institutions are the Japan Development Bank, Postal Savings, Export-Import Bank of Japan, Housing Loan Corporation, and Small Business Finance Corporation. Most of these government financial institutions were created after the end of World War II and currently play an important role in the financial operations of the nation.

The largest borrowers of funds in Japan are corporate business concerns, which dominate investment activities in the country. The biggest source of savings is private individuals who invest their money in Postal Saving accounts. This money, along with government trust and pension funds, is funneled into the government-owned lending institutions mentioned above. Large- and medium-sized Japanese corporations borrow from private Japanese banks or issue stocks and bonds to raise money; small companies (that are usually the subcontractors to the larger ones) get most of their loans from the government through the Small Business Finance Corporation.

The Central Bank.   The Bank of Japan was established in 1882. Since its establishment, the Bank has always served as the fiscal agent for the government. It provides the government with borrowing facilities and over the years has also assumed a wide range of activities, including handling the public receipts and payments, Treasury accounts, and government debt, and buying and selling foreign exchange.

The Bank of Japan also carries out a wide variety of activity with commercial banks and other institutions. These include receiving deposits, making loans, discounting bills and notes, and buying and selling Treasury bills. Commercial banks turn to the Bank of Japan as a source of funds similar to the way U.S. banks borrow from the Federal Reserve. Since the commercial banks depend upon the central bank for credit, discount policy has played an important and effective role in maintaining general economic stability. A restriction of central bank credit has an immediate and significant impact on commercial bank policy.

Commercial Banks.   Japan has become banker to the world. In 1986, Japanese banks held 31.6 percent of the worldwide assets of all banks; by 1990, they are expected to have around 50 percent.[25] Japanese banks are not only larger than their American counterparts; they are much larger. As Table 9-3 indicates, the ten largest banks in the world are Japanese; all are much larger than Citicorp, the largest U.S. banking institution. But it is not only the Japanese banks that are large. Nomura, the giant Japanese securities firm, has the highest market capitalization in the world. Its share of global equity trading volume is twenty times greater than Merrill Lynch, the leading American firm. The resources of the Japanese financial system give Japan unprecedented influence over how global resources are to be allocated. They also provide unlimited financial resources to Japanese industrial firms.

Government Financial Institutions.   The government itself is engaged in substantial financial activities through the ownership of a number of specialized credit institutions. Loans are provided for long-term industrial development, export financing, and agriculture as a part of government policy for stimulating economic growth in an economy where capital is scarce. These institutions obtain loanable funds from the special counterpart fund in the national budget and from individual savings in the form of postal savings, postal annuities, and postal life insurance. These

TABLE 9-3
The Largest Banks in the World

	Bank	Headquarters	Assets in Dollars
1.	Dai-Ichi Kangyo Bank Ltd., Tokyo	Japan	$388,937,333,376
2.	Sumitomo Bank Ltd., Osaka	Japan	$376,087,770,300
3.	Fuji Bank, Ltd., Tokyo	Japan	$364,043,947,200
4.	Sanwa Bank Ltd., Osaka	Japan	$348,357,955,888
5.	Mitsubishi Bank Ltd., Tokyo	Japan	$343,593,454,168
6.	Industrial Bank of Japan, Ltd., Tokyo	Japan	$257,577,924,532
7.	Norinchukin Bank, Tokyo	Japan	$241,947,349,684
8.	Tokai Bank Ltd., Nagoya	Japan	$225,121,125,836
9.	Mitsui Bank, Ltd., Tokyo	Japan	$219,666,258,008
10.	Mitsubishi Trust and Banking Corp., Tokyo	Japan	$210,485,840,188
24.	Citibank NA, New York	United States	$146,177,000,000

Source: American Banker, *July 25, 1989, Vol. 154, No. 143 (July 1989), p. 123.*

---

[25] Daniel Burstein, *Yen: Japan's New Financial Empire and Its Threat to America* (New York: Simon and Schuster, 1988), p. 127.

savings and the surplus funds from special budgetary accounts are deposited in a Trust Fund Bureau, which can use the funds for loans to public enterprises and financial institutions. Loans are also made to the private sector of the economy, particularly to industries that are export related. However, as a rule, private sector financing is undertaken in cooperation with private lending institutions.

The Export-Import Bank.   The Japan Export-Import Bank provides long-term loans at subsidized interest rates to exporters of Japanese products. For example, loans have been provided for the construction of tankers, textile machinery, and railroad cars. Loans have also been provided for the financing of projects, such as the development of iron ore mines in India and the construction of textile mills in South America. The Bank also provides financing and debt guarantees to attract foreign capital into Japan. To stimulate economic development in Southeast Asia, the government set up a special account with the Bank and called it the Southeast Asia Development Corporation Fund. Funds were provided out of the national budget. The fund was eventually transformed into an independent corporation and currently finances long-term investment in Southeast Asia.

Japan Development Bank.   Another important government-owned financial institution is the Japan Development Bank. The bank was created in 1951 to aid in the postwar reconstruction of the economy. Most of its loans were originally concentrated in the electric power, shipbuilding, and coal industries. However, in recent years its loans have been channeled into the petrochemical and rubber industries and also into the promotion of regional development, city transportation, and international tourism. The bank provides long-term loans at low interest rates to basic domestic industries. Through its control over loanable funds that are in the hands of official financial agencies like the Japanese Development Bank, the government is able to exercise some control over national investment and thereby exert some influence with respect to its national economic plans.

Another financial institution directly owned and operated by the government is the Small Business Finance Corporation, which provides long-term loans to small businesses when financing by ordinary financial institutions proves difficult. The government-owned Agriculture, Forestry, and Fisheries Finance Corporation provides long-term, low-interest loans for investment in agricultural equipment by agricultural cooperatives and individual farming enterprises. Loanable funds for both corporations are obtained from the national budget and from earnings on investments in securities and call loans.

The Ministry of Posts and Communications.   This is the prime savings institution in Japan, with total savings of over one trillion dollars. Every mama-san in Japan saves through the postal service. She gives her savings to the postman in her district for deposit in the post office. This money then goes to finance such government agencies as the Japan Development Bank. But the MPT does more than collect savings; it also regulates and structures the Japanese telecommunications industry. It is a prime source for the future leaders of Japan, because many Japanese politicians have worked for it at one time or another in their earlier careers.

Monetary Policy. The Bank of Japan has three instruments used to control the volume of credit and money—bank rate policy, open market operations, and reserve requirements. Bank rate policy involves the lowering or raising of discount rates and interest rates. The alteration of these rates is the most important monetary policy instrument in Japan because city banks rely heavily on loans from the Bank of Japan, and industries, in turn, rely heavily on bank loans. Costs in general and the availability of bank funds are highly responsive to changes in the discount and interest rates on commercial and export trade bills, overdrafts, and general secured loans. In addition, the Bank of Japan can place a ceiling on borrowing for each bank, above which it can impose a penalty rate or refuse to make loans. Open market operations are inhibited by the lack of a well-developed capital market and are not important as an instrument of monetary policy. Legal reserve requirements are far below the standard of reserve requirements in other major countries, and manipulation of these requirements by the Bank of Japan is a supplementary instrument of monetary control.

In Japan the function of monetary policy is more circumscribed than that of fiscal policy. In general, monetary policy has been expansionary to encourage a high rate of economic growth. Successive cuts in the official discount rate brought it down to an all-time low level of 4.25 percent in June 1972. However, in 1974 and 1975 the discount rate was raised to 9 percent because of inflation caused by the oil embargo. After 1975, the discount rate was lowered as inflation subsided. In 1988, the average Japanese discount rate was 2.5 percent.[26] The Japanese have relied more on monetary policy in recent years as an anti-inflationary device.

Labor-Management Relations

The distinctive feature of Japanese trade unions is that they are usually company unions. The typical Japanese labor union is made up of the employees of a single company or of a single operational unit within a company, regardless of their occupation. Approximately one-fourth of the Japanese labor force belongs to trade unions, with each union loosely tied to one of four central labor organizations. However, the central organizations have little authority over the company unions, which carry on the bargaining with employers. Negotiations between labor and management are conducted within each enterprise; however, there are several points of difference between Japanese labor practices and those of other countries.

Many Japanese firms, in particular the larger ones, provide lifetime employment for their employees. This makes for a very different balance of power between union and management in Japanese firms. The employees know that their future

---

[26] Deutsche Bundesbank, *1988 Annual Report* (Frankfurt; April 1989), p. 42.

depends on their company's future and that labor work stoppages could hurt their company's competitive position. Since it is difficult to obtain employment by leaving one company for another, the union will rarely press its demands so far as to seriously damage the company. Forcing a company into bankruptcy, for example, would put workers at the mercy of the labor market.

Positions within a company are determined largely on the basis of age and length of service. Japanese companies routinely provide a number of fringe benefits for their employees. Thus, negotiations between labor and management in Japan are limited primarily to wages. During February through April each year, unions begin what is called the *shunto*, "spring wage struggle," with their respective companies. If agreement is not reached, the union may go out on strike. But since there is one union for each company, industry-wide strike efforts are rare. Unions may also resort to public demonstrations to make the community aware of their demands.

This is not to say that Japanese labor-management relations are perfect. There is industrial conflict, as evidenced by the frequent wildcat strikes on the government-owned national railways. Worker-days lost through strikes, though much lower than in the United States, are higher than in Sweden or West Germany. The number of work stoppages is also high in comparison to West Germany and France. With the current emphasis on automation, the potential for labor conflict may well increase in Japan during the next few years. The failure of successive conservative governments to develop labor-oriented social welfare programs also provides a potential for labor unrest.

Japanese employers are also organized into several confederations, the largest of which is the Federation of Economic Organizations (*Keidanran*). It is made up of financial, industrial, and trading associations that include almost all of Japan's largest business firms. Membership in the federation is institutional, and its work is carried out by standing committees. Keidanran wields considerable influence in government economic policies because many business and political leaders are bound together by a common educational background and family ties. The Federation provides the Japanese with a mechanism for reconciling industrial policy objectives with political and social goals.

Government and Business Relations

The combination of free enterprise and government control in Japan dates back to the Meiji Restoration in 1868. The government was active during the Meiji era in introducing Western industrial methods into Japan and also took the lead in promoting the development of industries of strategic importance. Fundamental shifts took place in government policy during the 1930s. To counteract the effects of the worldwide depression, state intervention in the economy increased. The electric power industry was nationalized in 1938, and other strategic industries were brought under government control.

After World War II was over, the government continued its role in the economy as an expediter of business development. Policies to increase exports encouraged mergers that resulted in large-scale business operations and the revival of the zaibatsu combines. Special tax privileges, subsidies, and low interest loans were used to strengthen certain industries and certain types of economic activity. The Japanese government continues to exercise an important role in the nurturing of Japanese industry.

Ministry of International Trade and Industry—MITI.   MITI is probably the most important and powerful government agency in Japan, at least as far as Japanese business is concerned. It was created in the late 1940s to guide industrial modernization and promote exports. Its mandate was to determine a basic course of action to improve Japan's future comparative advantage and to mobilize each sector to make its contribution to the whole. Building a steel industry was one of Japan's most important postwar priorities. MITI encouraged Japanese banks to supply the capital that purchased steel-producing equipment and technology from the West, mostly from the United States. Tax incentives, low interest loans, and other financial incentives were also given to the steel industry. MITI has continued to restructure industry by concentrating resources in areas where it thinks Japan needs to be competitive in the future.[27]

MITI has a number of functions.[28] Its primary function is to offer guidance to Japanese industry. It provides the "big picture," so to speak, of where it thinks Japan as a nation should be heading. It develops an industrial policy for Japan and formulates and guides its implementation. It serves in a consultative capacity to other government agencies, and is responsible for the flow of funds to favored industries. It has the power to grant licenses and patents and to determine which firms will get them. No plant, supermarket, or department store in Japan can be built without notification to and authorization from MITI. It has the power to suspend the antitrust laws and create cartels, either for the purpose of aiding industries in recession or developing particular target industries. It has authority over electric power rates and other energy prices in Japan.[29]

Agency of Industrial Science and Technology—AIST.   AIST is another government agency involved with economic development. It is a semi-independent agency under the jurisdiction of MITI and is responsible for the promotion of technology. It monitors scientific and technical developments abroad and identifies new technology that will be important to Japanese industries. One of the strengths of Japanese industry is that it is well informed about worldwide scientific and technological developments. AIST consults with Japanese industry to encourage the use of new

---

[27] The U.S. equivalent of MITI would include the Departments of Commerce and Energy, the Office of the U.S. Trade Administration, the Export-Import Bank, the Small Business Administration, the National Science Foundation, the Overseas Private Investment Corporation, the Environmental Protection Agency, and parts of the Departments of Commerce and Justice.

[28] Prestowitz, *Trading Places*, p. 115.

[29] Prestowitz, p. 117.

technologies that will further the national interest; it sponsors research that will make the needed technology available. It is also responsible for the development of patents.

The Economic Planning Agency

Japanese economic planning is indicative rather than imperative and is similar to French planning in that it develops goals for industrial development, social welfare, labor relations, and related major economic and social sectors. Plans represent goals the Japanese government would like to see achieved. Plans, as announced, represent the consensus of not only government, but also of private groups, including business, labor, and the academic community. Each group is expected to fit its self-interest into a framework of national needs, national goals, and national aspirations.[30] This forces Japanese leadership groups to take responsibility for developing policies in the national interest. The private sector, therefore, has full knowledge through its government input of any government planning.

The Economic Planning Agency, established in 1955 when economic priorities shifted from postwar recovery to economic growth, provides indicative planning for the whole economy. It provides targets for long-term trends and specifies what is necessary for national economic and social development. It is responsible for coordinating the plans of other executive agencies of the Japanese government, analyzing and measuring national economic resources, and identifying future needs. Planning policies that involve foreign trade, agriculture, transportation, and labor are put into effect through cooperation with the ministries responsible for these activities. The Economic Planning Agency itself does not have the power of a ministry and can exercise little independent initiative or coordination.

The *Economic Council* is responsible for the development of the actual plan. It is composed of key members of the financial community, industry, and government, who are appointed by the prime minister to a two-year term. In addition, a number of experts on technical matters are used in formulating the plan. There is a General Policy Committee and a number of specialized committees, each of which is concerned with certain areas of the Japanese economy, such as agriculture, mining, and forestry. Their reports are integrated into a draft of the plan, which is sent by the Council to the prime minister for approval. Then the plan is returned to the Council for implementation.

To carry out its functions, which are not limited exclusively to long-term economic planning, the Economic Planning Agency must work with various executive departments and agencies. The Agency works with the Bank of Japan, whose support is crucial because it is the center of Japanese monetary policy formulation. It must also work with the Ministry of Finance because of its control over expenditures and the national budget, which affect the successful operation of any

---

[30] Drucker, "Behind Japan's Success," pp. 86–87.

plan. Planning policies that involve foreign trade, agriculture, transportation, and labor are put into effect through cooperation with the ministries responsible for these activities. The plan itself is more than just an estimate of the future, for the government is able through fiscal policies and control over financial institutions such as the Japan Development Bank to encourage or compel plan objectives.

AN APPRAISAL
OF THE JAPANESE ECONOMY

To much of the world Japan appears to be an economic colossus that will replace the United States as the dominant economic super power. There is much to justify this belief. Japan is the wealthiest country in the world and has the power to move markets anywhere. The Tokyo Stock Exchange is the largest in the world; the Osaka Stock Exchange is larger than Chicago's or London's. Seventeen of the 25 largest banks in the world are Japanese. The market value of Japanese real estate exceeds that of the United States. The Japanese have the resources to influence securities markets all over the world; they are held responsible for the 1987 worldwide stock market crash, not because they intended to do it, but because of the amount of their financial transactions. They are the world's leading creditor nation. The United States has come to depend on Japan to directly finance as much as 30 percent of the government's budget deficit.

Historical Background

For all practical purposes, the economic development of Japan began with the Meiji Restoration of 1868. At that time, Japan was at the same stage of economic development that the United States was in 1776. The Japanese had to start from scratch to catch up with the industrial West. In 1880, the real per capita GNP was one-twentieth of the United States and the United Kingdom and one-fourth of that for the Soviet Union.[31] To accomplish industrial development, Japan sent thousands of its students to foreign universities to learn science and engineering, and it imported scientists and engineers from abroad to provide technical assistance. The government also provided financial aid to business to further facilitate economic development. The defeat of the Russians at the naval battle of Tsushima Straits in 1904 made Japan a world power. The Treaty of Portsmouth in 1905 gave Japan valuable continental Asian holdings that provided raw materials for economic development.

By 1920, Japanese real per capita GNP had passed that of the Soviet Union and was one-fourth that of the United States. World War II interrupted the growth of the Japanese economy. At the end of the war, real per capita GNP in Japan had declined to one-twelfth of the real per capita GNP for the United States and was

---

[31] *Comparative Economic Statistics* (Tokyo Bank of Japan, 1984), p. 4.

lower than the Soviet Union's. But by 1970 it had passed the United Kingdom. In 1988, Japanese real per capita GNP was 75 percent of the U.S. GNP and 80 percent of West Germany's.

Japanese Economic Indicators

Table 9-4 presents key Japanese economic indicators for 1988. Using 1980 as a base, industrial production in Japan increased more rapidly than in any other major industrial country. Japan also had the lowest inflation rate of the industrial countries. Its gold reserves were the largest in the world, and it has maintained a surplus in its merchandise trade and current accounts.

Table 9-5 presents a comparison of real growth rates for Japan and other major industrial countries for the period 1980–1989 and for earlier time periods. As the table indicates, the growth rate of Japan was very high during the earlier time periods. However, during the 1980s the real growth rate of Japan slowed as the economy matured, and it was not much higher than that for the United States.

Table 9-6 presents the unemployment rate for Japan and other major industrial countries for the period 1980–1988. The rate is far lower in Japan than it is in the other industrial countries. A booming export economy and a guarantee of lifetime employment in the large Japanese corporations are part of the explanation. Japan also has an aging population, with an early rate of retirement set at 55. The percentage of women in the labor force, although increasing, is still low in comparison to the Western countries.

Table 9-7 presents the average annual rate of inflation for Japan and the other major industrial countries for two time periods, 1965–1980 and 1980–1987. The performance of Japan in this area has been quite good, particularly during the 1980s. A high volume of savings has been channeled into investment, and the

TABLE 9-4
Economic Indicators for the Japanese Economy, 1988

GNP (billions of dollars)	$2,576.841
Real GNP growth rate (percent)	5.7
Industrial production (1980 = 100 percent)	137.0
Labor productivity (1985 = 100 percent)	116.6
Bank of Japan discount rate (percent)	2.5
Consumer price under (1980 = 100 percent)	116.0
Unemployment rate (percent)	2.5
Exports (billions of dollars)	264.9
Imports (billions of dollars)	187.4
Trade balance (billions of dollars)	77.5
Current account (billions of dollars)	88.6
Gold reserves (billions of dollars)	86.8

Sources: World Bank, World Bank Atlas 1989, *p. 7; Central Intelligence Agency,* Handbook of Economic Statistics 1989 *(Washington: USGPO, 1989), p. 24;* Economic Report of the President 1990 *(Washington: USGPO), p. 416.*

TABLE 9-5

Growth Rates in Real per Capita GNP for Japan and Other Industrial Nations (percent)

Country	1971–75	1976–83	1984	1985	1986	1987	1988	1989
United States	2.2	2.5	6.8	3.4	2.7	3.7	4.4	3.0
Canada	5.2	2.7	6.3	4.8	3.1	4.5	5.0	2.9
Japan	4.3	4.4	5.1	4.9	2.5	4.5	5.7	4.8
France	4.0	2.5	1.3	1.9	2.3	1.9	3.4	3.4
West Germany	2.1	2.4	3.3	1.9	2.3	1.7	3.6	4.3
Italy	2.4	3.3	3.0	2.6	2.5	3.0	3.9	3.3
United Kingdom	2.1	1.7	2.2	3.7	3.4	4.7	4.2	2.3

Source: Economic Report of the President 1990 *(Washington; USGPO, 1990), p. 419.*

TABLE 9-6

Unemployment Rates for Japan and Other Industrial Countries (percent)

Year	U.S.	Canada	Japan	France	West Germany	Italy	United Kingdom
1980	7.1	7.5	2.0	6.4	2.9	4.4	7.0
1981	7.6	7.5	2.2	7.6	4.1	4.9	10.5
1982	9.7	11.0	2.4	8.3	5.8	5.4	11.3
1983	9.6	11.9	2.7	8.5	7.1	5.9	11.9
1984	8.5	11.3	2.8	10.0	7.4	5.9	11.7
1985	7.2	10.5	2.6	10.4	7.5	6.0	11.2
1986	7.0	9.6	2.8	10.6	7.0	7.5	11.2
1987	6.2	8.9	2.9	10.8	6.9	7.9	10.3
1988	5.5	7.9	2.5	10.4	6.3	7.9	8.1
1989	5.3	7.5	2.4	10.1	5.7	7.8	6.4

Source: Economic Report of the President 1990 *(Washington, DC: USGPO, 1990), p. 417.*

TABLE 9-7

The Inflation Rate in Japan and Other Major Industrial Countries (percent)

Country	1965–1980	1980–1987
Japan	7.8	1.4
Canada	7.1	5.0
United States	6.5	4.3
West Germany	5.2	2.9
United Kingdom	11.2	5.7
France	8.0	7.7
Italy	11.2	11.3

Source: The World Bank, World Development Report 1989 *(New York: Oxford University Press, 1989), p. 165.*

discount rate of the Central Bank of Japan has been low, reflecting an absence of inflationary pressures.

THE TWENTY-FIRST CENTURY: THE ASIAN CENTURY

There is a song in the movie *Cabaret* called "Tomorrow Belongs To Me." It was sung by a Hitler Youth and the meaning was obvious, although "tomorrow" did not belong to the Third Reich. But it might belong to Japan and the other East Asian countries. The performance of South Korea during the 1980s was even more spectacular than Japan's, and the economic growth rate of the People's Republic of China has averaged more than 10 percent a year during the 1980s. Singapore, Hong Kong, and Taiwan also have extremely viable economies. Japan, however, is the economic colossus of East Asia and the country with the financial resources. It should be the leader of the fastest developing area in the world.

Nevertheless, for all of its success at managing its economy, Japan lacks the ideology and moral commitment that goes with world leadership.[32] The Japanese have not exactly endeared themselves to their neighbors or to the world. Former prime minister Nakasone was quoted as saying that he believed that America's intellectual level was lower than Japan's because America had too many blacks, Hispanics, and Puerto Ricans.[33] He was also quoted as saying that Japan had to save the world by propagating its superior philosophy abroad.[34] A Japanese cabinet minister was quoted as saying that Japanese atrocities against China at Nanking in 1937 did not actually occur.[35] Japan does not have a world view like the British elite of the last century, who believed in their divinely appointed task of spreading Christian civilization and the Anglo-Saxon concepts of law to the farthest corners of the globe.

The Future as Seen by Japan

Table 9-8 presents future technological developments as seen by the Japanese. These are the goals that they have set and when they expect to achieve them. It may be that the Japanese have money without morals and power without purpose; nevertheless, these goals are formidable, and their attainment would make Japan even more powerful than it is now.

---

[32] R. Taggart Murphy, "Power: The Crisis of Japan's Global Financial Dominance," *Harvard Business Review*, Vol. 67, No. 2 (March–April 1989), pp. 71–83.

[33] *The New York Times* (September 24, 1986), p. 1.

[34] "Nakasone's World Class Blunder," *Time* (October 6, 1986), p. 21.

[35] Karen Elliott House, "Japan's Wealth Doesn't Guarantee Leadership," *Wall Street Journal*, January 30, 1989, p. A8. The incident referred to has been called "The rape of Nanking" and was well documented in the news and newsreels of that time. Eighty thousand Chinese civilians were estimated to have been killed by the Japanese at Nanking. For the Japanese to deny that atrocities occurred in Nanking is tantamount to the Germans claiming that they had no concentration camps.

TABLE 9-8
Japan's Long-Range Technology Goals and When It Expects to Achieve Them

1994	Use computer-aided design to make computer chips with more than one million gates
1996	Develop protocol technology to easily link communcitions networks.
1997	Remove sludge from the sea floor and purify fishing sites.
1999	Use artificial intelligence in aircraft management and control; develop a control system to prevent aircraft collision; develop technology to remove chemical pollutants from the air; employ nursing robots to help elderly and handicapped people.
2000	Reduce noise and vibration around train tracks.
2001	Develop artificial organs that the body won't reject.
2002	Prevent the spread of cancer in the human body; employ space robots with high-level artificial intelligence to perform difficult operations.
2003	Employ an international digital communications network world-wide; produce semiconductors and medicines on a commercial basis in factories in space.
2005	Correct the abnormal divisions of cancer cells and return them to normal cells.
2011	Develop superconducting materials for use in industrial and electrical equipment at near room temperature.

Source: Bernard Wysocki, Jr. "Technology, The Final Frontier," Wall Street Journal (Monday, November 14, 1988), Section 4, p. R 12.

Weaknesses of the Japanese Economy

In Japan a complicated set of reciprocal relations between groups has held the institutions of society together. Before World War II, these ties were centered in the nation as represented by the army, the zaibatsu, the state, and the emperor. The relations between groups were transferred after the shattering military defeat of World War II into the mundane tasks of economic reconstruction and growth. New groups developed after the war, and one foundation of Japanese society has been a willingness to compromise private ends for the public interest. The success of Japan up to now has been awesome. Its economy has performed better than those of Europe and the United States. If this success continues, Japan could well be the number one economic power in the world by the end of this century. However, the Japanese economy is not free from problems; it is vulnerable to forces over which it has little or no control.

Dependence on World Trade.   Japan is vulnerable to changes in the world economy. It imports a high proportion of resources required to meet its energy needs. High energy costs have made it difficult for certain Japanese industries—in particular aluminum, chemicals, and steel—to compete in world markets. Balance of trade deficits in the United States and Western Europe have created pressures to limit the flow of Japanese imports into these areas. There is also pressure from the United States and other countries on Japan to liberalize its restrictions on imports. For a country like Japan, which cannot survive without trade, these pressures have created serious problems. The very success of Japan has turned other countries against it. The maintenance of a stable world economy and continued foreign trade, particularly with the developed countries, are the basic conditions for the future development of the Japanese economy.[36]

A Change In Work Attitudes.   Although the Protestant work ethic may be associated with the United States and other Western industrial countries, the Japanese have their own legacy of the work ethic. It is in part predicated on Confucianism, which places a high value on education and hard work. Many Japanese believe work is the reason for living and pass up vacations in order to continue work. It appears that this "workaholism" has begun to abate, particularly among younger Japanese, who are opting for a more Western life style with an emphasis on consumption. Some older workers allege that younger Japanese have caught the "British disease," namely, a desire to substitute leisure for work.[37] What this will do to the Japanese work ethic remains to be seen.

Urban Growth.   Japanese economic growth has not been an unmixed blessing. The Japanese now realize that they have paid heavily for their obsession with economic growth. Tokyo, Osaka, Yokohama, and other metropolitan areas have become megapolitan nightmares, hopelessly congested and permeated with fumes. The Japanese have been forced to undertake a vast restructuring of the nation and its economy. To check pollution and urban congestion, factories have had to be dispersed to the countryside. Dozens of new towns have been created and linked together by networks of highways and express railways.

Export trade and a high rate of saving have been given high priority at the expense of investments in infrastructure. The potential demand for new housing is strong, and there is much room for such qualitative improvements as reconstructing old dwellings. Since Japan's infrastructure is inferior to that of the United States and Western Europe, it will need much more public investment.

Demographics.   The median age of the Japanese population has risen rapidly. Under the present national retirement system, the financing of pensions will inevitably face bankruptcy in the future. It will be necessary to refinance the whole public pension system and to raise the age, currently 55, at which a person can retire.[38] The

[36] "Problems Facing the Japanese Economy in the 1980s" (Tokyo: Keizai Koho Center, March 3, 1983).
[37] Takayoshi Hamano, "The Japanese Economy in the 1980s." In Rei Shiraton, ed., *Japan in the 1980s* (Tokyo: Kodansha International, Ltd., 1982), pp. 142–143.
[38] Workers for Japanese industries are required to retire at 55, though they may go on to hold other jobs. Social-security type pensions are paid at the age of 60.

demand for social services is increasing at the same time that a shortage of skilled workers has developed. An increase in transfer payments will result at a time that Japan is running a deficit in the national budget. In recent years, these deficits have amounted to one-third of the budget. The stimulative effects of Japanese tax policy may well have run their course, as more taxes are needed for government programs and services.

SUMMARY

The 1980s witnessed a dramatic transformation of the roles of the United States and Japan in the world economy. The United States started the decade as the world's leading creditor nation; now it is the world's leading debtor nation, and Japan is the leading creditor nation. There are those who feel that the United States has descended into second place behind Japan and that the descent will be permanent. The U.S. trade imbalance, the budget deficit, the loss of markets to Japan in industries ranging from consumer electronics to earth-moving equipment, can all be regarded as symptoms of a decline that has cost America its competitiveness. But there is more to this than losing industries to Japan; today, Japan is challenging the United States and the rest of the world in new ideas, innovations, and new technologies. It has caught up with the United States in old technologies; it is trying to pass the United States in new ones. It is embarking on new technological frontiers in space and in the seas.

However, there is no mandate from heaven that Japan will dominate the twenty-first century, despite its considerable accomplishments. It has been called a country with power but no purpose, meaning that it has no vision for world leadership. It has managed to antagonize its neighbors. It faces internal problems, such as the aging of the workforce. In 1989 the Japanese government ordered banks, insurance companies, stock exchanges and other financial institutions to close on Saturdays and give their employees both Saturday and Sunday off for the first time in Japanese history. The two-day weekend may eventually extend beyond the estimated two million people in the industries affected by the government edict. It remains to be seen whether or not the Japanese will substitute more leisure for less work. It also remains to be seen whether Japan or the United States will dominate the world economy in the future. That depends more on what will happen in the United States than in Japan.

REVIEW QUESTIONS

1. Comment on the Japanese system of lifetime employment with one firm. Would this system work in the United States?
2. The Japanese economic system involves management by consensus. Discuss. Would this system work in the United States?

3. Discuss the relationship between government and business in Japan.
4. What factors are responsible for the high rate of economic growth in Japan?
5. Discuss the objectives of Japanese economic planning.
6. Explain some of the factors that have been responsible for a high rate of personal savings in Japan.
7. Discuss the ways in which Japanese government provides financial support to business.
8. What is the role of the Japan Development Bank in the Japanese banking system?
9. What are some of the problems confronting the Japanese economy?
10. Discuss the role of the Ministry of International Trade and Industry (MITI) in the Japanese economy.
11. What is a keiretsu? What is a sogo shosha?
12. Will the next century be known as the Japanese century?

RECOMMENDED READINGS

Burstein, Daniel. *Yen! Japan's New Financial Empire and Its Threat to America.* New York: Simon & Schuster, 1988.

Christopher, Robert C. *The Japanese Mind.* New York: Simon & Schuster, 1982.

Fallows, James. *More Like US.* Boston: Houghton Mifflin, 1989.

Ferguson, Charles F. "From the People Who Brought You Voodoo Economics." *Harvard Business Review*, Vol. 66, No. 3 (May–June 1988), pp. 55–62.

House, Karen Elliott. "Japan's Wealth Doesn't Guarantee Leadership." *Wall Street Journal*, January 30, 1989, p. A1, A8.

Kennedy, Paul. *The Rise and Fall of the Great Powers.* New York: Random House, 1987.

McCraw, Thomas K., ed. *America versus Japan.* Boston: Harvard Business School Press, 1986.

Murphy, R. Taggart. "Power: The Crisis of Japan's Global Financial Domination," *Harvard Business Review*, Vol. 67, No. 2 (March–April 1989), pp. 71–83.

Ohmae, Kenichi. *Beyond National Borders: Reflections on Japan and the World.* Homewood, IL: Dow Jones-Irwin, 1987.

O'Rielly, Brian. "Will Japan Gain Too Much Power?" *Fortune*, Vol. 118, No. 6 (September 12, 1988), pp. 150–153.

Prestowitz, Clyde V., Jr. *Trading Places: How We Allowed Japan to Take the Lead.* New York: Basic Books, 1988.

Vogel, Ezra. *Japan As Number One.* Cambridge, MA: Harvard University Press, 1979.

Wysocki, Bernard, Jr. "Technology, The Final Frontier," *The Wall Street Journal.* Monday, November 14, 1988, Section 4, p. R 12.

Yoshihara, Kunio. *Japanese Economic Development.* New York: Oxford University Press, 1984.

CHAPTER TEN

THE UNITED KINGDOM

One hundred years ago England was at the apogee of its power. The British Empire extended from England to Africa, from India to New Zealand, and British interests owned and operated everything from diamond mines in South Africa to tea plantations in Ceylon and paper mills in Canada. Brittania ruled the waves, and British citizens throughout the world were able to apply the Roman words *civis Romanus sum*[1] to themselves and know that they would enjoy the protection of the British government.

However, the days of Kipling and the British Empire are long since gone, and the society that once produced Charles Dickens and Alfred Tennyson now produces author Barbara Cartland and comedian Benny Hill. The British economy has fallen on hard times. Slow growth, low productivity, inflation, unemployment, and balance-of-payments crises have plagued the British economy. Successive governments have had little success with these problems in anything but the short run. Prime Minister Margaret Thatcher's electoral victories and the policies she has adopted can be explained partly by the inability of previous governments to manage the economy successfully and, in particular, to restrain inflation.

It may well be that the United Kingdom represents a watershed in Western society. Oswald Spengler, a German philosopher, wrote a book called *Decline of the West* that forecasted the decline of Western civilization.[2] Spengler claimed to be able to discern the outline of a life cycle through which, he believed, all civilizations must pass. Western civilization was compared

---

[1] "I am a Roman citizen." Because one British citizen of Greek extraction was killed in a riot in Greece, the British declared war on Greece.
[2] Oswald Spengler, *Decline of the West* (New York, Alfred A. Knopf, Inc., 1939), pp. 1–7.

with Greco-Roman civilization in terms of form, duration, and meaning. His view of Western civilization was a gloomy one. The West, according to Spengler, had already passed through the creative stage of culture into a period of material comfort. The end of the creative impulse begins the process of decline. There is no prospect for reversing the decline, for civilizations blossom and decay like natural organisms, and true rejuvenation is impossible. He used a biological metaphor to describe the fateful trajectory of a civilization: "For everything organic the notions of birth, youth, age, lifetime, and death are fundamental."

The Industrial Revolution first began in the United Kingdom, and that may be part of its problem. An aggressive country (Germany and Japan are examples) entering later into the industrialization cycle is able to take advantage of newer technologies in plant layout and design, while countries that industrialized earlier have older and less efficient plants. The United Kingdom began to lose ground in areas of advanced technology, first to Germany and then to the United States. British economic dominance of the world crested in 1910, and eventually the economy began to live off the foreign earnings of its corporations. Many British industries today are in advanced stages of atrophy and need large amounts of capital to increase productive capacity. In many crucial areas, British industry has lost its advantage to the younger and more viable industries of Germany, France, and the United States. But these industries, too, face challenges from the Japanese and South Koreans.

The remainder of the chapter will be devoted to a discussion of the British economy in the 1980s. At the beginning of the decade, the British economy had fallen on hard times. It was plagued by slow growth, low productivity, inflation, unemployment, and a balance of payments crisis. Successive governments had little success with these problems in anything but the short run. Prime Minister Margaret Thatcher has focused on a different approach to these problems, and her approach will be presented in some detail.

THE ECONOMIC SYSTEM

The British economy is mixed. Although private enterprise is dominant, the government plays an important role in economic activity in three ways: through the nationalized sector of the economy, through social welfare measures aimed at achieving income redistribution and economic and social well being, and through fiscal and monetary policy measures used to pursue such macroeconomic goals as full employment.

Nationalization took place in the period immediately following World War II. The nationalization program of the Labour government involved the Bank of England, the railways, the coal mines, the steel industry, trucking, and the public utilities—especially the electrical and gas industries. The owners were compensated at approximately the market price of their holdings. In some cases, nationalization was not revolutionary or controversial. The Bank of England was already, in effect, a public institution; its changed status was hardly more than a change in title. The railroads and coal mines had been losing money for years, and their owners were perfectly willing to accept nationalization.

Apart from the nationalized industries, economic activity is organized pretty much in the capitalistic fashion. Business firms are free to organize in any of the traditional forms and may make their decisions on the usual capitalistic bases of price and cost. Through the use of monetary and fiscal policies, however, the government can exert indirect control on the activities of private enterprises. For example, the government has wide powers to encourage the development of industries in geographic areas that are depressed because of the dependence on a single industry, usually coal mining or shipbuilding. The government can also influence and control industrial, residential, and public construction.

Public Finance

The British budget is a powerful weapon for influencing the general level of activity in the economy. Its purpose is not only to raise revenue to meet government expenditures, but also to regulate the national economy. An important goal in determining the budget is to bring about a balance between the total goods and services that are likely to be available to the nation and the total claims that will be made upon them.

The budget does not include all public sector expenditures. It does not include either local governmental expenditures or nationalized industry investment, although it does cover grants to local authorities and loans and deficit grants to the nationalized industries, as well as the British government's contributions to the National Insurance Funds. The budget does include all national government expenditures other than payments out of the National Insurance Funds. The expenditure figures in the budget are one measure of the national government's share of the total demand for goods and services.

The nationalized industries, local authorities, and other public bodies often need to borrow to finance expenditures on capital projects. Most of this borrowing is done from the National Loans Fund, which is responsible for the bulk of domestic lending by the government. The National Loans Fund and the Consolidated Fund, which balances current revenue against current expenditures, are the two basic components of the budget.

The British Tax System.   Taxation in the United Kingdom is fairly evenly balanced between direct and indirect taxes. The most important direct tax is the personal income tax. No other European country, except Sweden, imposes personal income taxes to a greater degree than does the United Kingdom, nor do personal taxes account for nearly so high a percentage of gross national product in France, Germany, or the United States as they do in the United Kingdom and Sweden. There is also a heavy reliance on indirect excise taxes on tobacco, alcohol, and gasoline. The tax yield on these three commodities amounts to nearly 7 percent of the British gross national product, over half again as much as Sweden, twice as much as West Germany and France, and three times the U.S. proportion.

Personal Income Taxes. For many years the British income tax structure included an income tax and a surtax. However, in 1973 this system was replaced by a single graduated income tax. British income tax rates were among the highest in the world, exceeded only by the tax rates of the Scandinavian countries. A distinction was made between earned and unearned income, with rates as high as 98 percent on the latter. In 1980 minimum and maximum rates were lowered on both earned and unearned incomes. The minimum rate on earned income is now 27 percent on income up to £17,900 (approximately $25,000), and the maximum rate is 60 percent on income in excess of £41,200 (approximately $60,000). The top rate on unearned income is 30 percent.[3] There are exemptions for children that vary with ages, and flat exemptions for single and married taxpayers. In 1987 the personal income tax accounted for 10.7 percent of gross domestic product.[4]

Other Taxes. In addition to the personal income tax, there is also a corporate income tax. In 1988 a 35 percent tax rate was applied to corporate incomes.[5] Capital gains are taxed at a flat 30 percent rate. However, there are generous allowances for capital investment. Britain has experimented with a wide variety of subsidies to promote investment or regional development or both. It has used, at one time or another, accelerated depreciation, high initial depreciation allowances, investment tax credits, and investment grants.

There is also a value-added tax calculated at a single flat tax rate of 15 percent of the value of a good or service. Certain commodities, including drugs and medicines, are exempt from the value-added tax. As mentioned earlier, excise taxes are also levied on consumer goods, especially tobacco, alcohol, and gasoline. One feature of these excise taxes is the large proportion they represent of the total sales price. For example, the tax on cigarettes is 90 percent of the purchase price.

Finally, in the United Kingdom as in other countries, the social security system is financed largely from payroll taxes. At one time, contributions from both employees and employers were paid at a flat amount per employee per week. Since 1975 the social security tax has been levied as a percentage of the employee's earnings. In 1988 the rate was 9.0 percent for fully covered employees. Employers paid at a rate of 10 percent on the first £100 of earnings a week.

Government Expenditures. Total central government expenditures for 1988–1989 amounted to $215 billion. These expenditures can be further divided into two categories—current and capital. Current expenditures can be further divided into four categories: expenditures for goods and services, subsidies, current grants to the personal and public sectors, and interest on the public debt.[6] Capital expenditures include gross domestic fixed capital formation, capital grants, and loans.

[3] *Individual Taxes: A Worldwide Summary* (New York: Price Waterhouse and Co., 1988), p. 297.
[4] *The British Economy in Figures* (London: Lloyds Bank, 1988). p. 1
[5] *Corporate Taxes: A Worldwide Summary* (New York: Price Waterhouse and Co., 1988), p. 453.
[6] Central Statistical Office, *United Kingdom National Accounts 1988* (London: HMSO, 1989), pp. 58–59.

When local government and central government spending are added together, total public expenditures of all types are around 44 percent of the gross national product. One reason that the public sector contribution to investment is much higher in Great Britain than in the United States is the importance of public enterprises. This continues to be true despite the fact that the Thatcher government has privatized (denationalized) a number of enterprises that had been owned by the government.

The Welfare State.   The United Kingdom has a comprehensive social welfare system. It can be divided into two categories: the medical care and social security program, which includes family allowances; and the national health insurance program, which provides unemployment and sickness benefits, old age pensions, maternity benefits, and death grants. Both programs were developed partly as a result of deprivations sustained during World War II and partly as a remembrance of prewar British capitalism, which was characterized by high rates of unemployment as well as excessive and widespread inequalities in the distribution of wealth and income. In 1924, for example, two-thirds of the total wealth in the United Kingdom was held by 1.6 percent of all wealth owners (property owners—real estate, stocks, bonds).[7]

Medical Care and Family Allowances.   The best-known social welfare program is medical care, which is provided in the United Kingdom under the National Health Service as a free public service and is not a part of the regular social insurance program. All residents are eligible for health services. General practitioner care, specialist services, hospitalization, maternity care, and treatment in the event of industrial injuries are provided by the National Health Service. There are charges for some medical prescriptions and cost sharing by the patient for such devices as dentures and hearing aids. Most of the cost of the National Health Service program is financed by the British government out of general revenues from the budget. The employer and employee pay flat-rate weekly contributions that meet about one-fifth of the total cost of medical care.

In addition to medical care, there are family allowances, cash payments for the benefit of the family as a whole. They are financed out of general revenues rather than from taxes on employers and employees and are paid to families with two or more children under certain age limits.

National Insurance.   Separate and apart from the National Health Service, a comprehensive program of social security comes under the category of national insurance. This program provides fixed-rate sickness benefits for up to one year to working men and women and widows. Dissatisfaction with this program has led to a rapid increase in the number of individuals who purchase private medical insurance. Old-age pensions and unemployment benefits are similar in make-up to sickness benefits. As a corollary to regular old-age pensions, a graduated pension

---

[7] James Wedgwood, *The Economics of Inheritance* (London: Routledge & Kegan Paul, 1929), p. 42

scheme provides higher rates to higher-paid contributors. A maternity allowance is paid to women who give up paid employment to have a baby, and there is also a lump-sum maternity grant paid to most mothers. A death grant is payable on the death of the insured person or the spouse or child of an insured person. Finally, there are widows' and widowed mothers' allowances, the latter based on the number of dependent children.

The Banking System

The British banking system consists of the Bank of England—the central bank of the nation—and a few large commercial banks that have assumed an oligopolistic structure as as result of mergers and integration. Besides the commercial banks, whose primary function is financing the economy in general, there are other institutions whose activities are more specialized but whose aggregate importance is very great. These are the merchant bankers and the acceptance houses, whose primary concern is with the financing of foreign trade. The insurance companies and building societies are the most important suppliers of investment capital in the United Kingdom.

The Bank of England.   The Bank of England was chartered by an act of Parliament in 1694. In 1844 it was given the sole right of note issue. By the second half of the nineteenth century, the public service aspects of the Bank's activities began to eclipse its private banking business. It became the lender of last resort to the commercial banks and the regulator of the great international gold and capital market in London.

In 1946 the Bank was nationalized by an act of Parliament. The government acquired the entire capital stock of the Bank and was empowered to appoint the governor, deputy director, and directors of the Bank for fixed terms. The Treasury has the power to give directions to the Bank through consultation with the governor.

The Bank has responsibility for the overall management and control of the British monetary and financial system. It exercises monetary control through a combination of open market operations and discount policy, done on the basis of institutional arrangements peculiar to the British monetary system. Unlike the Federal Reserve System of the United States, the Bank does not lend to commercial banks, but only to discount houses, whose main business is to underwrite the weekly Treasury bill issue with call loans secured mostly from London clearinghouses.

Credit is restricted to selling Treasury bills or government bonds through discount houses and securities dealers, thus absorbing cash from the banking system. The discount market consists chiefly of 12 major houses that are members of the London Discount Market Association, the organization that is responsible for bidding on Treasury bills each week. To restore their cash and liquidity positions, banks can withdraw their call loans from the discount houses; the discount houses, in turn, may be forced to borrow money from the Bank of England at a penalty rate, which is set higher than the average yield from the discount houses' earning assets.

The Commercial Banks. The commercial banking system operates under private ownership and management. There are five major commercial banks—Barclays, Lloyds, Midland, National Provincial, and Westminster. Two other large banks are the District Bank and Martins. These banks undertake all normal types of banking business, such as deposits, advances, bill discounting, and foreign exchange. They do not participate directly in industry, their financing of industry is limited to short-term advances and overdrafts that are formally repayable on demand. British banks have a traditional preference for financing working rather than fixed capital expenditures.

Discount Houses. Discount houses play a very important role in the British financial system. Their most important function concerns the financing of Treasury bills. The discount houses purchase the Treasury bills on a weekly basis with loans obtained from the commercial banks or with their own funds. The proceeds of these purchases provide the government with day-to-day financing.

The discount houses are also the intermediary through which the Bank of England acts as a lender of last resort to the banking system. As mentioned above, the discount houses obtain a substantial amount of their funds to purchase Treasury bills from the commercial banks on a *call loan* basis. If loan repayment is demanded by the banks, the discount houses can borrow from the Bank of England through rediscounting bills or by advances against collateral. In this way, funds flow into the commercial bank. The minimum rate at which the Bank of England will make funds available to the discount houses is called the *bank rate,* and it is the key rate in the whole structure of interest rates in Great Britain.

Other Financial Institutions. Funds for investments are also provided through other sources, such as insurance companies, building societies, investment trusts, and pension funds. The insurance companies, pension funds, and building societies are the dominant sources of long-term loans. Insurance companies are privately owned and provide a supply of capital to the long-term market.

Building societies, also privately owned, are second only to the insurance companies as a source of long-term loanable funds. The building societies rely on the savings of the public, and they provide financing for about two-thirds of private home building. The societies offer both shares and deposits to the public. Shares are nonmarketable and pay a higher rate of interest.

Investment trusts are also an important source of long-term capital funds. In the past, trusts played an important part in the development of the Commonwealth countries. During the period from 1870 to 1914, they also contributed much to the economic development of the United States.

In investment banking, there is no doubt about the power of the government to exercise control. Under the Banking Control and Guarantee Act of 1947, the government has the power to regulate new issues of stocks and bonds and establish priorities that are deemed essential to the national interest. The act also empowered the Treasury to guarantee long-term loans made to facilitate industrial development.

Monetary Policy.   Monetary policy in the United Kingdom is used as a stabilization device and consists of several arrangements.

Hire purchase controls are used to regulate the volume of consumer expenditures. This type of control is selective in that it involves the amount of down payment required to consummate the purchase of consumer goods and also involves the maximum period of repayment. It has proven to be an important monetary policy instrument and has an advantage over other monetary and fiscal policy instruments in that it can be imposed immediately.

The use of the *bank rate* is also an important monetary policy device. The bank rate is the price the Bank of England will pay when rediscounting bills. It is a penalty rate that is usually set above the market rate of discount and has its impact on the discount houses. As mentioned previously, the discount houses occupy a special position in the market for Treasury bills, and from the standpoint of monetary policy the Treasury bill is a major instrument in the money market. The discount houses link the commercial banks to the Bank of England. They purchase Treasury bills with money borrowed at call from the commercial banks; if they have to borrow from the Bank of England, the bank rate, or "penalty rate," can be employed. Changes in the bank rate force changes in other interest rates.

Open market operations constitute another monetary policy instrument. This term refers to the buying and selling of Treasury bills and other short-term obligations in the money market by the Bank of England. These transactions affect the liquidity of the commercial banks by expanding or contracting their balances with the Bank of England.

A direct control, which takes the form of special deposits, can be imposed on commercial banks by the Bank of England. The purpose of this device is to alter the liquidity ratio of commercial banks. The *liquidity ratio,* which is the ratio of liquid bank assets to total assets, is set at 30 percent of total bank assets. Special deposits have the effect of reducing the liquidity ratio.

Supply-Side Economics and the Thatcher Government

Margaret Thatcher came to office in 1979 in the wake of the Labour government's unsuccessful attempts to use demand management and incomes policy to deal with the problems of the British economy. She espoused an economic program based on monetarist theories and belief in a freely operating market economy. Thatcher came to office committed to a policy of increasing aggregate supply by decreasing the role of the government in the economy and improving incentives for individuals in the private sector. To increase incentive and reward initiative, personal income tax rates were cut. Short-term stabilization policies used by previous governments were rejected in favor of policies considered necessary for reducing inflation and creating the conditions for an increase in total real output and employment in the long run.

The following policies were adopted by the Thatcher government.

1. The role of monetary policy became the linchpin of economic policy. Emphasis changed from the level of interest rates to control over the money supply through progressive deceleration, over the medium term, of the growth rate of one of the money aggregates. This aggregate, called M3, consists of notes and coins in circulation plus all sterling bank deposits held by the private and public sectors.
2. An attempt was made to increase total output by decreasing the interference of the government in the economy and by promoting the free operation of markets. As mentioned previously, the basic income tax was reduced, top rates on both earned and unearned incomes were reduced, and personal tax allowances were increased. The base of the corporate income tax was changed, and subsidies to industries in depressed areas were reduced. Foreign exchange controls were lifted and quantitative credit controls removed.
3. The government also intended to limit its role in the price and income determination process. It was believed that monetary policy would affect wages by influencing expectations in that a restrictive monetary policy would moderate wage demands. However, the government decided that public sector pay had to be restrained because high public sector wage settlements were contributing to excessive government expenditures.

The results of Prime Minister Thatcher's economic policies have been reasonably good. The rate of inflation has been reduced to well below the average annual rate of 10 percent that prevailed during the 1970s, but unemployment has averaged around 10 percent. The rate of economic growth was negative during 1980 and 1981, but the economy expanded at an average annual rate of 3.3 percent from the period 1983 through 1989. The growth rate during this period was higher than the growth rates for France, West Germany, and Italy. Industrial production increased at an average annual rate of 1.6 percent for the period 1980–1988, a rate higher than those for West Germany and France. Gross private domestic investment increased at an average annual rate of 4 percent. The government's success in decreasing wage and free inflation resulted in part from increases in the rate of unemployment and appreciation of the pound sterling.

Labor-Management Relations

Unions occupy a powerful position in the United Kingdom. During the post–World War II period, full employment contributed to the development of union power, and wages increased faster than productivity. In general, British labor-management relations have been rather acrimonious, with some of the worst labor disputes occurring in the public sector. Many labor unions are afflicted with a class struggle mentality, and there is no question that union intransigence on issues involving productivity has contributed to the general decline of the British economy during the postwar period. British unions are politically active and constitute the main base of support for the Labour party.

Union members account for a larger percentage of the labor force in the United Kingdom than in the United States. Approximately 45 percent of the British labor force belongs to unions, compared to less than 20 percent in the United States. In the political sphere, the British trade unions have been more militant than their counterparts in the United States. The trade unions are affiliated with the British Labor party and contribute much of its financial support, while American trade unions generally support the Democratic party. Class divisiveness exists to a much greater degree in the United Kingdom than it does in the United States, and the British unions are much more class conscious than are U.S. unions.

There are some 500 trade unions in the United Kingdom, and most belong to the British Trades Union Congress (TUC). Unions affiliated with the TUC vary in size and character and in the views they hold regarding organization. There are craft unions, industrial unions, general workers' unions, and nonmanual and professional organizations. Although the unions operate individually, they come together, industry by industry, through federations set up for the purpose of collective bargaining. A single union may have members in several industries and may therefore be affiliated with several federations.

Industrial relations in the United Kingdom are governed by two acts, the Trade Union and Labor Relations Act of 1974 and the Employment Protection Act of 1975. The Employment Protection Act is the more important in that it sets employees' rights. Under the provisions of the act, guaranteed minimum weekly wages and paid maternity leave became legal requirements, along with such things as time off with pay for union duties. Written terms for dismissal and redundancy (the British term for being laid off) have to be provided. Government intervention in all aspects of collective bargaining came to be an increasingly important policy priority. The Advisory, Conciliation, and Arbitration Service (ACAS) was created to adjudicate collective bargaining disputes. Decisions of the ACAS can be appealed to the Employment Appeal Tribunal.

Government and Business

The government has control over a number of industries, such as coal, inland transportation, and steel. The nationalized industries produce about 6 percent of gross domestic product. The steel industry was nationalized after World War II, denationalized by the Conservative party when it came to power in 1951, and nationalized again by the Labour government in 1966. Two industries were nationalized during the 1970s—shipbuilding and aerospace—and the British National Oil Company (BNOC) was formed chiefly on the basis of the North Sea oil assets previously owned by the National Coal Board.

Nationalization and Pricing Policies.   In 1967 explicit price and investment rules were established for the nationalized industries.[8] On pricing, marginal cost pricing was laid down, though accounting costs were to be covered by revenue. Unit prices proportional to marginal cost were recommended for the apportionment of fixed costs among consumers where necessary to cover total costs. Social cost-benefit analysis was proposed for investment appraisal, and it was stated that the returns on investment should be presented in terms of discounted net present value. A test discount rate of 8 percent was laid down for project appraisal. The government explicitly recognized the noncommercial operations undertaken by nationalized industries and stressed the need to distinguish social obligations from commercial operations. When social obligations were involved, subsidies from the government could be provided to cover costs.

In 1978 the government recognized that in many cases prices are market-determined, and even where this is not so, the difficulties of practical application of marginal cost pricing can be severe. The main focus of current policy was shifted from matters affecting individual services and projects to the opportunity cost of capital in the industry as a whole.[9] A real rate of return on assets was defined and was to be achieved by the nationalized industries on new investment as a whole. The real rate of return is principally related to the real rate of return in the private sector, taking into consideration questions of the cost of finance. It was set initially at 5 percent and is to be reviewed every three to five years. Thus the main ways over which the government has sought to exercise control since 1978 are the real rate of return and the financial target together with the general level of prices.[10] Individual prices and investment priorities are left largely up to the industries themselves.

Privatization of British Industry.   Margaret Thatcher and Ronald Reagan have a number of things in common. They are both conservative, good friends, and they want to reduce the role of government in their respective economies and rely more on market mechanism. Ronald Reagan is no longer President and the extent of reduction in government activities during his two terms in office can be debated. Margaret Thatcher had a much longer way to go when it came to get the British government out of business, but she has done this through the privatization of a number of activities that had been performed by government. Since she has been in office, she has overseen the sale of more than two dozen major state-owned businesses to private enterprise. Her economic objectives were to promote business efficiency and wider private stock share ownership.

---

[8] *Nationalized Industries: A Review of Economic and Financial Objectives,* Command Paper 3437 (London: HMSO, November 1967).

[9] *The Nationalized Industries,* Command Paper 7131 (London: HMSO, March 1978).

[10] Andrew Likierman, "The Financial and Economic Framework for Nationalized Industries," *Lloyds Bank Review* (October 1979), pp. 16–32.

In 1979, state-owned industries accounted for 10.5 percent of British gross domestic product and for one seventh of gross domestic investment. State-owned industries that have been privatized include the British telephone system, Jaguar Cars, British Aerospace, British Airways, sugar refineries, port facilities, freight transportation, Rolls-Royce, British Gas, and the state-owned shares of British Petroleum. Privatization reduced the participation of the British government in the economy in four ways. It reduced the share of state-owned industries from 10.5 percent of gross domestic product in 1979 to 5.1 percent in 1988. Second, it reduced the number of workers who were directly employed by state enterprises from 1.5 million workers in 1979 to around 800,000 in 1988. Third, it has more than doubled the number of British stockholders. Fourth it increased British Treasury revenues by an estimated $35 billion during the period 1979–1987.[11]

Table 10-1 presents a list of the more important state-owned industries that have been privatized by the Thatcher government. However, privatization has not ended with the firms listed in the table. In 1989 the government proposed the sale of its 51 percent ownership in the electric and water power industries. If its holdings in water companies, electricity distribution companies, and the electric generating

TABLE 10-1
Partial List of Firms Privatized by the Thatcher Government

Company	Dates[a]	Value in Pounds (million)[b]
British Aerospace	1981	390
Cable & Wireless	1981	1,021
British Sugar Corporation	1981	44
British Petroleum	1987	200
British Airways	1987	854
BAA	1987	1,160
British Gas	1987	5,080
Rolls-Royce	1987	1,020
Jaguar	1984	297
British Rail Hotels	1984	45
Britoil	1985	1,053
British Steel[c]	1988	2,500

[a] There are several dates of stock sale for many of these companies. For example, government-held shares of British Petroleum were sold in 1979, 1981, 1983, and 1987.
[b] Proceeds to the British Treasury from sales of government stock shares to the public.
[c] In December 1988 the government offered 2.5 billion pounds of its stock ownership in British Steel for sale to the public.
Source: Data provided by H.M. Treasury, London (April 19, 1989).

[11] The data on privatization were furnished by the Reference Services, Central Office of Information, London.

companies are sold, the Treasury could gain around £35 billion (approximately $50 billion). This privatization may not come about because the British public is opposed to it. In the case of water, it feels that water is a natural resource that belongs to everyone.[12]

AN APPRAISAL
OF THE BRITISH ECONOMY

By any economic standard, the performance of the British economy has been poor in comparison with other industrial market economies. In 1951, it ranked second only to the United States in per capita gross national product; in 1988, it ranked fifteenth in per capita GNP out of the 19 industrial market economies. In 1988, the United States had a per capital GNP of $19,780 compared to a per capita GNP for the United Kingdom of $12,800. France had a per capita GNP of $16,080; West Germany had a per capita GNP of $18,530; and Japan had a per capita GNP of $21,040.[13]

Growth Rates

The United Kingdom was the first country to industrialize, and it had export markets in its colonial possessions that were not available to latecomers to industrialization. Thus, though its economic situation in the long run was such that it could not hope to retain its early lead, it did experience a full century of prosperity. During the nineteenth century, every invention could be put to immediate use, either in agriculture or in industry. British industry was in a very strong position, and it was aided and encouraged by the government. There was no shortage of markets for British goods at prices that undercut competitors in the fields in which British industry specialized, primarily cotton textiles and machinery. However, by the latter part of the 1800s, other countries were undercutting the British prices. The Germans, starting late, had newer machinery and a spirit of enterprise that was beginning to falter in late nineteenth century Britain.

Table 10-2 compares average annual real per capita growth of GNP for the United Kingdom and other Western industrial countries for two periods, 1870–1913 and 1913–1950. In the first period, which ended before World War II, the performance of the German economy was best. This performance exacerbated a rivalry between the major world powers and was a factor contributing to World War I. The real annual average rate of growth for the United States during that period was a respectable 2.2 percent.[14] Although the growth rate of the United Kingdom

---

[12] Both water and electricity would be considered natural monopolies because they are unique and essential to the public interest. They have no competitors.

[13] The World Bank, *World Bank Atlas 1989,* pp. 6–9.

[14] Angus Maddison, *Economic Growth in the West* (London: George Allen & Unwin, Ltd., 1964), p. 21.

TABLE 10-2
Average Annual Real Per Capita Growth Rates
for Western Industrial Countries, 1870–1913,
1913–1950

Country	1870–1913	1913–1950
Belgium	1.7%	0.7%
Canada	2.0	1.9
Denmark	2.1	1.1
France	1.4	0.7
Germany	2.8	0.4
Italy	0.7	0.6
Netherlands	0.8	0.7
Norway	1.4	1.9
Sweden	2.3	1.6
United Kingdom	1.2	0.8
United States	2.2	1.7

Source: Angus Maddison, Economic Growth in the
West (London: George Allen & Unwin, Ltd., 1964), pp.
7–21.

was 1.2 percent, it was still the dominant world power before World War I. The
period 1913–1950 encompassed two world wars and the Depression of the 1930s.
All were particularly hard on the British economy. It was also during this time
period that the United Kingdom lost most of its colonial possessions—a source of
markets for British goods. The economies that performed the best were those that
were relatively unaffected by the two major wars.

The performance of the British economy during the 1950s, 1960s, and 1970s
was the poorest of all of the major industrial market economies.[15] During the period
1950–1960, the average annual rate of increase in real per capita GNP was 2.2
percent, compared to a high of 8.8 percent for Japan. Only the United States, with
an average annual real growth rate of 1.6 percent, had a rate lower than the United
Kingdom. During the 1960s and 1970s, the United Kingdom had the lowest rate
of economic growth of the major industrial market economies. The average annual
rate of increase in real per capita GNP for the 1960s was 2.8 percent, compared
to 10.6 percent for Japan and 4.0 for the United States. For the decade of the
1970s, the real average annual rate of increase per capita GNP was 1.8 percent,
compared to an average of 2.8 percent for the United States and 4.8 percent for
Japan. However, as Table 10-3 indicates, the performance of the British economy
in the 1980s has been quite good.

[15] Data obtained from Angus Maddison, *Economic Growth in the West* (London: George Allen & Unwin,
Ltd., 1964); The World Bank, *World Development Report 1989;* (New York: Oxford University Press,
1989); and the *Economic Report of the President 1990,* (Washington: USGPO, 1990).

TABLE 10-3
Average Annual Growth Rates in Real Per Capita GNP for the United Kingdom
and Other Countries, 1976–1989

Country	1976–1982	1983	1984	1985	1986	1987	1988	1989
United States	2.3%	3.6%	6.8%	3.4%	2.8%	3.0%	3.8%	3.0%
Canada	2.6	3.2	6.3	4.6	3.2	4.0	4.1	2.9
Japan	4.5	3.2	5.1	4.7	2.5	4.4	5.4	4.8
France	3.1	0.7	1.3	1.7	2.1	2.3	2.8	3.4
West Germany	2.3	1.9	3.3	1.9	2.3	1.8	2.9	4.3
Italy	2.9	1.0	3.2	2.8	2.9	3.1	3.1	3.3
United Kingdom	1.3	3.5	2.1	3.9	2.9	3.6	3.5	2.3

Source: Economic Report of the President 1990 *(Washington: USGPO, 1990), p. 419.*

Inflation and Unemployment

For many years Britain suffered relatively greater increases in both inflation and unemployment than comparable mixed economies such as France, Japan, and West Germany. A problem of stagflation, a combination of increases in inflation and unemployment coupled with low growth rates, led many people to speak of the "British disease" as if it were something that is contagious and to be avoided at all costs. Basically, the "British disease" meant a desire not to work hard but to rely on the welfare state. Some attributed the "disease" to inflexibility of both labor and management to compromise in the public interest, while others blamed it on alleged flaws in the British national character.

However, the performance of the British economy during the 1980s has improved dramatically. The British economy during the 1970s was an unmitigated disaster. The rate of inflation was around 15 percent a year and the rate of productivity was the lowest for all major industrial countries. Although unemployment was low, labor unrest was common. Wages increased at a rate far in excess of worker productivity. A turnaround occurred in the 1980s. In manufacturing alone during the 1980s, output per British worker increased at an average annual rate of 5 percent.[16] Inflation came down and the unemployment rate increased as a result of a tight monetary policy designed to reduce inflation. The results of the economic policies of the Thatcher government are presented in Table 10-4.

Income Redistribution

A hallmark of any welfare state is the redistribution of income from the "haves" to the "have nots." This is accomplished through taxes and transfer payments, with taxes reducing the incomes of some persons and transfer payments adding

[16] *United Kingdom National Accounts 1988* (London: HMSO, 1988), p. 122.

TABLE 10-4
Unemployment and Inflation Rates for the United
Kingdom, 1980–1989

Year	Unemployment Rate	Inflation Rate
1980	7.0%	9.9%
1981	10.5	9.4
1982	11.3	7.5
1983	11.9	4.4
1984	11.7	5.8
1985	11.3	6.4
1986	11.2	2.7
1987	10.2	4.8
1988	8.3	4.3
1989	6.4	8.5

Sources: Economic Report of the President 1990
*(Washington DC: USGPO, 1990), p. 417; Lloyds Bank
Review (London: First Quarter 1990), p. 53*

to the income of others. Income redistribution can be accomplished through the progressivity of the personal income tax by making rates higher on higher incomes. Tax revenues accruing from the personal income tax are then redistributed to lower-income groups in the form of income transfers. However, personal income taxes alone are insufficient to effect a complete transfer of income, so other taxes are used, including payroll taxes to finance social security.

Tax Policies of the Thatcher Government.   Margaret Thatcher and Ronald Reagan are ideological soulmates in more ways than one. They both wanted to get the government out of business and they are both supply siders. When they took office, they felt that high income tax rates were inhibiting economic growth in their respective countries, and both set about cutting them. When Margaret Thatcher took office in 1979, the United Kingdom had one of the highest personal income tax rates in the world. The top rate was 83 percent on salaries and 98 percent on investment income.[17] The personal income tax rate has been cut several times, the last in March 1988 when the rates on both wages and investment income were reduced to 40 percent.[18] The corporate income tax rate was reduced from 52 percent to 35 percent.[19] However, Thatcher's version of supply-side economics worked far better than Reagan's. Despite the tax cuts, corporate income tax revenues increased

[17] The maximum rate in the United States in 1979 was 70 percent on both wages and salaries and investment income. Capital gains were subject to a lower tax.

[18] The maximum rate in the United States in 1988 was 33 percent on both wages and salaries and investment income. In 1989 the maximum rate changed to 28 percent.

[19] The maximum rate of the corporate income tax in the United States was 48 percent; it was 34 percent in 1989.

from $7 billion in 1979 to $25 billion in 1987, and personal income tax revenues increased from $15 billion to $40 billion.[20]

Greater Income Equality.   A prime goal of the British welfare state when it was created in 1945 was a more equal distribution of income. This was to be accomplished by a progressive income tax levied on both earned incomes (salaries) and unearned (interest and dividends) income and an inheritance tax. However, the structure of the income and inheritance taxes has changed frequently since 1945 because the tax policies of the two major political parties, Conservative and Labour, differ markedly. Each party makes changes in the tax structure when it comes to power, and each party revises expenditure policies, with the Conservative government placing more stringent controls on expenditures, including income transfers, and the Labour government placing more emphasis on increasing transfer payments.

The economic policies of the Reagan and Thatcher governments have been criticized on the grounds that there has been a shift of income from the "have nots" to the "haves." There was some shift of income redistribution during the Reagan years. In 1979, the share of family income for the lowest quintile of American families was 5.3 percent; in 1987, the share had decreased to 4.6 percent.[21] In 1979, the share of family income received by the highest 20 percent of American families was 41.4 percent; in 1987, the share had increased to 43.7 percent.

Since Prime Minister Thatcher's economic policies have been similar to Reagan's, it is logical to assume that there has been some shift in income toward the upper-income groups in the United Kingdom. She privatized a number of government-owned industries by selling their stocks to the public. In addition to receiving dividends, British stockholders have also realized capital gains, which are taxed at a rate of 30 percent.[22] For example, the share price of Jaguar stock when issued to the public in 1984 has doubled, as has the share price of British Telecom, which was also sold to the public in 1984.[23] Dividends, interest, and rent, which would primarily accrue to middle and upper-middle income earners, increased from £6.4 billion ($10.5 billion) in 1979 to £19.4 billion ($29.4 billion) in 1987.[24]

On the other hand, transfer payments, which primarily benefit the lower-income groups, increased from £21 billion ($32 billion) in 1979, to £52 billion ($79 billion) in 1987.[25] Taxes on income increased from £25 billion ($38 billion) in 1979 to £56 billion ($84 billion) in 1987. Taxes on expenditures, including the value-

---

[20] *United Kingdom National Accounts 1988,* p. 77.

[21] See Table 6-16 in Chapter 6.

[22] The capital gains tax is less than half of what it was in 1979.

[23] Shares of other stocks have not done as well. For example, a stock share of Rolls-Royce, when sold to the public in 1987, was £170; in December 1988, the share was valued at £172.

[24] *United Kingdom National Accounts 1988,* p. 112.

[25] *United Kingdom National Accounts 1988,* p. 56.

added tax, increased from £23 billion ($35 billion) in 1979 to £51 billion ($77 billion) in 1987.[26] As Table 10-5 indicates, there has been a small income redistribution effect upward.

Inequality of Wealth.   Inequality in the distribution of wealth is perhaps more closely identified with the United Kingdom than with any other major industrial country because, after all, the Industrial Revolution really developed in this country. A concomitant of the Industrial Revolution was the concentration of property in the hands of a few persons. Vast fortunes were made, particularly during the development of the British Empire's markets and resources. These fortunes, for the most part, were not touched by taxation, but were allowed to accumulate and be passed down from generation to generation.

Studies of the distribution of wealth are not often made. One of the first studies of the distribution of wealth in the United Kingdom covered the years 1912 and 1924. In 1912, 43 percent of all wealth of the country was owned by only 0.8 percent of wealth owners. During the intervening 12-year period World War I occurred, causing some dislocations in the British economy. The tax structure was also revised considerably in 1914 and in subsequent war years by the imposition of a surtax on incomes exceeding a particular level—$7,200 in 1914 and $4,800 in 1918. Minor shifts occurred in the distribution of wealth. In 1924 two-thirds of the wealth was owned by 1.6 percent of all wealth owners, compared to 0.9 percent in 1912. Some 93 percent of all of the wealth was owned by 13.3 percent of the owners in 1912 and by 23.0 percent of the owners in 1924.[27]

TABLE 10-5
Distribution of Income for the Top 1 Percent and the Top 5 Percent before and after Tax

Fiscal Year	Before Taxes		After Taxes	
	Top 1%	Top 5%	Top 1%	Top 5%
1972/73	6.4%	17.2%	4.4%	14.2%
1973/74	6.5	17.1	4.5	14.3
1974/75	6.2	16.8	4.0	13.7
1975/76	5.7	16.4	3.9	13.6
1976/77	5.5	16.3	3.8	13.5
1977/78	5.5	16.1	3.9	13.7
1978/79	5.3	16.0	3.9	13.7
1981/82	6.0	17.6	4.6	15.3
1984/85	6.4	18.5	4.9	16.0

Source: The Distribution of Income in the United Kingdom *(London: HMSO, 1988).*

---

[26] *United Kingdom National Accounts 1988*, p. 57.
[27] Wedgwood, *Economics of Inheritance*, pp. 47–49.

TABLE 10-6
Percentage Distribution of Personal Wealth in
the United Kingdom

	1924	1976	1982
Top 1 percent	61%	25%	21%
Next 2 to 5 percent	21	21	20
6 to 10 percent	7	14	15
11 to 20 percent	5	17	18
21 to 100 percent	6	23	26

*Source: Commission on the Distribution of Income
and Wealth (Diamond Commission),* Report No. 7,
Command Paper 7595 (London: HMSO, July 1979);
Income and Wealth *(London: British Central Statistical
Office, 1985), Table 22.*

Considerable shifting in the distribution of wealth has occurred since 1924, as
is indicated in Table 10-6. The share of the highest 1 percent fell from 61 percent
in 1924 to 21 percent in 1982. The main influences at work on the distribution
of wealth have been an increase in real income, which has allowed many people
to buy their own homes and to accumulate other assets, and the impact of the
estate tax, which reduced wealth inequality directly and also encouraged wealthy
persons to distribute their incomes before death. However, the role of inheritance
in the creation of the largest wealth holdings remains large. Notice that the top 20
percent of the wealth holders still own 74 percent of the total personal wealth in
Britain.

 # SUMMARY

Prime Minister Margaret Thatcher has made some dramatic changes in the
British economy since she was first elected to office in 1979. The most important change was the privatization of industries that were formerly owned and
operated by the British government. Since she has been in office, she has sold
more than two dozen major state-owned businesses to private enterprise. She
has also attempted to stimulate economic growth and productivity by cutting
tax rates for both corporations and individuals. Inflation was a major problem when she took office in 1979. By following monetary policies similar to
those used by the Federal Reserve in the late 1970s and early 1980s in the
United States, the Thatcher government reduced the rate of inflation from 17.9
percent in 1980 to around 4.0 percent in 1988. The rate of unemployment increased from 6.8 percent of the labor force in 1980 to 11.7 percent in 1984 and
8.2 percent in 1988. The real rate of economic growth ranged from a low of 2.3
percent in 1980 to a high of 3.9 percent in 1985 and 3.5 percent in 1988.

REVIEW QUESTIONS

1. Discuss the economic policies of the Thatcher government.
2. Discuss the relationship of the Bank of England to the British banking system.
3. Discuss the role of fiscal and monetary policy as economic stabilization devices in the United Kingdom.
4. What trends have developed over time in the distribution of income and wealth in the United Kingdom?
5. The rate of economic growth in the United Kingdom has improved during the 1980s. What are some of the reasons for this improvement?
6. Discuss the supply-side economic policies of the Thatcher government.
7. What impact, if any, has supply-side economics had on income distribution?
8. Discuss some of the reasons for the denationalization of industries under the Thatcher government.
9. Discuss pricing policies in the nationalized industries.
10. Discuss the results of privatization.

RECOMMENDED READINGS

Black, John. *The Economics of Modern Britain.* Oxford: Martin Robertson, 1983.

Challen, D. W. *Unemployment and Inflation in the U.K.* New York: Longman, Inc., 1984.

Country Profile: United Kingdom 1988. London: Economist Intelligence Unit, 1988.

Elbaum, Bernard, and William Lazonick. *Decline of the British Economy.* Oxford: Clarendon, 1986.

Kennedy, Paul. *The Rise and Fall of the Great Powers.* New York: Random House, 1987.

Kirbland, Richard I. "The Great Rebound: Britain is Back." *Fortune,* May 9, 1988.

Lawson, Nigel. *Privatization, the U.K. Experience.* London: HM Treasury, December 1988.

Olsen, Mancur. *The Rise and Decline of Nations.* New Haven: Yale University Press, 1983.

Thompson, Graham. *The Conservatives' Economic Policy.* London: Croom Helm, 1986.

Walters, Alan. *Britain's Economic Renaissance.* New York: Oxford University Press, 1986.

CENTRALLY PLANNED ECONOMIC SYSTEMS

11
THE COMMUNIST WORLD IN DISARRAY

12
AN INTRODUCTION TO THE SOVIET
UNION

13
REFORMS AND PERFORMANCE IN THE
SOVIET UNION

14
EASTERN EUROPE: HUNGARY AND
POLAND

15
YUGOSLAVIA

PART FOUR

CHAPTER ELEVEN

THE COMMUNIST WORLD IN DISARRAY

Zbigniew Brzezinski, former director of the National Security Council during the Carter Administration, has written a book called *The Grand Failure: The Birth and Death of Communism in the Twentieth Century*.[1] He has proved to be rather prophetic, for massive changes happened in the communist world in 1989, changes that would make Marx and Lenin turn over in their graves. A rough chronology of events that occurred in 1989 can be presented as follows:

1. In April 1989 hundreds of thousands of Chinese demonstrated for democratic reforms in the Peoples' Republic of China, only to be massacred in Tiananmen Square.
2. An historic election was held in the Soviet Union as part of a crusade by Mikhail Gorbachev to create a new society. Even Gorbachev himself had to run for a second term in the April 1989 election for a New Congress of Peoples' Deputies.
3. Free elections were held in Poland, and for the first time in 40 years a noncommunist leader became president of the country. Poland has renounced communism and has opted for a free market economy.
4. In Hungary, the Communist Party was dissolved and renamed the Socialist Party, which vowed a commitment to a democratic system with free elections. Hungary has also opted for a free market economy.
5. Thousands of East Germans fled to the West in the summer and fall of 1989. The hardline communist regime of Erich Honecker collapsed, the Berlin Wall came down, the Brandenburg Gate was reopened, and East

---

[1] Zbigniew Brzezinski, *The Grand Failure: The Birth and Death of Community in the Twentieth Century* (New York: Charles Scribner's Sons, 1989).

Germans are now free to go to and from West Germany. Free elections were held in the spring of 1990.

6. In November and December of 1989 thousands of Czechs demonstrated against the communist regime in Czechoslovakia. The regime was toppled and in a dramatic irony, the dissident playwright Vaclav Havel and Alexander Dubcek, the deposed leader of Czechoslovakia who was outed by the Russians in 1968, were elected to lead the country.

7. In December 1989, Nicolae Ceausescu, the communist dictator of Romania for 24 years, was overthrown in a bloody revolution; he and his wife were executed.

For 40 years the United States and the West have been influenced by communism. U.S. foreign policy since 1947 has been based on containment of Soviet aggression as the world was divided into two spheres of influence—one democratic and capitalist, and the other communist and authoritarian. The NATO alliance was created to provide a military defense against the Soviet Union and its East European satellites, and the United States spent trillions of dollars on national defense. The lives of many, if not most, Americans were influenced by events that happened in the communist world, and the fear of an atomic holocaust was always present in both the capitalist and communist worlds. These events can be presented as follows:

1. In 1947 Winston Churchill declared that an "iron curtain" separated Eastern Europe from Western Europe.
2. In 1948 the Berlin Blockade occurred.
3. In 1950 North Korea invaded South Korea and the Korean War began. The United States entered the war in support of South Korea.
4. In 1956 the Soviet Union sent tanks into Hungary to crush the Hungarian uprising.
5. The Berlin Wall was erected in 1961, separating East Germany from West Germany.
6. In 1968 the Soviet Union and other Warsaw Pact countries sent tanks into Czechoslovakia to crush reforms that had been implemented.
7. The Vietnam War lasted more than a decade, divided America, caused many casualties, and was the first war the United States failed to win.

Like sand castles that are washed away by incoming tides, communism has appeared to have collapsed. Perhaps the whole edifice of communism was built on sand, held together only by authoritarian rule, only to be washed away by the tides of freedom. This makes this chapter and the ones that follow on the communist countries very difficult to write, for what is there left to compare? The institutional arrangements of central planning and a one-party political system appears to have been swept away. The only thing that can be done is to present a table that was used in the fourth edition to show the differences between capitalist and socialist economies and say that's the way it used to be. Who knows what the future will bring? Who knows what will happen in China and the Soviet Union?

EAST GERMANY: THE FORMER ROLE MODEL FOR COMMUNISM

It was said that if communism can't work in East Germany, it can't work anywhere. East Germany had that famous Prussian self-discipline, the Protestant work ethic, and other socioeconomic factors necessary to build a successful economy, and it achieved the highest standard of living of any communist country. Its leaders were slavish in their devotion to communism and to the Soviet Union. East German leaders wanted no part of glasnost or any other new reforms coming from Mikhail Gorbachev. Its former leader, Erich Honecker, once criticized the rehabilitation of Stalin's enemies in the Soviet Union as the "croaking of the petit bourgeois run wild."[2] Unfortunately for Honecker, his own people did the croaking and Honecker was deposed. He is now awaiting trial on charges of corruption in office. For one who denounced the petit bourgeois, Honecker enjoyed a very lavish lifestyle.

The remainder of this chapter has three objectives. The first is to discuss the East German economic system the way it was, at least up to 1990. The economy conformed to the role model of a centrally planned economy, with central planning and state ownership of the agents of production. The second objective is to compare the performances of the East and West German economies that have existed side by side for forty years. Direct comparison can be made more easily than comparing the economies of the United States and the Soviet Union. The final objective is to discuss the reunification of East Germany and West Germany into one united Germany. This is a subject which has caused much concern in Europe.

The Development of East Germany

East Germany was a part of the *Zusammenbruch* that occurred after Hitler's Third Reich was defeated in World War II. It was created out of the provinces of Prussia, Silesia, Pomerania, Brandenburg, and Upper Saxony, and was occupied by the Russian Army. Its industrial base was partially destroyed by the war, and what machinery and rail transportation remained was carted away to the Soviet Union. Much of East Germany was agricultural and was made up of large estates owned by the Junkers.[3] Walter Ulbricht, a German communist who had fled Germany when Hitler came to power, became the first president. Agriculture was collectivized and a Stalinist economic model was introduced into the country, which formally

---

[2] Barry Newman, "East German Leaders Recoil From Glasnost," *The Wall Street Journal* (Tuesday, January 31, 1989), p. A14.

[3] The Junkers were Prussian aristocrats who had large land holdings in eastern Germany for many centuries. They provided many of the officers in the German army.

became the German Democratic Republic in 1949. After millions of Germans had fled to the West, the Berlin Wall was built in 1961. East Germany became the most prosperous communist country and has adhered faithfully to communism.[4] Its economic arrangements can be considered as a framework for a centrally planned economy.

When East Germany, or the German Democratic Republic, was created in October 1949, the Kommunische Partei Deutschlands (KPO) became the official political party.[5] The Soviet contribution to the development of Communism in East Germany was enormous. The leading figures in the imposition of Communism, such as Walter Ulbricht and Wilhelm Pieck, received their training in the Soviet Union. When the war was over, Ulbricht and other German Communists were sent from the Soviet Union to supervise the integration of the Soviet part of the Third Reich into the Soviet system. The proximity of East Germany to the Soviet Union and the presence of Soviet troops and tanks in the country tended to make any overt opposition to the development of Communism unwise.

Economic Planning

Economic planning was formally introduced in 1949 with the creation of a comprehensive two-year plan. In 1950 the State Planning Commission was created, and a five-year plan was announced in 1951 with priority given to the development of heavy industry. East Germany, like other communist countries, had three sets of plans—a long-term plan of 15 years or longer, a five-year plan, and an annual operating plan. In these, East Germany was following the Soviet planning models. The economic plans consisted of physical input-output planning and financial planning. The physical input-output plan involves output targets for industrial and agricultural commodities, raw material allocation, and capital investment. The financial plan is a control mechanism. It includes the state budget and the credit and cash plans of the central bank.

It is unlikely, given the rapid changes that have happened in East Germany, that planning in its present form will continue. It is therefore important to present the goals of the East German five-year plan for 1986–1990 and the annual operating plan for 1987.

The East German Five-Year Plan for 1986–1990. The East German five-year plan was to run from 1986 to 1990. The plan indicators can be summarized as follows:[6]

---

[4] There were some contributing factors to East Germany's success. To a considerable degree its success was linked to West Germany and its contacts with the West. There was trade between the two countries, and East Germany received subsidies from West Germany. The Protestant work ethic remains strong in East Germany as does the vaunted Prussian discipline.

[5] Minority opposition parties were permitted in order to preserve a semblance of democracy.

[6] Gesetz über den Fünfjahrplan für die Entwicklung der Volkswirtschaft der DDR 1986–1990 (East Berlin: Panorama, 1986).

1. National income produced was to increase from 21 to 25 percent by 1990.
2. Construction output was to increase by 16.2 percent by 1990.
3. Exports to other socialist countries were to increase by 29 percent over the period.
4. Labor productivity in the industrial sector was to increase by 50 percent over the period.
5. Grain production per hectare of farmland was to increase by 5.1 tons.
6. The amount of milk delivered to the state was to increase by 7.4 million tons.
7. The amount of meat (beef) delivered to the state was to increase by 2.6 million tons.
8. A total of 1,064,000 dwellings were to be constructed by 1990.
9. Retail trade turnover was to increase by 21.7 percent.
10. Net monetary income of the population was to increase by 21.7 percent.

The East German One-Year Plan for 1987.   The one-year plan is an annual operating plan. It is a control mechanism to see that the yearly results of the five-year plan are being followed. The objectives and results of the one-year plan were as follows:[7]

1. Produced national income (physical output) was to increase by 4.0 percent over 1986.
2. Meat and meat products were to increase by 2.8 percent over 1986.
3. A state quota of 138 million eggs was set for 1987.
4. Coal and energy resources were set to increase by 2.1 percent for 1987.
5. Industrial robots were to increase by 7 percent to increase the total to 78,000.[8]
6. Net monetary income to workers was to increase by 4.6 percent in 1987.

Organization of Industry

In East Germany, as well as in other communist countries, the state has exercised monopolistic control over the basic economic structure and resources of the country. It owned and operated large-scale industries, mines, power plants, railways, and shipping. Private enterprise was of minor importance. The organization of industry had to be considered as a basic part of the economic and political organization of the state. Industrial organization in East Germany was divided into two categories: the state enterprise and the combine. State enterprises provided the foundation upon which the state economic organization was built, whereas the combine was more of an administrative and monitoring arrangement.

The Enterprise.   The enterprise, which was usually an individual firm, was the basic unit of industrial production. It was obliged to fulfill the physical output

---

[7] Mitteilung der Staatlichen Zentralverwaltung für Statistik der DDR über die Durchführung des Volkswirtschaftsplanes 1987, Dokumente zur DDR (East Berlin: Panorama, 1988).

[8] The plan also placed some emphasis on the development of computer technology. The manufacture of advanced capacity 32-bit computers was to be introduced.

and financial plans set down by the state, which specified target indicators to be achieved. For the most part, targets were stated quantitatively in terms of physical or monetary output. An enterprise had its own fixed and financial capital, derived in part by the state budget and in part from bank loans and retained earnings. The enterprise was strictly subject to state planning and was managed by state appointees who were usually members of the Communist Party. With most state enterprises, quantity was achieved at the expense of quality, and East German consumer goods were often shabby.

The Combine. The combine (Kombinat) was an important part of industrial organization in East Germany. It was the consolidation of different firms on the basis of economic and administrative functions. Individual firms belonging to a combine lost their juridical independence. The rationale for the use of the combine was the improvement of profit through a continuous production process and through decreases in costs resulting from large-scale production. It was responsible for the development of long-range and annual production plans and for coordination of the plans of the enterprises subordinate to it. In order to assess the production output of the enterprises, a production coefficient was used to cover the total of all industrial finished foods and services produced by the enterprises. In 1987 there were 126 combines in East Germany employing 98 percent of the industrial labor force and covering 3,423 state enterprises.[9]

Organization of Agriculture

There was a distinctive relationship between industry and agriculture in East Germany in that each was controlled by the state through economic planning. The supply and price of inputs, the share of output marketed, the prices paid for agricultural products, and farm income and expenditures were regulated by the plan. Overall procurement goals were set for agricultural products that were to be delivered to state purchasing agencies. The basic agriculture units were the state farm (Volkseigenes Gut) and the collective farm (Landwirtschaftliche Produktionsgenossenschaft). Some private farms existed, but they were considered a rarity. However, private plots of land that were farmed by members of collective farms were permitted.

State Farms.   State farms were owned by the government and were operated as regular industrial establishments with managers and hired workers. They were a part of industrial combines for the purpose of effective vertical integration. For example, a state farm producing livestock could be a member of a combine responsible for slaughtering and meat packing. One unit did the producing and the other the slaughtering. The state farms did their selling to government procurement offices for processing and distribution through state stores and for exports, and they were

[9] Staatliche Zentralverwaltung für Statistik, *Statisches Taschenbuch 1988*, p. 45.

expected to support themselves out of internally generated funds and from bank credit. In 1987 there were 485 state farms, primarily concentrated in livestock production, responsible for 15.1 percent of total farm output.[10]

Collective Farms.   The collective farm was the basic farm unit in East Germany. In 1987 there were 3,878 state farms that accounted for 83.8 percent of total agricultural output.[11] The collective farm was socially owned; that is, the land was held in perpetuity by the collective. Statutes permitted a collective farm to use all land, farm equipment, and livestock contributed by the members for meeting obligations to the state. Collective farms provided their own working capital and fixed investment funds from the income of farm operations. Minimum daily wages and bonuses either in cash or in kind provided the basis of labor income. Collective farms were headed by directors, who were responsible for their management. The distribution of income to members was based on land shares and work units.

Other Economic Arrangements

The institutional arrangements of a centrally planned economy will be discussed in more detail in Chapter 12 on the Soviet Union. It is sufficient to say that these arrangements were imposed on the East German economy during the Soviet occupation after World War II and have existed pretty much intact for 40 years. Not only was there centralization of control over agriculture and industry, but there was also control over domestic and foreign trade, both of which were conducted within the framework of the annual and longer-term plans. Retail trade was carried on by several types of establishments—state retail stores, consumer cooperatives, and some private stores. Wholesale domestic trade was handled by state distribution organs, which were responsible for virtually all commodity groups. The Ministry of Foreign Trade was responsible for coordinating foreign trade and economic planning, with the plan determining the availability of foreign exchange to be allocated to state enterprises engaged in foreign trade.

   As is true in all socialist economies, the state budget was of prime importance since it provided for the accumulation and distribution of much of the national income. The main function of the state budget was the reallocation process of not only the receipts of the central government but also the receipts of state enterprises. It was a component part of the financial plan and was integrated with the overall economic plan. Budgetary expenditures on investment, for example, represented a financial reflection of decisions pertaining to priorities that were established in the economic plan. In a planned economy, the state budget provides an excellent control mechanism over the flow of financial resources. Revenues and expenditures

[10] *Taschenbuch 1988*, p. 70.
[11] *Taschenbuch 1988*, p. 70.

in the East German state budget in 1987 amounted to around 260 billion Ostmark, which could be compared to a net national product of 526 billion Ostmark.[12]

A COMPARISON OF WEST GERMANY AND EAST GERMANY

West Germany (FRG) and East Germany (GDR) afford an excellent comparison of a capitalist country to a communist country, because both have existed side by side and both are developed countries. They also have a common heritage. The Federal Republic of Germany, or West Germany, was created out of the western portion of the German Reich, which portion had been divided in 1945 into a British, an American, and a French zone of occupation. Eastern Germany, which consisted of the provinces of Prussia, Silesia, Pomerania, Brandenburg, and Upper Saxony, fell under the Russian sphere of influence, and from these provinces the German Democratic Republic, or East Germany, was created. A third part of Hitler's Reich was given to Poland and is now a part of that country.

Almost from the beginning, the development of the two Germanies was different. Marshall Plan aid played an important role in the revival of West Germany. Some $4.5 billion were spent to help it recover from war losses. This aid supported the modernization of plants and equipment by supplying foreign exchange and investment funds. A contrary approach was taken by the Russians in East Germany. The Soviet economy, including much of its industrial base, had been severely damaged by the Germans during World War II. To compensate for their losses, the Russians wreaked havoc on East Germany after the war. They dismantled and hauled off to plants in the Soviet Union machinery, trains, railroad ties, and about everything they could lay their hands on. That was the Russian version of the Marshall Plan.

The two Germanies then went their separate ways. The West German economy relied on market forces and incentives to accomplish recovery from the devastation brought about by the war.[13] This policy was carried out by Ludwig Erhard who was later to be minister of economics when the Federal Republic of Germany was created in 1949. He gambled that the incentives of a free market economy would stimulate long dormant productive capacity. An opposite approach was taken in East Germany. At first, private enterprise was permitted and existed side by side with a socialized sector. However, as the communists under the direction of Moscow were able to gain control over the economy, industry and agriculture were placed under state control and the German Democratic Republic was created in 1951.

---

[12] *Taschenbuch 1988*, p. 25 and p. 108.

[13] Although split in two by the partition, the western part of Germany retained most of the prewar industrial base. This base was concentrated in the capital goods industries. These goods were needed not only for German reconstruction but for world markets in general.

Income Distribution

Decisions about equity in the distribution of income are a fundamental starting point for comparing economic systems. Under a market system, individual preferences expressed through spending determine market demand for goods and services, but these individual preferences are weighted by incomes. The distribution of ownership of productive resources is very unequal. A large part of the population owns only its labor power. An individual with no income or wealth has needs and desires, but he or she has no economic resources with which to satisfy them. This means that individual preferences will not be properly reflected by the market. This leads to a misdirection of production because inequality in the distribution of income sharply reduces the accuracy with which the prices of various goods measure the relative intensity of human desire for them.

It can be assumed that incomes are more evenly distributed in a socialist country than in a capitalist country. The Marxist goal that eventually all of society's goods should be distributed on the basis of human need would be reflected in income distribution. Socialist economic policy includes a guarantee of a minimum standard of living for everyone. Basic needs are subsidized, and these subsidies can be significant. In Poland, total subsidies amounted to 50 percent of government expenditures and created a drag on the Polish economy; also, subsidies contributed to food shortages in Poland. Housing and transportation are also subsidized in the socialist countries, and their wage structure is compressed to narrow income differentials between various occupational groups.

Table 11-1 presents a comparison of net income distribution in the FRG and the GDR. Although it can be assumed that incomes are more evenly distributed in a socialist economy than in a capitalist economy, it is necessary to point out the fact that Western capitalist governments have been involved in altering the distribution

TABLE 11-1

A Comparison of Net Household Income for the FRG and GDR by Quintiles, 1970 and 1983 (percent)

Quintile	1970		1983	
	FRG	GDR	FRG	GDR
1	8.3	9.7	9.8	10.9
2	12.7	16.1	14.7	16.3
3	16.8	19.7	18.3	19.7
4	22.3	23.4	22.9	22.9
5	39.9	31.1	34.3	30.2

Source: Deutscher Bundestag, Materialien zum Berichte zur Lage der Nation im geteilten Deutschland, 1987, Drucksache 11/11 (Bonn: Verlag Dr. Hans Heger, 1987), p. 503.

of income for a long time. They have altered the distribution of income through the uses of taxes and transfer payments. Since a government does not spend its money on the same goods and services that would be purchased by private individuals, a transfer of purchasing power from individuals to government yields a different distribution of income.

Figure 11-1 presents a Lorenz curve of income distribution for the FRG and GDR for 1983. The Lorenz curve is a device for showing concentration of income or wealth.[14] The diagonal line of the curve indicates complete equality in the

FIGURE 11-1
Lorenz Curve Comparing Income Distribution in East and West Germany (by quintiles) for 1983

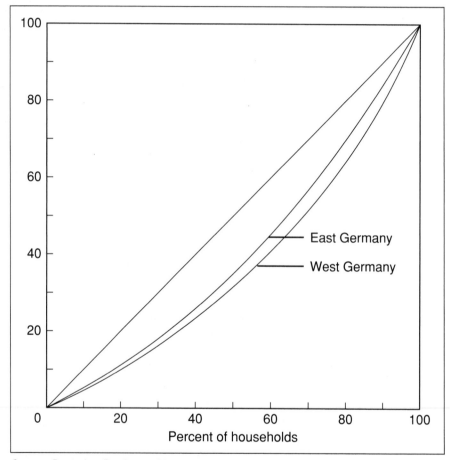

Source: Deutscher Bundestag, Materialien zum Berichte zur Lage der Nation im geteilten Deutschland, 1987 (Bonn: Verlag Dr. Hans Heger, 1987), p. 503.

[14] The Lorenz curve is not limited to measuring income or wealth inequality; it has other statistical applications.

distribution of income. Each quintile would be receiving the same share of income. The farther the curve is from the diagonal line, the greater the inequality in the distribution of income or wealth. As Figure 11-1 indicates, there is more income inequality in the FRG than in the GDR; however, the difference has narrowed since 1970. The Gini coefficient is approximately .35 for the FRG and .33 for the GDR.[15] Neither the table nor the figure takes into consideration the value that the nomenklatura system conveyed on the GDR elite.

Living Standards

The East German standard of living, although higher than the Soviet Union and the other Eastern European countries, is lower than West German living standards. Although living standards in the two Germanies were comparable before World War II,[16] East Germany has lagged behind West Germany since the end of the war. Initially, this lag could be attributed to the fact that East Germany had the greater transitional problem in that it had to contend with the dismantling and reparations policy of the Soviet Union. However, the lag has continued since the 1960s when the Berlin Wall was built and East German migration to the West was halted. In East Germany shortages of consumer goods developed in the 1960s but were alleviated to some extent when reforms provided added incentives more responsive to demand.

Although consumption of foodstuffs does not necessarily show an advantage in favor of the East or West German consumer, West Germans enjoy a far greater advantage in the quality and quantity of consumer goods, particularly automobiles and refrigerators. Automobiles are less available and more expensive in East Germany than in West Germany. As Table 11-2 indicates, in other areas that determine living standards, East Germany lags behind West Germany. For example, a woman's dress in West Germany would cost less than half what it would cost in East Germany. A man's suit would cost substantially less in West Germany than in East Germany. West German transportation costs are also less despite East German subsidies. The quality of housing in East Germany is generally inferior to the quality in West Germany.

Another way of comparing living standards in East Germany and West Germany is to compare nominal or real income. This can be done by comparing the purchasing power of the mark in East Germany to the purchasing power of the West German Deutsche Mark. Converting the mark into the Deutsche Mark gives a nominal average monthly income of 3,745 DM in West Germany to a nominal

[15] For a perfectly equal distribution, the Gini coefficient is zero; for a perfectly unequal distribution, the coefficient is one.

[16] If anything, living standards were probably higher in East Germany. Berlin was the capital of Germany and the center of financial activity. Many of the high-wage, specialized industries were located in East Germany. World leadership in the production of optical goods was held by the Zeiss firm in Jena, which was in East Germany. The great agricultural food basket of Germany was also located in East Germany.

TABLE 11-2

A Comparison of Living Costs in the FRG and GDR (Marks)

Consumer Goods	FRG	GDR
Food		
Potatoes, 5 kg	5.32	4.05
Tomatoes, kg	2.10	4.40
Apples, kg	2.10	1.40
Grapefruit, kg	2.95	4.40
Bananas, 500 g	4.10	18.50
Calves liver, kg	19.45	9.80
Pork cutlets, kg	14.99	10.00
Bratwurst, kg	9.90	11.00
Salami, kg	17.50	12.40
Rumpsteaks, por	15.00	5.40
Herring, 200 g	1.99	3.70
Edam cheese, kg	9.90	9.60
Camembert, 125 g	1.29	1.30
Butter, kg	8.76	9.00
Margarine, kg	3.96	4.00
Rye bread, 1.5 kg	4.59	2.93
Coffee, 250 g	5.25	25.00
Tea, 50 kg	1.98	4.75
Sugar, kg	1.72	1.59
Cocoa, 100 g	.99	4.00
Clothing and Shoes		
Men's pants	159.00	390.00
Men's jeans	59.90	135.00
Men's coat	259.00	1,600.00
Women's dress	69.50	174.50
Women's sweater	29.95	88.00
Women's coat	339.00	950.00
Men's socks	5.00	6.10
Women's hose	2.99	15.80
Boys' T shirt	10.90	30.80
Men's leather shoes	34.95	119.20
Women's leather pumps	89.00	224.00
Children's shoe	37.95	41.20
Children's T shirt	14.00	18.00

average income of 1,868 DM for East Germany. To put it another way, comparison can be of the amount of work time it takes in both East Germany and West Germany to buy consumer goods. Table 11-3 indicates the number of hours and minutes a worker in East Germany and in West Germany would have to work to obtain such consumer goods as television sets and cars. As the table indicates, the West German worker clearly has the superior purchasing power in terms of time invested. The table also indicates the fact that East Germany lags behind West Germany in the development of technology.

TABLE 11-2

(continued)

Consumer Goods	FRG	GDR
Durables		
Coffee service for six persons	179.00	345.00
Washing machine	869.50	2,750.00
Electric coffee maker	39.95	165.00
Light bulb, 40 watts	1.90	1.50
Electric handmixer	39.95	105.00
Lamp, table	49.95	84.60
Television set, black-white	339.95	1,610.00
PKW, Lada Nova, 1500 ccm	10,210.00	24,500.00
Auto batteries, 12 volts	109.00	185.00
Men's watch, quartz, digital	25.00	260.00
Dryer	369.00	1,435.00
Child's wagon	198.00	420.00
Radio and cassette recorder	199.95	1,160.00
Bedroom furniture	1,870.00	4,728.00
Living room furniture	1,495.00	4,275.00
Electric range with oven	389.50	815.00
Refrigerator	369.50	1,435.00
Vacuum cleaner with attachments	248.00	550.00
Color television, 56 cm	1,199.00	5.650.00
Time reflex camera	429.00	2,530.00
Slide projector	290.00	1,320.00
Motorscouter	1,490.00	2,050.00
Ladies bicycle, 26 inch wheels, no attachments	289.00	490.00
Rent and Transportation		
Month's rent, 2-room apt., kitchen without bath	190.00	33.00
Month's rent, 2-room apt., kitchen and bath	390.00	75.00
Electricity, consumer price for 75 kwh[a]	29.30	7.50
Gas, consumer price for 1000 cm	95.40	38.00
Railroad travel, second class, 50 km	9.20	4.00
Railroad, week pass, second class, 15 km	26.00	2.50
Streetcar or bus, local fare	1.93	.20
Streetcar or bus, monthly ticket	96.00	20.00
Day nursery, monthly rate	140.00	7.00
Round trip air fare with room and board, 14 days to Romania	926.00	1,196.00
Men's haircut	11.25	1.90
Women's permanent	45.00	9.90

[a] Two bedroom apartment with kitchen.

Source: Deutscher Bundestag, Materialien zum Bericht zur Lage der Nation in geteilten Deutschland 1987, *Drucksache 11/11 (Bonn: Verlag Dr. Hans Heger, 1987), pp. 732–735.*

TABLE 11-3

Purchasing Power in East Germany as Measured by Time Necessary to Make Purchase (hours & minutes)

Type of Purchase	West Germany	East Germany
Men's shirt	1.22	7.19
Men's shoes	5.20	24.01
Men's suit	10.49	59.30
Women's pantyhose	0.12	2.40
Women's dress	4.44	21.30
Children's shoes	2.35	7.21
Radio-cassette	13.36	207.09
Color TV	81.34	1,008.56
Washing machine	59.09	491.04
Refrigerator	29.54	272.19
Vaccuum cleaner	13.32	82.09
Car	694.33	4,375.00
Railroad fare, 15 kilometers	1.46	0.27
Dark bread, 1 kg.	0.12	0.07
Sugar, 1 kg.	0.07	0.17
Butter, 1 kg.	0.36	1.39
Eggs, dozen	0.10	0.36
Milk, litre	0.05	0.07
Cheese, 1 kg.	0.52	1.43
Pork cutlets, 1 kg.	1.01	1.47
Apples, 1 kg.	0.09	0.15
Lemon, 1 kg.	0.16	0.54
Coffee, 250 g.	0.21	4.20

Source: *Bundesministerium für Innerdeutsche Beziehungen,* Zahlenspiegel Bundesrepublik Deutschland/Deutsche Demokratische Republik, *Ein Vergleich, Bonn 1989, pp. 77–78.*

Agriculture

The development of agriculture in East and West Germany after the end of World War II followed diametrically opposite patterns of development. In the FRG, the development of family farms was furthered through various forms of farm subsidies. In the GDR the structure of agriculture was completely changed through the combination of many small farms into large-scale enterprises—the state and collective farms. In 1987 there were 465 state farms and 3,878 collective farms in the GDR.[17] Some private farms may exist but can be considered a rarity. State farms were owned and operated by the government and were operated as regular industrial establishments with managers and workers. The collective farm was the basic type of farm unit in East Germany and was socially owned; that is, the land was held in perpetuity by the collective and was farmed by its members. The

---

[17] Staatliche Zentralverwaltung fur Statistik, *Statistisches Taschenbuch Der DDR 1988* (East Berlin: Staatsverlag der DDR 1988), p. 70.

number of collective farms in the GDR declined from 9,009 in 1970 to 3,878 in 1987.[18]

Table 11-4 compares agricultural productivity in East and West Germany for two time periods (1970 and 1984). It is important to remember the fact that there are different farm entities involved: the private farm in the FRG as opposed to the state and collective farms in the GDR. The latter were very large units, comprising on the average, some 700 hectares of farmland.[19] The West German farm unit is

TABLE 11-4

A Comparison of Agricultural Productivity in East and West Germany for 1970 and 1984

Produce	Year	FRG	GDR	GDR As percent of FRG
All grains[a]	1970	33.4	28.2	84.4
	1984	53.6	45.1	84.1
Wheat	1970	37.5	35.6	93.9
	1984	62.6	52.3	82.5
Rye	1970	30.8	26.8	70.8
	1984	43.9	35.0	79.7
Barley	1970	32.2	30.1	93.5
	1984	51.3	47.8	93.2
Potatoes	1970	272.3	195.7	71.9
	1984	331.5	244.0	73.6
Sugar beets	1970	444.2	320.1	72.1
	1984	494.7	325.3	65.8
Clover	1970	78.1	72.8	93.2
	1984	84.5	115.1	136.2
Corn	1970	444.9	348.0	78.2
	1984	435.5	300.6	69.0
Milk[b]	1970	4,126.0	3,314.0	80.3
	1984	5,120.0	4,187.0	82.0
Meat (beef)[c]	1970	171.0	116.0	67.8
	1984	180.0	113.0	60.1
Meat (pork)	1970	146.0	94.0	64.4
	1984	160.0	107.0	66.9
Chicken (eggs)[d]	1970	220.0	168.0	76.4
	1984	265.0	217.0	81.9

[a] Kilos per hectare: A kilo is 2.2 pounds; a hectare is 2.471 acres.
[b] Kilos per milk cow.
[c] Kilos in beef and pork.
[d] Number of eggs per laying hen.

Source: Deutscher Bundestag, Materialien zum Berichte zur Lage der Nation im geteilten Deutschland, 1987, Drucksache 11/11 *(Bonn: Verlag Dr. Han Heger, 1987), pp. 441–442*

---

[18] *Taschenbuch 1988*, p. 70.
[19] One hectare equals 2.471 acres.

much smaller, averaging around 20 hectares. There are two conclusions that can be drawn about agriculture in the FRG and GDR. First, productivity per farm worker has increased at a much more rapid rate in the FRG than in the GDR. In 1987, around 10 percent of the East German labor force was employed in farming compared to 3 percent in West Germany. Second, in comparing agricultural yields in the FRG and GDR for the two time periods, there has been no real change despite the increased size of the East German farm units.

Comparisons of East and West German agricultural productivity can be made when each was a part of pre–World War II Germany. In comparing East and West German agricultural production, however, it is necessary to remember that East Germany was the most important agricultural area of Germany before World War II. Thus, East Germany had certain advantages in land fertility to begin with. The base for agriculture was established. Table 11-5 presents a comparison of agricultural productivity in pre–World War II East and West Germany and the more current data on agricultural productivity. As the table indicates, agricultural productivity was in

TABLE 11-5
Agricultural Production in East and West Germany for Selected Years

Year	FRG	GDR
All Grains[a]		
1935–1938	22.4	23.9
1970	33.4	28.2
1984	53.6	45.1
Potatoes[a]		
1935–1938	185.0	194.3
1970	272.3	195.7
1984	331.5	244.0
Sugar Beets[a]		
1935–1938	327.2	301.2
1970	444.2	320.1
1984	494.7	325.3
Milk[b]		
1935–1938	2,436.0	2,549.0
1970	4,126.0	3,314.0
1984	5,120.0	4,187.0

[a] Doppelzentners: 1 doppelzentner = 100 kilograms.
[b] Kilograms.
Source: Martin Schnitzer, East and West Germany: A Comparative Economic Analysis *(New York: Praeger, 1972), pp. 369–370;* Materialien zum Bericht zur Lage der Nation in geteilten Deutschland, 1987, *pp. 441–442.*

general higher in East Germany than in West Germany before the war; now West German agriculture is more productive.

Labor Productivity

A comparison can be made of productivity in East and West German industry. For each branch of industry, production is divided by employment to obtain comparable productivity values for the two countries. The results of the comparison are shown in Table 11-6. They are presented for four time periods. The results are as follows:

1. Labor productivity is lower in East German industry than in West German industry. This can be attributed in part to the fact that relatively more workers are employed in East German industry than in West German industry, causing diseconomies of scale. The difference in labor productivity varies considerably from industry to industry.
2. Those industries that were given priority in terms of the allocation of investment funds have not achieved productivity anywhere near the West German level. This can be attributed in part to the fact that the degree of automation is far greater in the FRG than in the GDR.
3. The East German economic plans contributed to a lack of flexibility in production. Production bottlenecks in certain industries occurred on numerous occasions.

The Environment

A new reality in the world economy is the emergence of ecology as an economic and social issue that transcends national boundaries. Concern for the ecology will

TABLE 11-6
Industrial Worker Productivity in East and West Germany (GDR as percent of FRG = 100)

Industry	1970	1976	1980	1983
Power and fuels	61	41	37	41
Chemicals, synthetic fiber, rubber	34	39	44	47
Metallurgy	41	41	39	45
Construction	44	46	44	41
Water production and use	62	55	56	65
Steel, machinery, vehicles	44	45	46	53
Electronic, precision, and optics	38	38	43	48
Textiles	53	55	57	57
Consumer goods	55	55	58	58
Food, beverages, and tobacco average	60	51	43	41
Average	48	45	44	47

Source: Karl C. Thalheim, Die Wirtschaftliche Entwicklung der beiden Staaten in Deutschland *(Berlin: Lesche Verlag, 1988), p. 88.*

increasingly have to be built into economic policy. The Summit meeting between the seven major Western industrial powers, which was held in Paris in July 1988, recognized the world environment as a major issue that needs to be addressed. What is endangered are the needs of the human race. It used to be that society had to be protected against the forces of nature; now, it is nature that has to be protected against society. Even the seas upon which the survival of the human race depends are polluted by agricultural runoffs of fertilizers, topsoil, and pesticides, and by waste water from factories and sewage treatment plants.

Pollution has a direct impact on the quality of life because it subtracts from real income. Thus, East and West Germany can be compared economically by the extent to which each country pollutes its environment. Both countries have problems of pollution. There is some overlap in their pollution in that water pollution in West Germany impacts upon East Germany through emission into the North Sea, and air pollution in East Germany carries over into West Germany. In West Germany 8 percent of forest lands have been damaged or destroyed by some form of pollution. Table 11-7 compares pollution in East and West Germany for 1982. Sulphur dioxide pollution was worse in East Germany because of the burning of coal for energy; nitrous oxide pollution was worse in West Germany because of the number of cars.

GERMAN REUNIFICATION

Robert Mitchum, the well-known actor, once said that he didn't think communism was much good because he didn't see anyone beating down the door to get into Bulgaria. Conversely, capitalism, or at least democracy, must be good as demonstrated by the fact that in the summer and fall of 1989 thousands of East Germans literally beat down the doors to get out of East Germany and into West Germany. This exodus could not have come at a more inopportune time for East Germany and for communism as a whole, and, to add insult to injury, it came at a time when East

TABLE 11-7
Sulphur Dioxide and Nitrous Oxide Pollution in East and West Germany, 1982 (1000 tons)

	SO_2		N_2O	
Source	**FRG**	**GDR**	**FRG**	**GDR**
Power stations	1,861.0	2,911.0	860.0	279.0
Industry	750.0	1,084.0	430.0	157.0
Housing and living	260.0	950.0	110.0	38.0
Traffic	110.0	16.0	1,700.0	96.0
Kilograms per person	48.7	296.0	50.3	34.1

Source: Karl C. Thalheim, Die Wirtschaftliche Entwicklung der beiden Staaten in Deutschland *(Berlin: Leske Verlag, 1988), p. 56.*

Germany was in the process of celebrating the fortieth anniversary of its creation. The exodus probably catalyzed the events that led to the changing of governments in Czechoslovakia, Bulgaria, and Romania.

Probably the most dramatic act symbolizing the end of the Cold War was the opening of the Berlin Wall to permit traffic between the Germanies. The opening of the Brandenburg Gate, for years the main East-West axis, portends the eventual reunification of the two Germanies. This will create potential problems. For one thing, the spectre of a unified Germany still haunts Europe, because Germany is blamed for World War I and World War II, particularly the latter. Second, German reunification would make Germany the economic powerhouse of Europe. This could have a disruptive effect on the creation of the European Community of 1992. Third, there is the issue of the effect of reunification on the Soviet Union and the Warsaw Pact alliance, which is a defense counterpart of NATO.

ECONOMIC AND POLITICAL REUNIFICATION

It is obvious that two different economic and political systems cannot exist side by side in the same country. There has to be a closed society for central economic planning to work, because the government must have complete control over all resources. With resources and labor flowing back and forth between the two Germanies, where does the East German economy go from here? Also, a one-party system can work only in a closed society where opposition parties are either banned outright or tolerated in order for the Communist Party to pretend that a democracy exists. However, East Germany is no longer a closed society and free elections were held in March 1990. There was sentiment for reunification in both East and West Germany, which has now occurred.

Table 11-8 compares some of the institutional arrangements that make the two Germanies different. It will be interesting to see what will happen with all barriers removed between the two countries. What will happen to central planning in East Germany? The answer is that it will be abandoned. West Germany has economic planning, but it involves the use of budgetary revenues and expenditures. Both East Germany and West Germany have a developed welfare system and their basic educational systems are similar. The comparisons made in the Table 11-8 are subject to change at any time.

Table 11-9 presents the economic effects of German reunification by comparing gross national product and value of exports for East and West Germany before and after reunification to gross national product and value of exports for other major countries for 1988. As the table indicates, a combined Germany would become even more economically powerful than West Germany is today. There would be the fear of German domination of the European Community of 1992. Although history is unlikely to repeat itself, economic rivalry between Germany and England contributed to World War I.

TABLE 11-8
A Comparison of East German and West German Economic and Political Institutions

Type of Institution	East Germany	West Germany
Economic Institutions		
Resource allocation	central planning	free market
Resource ownership	state	private
Pricing	state	free market
Profit determinates	state guidelines	competition in free markets
Individual worker	cooperation	competition
Other Institutions		
Banking	centralized, state owned	basically private
Industrial organization	combines	large firms in most industries
Taxes	turnover	value added
	income tax unimportant	progressive income tax
Agriculture	state & collective farms	small privately owned farms
Labor unions	controlled by government	independent of government
Political Institutions		
Government structure	centralized	federal republic similar to U.S.
Political parties	Communist Party	two major parties
Legal Institutions		
Laws	centralized legal system	contract law
	no business laws, private	tort law
	property laws	bankruptcy law

Accessible now through East Germany, Eastern Europe provides a potentially large market not only for consumer goods for their long-deprived peoples, but also for capital goods for future economic growth. This is an area where West Germany excels. In return, West Germany can get supplies of raw materials from Eastern Europe and an educated East German labor force. Second, the West German DM (Deutsche Mark) is one of the world's strongest currency units. It can be expected that the Eastern Europe countries will tie their currencies and economies to the West German DM. Thus, there will be a DM standard which gives an economic and psychological boost to West Germany. West Germany is one of the world's largest exporting countries. What all of this means for the world is that a new power will challenge the United States and Japan.

EAST GERMAN ELECTIONS

Free elections were held in East Germany on March 17, 1990, and an alliance of conservative parties favoring immediate reunification and backed by the ruling

TABLE 11-9

A Comparison of Gross National Product and Exports for East and West Germany and Other Major Countries for 1988 (millions of dollars)

Country	GNP	Exports	Current Account
United States	4,864.3	321.6	−126.6
Japan	1,758.4	264.9	79.6
France	762.0	167.8	−3.6
United Kingdom	755.3	145.2	−25.9
Italy	753.8	128.5	−1.5
Soviet Union	2,535.3	110.7	2.6
	Combined West and East Germany		
West Germany	870.0	323.4	48.5
East Germany	207.2	30.7	−0.4
	1,077.2	354.1	48.1

Source: Central Intelligence Agency, Directorative of Intelligence, Handbook of Economic Statistics 1989 *(Springfield, VA: NTIS, 1990), pp. 24–25; World Bank,* World Debt Tables, *p. 61.*

West German political party, the Christian Democrats, won a major victory. The Alliance for Germany received 48 percent of the popular vote and won 193 seats in the new East German Parliament.[20] The Social Democrats, supported by the West German Social Democrat party, received 22 percent of the popular vote and 65 seats in the parliament. All together, there were 24 parties, including the German Beer Drinkers' Party,[21] competing for seats in the parliament, which is to hold office for a four-year period. Lothar de Maiziere, leader of the East German Christian Democrats, a part of the conservative alliance, was elected Prime Minister.

July 2, 1990 was named the day for the economic and social, but not political, reunion of the two Germanys. A major development that will facilitate economic reunion was the decision of the West German government to exchange the West German mark, which is one of the world's strongest currencies, for the East German mark, which has no foreign exchange value. This will be done on a 1-to-1 rate applied to wages, pensions, and savings accounts of East Germans up to 4,000 West German marks ($1,300). There were two reasons for this 1-to-1 rate. The first was to keep East Germans from migrating to West Germany at the current rate, which was more than 4,000 a week in the first three months of 1990. The second reason was to protect East German workers from higher living costs in a united Germany and the loss of subsidies that existed in the former communist system.

---

[20] There are two major political parties in West Germany: the Christian Democrats and the Social Democrats. Both parties campaigned for their counterparts in East Germany.

[21] Who said the Germans lacked a sense of humor?

OTHER PROBLEMS
OF REUNIFICATION

Reunification of what was divided for over 40 years will not be a smooth operation. Take, for example, ownership reform. Almost all the entire industrial production of East Germany comes from the combines (*Kombinats*), which have been controlled by various ministries and have been instruments through which economic plans have been implemented. These combines have to be privatized and divided into smaller units of manageable size. Then the units have to be incorporated into corporate enterprises in order to create the incentive structures necessary for effective business management. Market economies and private ownership must be learned and experienced. In this respect, East Germany will be starting from scratch. Entrepreneurship and management skills are something that also have to be learned.

Price reform is also very important because price relations in East Germany are distorted. Essential goods such as rent and food are extremely cheap and thus require high levels of subsidies from the state budget. Higher-value goods are very expensive. Prices do not reflect the scarcity of the goods and thus do not give the right signals either for production or consumption. Price reforms will be successful only when East Germany is exposed to free market competition, which will require the breaking up of the combines, the establishing of new business, and the introduction of foreign competition. The effects of lifting price controls and other subsidies will be considerable, but it can be done in stages. In the initial stages, at least, many groups could lose out in comparison to others.

Another problem that needs to be addressed is the transportation infrastructure, which is outdated. Many of the highway and railroad systems were built before World War II. Because of the inadequate road system, the railroads have become the backbone of East German transportation. However, the railroad system is antiquated by West German standards. The rolling stock is obsolete, and the network of rails is mostly from West to East to facilitate trade with the Soviet Union. Only 16 percent of the railway network is electrified, compared to 94 percent in West Germany; this has contributed to the environmental problems in East Germany. Financial support for the restructuring of the transportation system will have to come from West Germany.

SUMMARY

East Germany has been the prototype of a centrally planned socialist economy. The state exercised virtual monopolistic control over all economic resources. It owned and operated large-scale industries, mines, power plants, railways, shipping, and various communication media. It engaged in farming on its own account through state farms, and it largely controlled agriculture through collective farms. It had an exclusive monopoly on banking and foreign trade, and it had controlled its domestic channels of distribution in its role of manufacturer, farmer, merchant, shipper, and banker. In the field of labor relations, it was the sole employer of note, and as such dominated collective bargaining between itself and its employees. In the absence of the market mechanism, economic planning was used to allocate resources and to make the complex of state enterprises function.

But change has come to East Germany in a dramatic fashion. Thousands of young East Germans fled the country, preferring freedom to rigid state control. Erich Honecker, a hard-line ideologue of the old school, was replaced by Egon Krenz, also a party hard-liner, who opened dialogue with dissidents who advocated more economic and social reform. Egon Krenz was then replaced by Gregor Gysi, who became Communist Party chairman. The Prime Minister was Hans Modrow, who headed a government of both Communists and non-Communists. Free elections held in March 1990 were won by the Conservative Alliance. The Berlin Wall is down, the Brandenburg Gate is open, and German reunification has occurred.

REVIEW QUESTIONS

1. Compare the process of income distribution in a market economy and a centrally planned economy.
2. What was the purpose of the East German annual plan?
3. What was a combine?
4. Compare East and West German living standards.
5. Compare agricultural productivity in East and West Germany.
6. What were the major reasons for thousands of East Germans to leave their homeland for a new life in West Germany?
7. What are some of the problems confronting German reunification?
8. There are fears that a united Germany will dominate Europe. Are these fears groundless?

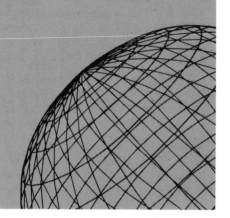

CHAPTER TWELVE

AN INTRODUCTION TO THE SOVIET UNION*

Lenin once reduced the past and future alike to two pronouns and a question mark: "Who-whom?" He meant: Who would prevail over whom? To the Communist Party the answer was never in doubt: Lenin and those who came after him in the Soviet Union would prevail over "whom"—whoever they were. But Lenin failed to reckon with Ronald McDonald. On NBC nightly news, a report from Moscow showed long lines of Russians waiting to get into the newly opened McDonald's where they could get quality food that was unavailable elsewhere.[1] Then the report shifted to Lenin's crypt in Red Square, long regarded as a shrine by the Russian people. The line waiting to view Lenin's crypt was not nearly as long as the line waiting to get into McDonald's.

The Soviet Union has interrelated economic and political problems. The economy has problems of declining growth in output, serious inflationary pressure, slow technological growth, and accumulated deficiencies in housing and other needs. Attempts to alleviate these problems have usually encountered resistance from party ideologues and bureaucrats. Moreover, an imbalance in the economic system has been created by an orientation toward military spending. Even though the Soviet Union is one of the richest countries in the world in terms of natural resources, resource constraints based in part on geographic impediments to transportation limit the growth of the Soviet economy. The cost of obtaining and using natural resources

*Given the rapidity of change in the Soviet Union, the author wishes to attach a caveat to this chapter. Basically, these have been the economic and political institutions of the Soviet Union, at least up to July 1990. There have been some modifications. It is the opinion of the author that dramatic change will happen, perhaps by the time the book is published.
[1] NBC Evening News, February 7, 1990.

has risen as high-grade well-located resources have been depleted and less accessible supplies have to be used.

The Soviet Union is also going through a very turbulent political phase. Moving voluntarily to catch up with political change in Eastern Europe, the Soviet Communist Party leadership voted on February 7, 1990, to voluntarily surrender its 70-year monopoly on political power. This came at a time of political ferment within the Soviet Union. This ferment is based in part on the fact that the country is a melange of different ethnic and racial groups. The people of the Soviet Union can be classified as Russian or non-Russian or as Slavic or non-Slavic. There are in fact more than 170 nationalities and 200 languages and dialects spoken in the Soviet Union. Racial and religious animosities run deep, as exemplified by the bloody clashes between Christian Armenia and Moslem Azerbijan. There are also the Baltic states of Estonia, Lithuania, and Latvia, which were grabbed by the Russians during World War II and which are trying to break away from the Soviet Union.

THE POLITICAL SYSTEM

The Soviet Union consists of 15 socialist republics. The largest is the Russian Soviet Federated Socialist Republic, which comprises 79 percent of the total area and around half of the population of the country. The second largest republic in terms of land area and population is the Ukrainian Soviet Socialist Republic. Within a republic, there are autonomous republics and regions that reflect the ethnic diversity of the country. For example, within the Russian Soviet Federated Republic is the autonomous Soviet Socialist Republic of Yakutia, which has a land area of more than a million square miles but is very sparsely populated and far removed from Moscow. Its autonomy is largely a matter of administrative convenience. An example of an autonomous region is the Jewish Autonomous Region in the Asiatic part of the Russian Soviet Federated Socialist Republic.

The Communist Party

Any history of the Communist Party has to begin with Vladimir Lenin, the founding father of the Soviet state. Lenin championed the "dictatorship of the proletariat" before the Russian Revolution of 1917 and was the leader of the Bolshevik faction that overcame the Menshivik faction after the Revolution to become the sole rulers of the Soviet Union.[2] Lenin said that the proletariat should only be led by a small dedicated core of communists who would direct society like an orchestra, dictating who would play each violin and discovering who plays a false note. Lenin also declared the undivided political supremacy of the Communist Party that would rule in the name of the proletariat. The institution of the Politburo, a handful of top party leaders who collectively set national policy, was also created by Lenin.

---

[2] The Russian Social Democratic Party split into two factions before the Revolution—the Bolsheviks and the Mensheviks. The latter favored social democracy with free elections.

Joseph Stalin became the leader of the Soviet Union after Lenin's death in 1924. He progressively centralized power by crushing his rivals. He launched the first five-year plan for economic development in 1927 and forced the collectivization of agriculture.[3] His great purges of the 1930s, in which millions of persons lost their lives or were deported to Siberia, reinforced the totalitarian system. Three years after Stalin's death, he was succeeded as Party leader by Nikita Khrushchev who made some reforms but was ousted in 1964 and replaced by Leonid Brezhnev, who was Party leader for around 18 years. Although the Soviet Union made economic gains and living standards improved under Brezhnev, there was also corruption and cronyism. The economy became stagnant during the 1980s.

Control of the government machinery in the Soviet Union is in the hands of the Communist Party. Moreover, it reaches into nearly every aspect of Soviet life, from management of industry to control of the Bolshoi Ballet. It has 440,000 cells in every factory, farm, school, and military unit—organizations that convey instructions from the top of the Party pyramid to the bottom and that keep tabs on the performance and advancement of people throughout the system. Party committees parallel government structures at every level from the village councils through the provincial party bosses. Cells consist of at least three members and are responsible for the recruitment of members and for selection of delegates to the local Party conferences, which in turn select delegates to conferences covering a somewhat wider area, and the process continues until, finally, in district and regional congresses, delegates are selected to the National Party Congress, which is supposed to be the highest body of Party authority. Power actually rests in the Central Committee, the Politburo, the Secretariat, and the various staff departments of the central apparatus in Moscow.

The Central Committee.   The Central Committee is elected at the meeting of the National Party Congress. It is composed of the Politburo, Secretariat, Party Control Committee, and a number of individual sections including those called Cadres Abroad, Economic Relations with Socialist Countries, International Affairs, and Relations with Bloc Parties. The Central Committee has no effective role as a decision maker; that function is performed by the Politburo. It does, however, provide a forum for the elaboration of the major policies of the Communist Party and its top leaders. It is also responsible for the dissemination of the aims and objectives of the leaders to officials in various departments in the central apparatus and also downward to the various party committees in the republics and lower levels.

The Politburo.   The *Politburo* is the supreme instrument of political power in the Soviet Union. When the Central Committee is not in session, the Politburo

---

[3] Millions of landowners, called *kulaks*, were forcibly removed from their land, which was expropriated by the state. Many landowners were shot.

is responsible for all phases of national life—foreign policy, domestic economic policy, and military policy. There will be 27 full voting members (changed from 12 in July 1990) who exercise the prerogatives and responsibilities of national policy making and nine candidate members who participate in varying degrees in the policy-making process.[4] Most members of the Politburo have collateral duties, meaning that they serve in other capacities in addition to their positions as party administrators.

Party and Government Structure.   Party and government structure parallel each other. For example, at the national or U.S.S.R. level, the basic Party administrative units are the Central Committee, Politburo, and Secretariat; the basic governmental administrative units are the Supreme Soviet and the Council of Ministers with their respective presidiums. The leaders of the party are members of both units. At the union republic level, the Party administrative unit consists of the Central Committee and Secretariat, and the governmental administrative unit consists of the Republic Supreme Soviet and Council of Ministers. This interlocking relationship continues down to the rural soviet level. Although inefficiency may result at lower administrative levels because of communication problems, there is no question that the interconnection of Party and government, and Party domination of the government, confer on Soviet public administration exceptional unity of control and uniformity of ideological perspective.[5]

Nomenklatura System

There is a famous quotation from George Orwell's classic *Animal Farm:* "All animals are equal, but some are more equal than others." [6] Supposedly workers are "first among equals" in the Soviet Union and the other socialist countries, but this is hardly the case. To the contrary, there is an ideological imperative that is simply that party leaders have to maintain a monopoly of political, ideological, and economic power. This is done through the *nomenklatura system.* Nomenklatura is simply patronage designed to ensure party loyalty. Party leaders determine the staffing of government and industrial posts beneath them. In turn, those in subordinate positions exercise the same influence over those beneath them. This ensures control from the top down. Promotions and rewards are more likely attached to party membership and one's position within the nomenklatura system than to merit.

---

[4] The Communist Party in the Soviet Union is rapidly losing its grip. It will be challenged by other parties (for example, Boris Yeltsin has already announced that he will form an independent party).

[5] This does not mean, however, that party and government organs function as two perfectly synchronized parts of a smoothly working administrative machine. To the contrary, there are cliques within the party and the governmental bureaucracies that often cause power rivalries or power disputes. These cliques have a vested interest in maintaining the status quo.

[6] George Orwell, *Animal Farm* (New York: Harcourt Brace, 1954), Chap. 10.

Nomenklatura gives a person both power and privileges. A member of the system is able to enjoy the best things in life, to travel to Paris and New York. He or she is able to shop at special state-run stores intended for foreigners with hard currency. These stores exist not only in the Soviet Union but in other socialist countries as well; they are off-limits to ordinary citizens. The stores contain many luxury items as well as basic consumer goods that are usually in short supply in the regular state stores. Membership in the nomenklatura elite also provides access to larger apartments and cars. Those who are higher up in the nomenklatura system have villas and summer homes. Privileges also extend to the family members. Admission to the best colleges and opportunities for better-paying jobs are examples. Even after retirement, a member of the system gets a special pension and retains the privilege of shopping at the special stores.[7]

Organization of the Government

The governmental administrative apparatus of the Soviet Union is a multitiered arrangement, with control extending from Moscow down to the rural soviets (elected government councils). The current arrangement is essentially as follows.

Territorial Administration.   From a territorial administrative standpoint, the Soviet Union can be divided into several categories. First, there is the Soviet Union itself. As a federation of constituent republics, it has its own constitution. Then there are the 15 theoretically independent union republics that form the federation. Each republic has its own constitution, government, and party hierarchy. The republics are similar to American states, though they are generally larger in size. A distinctive feature of Soviet public administration is the fact that most of these republics were formed primarily on the basis of nationality. The federalist structure of the Soviet Union can be regarded as a concession to the non-Slavic peoples' nationalistic sentiments. However, administrative safeguards modify the formal federalism of the constitutional structure of the Soviet Union. The Communist Party itself is a single, unified organization that exerts a countervailing centralism to ethnic federalism. Moreover, the highest administrative organs of the country are centralized in Moscow.

National Policy Administration.   The state apparatus through which national policy is administered can be divided into two pyramidal hierarchies—the Council of Ministers of the U.S.S.R. and the Supreme Soviet of the U.S.S.R. The Council of Ministers is the executive branch of the Soviet government; the Supreme Soviet, the legislative branch.

---

[7] Michael Voslensky, *Nomenklatura* (New York: Doubleday & Co., 1984).

The Council of Ministers.   The Council of Ministers is responsible for the development of economic policy and the enforcement of laws passed by the Supreme Soviet. It is also responsible for exercising general guidance in the sphere of relations with other countries and for directing the general organization of the country's armed forces. It is elected by and is responsible to the Supreme Soviet. The Presidium of the Council of Ministers, which consists of a chairperson and six deputies, one of whom represents each of six committees mentioned below, is the policy-making body. There is also a Council of Ministers in each of the 15 constituent republics.

To assist the Council of Ministers in coordinating economic activity, there are a number of committees whose responsibilities are to provide the information needed for decision making. One important committee is the State Planning Committee (Gosplan), which is responsible for the development of the national economic plans. There are five other committees—the All-Unions Agricultural Committee, the State Committee for Science and Technology, the State Committee for Material and Technical Supply, the State Committee for Construction, and the CEMA Commission.[8]

The Supreme Soviet.   The Supreme Soviet of the U.S.S.R. is the most important legislative branch in the Soviet Union. It is formally a bicameral legislature with coequal houses—the Soviet of the Union, whose deputies are elected on the basis of population, and the Soviet of Nationalities, whose deputies are elected on a territorial basis by nationality. The responsibilities of the Supreme Soviet are stronger in theory than in practice. In terms of real decision making it has little power; it passes the bills that are submitted to it. A law is considered enacted if passed by both houses by a simple majority vote in each. There are standing committees for each house in areas of credentials, plans and budgets, industry, transportation and communication, building and the building materials industry, agriculture, public health and social security, public education, science and culture, trade and public services, legislative proposals, and foreign affairs.

Gorbachev's Political Reforms

In February 1990 the Central Committee of the Communist Party voted to end its monopoly on political power and to permit a multiparty system. Section 6 of the Soviet Constitution, which states that the Communist Party has a sole monopoly of power in the Soviet, is to be eliminated. Also contemplated is the disbanding of Party organizations in state enterprises, the army, police, and the KGB. These reforms are the latest in a series of changes that have taken place since Gorbachev took power in March 1985. They may be briefly summarized as follows:

---

[8] The Council for Mutual Economic Assistance (CEMA) was the consultative organ that coordinated the domestic and foreign economic policies of the U.S.S.R. and the European satellite countries.

1. In June 1987 experimental multicandidate elections were held in some local districts.
2. In June 1988 a special Party conference approved political reforms that promised a shift of Party power to government and the creation of a new legal system. Gorbachev suggested that local Party leaders seek and win election to the corresponding government post.
3. In October 1988 constitutional amendments were proposed to provide for multicandidate elections. These elections to parliament were held in March 1989 with many Communist leaders voted out of office.
4. In May 1989 the first Congress of People's Deputies opened. In July 1989 a parliamentary opposition group, the Interregional Group, was formed. In December 1989 Lithuania approved a multiparty system. Lithuanian Communists voted to create a party independent from the Soviet Communist Party.
5. In January 1990 reform Communists met in Moscow to write an alternative party platform. In February a mass demonstration in Moscow demanded the end of a one-party political system. A three-day Central Committee meeting was held that agreed to a platform proposed by Gorbachev calling for an end to the Party's constitutional guarantee of power.

THE ECONOMIC SYSTEM

The leaders of the Soviet Union are committed to the view that the future of the country depends upon the Soviet economy's productivity and efficiency. Emphasis is placed on the organization of production. The organization is based on two fundamental characteristics of the Soviet economy: (1) the allocation of resources is accomplished by administrative decision rather than by a market mechanism; and (2) resource allocation is governed by a priority system that over the years has given preference to capital goods and military and scientific development over consumer goods. Because of these characteristics, consumer sovereignty, which exists when the production of goods is determined by the individual decisions made in the marketplace by millions of consumers, cannot function in the Soviet Union. Through its control over economic resources, the state can manipulate the share of gross national product allocated to consumption; through its investment policies, the state can control the amount of inputs for those sectors of the economy that supply the consumer. Nevertheless, in recent years Soviet leaders have heeded to some extent the expectations of the consumer for a higher living standard.

Economic Planning

The distinctive feature of the economic system of the Soviet Union is that it operates on the basis of comprehensive economic planning. Fundamental to centralized economic planning is public ownership of the factors of production. Public ownership has joined the multitude of industrial, agricultural, and trading enterprises together in a single economic unit. Since there is no competition among rival firms, there is no meaningful price competition. This, in turn, renders the profit motive impotent as an automatic economic regulator, which is its role in the market system of a capitalistic country. In the absence of the market system, economic planning is necessary to make the complex of Soviet enterprises function. To organize the uninterrupted operation of these enterprises, full and exact account must be taken of the national requirements and distribution channels for their particular products. Conversely, every enterprise must be constantly supplied with raw materials, fuel, plant and equipment, and trained workers, the amounts of which must also be commensurate with national needs.

An important principle of economic planning in the Soviet Union is the priority given to the development of industries that will contribute the most to the attainment of national economic and political goals. Economic plans provide for the maximum possible rate of development of targeted areas of the economy through priorities in investment, materials, labor, and financial resources. It is assumed that expansion of certain key industries, such as the chemical, oil, gas, and power industries, makes it possible to increase the overall rate of growth in industrial and agricultural production. Economic planning also has political as well as economic overtones in that priorities in past and current plans have been given to industries that make the Soviet Union strong from a military standpoint.

It is necessary to stress the fact that there is a difference between formal and actual economic plans. In practice, plans are changed often and some plans reflect simple aspirations. Targets are constantly revised to reflect changing economic conditions. As the socialist countries enter higher stages of economic development, the number of alternative uses for resources and the complexity of economic processes have greatly increased. Consequently, the negative results of errors have multiplied, threatening the economies with greater waste and dislocation than before. So the longer the planning period, the less precision can be introduced in terms of plan targets. What happens then is that planning, particularly for periods of five years or longer, is continuous; the plans are constantly supplemented and extended in the process of their implementation.

Types of Plans.   The economic plans differ in their functional character. There are physical output plans, which involve production, distribution, and investment goals; and financial plans, which are derivatives of the physical output plans. Then, too, plans differ in terms of time. Long-range plans extend for 15 to 20 years. These plans usually deal with a particular aspect of the economy, such as electrification. Medium-term plans, which cover a period of 5 to 7 years, develop targets or goals to be accomplished during this time. There are also annual plans involving production plans to be followed by Soviet enterprises and other organizational units during the year.

The annual plan can be considered an operational plan. Annual plans can be broken down further into quarterly or monthly periods. All of these plans are interconnected and related, and it is important and necessary for planning agencies to ensure their unification in order to establish a proper relationship between production and consumption and between national requirements and resources. In terms of a frame of reference for the presentation of the methodology of Soviet planning, economic planning refers primarily to physical planning, which involves product output and distribution, labor force utilization, and investment and which is developed annually. Table 12-1 illustrates an annual physical output plan.

The organization of economic planning can be divided into the following stages.

1. Drafting of the plan in conformity with the objectives of the Communist Party and the Soviet government.
2. Endorsement of the plan by relevant government administrative units.
3. Organization and control over the execution of the approved plan.

Planning in the Soviet Union is directed by the Supreme Soviet and the Council of Ministers. The actual plans are drawn up by planning bodies that may be divided into three groups—state planning bodies, ministries and departments, and the planning bodies of enterprises and organizations. The state planning bodies are the State Planning Committee (Gosplan), which is a part of the Council of Ministers of the U.S.S.R.; the state planning committees of the union and autonomous

TABLE 12-1

1985 Physical Output Plan for the Soviet Union

Type of Physical Output	Units of Output
Electricity (billions of kilowatts)	1,540
Petroleum (millions of tons)	628
Coal (millions of tons)	726
Steel pipes (millions of tons)	20
Cement (millions of tons)	132
Robots (thousands)	14
Meat (millions of tons)	9
Butter (millions of tons)	1
Milk (millions of tons)	29
New railroad lines (kilometers)	700
New hard-surfaced roads (thousands of kilometers)	12
Rolled ferrous metals (millions of tons)	109
New hospital beds (thousands)	60
Irrigated land (thousands of hectares)	663
Drained land (thousands of hectares)	695
Mineral fertilizers (millions of tons)	48

Source: John L. Scherer, U.S.S.R. Facts and Figures Annual 1985 *(Gulf Breeze, FL: Academic International Press, 1985), p. 138.*

republics; regional planning committees; and district and city planning committees. These committees draw upon the economic and cultural plans for the country as a whole and for individual republics, regions, and districts. In the ministries and departments, plans are compiled by planning boards and sections; at the enterprise level they are the responsibility of planning departments.

Gosplan. Gosplan is the agency that translates broad policy decisions made by the Council of Ministers and the Central Committee of the Communist Party into concrete programs. It is responsible for working out national economic plans of all kinds and for presenting them for review by the Council of Ministers. It is also responsible for the supervision of the plans. Gosplan is organized into various economic planning sections for the branches of the national economy. One section is responsible for sector planning and is divided into the following sectors: machine building, transportation and communications, consumer goods, agriculture, heavy industry, and electrification. Another section is responsible for the supply and distribution of materials, such as coal and metal products. This section monitors the supply of key materials.

Gosplan is also responsible for setting wholesale prices for industrial and agricultural products and for setting retail prices. Through an affiliated institute, the Scientific Research Institute of Economics, it also plays a leading role in theoretical economic research.[9] To check on Gosplan and its activities, various departments within the Secretariat of the Communist Party serve as watchdogs.

Since the Soviet economic plan covers the entire economy, it is necessary to have planning units extending down to the lowest administrative units of government. Below the national Gosplan, and subordinate to it in terms of planning, are the republic Gosplans. These Gosplans are responsible for the preparation of plans for all of the industries under republic supervision. They are also responsible for developing recommendations pertaining to the production plans of all enterprises located within their respective republics. There are also the Gosplans of the autonomous republics and regions. They are responsible for drawing up plans for industry and transportation, agriculture, social and cultural development, and regional housing and public construction. They base their summary plans on plans developed at the rural soviet levels. The planning bodies at the autonomous region and republic levels draft the plans for enterprises under their direct control and check to see that they are implemented. In addition, industrial enterprises, state farms, and transport and trading enterprises have planning departments. Their activities are guided by targets set forth in the national plan.

Gossnab. Gossnab is the State Committee on Material-Technical Supplies and is responsible for handling the distribution end of the plan. It is supposed to tie customers to suppliers at both the republic and local levels. Subject to general guide-

---

[9] Alec Nove, *The Soviet Economic System*, 2d ed. (London: George Allen & Unwin, 1981), pp. 37–40.

lines and within the limits set by central allocation, the local units of Gossnab make detailed arrangements for supplies, sometimes from warehouses they administer. Managers of enterprises are supposed to negotiate for supplies with the local Gossnab unit. Gossnab has 22 central distribution sections and each has the following responsibilities:

1. Identify special supply needs and assign priorities to such needs.
2. Make the most economical assignment of each supplier to a group of users.
3. Decide on long-term, direct supplier-user contacts among plants or enterprises.
4. Regulate the flow of products according to assigned priorities in the plan.[10]

Drafting of the Plan.   Control figures are drawn up by Gosplan before the five-year plan is drafted. These figures determine the principal trends and general scale of economic development planned for the duration of the plan. They cover the volume and distribution of national income, the overall volume of capital investment and industrial production in the more important branches of industry, the volume of output and state purchases of farm produce, the volume of retail trade, expected increases in labor productivity, and the monetary income of the population. These control figures are based on the economy's achievements in preceding time periods and on estimates of future labor availability and progress in technology and labor productivity.

Stages of the Planning Cycle.   When the plan is designed, it is a draft plan that outlines the basic economic development tasks for the plan period. This drafting phase transforms government and party objectives into numerical targets that determine the amount of resources to be allocated for specific purposes.

When the draft plan has been completed, it is sent for approval to the Central Committee of the Communist Party and to the Council of Ministers of the U.S.S.R. After the plan is approved, it is broken down by sections and sent to the appropriate national ministry or department for consideration. It is also sent to the Gosplans of the republics, which are supposed to prepare plans for the economic programs of their particular republics and ministries. The draft plan is then sent to the regional and local planning commissions and to enterprises. The purpose of this dissemination is to provide information that can be used as a basis for plan formulation at the enterprise level and at the various local, regional, and national administrative levels. An enterprise, for example, would receive information as to the kinds, quantities, and qualities of goods it was expected to produce, quantities and kinds of labor, power, materials, and capital goods that would be supplied to it, estimates of the productivity the workers should achieve, and estimates of the workers' incomes and living standards.

---

[10] Sumer C. Aggerwal, "Managing Material Shortages: The Russian Way," *Columbia Journal of World Business* (Fall 1980), pp. 26–37.

After the control figures have been made available to the various economic units and the lower echelons of government, there is a plan counterdesign that starts with the formulation of plans by industrial and trade enterprises, state farms, and other local economic units. These plans cover all phases of their operations in great detail. For example, plans of enterprises set forth what they are to make, in what quantities, and by what combinations of labor and capital. These are target plans that are supposed to serve as a framework for annual operating plans. The plans then travel upward to their eventual integration in the national plan by Gosplan. At each administrative stage the plans cumulate into a larger whole. From the primary producing units—industrial, agricultural, and trading enterprises—the plans move through local soviets and the various ministries and planning agencies at the union republic and national level. Gosplan has the final responsibility for the preparation of the overall national plan. The problem is reconciling all draft plans into one national plan.

The process of reconciliation is the third stage of the planning cycle. Gosplan must adjust Politburo objectives from above with the aggregation of plans from below. It is also at this stage that various financial plans are developed; they represent a counterpart to the main economic plan, which is expressed in physical terms. The major financial plans are the state budget and the cash plan and credit plan of Gosbank. Each plan exercises important control functions that will be discussed later in the chapter.[11] The financial plans are approved and developed by the Ministry of Finance and Gosbank and are reviewed by Gosplan in its preparation of the national economic plan. When the plan is prepared, it is sent to the Council of Ministers and the Central Committee of the Communist Party for ratification. Finally, the plan, with its tasks for each administrative and economic level, is passed down the line until it reaches the enterprise. The whole Soviet planning process is complex, for there has to be a flow of operational directives to the thousands of operating enterprises. Plans for various sectors must be coordinated with those of other sectors.

The Use of Material Balances.   The basic method of Soviet economic planning has involved the use of material balances. These balances, usually presented in physical terms, represent an intended relationship between supplies and their allocation for particular commodities. Material balances are drawn up for all important types of industrial and agricultural products. An example of the use of material balances is presented in Table 12-2.

However, given the complexities of the production and distribution process, the material balance method has become cumbersome. Thus it has been replaced to some extent with input-output analysis, which consists of working out a matrix

---

[11] There is also the consolidated financial plan, which includes the state budget and the cash and credit plans of Gosbank. In addition, it includes the profits of all state enterprises and allowances for depreciation, increases in savings bank deposits, and other financial resources.

TABLE 12-2

Example of a Material Balance Sheet[a]

Product:
Resources:

1. Stocks at the beginning of the year
2. Output, total
    a) State-owned enterprises (subdivided by government department, i.e. ministries or county authorities)
    b) Cooperative enterprises
    c) Capitalist enterprises
    d) Individual production
3. Imports
    a) From socialist countries
    b) From nonsocialist countries
4. Other resources
   Resources, total

Amounts:
Distribution:

1. Productive consumption (by government department, i.e. by ministries or county authorities)
2. Investment
3. Consumer needs
4. Public consumption
5. Exports
    a) To socialist countries
    b) To nonsocialist countries
6. Balance reserves
7. Stocks at the end of the year
   Distribution, total

---

[a] The balance sheet is broken down to the level of three-month periods for the management of plan execution.

of flows. These flows represent an array of relationships among economic sectors. The economy is divided into many sectors, each supposed to achieve an annual output of a given quantity. Each sector uses a certain portion of its annual output, and the remaining portion is available to be used as inputs for other sectors. The part of production over and above that used in the economic sector during the year constitutes net material production. This amount is used for production of final goods for consumption and capital investment.

Economic planning has to reconcile a number of flows, including production, consumption, and saving; the use of labor resources; the distribution of national income; and personal money income and expenditure. The total amount of wages to be paid and the production necessary to support the wages depend on the division of national income between savings and consumption and, further, of consumption between social consumption and wages. This leads to the problem of relating the total flow of wages to the total value of consumer goods and services. The maintenance of balance between incomes from work and the resources allocated to personal consumption is a part of distribution policy and especially of wage planning. Because prices of consumer goods and services may change, this also involves the problem of maintaining the purchasing power of wages and the relationship between nominal and real wages.

Conditions for Planning.   The essential requirements for centralized planning are present in the Soviet Union. The state is in full control of the land, factories, transportation, and raw materials necessary for the production of all commodities. It controls the quality and quantity of the labor force, which enables it to supply the economy with the necessary labor to fill planned targets. Through control of money and credit, it finances construction and the operation of enterprises in accordance with the financial plan. The state, through Gosplan, Gosbank, and other organizations, can maintain control over the plan's execution. Gosplan in particular has the responsibility for checking on the progress made in implementing the plan. This is done through the hierarchy of planning offices that exist from the top to the lower administrative levels of government. The Communist Party also performs a control function in that its members hold positions of authority in all enterprises; they can supervise the implementation of the plan at the enterprise level.

Limitations of Planning.   Nevertheless, the whole process of planning has its limitations. The plan may estimate that workers, given certain supplies of machinery, land, equipment, materials, and energy, will turn out a specific number of units of product of definite quality in a given period, but the results of the workers' activities may be anything but the expected results. There is also a certain lack of coordination and inefficiency in planning that can be attributed to the comprehensive bureaucratic structure. Enterprises are separated from the decision-making agencies at the top by a number of intermediary agencies. This means that they are separated from other enterprises by agencies that must check purchase and sales requests and disburse funds. Another defect in planning is that the setting of general production norms or indexes fails to take consider differences in the characteristics of various enterprises. Also, over the years since planning was developed, the Soviet Union has grown into a complex and modern industrial nation with increasingly sophisticated production techniques and greater demands for quality specifications of materials. This, in itself, has complicated the central planning process and has caused a need for more detailed microplanning.

Public Finance

The operation of any modern state requires the collection of large sums of money to finance public services and pay for the general administrative expenses of government. This is as true of the Soviet Union as it is of any capitalistic country. However, there are great differences in the ways in which the two forms of economic organization acquire and dispose of their revenues. Both the Soviet and Western capitalistic governments necessarily devote substantial portions of their national incomes to general administrative expenses, to war and defense measures, and to various forms of social services, but in the case of the Soviet state, additional sums must also be made available to finance industry operation.

The Soviet State Budget.   In the Soviet Union the national budget is of paramount importance because it provides for the accumulation and distribution of so much of the national income. The national budget, or Soviet State Budget, is a consolidated budget that provides for the revenues and expenditures of the national, republic, and local units of government. It is also closely related in terms of revenues and expenditures to the national economic plan. It performs an important allocative function in that it is the major instrument for financing many types of investment and for controlling the use of investment in accordance with planning objectives. The budget is also instrumental in decisions to divide the national product between consumption and investment.

The Soviet State Budget is prepared annually by the Ministry of Finance. It includes the all-union or central budget, the budgets of the autonomous republics, and the budgets of regional, urban, and rural administrative entities. Republic and local authorities prepare their own budgets in conformance with the objectives of the national economic plan.[12] When the tentative budgets are prepared, they are transmitted upward—local government budgets to their respective republics' ministry of finance and republic budgets to the Union Ministry of Finance—and coordinated at each step with the national economic plan. When the total budget—national, republic, and local—is integrated, it is sent by the Ministry of Finance to the Council of Ministers of the Soviet Union for approval. After the Council of Ministers has made changes and recommendations, the Soviet State Budget is then presented by the Ministry of Finance to the Supreme Soviet for final approval before it becomes law and is published. The budget often provides an indication of Soviet economic policies for the coming year, for it is a part of the country's overall economic and financial plan and reflects yearly priorities for resource allocation.

Government Revenues.   Table 12-3 presents the principal sources of revenue for the state budget. Most of the revenue of the budget is derived from national output rather than from direct taxes on the incomes of individuals. The two most important sources of revenue are the turnover tax and deductions from the profits of state-owned enterprises. Revenue is obtained by setting the prices of goods at levels higher than the cost of production and appropriating the difference.

The Turnover Tax.   The turnover tax is the largest single source of revenue in the state budget. It was established in 1930 when Soviet industry, unable to support

---

[12] Only the principal headings or expenditures in the budgets require ultimate approval at the top of the budgetary hierarchy. Local and republic governments have some autonomy concerning expenditures for specific items such as fire protection and repairs of drains.

TABLE 12-3
Planned Revenues of the Soviet State Budget for 1985 (billions of dollars)

Social Sector		$612.0
Turnover tax	$175.1	
Payments from profits	171.7	
Income tax for collective farmers	2.0	
Other receipts, including social insurance taxes	263.2	
Private Sector		53.5
State income taxes	$51.5	
Other receipts	2.0	
Total Revenues		$665.5

Source: John L. Scherer, U.S.S.R. Facts and Figures Annual 1985 (Gulf Breeze, FL: Academic International Press, 1985), p. 148.

itself, needed additional revenue for further expansion. The tax is a flexible and varied portion of the price and is delivered directly to the state budget in accordance with sales of goods on which the tax is levied. The tax is collected by wholesale distributing organizations, individual enterprises, and procurement organizations dealing with consumer goods and foodstuffs. The burden of the turnover tax falls ultimately on the Russian consumer, so it represents a part of the flow of funds between the state and households.

The Soviet turnover tax performs several important economic functions. In addition to being a principal source of revenue for the government, it also absorbs the excess purchasing power of consumers. The national production plans provide that a given amount of goods be made available to consumers annually. On the other hand, in order to maintain incentives and partly because of errors in planning, consumers may receive more purchasing power than can be absorbed by the goods made available to them at controlled prices. This excess of purchasing power is siphoned off by the turnover tax, which has the impact of an excise or sales tax as it is applied primarily to consumer goods. It is not a fixed-rate tax, but rather a tax where the desired yield determines the rate. It is varied in response to particular supply and demand conditions. Since the turnover tax is tied to output and is collected either directly at factories or at wholesale distribution outlets, it guarantees a steady flow of funds to the government and is easy to collect and inexpensive to administer. Moreover, it is a flexible device for establishing equilibrium prices on the basis of the level of output of consumer goods and disposable income.

Payments from Profits. Another important source of revenue in the state budget is payments from profits of state-owned enterprises and organizations. In fact, the turnover tax and payments from profits account for more than one-half of the total government revenues. In 1985, for example, the turnover tax accounted for $175.1 billion and payments from profits accounted for $171.7 billion out of planned total budget revenues of $665.5 billion. Thus, most of the Soviet tax burden can be seen as equal to the total difference between production cost and final sales prices of all goods and services.

Payments from profits are paid on actual rather than planned profits of enterprises, and payments vary from industry to industry. Most state enterprises operate on the basis of what is called *khozraschet financing*.This means that they sell their products for money and use the resulting proceeds to finance normal operating expenses. However, the typical enterprise receives extensive support, including the major share of all capital investment, from the state budget. The rate for a particular enterprise is fixed on the basis of its financial plan for the year. Each enterprise has the right to retain part of its profits for such purposes as expanding its fixed and financial capital, and the government takes this into consideration. Nevertheless, the amount of profits returned to the state is high; it can be as much as 80 percent of total profits.

Retained profits can be used to finance an enterprise's material incentives fund, which is a part of the new economic reforms that have taken place in the Soviet Union. Their purpose is to provide an incentive system of bonuses to workers as a reward for increased productivity. Retained earnings are also used to finance an enterprise's social-cultural and production development funds. The former is used to support various services provided to workers by an enterprise, and the latter provides a source of revenue for the expansion of fixed capital. Depreciation deductions also provide revenue for the same purpose.

Social Insurance Taxes.   The remainder of the revenues obtained from the operation of the national economy comes from social insurance taxes paid by enterprises, taxes levied on organizations such as collective farms, and income taxes levied on individuals. The social insurance taxes are levied as a percentage of wages and salaries and vary from industry to industry. The revenue is paid into a state social insurance budget administered by the trade unions. This budget is consolidated with the state budget, and revenue is transferred to republic and local budgets.

Personal Income Tax.   Direct taxes on the population are relatively unimportant in the Soviet revenue system. The personal income tax accounted for only 7.8 percent of the planned total state budget revenues in 1985. The tax is progressive in nature; in 1983 it ranged from a minimum of 0.35 percent to a maximum of 13 percent of monthly earnings. It is withheld by the enterprises and paid to the Ministry of Finance. The income tax is differentiated between economic groups, with certain groups, such as workers and salaried employees, paying a lower tax than others, such as doctors, lawyers, and artisans with incomes from private practice. The personal income tax was supposed to have been abolished in the Soviet Union by 1965; however, this has not yet occurred. In 1983 the amount of income exempted from the tax was 70 rubles ($118) a month.

There is a rural counterpart to the income tax, a so-called agricultural tax levied on farmers who earn an income from their private plots of land. Its purpose is to discourage farmers from spending too much time on their own land at the expense of their work on collective farms.[13] The tax rate is progressive and is based on the quantity of land in use rather than on the return on the land. As a source of revenue, the agricultural tax is of little importance, but it has a control function of regulating work.

Government Expenditures.   Expenditures of the state are presented in Table 12-4. There are four main categories of expenditures—expenditures to finance the national economy, social-cultural measures, national defense, and administration. Expenditures for financing the national economy and social-cultural expenditures account for almost 90 percent of total outlays.

Financing the National Economy.   Expenditures to finance the national economy accounted for approximately 56 percent of planned total budget expenditures in 1985. These expenditures include allocations to enterprises for capital investments and financial capital. Capital goods and construction industries are the major recipients of budget funds for investment purposes, for the government concentrates on growth-inducing investment in areas that constitute the base of economic power. Appropriations from the state budget are used to finance the construction of transportation facilities, investment in state farms, and housing construction. State farms are government-owned and -operated and are a major recipient of budgetary funds.

TABLE 12-4
Planned Expenditures of the Soviet State Budget for 1985 (billions of dollars)

Financing the national economy		$377.4
Social-cultural measures		210.0
Education, science, and culture	$84.3	
Health and physical culture	29.0	
Social security and social insurance	98.0	
Defense		33.3
Administration		5.1
Residual[a]		39.1
Total expenditures		$664.9
Budget surplus		$ 0.5

[a] This includes such items as budget allocations for increasing credit resources of long-term investment banks.
Source: John L. Scherer, U.S.S.R. Facts and Figures Annual 1985 *(Gulf Breeze, FL: Academic International Press, 1985), p. 148.*

---

[13] If farmers fail to work the stipulated minimum number of labor days or workdays on the collective farms, the agricultural tax can be increased by as much as 50 percent.

Housing construction also enjoys a high priority in terms of allocation of budgetary funds because there is an acute housing shortage in the Soviet Union, particularly in the large cities. Funds are allocated to housing construction in two ways: to construction enterprises for building apartments and other dwellings and to individual home builders in the form of credits.

The state budget redistributes income within the economy. Payments from profits represent a withdrawal of income from the economy, but the funds reenter the economy through the budget as expenditures used to finance capital investment, increases in financial capital, and housing. The turnover tax can also be considered a device used to reallocate resources from consumption to investment.

Social and Cultural Measures.   Expenditures for social and cultural measures, including education and training, public health, physical culture, and social insurance benefits, accounted for 32 percent of total expenditures in the 1985 planned state budget. A wide variety of social services are financed under the three subcategories of social and cultural measures—education, science, and culture; health and physical culture; and social welfare measures.

Expenditures on education, science, and culture include building and maintaining schools, paying teacher's salaries, and providing financial support for students. Expenditures for science include the support of scientific research. Certain defense expenditures are included under this category. Expenditures on culture include support for museums, expositions, and the performing arts. Other expenditures that are financed under education, science, and culture include the costs of disseminating Soviet propaganda throughout the world.

The second subcategory of social and cultural expenditures includes spending on health and physical culture. Health expenditures cover outlays for medical and hospital facilities, medical personnel training, and medical research. Physical culture expenditures support athletic programs that are carried on throughout the Soviet Union. Unlike the United States, the Soviet Union subsidizes sports activities and provides special support for its better athletes. In fact, success in sports, particularly in the Olympic Games, is of prime value to the Soviet Union from the standpoint of propaganda. Special sports schools are maintained throughout the Soviet Union.

The third subcategory, social security and social insurance, represents expenditures for old-age and disability pensions, sickness and maternity benefits, and family allowances. The retirement age is 60 for male industrial workers with 25 years or more of work experience and 55 years for women workers with at least 10 years of work experience. Sickness and maternity benefits are also payable to all persons under the Soviet social insurance program. Paid vacations cover 15 working days as a minimum. Pensions are also paid to Russian workers, including those on collective farms, who become disabled as a result of work injuries. Temporary disability benefits are paid from the first day of injury until recovery. Finally, family allowances are paid to families with two or more children, and there is an income supplement for those whose per capita income falls below 50 rubles a month.

National Defense.   Outlays for national defense account for about 5 percent of planned total budget expenditures in 1985. However, the amount of $33.3 billion understates the amount that will actually be spent for defense-related activities because a substantial proportion of military-space research is carried out under expenditures for science. These expenditures include outlays for research and development for complex military equipment, such as aircraft and missiles, and for nuclear energy and space activities. The general defense category includes monetary and material allowances for armed forces personnel, payment for supplies and repair of combat equipment, maintenance of military institutions and schools, and military construction. When general defense expenditures are added to outlays for scientific research related directly or indirectly to national defense, total defense expenditures have been about 20 percent of the state budget and around 14 to 18 percent of Soviet gross national product.[14]

Soviet defense expenditures have placed a burden on the economy. For one thing, the best human and material resources are channeled into defense-related activities. The huge amounts of human and material resources claimed by the military and space establishment have been particularly detrimental to agriculture. Outside of defense activities, the economy has generally been inefficient. With a labor force 45 percent larger and about equal real capital investment, the Soviet Union provides its population with less than half the goods and services available in the United States. The resources foregone for defense could have resulted in a higher standard of living for the Soviet consumer. The most apparent tradeoff has been between defense weapons and producer durable goods, with decreases in the latter resulting in a smaller capital stock, one of the primary ingredients in the growth process. So it can be argued that Soviet defense expenditures have had an adverse effect on the country's economic growth rate.[15]

Administration.   Expenditures for administration is the final major category of expenditures. It includes financing for local and central government agencies including planning and financial bodies, ministries, government departments, and the courts and judicial organs. The Soviet state budget covers a scope of activities that is much broader than equivalent activities financed in the budgets of capitalistic governments. The state budget covers the planned expenditures for all of the national, regional, and local Soviet governments.

Money and Banking

Money plays a subordinate role in the Soviet economy. To some extent this reflects the traditional Marxist view of money, which largely represented a reaction against

---

[14] Central Intelligence Agency, National Foreign Assessment Center, *Handbook of Economic Statistics* (Washington: USGPO, 1985), p. 64.

[15] Henry F. Becker, "Soviet Power and Intentions: Military-Economic Choices," *Soviet Economy in a Time of Change* (Washington: Joint Economic Committee, 1979), pp. 341–45.

capitalism, where money reaches its peak of development and influence. Moreover, primary reliance on planning is in real terms; investment funds are channeled through the state budget rather than through financial markets. As long as plan balancing is done in physical terms, there is little need for prices in planning. Since prices are generally fixed, money values rarely indicate the value of goods in terms of real cost, and are therefore an uncertain guide to investment decisions. Money also does not provide automatic access to goods in the capital investment market. First, there must be authorization for the goods to be produced; second, in addition to money there must be plan authorization to acquire the goods. The Gosbank, acting as the agent of the planning authorities, allocates credit to enterprises in conformance with the plan.

This is not to say, however, that money is of no importance. Soviet money has many of the same functions as money in a market system. Within and outside the state sector, money serves as a unit of account; that is, all goods and services that are bought and sold are valued in monetary units. Money also functions as a medium of exchange in the Soviet Union in that wages and salaries are paid in terms of currency, and receivers of money can use it to purchase goods and services. However, the ownership of money does not give individuals command over the allocation of resources as it does under a market system, for resource allocation is determined by the national plan and not by the price system. Economic reforms, even to the limited extent they have been implemented, imply a more important role for money, particularly in the area of pricing.

Similar to the control over other sectors of the Soviet economy, there is a plan to control the monetary aspects—the financial plan—that parallels and is co-ordinated with the production and distribution plans for each period of time. The three essential components of the financial plan are the following: the state budget, which is responsible for resource allocation between consumption and investment; the credit plan, which regulates the granting of credits by the banking system to enterprises during a stipulated period of time; and the cash plan, which controls the supply of money in circulation. Through the financial plan, the planners seek to coordinate the operations of the monetary and financial aspects of the economy with the production of physical goods and services. The financial plan is calcu-lated prior to the production plan because it determines the income and expenditure patterns of all important sectors of the Soviet economy.

The Soviet banking system has the following characteristics.

1. Banking is centralized as a monopoly of the government. Through the direct operation of the banking system, the government determines the volume of credit and hence the money supply.
2. The banking system is subordinate to the economic plan. It serves as an in-strument of control through the verification of planned transactions.
3. Banks specialize according to functions. There are banks for savings and for investment. There is, however, a trend toward bank consolidation, and savings banks have become a part of the State Bank (Gosbank). For all practical pur-

poses, Gosbank is the banking system of the Soviet Union because it provides the cash and credit needs of the country.

The State Bank (Gosbank).   The Gosbank is the keystone of the Soviet banking system. Within the framework of the centrally planned economy, it performs a number of functions.

1. It acts as the fiscal agent of the government in that it receives all tax revenues and pays out budgetary appropriations to enterprises and institutions.
2. It is responsible for granting short-term or commercial credit to all types of enterprises.
3. It carries the accounts of all business enterprises in the country. Each enterprise has an account in the Gosbank that is supposed to supply it with financial capital. When a sale is made between two industrial enterprises, the bank simply deducts the amount of the sale from the buyer's account and adds it to that of the seller. This, as will be explained later, gives the central government control over the performance of each enterprise within the economic system.
4. It is responsible for the preparation of the credit and cash plans that are a part of the financial plan prepared by the Ministry of Finance. In this capacity, the bank is exercising a planning function for currency needs and credit expansion.
5. It is also responsible for providing currency and for holding all precious metals and foreign currencies owned by the Soviet government. As the bank of issue, it can issue money and withdraw it from circulation, thereby helping to regulate the supply of money available to enterprises and individuals in accordance with the cash plan.

Planning Function.   One of the most important functions of the Gosbank involves economic planning. The Gosbank has the responsibility for the preparation of the credit and cash plans. Loans made by the bank are carried out in connection with the credit plan and are granted for the fulfillment of the production and distribution plans. Through its quarterly cash plans, the bank has a significant influence in determining the extent and composition of note issue. The purpose of the credit and cash plans is to adjust the supply of money to the real output goals of the national economic plan and to prevent expenditures outside of planning purposes. The credit and cash plans are used to implement the physical output plan and to preserve price stability. Both types of plans are used not only by the Soviet Union but by the other centrally planned economies of Eastern Europe and by China.[16]

The *credit plan* determines the amount of short- and long-term credit allocated to all enterprises and collective farms in the economy during the period of the

---

[16] The banking system of the Soviet Union is a model followed by other Eastern European Communist countries, with the exception of Yugoslavia.

national economic plan. Both types of credit plans involve the preparation of a statement showing the sources and uses of funds.

The short-term credit plan is designed to provide loans for such purposes as financing the acquisition of inventories by enterprises. Other uses of funds include loans for the payment of wages, loans for temporary needs, loans against drafts in the process of collection, and loans for technological development. The sources of funds used to provide short-term credit are state budgetary contributions, bank reserves and profits, balances of credit institutions such as savings banks, deposit balances of enterprises, and net changes in currency in circulation. It can be seen that the purpose of the plan is to collate the short-term needs of enterprises and collective farms with the supply of credit. This collation is carried down to the regional and local levels of the economy through the use of regional credit plans.

The long-term credit plan is prepared annually and is designed to provide loans for both productive and nonproductive investments with completion dates of several years or longer. The funds to finance fixed investment are obtained from three sources: loan repayments by collective farms, individuals, consumer cooperatives, and municipal enterprises; funds from the state budget, which include allocations for such purposes as construction, home building, and agriculture, and also temporary Treasury loans; and subsidies from the union republics, used to defray the cost of home building. The funds are used to provide loans to collective farms, individuals, consumer cooperatives, and municipal enterprises, and to repay temporary Treasury loans.

The *cash plan* controls the amount of currency in circulation. It is prepared quarterly and consists of a statement showing the inflows and outflows of money. The inflow of money represents deposits in the Gosbank. These deposits represent currency receipts from a wide variety of sources—tax payments, deposits to the accounts of collective farms, receipts from municipal services, receipts from retail sales, receipts from amusement and personal services enterprises, post office and savings banks receipts, and receipts from railroad, water, and air transportation. Monetary outflows under the cash plan go for wage payments, pension allowances and insurance payments, payments for agricultural products and raw materials, consumer loans, expenditures for individual housing construction, and cash disbursements by various economic organizations. The outflow side of the balance statement represents most of the money income payments of the Soviet Union. Wage payments constitute four-fifths of total monetary outflows of the cash plan. Inflows into the Gosbank represent the deposit of receipts from consumer expenditures that result from wage and other income payments on the outflow side. Thus, the cash plan is an instrument used to control the performance of the consumer sector of the Soviet economy in terms of the disbursement and use of money.

Control Function. The Gosbank also exercises important control over the operations of Soviet enterprises. All financial transactions of enterprises are legally required to be accomplished through the Gosbank. This affords the bank an opportunity to view the economic performance of an enterprise with regard to real and financial plan fulfillment. Inasmuch as most transactions between enterprises are concluded in terms of bank transfers, the flow of goods is necessarily accompanied by a counterflow of funds. The very status of an enterprise's account at the bank is an indicator of its efficiency and production. If it breaks even on its operation, its account should neither increase nor diminish. If it makes planned or unplanned profits, its balance at the bank will grow; but if it operates inefficiently and sustains losses, its balance will decrease.

Financial transactions must be executed through accounts established in the Gosbank where not only the transactions but also the performance of the units carrying out the transactions comes under the close scrutiny of bank officials. This procedure is not in reality basically different from capitalistic bank settlement procedures; most transactions in capitalistic countries are also carried out through bank accounts, though these transactions are not as closely examined by capitalistic commercial banks. In the Soviet Union, every purchase or sale of goods and raw materials must be reflected in changes in the accounts of the enterprises involved. This settlement process gives the Gosbank its unique position to carry out many of its control functions.

Provision of Credit.   Short-term credit accounts for an overwhelming percentage of the total credit granted by the Gosbank. The most important purpose of short-term credit is to finance accumulations of inventories by enterprises. Another important use of short-term credit is to finance accounts receivable, which provides financial capital to the seller of goods while payments are being collected. Short-term loans must be secured by real assets, such as goods in process or finished goods, and must carry a fixed maturity date.

Interest rates, which are practically uniform as to borrower, are applied to all short-term loans, and penalty rates are charged on overdue loans. Interest proceeds are a source of revenue to cover the operating expenses of the Gosbank. Since short-term loans can be made only for purposes consistent with the credit plan, interest does not play an important role as an allocator of resources in the Soviet Union.

The Investment Bank.   The Investment Bank is an agent for the disbursement of budgetary funds in the form of grants to enterprises in accordance with their investment plans. Although most of its financing is long term, it provides short-term working capital loans to the construction industry. The Investment Bank derives its funds from state budget grants, which constitute the bulk of its investment assets, and from depreciation allowances and profits of enterprises. It is also responsible for the following functions.

1. Financing cooperative housing construction and the long-term credit for individual housing construction and repair of houses in urban areas.
2. Financing the construction of schools, hospitals, and the like in urban areas.

3. Investment financing in all state-owned sectors of the economy, except agriculture, transportation, communication, and state-owned housing construction.
4. Providing short-term credit for contract organizations working on construction projects for which it handles budget grants.
5. Controlling the accounts and expenditures of funds for capital repair and maintenance by contract organizations in the construction field.

The Foreign Bank.   Another Soviet financial institution is the Foreign Bank, which has been in operation since 1924. It is responsible for financing Soviet foreign trade and for carrying out a large part of Soviet international settlement operations. It is also designated as an agent for the Gosbank in many dealings with regard to gold and foreign exchange. It provides the state budget with any surplus of export proceeds over the amount export producers would receive based on the domestic value of their products and pays subsidies to producers when export prices are below domestic costs. The Foreign Exchange Bank is organized as a shareholding bank with the Gosbank owning two-thirds of the shares. It has few offices of its own in the Soviet Union and, therefore, carries out its operations in the offices of the Gosbank; abroad, it carries out its business through local correspondence banks.

The Soviet Enterprise

The enterprise is the basic link in the general system of Soviet production management and operates as a legal entity engaged in production activity under the national economic plan. It is obligated to fulfill its own production plan, which contains certain targets or success indicators that should be attained. It is required to operate under a profit-and-loss accounting system, and it has fixed and financial capital that form the basis of its statutory fund, the size of which is shown on its balance sheet. It can decide how best to use the fixed and financial capital assigned to it, providing that each is used for purposes stipulated in the production plan. An enterprise also has the right to make capital investments from funds that are set aside for amortization purposes and to fix the prices of its products within the limits set by the economic plan.

Organization of an Enterprise.   In general, a Soviet enterprise is organized along the following lines.[17] There is a director appointed by the state to run the enterprise. This director is governed from above by directives and rules of behavior that guide all decisions. However, the director is not rigidly circumscribed as to what can be done, but rather is somewhat free to operate in any manner as long as it is within the general framework of the national economic plan and the enterprise's op-

[17] The Communist Party controls all appointments to important positions through the nomenklatura (patronage) system, meaning appointees have to be either members of the Communist Party or in good standing with the party.

erating plan. The director can influence the contents of the operating plan through familiarity with the resource needs and product specifications of the enterprise. The Soviet planning system, of necessity, has to permit a certain degree of managerial autonomy, for it is impossible to supervise in detail the operation of thousands of enterprises. Caution, rather than risk taking and innovation, appears to be an important characteristic of Soviet enterprise directors; it is easier and safer to work within established production procedures in the fulfillment of the operating plan.

Since the Soviet reward system has favored directors who fulfill or overfulfill their plans, there have been frequent unfavorable results. Directors have often claimed overall plan fulfillment when in fact the production included subquality output, incomplete items, or an incorrect assortment of goods. To fulfill their plans, directors have often concentrated on goods of high value or items that are easy to produce. This subterfuge is fairly difficult to detect, but the Soviet authorities are aware of it. Economic reforms have drastically reduced the number of targets or success indicators with which a director has to contend. Nevertheless, there is a community of interest, which tends to favor plan fulfillment regardless of the method involved, that binds the director and others who are directly associated with the enterprise.

The Tekhpromfinplan.   Each Soviet enterprise has to prepare what is called a *tekh-promfinplan*, which is its operating plan for the year.[18] The tekhpromfinplan is a consolidated plan that includes the financial, output, and investment plans of the enterprise. It is prepared twice. The first is a preliminary draft and the second is a formally approved economic document. It is supposed to be developed within the framework of the long-term or five-year plan, which is not only developed for the economy as a whole, but for each enterprise as well. However, operational targets and the allocation of resources for an enterprise are determined for the most part in the annual plan. The plan also functions on a quarterly and monthly basis.

In terms of success, an enterprise is judged primarily by the volume of its sales and amount of its profit, which includes savings made from economies in production. Constraints are placed on an enterprise in the form of fixed prices for both inputs and outputs and in limitations in the selection of inputs allocated to it. All prices, with the exception of those in the free agricultural market, are set by the government. In setting prices, an allowance is made for profits expressed as a percentage of average production cost for an entire industry. Individual enterprises will have differing rates of profits because of differences in production costs. *Profits*, then, can be defined in terms of the Soviet enterprise as the difference between its total income from sales and its cost of production. In its annual operating plan, an enterprise lists its expected or planned profits as a percentage of total production costs. Its planned profits may be more or less than its actual profits.

---

[18] David Lane, *Soviet Economy & Society* (London: Basil Blackwell, 1985), p. 21.

AGRICULTURE

Agriculture is controlled by the government through national economic planning. The supply and price of inputs, the share of output marketed, and the prices paid for agricultural output, as well as farm income and expenditures, are regulated by the plan. Overall output goals are established for agricultural products that are to be delivered to the government. These goals are disseminated downward by Gosplan to the Ministries of Production and Procurements in each republic and to lower administrative units in the provinces and districts. Given the goals, which are supplemented by local requirements, each state farm and collective farm has to formulate a production plan. When this is done, each plan goes up the administrative line—district, province, and republic—to be examined and combined with other plans. Finally, the combined plans reach Gosplan for approval. Gosplan is also responsible for the determination of the production and use of such agricultural inputs as machinery and fertilizer.

State Farms

As originally set up, the state farms were extremely large. They were intended to increase agricultural production through economies of scale by utilizing modern, efficient farming techniques and by serving as experimental stations and model agricultural centers. The state farm remains the highest form of a socialized agricultural unit and enjoys a favored position in Soviet agriculture. In recent years the number of state farms has increased considerably because some collective farms have been converted into state farms. Also, a number of specialized meat, dairy, and vegetable state farms have been created around major urban centers. In terms of physical output, they account for one-fourth of total agricultural output—an amount adversely affected by the fact that many state farms are established in areas of low productivity.

State farms sell their produce to the government for processing and distribution through state stores, for stockpiling, and for export. The arrangement between state farms and the government is a contract that specifies the price to be paid for the commodity produced and the delivery date. There is usually a basic procurement price, subject to some regional variation, for each commodity. Prices are used as incentives for changes in production. For example, if an increase in the production of dairy products or meat is desired, prices are raised. In this way, prices perform a function in allocating resources that is similar to their role in a market economy. Prices are also set at levels that reflect, at least in part, differences in average production costs on state farms operating in different areas of the country. Lower prices are paid in areas with more productive land, reflecting the fact that no charge is made for land rent.

Collective Farms

Members of a collective farm are not paid wages, but share in the income of the individual collective farm. This income depends directly upon the crops produced.

After certain deductions are made from the harvest, the remainder is distributed in kind among the collective farmers or is sold for cash, which is then distributed. However, with recent agricultural reforms, there has been a shift to a regular cash wage paid on a monthly basis. This reflects an attempt on the part of the government to use similar methods of wage payments for both collective and state farm workers.

Investment in collective farms is not financed out of the state budget, but from the income of the individual collective farm. From this income, the collective farm must pay an income tax and various current expenses, including those for administrative, educational, and cultural purposes. An undivided surplus must also be set up to cover necessary capital expenditures.

Private Plots

Private plots represent the third form of agriculture in the Soviet Union. They can be divided into three categories: plots operated by state farm workers, plots operated by collective farm workers, and plots operated by workers in urban areas.[19] Although dwarfed in physical size by the state and collective farms, the private plots account for an inordinately large share of agricultural output. They account for less than three percent of the land under cultivation, but contribute substantially to the production of livestock, dairy, and truck garden products. Most of the products produced in the private plots are high-value products. Approximately one-third of the total Soviet Union production of meat and milk and two-thirds of the eggs and potatoes come from private plots.

SUMMARY

At the time that the author finished this chapter, politics in the Soviet Union was in such a state of flux that it was difficult to keep up. One thing that can be said for sure is that the Communist Party is rapidly losing control of the country. Opposition parties are being formed, and the general public is becoming increasingly more hostile to the Communist Party. Gorbachev may hold it together for a while, but its future is in doubt.

In the Soviet Union central economic planning is responsible for resource allocation based on the public ownership of the factors of production. However, the size and complexity of the Soviet Union make it difficult for planning to operate efficiently. Economic planning consists of a system of plans. There is a single national plan for the economic development of the country and a subset of plans for different sectors of the economy and for different geographic areas.

Economic planning can be divided into long-term and annual planning. The basic form of long-term planning is the five-year plan, in which important tar-

---

[19] There are limits on the size of private plots held and operated by individuals. For example, workers in collective farms are entitled to private plots up to 1.25 acres, and workers in state farms are entitled to plots up to 0.75 acres. These limitations are subject to change with reforms.

gets are established. The long-term plan is the principal form of state economic planning. Long-term economic planning is essentially investment planning, and annual planning is basically production planning. These operational plans are particularly important at the enterprise level.

Public finance in the Soviet Union occupies a much more prominent role in the economy than it does in the economies of the United States and Western Europe. The state budget is very important, for through it flows a large part of national income. The budget is related to the financial plan of the Soviet Union, which it uses primarily as a check on the operation of the basic plan, which is expressed in physical value terms. The two main sources of state budget revenues are the turnover tax and payments from the profits of state-owned enterprises. The turnover tax is used to regulate profits and to maintain a balance between aggregate demand and the available supply of consumer goods. Budgetary expenditures include allocations for capital investment and for financial capital for enterprises. Expenditures on social welfare measures also constitute a major expenditure item in the state budget.

Gosbank is the principal instrument of the banking system in the Soviet Union and can be called a monobank because it performs the functions of both central and commercial banks. It is the collection agent for the payment of taxes and other revenues by state enterprises and other organizations. It also serves as a control mechanism to ensure that the flow of funds between enterprises accords with the objectives of the national plan. Gosbank plays an important role in economic planning in that it prepares the credit and cash plans, which are a part of the financial plan.

REVIEW QUESTIONS

1. Distinguish between the roles performed by the Council of Ministers and the Supreme Soviet of the U.S.S.R..
2. Discuss the interlocking relationship maintained between the Communist Party and the administrative units of the Soviet government.
3. Distinguish between Gosplan and Gossnab.
4. What is the role of the state budget in the Soviet economy?
5. The turnover tax performs several important economic functions in the Soviet Union. What are those functions?
6. Discuss the role of money in the Soviet economy.
7. In addition to performing central and commercial banking functions, Gosbank also performs control functions. Discuss.
8. What is the purpose of the credit plan?
9. What is the purpose of the cash plan?
10. Distinguish between state farms and collective farms.

RECOMMENDED READINGS

Aslund, Anders. *Gorbachev's Struggle for Economic Reform*. Ithaca, NY: Cornell University Press, 1989.

Garvey, George. *Money, Financial Flows and Credit in the Soviet Union*. Cambridge, MA: Ballinger, 1977.

Goldman, Marshall I. *Gorbachev's Challenge*. New York: W. W. Norton, 1988.

Hewett, Ed A. *Reforming the Soviet Economy*. Washington, DC: Brookings, 1988.

Linz, Susan J., and William Moskoff, eds. *Reorganization and Reform in the Soviet Union*. Armonk, NY: M. E. Sharpe, 1988.

Roucek, Libor. "Private Enterprise in Soviet Political Debates." *Soviet Studies*. Vol. 40, No. 1 (January 1988), pp. 44–63.

Schroeder, Gertrude E. "Soviet Economic Reforms: A Study in Complications." *Problems of Communism*. Vol. 40, No. 3 (July 1988), pp. 1–21.

Shelton, Judy. *The Coming Soviet Crash*. New York: Free Press, 1989.

CHAPTER THIRTEEN

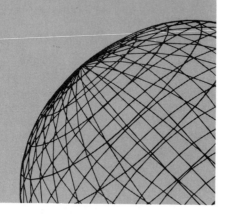

REFORMS AND PERFORMANCE IN THE SOVIET UNION

The following joke is popular in Moscow and sums up the conditions that exist in the Soviet economy:

> *Ivanov had finally saved enough money to purchase a car. He went to the appropriate office and paid the money. "Your car will be delivered exactly ten years from today," the clerk advised Ivanov. "Morning or afternoon?" Ivanov asked. "What difference does it make?" asked the clerk. "Because the plumber is coming in the morning," Ivanov replied.*

General Secretary Mikhail Gorbachev was named *Time*'s "Man of the Decade," and rightfully so, because no man had a greater impact on the world during the 1980s than he. He is responsible for the developments that have happened in Eastern Europe; no Eastern European country would have dared break away from the Soviet Union under his predecessors, particularly Leonid Brezhnev. Relations between the United States and the Soviet Union have improved immensely; armaments have been reduced; and the prospects for a third world war are remote. Gorbachev has charmed Western Europe, and his popularity there exceeds that of President Bush.

But Gorbachev has his problems at home. Four years of economic reforms have failed to produce economic gains for the populace. Food and other consumer goods are in short supply, and people have to queue up as they always have. Social unrest that threatens to tear apart the fabric of Soviet society is endemic. It begins in the Baltic countries—where Lithuania, Latvia, and Estonia (occupied by the Soviet Union only since World War II)[1] have never lost their sense of distinctive

---

[1] They were occupied as a result of an arrangement between Hitler and Stalin where Hitler took half of Poland and Stalin took the other half. The three Baltic countries were created after World War I.

identity and desire for independence—and extends to central Asia with its 50 million Moslems who share a common desire to loosen ties imposed on them by Moscow. Ethnic conflicts also create a potential for disruption because no love is lost among some of the non-Russian nationalities. Historically, the Georgians, Armenians, and other peoples have feuded for centuries over religion and territories. Finally, demographics works against the Russians and in favor of the non-Russians, with the latter eventually constituting the majority of the populace while the Russians continue to wield political power.[2]

The Soviet Union, which was supposed to become the fountainhead for the creation of a Marxist utopia, also has more than its share of economic problems. Its economy has entered into a period of declining growth in output, serious inflationary pressures, slow technological progress, and accumulated deficiencies in housing and other public needs. But the problems do not end there. Coal miners, from the Ukraine to Siberia, walked off of their jobs in protest over lost pay and poor living conditions. Strikes are not technically illegal in the Soviet Union; the Marxist tenet that they are unnecessary in a proletariat society has not kept them from happening. In the past, Communist leaders used bullets to control unruly workers, but under perestroika and glasnost work stoppages have become a part of the Soviet political and economic landscape.

It remains to be seen if Gorbachev is living on borrowed time. He has a long way to go before the Soviet Union can become a viable economy. He has to deal with an entrenched bureaucracy that wants to maintain the status quo. It is the dead hand of Moscow's ministries that has to be overcome before any successful attempt at reform can occur. At least free elections have been held for the Congress of Peoples' Deputies, and Gorbachev has been able to demote those who oppose his reforms from the Communist Party's ruling Politburo. Nevertheless, he has a long way to go before the Soviet Union becomes free from the political and economic encrustation that has existed for many decades.

ECONOMIC AND POLITICAL REFORM

The Gorbachev reforms come under three broad categories: perestroika, glasnost, and demokratizatsiia. They represent an attempt to break from the past and to chart a new course for the future. Since he has been in office, Gorbachev has undertaken many initiatives. He has cracked down on corruption, which has been a serious problem in the Soviet Union. To reduce alcoholism in the Soviet Union, he restricted the hours during which alcohol can be sold.[3] A charismatic leader, he has dramatically improved relations with the West to the point where he is more

---

[2] There are in fact more than 170 different nationalities and 200 languages and dialects spoken in the Soviet Union.

[3] This worked about as well as Prohibition in the United States. The Russians made "bathtub vodka" instead of "bathtub gin." Gorbachev has had to rescind his proscription on store hours because, in making "bathtub vodka," the population used up the Russian sugar supply.

popular in Western Europe than either Bush or Reagan. But his reforms are much broader in scope and have to be examined in some detail.

Perestroika

Perestroika means restructuring of the Soviet economy. Its concept did not begin with Gorbachev; rather, it was first used before the Revolution of 1917 by some political groups that wanted a restructuring of Russian society. It was also a concept used in the early Stalinist period, when it meant some form of reorganization in culture, education, and economics. Under Gorbachev, it represents an attempt to modernize Soviet society, which means less bureaucracy, central planning, and coercion in the economic field; more reliance on private initiative and incentive; and an attempt to rekindle the spirit of the masses to build a better and more energetic socialist society within the Marxist-Leninist framework.[4] The old economic system—where only quantity of output counted and where payment was made according to whether the plan was fulfilled, not whether the products were needed by anyone—simply was very inefficient.

Gorbachev's initial approach to improving Soviet economic performance was to increase worker and bureaucratic responsibility and to improve discipline. An attack was made against alcoholism and corruption. A number of heads of economic ministries were fired and replaced by people more attuned to Gorbachev's objectives.[5] The crackdown on alcoholism did result in a decline in absenteeism, fewer industrial accidents, and increased productivity.[6] There were also trials involving corrupt officials, including the son-in-law of former General Secretary Leonid Brezhnev. Efforts were made to reequip Soviet industry with more modern machinery and to increase investment necessary to retool existing enterprises. However, the attempt to modernize machinery did not live up to expectations. But reforms have continued, and some of them are summarized in Table 13-1.

Joint Ventures.   The Soviet Union needs to modernize its technology if it is to have any hope of being competitive in today's global economy. A joint venture arrangement between Soviet and foreign enterprises was approved by Gorbachev in order to improve the quality of goods and productivity of resources in the economy. An original joint venture plan, which insisted on majority Soviet state ownership, was revised to accommodate the demands of Western investors. The arrangement has encouraged some foreign investment, particularly on the part of West German

---

[4] Walter Laquer, *The Long Road to Freedom: Russia and Glasnost* (New York: Charles Scribner's Sons, 1989), p. 52.

[5] Thane Gustafson and Dawn Moore, "Gorbachev's First Year: Building Power and Authority," *Problems of Communism* (May–June 1986).

[6] Central Intelligence Agency and the Defense Intelligence Agency, *The Soviet Economy in 1988: Gorbachev Changes Course* (Report to the Subcommittee on National Security Economics, Joint Economic Committee, Congress of the United States, 1989), p. 5.

TABLE 13-1
Soviet Economic Reforms

Reform	Purpose
Reduce the number of centrally mandated output targets	To give state enterprises more authority to make output decisions
Reduce the central rationing of supplies & replace it with a system of whole-sale trade	To allow enterprises to freely buy their supplies from other enterprises and wholesalers
Institute a system of economic account-ability or self-financing	To allow enterprises to keep a larger share of their profits
Encourage the formation of independent business cooperatives	To improve the quality and avail-ability of consumer goods
Expand long-term leasing arrangements in agriculture	To encourage greater individual initi-atives & responsibility in agriculture
Relax regulations pertaining to foreign trade	To allow ministries & enterprises to engage directly in foreign trade
Overhaul wage and salary structure in the production sector	To increase worker productivity: also linked to enterprise performance
Republic and regional autonomy in self-financing	To provide more local latitude in forming budgets & covering expenditures

Source: Central Intelligence Agency and the Defense Intelligence Agency, The Soviet Econ-omy in 1988: Gorbachev Changes Course *(Report to the Subcommittee on National Security Economics, Joint Economic Committee, Congress of the United States, 1989), pp. 7–9.*

business firms, in the Soviet Union. Several American firms, including Chevron and Eastman Kodak, have signed an agreement with the Soviet Union for 25 joint ventures involving about $10 billion over the next 20 years. However, a problem with the joint venture arrangement is the desired repatriation of profits in hard currency rather than their being held in rubles.

Industry.   A new State Enterprise Law went into effect in 1988, resulting in greater management responsibility and control over the financial fate of enterprises. Man-agers were given increased control over the use of profits for reinvestment or bonuses for workers. They could set their own production plans, choose their sup-pliers, and to some extent set their own prices. They also can sell to each other and sell abroad without many of the restrictions that were formerly placed on them by the industrial ministries. They can also provide an employee stock-ownership plan. The law also requires enterprises to free themselves from reliance on government subsidies. But the reform in itself is not going to make Soviet industry that much more competitive, because there is still bureaucratic control. The prices of labor and raw material are kept artificially low, so managers don't know the true costs of production.

Cooperatives. Cooperatives and other small-scale private enterprises are also a part of Gorbachev's economic reforms. In 1987 he proposed the formation of privately owned, profit-oriented cooperative enterprises to supplement and even compete with state-owned enterprises. The primary goal of his proposal was to inject vitality into the Soviet Union's laggard consumer goods and service industries. In addition, the new co-ops would pay taxes and employ workers who could lose their jobs in a restructuring of industry. Loans are made available for resourceful citizens who want to open up restaurants, fashion boutiques, repair shops, night clubs, and other enterprises. Many cooperatives have proved to be successful, a contradiction and a source of envy in a society that officially scorns materialism but can't even produce enough basic goods to satisfy the needs of consumers. There is always the possibility that taxes will be raised or that bureaucrats will crack down on the cooperatives.

Price Reforms. The problem of pricing in a centrally planned economy is a different order of magnitude from that in a market economy. For one thing, prices do not determine the allocation of resources to the same extent as in a market economy. Moreover, pricing is not merely a matter of economics, but also of ideology and politics. Value in the communist frame of reference is the amount of labor embodied in particular goods and services; that is, labor is the only source of value. Thus, the price or value of any commodity is determined by the amount of the labor required to produce it. However, trying to set prices based on the labor theory of value has caused the communists all kinds of pricing problems. For one thing, the theory virtually denies the role of demand in the determination of value. Moreover, the factor of scarcity has been ignored.

However, pragmatism has transcended ideology and prices have been arrived at through the use of different plan variants that do recognize the scarcity of resources and the significance of demand. But the fact remains that no fully workable price system has been devised, and in the Soviet Union all prices have been regulated directly or through calculated rules, based on all costs plus a profit markup. Some attempts have been made a price reforms on a piecemeal basis. For example, a shoe factory was allowed to operate without a plan and with market-oriented[7] prices. Free markets have been permitted in certain service areas and for some agriculture produce, but basic foodstuffs are subsidized by the state budget, even though the introduction of a market-clearing price system is a necessary condition for a successful market-oriented reform.

Achievements of Perestroika

When Gorbachev took over the leadership of the Communist Party, he stated that his goal would be to reform the Soviet economic and political life. While his efforts at political liberalization have been enormously successful, probably much to his

---

[7] Anders Aslund, *Gorbachev's Struggle for Economic Reform* (Ithaca, NY: Cornell University Press, 1989), p. 35.

chagrin,[8] his attempts to revitalize and reform the Soviet economy so far have been ineffective. Economic reform was supposed to make the Soviet Union more competitive in the production of conventional products, such as machine tools, and also in the production of high technology products. He also promised to raise the living standards of the Soviet people. He has failed on both objectives, particularly the latter. The per capita real standard of living has shown a decline during the five years he has been in power. Many goods are in short supply because he has done little to stimulate the production of consumer goods, and the rate of inflation has increased. Rationing of such basic products as sugar has been initiated.

Table 13-2 presents the performance of the Soviet economy during the 1980s, including the Gorbachev period, which began in 1985. In fairness to Gorbachev, he inherited a rather poor economic situation. From 1979 through the early 1980s, there was a drop in the real rate of economic growth and a decline in the production of many industrial goods. Problems in agriculture had been compounded by a succession of six years of bad harvests. But there has been little or no improvement in the Soviet economy since he has been in office, and he has to assume a major share of the responsibility for the current performance. Too much emphasis was placed on the production of machine tools and too little emphasis was placed on consumer goods production.

TABLE 13-2
Soviet Economic Performance for Selected Years
(annual rate of growth in percent)

Year	Real per Capita GNP	Industry	Agriculture
1981–1985	1.0	2.0	1.2
1984	0.5	2.5	−0.5
1985	0.0	2.0	−3.9
1986	3.1	2.7	10.3
1987	0.2	2.9	−4.0
1988	1.5	2.4	−3.2
1989	0.5	0.2	3.1

Source: Central Intelligence Agency, Handbook of Economic Statistics 1989, *(Springfield, VA: NTIS, 1990), pp. 34 and 58; Central Intelligence Agency and the Defense Intelligence Agency,* The Soviet Economy Stumbles Badly in 1989 *(Report to the Technology and National Security Subcommittee of the Joint Economic Committee, Congress of the United States, 1990), pp. 4 and C 11.*

[8] On May Day (May 1) 1990, the holiest of days on the Communist calendar, Gorbachev was booed by marchers in the Moscow parade. They displayed placards calling him a fascist and telling him to get out of Lithuania.

Industrial Performance. A major part of Gorbachev's economic reforms has involved the modernization of Soviet industry, and the results have been mixed. The proportion of state investment that has gone to re-equip and retool state enterprises has increased, and newly introduced machinery models increased in 1988 over 1987.[9] However, the percent of industrial output for both producer and consumer goods declined in 1987 over 1986 and showed little increase in 1988 and 1989.[10] There has been an inability to achieve a shift in investment in favor of modernization in existing facilities. New advanced technology is needed to modernize Soviet industries, increase the competitiveness of its exports in world trade, and promote economic growth. Investment policies have led to a failure of industrial modernization and have not contributed to increasing the rate of economic growth.

One problem that has confronted the Soviet economy is the quality of output, which has been long overlooked in the effort to increase economic planning goals. Most goods fail quality-control standards. In 1987 only 15 percent of the machinery used to produce consumer goods met world standards. Soviet mass-produced goods cannot meet world standards. Gorbachev has attempted to improve the quality of Soviet goods by creating *Gospriemka*, the State Quality Acceptance Committee. However, there has been no real improvement in the quality of consumer and producer goods.[11] So a contradiction has occurred in that the attempt to improve quality standards has actually led to a decline in output because many goods have been rejected as being of inferior quality.

Even more important is the Soviet lag in the coming informational society of the future. In key technologies, the Soviet Union is far behind the United States, which is itself behind Japan. These technologies—which include computers and electronic components and instruments—offer the promise of future economic growth. Increasing international competition and these technologies are transforming the world and threaten to leave the Soviet Union far behind. The Soviet Union is six years behind the United States in the production of mainframe computers, seven years behind in the production of fiber optic equipment, six years behind in the production of minicomputers, and five years behind in the production of supercomputers.[12] Rapid change, particularly in the Soviet Union, is difficult to accept and even more difficult to implement. Advanced technology is needed to modernize Soviet industries; without it, the Soviet Union may lose out entirely as a major world power.

Agriculture. Agriculture is an area of concern for the Soviet Union. There are many problems confronting Soviet agriculture. Geography and nature have not been kind

[9] Aslund, *Gorbachev's Struggle*, p. 5.

[10] Central Intelligence Agency and the Defense Intelligence Agency, *The Soviet Economy Stumbles Badly in 1989* (Report to the Technology and National Security Subcommittee, Joint Economic Committee, Congress of the United States, 1990), Table C-1.

[11] Marshall I. Goldman, "Gorbachev the Economist," *Foreign Affairs*, vol. 69, no. 2 (Spring 1990), pp. 32–34.

[12] CIA, *The Soviet Economy in 1988*, p. 6.

to the country. Despite the largest land area in the world, only a small fraction of the country has a long enough growing season and enough moisture to support agriculture. Storage and transportation facilities are inadequate. The overwhelming majority of Soviet farms have no paved roads at their disposal to bring supplies and to take out their harvests. Agricultural products are inefficiently produced and are expensive to the Soviet government in that annual subsidies have averaged around $100 billion a year. Despite perestroika, consumers are no better off than before and must still spend many hours standing in line to buy basic food products. The overall performance of Soviet agriculture is presented in Table 13-3.

On March 15, 1990, Gorbachev proposed a complete reorganization of the state-managed agricultural system.[13] He called for a new highly-decentralized system that would encourage the country's farmers to work in small cooperatives and on independently owned farms in an effort to solve the problems of food shortages that have become endemic in the Soviet Union. He proposed to lease the land, the livestock, the equipment, and most of the other productive assets of the country's 49,200 state and collective farms to groups of farmers and individuals on the basis of negotiated contracts. These contracts, which would run for as long as 50 years, with a son inheriting the land from his father, will require rental payments and, initially, delivery of specified amounts of produce. Farmers would be freed from the supervision of the multilayered bureaucracy that administers Soviet agriculture and permitted to sell on the open market whatever they produced over contractual agreements with the state. They would also receive higher payments for the produce they sell to the state as an incentive to increase output.

Foreign Trade.   The Soviet Union's lack of export competitiveness continues to be an important impediment to the success of perestroika. Its inability to increase its export earnings from manufacturing goods is reflected in the commodity composi-

TABLE 13-3

Indicators of Soviet Agricultural Output for Selected Years
(million metric tons)

Commodity	1970	1975	1980	1985	1986	1987	1988	1989
Grain	186.8	140.1	189.1	191.7	210.1	211.3	195.0	211.1
Potatoes	96.8	88.7	67.0	73.0	87.2	75.9	62.7	72.0
Sugar beets	78.9	66.3	81.0	82.4	79.3	90.4	87.8	97.5
Cotton	6.9	7.9	9.1	8.8	8.2	8.1	8.7	8.6
Vegetables	21.2	23.4	27.3	28.1	29.8	29.2	29.3	28.5
Meat	12.3	15.0	15.1	17.1	18.1	18.9	19.7	20.0
Milk	83.0	90.8	90.9	98.6	102.2	103.8	106.8	108.1

Source: Central Intelligence Agency and the Defense Intelligence Agency, The Soviet Economy Stumbles Badly in 1989 (Report to the Technology and National Security Subcommittee of the Joint Economic Committee, Congress of the United States, 1990), p. C 9.

[13] *The Washington Post*, (March 15, 1990), p.1.

tion of its exports, which basically consists of military hardware, crude and refined oil, and natural gas. For example, Soviet trade with the Third World countries comes from the export of arms. Arms exports to the Third World countries were sold mainly on credits, so that any hard currency surplus appears only on paper. Earnings from exports to the developed countries of the West come from selling oil and natural gas. Machinery and other durable goods are not competitive in world markets. In 1986 only 15 percent of Soviet-produced machinery met world standards; in 1987 the percentage was lower.[14]

Import strategy has been directed toward running a surplus in the merchandise trade account. This has been done through cutbacks in imports from the developed countries, which has had an adverse effect on the modernization of Soviet industry because imports were cut in Western machinery and equipment.[15] It affected Soviet ability to improve the quality and assortment of its manufactured products and to compete in world markets, where it has to earn more hard currency to service the interest on its foreign debt and to purchase advanced technology. Cutting imports has also had a negative effect on domestic consumption and living standards of Soviet citizens. Soviet industry is incapable of satisfying the growing demand for consumer goods. Table 13-4 presents a summary of Soviet foreign trade for the period 1984–1989.

The net hard currency debt of the Soviet Union to the West has almost tripled during the 1980s, with most of the increase in the debt occurring from 1985 to 1988. The increase in the hard currency debt can be attributed to a number of factors. One is a higher quantity of grain imports coupled with rising world grain prices.

TABLE 13-4

Hard Currency Balance of Payment for the Soviet Union (millions of dollars)

	1984	1985	1986	1987	1988	1989
Merchandise trade balance	4727	519	2013	6164	2647	−1400
Exports	32173	26400	25111	29092	31165	33600
Imports	27446	25881	23098	22928	28518	35000
Net Interest	−1163	−1481	−1737	−2191	−2575	−2993
Capital account balance	−124	1869	1794	−738	1378	4348
Changes in gross debt	226	6804	6811	5011	1990	4120
Change in assets held in western banks	−664	1787	1595	−527	1119	−505

Source: Central Intelligence Agency and the Defense Intelligence Agency, The Soviet Union Stumbles Badly in 1990 *(Report to the Technology and National Security Subcommittee of the Joint Economic Committee, Congress of the United States, 1990), Table C 7.*

[14] *U.S. News & World Report* (April 3, 1989), p. 44.

[15] Import substitution has been used as a development strategy by Mexico and Brazil with some success. They have built world class steel industries.

There has also been an ⌐ ⌐rease in imports of machinery from West Germany, Austria, and Japan. Working against the Soviet Union has been a decline in hard currency from export earnings resulting from lower world oil prices. Net foreign debt increased as the Soviet Union borrowed more from West German and Swiss banks. As Table 13-5 indicates, net interest payment on the foreign debt has also increased dramatically during the period 1984–1989. Gold sales have also increased to finance imports.

Consumer Living Standards.   A number of criteria can be used to evaluate the overall living standards of Soviet citizens. One standard is health, which has actually showed a decline during the 1980s. There is a high rate of infant mortality, and life expectancy—particularly for males—has declined.[16] Hospitals often lack adequate facilities for patients, and staffs are often poorly trained. Alcoholism is rampant. Many state primary and secondary schools do not have central heating, running water, or sewage systems. Pollution is reported to be worse in the Soviet Union than in any other major industrial country. In Leningrad, sewage seeps into the drinking water, and in 104 Soviet cities, air pollution exceeds the minimum health standards by 1,000 percent.[17] Pollution in the Aral Sea has led to serious diseases, such as typhoid fever, and an increase in infant mortality. Over 30 million Soviet citizens drink polluted water, and 65 percent of rural hospitals have no hot water.[18]

Poverty.   The Soviet Union and other communist countries have always denied any possibility that poverty could exist under communism and pronounced it an evil of capitalism. However, poverty is a reality in the Soviet Union; Soviet authorities

TABLE 13-5
Hard Currency Debt of the Soviet Union to the West (billions of dollars)

	1980	1984	1985	1986	1987	1988	1989
Gross debt	20.5	22.2	29.0	36.0	40.8	41.7	47.0
Less assets in Western banks	10.0	11.5	13.3	14.9	14.4	14.4	15.0
Net debt	10.5	10.7	15.7	21.1	26.4	27.3	31.0
Net interest	−1.2	−1.2	−1.5	−1.7	−2.2	−2.4	−3.0
Gold sales	1.6	1.0	1.8	4.0	3.5	3.8	3.6

Source: Central Intelligence Agency and the Defense Intelligence Agency, The Soviet Economy Stumbles Badly in 1989 (Report to the Technology and National Security Subcommittee, Joint Economic Committee, Congress of the United States, 1990), Table C 8.

[16] The World Bank, *World Development Report 1989* (New York: Oxford University Press, 1989), p. 215.
[17] *U.S. News & World Report* (April 3, 1989), p. 43.
[18] The Soviet Union has 62 CAT scanners compared to 4,800 in the United States.

have admitted that at least 20 percent of the population live in poverty, compared to 14 percent in the United States.[19] Officially, the poverty level in the Soviet Union for an urban family of four is 205.6 rubles a month ($339.24) at an exchange rate of $1.65 to the ruble. Other calculations place the urban poverty level at 300 rubles, or around $496 a month. More than 43 million people are living in families with incomes of less than 300 rubles a month, but there is no state agency to deal with the poor because the word "poverty" does not exist in the Soviet lexicon.[20]

Income Distribution.   Soviet society is far from egalitarian. The nomenklatura system ensures that the Party elite will have the best jobs, the best education, and access to the finer things of life. But the great majority of people do not belong to the Communist Party and, with or without nomenklatura, incomes are unequally distributed. It has been estimated that in 1979 the 10 percent of Soviet households with the highest average income per household received 33.4 percent of all income.[21] The share for the lowest 10 percent of households was 3 percent of the income. The highest 20 percent received 46.4 percent of all of the income; the lowest 20 percent, 7.4 percent.[22] Income inequality is affected by the fact that some Soviet workers (e.g., doctors, mechanics) can also earn income from private practices, with earnings from private activities often much greater than earnings from public employment.

Wealth distribution in the Soviet Union is also far from equal (see Table 13-6). The top 10 percent of households own more than 40 percent of the total sum of wealth and approximately 45 percent of the total financial assets. Conversely, the lowest 50 percent own only 8.9 percent of wealth and 5.9 percent of financial assets.

Food and other Consumer Goods and Services.   An abundance of food and other goods and services is the most important measure of living standards. Gorbachev has failed to deliver in this area despite his promises to increase their availability, especially food. A Soviet survey in early 1988 showed that only 23 out of 211 varieties of foodstuffs were readily available in Soviet shops.[23] Even bread has

---

[19] *The New York Times* (January 22, 1989), p. A3.

[20] As is also true in the United States, there is the feminization of poverty in the Soviet Union. Single women and mothers with children are much more likely to be found among the poor. In the Soviet Union, women earn between 18 to 29 percent less than men, in part because of occupational segregation, which also exists in the United States, but mainly because women are paid less than men, even when both have similar education, experience, and responsibility.

[21] James R. Millar and Peter Donhowe, *Life, Work, and Politics in Soviet Cities: Results of the Soviet Interview Project*, Working Paper No. 30 (University of Illinois, 1987), p. 18.

[22] Given the fact that income distribution in the Soviet Union is based on estimates, it would appear that there is not that much difference in income distribution between the Soviet Union and the United States. Bureau of the Census statistics for 1979 indicate the top 20 percent in the United States received 42.7 percent of income and the bottom 20 percent received 5.5 percent of income.

[23] Goldman, "Gorbachev the Economist," p. 29.

TABLE 13-6
Wealth Distribution in the Soviet Union (percent)

	Gross Wealth	Financial Assets
Lowest 25 percent	0.3	0.0
Lowest 50 percent	8.9	5.9
Highest 1 percent	7.0	11.5
Highest 5 percent	28.7	28.6
Highest 10 percent	42.0	43.1
Highest 25 percent	69.5	72.8
Gini coefficient	.61	.64

Source: Aaron Vinokur and Gur Ofer. Inequality of Earnings, Household Income and Wealth in the Soviet Union in the 1970's *(University of Illinois: Soviet Interview Project, 1987), p. 43.*

been in short supply, and rationing has been imposed on products such as meat. Real per capita living standards have decreased and the rate of inflation has increased.[24] Even including imports of grain and meat, the availability of consumer goods has fallen far short of the population's demand. Consumer goods that were produced in the Soviet Union have been of inferior quality. Meanwhile, wage reforms that have been implemented have allowed enterprises much more latitude in increasing wages. Money income increased by an estimated 13 percent in 1989, while shortages of consumer goods increased.[25]

Defense and the Economy. The Soviet Union met its Viet Nam in Afghanistan and eventually had to withdraw after a useless expenditure of money and human resources. These expenditures and also Soviet response to the military buildup of the Reagan administration drained resources that could have been applied to Gorbachev's economic reforms. Military expenditures increased the deficit in the Soviet state budget from 2 percent of Soviet gross national product in 1983 to around 11 percent in 1989.[26] Gorbachev came into office intent on accelerating growth and modernizing the economy, but to do this he needed to stabilize the external military threat. Improved relations with the West enabled Gorbachev to make cutbacks in military spending. Defense, which has a large share of the output of the machine building industry and larger shares of the highest quality materials,

---

[24] CIA estimates place the rate of inflation at 6 percent for 1990, up from the rate of 3.1 percent in 1988. Soviet estimates place the rate of open inflation in 1989 as 5 percent and the rate of repressed inflation at 5.5 percent. See Central Intelligence Agency and the Defense Intelligence Agency, *The Soviet Economy Stumbles Badly in 1989* (Report to the Technology and National Security Subcommittee, Joint Economic Committee, Congress of the United States, April 20, 1990), pp. 6–7.

[25] Marketing, distribution, and storage problems, which are hardly new in the Soviet Union, also have led to shortages and an increase in consumer complaints.

[26] On a percentage basis, the deficit in the U.S. federal budget was around 4 percent of U.S. gross national product in 1989.

became a candidate to support Gorbachev's modernization program. It is a matter of shifting resources from guns to butter.

Some resources are readily transferable to the consumer goods sector. Materials used in weapons production (steel, construction materials, and engineering fibers) are transferable and are in demand in the civilian sector.[27] Robots manufactured by the defense sector are installed in many civilian factories. The Ministry of Aviation has transferred food processing equipment for fruit and vegetable production. Enterprises under the Ministry of Defense have transferred heavy duty tractors, irrigators, and mineral fertilizers; the missile-space industry has transferred tractors and seed drills; and enterprises under the jurisdiction of the Ministry of Medium-Machine Building have supplied equipment for making dried milk. The defense-related Ministries are supposed to transfer 17.5 billion rubles of machinery to the food processing industries between 1988 and 1995.[28] However, technology transfers from the military to the civilian sector are not likely to have any immediate impact on the economy.

The Future of Perestroika

The Soviet Union remains sclerotic even after five years of perestroika. Industrial failures drove Gorbachev to attempt industrial modernization but little has been accomplished. He has had to face an entrenched bureaucracy and hard-line conservatives in his party who are resistant to change. However, he has made his share of policy mistakes. For one thing, he has emphasized the development of the industrial goods industries over the consumer goods industries, a policy followed by his predecessors.[29] He probably should have focused on the development of a grass-roots agricultural and consumer goods sector as the Chinese have done. Another thing that went wrong was unrealistic planning. Production of consumer goods was set to increase by 7 percent in the 1989 plan; it actually increased by less than 2 percent. The state budget deficit increased from 4 percent of GNP in 1985 to 11 percent in 1989.[30] This deficit was created by several factors, including subsidies on consumer goods, which amounted to 110 billion rubles in 1989, and spending on investments that have had little payoff.[31]

The support of the Soviet populace is critical to the success of Gorbachev and perestroika. There has to be the perception on the part of the Soviet citizen that

---

[27] Julian Cooper, "Technology Transfer Between Military and Civilian Industries" in *Gorbachev's Economic Plans*, vol. 1, Joint Economic Committee, Congress of the United States (Washington: USGPO, 1987), pp. 398–400.

[28] CIA, *The Soviet Economy in 1988*, p. 21.

[29] Goldman, "Gorbachev the Economist," p.31–32.

[30] CIA, *The Soviet Union Stumbles Badly in 1989*, p.19.

[31] On the revenue side of the budget, turnover taxes declined as a result of Gorbachev's anti-alcohol campaign, and receipts from profits declined because of reforms allowing enterprises to retain a larger share of profits.

somehow he or she is better off as a result of perestroika. Often perception does not match reality. In 1988, for example, popular perception of improvements in consumer welfare for 1988 and the two previous years was negative, when actually there was an improvement in certain areas such as health care, personal care, and housing. Table 13-7 compares the popular perceptions of performance in various areas of consumer welfare and the actual performance measures of the economy in 1988 for the same measures. There is a considerable disparity.

Support for perestroika comes from the younger and better educated segments of Soviet society. These segments want material and measurable performance now. If it does not come soon, this could create problems for the Soviet leadership. Many persons who are among the best educated and best paid members of Soviet society express the greatest desire for change.[32] Conversely, the level of support for traditional state control of the economy increases as the level of education declines. The older generation that has experienced one or more of the many traumatic events in Soviet history is more philosophical about the failures of the Soviet economic system. After all, success is relative and many persons feel that they are better off today than they were under Stalin, even though there are food and housing shortages and the quality of services is very poor. The drive to modernize the Soviet economy can also carry with it some side effects, such as the creation of an elite class that is of increasing importance in the area of science and technology. This class is necessary to facilitate economic growth.

TABLE 13-7
A Comparison of Performance and Consumer Perceptions of Welfare Indicators for 1988[a]

Welfare Indicators	Performance	Perception
Total consumption	0	—
Meat	0	—
Other foods	—	—
Durable goods	0	0
Clothing	0	0
Personal care and services	+	0
Housing	+	0
Health care	+	0
Inflation	—	—

[a] + = improvement, 0 = no significant change, − = decline.
Source: Central Intelligence Agency and the Defense Intelligence Agency, The Soviet Economy in 1988: Gorbachev Changes Course *(Report to the Subcommittee on National Security Economics, Joint Economic Committee, Congress of the United States, 1989), p. 13.*

[32] Elizabeth Clayton and James R. Millar, "Quality of Life: Subjective Measures of Relative Satisfaction," Soviet Interview Project (Urbana: University of Illinois, 1987), pp. 2–8.

Glasnost

In July 1989 Americans and people in other countries witnessed the picture of striking Soviet coal miners on the nightly news. The coal miners wanted better pay, better working conditions, and more food. In many respects it was like a labor strike in the United States, except for the fact that Soviet labor unions have no power. Representatives of the government would be sent from Moscow to negotiate with the coal miners. Gorbachev himself put in a personal plea for the coal miners to end their strike, lest they jeopardize the Soviet economy. Television reporters from the United States and foreign networks interviewed individuals coal miners to find out why they were striking. The same reasons were given: low pay, poor working conditions, and inadequate food. They also complained about the big shots who would come down from Moscow in their chauffeur-driven limousines and who lived in comfort while they had to work in the mines.

None of this would have happened in the days of Stalin and Brezhnev. First of all, there would have been no pictures or interviews shown on the nightly news. Second, the world would have never learned that a strike had actually taken place. Third, had the strike occurred when Stalin was in power, he would have had the workers shot or deported to Siberia, and he would also have shot the local party leaders for letting the strike occur. Brezhnev probably would have increased food supplies as a temporary palliative and then deported some miners to Siberia. But glasnost now exists in the Soviet Union, and society is much more open and events are reported to the world.

Glasnost means openness about public affairs in every sphere of life.[33] When it was first introduced in 1985, it involved an exposé of bureaucratic inefficiencies and waste and mismanagement in the economic system. Glasnost is interrelated with perestroika because, through popular support, Gorbachev has been able to initiate a series of changes that have focused on the restructuring of the Soviet economy.[34] It is considered an effective form of public control over the activities of all public entities and a lever in correcting shortcomings. It marks an enormous step forward in comparison with the dismal state of affairs that prevailed before Gorbachev. If nothing else, it allows Russians to let off steam and to give vent to their frustrations. But the Soviet Union has as yet a long way to go toward true political and cultural freedom.[35]

Glasnost and the Soviet Economy.   Glasnost has, for better or for worse, had a direct impact on the Soviet economy. It has revealed much about the state of the

---

[33] Mikhail Gorbachev, *Perestroika* (New York: Harper and Row, 1987), p. 66.

[34] Gorbachev, *Perestroika*, p. 63.

[35] Glasnost is not a new concept in Russian history. Gorbachev quotes Lenin as saying: "More light! Let the Party Know Everything!" However, it goes back long before Lenin. The author Gogol wrote *Dead Souls* about corruption and tax evasion in the time of the Tsars. The term itself was used in the Russian periodicals of the last century.

economy, particularly its shortcomings. For example, glasnost has attacked official statistics, which have been notoriously untrustworthy. Some attempts have been made to supply more valid statistical data, such as grain harvests, but other data on crime and alcoholism is not published.[36] There is also more openness when it comes to a discussion of the Soviet supply system. Seventy years after the 1917 Revolution, the Soviet Union still has not created the good life. Cars produced in the 1950s were better made than cars of today. Shoddy goods and the absence of services have been a topic for discussion under glasnost. At least complaints were heard and suggestions made by economists on how to improve the quality of consumer goods.

Glasnost has also led to a more open discussion of agricultural problems. Various explanations have been advanced for the failure of agriculture. Some blame overly rigid central planning, while others have argued that there were no incentives or blamed an orientation toward quantitative output. Gorbachev has viewed bureaucracy, with its organization along narrow departmental lines, as an obstacle to agricultural reforms. He created *Gosagroprom*, a supercommittee that would supersede the many ministries and bureaucracies that were supervising the state and collective farms. Gosagroprom merged five ministries and one state committee. As the central organ of agriculture, it was given the authority to coordinate and plan the activities of all branches of industry concerned with the production and processing of food and natural fibers.[37]

Glasnost and Soviet Society. Glasnost has revealed the bad side of Soviet society, from alcoholism to pollution, failings that the Soviet Union had refused to admit when it held itself as a country that had solved all social problems. There was a fundamental reason for an open discussion of the shortcomings of Soviet society. It could be used by Gorbachev as a moral crusade to cut down on alcoholism, corruption, drugs, and prostitution. Initiatives were taken against alcoholism by reducing the number of hours that state liquor stores remained open,[38] and those who were found guilty of corruption were punished. It was maintained that admission of shortcomings in society was a sign of strength, that the problems were real, and that Gorbachev was going to handle them.

But glasnost has not just been limited to the exposure of alcoholism and corruption. It also has to do with the role of women in society. Despite long-standing Soviet proclamations about the equality of women in Soviet society, women are anything but equals. Few women serve in positions of authority, and the Soviet

---

[36] Laquer, pp. 197–205.

[37] Penelope Doolittle and Margaret Hughes, "Gorbachev's Agricultural Policy." In *Gorbachev's Economic Plans*, vol. 2, Joint Economic Committee, Congress of the United States (Washington: US-GPO, 1987), pp. 34–36.

[38] It has been reported that there has been a decline in drink-related crime and a reduction in traffic accidents by drunken drivers. On the other hand, there has been an increase in the production and sale of bootleg vodka.

Union is a male-dominated society. Raisa Gorbachev is the first wife of any Soviet leader who has traveled in public with her husband. That in itself is an example of glasnost. Complaints by women have become public. They ask how they can do an effective job at work, wait in queues for hours to buy food and necessities, take care of the children, and do the housework without the help of Soviet men who are not noted for doing domestic chores.

The intelligentsia has probably become the greatest beneficiary of glasnost. The Soviet Union has long been a society where culture has been stultified. Culture has served as an instrument to glorify the achievements of the workers and the state, for example, operas that hailed the achievements of coal miners. The response to the demand for open and free debate has come from many cultural sources, and subjects ranging from the brutality of Soviet labor camps to the disillusionment of Soviet veterans of the Afghan war have been covered by filmmakers and writers. Soviet writers long in disfavor in the Soviet Union now are being read. An example would be Boris Pasternak's *Dr. Zhivago*. Soviet theater has also become more open in discussing issues such as prostitution and alcoholism and the excesses of Stalinism. Popular music is more open in terms of expression, even though it represents a hybrid of Western music.

Glasnost and Nationalism.   Glasnost and perestroika are linked together in that the free, public discussion of problems and events and the restructuring of the Soviet economy are compatible ideas and that either one leads to the other. However, glasnost has also contributed to ethnic nationalism in the Soviet Union. Nowhere is this more apparent than in the Baltic republics of Latvia, Lithuania, and Estonia, who have taken "openness" literally to demand autonomy or independence from Moscow.[39] But nationalism is not just limited to the Baltic republics; it has spread to the Ukraine, which also wants more autonomy from Moscow.[40] The small province of Moldavia, which was also annexed by the Soviet Union, has pressed for autonomy. But it is in Central Asia where nationalism can cause the greatest problem to the Soviet Union. There religion is the driving force for nationalism, and glasnost has aroused Moslem aspirations for autonomy.

Demokratizatsiya

Demokratizatsiya, or democratization, is the third prong in Gorbachev's approach to reform the Soviet economy. Perestroika was to be reinforced and driven by glasnost, which would in turn be stimulated by democratization. This would have

---

[39] Lithuania already has declared its independence.

[40] When Hitler invaded the Soviet Union in 1941, he received much support from the Ukrainians who wanted their independence from Moscow. Had Hitler played on this sentiment and allowed their autonomy, he would have won the war.

encouraged bottom-up pressure to spur reforms, and not the top-down approach that had characterized the traditional Leninist emphasis on total control from above. Gorbachev felt that continued reliance on the traditional approach would doom his reforms to failure for the simple reason that he would be opposed by a party structure of power and privilege. Even limited democratization from above meant concessions that were bound to be repugnant to a ruling elite steeped in the self-serving Marxist-Leninist notion that it alone was the repository of historical proof and political wisdom.[41]

In an election that was free by Soviet standards, but would hardly have been considered free in the Western democracies, changes were made in the Congress of Peoples Deputies. Communist Party officials from Lithuania to Siberia were defeated by newcomers. There were 1,500 candidates who were up for reelection.[42] They were joined by 750 selected by public organizations, including the Communist Party. The two groups were to select 544 persons for a new Supreme Soviet. This new legislature will challenge the authority of the Communist Party hierarchy. It is through the Congress of Peoples Deputies and the Supreme Soviet that democratization is implemented. Here in open debate the reforms necessary to implement perestroika can be discussed. One of Gorbachev's goals in the election was to get people talking about his reforms, and this he did. Elected to the Congress of Peoples Deputies were a wide variety of people from army officers and shipyard workers to Boris Yeltsin, who had been kicked out of the Politburo.

THE FUTURE OF SOVIET-STYLE COMMUNISM

The Soviet Union is in trouble. There has been a breakdown in authority, as exemplified by the handling of the coal miners strike and exacerbated by Gorbachev's efforts to address the failures of the Soviet economic and social system. He has attempted to transfer power from an intransigent Communist Party set in its ways and opposed to change to a hierarchy of popularly elected councils, headed by the Supreme Soviet. The party itself is in trouble as represented by the fact that a number of party leaders failed to get themselves elected to the new Council of People's Deputies in elections held in March 1989—even though most of them had contrived to run unopposed and needed only 50 percent of the voters to win.

---

[41] This is the nomenklatura, or ruling class, of which there are around 18 million members. They could lose their jobs and, worse, the special stores, food sources, and all the perks that make them the ruling elite.

[42] Gorbachev did not have to run for election because he had secured one of the seats reserved by top party officials.

Will the Communist System Be a Thing of the Past?

Zbigniew Brzezinski lists five major developments that have contributed to the crisis that exists in the communist world, which are as follows:[43]

1. The Soviet Union can no longer be used as a role model for other communist countries. It has failed to deliver on its promise to create a better and more prosperous society. In fact, the economy seems to be going in reverse. Lenin and Stalin perverted Marxism to a justification for arbitrary and dictatorial power, with millions of lives being sacrificed in the process.
2. In the Soviet Union and also in China it has been demonstrated that economic success can only be created at the expense of political stability, and political stability can only be bought at the expense of economic failure.
3. In Eastern Europe the monopoly of power by the Communist Party could be maintained by Soviet dominance. The elimination of Soviet and Party dominance is regarded as a precondition for economic reform.
4. The era of a communist world movement based on the same Marxist-Leninist dogma is a thing of the past. At least for the present, communism is on the wane throughout the world. It is no longer the powerful political force it once was in France, Italy, and many other countries. There has been a continuous defection of new countries from the Soviet-influenced model.
5. There has been an intensification of internal instability and decay in the communist countries, as manifested by political unrest in the Soviet Union, a constant failure to effectively utilize productive capacity, and low rates of production growth. There has also been a weakening of the ability of the communist countries to compete with advanced, free-enterprise democracies in world markets.

A Post-Communist World

The standard Marxist postulate has been that socialism was the inevitable concomitant of the crisis of capitalism within industrialized society. The twentieth century was supposed to be the century of communism. There would be a continuous defection of countries from capitalism, with the instability and decay of the capitalist countries manifested in low rates of economic growth and chronic unemployment. However, the reverse has occurred, as the capitalist countries have demonstrated their viability in adapting to changing circumstances and communism has become increasingly irrelevant in a rapidly changing world. It may well be that capitalism and democracy will be the result of the crisis in socialism. Thus, the question can be raised concerning the future of communism as the world prepares to enter the twenty-first century. Brzezinski suggests four phases in the retreat from communism which are as follows:[44]

---

[43] Brzezinski, pp. 232–235.
[44] Brzezinski, p. 255.

Phase 1: Communist totalitarianism, where the Communist party controls the political system, which in turn controls society and the economy. China is a case in point. Then there is a transition to phase 2, which results from struggles that divide the Communist party and increase pressures for socioeconomic changes.

Phase 2: Communist authoritarianism, where the party controls the political system but society contests it, and political supremacy in the economy is on the defensive. A transition to phase 3 occurs as a result of rising social pressures. This can result in a top-level coup. Romania is an example.

Phase 3: Postcommunist authoritarianism. An authoritarian regime is based on nationalist appeal and ideology is ritualized. Civil society becomes political society, and political supremacy over the economy is in retreat. Yugoslavia is in phase 3. The transition to phase 4 is likely to be turbulent, although peaceful evolution is possible.

Phase 4: Postcommunist pluralism. Political and socioeconomic systems become pluralistic. Hungary and Poland are examples.

SUMMARY

Under Gorbachev a number of economic reforms have been introduced into the Soviet Union, including the proposed legalization of private ownership of homes and residential lots. However, the Soviet economy has not improved despite this *perestroika*. Shortages of consumer goods and inequalities in their distribution remain economic facts of life. The Soviet Union continues to fall further behind the West in advanced technology as well. In the minicomputer industry, technological lags with the United States are estimated to range from seven to ten years. The development of and applications for mainframe computers lag nine to fifteen years behind the United States. Industrial production had stagnated, with 1989 representing the worst performance of the Soviet economy since World War II. Although GNP increased by 1.5 percent in 1989, the gap between what consumers want and what is produced widened. Poverty, which is not officially acknowledged, increased. Soviet sources estimate that 15 to 20 percent of the people live below the poverty line. Foreign debt increased an average of 38 percent per year over the last five years, from $11 billion in 1984 to $32 billion in 1989.

For the present, it would appear that Gorbachev is rearranging desk chairs on the Titanic, for things are getting worse instead of better. Arguably Gorbachev's most important economic reform has been to reduce government expenditures on armaments. Savings resulting from reduced expenditures on arms may now be diverted to the production of more consumer goods. *Perestroika*, however, has been overshadowed lately by both external and internal events. Anticommunist revolutions have swept through the countries of Eastern Europe. Formerly reliable trading partners may now become more aligned with the West. Gorbachev faces serious political and social problems at home, with Estonia, Latvia, and Lithuania demanding more independence from Moscow. Ethnic violence occurring in other parts of the Soviet Union also pose threats to Gorbachev's leadership in the economic arena.

REVIEW QUESTIONS

1. What is perestroika and how has it been implemented by Gorbachev?
2. It is said that poverty exists in the Soviet Union. Discuss.
3. Compare income distribution in the Soviet Union to income distribution in the United States.
4. What are some of the shortcomings of the Soviet Economy?
5. Have living standards in the Soviet economy improved any in the 1980s.
6. What is glasnost? How has it worked?
7. What is demokratizatsiya?
8. Is Soviet-style communism a thing of the past, and if it is, what will replace it?
9. Brzezinski suggests four phases in the departure from Soviet-style communism to a different type of system. Discuss.
10. In your opinion, has communism been a failure, and if so, why?

RECOMMENDED READINGS

Bergson, Abram. "Comparative Productivity: The U.S.S.R., Eastern Europe, and the West." *American Economic Review*, Vol. 77, No. 3 (June 1987), pp. 342–357.

Brzezinski, Zbigniew. *The Grand Failure: The Birth and Death of Communism in the Twentieth Century*. New York: Charles Scribner's Sons, 1989.

Central Intelligence Agency and the Defense Intelligence Agency. *The Soviet Economy Stumbles Badly in 1989*. Report to the Technology and National Security Subcommittee of the joint economic Committee, Congress of the United States, 1990.

Clayton, Elizabeth, and James. R. Millar. *Quality of Life: Subjective Measures of Relative Satisfaction*. University of Illinois: Soviet Interview Project, 1987.

Czath, Magda. *The Achievements of Perestroika in its Early Stages*. Unpublished paper, 1988.

Friedberg, Maurice, and Heyward Isham, eds. *Soviet Society Under Gorbachev*. Armonk, NY: M.E. Sharpe, 1987.

Goldman, Marshall I. *Gorbachev's Challenge*. New York: W.W. Norton, 1987.

Goldman, Marshall I. "Gorbachev the Economist." *Foreign Affairs,* Vol. 69, No. 2 (Spring 1990), pp. 28–44.

Gorbachev, Mikhail. *Perestroika*. New York: Harper and Row, 1987.

Laquer, Walter. *The Long Road to Freedom: Russia and Glasnost*. New York: Charles Scribner's Sons, 1989.

Linz, Susan J., and William Moskoff, eds. *Reorganization and Reform in the Soviet Union*. Armonk, NY: M.E. Sharpe, 1988.

Mathews, Mervyn. *Poverty in the Soviet Union*. New York: Cambridge University Press, 1988.

Millar, James R. *Perestroika and Glasnost: Gorbachev's Gamble on Youth and Truth*. University of Illinois: Soviet Interview Project, 1988.

"Overcoming the Information Society Lag." *Current Digest of the Soviet Press*. Vol. 34, No. 4 (February, 1987), pp. 12–43.

Ruble, Blair. "The Social Dimensions of Perestroika." *Soviet Economy*. Vol. 3, No. 2 (1987), pp. 171–183.

"The New U.S.S.R." *Time*. April 10, 1989, pp. 48–129.

U.S. Congress, Joint Economic Committee. *Gorbachev's Economic Plans*. Vols. 1 and 2, 100th Congress, 1st Session, Washington: USGPO, 1987.

Vinokur, Aaron, and Gur Ofer. *Inequality of Earnings, Household Income and Wealth in the Soviet Union*. University of Illinois: Soviet Studies Project, 1987.

CHAPTER FOURTEEN

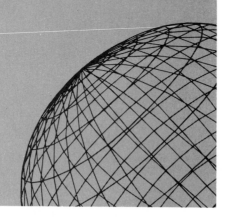

EASTERN EUROPE: HUNGARY AND POLAND

Events have happened with such rapidity in Eastern Europe that to stay current is about as impossible as trying to catch lightning in a bottle. Consider the following: In late fall 1989 four formerly hardline communist countries—Bulgaria, Czechoslovakia, East Germany, and Romania—opted for democratic reforms, free elections, and less state control over their economies. In Romania the dictator, Nicolae Ceausescu, was overthrown in a bloody revolution. He and his wife were executed by a firing squad, and a provisional government was created with elections scheduled in 1990. The role of the Communist Party has been abolished, and the Communist symbol has been removed from the Romanian flag. Hungary and Poland are well on their way to becoming democratic countries with free market economies.

Why has communism failed? Its quick repudiation in Eastern Europe leads one to believe that it was a hollow ideology, full of hypocrisy and cant, that failed to deliver what it had promised—a better society for all. That it delivered a better society for a select few is self-evident. Pictures on nightly television in the fall of 1989 showed compounds with swimming pools, special shopping stores filled with the finest products from the West, theaters, and chauffeur-driven limousines—all for the Communist Party elite, none of whom had been elected to office in free and open elections.[1] All of these occurred in supposedly classless societies at a time when the average East German or Czech had to wait 15 years to get an apartment and 10 years to get a car. Moreover, corruption

---

[1] Ceausescu had a mansion with 150 rooms, including bathrooms with gold fixtures, and a villa on the Black Sea manned by 80 servants, some of which had the responsibility of sifting the sand to keep it clean.

among Communist Party leaders was widespread. These were hardly the dreams upon which to base a classless society.

It is the most dramatic of ironies that Vaclav Havel, the dissident Czech playwright who repeatedly went to jail for writing plays that demonstrated a belief in democratic values, became the first non-Communist president of Czechoslovakia in 41 years, and that Alexander Dubcek, the leader of Czechoslovakia's 1968 "Prague Spring," which was crushed by Russian tanks, became Chairman of the Federal Assembly. Dubcek, who had been declared a nonperson by the Communist Party, spent 20 years in obscurity working as a gardener. His political resurrection illustrates the triumph of the human spirit in the face of adversity. Communism failed because it denied the basic right of freedom to the people who lived under it. It ruled through fear—the loss of one's livelihood and jail sentences for those persons who spoke out. There is the example of Czech police beating student demonstrators over the heads with clubs, an incident that became the catalyst in the downfall of the communist regime in Czechoslovakia.

Shakespeare once wrote that "a rose by any other name would smell as sweet."[2] In East Germany and Hungary, the Communist Party had tried to change its sour smell to sweet by changing its name to the Socialist Unity Party and the Socialist Party. In free elections that were held in the spring of 1990, the former Communist Party did not do well. The Communist Party did not fare well in elections held in Poland in the summer of 1989. In Romania, after the bloodbath that occurred, hostility toward the Communist Party in any form runs deep, and the Salvation Front, a combination of groups that opposed Ceausescu, has emerged as the decision-making body behind the new government.

HUNGARY AND POLAND: TWO COUNTRIES IN CHANGE

Both Poland and Hungary became a part of the Soviet sphere of influence when the Russian armies conquered and occupied their territories in 1945. Free elections were supposed to have been held according to the terms of the Yalta agreement, but when they were held they were dominated by the Communists, and opposition leaders were either jailed or murdered. In 1956 there was an uprising in Budapest against the Soviet domination of Hungary. The Soviets sent in their tanks and the uprising was crushed, with thousands of Hungarians being killed or executed, while thousands more fled the country. Hungarian Premier Imre Nagy, who had sponsored economic and social reforms, was executed by the Soviets and a puppet was put in his place to rule Hungary.

The tragedy of Poland is its geographic location. It has the unique misfortune of being located between Germany and the Soviet Union. An historian once wrote: "It is easier to lecture the Poles than to live their lives between Berlin and

---

[2] *Romeo and Juliet, II,ii.*

Moscow."[3] However, long before Germany and the Soviet Union became countries, Poland was a common battleground for invaders ranging from the Mongol hordes of Genghis Kahn to the Magyars and Swedes. In addition to suffering repeated foreign invasions, Poland was partitioned in the eighteenth century and was eliminated as a political organization until 1848. From 1918 to 1939 Poland was recreated as a country out of territory that had been taken from Germany, the Austro-Hungarian Empire, and Russia. During World War II, Poland was again partitioned between Germany and the Soviet Union. Some six million Poles were killed during World War II, the highest casualty rate relative to population for any country involved in the war.[4]

Both Hungary and Poland have made a complete break with communism and are charting a path toward a democratic political system and a free market economy. The pitfalls are many, not the least of which is the future of the Gorbachev reforms in the Soviet Union and of Gorbachev himself. The preconditions for economic reform look much better today than in the past, because the economic situation in both Hungary and Poland has deteriorated and communist illusion has faded away. However, for economic reforms to be successful in Hungary and Poland—and, for that matter, in the Soviet Union—the power of the bureaucracy with a vested interest in perpetuating its own interests must be broken. To accomplish this there has to be a far-reaching democratization process with popular pressure balancing the bureaucracy. In both Hungary and Poland that democratization process is going on.

The remainder of this chapter will examine the economic and political reforms that are going on in Hungary and Poland. Both countries are going to serve as economic and political laboratories for the future of Eastern Europe. Will it be possible to make a successful transition to a market economy after years of a state-directed and -planned economy? It is easier said than done, and the help of the West is needed. How will the process of democratization work in the two countries, neither of which has had much experience with democracy? It is difficult to believe that sensible reforms can be both legislated and implemented without a clear majority of reformists in power. Political resistance by those persons who want to maintain the status quo will be strong.

THE ECONOMIES
OF HUNGARY AND POLAND

The performance of the Polish economy during the 1980s has been poor. The level of industrial production has been about the same as it was in 1975, real per capita income has shown a decline, and agricultural production has declined to the

---

[3] Salvador de Madariaga, *Victors Beware* (London: Jonathan Cape, 1946) p. 214.

[4] About 20 percent of the Polish population were killed in fighting or in concentration camps, compared to a death rate of 12 percent for the Soviet Union and 9 percent for Germany.

point where most food products are in short supply. Moreover, Poland has serious environmental problems. Ninety-five percent of its river waters are now unfit for drinking, half of its lakes have been irreversibly contaminated, and more than three-fourths of drinking water sources do not meet official standards of purity.[5] By any criterion that can be used, the quality of life in communist Poland declined in the 1980s despite attempts by Party leaders to blame this poor performance on social unrest caused by the Solidarity movement. The simple fact is that after 40 years with a monopoly on power, the Communist regime was not able to fulfill its economic promises to the people of Poland.

Hungary offers a contrast to Poland in that it has been in the vanguard of East European reforms. In essence, it has attempted to reform its economy by developing something of a market-socialist economic system while maintaining its political allegiance to the Soviet Union. Given the emphasis that Soviet leader Mikhail Gorbachev has placed on revitalizing the Soviet economy, Hungary has been given more latitude to experiment. Prices were freed on many consumer products, and regulation was eased on the private and semiprivate sectors of the economy. However, the performance of the Hungarian economy during the 1980s was not much better than the performance of the Polish economy. Real per capita income and industrial production showed only modest increases and inflation developed. Pollution is also a problem, as it is in the other Eastern European countries and the Soviet Union. One in 17 deaths in Hungary is related to air pollution, and the Danube River immortalized in song is not blue but brown from pollution.[6]

Real Per Capita Growth

Table 14-1 presents real per capita growth for the Eastern European countries, including Hungary and Poland, for selected time periods, including the 1980s. As

TABLE 14-1
Real per Capita Growth in GNP for Eastern Europe (Average Annual Increase)

Country	1971–1980	1981–1985	1984	1985	1986	1987	1988
Bulgaria	2.8	0.8	3.3	−3.0	4.9	−0.9	2.0
Czechoslovakia	2.8	1.2	2.4	0.7	2.1	1.0	1.4
East Germany	2.8	1.9	2.8	3.1	1.5	1.8	1.8
Hungary	2.6	0.7	2.6	−2.5	2.2	1.1	1.1
Poland	3.6	0.6	3.7	0.9	2.7	−1.7	2.1
Romania	5.3	−0.1	4.4	0.8	2.9	−0.9	−1.5

Source: Central Intelligence Agency, Handbook of Economic Statistics 1989 *(Springfield, VA: National Technical Information Service, 1989), p. 33.*

_____

[5] Jackson Diehl, "New Face of East Bloc is Pitted by Pollution," *The Washington Post* (April 18, 1989), pp. A1, A20.

[6] Diehl, p. A20.

the table indicates, the economic performance of the Eastern European countries was not good. Productivity was low, and the Eastern bloc countries began to lag further behind the Western European countries in living standards. Agricultural production was poor, with some countries—notably Bulgaria and Poland—showing little gain in output during the 1980s.

Industrial Production

Table 14-2 presents an index of industrial production for Eastern Europe as a whole and for each of the countries. As the table indicates, the index shows that Polish industrial production has actually declined from a base year of 100 percent in 1980. Hungarian industrial production has been about average for Eastern Europe.

Inflation

A well known assertion in the socialist economies is that inflation cannot occur. This contention is based on the assumption that state planning can achieve a balance between production and spending to ensure price stability. As Table 14-3 indicates, this mechanism has not worked that well in practice because money in a socialist economy is an imperfect measure of value, and changes in its purchasing power are selectively restricted. There is no conventional market for the factors of production and no secure labor for hire unless prearranged through planning. The prices of consumer goods are not indicative of their value because a seller's market means that the official prices are understated. As Table 14-3 indicates, inflation has become a serious problem in Hungary and Poland.

POLAND

Joseph Stalin, who was not known for his sense of humor, once said that it was easier to saddle a bull than it was to impose communism on Poland. Although he has been dead for many years, subsequent events have proved him right. Solidarity,

TABLE 14-2

Index of Industrial Production of Eastern Europe (1980 = 100 percent)

Country	1975	1980	1983	1984	1985	1986	1987	1988
Eastern Europe	88	100	101	104	105	107	110	107
Bulgaria	85	100	107	110	108	110	112	113
Czechoslovakia	87	100	105	106	109	111	112	117
East Germany	86	100	104	108	111	114	118	120
Hungary	90	100	104	106	107	108	111	112
Poland	97	100	91	93	95	96	98	99
Romania	80	100	94	95	96	97	93	90

Source: Central Intelligence Agency, Handbook of Economic Statistics 1989 *(Springfield, VA: National Technical Information Service, 1989), p. 37.*

TABLE 14-3
Consumer Price Index for Eastern Europe (percent)

Country	1975	1980	1983	1984	1985	1986	1987	1988
Bulgaria	72	100	109	111	114	117	119	120
Czechoslovakia	88	100	105	106	109	109	110	111
East Germany	91	100	104	106	109	111	112	113
Hungary	73	100	123	133	144	152	167	193
Poland	64	100	285	330	386	467	600	1020
Romania	83	100	134	135	129	135	135	N.A.

Source: Central Intelligence Agency, Handbook of Economic Statistics 1989 *(Springfield, VA: National Technical Information Service, 1989), p. 39.*

the opposition trade union, outlawed in 1980, was legalized in 1989 when Poland's Communist Party agreed to share the power it had held for 40 years. In elections that were held in June 1989, Solidarity captured 99 seats out of 100 in the lower house of the *sejm*, which is the Polish parliament. However, under an agreement with the Communist Party, the majority of the seats in the upper house of the sejm was reserved for members of the Communist Party. In July 1989, Communist Party leader and President of Poland Jaruzelski invited Solidarity to form a coalition government, and in August 1989, Tadeusz Mazowiecki, a high-level Solidarity leader, became Poland's first non-Communist Prime Minister since World War II.

There are four reasons why the Poles have proved to be so intractable to communism. First, Poland had no tradition of communism before World War II. In East Germany and Hungary, communist parties were well established between World Wars I and II. Second, Poland has been occupied by foreign powers throughout most of its history. Third, there is a resentment of any outside power, particularly the Soviet Union.[7] Fourth, the Roman Catholic Church has always been a viable part of the life of Poland and a bulwark against change. Finally, there is the Polish national character itself, a romantic fatalism which has been created by many centuries of being the national battleground for neighboring powers. Poles have revolted countless times against their oppressors, with these revolts usually ending in failure.

Religion, History, and Economics

Modern Poland was created as a result of agreements reached at the Yalta Conference of 1945. At the end of World War II there were two rival factions in Poland, both of which had been resistance groups during the German occupation. One faction was the so-called National Army of Liberation, and the other was the

---

[7] While visiting Warsaw in 1985, the author was told the following joke: A sergeant in the Polish army asked a new recruit, "If the Germans and Russians invaded Poland at the same time, who would you shoot first, a German or a Russian?" The recruit replied, "The German." "Why?" the sergeant asked. "Business before pleasure," the recruit replied.

Communist People's Army.[8] The agreements of the Yalta Conference allowed the Soviet Union to extend its sphere of influence over Poland. Although free elections were called for, the Soviet Union had already created a provisional government, and it was only a matter of time before Communist Party influence was firmly established. When free elections were finally held in 1946, the outcome was pre-ordained. The Communist Party and its affiliated groups received 89.8 percent of the vote. Members of the National Army groups were either eliminated or left the country. In 1949, the Communist Party became the only political party in Poland, and in 1952 a constitution based on the Soviet constitution was promulgated.

Certain contradictions developed in the Polish economy and society despite attempts to impose a Soviet-type economic and social model. In the Soviet model, agriculture is collectivized, management and labor relations are controlled by the state, and resources are allocated on the basis of centralized economic planning. Religion was regarded by Marx as the opiate of the masses, so it would be eliminated (or at least severely discouraged). The application of the Soviet model was more difficult to implement in Poland than in the other Eastern European countries. For one thing, Poland is a larger country in both population and physical size. Poland is a Roman Catholic country, with strong attachments to the Church that go back a thousand years. The tradition of Polish agriculture runs counter to the establishment of collectivized agriculture. The Polish farmer has a deep-rooted sense of private property, individual freedom, religious feeling, and family farming. Attempts by the state to alter these institutions have not been successful.

Religion

The Catholic Church has been an integral part of Polish life ever since the baptism of the nation's first ruler, Prince Mieszko I, in 966. It helped keep the Polish language and culture alive during periods of occupation. After the communist takeover of Poland in 1945, religion remained largely untouched. The Roman Catholic Church was too much a part of Polish history and a repository of its culture for the state to eliminate it. A policy of accommodation developed between Church and state in Poland. The Church did not criticize the communist regime directly, and the regime ignored the Church as best it could. The Primate of Poland from 1948 to his death, Stefan Cardinal Wyszynski set Church policy based on moral criticism and ethical guidance to the faithful. The essence of the Church was its religious mission. It would not identify itself directly with any opposition movement, but it would also defend every persecuted opposition movement. However, the Church was not submissive to the state. Bishop Karol Wojtyla, who later became Pope John Paul II, was a critic of the temporal power of the state. The viability of the

---

[8] The National Army of Liberation was a part of the Free Polish group that was based in London during World War II. During the Warsaw uprising against the Nazis in 1944, the Russian army, though just across the Vistula River from Warsaw, did nothing to help the Poles.

Catholic Church is evidenced by the fact that 88 percent of the people of Poland today are communicants.

Problems of the Polish Economy

The Solidarity government has presented the most far-reaching free-market reforms in the postwar history of Eastern Europe. It proposes to sell off state enterprises, rewrite banking laws, overhaul the tax code, make the *zloty* (the Polish currency unit) fully convertible, end subsidies to state enterprises and state farms, and create new forms of state government. The government expects its program will force a 20 percent drop in real income, a 2 to 3 percent contraction in real gross national product, and a loss of some 600,000 jobs. The latter is rather drastic in an economy that has guaranteed employment or, as it has been described, an economy in which people pretend to work and the government pretends to pay.

However, economic and social problems confront the Polish economy. The rate of inflation has been estimated at 900 percent for 1989. There are chronic shortages of gasoline and consumer goods. The young people are migrating to the West in search of better jobs, and there is an ecological crisis of the worst order with polluted rivers and lakes and air pollution causing damage to health. These problems, however, can be considered of lesser importance than the three major problems of agriculture, the foreign debt, and industrial productivity. Each of these problems have to be addressed before Poland can have a viable and competitive market economy.

Agricultural Problems. Poland was the only centrally planned economy in Eastern Europe that has relied principally on private farming for the bulk of agricultural production. The Communists never succeeded in collectivizing the bulk of Polish agriculture; even at the outset of Communist Party rule, its hold on the allegiance of the people, especially in the heavily Catholic countryside, was simply too tenuous. Communist efforts to collectivize all forms of agriculture, often against the armed opposition of the farmers, resulted in many deaths. In 1956 the government formally postponed the political efforts required to enforce the collectivization of agriculture. The result is that 75 percent of the country's arable land is farmed by independent small farmers who account for around 75 percent of the country's agricultural output.

During the 1970s poor agricultural harvests and government inefficiency played havoc with agricultural production in one of the premier agricultural countries in Europe. Meat exports to the West, which were an important source of hard currency earnings, declined to the point where meat eventually had to be imported and rationing was imposed as early as 1977. A shortage in the potato crop, a major source of feed for hogs, forced farmers to purchase livestock feed from the state. This resulted in an increase in Polish grain imports, which heavily affected the trade deficit with Western countries. The cost of the grain imports was passed on to farmers, but it was not matched by higher prices for livestock.

Agricultural production in the 1980s did not improve. Agricultural prices were kept artificially low because almost every attempt to raise them to their true level provoked worker protest. The problem was that the centrally mandated lower prices reduced supplies because farmers reduced production or sold on the black market. Productivity plummeted and food lines grew longer as goods became scarcer. Table 14-4 provides some agricultural indices for the period 1975–1988. As the table indicates, in many respects Polish agricultural output was higher in 1975 than it was in 1988. For example, meat production was higher in 1975 than it was in 1988, and meat shortages have become epidemic in the Polish economy.

There are several reasons for the erratic performance of Polish agriculture. First, most Polish farms are too small to achieve economies of scale. Incomes are too low on most farms to afford investment in equipment for mechanizing farm tasks. Second, government policy toward agriculture has not been consistent. The government has subsidized consumers at the expense of farm income. Investment in agriculture has been generally low, as the government has favored development of the industrial sector. Third, processing facilities such as slaughter houses and meat processing plants have been controlled by inefficient state monopolies. Fourth, the distribution system is inefficient, so there is much waste and spoilage before farm goods get to consumers. Fifth, Polish agriculture produces little high-protein feed. This means that imports must be relied upon for its livestock sector. When imports are low or unavailable, feed utilization is very inefficient.

Table 14-5 compares agricultural efficiency in Poland to efficiency in other Eastern European countries and West Germany. While Poland ranks near the top in total production of farm crops, its yields are relatively low. It has the capacity to produce much more than it does. For years, private farmers have suffered from neglect, and government policies discouraged expansion and limited growth in productivity. As Poland enters into a new era of far-reaching, free market reforms,

TABLE 14-4

Indices of Agricultural Production in Poland

Type of Agricultural Production	1975	1980	1983	1984	1985	1986	1987	1988
Potato production[a]	46.43	26.39	34.47	37.44	36.55	36.25	36.30	36.25
Cattle numbers[b]	12.82	12.16	11.02	11.09	10.91	N.A.	10.52	N.A
Hog numbers[b]	21.71	20.98	17.56	15.86	17.21	18.90	19.62	18.90
Meat production[c]	3,062	3,032	2,407	2,435	2,696	2,083	3,022	2,983
Milk production[c]	16,377	16,499	15,990	15,750	15,626	15,078	15,593	15,078

[a] Millions metric tons
[b] Million head
[c] Thousand metric tons

Source: Central Intelligence Agency, Handbook of Economic Statistics 1990 (Springfield, VA: National Technical Information Service, 1990), pp. 72–74.

TABLE 14-5

A Comparison of Crop Yields for Poland and Other Eastern European Countries for 1988 (tons/hectares)

Country	All Grains	Wheat	Rye	Barley	Potatoes	Sugar Beets	Rapeseed
Bulgaria	3.9	4.1	1.7	3.7	11.0	10.0	–
Czechoslovakia	4.7	5.4	3.5	4.1	17.2	3.6	2.9
East Germany	4.1	5.1	2.8	4.2	25.8	2.3	2.6
Hungary	5.2	5.4	2.1	3.9	15.4	3.8	2.0
Poland	2.9	3.4	2.4	3.3	18.6	3.4	2.4
Romania	4.8	3.6	2.0	3.3	22.3	2.5	0.6
West Germany	5.7	6.8	4.2	5.2	31.7	4.8	3.1

Source: Data provided by the U.S. Department of Agriculture.

market institutions for guiding production, distribution, and consumption do not exist. Yet the pressures for their development and for them to deliver increasing supplies of consumer goods at reasonable prices are enormous.

Agricultural Reform. On December 20, 1989, the Polish Parliament voted 284 to 1 to convert agriculture into a free market system. This will be easier said than done. It will mean dismantling the state-set procurement prices, the state farms (which have received most of the government's financial support for agriculture), the state-owned processing plants, and the state-run food distribution system. There is also a jurisdictional problem over which government ministry, the Ministry of Agriculture or the Ministry of Science, will control research. No plan or procedure exists for concentrating research (weed control, disease control, fertilizer responses) on particular crops in order to obtain improved yields. Most agricultural research never gets disseminated, and an inadequate extension service manned by poorly trained people is regarded as the weakest link in the agricultural production systems.

Considerable outside aid for Polish agriculture is needed, part of which will be provided in an aid package approved by the U.S. Congress to assist Poland and Hungary.[9] There is much that has to be done before a free market can be instituted because market institutions for guiding production, distribution, and consumption do not exist. It is not as though Poland cannot produce food; the 1989 harvest was abundant, with a record of 27 million tons of grain produced. The paradox was the food queues in all of the stores, illustrating the complete ineptitude of the state-run distribution system, the waste on the farms and the drawback of state-set prices that encourage farmers to feed grain to livestock rather than sell to the state. A major argument for freeing farm prices is the need to improve incentives for farmers to sell more in the market, higher volume eventually lowering food prices.

---

[9] See S. 1582, September 6, 1989, 10125 Congress, 1st Session.

On the other hand, free pricing might instead decrease prices, discourage increased production and eventually raise prices.[10]

The Polish Foreign Debt. The Polish foreign debt is a major economic problem. Most of this debt was incurred during the 1970s when Edward Gierek was leader of Poland. He promised massive gains in the nation's standard of living, to be achieved by making Poland more competitive in world markets. To do this, he imported large amounts of capital goods from the West, paid for with credit from Western banks and governments. The Poles expected to pay off their debts with expanded exports to the West in the form of goods produced with their new technology. However, much of the borrowed money was wasted on a wide variety of things, including villas and Mercedez-Benzes for Communist Party officials. Little or nothing was done to enhance the Poles' ability to earn hard currency in order to finance foreign loan payments to Western banks.

The growth of exports to the West has not kept pace with the growth of imports and the increase in the foreign debt, as Table 14-6 indicates. As borrowing has increased, Poland has become more dependent on private credit from Western commercial banks. In 1970, debt to Western commercial banks and governments amounted to $1.3 billion; by 1989 the debt amounted to $42.6 billion. An increase in debt service payments has forced Poland to seek easier credit terms in the West, but Western banks have been reluctant to lend money. Debt payments are going to have to be liberalized if Poland is going to have any chance of succeeding in its transformation to a market economy. Interest payments and debt service exceed hard currency earnings from Poland's exports, much of which has to pay for imports.

TABLE 14-6
Poland's Foreign Debt, Exports, and Gross National Product 1982–1989 (millions of dollars)

Year	Foreign Debt	Exports	Debt/Exports	GNP	Debt/GNP
1982	29.1	14.2	205.0%	72.3	39.1%
1983	30.2	13.8	219.9	74.0	40.8
1984	32.2	13.9	231.1	74.4	43.2
1985	33.1	13.2	250.3	69.8	47.4
1986	36.6	14.1	259.3	72.8	50.3
1987	42.1	13.4	314.1	63.8	66.0
1988	42.8	8.6	498.6	68.8	62.3
1989	42.6	9.6	444.1	73.6	58.0

Source: The World Bank, World Debt Tables, 1988–1989, *(Washington, DC: The World Bank, 1989), p. 49.*

[10] For an excellent analysis of Polish agriculture, see J.B. Penn, "Poland's Agriculture: It Could Make The Critical Difference," *Choices,* Vol. 4, No. 4 (Fourth Quarter 1989), pp. 3–7.

Low Industrial Productivity. Industrial productivity is a third major problem confronting the Polish economy. As Table 14-2 indicated, the index of industrial production in Poland was lower in 1988 than it was in 1975. There has been a reduction in both capital and labor productivity. There has been a lack of economic motivation and pressure to economize on the use of fuels and raw materials. Technology is obsolete, and many industries are simply uncompetitive even by Eastern European standards. The Lenin shipyard in Gdansk, the birthplace of Solidarity, is bankrupt. The present industrial structure was created during the time of Stalin, with priority given to the development of the iron and steel industry, heavy machinery, and other producer goods. In the 1970s, efforts were made to restructure these industries with the help of Western capital and technology. These efforts failed and economic stagnation coupled with the problem of foreign debt repayment resulted in a decline in consumption and investment during the 1980s.

Table 14-7 presents a comparison of the level of productivity in Poland for 1987 compared to 1978. The statistics imply a decline in both capital and labor productivity.[11] Productivity changes are obtained by comparing changes in the level of Produced Net Material Product (PNMP) with changes in employment and gross capital stock.[12] In 1987, PNMP at constant prices with changes in employment and gross national stock represented 94.6 percent of its 1978 level. Gross national stock showed an increase over 1978, but productivity declined, showing a misuse of resources. There is also the use of outdated highly fuel-intensive technologies, particularly in the production of steel and cement.

Solidarity and Lech Walesa

In July 1980, workers in the Lenin Shipyard in Gdansk walked out in protest of the government's decision to raise meat prices. The protest appeared to be going nowhere when an unemployed electrician named Lech Walesa, who had been fired for trying to create an independent union, climbed over the shipyard fence and became the catalyst in a labor movement that was to shake Poland and the world. That he was able to do what he did in a shipyard named for one of the saints of communism has some irony, for the last thing in the world Lenin wanted, or would tolerate, was any movement that would mitigate the dictatorship of the Communist Party.

Walesa assumed control over the protesting shipyard workers and the protest movement began to spread to other parts of Poland. A link was formed between

---

[11] See Zbigniew Fallenbuchl, "Poland: The Anatomy of Stagnation." In *Pressures for Reform in the East European Countries*, Vol. 2, Joint Economic Committee, Congress of the United States (Washington, DC: USGPO, 1989), pp. 102–136.

[12] Net Material product includes all activities that create material goods or help in productive processes, less depreciation. Material production can be divided into six major divisions: industry, construction, agriculture, transport, trade, and other material production.

TABLE 14-7

Net Material Product Employment and Capital Stock and GNP (1987/1978 with 1978 = 100 percent)

	1978	1987
Produced NMP		
Total	100	94.6
Industry	100	96.3
Construction	100	63.7
Agriculture	100	95.1
Distributed NMP		
Total	100	88.5
Total consumption	100	106.0
Total net capital formation	100	48.9
Net fixed capital formation	100	52.4
Employment		
Total material sphere	100	95.5
Industry	100	95.6
Construction	100	82.7
Agriculture	100	97.1
Gross Capital Stock		
Total material sphere	100	131.5
Industry	100	132.7
Construction	100	127.5
Agriculture	100	132.1
GNP	**100**	**98.7**

Source: Zbigniew Fallenbuchi, "Poland: The Anatomy of Stagnation." In Pressures for Reform in the East European Economies, *Vol. 2, Joint Economic Committee, Congress of the United States (Washington, DC: USGPO, 1989), p. 108.*

intellectuals and workers that led to the creation of Solidarity. The Lenin Shipyard became the focal point of the Solidarity movement; in August, 1980, Walesa and other Solidarity officers met with members of the Gierek government to hammer out the Gdansk agreement. The government agreed to allow the workers the right to strike—something unheard of in a communist state, where Marxist theory holds that there are no contradictory class interests to cause labor conflicts. Workers were also given the right to form their own unions. Censorship was reduced and access to the state broadcasting networks was given to the unions and the Catholic Church.

After the Gdansk agreement, the Solidarity movement spread like wildfire across Poland. Solidarity evolved into a loose-knit federation to which some 10 million Poles belonged. Everyone from coal miner to college professor belonged to Solidarity, which was divided into 30 semiautonomous regional chapters throughout the country. Problems of policy and strategy developed because some members wanted a union federation concerned with labor goals, while other members wanted to mount opposition to the state. Cross-currents were at work in Solidarity, and the federation was increasingly forced into the path of contentious political activism by its various factions. Elements within Solidarity eventually gave the goverment the excuse it was looking for when they called for a national referendum on the future of the communist government in Poland and reexamination of Polish military ties with the Soviet Union. In December 1981, martial law was declared in Poland and Lech Walesa and thousands of other Poles were arrested.

Return of Solidarity

Economic and social conditions continued to unravel in Poland in 1988, and Solidarity was able to mount a comeback. Strikes broke out over higher food prices announced by the Communist regime. In August 1988, coal miners in Silesia went out on strike, and the shipyard workers in Gdansk, the birthplace of Solidarity, also went out on strike. Social unrest continued into 1989. Roundtable discussions began between Communist Party leaders and members of Solidarity, and the latter was eventually legalized. Parliamentary elections were held in June 1989 for 100 seats in the Senate and 161 seats in the lower house, with Solidarity winning 260 of the 261 seats it was contesting.

When the elections were over, a new government had to be formed. Jaruzelski became President after receiving a parliamentary majority of only one vote. The more important position of Prime Minister went to a non-Communist, Tadeusz Mazowiecki, who had the support of Lech Walesa. As Prime Minster, he has had to deal with a mountain of economic and social troubles. The zloty is virtually worthless as a medium of exchange because there is little to buy and it has been depreciated to the point where twenty thousand zlotys is worth two and a half dollars at its true black market rate of conversion. Many people have stopped working because they cannot afford to tie up their hours at jobs where they are paid in depreciating zlotys.

HUNGARY

Hungary was a part of the Austro-Hungarian empire that existed before World War I. There was an uneasy relationship between the Magyars, who were dominant in Hungary, and the Germans, who dominated the Austro-Hungarian empire as a whole.[13] The Treaty of Versailles in 1919 created a separate Austria and Hungary.

---

[13] There were two capitals in the Austro-Hungarian empire—one in Vienna and the other in Budapest.

Hungary was largely an agricultural country ruled by aristocratic landlords with little pretense of a democracy. During World War II, Hungary had little choice but to become an ally of Nazi Germany, and after the war it became a part of the Soviet sphere of influence. It formerly became a communist country in 1949, but in 1956 the government sponsored by the Soviet Union was replaced in a spontaneous uprising that was crushed by the Russians, with many casualties. The economic approach used in Hungary was basic Stalin: the creation of an iron and steel industry in an agrarian country with few natural resources.

Janos Kadar was installed by the Russians to govern Hungary after the 1956 uprising had been put down. He governed Hungary for 32 years and, to his credit, was more flexible in his rule than his counterparts in the other Eastern bloc countries. He was willing to allow some experimentation with economic reforms, and Hungarians were pretty much free to travel to other countries. Despite these reforms, the performance of the Hungarian economy during the Kadar years was about average in comparison with the other Eastern European countries, yet Hungarians enjoyed a relative abundance of consumer goods that made them the envy of their neighbors.

Problems of the Hungarian Economy

Although Hungary was the most progressive of all the communist countries, it is not free from economic problems. There is persistent economic stagnation and a rapidly growing foreign debt, which in 1988 amounted to $18 billion. Its current balance-of-payments account was negative for the third straight year, and the debt service amounted to 30 percent of its exports.[14] It has had to borrow from the International Monetary Fund (IMF) to make debt service payments. The rate of economic growth in Hungary during the 1980s has been low in comparison to some of the other Eastern bloc countries. To some extend, there are extenuating circumstances. For example, the fall in world oil prices has not helped energy-importing Hungary, since the price it has had to pay the Soviet Union for its oil has been based on a five-year moving average of world oil prices.

The Hungarian economy has to become more efficient in order to export more to the West and earn the hard currency necessary to reduce its foreign debt. Although living standards are above most of the other Eastern bloc countries, and dynamic agricultural and consumer sectors exist, Hungary has to make its industrial sector more efficient. In the past, huge subsidies were paid to state enterprises so that they could operate. These and other subsidies amounted to as much as 50 percent of the state budget, which left the government with little financial latitude when it came to importing technology from the West. That is why the Hungarians are trying to create a market-based economy with prices and profit-oriented competition similar to that of the West.

---

[14] The World Bank, *World Debt Tables: External Debt of Developing Countries, 1988–89* (Washington, DC: The World Bank, 1989), p. 182.

The Foreign Debt. The foreign debt also presents a problem to Hungary. During the 1980s there has been an increase in the debt service at a time when hard currency earnings have shown little or no increase. There has been a continued current account deficit and an imbalance in the balance of payments, which forced the government in 1987 to respond with a series of austerity measures. These measures had no impact on the current account deficit. The government used import and investment controls and even recourse to IMF aid. The Hungarian economy struggled with a low rate of economic growth during the 1980s and an increasingly obsolete and uncompetitive industrial base, which made it more difficult to increase exports to earn the hard currency necessary to service the foreign debt.

Table 14-8 presents exports of goods and services, gross national product and foreign debt to exports, and foreign debt to GNP ratios for Hungary for the period 1980–1989. Hungary had a negative balance in its current account in nine of the ten years, as the table also indicates.

Low Productivity. There has been a slowdown in economic growth in Hungary during the 1980s, with real per capita growth in GNP averaging about 1 percent a year. In part this slow growth can be attributed to financial constraints imposed by the foreign debt, particularly import and investment cuts. There has also been a fall in factor productivity and a misallocation of investment that resulted in wastage. Modernization efforts were hindered by the fact that an increasing share of resources was allocated to inefficient enterprises in the heavy industry sector. Productivity increases have also been retarded by the declining health of the population, which has contributed to increased absenteeism and prolonged illnesses. There is also a

TABLE 14-8
Hungary's Foreign Debt, Exports, GNP, and Current Account Balance 1980–1989 (millions of dollars)

Year	Foreign Debt	Exports	Debt/Exports	GNP	Debt/GNP	Current Account
1980	10.3	10.1	101.1	21.8	47.3	−631
1981	10.0	10.3	97.1	21.9	46.4	−943
1982	9.0	10.5	91.4	22.5	40.0	−482
1983	9.6	10.3	93.5	20.6	46.8	−19
1984	10.1	10.5	96.6	19.8	51.1	199
1985	13.0	10.4	125.1	19.9	65.5	−116
1986	16.3	11.0	148.6	22.9	71.2	−1,365
1987	19.0	12.1	157.1	25.1	75.5	−676
1988[a]	18.8	6.3	296.3	26.7	70.2	−1,402
1989[a]	18.4	6.9	267.0	28.1	65.5	−1,333

[a] Estimates

Source: The World Bank, World Debt Tables, 1988–1989, *(Washington, DC: The World Bank, 1989), p. 29.*

shortage of skilled labor as many workers either emigrate or go to work for themselves. As Table 14-9 indicates, low productivity has adversely affected production and resource utilization.

Foreign Trade. A third problem confronting the Hungarian economy is its declining competitiveness in foreign trade, which adversely affects its current account and its overall balance of payments. All the Eastern European countries are losing world market shares to the developing countries of East Asia. This has reduced hard currency earnings in many Hungarian export sectors. The bulk of Hungarian exports are primary products whose prices have declined in world markets, and imports consist in part of manufactured goods whose prices have gone up in world markets. Hungary had negative terms of trade during the 1980s. Hungary also lost a major source of hard currency, namely, its reexporting of Soviet oil for hard currency, which the Soviet Union would spend in Hungary for grain and meat products. Lower world prices for oil reduced Soviet hard currency earnings, which meant less hard currency for Hungarian products.

Table 14-10 presents changes in the prices of hard currency from Hungary during the period 1981–1987. Also presented is the terms of trade for Hungary during the same period. The terms of trade means that quantity of imports that can be bought by a given quantity of exports. In the case of Hungary, it is giving up more exports than it is getting in imports.

TABLE 14-9

Estimates of Production and Resource Utilization in Hungary 1981–1987 (percent change over previous year)

	1981	1982	1983	1984	1985	1986	1987
Hungarian Estimates							
NMP produced	2.5	2.6	0.3	2.5	−1.4	0.9	4.1
NMP used	0.7	−1.1	−2.7	−0.6	−0.6	3.9	3.0
Consumption	3.0	1.4	0.6	0.9	−1.2	2.9	3.1
Net capital formation	−8.6	−12.4	−20.4	−11.3	−15.0	21.4	2.7
Western Estimates							
GNP	0.7	3.6	−1.0	2.6	−2.6	2.1	1.2
GNP, final use	−0.7	0.7	−3.4	0.3	−2.1	4.4	1.0
Consumptions, private	2.1	0.5	−0.7	0.3	0.4	1.4	1.5
Investment	−5.5	0.9	−9.3	−0.4	−7.8	11.5	−0.5

Source: Central Intelligence Agency, "Hungary: Economic Performance in the 1980's, Prospects for the 1990's." In Pressures for Reform in the East European Economies, Vol. 2, Joint Economic Committee, Congress of the United States (Washington, DC: USGPO, 1989), p. 24.

TABLE 14-10
Changes in Price of Hungarian Exports and Terms of Trade 1980–1987 (percent change from previous year)

	1981	1982	1983	1984	1985	1986	1987
Price							
Energy products	12.9	−11.6	−9.2	−8.3	0	−43.0	11.4
Raw materials	−7.1	−7.0	−8.5	−3.4	−1.2	5.3	7.3
Machinery	−2.6	−3.6	−5.6	−5.2	0.6	13.5	7.9
Consumer goods	−3.2	−6.5	−8.2	−4.9	−1.1	17.4	7.7
Food & agricultural products	2.2	−10.0	−12.4	−9.6	−9.0	4.9	3.7
Terms of trade	2.2	−1.1	−2.5	−2.3	−1.1	−6.9	−0.2

Source: Central Intelligence Agency, "Hungary: Economic Performance in the 1980's, Prospects for the 1990's." In Pressures for Reform in the East European Economies, Vol. 2, Joint Economic Committee, Congress of the United States (Washington, DC: USGPO, 1989), p. 32.

Economic Reforms in Hungary

Hungarian administrative and economic reforms have been designed to promote efficiency. Some effort was made during the 1950s to effect a liberalization of the bureaucratic and administrative framework. In 1957, for example, individual enterprises were relieved of the obligation to submit monthly and quarterly plans for the approval of higher authorities. In 1963 the guidance and control of enterprises, previously exercised by ministerial industrial boards, was turned over to newly organized trusts operated to maximize profits, with the component enterprises defraying the expenses. Another significant reform was made in 1964 with the introduction of capital charges in industry. Capital charges were annual payments made by enterprises to the state on fixed and circulating capital in their possession. It was recognized that interest can be ideologically justified because capital is nothing else than materialized labor, and as such it should be rationally distributed because it represents a means of economizing on live labor.

The New Economic Mechanism, 1968.   However, the most important reforms took place in 1968 with the introduction of the New Economic Mechanism, which substantially reduced central government intervention in the economy at the enterprise level. Enterprises were made independent economic units with the right to determine the structure of their production and sales. This policy conformed to one basic objective of the reforms, namely, to relieve the planning authorities of the task of preparing intricate economic plans. Instead, broad guidelines were provided for enterprises to follow. Enterprises were given latitude with respect to quality, styling, and pricing. They were then given the right to determine their own production mix on the basis of their preferences. A modified market economy was permitted in which enterprises could react to consumer preferences. Nevertheless, the central planning authorities were able to exercise some control over enterprise production through the use of economic levers designed to induce cooperation by making it more profitable to produce certain items. However, all major macroeconomic decisions concerning economic development, living standards, and investment and consumption remained in the hands of the state.[15]

However, enterprises and individuals discovered that indirect regulators and controls exercised by the state provided constraints that manipulated the market framework. Moreover, there were no political reforms to accompany decentralization of economic decision making at the enterprise level. Although there was an effort to achieve decentralization of decision making, there was no corresponding effort to provide more autonomy in terms of political rights. All economic decisions had to be made within the constraints of a highly circumscribed political framework. Inevitably, the reforms came into conflict with ideological and political issues. Subsequent reforms have aimed at reducing the amount of state control over enterprises.

Later Reforms. Reforms introduced in 1984 and 1985 were aimed at increasing the efficiency of state enterprises. A compulsory reserve fund, introduced in 1968, was eliminated. The reserve fund was a prescribed percentage of after-tax profit; as a result, disposable enterprise income was reduced. In its place, reserves held from pre-tax profits were to be allowed, based on the decisions of individual enterprise managers. Bonds may now be issued by state enterprises and sold to the general public to raise capital. Another reform, introduced in 1985, was a new form of management. Rather than being chosen by the Communist Party, the director and management staffs of small and medium-sized state enterprises were to be selected by the workers, who were also given the right to recall them. Enterprise councils were introduced in the same year as a new form of management of large state enterprises. The enterprise council has the following responsibilities.[16]

1. Approval of the company's annual budget, strategic plan, and financial statements.
2. Approval of capital budgets, major resource allocation decisions, and changes in the company's line of business.
3. Approval of mergers, acquisitions, or any other major corporate reorganization decisions.
4. Election and evaluation of the performance of the managing director.

---

[15] For discussions of the reforms see Barnabas Buky, "Hungary on a Treadmill," *Problems of Communism* (September–October 1972), pp. 31–39; also Harry G. Shaffer, "Progress in Hungary," *Problems of Communism* (January–February 1970), pp. 45–59.

[16] Magdolna Czath and Thomas H. Naylor, "The Hungarian Experience with Deregulation," *Technovation*, Vol. 5 (1986) Elsevier Science Publishers, Amsterdam, The Netherlands, pp. 95–113.

An enterprise council is composed of elected representatives of a company's employees and representatives of management. A management director, who used to be appointed by the appropriate industrial ministry, but is now elected by the enterprise council, is responsible for the day-to-day operations of the enterprise. The enterprise council is the strategic decision-making body of an enterprise and exercises the property rights transferred to it by the state. It should be emphasized, however, that the state through the appropriate branch within the Ministry of Industry is able to exercise some control over an enterprise. The Ministry of Industry has veto power over the appointment of the managing director of an enterprise, as well as over decisions involving the creation of an enterprise.

The Cooperative.   Another form of management organization is the cooperative. Cooperatives are very decentralized and are in widespread use in agriculture but have also evolved in such areas as engineering design, computer software, and management consulting. The state provides considerable latitude when it comes to forming a cooperative; almost anyone can form one. The state can intervene in the appointment of a director, and it has the right to approve or disapprove the creation of a cooperative. Most Hungarian farms are managed by cooperatives, which cultivate 80 percent of the farm land. Production quotas are to be fulfilled, but private plots are permitted.[17] On these plots of land, farmers produce half of the pigs, a third of the beef and dairy cattle, three-fourths of the poultry, and half of the fruit produced in Hungary.[18]

Stocks, Bonds, and a Rotary Club.   Perhaps the most radical of Hungarian economic reforms include the creation of a stock market and a bond market. Since January 1, 1989, any company in Hungary can issue and sell stock to the public. Hungarian firms that were formerly subsidized by the state are now encouraged to raise money through the sale of stocks and bonds. There is, of course, the problem of persuading Hungarians, most of whom have never heard of a stock market, to buy stock. To sell stocks in the market there have to be investment bankers, rating agencies, accountants, and brokers, but this is in the process of being done. In what must be the irony of all ironies, one Hungarian brokerage firm is planning to rent a room in Karl Marx University to use as an office.[19] As for Rotary, the Budapest Rotary

---

[17] The reforms have reduced production quotas and have provided more latitude for cooperatives to manage the farms as they see fit. Most cooperatives are now independent from state control. The state rents equipment to them and they may also buy equipment.

[18] There are also some state-owned farms, which are decreasing in number and importance. There are also some privately owned farms that work in conjunction with the cooperatives. For example, nearly all of the high-quality paprika in Hungary is produced by private farmers and then processed by cooperatives for shipment abroad.

[19] Barry Newman, "Hungary Unveils Its Own Stock Market," *The Wall Street Journal* (Thursday, April 20, 1989), p. 10.

Club has been chartered, marking the first time any capitalist civic club has been created in a communist country.[20]

Joint Venture. In 1988 the Hungarian government passed laws to encourage more foreign direct investment in Hungary. In particular, the laws pertained to the creation of joint ventures that involve foreign Hungarian enterprises. A 1989 law permits the setting up of 100-percent foreign-owned firms.[21] A number of benefits have been provided to encourage the formation of more joint ventures. First, a foreign firm is permitted to have a majority interest in the joint venture. Second, income taxes can be eliminated for a period of five years.[22] Third, restrictions have been reduced on the amount of earnings that foreign firms can repatriate from Hungary. Fourth, foreign enterprises, joint ventures, and Hungarian-owned enterprises may hire up to 500 private workers. Fifth, custom-free zones are to be set up to exempt foreign investors from customs duties and exchange controls. Priority in joint ventures is given to such areas as electronics, vehicle component production, farm and food production, packing technology, and tourism.

Political Reforms

On June 24, 1989, while the Chinese Communist Party was purging moderates and electing hardliners to run China, the reverse was true in Hungary. In fact, a moderate Karoly Grosz, who had led the Hungarian Socialist Workers' Party for 13 months, was replaced when the Central Committee elected a four-member Presidium dominated by reformers. The Presidium will direct Hungary's political reforms until October 1989 when a new party leader is elected. National elections are to be held in 1990. The election will be a referendum on the results of 40 years of communism in Hungary, which have been rather dismal. The reformers are hoping to create a new Communist Party based on Western-style socialist and social democratic ideals. This comes at a time when public opinion polls show that the Communist Party would get less than 30 percent of the vote in a multiparty election.

CAN DEMOCRACY AND FREE MARKETS BE ACHIEVED?

Unlike the fairy tales where fairy godmothers could wave magic wands and transform a scullery maid into the belle of the ball or an evil stepmother into a toad, no quick fix can transform Hungary and Poland into democratic societies overnight.

---

[20] A Rotary Club has also been chartered in Warsaw, Moscow, and Prague.

[21] The law is Act 24 on Foreign Investment in Hungary. See "New Hungarian Law Will Boost Joint Ventures in Hungary," *Business Eastern Europe* (January 16, 1989), p. 1.

[22] The profits tax rate is 40 percent in Hungary.

There is no fail-safe recipe for democracy, and neither Hungary nor Poland has had any experience with it. In Poland, Solidarity has had a hard time enforcing party discipline. Moreover, Solidarity has to bump up against the realities of life, including how to deal with an entrenched communist bureaucracy that is going to resist change. Then there are also the economic problems that have to be confronted. One problem is chronic food and fuel shortages, and another is already inadequate salaries that are declining in purchasing power. Budget deficits and the $40 billion debt to the West place constraints on Solidarity's handling of economic reforms.

It is difficult to introduce a free market economy into Hungary and Poland where there is no experience with free markets and free enterprises. In a free market, prices determine resource allocation; in a planned economy, it is the state that allocates resources. In a free enterprise economy, there is an element of Social Darwinism in that competition is supposed to eliminate inefficient businesses, whereas under a planned economy, failing enterprises are subsidized by the state. When a free enterprise system is introduced into Hungary and Poland, there will be inevitable chaos—including high unemployment, which would not be permitted in a planned economy even at the expense of inefficiency. In addition to plant closings, prices will have to rise to reflect the true costs of production, and austerity measures will have to be imposed to control inflation. So how do you make capitalists out of communists? It is easier said than done. Here are some of the problems.

Bureaucracy

The Czech writer and political dissident Vaclav Havel wrote a play called *The Memorandum* (New York: Grove Press, 1980) for which he was thrown in jail by his government. The theme of the play is that the communist system is based on an *a priori* assumption that the state can do no wrong. Since the bureaucracy represents the state it, too, can do no wrong. If the institutions of the state can never be in error, then anybody criticizing their actions is logically defined as an enemy. No matter how absurd things are, the party is never wrong. In the play, a new form of language communication is introduced into the bureaucracy. It makes no difference that it makes no sense, everyone must learn it and spies covertly see that it is being learned. Those who don't want to learn it are demoted and replaced by their subordinates. Then another language form is introduced to replace the first language change, and those who learned the first are replaced by those they had replaced.

Like bureaucrats all over the world, Communist bureaucrats will resist change, particularly when they feel threatened. However, communist bureaucrats are going to be more likely than other bureaucrats to resist change, because a reform reduces their power by definition. Therefore, to be successful, a reform must break the power of the bureaucracy, and that is easier said than done. It is difficult to perceive any other solution than a far-reaching democratization with strong popular pressure and openness balancing the bureacracy. Bureaucratic conservatism and dogmatic orthodoxy tend to reinforce each other, with dogma legitimizing established power, and power protecting the established dogma. Then there is the system of nomenklatura, with its vast structure of overlapping privileges, controls, rewards, and vested interests.[23]

Changing the Economic System

An economic system must be reasonably consistent to be effective. No chain is stronger than its weakest link. The problem with reforms in Hungary and Poland, as well as other communist countries, is that they have been limited and inconsistent. There have been attempts to graft certain elements of a market economy onto a command economy, where the grafting doesn't take. One problem has been that often, when enterprise managers have been given more authority to set prices, there was not a corresponding reduction in the power of regulatory and central planning commissions. Sometimes reforms were applied to certain economic sectors, while other sectors were left untouched. Reforms also bumped into Marxist-Leninist ideology pertaining to central planning and socialist ownership of the means of production. Any complete break with this ideology would have amounted to a basic redefinition of the Communist Party, its legitimacy, and its infallibility.

Comecon.   One problem that confronts both Hungary and Poland in their attempts to move toward more open market economies is their association with Comecon, which is the Eastern bloc's version of the Common Market. Comecon, or Council for Mutual Economic Assistance, was created in the 1950s to link the economies of the Soviet Union and Eastern Europe. Comecon calls for individual member countries to specialize in the manufacture of specific goods and sets production quotas to meet the bloc's needs. The common currency denominator is the ruble. Most foreign trade of each country goes to other bloc countries. Comecon has built a wall around itself that promotes inefficiency and the production of goods that are not competitive in world markets. Soviet energy supplies and raw materials are sold at subsidized prices to other member countries.

Currency Reforms.   Both the Hungarian forint and the Polish zloty are incovertible currencies, which means that they cannot be denominated against Western hard currencies such as the dollar, but only against the ruble. The problem with the forint and the zloty is that they are not true measures of value. There is no conventional market for the pricing factors of production; thus, money cannot buy the means of production or secure labor for hire. But even the prices of consumer goods are not indicative of their value. Traditionally, there has been an almost complete insulation of domestic from foreign prices. Also, in market economies, foreign exchange rates normally relate domestic to foreign prices, and they roughly indicate the

---

[23] It is easy to identify who are the communists in a bureaucracy. They are the ones with the private offices and secretaries.

purchasing power of the national currency in terms of foreign currencies. Exchange rates directly influence the profitability of foreign trade, and they largely influence the size and direction of trade. The currencies of Hungary, Poland, and other Eastern bloc countries have been artificially overvalued relative to Western hard currencies.[24]

Private Enterprise.   In both Hungary and Poland, there is a transition from a repressive system that is predictable to one that demands personal initiative. There is bound to be social unrest as inefficient state enterprises are abandoned and private enterprise is introduced into countries that have had little or no experience with it. Under communism the tradeoff was simple. People could not speak freely and were constantly under surveillance, but they had a roof over their head, a job, food in their stomachs, and medical attention when they needed it. But there was poverty, alcoholism, and pollution. In Hungary, current government estimates place 20 percent of the population living in poverty. So as Hungary and Poland make the transition from communism to capitalism, real impediments exist.

Both the United States and West Germany are providing financial assistance to Hungary and Poland.[25] This financial assistance takes many forms, one of which involves an attempt to export entrepreneurship. The United States is sponsoring a new version of the Peace Corps where retired business executives teach the locals how to become entrepreneurs. Also included in the assistance are financial grants to Hungarian and Polish students for study in management programs in the United States. Scientific and technical assistance will be provided to Hungarian and Polish universities. The assistance will also cover environmental cleanup; both Hungary and Poland are among the most polluted nations in Europe. U.S. aid also includes resumption of most-favored-nation treatment for Poland. West German aid includes the formation of joint ventures with Hungarian and Polish enterprises.[26]

In short, the following requisites will be necessary to create a free market economy in Hungary and Poland.

1. A convertible hard currency at a uniform exchange rate.
2. A disciplined and balanced state budget with no subsidies for inefficient enterprises or on consumer goods.

---

[24] The Soviet ruble has been devalued from an exchange rate of $1.46 = 1 ruble to 6 rubles = $1, which is the black market rate. The official exchange rate for the Polish zloty is around 40 zlotys = $1. The official exchange rate for the Hungarian forint is 60 forints = $1, but the black market rate is 95 forints = $1.

[25] U.S. aid to Hungary and Poland will amount to around $750 million. By contrast, West German aid will amount to around $10.1 billion. However, much of that amount will go to the Soviet Union with whom West Germany has important ties.

[26] Both Hungary and Poland have liberalized joint venture laws to the extent that foreign firms can have a controlling interest. The joint venture arrangement is a good way for Eastern European countries to gain technological know-how.

3. A free financial system, including banking and other financial institutions.
4. Recognition of private enterprises: In Poland, over 80 percent of production is in the state sector.
5. Recognition of private property rights.
6. Joint stock companies, including a stock exchange.
7. Revision of the tax system to encourage investment, not to tax away wealth.

Polish Reforms

On December 29, 1989, the Polish government announced a series of economic reforms that were designed to move Poland toward a free market economy. The reforms called for removing most price controls, converting many state enterprises to private ownership, ending subsidies to other state enterprises, and allowing layoffs and bankruptcies. An unemployment insurance system is to be created that will pay 70 percent of an unemployed worker's former wages for three months, 50 percent for the next six months, and 40 percent after nine months. The banking system is to be reformed, with banks allowed to make loans to enterprises based on their profit potential and to deny loans to enterprises that owe their existence to state subsidies. The Polish zloty is to be made convertible into Western currency.

SUMMARY

Hungary has been the most reformist oriented of all the Eastern European countries, and it is often looked at as a role model for the other countries to emulate. It has attempted to reform its economy on a broad scale, and it is in the process of transforming it into a more open market economy. It has also declared itself a democracy after 41 years of Communist rule. It has also formally changed its name and form of government. It has been renamed the Republic of Hungary, and amendments have been passed providing for a multiparty system and free elections by the summer of 1990 and creating the office of state president. The Communist Party has been dissolved and has been replaced by the Hungarian Socialist Party. However, it will take more than name changes to resolve Hungary's problems. The people are unused to democracy, having lived under a bureaucratic structure with set rules. More important is the transition from a repressive but predictable system to a market system that demands individual initiative.

The road for Poland will be even more difficult because the Polish economy is in worse shape than the Hungarian economy. It continues to have problems, including a decline in overall living standards and a large external debt to the West. In 1989 General Wojciech Jaruzelski, who had governed Poland since the military crackdown on Solidarity in 1981, stepped down from his position, and free elections dominated by Solidarity were held and a non-Communist became leader of Poland. Poland is attempting to turn itself into a free market economy but needs much financial assistance from the West in order to succeed. Like Hungary, it has had little experience with democracy after years of control by the Communist Party.

REVIEW QUESTIONS

1. Why have Hungary and Poland been in the vanguard of economic reforms?
2. Why did the Solidarity movement revolt against the communist party system in Poland?
3. What role has religion played in the life of Poland?
4. Discuss some of the problems of Polish agriculture.
5. What are some of the problems involved in introducing a free market economy in Poland and Hungary?
6. What is Comecon?
7. What can the United States do to further the creation of free enterprise in Hungary and Poland.
8. What currency reform is needed to make Hungary and Poland more competitive in world markets?

RECOMMENDED READINGS

Adams, Jan. *Economic Reforms in the Soviet Union and Eastern Europe Since the 1960's.* New York: St. Martin's Press, 1989.

Brezinski, Zbigniew. *The Grand Failure: The Birth and Death of Communism in the Twentieth Century.* New York: Charles Scribner's Sons, 1989.

Central Intelligence Agency. "Hungary: Economic Performance in the 1980's: Prospects for the 1990's." In *Pressures for Reform in the East European Economies,* Vol. 2, Joint Economic Committee, Congress of the United States, 101st Cong., 1st Sess. Washington, DC: USGPO, 1989, pp. 20–41.

Diehl, Jackson. "New Face of East Bloc is Pitted by Pollution." *The Washington Post,* April 18, 1989, pp. A1, A14.

Fallenbuchl, Zbigniew. "Poland: The Anatomy of Stagnation." In *Pressures for Reform in the East European Economies,* Vol. 2. Joint Economic Committee, Congress of the United States, 101st Cong. 1st Sess. Washington, DC: USGPO, 1989, pp. 102–136.

Hardt, John and Jean P. Boone. "Perestroika and Interdependence: Implications for Eastern Europe." In *Pressures for Reform in the East European Economies,* Vol. 1, Joint Economic Committee, Congress of the United States, 101st Cong., 1st Sess. Washington, DC: USGPO, 1989, pp. 27–39.

Marer, Paul. "Hungary's Political and Economic Transformation (1988–1989) and Prospects After Kadar." In *Pressures for Reforms in the East European Economies.* Vol. 2. Joint Economic Committee, Congress of the United States, 101st Cong., 1st Sess. Washington, DC: USGPO, 1989, pp. 42–51.

Nargoski, Andrew. "Uncharted Territory: Dismantling Communist Rule." *The Washington Post,* May 30, 1989. pp. A1, A12.

Penn, J.B. "Poland's Agriculture: It Could Make The Critical Difference." *Choices,* Vol. 4, No. 4 (Fourth Quarter, 1989), pp. 3–7.

Sachs, Jeffrey and David Lipton, "Polands' Economic Reform." *Foreign Affairs*, Vol. 69, No. 3 (Summer 1990), pp. 47-66.

CHAPTER FIFTEEN

YUGOSLAVIA

The Federal Republic of Yugoslavia represents a rather distinct brand of socialism that is different from the Soviet Union. The Yugoslav economy is a synthesis of central planning and a market economy. It contains many features of a market economy, including decentralized management, small-scale private enterprises, advertising associations to promote the distribution of products, and personal incentives to accomplish desired economic objectives. There is also a constitutional guarantee of private peasant landholdings of up to 25 acres of arable land. There is decentralized economic decision making and virtual autonomy of individual producing units, which leads to the use of the term *decentralized socialism* to describe the economy of Yugoslavia.

Yugoslavia was formed in 1918 from the countries Serbia and Montenegro. The population included five Slavic groups—Serbians, Croats, Slovenes, Macedonians, and Bosnians—as well as Hungarians and Albanians. A centralized monarchy was created with the support of the dominant Serbian elements in the population and against the wishes of the Croats, who wanted a federal system of government with a certain amount of regional and ethnic autonomy. Antagonism between the Serbs and Croats characterized the internal history of Yugoslavia between the two world wars. Although considerable autonomy was given to the Croats by the time of World War II, rivalries persist between Serbs and Croats that even today the present government finds difficult to dissipate.

During World War II, Yugoslavia was occupied by the Germans. Resistance forces were split into two groups—the Chetniks, representing the exiled monarchy of King Peter, and the Partisans, led by Tito, a member of the Communist party.[1] The Partisans emerged as the stronger of the two groups and received the bulk of Allied (including Soviet) military support. Those forces that had identified with Tito formed an independent base for the establishment of a communist regime in Belgrade at the end of the war. Since the liberation of Yugoslavia owed nothing to the Russian army but much to Tito and his supporters, there was no reason to be grateful or subservient to Moscow. For this reason, Tito could assert the independence of his regime from Russian domination. In 1948 Yugoslavia was expelled from the Soviet-dominated Cominform for pursuing both domestic and foreign policies independently of Moscow's influence.

After the split with Moscow, Yugoslavia effected a rapprochement with the Western countries based on trade and aid and the desire to secure an alliance in the event of Russian aggression. However, in terms of foreign policy, it has pursued an independent line between East and West and has attempted to project itself as the leader of nonaligned nations, eschewing proximity to either the Eastern or Western military bloc. Although relations with the Russians have improved since the hardline Stalinist days, Yugoslavia's economic ties are primarily with the West, and Yugoslavia participates in such Western economic organizations as the Organization for Economic Cooperation and Development (OECD) and the European Economic Community.

Politically, the country is divided into six republics and two autonomous regions. Each has a president, republic assembly, and numerous specialized administrative agencies. Over the years, greater authority has been given to republics, as the federal government has sought to decentralize decision making and to encourage wider popular participation in economic affairs.

The commune (which has nothing in common with the Chinese institution of the same name) is a local government unit that forms the basic self-governing entity in Yugoslavia. It would roughly correspond to a small city or county in the United States and has three basic responsibilities: guiding economic affairs, including planning, investment, and supervision of enterprises; providing municipal services; and managing various social welfare activities.

Yugoslavia is a communist country, and the Communist Party (League of Communists of Yugoslavia, LCY) is the only political party. Despite the institutional arrangement of the Yugoslav economic and political system, the LCY is the final authority over and above all other decision makers. It participates directly in the institutions of the state and of self-management, all the way down to the lowest level of enterprise organization. In these respects the LCY is no different from communist parties in the Soviet Union and the People's Republic of China.

---

[1] The *Chetniks* were Serbian nationalists who desired an independent Serbia. The *Partisans* were primarily Croats and were led by Josip Broz (Tito), a Croat who was a Communist. Although Communists controlled at the top, considerable support was obtained from people and groups of differing political opinions who believed in Tito's call for national unity.

THE ECONOMIC SYSTEM

Yugoslavia has a unique, complex economic system combining elements of both a centrally planned and a free market economy. One special feature of the Yugoslav economy is the workers' council, which is elected by all workers in each enterprise. The workers' council has extensive management powers concerning the operation of an enterprise. It approves the production plan, the hiring and firing of workers, the distribution of income to workers, and the annual financial statement. It also has control over the division of production and the use of investment funds from outside sources. The workers' council functions through a management board, which it elects from its members to perform the necessary decisions involving the day-to-day operations of the enterprise.

Other unique characteristics of the Yugoslav economic system are the use of decentralized economic decision making and dependence on the free market to allocate resources. Within the limits dictated by national and international competition, enterprises are free to set prices, to decide what and how much to produce, and to distribute revenue from sales from their products. Enterprises are legally independent in that their property is not owned by the government, but the property is held in trust by the enterprises for society as a whole.

Economic Planning

Yugoslavia has moved from centralized planning, which copied that of the Soviet Union, to decentralized planning. The process of decentralization began at the time of the political split with Russia in 1948 and has continued to the present. During the first Five-Year Plan (1947–1951)[2], the dominant theme was the elimination of the market system and its replacement by a system of central economic planning. The early economic plans gave definite instructions to each Yugoslav enterprise pertaining to the methods and scope of production and distribution. Subsequent economic plans shifted from a centralized command arrangement to a more decentralized form of planning that came to resemble French economic planning more than Russian economic planning. The system of fixed production quotas and prices was abandoned, and planning control was transferred to local authorities. Enterprises were given more latitude in price setting and in the distribution of their income.

Formulation and Implementation of Yugoslav Plans.   There are actually three levels of plans in Yugoslavia—national, republic, and commune plans. Communes are subunits within the republics. The Yugoslav national plan lays down the basic guidelines, targets, and aims of economic policy. Within the guidelines and objectives determined by the national plan and plans of the republics and communes, Yugoslav enterprises and other economic organizations are free to formulate their

---

[2] There are annual and middle-term (five-year) plans and also a ten-year plan. The fundamental elements of the policy of Yugoslav development are expressed in the five-year plans.

own production plans. This is in keeping with the decentralization policies of the government and reflects the Yugoslav view that it is necessary to turn more and more economic authority from the government to the enterprises and communes. It also reflects the view that the workers, rather than the state, must decide on the allocation and use of the goods that they produce. This is done, as will be discussed later in the chapter, through the election of the workers' councils, who have vested control over the operations of all enterprises. Worker self-management fits in with the process of decentralized planning.

The national plan is prepared by the Federal Planning Institute and is approved by the Federal Assembly. The Federal Planning Institute consists of a number of technical divisions, each of which is responsible for the preparation of a certain part of the plan. These divisions include agriculture; forestry; transportation and communication; regional development; personal consumption and social welfare; investment; domestic trade and tourism; industry, power, and mining; and national income.

The republic plans set the same objectives embodied in the national plan, allowing for special features of the republic economies. Republic plans refer only to segments of the economy and do not involve national concerns such as foreign trade or balance of payments. The republics are free to set goals that go beyond the scope of the federal plan and are under no legal obligation to harmonize their plans with the federal plan. As the commune has emerged as the basic unit of government, republic plans have come to play a more limited role.

After the republic plans are completed, the communes prepare plans. The plans of the communes are more comprehensive and detailed than the republic plans and are prepared after consultations with various workers' organizations. They encompass such concerns as planned tax policies and social welfare services. The communes, as well as the federal government, can influence compliance with planning objectives through control over policy instruments in the fields of credit, finance, and taxation. Neither the republic nor the commune plans must agree in detail with the national plan; nevertheless, the lower administrative units are expected to consider the overall frame of reference provided by the national plan.

Public Finance

During the period just following World War II the state was preeminent in all economic activities. All phases—production, distribution, exchange, and consumption—were included in government planning. Of all instruments of control available to the state during this period, the general state budget was the most important. It was composed of the federal budget, the budgets of the national republics, and local commune budgets. The general state budget was, for all practical purposes, one fund established by one authority, the national government. The general state budget served as the main distributor of investment funds. Its main sources of revenue were the sales tax, a form of profits tax from the socialist sector, and an income tax from the private sector. The state budget has become less important relative to the budgets of the republics.

Over the years, the Yugoslav budgetary system has been decentralized and jurisdiction for expenditures has been transferred from higher to lower administrative units. As a result, the size of the budgets of the communes has been increased. All sociopolitical units, with the exception of the autonomous provinces and districts, are independent in determining their revenue needs and the required tax rates.

Government units in Yugoslavia rely on several types of taxes as revenue sources. The sales tax is an important source of revenue for the operating budget of the federal government. A general tax rate of 14 percent is normally charged at the time of purchase of all items bought at the retail level. Special taxes on luxury goods can range up to 100 percent of the purchase price, while some essential goods are not subject to taxation. Communes and republics also levy sales taxes. The sales tax imposed by both is confined to retail trade, is uniform within each territorial district, and has a maximum limit prescribed by federal regulation.

There are also fixed capital and income taxes. The fixed capital tax is levied on the fixed assets and buildings owned by an enterprise. The federal government is the sole recipient of revenue from this tax source and uses the revenue to finance economic development in the less developed areas of the country and to finance infrastructure (social overhead capital) investments that benefit the nation as a whole. Income taxes are levied by the federal government and are shared with communes and republics. The range of tax rates varies; the average Yugoslav worker pays at a rate of 12 percent and private enterprises pay as high as 35 percent.[3] Foreign firms, which are allowed to have joint ventures with Yugoslav enterprises, are also subject to a 35 percent federal income tax. The rate is reduced to 10 percent if the income is reinvested in Yugoslavia.

Social welfare taxes and expenditures are excluded from budgetary accounts and are collected and distributed by the communes and autonomous districts. Yugoslav workers have to pay various social security taxes, which average about 25 percent of their gross income. The social security system itself includes old-age and survivors pensions, sickness and maternity benefits, unemployment compensation, work injury disability benefits, and family allowances. All wage and salary earners are eligible for full coverage under the social security system, while limited benefits are available to the remainder of the population. Although private farmers, craftspeople, and shopkeepers are eligible for health and old-age benefits, they are not eligible for family allowances.

The Banking System

Banking laws passed in 1976 and 1977 applied the provisions of the 1974 constitution to the banking system. The current system includes the National Bank,

---

[3] Private enterprise is permitted in Yugoslavia. Business owners are allowed to employ up to 500 workers. Private enterprise is important in the service areas—restaurants, dry cleaning, and hotels. There are also craftspeople.

which is responsible for general central banking operations; regular banks; and specialized banks. Regular and specialized banks are not intended to function as profit-making institutions, nor are they instruments of the state. Accordingly, banks may be funded by enterprises, but not by local governments or government agencies. Each organization or member associated with a bank has a delegate in the bank's assembly. Management of the bank is entrusted to the bank assembly. Apart from participating in the bank management, the members also have the right to share in any profits of the bank. The members also jointly carry the liability for all bank obligations.

The National Bank of Yugoslavia. The National Bank is the central bank of Yugoslavia. It has branches in the republics and autonomous provinces, and governors of these banks constitute the Board of Governors of the National Bank. In addition to issuance of bank notes as legal tender, it is also responsible for the monetary policy of Yugoslavia. The National Bank is authorized to regulate the money supply by using minimum reserve ratios and by conducting open market operations in treasury and commercial bills. It utilizes instruments of qualitative credit control, such as rediscounting, to exert a selective influence on the structure of short-term investments by basic and associated banks. However, it cannot extend long-term loans, except to the national government to finance budget deficits or to guarantee foreign loans.

Regular Banks.   There are three kinds of regular banks: internal, basic, and associated. *Internal banks* are established by groups of enterprises for their own use and do not serve the general public. They can perform all banking transactions for their members. Since they do not deal with the general public, they do not create money and are not subject to monetary regulation. Their main function is to facilitate pooling of resources among the member enterprises. *Basic banks* are conventional commercial banks that can be created by enterprises, communes, and other social-legal entities. They are all-purpose banks largely continuing the activities of the former commercial banks, which were eliminated by new bank laws.[4]

Associated banks are formed by basic banks for tasks that exceed their legal responsibilities and are authorized to engage in foreign exchange operations. They specialize in loans for investment to increase foreign trade in particular sectors such as manufacturing or mining. Interest rates on loans extended by the associated banks are determined by individual agreements with the borrowers, while interest rates on deposits are determined by interbank agreements. Each republic and autonomous region also has its own associated bank.[5]

---

[4] Martin Schrenk, Cyrus Ardalan, and Nawal E. Tatawy, *Yugoslavia: Self-Management Socialism and the Challenge of Development* (Baltimore: Johns Hopkins University Press, 1979), pp. 140–141.
[5] Schrenk et al., pp. 140–141.

Specialized Banks. In addition to the main banking system, there are three special-ized financial institutions. The Yugoslav Foreign Trade Bank is responsible for hold-ing foreign exchange and providing long- and short-term foreign exchange credits. The United Agricultural Bank is responsible for extending long-term agricultural loans. The Yugoslav Bank for International Economic Cooperation is authorized to finance exports of capital goods as well as the construction of overseas projects, to provide export insurance against noncommercial risks, and to promote cooperation between Yugoslav and foreign firms in third-world markets. The bank's operations are financed by other banks and enterprises, but not by the federal government.[6]

The Role of Interest. Under a capitalistic system, when quantities of capital funds are available for investment, the question of how they should be allocated is deter-mined by the amounts of interest firms in various fields of production are willing to pay for their use. The rate of interest will be determined in the market by the forces of supply and demand, and the rate plays the role of an allocator of re-sources. The underlying assumption is that if an economic entity is willing to pay more for the use of capital resources, the productivity of that entity is expected to be higher.

In Yugoslavia, interest is also used as a device to allocate investment funds. Enterprises have to pay interest on borrowed funds as well as on their fixed and financial capital. Almost all real capital is owned by society, and enterprises are only entrusted with its use. It is to society's benefit to have full and efficient utilization of these capital resources. This is ensured by charging interest for the use of fixed and financial capital, the idea being that those who have no use for the capital will hesitate to hold it if they have to pay a certain price to do so. By granting loans to those who are willing to pay the highest rate for the privilege, the rate of interest plays the role of allocator of financial and capital resources. This role of interest is not only applicable at the enterprise level, but also at the personal level for consumer credit.

Agriculture

Agriculture in Yugoslavia (and Poland) departs from the typical pattern found in the Soviet Union and its Eastern European satellites. The ownership and manage-ment of farms in Yugoslavia remains overwhelmingly in private hands, organized in many small family farm units. State farms and collective farms, which are the dominant forms of agricultural production in the Soviet Union, control only about 16 percent of the productive farm land in Yugoslavia.[7] The Yugoslav government

---

[6] Data provided by the U.S. Embassy in Belgrade, Yugoslavia, 1988.

[7] Gregor Lazarcik, "Comparative Growth of Agricultural Output, Inputs, and Productivity in Eastern Europe, 1965–1982." In *East European Economies: Slow Growth Rate in the 1980's,* Vol. 1, U.S. Congress, Joint Economic Committee, 99th Cong., 1st Sess., 1985, pp. 389–393.

has actively supported private farming by providing a number of incentives to stimulate the expansion of farm output:

1. Increasing prices paid by government to farmers for their products.
2. Expanding agricultural loans to private farmers on favorable terms.
3. Greatly expanding the use of fertilizers by private farmers.
4. Encouraging specialization and interfarm cooperation in the use of machinery.
5. Abstaining from further forced collectivization of agriculture.

State Farms. Farms that are managed by the government in Yugoslavia emphasize large-scale production of grains and potatoes. Both state-supported and private agricultural sectors can be regarded as largely complementary: The state sector produces the bulk of industrial crops and grains, while the private sector produces most of the vegetables, fruits, and meat products that supply the population with food. The private sector is important during the current plan period because of the continuing emphasis on livestock breeding to achieve both improved domestic diet and export goals. The goal of the plan is to shift the national diet away from cereals and toward higher quality foodstuffs, especially meat. In the state sector, which accounts for around 25 percent of real agricultural output, more intensive efforts are to be placed on the production of grain.

Collective Farms. Land on the collective farms is state owned and is worked by the farmers in common. The produce is distributed according to the contribution of each member. They function and operate in a fashion similar to Russian collective farms. The government encourages cooperation between the collective farms and private farmers; in some instances, private farms are worked by a collective farm on a sharecrop or cash basis. In this way farmers may retain possession of their land and benefit from the use of agricultural machinery, fertilizer, and farming techniques provided by the collective farm.

Cooperatives. There are also general agricultural cooperatives jointly managed by the farmers and their own employees. The land is owned by the cooperatives and farmed by private farmers who are paid in cash. The cooperatives provide the machines, implements, seed, and fertilizer. They are also responsible for the marketing and sale of farm produce produced on cooperative land. The private farmers neither subscribe to business shares in a cooperative nor are they liable for its debts. Cooperatives and individual farmers may produce jointly, with profits shared in proportion to the contribution made by each partner, or the cooperatives may be responsible only for participation in the production process—furnishing services and equipment—and, in return, receive a fixed share of the profits of the farmers. In most cases, the cooperatives and the private farmers conclude, in advance, contracts on production and the purchase of farm produce at fixed prices or at prices found on the market at the date of delivery.

The Yugoslav agricultural sector is caught in a bind. Productivity is lower than it would be with larger-scale operations, but ideology and inheritance customs in the country have caused private farm holdings to be too small to effect economies of scale. Private farms are limited by law to a maximum of 10 hectares (24 acres), but most private farms are smaller. Farmers have subdivided their farmland between their heirs, constricting the size of private farm holdings. Also, private enterprise, including private farms, is constrained by rules limiting the number of hired workers they may employ. Attempts by the state to encourage the movement of farmers from their private holdings into labor-managed collective farms have failed. The difference in ownership rights evidently has discouraged many farmers from leaving their own farms, no matter how small they are.

The Yugoslav Enterprise

The Yugoslav enterprise is the basic economic unit and may be started or expanded in several ways.

1. It may be formed by any governmental unit—commune, republic, or the national government.
2. It may be formed by a group of five or more individuals who have pooled their assets.
3. It may be formed by the division of an existing enterprise or by the merger of two or more existing enterprises.

When the enterprise starts operation, it acquires an independent status even though its sponsors have committed considerable resources to its formation. Its assets become social property and the people that it employs have the right to self-government and to participate in the income of the enterprise on the basis of work done. It may merge with another enterprise provided that a majority of workers in both enterprises approve the merger. As a matter of economic policy, mergers have been encouraged in order to improve productivity and make Yugoslav firms more competitive in international markets.

Yugoslav enterprises have certain similarities to their U.S. counterparts. Profit is the basic criterion of success for enterprises in both countries, and each enterprise acts independently in the pursuit of its business and development policies. Each can determine the volume and assortment of production according to its assessment of the market, and each can determine its pricing policies. Although economic planning exists in Yugoslavia, the government does not direct that specified quantities of products have to be provided by each enterprise, but instead relies on more indirect controls, including relying on money incentives (wages and bonuses), to encourage compliance with national economic objectives.

Management of an Enterprise.   Management of all Yugoslav enterprises was given to their workers under terms of a law passed in 1950. That is, all factories, mines, and other enterprises that had been under state ownership since the Communist Party came to power in Yugoslavia were turned over to the workers of these enterprises to manage. The ownership passed from the state to society in general. Enterprises were defined not as state property, but as social property, and workers were given the right to manage them, but not to own them. The key instrument through which this management would be accomplished was the workers' council that, in essence, became the trustee of social wealth and the method of self-management for an enterprise. Through the system of workers' councils, the workers, in principle, exercise ultimate control over economic policy, including the formulation of economic plans.

Figure 15-1 presents the organization and the process of decision making of a Yugoslav enterprise. At the top is the workers' council, which decides on all of the most important matters affecting strategic planning and the operation of the enterprise. The management board, elected by the workers' council, is responsible for drafting the operating plan of the enterprise. Its jurisdiction includes the tactics involved in running the enterprise and the enforcement of the plan. The general manager implements the decisions of the workers' council and the management board. The working unit councils consider the plans and tasks of each work unit and implement the policies of the workers' council.

Workers' Councils. Workers' councils are composed of delegates elected by secret ballot from within the work organization and from a list of candidates prepared by unions.[8] The authority of workers' councils is substantial. Within the limits set by the government, they have the right to decide what to produce and in what quantity, and they are also responsible for setting prices, determining wages, and distributing profits. The last responsibility is one of their most important functions. They distribute enterprise profits in the form of wage bonuses to the various investment and social welfare funds of the enterprises. They also choose a management committee, which is their executive organ. The management committee is responsible for the development of the production plans of the enterprise, the appointment of workers to important administrative positions, the specification of wage and production norms, and the development of methods designed to increase productivity.

Council of the Working Units. This body is elected by members of each work unit within the enterprise. For example, an integrated textile mill could be divided into work units for spinning, weaving, finishing, final processing, and retail supply. The council represents workers linked together by a common working interest. To be valid, the plan of each enterprise must be accepted by all constituent councils. Profits to be distributed are computed for each work unit in the enterprise on the basis of its business success and by the contribution of each work unit as determined on the basis of an agreement between its council and the enterprise.

Enterprise Managers. Administration and management of the enterprise is the responsibility of the manager (or management board), who is appointed by the

---

[8] The Communist Party is heavily represented on each workers' council.

FIGURE 15-1 Organization of a Yugoslav Enterprise

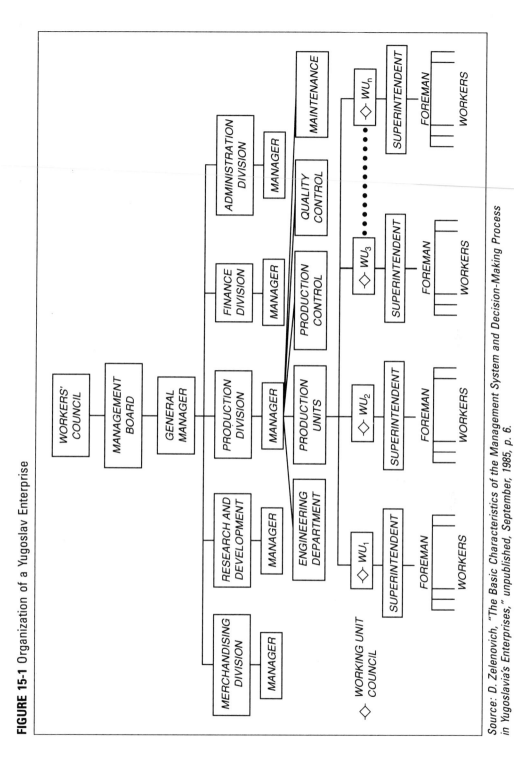

Source: D. Zelenovich, "The Basic Characteristics of the Management System and Decision-Making Process in Yugoslavia's Enterprises," unpublished, September, 1985, p. 6.

workers' council and the Communist Party of the local commune. Management positions must be publicly advertised, and the manager (or management board) is appointed on the basis of a competitive examination. Friction between the workers' council and the management often arises over the distribution of profits; the workers' council tends to favor higher wages out of profits, while the manager or board strives for increased investment. Management is responsible for carrying out the decisions of the workers' council and for handling the day-to-day affairs of the enterprise according to its plan and business policy. Management is subject to recall at any time by either the workers' council or the assembly of the local commune. It is excluded from personnel relations in that it does not have the right to hire or fire workers, take disciplinary action, or determine the final internal distribution of income.

The Operation of an Enterprise.   An enterprise can draw up its own plans for production independent of the national plan, but within limits prescribed by the plan of the commune. The production plan is approved by the workers' council after being put forward by the management committee of the enterprise. Once passed, the plan may be amended by the workers' council. Usually the enterprise is free to make its own decisions pertaining to what to purchase and what to sell, and it can establish prices for its products unless they are subject to some form of price control. Distribution is not regulated, and an enterprise can offer its goods in a comparatively free market.

In a Yugoslav enterprise, wages are not deducted from revenue as a cost of production. Instead, after raw material costs and other operating expenses are deducted, the resulting net income is divided between a fund for personal income (wages) and a fund for reinvestment. Income set aside in the wage fund is shared among the workers as base pay and supplements in accordance with a wage schedule adopted by the workers' council. To start with, a guaranteed minimum wage is ensured for all workers, and no worker can be paid less than this amount. Actual earnings, however, normally exceed the guaranteed minimum by a substantial amount, and the minimum assumes importance only when it cannot be covered out of the earnings of an enterprise. If this situation occurs, then the commune is required to make up the difference between the actual wage and the guaranteed minimum wage.

However, the use of workers' councils in decision making in Yugoslavia also has its drawbacks.[9] In particular, because workers receive a share of the firm's profits only as long as they are members of the organization, the incentive of workers to invest in capital with long-term payoffs decreases as they approach retirement or anticipate leaving the enterprise for some reason. The bias is toward projects with short-term payoffs to the exclusion of some investment projects that would be socially beneficial. This is not a problem in capitalist firms because

---

[9] Late 1989 reforms have reduced some of the power of the workers' councils.

the potential value of long-term investments will be reflected in the value of the firm's stock, which owners can sell to capitalize the value of current investments. In addition, since all workers must share in the residual profits of the Yugoslav enterprise, the incentive for a single individual to innovate or institute a new production idea is substantially reduced.

AN APPRAISAL OF THE YUGOSLAV ECONOMY

From the beginning of its history, Yugoslavia has been confronted by a seemingly insoluble nationality problem. It is really a confederation of diverse ethnic groups that are difficult to weld into a homogeneous unit. Rivalries exist between regions and are exacerbated by extremely uneven economic development between regions. The hope that surplus capital would flow to the less developed regions of the country has not been realized. Neither Croatia nor Slovenia, which are among the most developed and richest republics of Yugoslavia, has shown much interest in investing in the underdeveloped areas of the south. Chauvinistic sentiment is a key deterrent to the free flow of capital between regions.

Much of Yugoslavia's success over the last several decades was derived from the unifying force of President Tito's leadership. Tito's charisma helped prevent the country's political disintegration into a number of regional special-interest groups. His death in 1980 has intensified regional rivalries that appear to be an ineradicable feature of the Yugoslav political and economic system. The problem the current leaders of Yugoslavia have is to prevent a renewal of regional nationalism and separatism. To achieve this goal, they must create a viable economy that continues to improve living standards and reduce the income disparities between prosperous and less prosperous republics. Antagonisms, ethnic differences, and other sources of discord in Yugoslavia are likely to continue in the future because even adherence to communism as a unifying factor has not united the people.

Economic Problems

At the start of the 1980s Yugoslavia began to place emphasis on achieving economic stability to improve its balance of payments and to curb inflation. In the Five-Year Plan for 1981–1985, the government sought to restrict consumption, to channel investment into the most productive sectors of the economy, and to solve the country's recurring trade imbalances by improving export performance and reducing imports to essential goods and services. Yugoslavia amended its joint venture laws to allow foreign firms to make contributions to a joint venture exceeding 49 percent of its equity and to guarantee repatriation of profits.[10] The major goals of the 1986–1990 Economic Plan have been to gradually slow the rate of inflation to more

---

[10] A new law in 1988 permits joint ventures with a majority of foreign managers on their boards.

acceptable levels, to increase exports, and to reduce the debt service ratio in its foreign debt.

However, the Yugoslav economy is in a state of crisis. It suffers from a protracted economic downturn. Its economy suffers from low productivity, labor unrest, and high inflation. The average rate of inflation for 1988 was 260 percent.[11] The dinar, worth 35 to the dollar in 1981, rose to 3,000 to the dollar by late 1988. There are also balance-of-payments and debt service problems. The high rate of economic growth that Yugoslavia was able to maintain from the end of World War II to the 1970s has fallen victim to a number of problems, both external and internal, and is one of the lowest in Europe. Productivity has declined and there are marked variations among regional rates of development. The rate of unemployment was around 14 percent for 1988, and many households have suffered growing poverty.

Throughout the social sector, work discipline is at a low level. The quality of Yugoslav exports is not internationally competitive, and many firms are unable to meet the demands of their customers because of a lack of raw materials and spare parts for their machinery.[12]

Table 15-1 presents the objectives of the 1988 economic plan and the actual results. The table indicates that there was a wide gap between the set of targets in the plan and the actual results. The data represents change in volume over 1987.

Inflation.   Probably the most important problem confronting the Yugoslav economy is inflation. The 1980s have been highly inflationary as the result of the lessening of control over the economy and the move to a freer price structure. During the period 1965–1980 consumer prices increased at an annual rate of 15.3 percent, but during the period 1980–1987 consumer prices increased at an average annual rate

TABLE 15-1
The 1988 Yugoslav Plan and Actual Results
(percent)

	Plan Target	Result
Consumer expenditures	0.5	−4.0
Public expenditures	−3.2	1.0
Fixed investment	0.5	−7.0
Exports of goods and services	5.4	3.5
Gross social product	1.0	−1.5
Industrial output	2.0	−2.5

*Source: The Economist, Economic Intelligence
Unit,* Country Profile 1989–1990, Yugoslavia *(London:
Economist, 1989), p. 13.*

[11] OECD, *Economic Survey of Yugoslavia* (Paris: OECD, 1989), p. 2.
[12] Harold Lydall, *Yugoslavia in Crisis* (Oxford: Clarendon Press, 1989), pp. 32–34.

of 57 percent in spite of the government imposition of wage and price controls and attempts to limit the money supply.[13] Inflation continued to accelerate in 1988 with retail prices increasing by 199.0 percent over 1987.[14] The projection for 1989 is even worse, with retail prices estimated to increase by 600 percent over 1988. For the tenth year in a row, real income of Yugoslav workers continued to decline.

Economic Growth.   The Yugoslav economy is one of contrasts. With a mixture of a planned and a market economy and a policy of accelerated industrialization, the government has transformed Yugoslavia from an agrarian society to a position just short of the less developed Western European countries such as Portugal. In 1988 the per capita income of Yugoslavia was $2,688 compared to $3,670 for Portugal.[15] However, growth rates have been negative during the 1980s except for 1984 and 1986. Real increases in gross social product were a negative 0.9 percent in 1987 and a negative 2.7 percent for 1988.[16] The rate of economic growth for Yugoslavia during the 1980s was below the average for all of the OECD countries, of which Yugoslavia is a member, but about on a par with the average for the Eastern European countries.[17]

Foreign Debt.   The foreign debt of Yugoslavia as of 1989 was $21.7 billion.[18] This debt creates a serious burden for the Yugoslav economy: Some 50 percent of its hard currency earnings have to be used to meet principal and interest payments, thus limiting the ability to import critically needed merchandise. The merchandise trade account has been negative for each year in the 1980s, which is a serious problem because increased exports to the Western European countries is a key component of Yugoslavia's development strategy for reducing the foreign debt. Table 15-2 presents Yugoslav foreign debt, interest payments on the debt, and the merchandise trade balance for 1983 to 1988.

Regional Economic Differences.   Adding to the complexity of Yugoslav economic problems are the enormous regional disparities in income that remain despite several decades of regional development efforts. Although the Yugoslav per capita gross national product is around $2,700, the highly industrialized Republic of Slovenia enjoys a per capita income more than five times higher than that of the Province of Kossovo in the southeast. This north-south disparity of income and economic development and living standards is a very sensitive issue with important political and social effects. Despite efforts to transfer wealth from north to south, the

---

[13] The World Bank, *World Development Report 1989*, p. 165.
[14] The Economist, Economic Intelligence Unit, *Country Profile 1989–1990, Yugoslavia*, p. 15.
[15] The World Bank, *World Development Report 1989*, p. 165.
[16] Gross social product is material product or total material production. It does not include services.
[17] Central Intelligence Agency, Directorate of Intelligence, *Handbook of Economic Statistics, 1989* (Springfield, VA: NTIS, 1989), p. 34.
[18] The World Bank, *World Debt Tables, 1989* (Washington DC: World Bank, 1989), p. 65.

TABLE 15-2
Foreign Debt, Interest Payments, and Trade
Balances for Yugoslavia 1983–1988 (millions of
dollars)

	Foreign Debt	Interest Payments	Trade Balance
1983	20,472	−1,469	−1,690
1984	19,521	−1,579	−1,205
1985	20,426	−1,610	−1,771
1986	21,220	−1,870	−2,490
1987	23,518	−1,670	−1,035
1988	22,258	−1,734	−588

Source: *The World Bank,* World Debt Tables, 1983–1988
(Washington DC: World Bank, 1989)

development gap has continued to widen over the past two decades. In periods
of economic retrenchment, the poorer areas are the ones that suffer the most. The
resumption of sustained economic growth, which has been absent in the 1980s, is
of vital importance to maintaining domestic economic and political stability.

Economic Reforms

A number of economic reforms have been introduced in Yugoslavia since it declared its economic and political independence from the Soviet Union in 1948.
These reforms have included administrative decentralization, indirect regulation, a
substantial role for market forces, and self-management. The Yugoslav economy
has become a hybrid resource allocation model, partly planned and partly market.
This hybrid relationship has not worked well for several reasons.[19]

1. Inefficiency in allocations occur because prices for many goods are either ad-
   ministratively fixed or set by self-management or social contracts, thus circum-
   venting market forces. Also, large enterprises create an oligopoly or monopoly
   market.
2. Allocative inefficiencies are also created by the fragmentation of markets along
   political divisions. There are six republics and two autonomous regions that
   together do not form a politically cohesive unit; each of them uses some form
   of economic protection against goods shipped into their areas.
3. Unclear ownership relations exist, with no one ultimately held responsible
   for mistakes or inefficient deployment of resources. The penalties (e.g.,
   bankruptcy) for losses are missing. Socialization of losses is a corollary of
   social owership and encourages irresponsible risk taking.

---

[19] Dennison Rusinow, "Yugoslavia: Enduring Crisis and Delayed Reforms." In *Pressures for Reform in
the East European Economies,* Vol. 2, Joint Economic Committee, Congress of the United States
(Washington, DC: USGPO, 1989), pp. 58–61.

4. Allocative inefficiencies are created by inelasticities of substitution among factors of production. These are created by an imperfectly competitive commodity market, with no markets and therefore no scarcity-value public price for labor and capital.

In the latter part of 1988, far-reaching reforms were introduced into the Yugoslav economy. One reform split banks from firms with intent to give banks more independence and to make firms raise capital based on expected rates of return and profit. Another reform was to redefine self-management of enterprises. Workers councils are to have less voice in management strategic decision making. A third reform is to reduce the role of the Communist Party and the bureaucracy in the economy. The party and the state are to be separated in order to enable the federal government to push through reforms that are above regional and party interests. Foreign trade reforms include a new joint venture law that will allow foreign firms to repatriate profits, select their own management, and disregard workers' self-management limitations. Limitations on the ownership of private property have been abolished.[20] Bankruptcy laws have been introduced and profit is to be the basic motivator for enterprises.

Comparisons with Socialist Economies

Comparisons of Yugoslavia with the socialist economies[21] of Eastern Europe are somewhat difficult to make. For one thing, there are differences in the kind of economic development and resource availability. Moreover, some countries were more adversely affected by World War II than others. East Germany had a pre–World War II industrial base on which to rebuild its economy. Czechoslovakia was also an advanced industrial country, particularly in comparison to Bulgaria and Romania. Soviet influence over the economic process also affects comparisons. Soviet control and influence over industrialization policies fall more heavily on countries that are closer to its sphere of influence. Additionally, comparisons can be difficult because a comparatively good performance in one area of the economy may be achieved at the expense of a concurrent or postponed weaker performance in another area.

Table 15-3 presents the real growth rates of real per capita GNP for Yugoslavia, the Soviet Union, and Eastern Europe for selected periods. The performance of the Yugoslav economy during the 1960s and 1970s was quite good in comparison to the Soviet Union and Eastern Europe. During the 1980s, Yugoslavia has encountered the same problems that have affected other socialist countries—declining growth rates, large hard currency debts, and falling investment.

The economic stagnation that has plagued the Eastern European countries during the 1980s has also plagued Yugoslavia, as is indicated in Table 15-4. Hard

---

[20] An exception is that ownership of arable land is limited to 30 hectares (75 acres).

[21] The economies of Eastern Europe were socialist when the comparsions were made.

TABLE 15-3
Growth in Real Per Capita GNP (average annual rate of growth)

	Yugoslavia	Soviet Union	Eastern Europe
1961–1970	3.2	3.4	3.4
1971–1980	4.1	1.8	2.7
1981–1985	0.6	1.0	0.5
1984	1.7	0.5	2.9
1985	−0.1	0.0	0.0
1986	3.1	3.0	3.0
1987	−1.1	0.2	0.2
1988	−0.5	0.5	0.5

Source: Central Intelligence Agency, Directorate of Intelligence, Handbook of Economic Statistics 1989, (Springfield, VA: NTIS, 1989), p. 34.

currency debt is one problem common to most of these countries. Resources that could have been marked for investment and consumption have been diverted to serving foreign debt. Foreign loans were spent in inefficient investments that were based on ideology or political expediency. Development strategy was based on the importation of Western technology, with the goal of modernizing the domestic economies through the use of high technology imports to manufacture products of higher value for exports. Higher earnings from exports would be used to repay foreign creditors.

Labor Productivity.   Comparisons can also be made of labor productivity. As Table 15-5 indicates, there has been a low and declining rate of labor productivity. This can be attributed to several factors including technological obsolescence, a lack of incentives for innovation and initiative on the part of enterprises, and declining allocation of resources for investment.

TABLE 15-4
Yugoslavia and Selected Eastern European Countries (average annual rate of growth)

Country	1971–1980	1981–1985	1984	1985	1986	1987	1988
Yugoslavia	4.1	0.6	1.7	−0.1	3.1	−1.1	−0.5
Bulgaria	2.4	0.6	3.3	−3.0	4.3	−0.8	1.8
Czechoslovakia	2.1	0.9	2.2	0.4	2.3	0.3	0.7
East Germany	3.1	2.0	3.0	3.2	1.8	1.8	1.8
Hungary	2.3	0.8	2.8	−2.3	2.4	1.0	1.1
Poland	2.7	−0.3	2.8	0.2	2.0	−2.3	1.6
Romania	4.4	−0.5	4.1	0.4	2.4	−1.4	−2.0

Source: Central Intelligence Agency, Directorate of Statistics, Handbook of Economic Statistics, 1989, (Springfield, VA: NTIS, 1989), p. 34.

TABLE 15-5
Growth Rates of Labor Productivity in Overall GNP for Eastern Europe (percent per year)

Country	1980–1985	1981	1982	1983	1984	1985	1986	1987
Bulgaria	0.7	1.8	3.1	−2.1	4.1	−3.2	4.9	−1.0
Czechoslovakia	0.5	−1.1	1.6	0.9	1.5	−0.2	0.9	0.2
East Germany	1.1	1.1	−1.3	1.0	2.0	2.7	1.3	1.6
Hungary	1.5	1.6	1.6	−0.1	3.0	−2.5	2.5	1.5
Poland	0.5	−5.5	1.6	5.2	3.5	0.2	2.1	−2.1
Romania	0.3	1.1	2.0	−1.7	2.5	−5.1	1.6	0.8
Yugoslavia	1.0	2.0	0.2	0.4	2.5	−0.2	2.0	−2.2

Source: Thad P. Alton, "East European GNPs, Domestic Final Uses of Gross Product, Rates of Growth, and International Comparisons." In Pressures For Reform In The East European Economies, Vol. 1, Joint Economic Committee, Congress of the United States (Washington, DC: USGPO, 1989), p. 92.

Agricultural Productivity.   The performance of agriculture in the Eastern European countries has been mixed at best. During the 1970s, the countries made gains in consumption and living standards despite the inefficiency of centrally planned agriculture.[22] Growth policies in the early 1980s tended to undermine agriculture because emphasis was placed on import-led growth financed by borrowing from abroad, which was supposed to improve technology, which in turn was supposed to lead to the export of high–value-added products in world markets. Investment resources were concentrated on industry, not agriculture. This development strategy failed to work for two reasons: declining world prices for industrial goods; and more important, competition from the newly industrialized countries (NICs) such as South Korea and Taiwan, who made better products at lower costs.[23] In the early 1980s the East European countries became net importers of grain, so East European leaders responded with a variety of agricultural reforms, primarily based on monetary incentives to encourage individual initiative.[24]

Table 15-6 presents the net productivity of workers employed in agriculture in Yugoslavia and the other East European countries. The table reflects improvement in agricultural productivity per person employed in agriculture in Yugoslavia. This can be explained by a drastic drop in the labor force employed in agriculture in Yugoslavia. In 1965, 50 percent of the labor force in Yugoslavia was employed in

---

[22] Nancy J. Cochrane and Miles J. Lambert, "East European Agriculture: Pressures for Reform in the 1980s." In Pressures for Reform in the East European Counties, Joint Economic Committee, Congress of the United States, (Washington DC: USGPO, 1989), pp. 236–247.

[23] A good example is the Yugo car, a low-priced car that was made in Yugoslavia and sold in the United States in the middle 1980s. It was poorly made and was a flop salewise. On the other hand, the South Korean cars, particularly the Hyundai, were introduced in the United States and proved to be popular.

[24] These reforms varied by countries.

TABLE 15-6

Net Product per Person Employed in Agriculture in the East European Countries (percent)

Country	1971–1975	1975–1980	1981–1985	1986–1987
Eastern Europe	100	100	100	100
Bulgaria	112	120	102	101
Czechoslovakia	121	142	129	125
East Germany	284	263	261	254
Hungary	154	140	137	137
Poland	100	83	77	75
Romania	51	59	56	62
Yugoslavia	87	96	120	120

Source: Gregor Lazarcik, "Comparative Agricultural Performance and Reforms in Eastern Europe, 1975–1988." In Pressures For Reform in the East European Economies, *Vol. 1, Joint Economic Committee, Congress of the United States (Washington, DC: USGPO 1989), p. 267.*

agriculture; in 1987, 22 percent was employed. In Poland, comparable statistics were 38 percent and 29 percent. This means that there has been a greater reduction of disguised unemployment in Yugoslavia by transfer of labor to nonagricultural sectors of the economy.

SUMMARY

Yugoslavia is a country with many contradictions. It broke away early from the Soviet Union and Stalinism and has abandoned central planning and collectivization. It has created a market economy with some state control and has actively courted foreign investment. Its citizens are free to work in other countries; many of them do and their remissions back to Yugoslavia are an important source of hard currency. It has also allowed its workers some participation in self-management. On the other hand, Yugoslavia is still a one-party state, and there are no free elections. In this area Hungary, Poland, and the Soviet Union are well ahead of Yugoslavia. The Communist Party dominates all positions of importance in government, education, the trade unions, and the press, but it is generally out of touch with the population.

Yugoslavia is also a country in crisis; not the least of its problems are deep political and social differences between the regions that make up the country. Living standards have decreased. Worker self-management has resulted in excessively capital-intensive investment decisions, the immobility of labor and capital, and internal organizational inefficiency, resulting specifically from a lack of managerial authority and declining labor discipline. Inflation has become a very serious problem and unemployment is high. There are balance-of-payments problems, particularly in the current account, with merchandise imports exceeding merchandise exports during most of the 1980s. Net interest on the external debt has increased from $289 million in 1975 to $1.7 billion in

1987, and export earnings are not sufficient to cover annual interest payments. Most repayments of principal have been deferred, either by debt rescheduling or by raising new loans, the latest of which was a $1.4 billion loan from the International Monetary Fund.

REVIEW QUESTIONS

1. Compare the roles of economic planning in Yugoslavia and the Soviet Union.
2. What are the responsibilities of a workers' council?
3. Discuss the role of the Bank of Yugoslavia in the monetary system.
4. How do the foreign debt and interest payments have an adverse impact on the Yugoslav economy?
5. How may Yugoslav enterprises be formed?
6. What is the role of the commune in the Yugoslav economic and political systems?
7. Yugoslavia has a problem of national identity. Discuss.
8. Yugoslavia can be called a nation in crisis. What are the causes of this crisis?

RECOMMENDED READINGS

Alton, Thad P. "East European GNP's, Domestic Final Uses of Gross Product, Rates of Growth and International Comparisons." In *Measures for Reform in the East European Economies,* Vol. 1, Joint Economic Committee, Congress of the United States, Washington, DC: USGPO, 1989, pp. 77–96.

Estrin, Saul. *Self-Management: Economic Theory and Yugoslav Practice.* New York: Cambridge University Press, 1984.

Flaherty, Diane. "Plan, Market and Unequal Regional Development in Yugoslavia." *Soviet Studies,* Vol. 40, No. 1 (January 1988), pp. 100–124.

Lydall, Harold. *Yugoslavia in Crisis.* Oxford : Oxford University Press, 1989.

OECD. *Economic Survey of Yugoslavia 1988.* Paris: OECD, 1989.

Prasmikar, Janez, and Jan Sveynar (eds.). "Economic Behavior of Yugoslav Enterprises." *Advances in the Economic Analysis of Participatory and Labor-Managed Firms,* Vol. 3, Greenwich, CT: JAI Press, 1988.

Rusinow, Dennis. "Yugoslavia: Enduring Crisis and Delayed Reforms." In Joint Economic Committee, Congress of the United States, *Pressures For Reforms in the East European Countries.* Vol. 2, Washington DC: USGPO, 1989, pp. 52–69.

The Economist, Intelligence Unit. *Country Profile Analysis: Yugoslavia 1988–1989.* London: The Economist, 1989.

ECONOMIC SYSTEMS OF THE LESS DEVELOPED COUNTRIES

16
PROBLEMS OF THE LESS DEVELOPED COUNTRIES

17
THE PEOPLE'S REPUBLIC OF CHINA

18
MEXICO

19
NIGERIA

PART FIVE

CHAPTER SIXTEEN

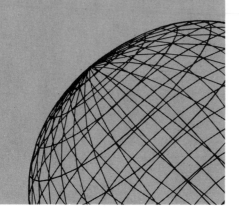

PROBLEMS OF THE LESS DEVELOPED COUNTRIES

The countries of the world can be classified into more developed and less developed, or haves and have-nots, and there are a few that are somewhere in between. Unfortunately, a majority of countries can be classified as less developed—including China and India, which have more than a third of the world's population between them. Mass poverty exists in the less developed countries and basic consumption needs remain unfulfilled. The magnitude of poverty is all too apparent. We read about it in newspapers and see it on television. A drought in Ethiopia and other parts of Africa was responsible for the death by starvation of thousands of people. Anyone who has been to a less developed country is struck by the squalor and the number of beggars in the large cities. The enormous gap between more and less developed nations increases the potential for social conflict in the world.

This chapter is divided into several parts, the first of which examines the subject of economic development. The second part discusses the characteristics of the less developed countries. It looks at population—the causes and consequences of population growth and its link to economic development and performance. The third part explores some theories of economic development. Many economists are concerned with the conditions necessary for economic development. The fourth part presents some of the obstacles to economic development confronting the less developed countries, and there are many. Possible solutions to the problems of economic development make up the last part of the chapter—but solutions will not come easily. The problems of the less developed countries can be attributed in part to the economic and financial policies of the developed countries.

ECONOMIC DEVELOPMENT

Economic growth and economic development are often used interchangeably. However, the two terms have different meanings. *Economic growth* can be defined most simply as the ability of a nation to expand its capacity to produce the goods and services its people want. It represents an increase in the real output of goods and services. *Economic development* means not only more real output but different kinds of output than were produced in the past.[1] It includes changes in the technological and institutional arrangements by which output is produced and distributed. There can be economic growth without economic development. For example, a country that relies on the production of oil for export can have its growth rate increase as greater inputs lead to greater output of oil, while its economic development may be minimal. However, the process of economic development almost necessarily depends on some degree of simultaneous economic growth.

There are a number of requisite factors that must exist before economic development can take place in any country. Most of the developed countries in the world have at least several of them, which are listed here.

1. The quantity and quality of a country's labor force has an impact on its economic development. However, the existence of a large labor force does not guarantee economic development. India is an excellent case in point. A labor force has to have education and job skills, both of which are lacking in India because it is a poor country.

2. The quantity and quality of real capital is important for economic development. Real capital is capital goods or inventories in the form of raw materials, machines, and equipment used for the ultimate purpose of producing consumer goods. The supply of real capital depends upon the level of savings in a country, which is the difference between its income and its consumption. In countries at a subsistence level, there is little difference between income and consumption.

3. The level of technological attainment in a country has to be considered. Technology as a concept deals more with the productive process than with the introduction of new goods. It involves the relationship between inputs of economic resources of land, labor, and capital. The combination of these inputs will determine both the level and type of technology.

4. The quantity and quality of a country's natural resources is also important. Great natural resources contributed to the economic development of the United States. However, it is possible to develop without adequate natural resources. Japan has attained a high level of economic development by importing what it needs.

---

[1] Bruce Herrick and Charles F. Kindleberger, *Economic Development*, 4th ed. (New York: McGraw-Hill Book Co., 1983), pp. 21–23.

5. Sociocultural forces also affect economic development. Religion is an example. The role of religion as an economic force can vary considerably among countries. The theocratic society of Iran offers a case in point, where modern ways are resisted. Other sociocultural forces are the underlying competitive nature of an economy, the distribution of income and wealth, the pattern of consumer tastes, the dominant forms of business organization, and the organization of society.

CHARACTERISTICS OF THE LESS DEVELOPED COUNTRIES

Three-fourths of the world's population live in the less developed countries. Most of the nations of Latin America, Africa, and Asia fall into this category.[2] However, the less developed countries are by no means all alike, for some countries are in different stages of economic development from others. There is a vast degree of difference between the lives of, say, the typical slum dweller of Mexico City and an average peasant in Bangladesh or Ethiopia. Although Mexico's per capita income is one-sixth that of the United States, it is 15 times that of Bangladesh or Ethiopia. Nevertheless, the less developed countries possess some common characteristics, and a discussion of each is in order.[3]

Per Capita Income

Whether a country can be classified as developed or less developed is often determined by the size of its per capita gross national product (GNP), which is a rough measure of the value of goods and services produced and available on the average to each country. Among the poorest countries of the world are China, India, Bangladesh, and Pakistan, which account for 40 percent of the world's population but less than 2 percent of the world's gross national product. The per capita GNP for each of these countries is less than 5 percent of the annual United States figure, which was $19,780 for 1988, and the average of $17,020 for the developed countries.[4] Bangladesh had a per capita income of $170 in 1988, which was less than 1 percent of the per capita income for the United States. The poverty this figure represents shows up in nutritionally inadequate diets, primitive and crowded housing, an absence of medical service, and a general lack of educational facilities.

---

[2] The United Nations classifies countries on the basis of more developed and less developed. More developed regions comprise all of Europe and North America, plus Australia, Japan, New Zealand, and the USSR. All other regions are classified as less developed.

[3] See Harvey Leibenstein, *Economic Backwardness and Economic Growth* (New York: Macmillan, 1957), pp. 40–41.

[4] The World Bank, *The World Bank Atlas 1989*, p. 10.

Table 16-1 is a summary table that breaks down the per capita incomes for most countries on the basis of income categories. In 1988, there were 50 countries with a per capita GNP of less than $500. These countries account for around 60 percent of the world's population, but their total GNP is around 6 percent of the total GNP for the world. Their average per capita GNP is less than 2 percent of that for the developed countries. Conversely, there are 46 developed countries, including those that are considered new industrialized countries (NICs). They have about 16 percent of the world's population but more than 80 percent of the world's gross national product. The in-between countries range from countries considered poor (as opposed to poorest) to countries that are in various stages of industrial development.

Table 16-2 presents a breakdown by categories of GNP for countries ranging from the poorest to the most developed. The first category includes the poorest countries in the world, those with per capita incomes of $500 or less. Then there are poor countries that have a per capita income above $500 but are not much better off than the poorest countries. A third category of countries includes Mexico and Brazil, which are relatively better off in terms of per capita income, have some industrial base, but are at the lower stage of economic development. A fourth category of countries includes those that are in the upper stage of economic development. The fifth category includes the developed countries. The Soviet Union qualifies even though its per capita GNP is not much higher than that of some countries that are in the upper stage of economic development.

Overpopulation

Although the overall rate of population growth in the world has been declining since the late 1970s, annual world population figures have increased each year. In 1988 the world population increased by 100 million persons, bringing the total to 5.1

TABLE 16-1
Summary Data for Per Capita GNP for Countries for 1988
(GNP and population in millions)

Per Capita GNP	Countries	GNP	Population	Average per Capita Income
Less than $500	50	$ 909,000	2,881	320
$500–1,499	36	359,000	403	890
$1,500–3,499	31	1,223,500	543	2,100
$3,500–5,999	13	296,000	74	4,000
$6,000 or more	46	13,345,000	784	17,200
No data	10		388	

Source: The World Bank, The World Bank Atlas, 1989 *(New York: Oxford University Press, 1989) p. 10.*

TABLE 16-2
Per Capita Incomes for Countries in Various Stages of Economic Development (dollars)

Poorest Countries		Poor Countries		Lower-stage Development	
Ethiopia	$120	Bolivia	$570	Mexico	$1,820
Bangladesh	170	Phillipines	630	Malaysia	1,870
Zaire	170	Egypt	650	Brazil	2,280
India	330	Morocco	750	Hungary	2,460
China	330	El Salvador	950	Argentina	2,640
Pakistan	350	Ecuador	1,050	Yugoslavia	2,680
Kenya	360	Turkey	1,230	Venezuela	3,170
Haiti	360	Colombia	1,240	Trinidad	3,350

Upper-stage Development		Developed	
South Korea	$3,530	United Kingdom	$12,800
Portugal	3,670	Italy	13,320
Greece	4,790	France	16,080
Ireland	7,480	Canada	16,760
Spain	7,740	West Germany	18,530
Israel	8,650	Sweden	19,150
Singapore	9,100	United States	19,780
Hong Kong	9,230	Japan	21,040

Source: The World Bank, The World Bank Atlas, 1989 *(New York: Oxford University Press, 1989) pp. 6–9.*

billion, or twice the level of 20 years ago.[5] Given current projections of population increase, the world population is estimated to be around 6.5 billion by the end of this century, with almost all the increase taking place in Latin America, Africa, and Asia, where birth rates are high and mortality rates are declining. Moreover, the bulk of the population increase will take place in the countries that can afford it the least. For example, the populations of China and India, two of the poorest countries in the world, are projected to increase by 450 million persons each by the year 2000, and the populations of Bangladesh and Pakistan are projected to increase by 150 million each.

Table 16-3 presents the population, birth and death rates, and population-doubling time for selected less developed countries that together have over half of the world's population. (Population-doubling time is found by dividing 70 by the population growth rate.) It is well to remember that for these countries the more

[5] Mary M. Kent and Carl Haub, *1988 World Population Data Sheet* (Washington, DC: Population Reference Bureau, 1988)

TABLE 16-3
Population Data for 1988

	Population (millions)	Birth Rate (per 1,000)	Death Rate (per 1,000)	Population Doubling Time (years)
Bangladesh	109	43	17	26
Ethiopia	48	46	15	23
India	817	32	13	35
China	1,087	21	7	49
Pakistan	107	43	15	24
Kenya	23	54	13	17
Sudan	24	45	16	24
Philippines	63	35	7	26
Egypt	53	38	9	24
Indonesia	179	27	10	40
Nigeria	112	46	17	24
Malaysia	17	31	7	28
Burma	41	34	13	33
Thailand	55	29	8	33
Brazil	144	28	8	34
Mexico	83	30	6	29
United States	246	16	9	99
Sweden	8	12	11	6,930
W. Germany	61	10	11	—

Source: Mary M. Kent and Carl Haub, 1988 World Population Data Sheet (Washington, DC: Population Reference Bureau, 1988).

people there are, the less will be the real capital and natural resources per capita. India, which is one of the poorest countries in the world, had a 1988 population of 817 million and will double its population in 35 years. Mexico, with a birth rate of 30 per 1,000 persons and a death rate of 6 per 1,000 persons, will double its population in 29 years. China will double its population in 49 years, while Nigeria, with one of the highest birth rates in the world, will double its population in only 24 years. Conversely, the United States, with a birth rate of 16 per 1,000 persons and death rate of 9 per 1,000 persons, will double its population in 99 years. West Germany, with a negative rate of population growth, will never double its population.

Agriculture

One of the most fundamental characteristics of the less developed countries is that a very high percentage of the population is employed in agriculture. There is absolute overemployment in agriculture; that is, it would be possible to reduce the number of workers and still retain the same total output. The level of agrarian technology is low; tools and equipment are limited and primitive. Opportunities for sale of agricultural products are limited by transportation difficulties and the absence of local demand. Agricultural output in the less developed countries is made up mostly of cereals and primary raw materials, with relatively low output of protein foods. The reason for this is the conversion ratio between cereals and meat production; that is, if one acre of cereals produces a certain number of calories, it would take more than one acre to produce the same number of calories from meat products.

Table 16-4 presents the percentage of the labor force employed in agriculture, industry, and services for less developed countries with a per capita gross national product of less than $500 a year, other less developed countries, and, as a frame of reference, developed countries such as the United States and West Germany. In Chad, one of the poorest countries in the world, 85 percent of the population of working age is employed in agriculture (compared to 2 percent in the United States and 4 percent in West Germany). Note also that as countries develop industrially they eventually reach a point where employment in the service industries exceeds employment in manufacturing. The United States is an example of what is called

TABLE 16-4

Labor Force Participation in Agriculture, Industry, and Services for Selected Countries (1987)

	Per Capita GNP (1988)	Agriculture (1987)	Industry (1987)	Services (1987)
Chad	$ 160	83%	5%	12%
Bangladesh	170	75	6	19
Ethiopia	120	80	8	12
India	330	70	13	17
China	330	74	14	12
Niger	310	91	2	7
Pakistan	350	55	16	29
Kenya	360	81	7	12
Sudan	340	71	8	21
Indonesia	430	57	13	30
Thailand	1,000	71	10	19
Syria	1,670	32	32	36
Brazil	2,280	31	27	42
Mexico	1,820	37	29	34
Yugoslavia	2,680	33	33	34
Japan	21,040	11	34	55
W. Germany	18,530	6	44	50
United States	19,780	3	31	66

Sources: The World Bank, The World Development Report 1989 (New York: Oxford University Press, 1989), pp. 282–283; The World Bank, The World Bank Atlas 1989, p. C 9.

a *postindustrial country*, with employment in services far exceeding employment in industry and agriculture.[6]

The Status of Women

Table 16-5 presents the life expectancy, mortality rate at childbirth, and educational attainment of women in the less developed and developed countries. Women who live in the poorest countries of the world have a life expectancy lower than men. Their mortality rate at childbirth is much higher than for women in the developed countries, and their level of education is lower than for males in the poorer countries. There are a number of factors that contribute to the lower status of women in the less developed countries. Religion is one factor in that there may be proscriptions against the use of birth control measures. A large family is considered

TABLE 16-5
A Comparison of Life Expectancy, Maternal Mortality rate and the Educational Levels of Women in Less Developed and Developed Countries

Country	Life Expectancy (years)	Mortality Rates (for 100,000 live births)	Secondary School (females per 100 males)
Ethiopia	48	2,000	64
India	56	500	51
Sudan	51	607	40
Kenya	56	510	62
Pakistan	51	600	34
China	70	44	67
Nigeria	52	1,500	51
Bangladesh	50	600	38
Egypt	63	500	51
Mexico	71	92	86
Brazil	68	154	85
Venezuela	73	65	99
Portugal	76	15	92
Japan	81	15	99
Canada	80	2	95
West Germany	78	11	98
United States	79	9	95

Source: The World Bank, World Development Report 1988 *(New York: Oxford University Press, 1988) pp. 281–283.*

[6] Daniel Bell, *The Coming of Post-Industrial Society* (New York: Basic Books, 1976). An industrial society is defined by the quantity of goods as marking a standard of living; a postindustrial society is defined by the quality of life as measured by the services and amenities—health, education, and the arts—deemed desirable for everyone.

an asset in many countries because there are more breadwinners. Also, more importance is attached to educating males, even in industrially advanced countries such as Japan.

Income Distribution

Incomes are distributed far more unequally in the less developed countries than in the developed countries. There is generally no middle class, particularly in the poorest of the less developed countries, and an enormous income gulf between rich and poor creates a potential for economic and political instability—El Salvador is a case in point. Low incomes in the less developed countries can be explained by the large agricultural labor force and the absence of skilled workers in manufacturing. Economic growth and the development of technology lead to a greater equality in the distribution of income and wealth over an extended period. However, time is one thing the less developed countries do not have on their side, while rapid population growth and other factors make economic development extremely difficult.

Table 16-6 compares the distribution of household income for selected less developed countries. Although statistical comparisons of income distribution by countries are difficult to make, the table does indicate that incomes are distributed far more unequally in the less developed countries than in the developed countries, some of which are used as a comparison in the table. In Brazil, for example,

TABLE 16-6
Income Distribution for Selected Countries (share of total household income by quintiles)

		First Quintile	Second Quintile	Third Quintile	Fourth Quintile	Fifth Quintile	Top 10 Percent
India	1976	7.0%	9.2%	13.9%	20.5%	49.4%	33.6%
Kenya	1976	2.3	6.6	11.5	19.2	60.4	45.8
Peru	1972	1.9	5.1	11.0	21.0	61.0	42.9
Malaysia	1973	3.5	7.7	12.4	20.3	56.1	39.8
Panama	1970	2.0	5.2	11.0	20.0	61.8	44.2
Brazil	1972	2.0	5.0	9.4	17.0	66.6	50.6
Mexico	1977	2.9	7.0	12.0	20.4	57.7	40.6
Argentina	1970	4.4	9.7	14.1	21.5	50.3	35.2
United Kingdom	1979	7.0	11.5	17.0	24.8	39.7	23.4
Japan	1979	8.7	13.2	17.5	23.1	36.8	21.2
Finland	1981	6.3	12.1	18.4	25.8	37.6	21.7
West Germany	1978	7.9	12.5	17.0	23.1	39.5	24.0
Sweden	1981	7.4	13.1	16.8	21.0	41.7	24.8
Norway	1982	6.0	12.9	18.3	24.6	38.2	22.9
United States	1980	5.3	11.9	17.9	25.0	39.9	23.3

Source: The World Bank, World Development Report 1988 *(New York: Oxford University Press, 1988) pp. 272–273.*

50.6 percent of total household income was received by the top 10 percent of all households, compared to 16.4 percent of total household income for the bottom 60 percent. Moreover, the statistics do not show the enormous difference in living standards between the few at the top and the many at the bottom of the income ladder. The absence of a comprehensive welfare system does little to transfer income from the haves to the have-nots in the less developed countries.

Table 16-7 presents real rates of economic growth and inflation rates for selected Third World countries. Many Third World countries, in particular the African and Latin American countries, are suffering from a combination of low growth rates and high rates of inflation. Forty-seven countries, most of which had a per capita income of less that $500 a year, had negative per capita growth rates during the period 1980–1988, while another 14 countries had growth rates of less than 1 percent over the period. Conversely, the developed countries had per capita growth rates of two to three percent from 1980 to 1988.

Technological Dualism

Technological dualism is a prominent feature of many less developed countries. It is the coexistence in a society of two modes of production. One is generally categorized as modern, capital intensive, export oriented, and often foreign owned and managed; the other is traditional, labor intensive, dedicated to producing for the home market or for the family itself, and domestically owned. The second

TABLE 16-7
Real Growth Rates and Inflation Rates for Selected Third World Countries

	Real Growth Rate (percent)		Inflation Rate (percent) 1980–1987
	1980–1988	1986–1988	
Argentina	−1.6	−2.0	298.7
Bangladesh	0.8	0.4	11.1
Brazil	1.2	−0.3	166.3
Greece	0.1	1.1	19.7
Haiti	−2.1	−2.3	7.9
Mexico	−1.4	0.8	68.9
Nigeria	−4.3	−3.6	10.1
Sudan	−4.2	−2.6	31.7
Tanzania	−1.3	−1.0	24.9
Uganda	−0.3	0.5	95.2
Venezuela	−2.4	0.9	11.4
Yugoslavia	−0.1	−2.2	57.2
Zaire	−4.9	4.0	28.7
Zambia	−4.9	4.0	28.7

Source: The World Bank, The World Bank Atlas 1989 *(New York: Oxford University Press, 1989) pp. 6–9.* World Development Report 1989 *(New York: Oxford University Press, 1989) pp. 164–165.*

mode may involve small cottage industries where each worker performs all of the production operations. The first mode of production operates in a sector of the economy that is technologically well advanced and highly productive, while the second mode of production involves a sector that has old technology and low productivity. Technological dualism can lead to social dualism because new products and production methods often cause people to change their beliefs and ways of living. Workers accustomed to the two different modes of production will have different and often conflicting social values.

THEORIES OF ECONOMIC DEVELOPMENT

Economic development involves changes in the composition of a country's outputs and inputs. Economists have been concerned with the conditions necessary for economic development, and over time a considerable number of economic development theories have evolved.[7] The "big push" theory is seen as a way to break the circle of low income resulting from low productivity, which is caused by a low rate of capital formation, which in turn comes from a low rate of saving resulting from low income. According to this theory, a large, balanced wave of investment in different industries will enlarge markets, create support industries, increase growth because the industries will buy from each other, and lead to increases in income and saving. Thus the circle will be broken.

The "dependency" theory of economic development is in a way related to colonialism and imperialism. Most less developed countries were at one time possessions of Spain, England, France, or other European countries. These countries hindered the development of their colonies by exploiting their natural resources and denying them access to technological development. When independence was achieved, these former colonial possessions remained economically and psychologically dependent on their former owners.

Marxist Theory of Economic Development

One approach to explaining economic development is the Marxist theory of development. Marx contended that economic conditions were the basic causal forces shaping society. Economic development occurs in stages beginning with the evolution of medieval feudalism into industrial capitalism. Marx considered technological change the prime mover in the process of development. The transition from feudalism to capitalism is a result of technological change. But capitalism is merely a stage in the evolution of society toward the communist state, which is the inevitable final form of economic and social organization. According to Marx, economic development under capitalism results from technological progress, which

---

[7] Herrick and Kindleberger, *Economic Development*, Chapter 2.

depends on investment. The latter depends on profit, which, in turn, is affected by wages. The key proposition in Marxian economics is that all value comes from labor; for that reason, the profits of capitalists arise from the exploitation of labor. Capitalists pay a subsistence wage to the workers and claim the surplus value, that is, the value created by the workers less their wages. This eventually causes consumption to decline and economic crisis to develop.

The buying power of the home markets decreases because the workers are earning subsistence wages and their purchasing power is insufficient to take all of the goods that the capitalists produce. Inventory accumulates which causes the rate of profit to fall for the amount of money invested. The capitalists must turn to foreign markets to absorb their excess goods. But foreign markets are limited in number and imperialistic wars result. Eventually, within the colonies, liberation movements will occur that are directed against the mother country. India, Kenya, and Rhodesia (now Zimbabwe) are examples of former British colonies that have achieved their independence.

The result of imperialist wars and liberation movements, the Marxists say, will be the downfall of capitalism. Then the less developed countries will develop along Marxist lines. In the Marxist scheme of things, the less developed countries are simply precapitalist and would have to go through the capitalist phase before they could enter the optimum state of communism.

Rostow's Theory of Economic Development

Probably the most recent prominent theory of economic development is Walt Rostow's "takeoff" theory.[8] According to Rostow, in the process of economic development nations pass through five stages:

1. *The Traditional Society.* In the first stage, the nation's society is a traditional (or feudal). All societies before the Renaissance were traditional societies with little upward social mobility. Most resources were concentrated in agriculture. A crucial attribute is the absence of any cumulative, self-reinforcing process of material improvement.
2. *Prerequisites for Takeoff.* In the second stage, the prerequisites for sustained and systematic change are created. Chief among the prerequisites is an abandonment by at least part of the population of the philosophy of fatalism and determinism. There must be entrepreneurs in finance and manufacturing who are willing to take risks. Other changes in attitude and philosophical values must take place, including a respect for the individual, not on the basis of inherited status, but because of economic efficiency. Finally, a leading sector (e.g., mining, petroleum), is necessary for the takeoff.

---

[8] Walt Whitman Rostow, *The Stages of Economic Growth: A Non-Communist Manifesto* (New York: Cambridge University Press, 1971).

3. *The Takeoff.* In this stage, which lasts for 20 to 30 years, the pace of social and economic change suddenly accelerates. An important part of this acceleration is an increase in the percentage of the gross national product that is saved and invested in capital goods. Another important step is the establishment of manufacturing. There is also continued change in such things as customs of the people, governmental forms and practices, and kinds of economic units in existence.

4. *Drive to Maturity.* This stage is a period of self-sustaining increases in both total and per capita gross national product. During this stage of some 60 years, industry comes to employ the most advanced technology available anywhere and becomes capable of producing whatever it wishes, being constrained only by market conditions and availability of resources.

5. *Mass Consumption.* The last stage is mass consumption of consumer durable goods and services. The production of these goods and services enables the majority of the population to attain high living standards.

Rostow's theory of the stages of economic growth has been criticized on a number of counts. Included among these is the charge that it fails to fit with historical fact. Some countries did not have a takeoff at all; rather, they developed steadily over a long period. The theory is also criticized because it fails to specify what makes each of the stages peculiarly distinctive relative to each of the others. It is further criticized for its failure to include forces that may be important to causing growth. However, Rostow's theory does indicate that important changes must occur before a nation in the traditional stage can advance in its development.

OBSTACLES TO ECONOMIC DEVELOPMENT

Economic growth and development have been occurring slowly or not at all in many of the less developed countries. In Chad, for instance, the average annual economic growth rate was negative for the period 1960–1982; for Bangladesh, the average annual economic growth rate was 0.3 percent. Per capita income is not only very low, it is not increasing very much. The people of the less developed countries want higher living standards. Given the communications revolution that has been developing throughout the world, people in even the remotest villages in Latin America and Africa have some idea of what the good life is. However, it turns out that economic development is an extremely elusive objective. The obstacles to its achievement are many, and the task of converting backward, poor people into at best moderately well-off ones is far from easy. There are many obstacles to economic development and a review of some of them is in order.

Population

In 1798 the English clergyman Thomas Malthus published his book *An Essay in the Principles of Population* (London: J. M. Dent & Sons, 1951). His world outlook was pessimistic; it suggested that population grows faster than the food supply. Based on scattered empirical evidence, including the colonizing of North America, Malthus calculated that population tended to double every 25 years in a geometric progression, whereas food supplies tended to increase in an arithmetic progression. An example is shown in Table 16-8.

His proposition was based on two assumptions: Technological change could not increase food supply faster than population, and population growth would not be limited by fewer births, only by more deaths. Although both assumptions have proved to be wrong, there is an element of truth in his predictions. It took more than 4,000 years of recorded history for China to have its first 500 million people, but only a little more than three decades to increase the population to one billion. Regardless of a country's size, natural resources, or level of development, countries with large populations and high birth rates face increasing problems. At current rates of population increase, the population of developed countries will double in 120 years and the population of less developed countries will double in 33 years. [9]

Urbanization. Urbanization and congestion are population-related problems. Often peasants are driven off the land into the cities by poverty or takeovers of the land by rich landowners or foreigners. Overcrowding can lead to increased population, unemployment, stress, and a demand for human services that can be greater than the capacity of the urban area to provide. Overcrowding can lead to an increase in health costs, not only from communicable diseases, but also from heart disease, cancer, and other ailments caused by a stress-related breakdown in the body's immunity. Urbanization problems are particularly acute in less developed countries because they lack the financial resources to provide the necessary services to cope with their problems. By the end of the century, at least 22 cities in the world will have a population of more than 10 million; 60 will have more than 5 million. Most are located in the less developed countries. Mexico City, which has become the largest city in the world, is projected to have a population of 27 million by the end of the century. [10]

TABLE 16-8
Malthusian Progressions for Population and Food Supply

Year	0	25	50	75	100	125	150	175	200
Population size	1	2	4	8	16	32	64	128	256
Food supply	1	2	3	4	5	6	7	8	9

[9] Mary M. Kent and Carl Haub, *1988 World Population Data Sheet* (Washington: Population Reference Bureau, 1988).

[10] United Nations, Department of International and Social Affairs, *Population Bulletin of the United Nations*, No. 14 (New York: Author, 1984), p. 24.

Food Shortages. The larger the population of a country, the greater the demand for adequate food. Both a rural overpopulation and a rising tide of urban consumers compete for a limited agricultural output. In most less developed countries the need to satisfy the demand for food has prevented the allocation of resources to economic development. As a result, the inability to industrialize reduces the potential to earn money from exports to pay for the import of food products. It is a vicious cycle of hunger.

Food shortages can also have a deleterious effect on the health of a country's workers. A case in point is Ethiopia, where famine has resulted in the death of countless thousands of persons. Other African countries have also been affected by famine. Nutritional deficiencies in the less developed countries lead to a lower level of worker productivity, with subsequent lower agricultural and industrial output as a result.

Although food production in the less developed countries has increased in recent decades, it has just kept pace with population growth in some countries and has failed to do so in others, including 27 African countries. In Nigeria, the largest country in Africa, the average annual rate of agricultural production declined during the period 1970–1980.[11] The output of food in China and India has exceeded population growth, but only by a narrow margin.

Moreover, in the less developed countries, increases in agricultural acreage have been relatively small over the last two decades. In the main, further growth of the land frontier is constrained in many countries. In Africa, for example, the expansion of farm land is limited by the Sahara desert, rivers, jungles, and mountains and also by diseases that destroy livestock and farm products. Insecticides used to try to control the diseases have had undesirable effects on the environment.[12] In India the number of rural households and people trying to earn a living in agriculture has increased at a rate far in excess of cultivated land.

Infrastructure

Capital can be classified in two ways—social overhead capital and physical capital. The former includes the structures and equipment required for shelter, public health, and education, and the latter consists of plants and equipment used in industry and agriculture. Poor countries are deficient in both forms of capital because savings and incomes are low. They cannot afford the medical services and educational facilities necessary to improve the quality of the labor force. This fact becomes evident in Table 16-9. In Bangladesh, for example, there is one physician for every 10,940 persons; in the United States there is one physician for 520 persons.[13] In

---

[11] The World Bank, *World Development Report* 1988, pp. 84–88.

[12] World Bank, 1988, p. 90.

[13] In Chad there is one physician for every 47,530 persons. Only 3 percent of the secondary school age group are in school and less than one percent are in college.

TABLE 16-9
Health- and Education-Related Indicators for Selected Countries

	Population Per Physician	Percentage of Age Group in Secondary Schools	Percentage of Age Group in Higher Education
Bangladesh	9,690	18%	5%
Ethiopia	88,150	12	1
Uganda	21,270	9	1
India	3,700	35	8
China	1,730	39	2
Pakistan	2,913	17	5
Kenya	10,120	20	1
Indonesia	12,330	39	7
Nigeria	9.400	29	3
Mexico	1,210	55	16
Italy	250	75	26
Japan	740	96	30
United States	500	99	57
Sweden	410	83	38
U.S.S.R.	270	99	21
Canada	550	99	55

Source: The World Bank, World Development Report 1988 *(New York: Oxford University Press, 1989) pp. 278–279 and 280–281.*

Uganda, only 5 percent of people of secondary school age are in school and only 1 percent of those in the college age group are in some form of higher education. In Japan, the corresponding statistics are 92 percent and 30 percent. Only 1 percent of the relevant age group attends college in China; however, this is a legacy of the Cultural Revolution, when universities were closed down.[14]

Infrastructure, or social overhead capital, is a descriptive economic concept that refers to the existence of highways, railways, airports, sewage facilities, housing, schools, and other social amenities that indicate the development or lack of development of an area or region. Once an infrastructure is in place, it encourages both economic and social development. Developed countries have developed infrastructures; less developed countries generally do not. This creates a problem for economic development, because industry will not normally locate plants in areas where there is a poor infrastructure. In particular, mass consumption products require the existence of skilled labor, sewage disposal facilities, transportation and communication facilities, and other amenities for their marketing.

---

[14] The colleges were closed during the Cultural Revolution for ideological reasons, and professors and students were put to work in the fields with the peasants to learn humility and to ponder socialist ideals. Working side by side in a manure pile was considered a good way to eliminate class distinctions.

Education. Educational facilities are a key component in the infrastructure of any area or region. Education itself is directly related to the quality of life and constitutes a form of human capital. Literacy, or rather the lack of it, is not as directly related to a country's population as it is to the country's stage of economic development. There is a positive correlation between a lower standard of living and a higher rate of illiteracy. It has been estimated that one-third of the world is illiterate. Most of this illiteracy is concentrated in countries with high birth rates, large populations, and the least to spend on education. A lack of educational opportunities maintains the distinction between the haves and have-nots in society and perpetuates class differences. It also reduces the base of educated labor upon which the economic development of the country depends.

Roads. A requisite for the economic and social development of a country is an adequate system of roads. Few countries can depend exclusively on other forms of transportation. Air transportation is too expensive for most products, and railroads are limited to specific routes between main access points. Poor countries do not usually have the resources to maintain an adequate road system. Physiography also works against the development of an adequate highway system. Most of the less developed countries are located in geographic areas of the world with barriers to transportation. For example, the Sierra Madre and Andes mountains have inhibited the east-west development of Mexico, Bolivia, and Peru. Transportation is also hard to develop in countries dominated by tropical jungles because vegetation overtakes roads in only a short time.

Other Facilities. Dams, bridges, sewage disposal, and other facilities are a vital part of a region's infrastructure but are usually inadequate in the less developed countries. Dams control flooding and provide the water supply and electric power necessary for economic and social development. Bridges create more efficient transportation by linking areas that are separated by bodies of water. Inadequate sanitary facilities can result in the spread of communicable diseases such as cholera and typhoid fever. Garbage and waste materials dumped in city streets attract rats and other animals, which increase the possibility of epidemics. Communication facilities have to be adequate to handle the needs of a region. The cost and efficiency of service have to be considered. Government-owned telephone and postal services are notoriously inefficient in less developed countries.

Low Savings Rate

As mentioned above, there is an extreme imbalance in the distribution of income in less developed countries, exacerbated in part by the existence of a large component of unskilled labor. The vast majority of workers do not earn enough to do any saving; moreover, a minority of households get most of the income. In Mexico, for example, in 1977 the top 10 percent of income earners received 40.6 percent of national income; in Brazil in 1972, the top 10 percent received 50.6 percent of national income. This group should provide much of the saving necessary for capital formation. However, savings are usually invested out of the country or in real estate, where there is a quick and high rate of return. Political instability provides a good reason to invest one's income in, say, Swiss bonds, which will be safe from possible expropriation by a new government. El Salvador is a case in point.

Savings is a necessary requisite for capital formation, for without it investment for capital formation cannot take place. Inadequate amounts of capital and the inability to increase the capital are obstacles to economic development. It can be said that less developed countries are caught in a vicious circle. Because savings is small, investment is low and the capital stock is small, and the real gross national product is small. Nations that save little grow slowly and are locked into a circle of poverty.[15]

Limited Range of Exports

Less developed countries usually depend on the export of agricultural products, fuels, minerals, or metals such as oil or copper. Many depend on the export of a single product for the bulk of national income. Nigeria depends on the export of oil for around 80 percent of its total export earnings. Thus the drop in the world market price of oil has created problems for the Nigerian economy. When oil prices were high during the early 1970s, Nigeria benefitted. It ran a surplus in its balance of payments, and it could use foreign earnings to improve living standards. Government spending increased to improve the infrastructure of the Nigerian economy. However, during the early 1980s, the world demand for oil declined, and oil prices fell from a peak of $35 a barrel in 1980. Revenues from oil exports declined, Nigeria had a deficit in its balance of payments, and it now has a problem of a large foreign debt incurred when oil prices were high and earnings were good.

Countries that depend on exports of agricultural products and minerals are usually subject to a disadvantage in trade with the developed countries. The terms of trade, the real quantity of exports required to pay for a given amount of real imports, favor the developed countries. Brazilian coffee and Mexican oil are much more subject to shifts in world prices than are American computers and Japanese cars. When prices decline for coffee or oil, Brazil and Mexico will have to give up more income to import computers and cars. Conversely, America and Japan will have to give up less income to acquire coffee and oil. There is an inelastic demand for many products exported by the less developed countries. When prices for a product fall, there is no offsetting increase in revenue resulting from a more than proportionate increase in demand.

---

[15] Ragnar Nurkse, *Problems of Capital Formation in Underdeveloped Countries* (New York: Oxford University Press, 1953).

Terms of Trade

A country's terms of trade is a measurement of the quantity of imports that can be bought by a given quanity of its exports. If a country's terms of trade is less than 100 percent, it has to give up more in exports than it gets back in imports; conversely, if a country's terms of trade is above 100 percent, it is getting more back in imports than it is giving up in exports. As Table 16-10 indicates, the terms of trade for many less developed countries is less than 100 percent. Mexico and Nigeria are good examples. Both rely heavily on oil exports. As the price of oil has fallen in world markets, Mexico and Nigeria have to give up more oil in order to import the same of amount of manufactured goods. The price for manufactured goods is less subject to world market fluctuations.

Foreign Debt

Many less developed countries have a serious foreign debt problem. For dozens of countries, foreign debt has set back their economic development. Poverty has intensified as countries have had to struggle against an enormous foreign debt burden. Moreover, the world financial system has been disrupted by the prospect of widespread default on the foreign debts of the developing world. Almost all of the debtor nations are unable to borrow in the international financial markets on normal market terms. Table 16-11 presents the debt ratios of selected less developed countries for 1988. As the table indicates, the foreign debt of these countries exceeds their exports as much as eight to one.

TABLE 16-10
Terms of Trade for the Less Developed Countries
(1980 = 100 percent)

Country	1980	1987
Argentina	90	81
Brazil	89	97
China	95	87
Colombia	98	70
Indonesia	94	69
Kenya	92	80
Mexico	98	73
Nigeria	90	54
Tunisia	83	79
Venezuela	91	54
Zaire	82	74
Zambia	72	79

Source: The World Bank, World Development Report, 1989 *(New York: Oxford University Press, 1989) pp. 191–196.*

TABLE 16-11
Debt Ratios for Less Developed Countries for
1988 (percent)

Country	Debt to Exports	Debt to GNP
Argentina	527.9	74.6
Bangladesh	434.1	52.1
Bolivia	776.1	133.9
Brazil	325.3	34.5
Indonesia	263.4	72.4
Kenya	314.3	74.4
Mexico	312.2	105.9
Morocco	400.0	117.7
Nigeria	410.1	114.0
Phillipines	271.3	74.6
Senegal	290.3	80.5
Sudan	970.7	130.1
Tanzania	868.3	199.8
Zaire	569.0	155.1
Zambia	570.6	243.1

Source: The World Bank, World Debt Tables: External
Debt of Developing Countries, 1989 *(New York: Oxford
University Press, 1989).*

Sociocultural Factors

Sociocultural factors can also provide an obstacle to economic development.[16] Culture involves interaction between individuals and groups. It consists of behavioral patterns and values of a social group. It is culture that influences individual and group behavior and determines how things will be done, at least in theory if not in practice. It includes a number of features such as the status distinction, based on education, caste, politics, religion, or sex, between members of a social group. Culture may also assume the form of language differences identifying a group or region. It also may extend to production, with the use of machinery and equipment in an industrial society creating a culture that is alien to agrarian societies. Cultures need a certain amount of conformity to keep groups of people working together, but they also need new ideas to promote progress.

Religion. Religion can provide the spiritual foundation for a culture. It can also exacerbate the problems of economic development. Cultural conflicts in the area of religion can be quite serious, as anyone familiar with the Middle East can testify. Conflicts between Hindus and Moslems created such severe problems in governing

---

[16] For a discussion of sociocultural factors and their impact on development see Edmund Leach, *Social Anthropology* (New York: Oxford University Press, 1982).

India after it gained its independence from the United Kingdom that Pakistan was made a separate Moslem country. The assassination of Indian Prime Minister Indira Gandhi involved a religious conflict between Hindus and Sikhs culminating over the alleged defiling of the latter's holy temple at Amritsar by Indian troops. Several days of rioting resulted in threats and destruction of property. The revolt against the Shah of Iran was led primarily by fundamentalist Moslem clergy who felt that traditional religious values were being replaced by Western values of materialism. Religion can place moral and economic norms on a culture by prescribing limits, particularly the subordination of impulse, on acceptable conduct.

Fate. A fatalistic view of life is one of the differences between Western and Eastern cultures. Fate is called *karma* in the Hindu and Buddhist religions and *kismet* in the Moslem religion. Karma holds that every action carries with it a reward or punishment. One literally has little control over one's life; it is controlled by destiny. Good fortune is the result of some action in the past, even in a previous life, that was good. Conversely, bad fortune is also the result of some bad act committed at some time in the past. A person is unaware of past actions, good or bad; it is simply his or her karma at work.

Social Organization. The social organization of a society refers to the roles of men, women, and children within a system. Employment, manners, dress, and expectations are virtually dictated by each culture to its members. Certain actions may be permitted or denied through a legal process, but the majority of actions are learned through interaction in the culture or from the training by those familiar with the culture. A social organization functions within the cultural system of the society in which it is located. The component parts—that is, the people—function and work together through patterns of interaction that develop among the members. These interactions take many forms of interpersonal relationships that can have an effect on economic development.

Classes. Each social system has a demarcated class system. Class distinction may be based on religion. An example is the Hindu religion, with its caste system. At the top are the Brahmins, who are members of the priestly class; at the bottom are the untouchables. Social classes may achieve distinctiveness based on hereditary titles or through being arbiters of taste and refinement. Class may be based on educational attainment, particularly in societies where education is limited to the select few. Class systems can inhibit economic development; in some societies, business is regarded as a lowly occupation, something done by the lower classes or foreigners.

Family. In all cultures, men, women, and children live together in families. The family is the one basic institution found everywhere. It represents a sort of social insurance and insulation against the trials and tribulations of life. However, the role of the family varies in different countries. In Japan it represents stability in a country that prizes consensus. It is probable that the group ethic, including family solidarity, has contributed to the economic development of Japan. The role of the family can also work against economic development. Large families are regarded as an economic asset in many parts of the world. The children can be put to work in the fields when they are young and contribute to family income. They are also expected to take care of their elderly parents. Birth control methods designed to limit family size are often resisted in the less developed countries, even though the population is greater than the food resources available to feed it.

Physiography

The physiography of a country can have an impact on its economic and social development for better or worse. Flat, fertile soil, supported by water and a suitable climate, provides the basis for agriculture. Dense forests provide a renewable resource—wood—and also furnish a refuge and habitat for wildlife as well as a root base that prevents soil erosion. Fast-running rivers and streams offer a potential for hydroelectric development. Water is vital to the support of life and forms a primary source of transportation. Deserts, which were once a barrier to economic development, are now less formidable, given the state of world technology. In many of the less developed countries, a combination of physical forces has had an adverse effect on economic and social development.

Soil. Because humans must eat in order to survive and because nearly all of our food is either directly or indirectly a product of the soil, agriculture is probably the most important activity on the earth. A shortage of productive land is one of the major problems facing the world and its rapidly growing population. Although this problem hardly exists in the United States, it is endemic in most of the less developed countries. The ratio of arable lands to people is basic to agricultural productivity and consumption rates. As the maximum productivity per unit of agricultural land is achieved, the per capita amount of food available must decrease as the population continues to increase. Maintenance of soil fertility, vital to productivity, is a growing problem as soils are becoming more and more exhausted throughout the world.

Less than 5 percent of the total land area of Latin America and Africa has the combination of climate and physiographic conditions necessary for agricultural production.[17] The mountainous nature of Bolivia and Peru makes cultivation of most of the land impossible. In most of Latin America, climatic variations run to the extremes of either too much or too little rain; the Amazon basin of Brazil, for

---

[17] Bernard Gilland, "Considerations on World Population and Food Supply," *Population and Development Review* (July, 1983), pp. 203–211.

example, receives too much rainfall, resulting in the rapid leaching of nutrients from the soil. The tropical lands of Africa have sufficient moisture and are very fertile, but the presence of human and botanical tropical diseases results in low agricultural productivity. The remaining lands, which occupy an enormous expanse, are semidesert or desert and can produce little without irrigation.

Mountains. While mountains provide a basis for tourism and winter sports, they are a barrier to economic development. Mountainous terrain makes farming difficult if not impossible, makes mining expensive and hazardous, and inhibits the construction of transportation facilities. The forests that cover many mountain slopes are a valuable resource, but harvesting is difficult. Transportation is hard to develop in countries such as Guatemala, Bolivia, and Peru that are dominated by mountain ranges. In Asia, the Himalaya range makes a large land area inaccessible and unavailable for development. In China, economic development of the whole country is difficult because much of the land area is isolated from the main population centers by insurmountable mountains.

SOLUTIONS FOR ECONOMIC DEVELOPMENT

There are no easy solutions that will enable less developed countries to become developed. Many have nothing of value to export and little potential for industrial development. They are hamstrung by hostile social, cultural, and political institutions. The average annual growth rate of the poorest countries in the world, those with half of the world's population and with a per capita income of $500 or less, was 1.5 percent over the period 1965–1987.[18] The average annual growth rate of India was 1.8 percent, and its per capita income for 1987 was $300. At that rate of growth, it would take more than 50 years for India's per capita income to double. The rate of investment in India and other of the poorest countries is constrained in three ways: the capacity of the country to absorb additional capital, the level of domestic savings, and foreign exchange rates that affect trade with other countries. Even so, India is far better off than Bangladesh, which had an average annual growth rate of 0.3 percent for 1965–1987, or Chad, which had a negative rate of growth and a negative rate of investment for the same period.

Foreign Aid

Foreign aid involves a transfer between the more developed nations and less developed nations for the purpose of promoting economic development. The transfer may be in the form of grants that do not have to be repaid or loans that carry lower

---

[18] World Bank, *World Development Report 1989,* pp. 222–223.

rates of interest and longer periods of repayment than normally would prevail for the borrowing country. Foreign aid may also come in a variety of physical forms. Technical assistance and supplies of foods are examples of physical aid.[19] However, foreign aid cannot be considered a panacea for economic development. It may concentrate benefits in a few hands and may fail to change incentives and responses needed for broad economic development. Foreign aid can be used for consumption purposes, generating a one-time increase in well-being for those lucky to get it but leaving no lasting benefits. Many foreign aid projects have long gestation lags before their output is directly marketable. This can conflict with public expectations of immediate success.

Internal Policies

Certain development policies that do not involve outside assistance have been used with varying degrees of success by a number of countries. These policies rely on the notion that a less developed country can pull itself up by its bootstraps. The communist countries have followed a policy of unbalanced growth, where resources are channeled away from the production of agriculture and consumer goods and into the development of heavy industry. By following this policy, the Soviet Union was able to transform itself from an agricultural to an industrial country, although at considerable cost.[20] Then there are policies based on trade to achieve development. The inward-looking or import-substitution policy promotes the development of home industries by restricting the import of outside products.[21] This policy has its drawbacks, but has been used by some countries, notably Mexico and Brazil, to achieve some economic development. There is also an outward-looking trade policy that relies on exports of products to achieve development. Internal resources are used to develop export industries, and exports are subsidized by the government.

Government Monetary and Fiscal Policies. Government monetary and fiscal policies are also used to promote economic development. Central banks use monetary policy to control the level of national output and the price level through changes in the money supply. Increasing the money supply can have a stimulative effect on an economy, as witnessed by the development of Spain as the world's leading country during the sixteenth century. The flow of gold and silver from the New World stimulated the economic development of Spain and provided the base for

---

[19] The World Bank makes loans to less developed countries to improve their economic and social infrastructures. The United States and other developed countries have their own programs of capital and technical assistance for the less developed countries.

[20] This industrialization was achieved in its early stages largely at the expense of the landowners and the peasants. The former were liquidated and the latter were literally starved to provide a surplus of foodstuffs for the support of workers in the factories.

[21] For example, to build a domestic automobile industry one could restrict the import of automobiles.

"easy money" policies in the Dutch and German banking houses of Western Europe.[22] However, the problem with an "easy money" policy is that less developed countries are inflation prone. Shortages of goods develop as a result of bottlenecks in production, and prices rise. Investment on the part of the rich is directed toward speculative holdings, such as real estate, rather than toward the creation or expansion of productive enterprises. A constantly rising price level tends to aggravate this tendency by making speculation all the more profitable.[23]

Fiscal policy affects aggregate demand through changes in government spending and the level of taxation. An expansionary fiscal policy can stimulate economic growth and development through an increase in government spending, various tax breaks, or both. The problem with fiscal policy is that it is far more adaptable to the developed countries, where income, output, consumer spending, taxation, and investment are high enough to be manipulated. Many less developed countries rely on sales taxes as a major source of revenue. Income taxes are often not feasible because there is little income to tax or tax avoidance is easy. Countries may also resort to deficit financing—expenditures that are greater than revenues—to stimulate the economy. The deficit is financed by borrowing from the central bank or through the sale of debt to the public. However, in the less developed countries, there are no money markets for the sale of the debt and the public does not have the money. Thus, borrowing is done primarily through the central bank.

Market Mechanisms. Some economists feel that the problems of the less developed countries can be solved by market forces coupled with a nineteenth-century government policy of laissez faire. All developed countries began by being underdeveloped; they developed naturally without state intervention through the market application of capital, entrepreneurial and technical skills, and labor. Essentially, market mechanisms consist of permitting individual buyers and sellers to make economic decisions for themselves and letting things be as they are or will be. Market mechanisms can play an important role in the conversion of a less developed country into a developed one. The ideas of how they can do so have been formulated from the British experience and from other developed countries such as the United States and Japan. But it is unlikely that market mechanisms alone will achieve economic development for the less developed countries. Moreover, there are tremendous differences between the situations of England and the United States over the last two centuries and the less developed countries of today. Some of them may summarized as follows.

---

[22] It might be added that gold and silver proved to be the ruination of Spain. The Spanish kings spent the wealth on military conquests. Gold and silver increased the money supply in Spain, creating inflation that eventually destroyed the economy.

[23] Inflation also worsens income inequality between rich and poor and increases the potential for social unrest.

1. Sociological forces favored development of the United States and other Western countries. The Protestant work ethic emphasized thrift.[24] This attitude helped produce a flow of savings sufficient to finance the introduction of new commodities and new techniques brought on by the Industrial Revolution.

2. Technological factors were more favorable to development in the Western world than they are to the less developed countries of today. The simplest of these factors is the extent of resource endowment. If one compares the resource endowment of the United States to that of Bangladesh or Pakistan, the contrast is apparent. The proportions in which land, labor, and capital are available are a drag on development in the latter two countries. The proportions favor agriculture against industry; labor is abundant; land is relatively limited; and capital is very scarce.[25]

3. Political factors also favored economic development of the Western countries. In the United States, for example, nationalism did not manifest itself in a hostility toward the inflow of foreign capital. There was a large and continuous flow of foreign capital into the country during the period 1865–1900 when the United States became a world industrial power. In many of the less developed countries today, foreign investment may be threatened with outright expropriation. Foreign investment is limited because risks of unpredictable government action, often based on nationalistic sentiment, are added to the normal risks attendant in investment abroad.

Success in East Asia

Although there are many factors over which the less developed countries have no control, some East Asian countries, notably South Korea and Singapore, have succeeded in developing their economies through a combination of government policies and private enterprise initiative.[26] Exports have been promoted by keeping exchange rates competitive. This has enabled South Korea and Singapore to expand exports, while restricting imports on the basis of price. Second, these countries have maintained high real interest rates, which has encouraged domestic savings and ensured that investment is directed into the areas of highest return. Third, they have relied on market mechanisms for resource allocation.

In the following chapters, three countries will be examined from the standpoint of their approaches to economic development. They represent Asia, Latin America, and Africa. China is the largest less developed country in the world and is

---

[24] R. H. Tawney, *Religion and the Rise of Capitalism* (New York: Harcourt, Brace and World, 1926), Chapters 1 and 2.

[25] Colin Clark, *The Conditions of Ecomonic Progress* (London: Macmillan & Co., Ltd., 1951).

[26] Japan is the prime example of a successful East Asian country. However, Japan was a developed industrial nation before World War II.

also one of the poorest. It is a socialist country in the process of experimenting with market mechanisms of capitalism to increase productivity. Mexico is at a lower-middle stage of economic development. Its per capita income is one-sixth that of the United States, but is eight times larger than China's. Nigeria, the largest country in Africa, has a per capita GNP higher than most African countries but lower than most Latin American countries. It is a country in the lower stages of economic development.

SUMMARY

More than half of the world's people live in countries with a per capita gross GNP of $500 a year or less; another 500 million people live in countries with a per capita income between $500 and $1500 a year. These countries are at the lowest stages of economic development. Many countries with higher per capita incomes, such as Mexico and Brazil, can hardly be called modern industrial economies. This is also true of the oil-exporting countries, whose per capita incomes are high but whose level of economic development is low. These less developed countries are committed to economic development as a way to improve living standards, but face many obstacles in achieving a rate of investment that will provide a satisfactory rate of economic growth. One major obstacle is the lack of an adequate infrastructure to provide the services necessary for industrial development. Sociocultural factors can also inhibit development. Probably the most important obstacle to economic development is population. When population grows rapidly, the bulk of domestic investment is simply devoted to maintaining the current level of per capita income.

REVIEW QUESTIONS

1. Upon what basis is a country classified as less developed?
2. What are the typical economic features of a less developed country?
3. Distinguish between economic growth and economic development.
4. What is Rostow's theory of the stages of economic development?
5. In traditional societies, what is the typical attitude toward family size? Why does this attitude exist?
6. Discuss the concept of technological dualism.
7. What are some examples of sociocultural factors that block economic development?
8. Why do less developed countries have a disadvantage in their terms of trade with developed countries?

RECOMMENDED READINGS

Brown, Lester R., ed. *State of the World*. New York: W. W. Norton, 1989.

Dornbusch, Rudiger. *The World Debt Problem: Anatomy and Solutions*. New York: Twentieth Century Fund, 1987.

Herrick, Bruce, and Charles P. Kindleberger. *Economic Development*. 4th ed. New York: McGraw-Hill, 1987.

Inter-American Development Bank. *Economic and Social Progress in Latin America, 1989 Report*. Washington, DC: 1989.

Kent, Mary M., and Carl Haub. *1989 World Population Data Sheet*. Washington DC: Population Reference Service, No. 1 1989.

Leach, Edmund. *Social Anthropology*. New York: Oxford University Press, 1982.

Miller, G. Tyler. *Living in the Environment*. Belmont, CA: Wadsworth Publishing Co., 1985.

Rostow, Walt W. *Why the Poor Get Richer and the Rich Slow Down*. Austin: University of Texas Press, 1980.

Sacks, Jeffrey, ed. *Developing Country Debt and the World Economy*. Chicago: University of Chicago Press, 1989.

Tinker, Irene. *Persistent Inequalities: Women and World Development*. New York: Oxford University Press, 1989.

CHAPTER SEVENTEEN

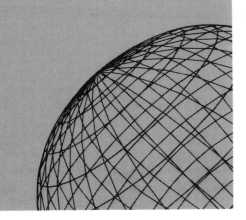

THE PEOPLE'S REPUBLIC OF CHINA

There is dramatic irony in China's national title as "People's Republic" because the Chinese government decided to shoot some of the people it claims to represent. The Chinese Communist Party, which has claimed a moral mandate to rule with a power monopoly for four decades, suddenly had its power challenged by Chinese university students who wanted a more democratic society. In 1949 the Chinese Communists drove the Nationalist government from office and created the People's Republic of China. Its authority has been absolute and unchallenged since that time, but in May 1989 an upheaval occurred. The people who lived under its rule rose up and asserted themselves in one of the more awesome political displays of this century. Night after night world television viewers watched hundreds of thousands of Chinese students and their supporters demonstrating in Tiananmen Square in Beijing. In a juxtaposition of political opposites, the students created a styrofoam copy of the Statue of Liberty and paraded it around the square under the pictures of Lenin and Mao.

It is necessary to emphasize the fact that the students were not advocating the overthrow of communism or the Communist party; they were advocating democratic reforms that would allow more participation by the people in the political decision-making process. A weakness of communist governments, including the Chinese, is that they will brook no challenge to their authority. So on June 3, 1989, the government sent troops and tanks to crush the student demonstrators. Many were killed by gunfire or run over by tanks. The hard-liners in the government dominate the government, at least for the present. In the tradition of all authoritarian societies, their solution to the problem of the students was simply to bash a few heads.

However, the problems of the government will not disappear that simply. The students called attention to the moral bankruptcy of the government. As is true in other communist countries, nomenklatura is a big political and moral issue. Chinese political elites, who claim to be the moral guardians of the people, enjoy the same privileges that their counterparts enjoy in the Soviet Union. They attend the best schools, get the best jobs, live in the best apartments, and drive Mercedes Benzes[1] to shop in special stores. All of this in a country that by any standard is one of the poorest in the world with a per capita income of around $330 a year.

It is hard to predict what will happen to China in the future. If the government proves too inflexible to change to meet the times, it will lose the future. Given modern communication and technology, it has become more difficult for any government to suppress freedom, much less eradicate it. The one thing that China has to do as it prepares to enter the 21st century is to improve its living standards. To do this, it has to modernize its technology and permit more interchange of ideas. This will be impossible if the Communist party maintains an ideological mindset that is rooted in the past. Killing students is one way not to attract the foreign capital and technology necessary to make China competitive in the 21st century.

DEVELOPMENT OF
THE ECONOMIC SYSTEM

At the end of World War II, China was split into two factions, the Nationalists and Communists, both of which had resisted Japanese incursions since the beginning of the Sino-Japanese War in 1937. Japan's defeat set up a struggle for control of occupied China extending from Manchuria in the north to Canton in the south. Mediation was attempted by the United States, and a tripartite committee consisting of Nationalists, Communists, and the United States was set up to work out conditions for a coalition government. These efforts proved short lived and a civil war broke out in 1946. The Nationalists' initial advantages in territory and logistics were lost, and the Nationalist government was driven from the Chinese mainland to Taiwan by the Communists in 1949.

The Period of Consolidation, 1949–1952

When the Communists formally announced the creation of the Chinese People's Republic on October 1, 1949, they were able to begin the consolidation of power and the development of a new type of economic system. Certainly the task was not easy. Years of fighting and inflation had debilitated the economy. Widespread corruption had been rampant under the Nationalist government. The masses of the

---

[1] For a good discussion of nomenklatura Chinese style, see "Too Much All in the Family," *Time* (June 5, 1989) p. 28.

people were illiterate and had to be trained and educated to fit into an industrial base that was to be the fountainhead for the development of the communist economic system.

During this period, Chinese industry was also placed under the control of the government. In 1949, the Communist government took over those state organizations it identified as bureaucratic capital. During 1951 and 1952, the government took over all foreign-owned businesses. In 1952 and 1953, private enterprises were placed under government control.[2]

The First Five-Year Plan, 1953–1957

The First Five-Year Plan marked the second stage in the economic development of the People's Republic of China. To implement the plan, the Chinese relied heavily on Russian expertise. Soviet technicians were imported to develop the plan and to run the factories. Agreements were reached providing for Russian aid in building or expanding electric power plants and supplying agricultural, mining, and chemical equipment. Soviet financial aid took the form of low-interest loans. The Russians also contracted for the construction of factories producing a wide variety of products, including chemicals, synthetic fibers and plastics, liquid fuel, and machine tools. The Soviets also built modern iron and steel complexes, nonferrous metallurgical plants, refineries, and power stations and trained Chinese technicians to operate them. Sets of blueprints and related materials giving directions for plant layouts were also provided for the Chinese.

The land reforms of 1949–1952 were followed by a series of organizational reforms beginning with the simplest form of social enterprise, the *mutual aid team* and progressing through successive stages of producer cooperatives to complete collectivization of the farms in 1957. At that time the peasants lost all title to the land. This same organizational pattern was followed for craftspersons and small retailers. By 1957, practically all industrial enterprises were state owned or collectives.

The Great Leap Forward, 1958–1960

In 1958 the Chinese departed from the pattern of economic development set by the First Five-Year Plan and moved to a new approach that relied on the idealistic fervor of the masses of workers and peasants to drive the economy ahead much more quickly. This approach was called the *Great Leap Forward*. It is an example of idealistic extremism that substituted zeal for the material incentives developed under the First Five-Year Plan. China's enormous population was regarded as an economic asset and not a liability—the more people, the more hands to build to communism. Emphasis was placed on indigenous methods of production and the

---

[2] Gregory Chow, *The Chinese Economy*, (New York: Harper & Row, 1985).

development of labor-intensive investment projects. To put the basic objective of the Great Leap Forward simply, the population was to be harnessed to increase production and make China a world power.

Agriculture. In agriculture, economic policy involved the formation of communes. The communes marked the final stage in the transition of agriculture away from private enterprise, which had existed during the first years of Communist rule. Under communal organization, all vestiges of private property were eliminated. The peasants were not only deprived of the private plots, livestock, and implements that had been left to them through previous collectivization; they also had to surrender their homes. The purpose was to turn the peasants into mobile workers ready for any task in any area to which they might be assigned.

Industry. In industry, economic policy emphasized the use of labor to create thousands of tiny industrial units throughout the country. Again, the Communists planned to capitalize on the presence of a large labor surplus to accomplish rapid industrialization, particularly in rural areas. During that part of the year when the rural population was underemployed, labor could be used for useful output. Small indigenous industrial plants were created to harness the energies of the labor force. These plants included handicraft workshops, iron and steel foundries, fertilizer plants, oil extraction, machine shops, cement manufacture, coal and iron ore mining, and food processing. The capital used to build the small plants came from the local communes and from taxes on state enterprises. Labor, however, was the key factor employed in the development of local industry.

Top priority was given to the iron and steel industry. Lack of technology and equipment was replaced by mass fervor. This has been called facetiously "the steel mill in every backyard" policy. Some 80 million people were involved in an attempt to create a do-it-yourself steel industry. Two million backyard furnaces were developed throughout China. Many millions of Chinese worked day and night turning out steel, while millions of others labored in the extraction of iron ore and coal. The result was the development of labor-intensive, small-scale steel production with a low capital-output ratio. Although the output of iron and steel was increased by the backyard furnace method, much of it was of poor and often unusable quality, reflecting the absence of quality control standards and the necessary technical expertise. Production in other areas suffered as well because more than one-tenth of the population was diverted from other pursuits into the production of steel.

Failure of the Great Leap Forward. The Great Leap Forward was not a success. Although industrial and agricultural output rose sharply in 1958, much of the gain was spurious. The output was often of such poor quality that most of it had to be scrapped. Production costs were high, reflecting an indiscriminate development of small plants in almost all industries. There was also a disregard for cost considerations at the level of the local plant because the most important success indicator was the degree to which the local cadre (leaders) could fulfill or overfill physical quotas. Output was maximized at the expense of quality and cost, and inputs of labor and raw materials could have been more effectively employed elsewhere. A shortage of fuel and raw materials caused by the waste involved in the backyard furnace method of production and a lack of adequate transportation facilities was responsible for the demise of many plants.

Sino-Russian Relations. The Great Leap Forward also caused a rift in the relationship between the Chinese and the Russian advisers and technicians that had been sent to help them. In essence, the Russian blueprints for making China a self-sufficient world power were set aside in favor of a development program that made little economic sense. The Chinese persisted in ignoring the advice of their Russian technicians despite the fact that Russia intimated that support would be withdrawn unless the Great Leap Forward was discontinued. In 1960 the Soviet technicians were withdrawn from China. With them went the equipment, financial aid, and blueprints that had played a paramount role in the development of the Chinese economy during the First Five-Year Plan. This departure *en masse* of the technicians had a negative effect on China because it could not replace their expertise.

Proletarian Cultural Revolution, 1966–1969

The Third Five-Year Plan, which began in 1965, was eclipsed by a political aberration of the first magnitude called the *Proletarian Cultural Revolution*. This was an attempt by Mao Tse-tung to mold Chinese society into his prescribed pattern. It placed primacy on ideological cant over scientific expertise and reverted to the Great Leap Forward period in its attempt to replace material incentives with political ideology and to denigrate any emphasis on technical excellence.[3] It aimed at annihilating, throughout China and particularly in the universities, any tendency towards a moderate or revisionist viewpoint concerning the role of communism in world affairs. Intransigence toward the Western countries in general and the United States in particular was to be maintained until Western influence was eliminated from Asia. The Russians did not escape the general opprobrium that the Chinese engendered toward the West, because Mao was furious with them for drawing back from war and subversion with the West in the interest of coexistence.

The rationale of the Cultural Revolution was political as well as economic. It involved Mao's attempt to develop a new socialist morality that would place public interest above private individualism. He believed that Stalin had permitted the

---

[3] A poster in a Peking park proclaimed, "We do not need brains! Our heads are armed with the ideas of Mao Tse-Tung."

development of a new class structure in the form of a state bureaucracy that differed little from a capitalist class structure. Soviet claims of egalitarianism ignored the special privileges for this small bureaucratic and technical elite. Moreover, Mao believed that Russia and other socialist countries had moved away from the utopian idea of an egalitarian society by introducing material incentives and bonuses, which tended to differentiate among workers. An ethical revolution was needed, for people had to be changed in order to create a new order of society.

The Cultural Revolution represented a step backward in terms of economic growth. The average annual rate of growth of gross national product during the period 1966–1968 was −2.5 percent, reflecting a general decline in industrial output of around 15 to 20 percent in 1967. More importantly, the Cultural Revolution encouraged an ideological polarization within the regime and weakened consensus on the nation's fundamental values and priorities. The regime faced the task of rebuilding a stable institutional structure and working out a new pattern of relationships among various groups.

The Post–Cultural Revolution Period, 1970–1976

The end of the Cultural Revolution ushered in another stage of Chinese economic development. For one thing, central economic planning in the form of a Fourth Five-Year Plan was reintroduced. Both the Second and Third Five-Year Plans were largely shunted aside by sudden shifts in Chinese ideological policies—the former by the Great Leap Forward and the latter by the Cultural Revolution.

However, there were additional political interruptions during this period. The leaders began jockeying for power as it became evident that both Chairman Mao and Premier Chou En-lai were in failing health. Radical elements in the Communist Party wanted to continue the Cultural Revolution. They denounced material incentives, orderly economic planning, and reliance on foreign technology; and they brought disorder into production by opposing rules and regulations. Toward the end of 1975 and the beginning of 1976, the radicals increased their attacks on government bureaucrats and party leaders who were in favor of economic modernization. Serious riots occurred in some of the larger Chinese cities.

The year 1976 was a momentous one for China. Premier Chou died in February and Chairman Mao died in September. With the death of the two major political leaders, a struggle for succession developed between those who wanted to maintain a rigid ideological status quo, with collective behavior and control and a closed door to the outside world, and those who wanted to modernize the economy and increase the rate of economic growth. The latter faction won out, and Deng Xiaoping was elected party leader.[4]

---

[4] The so-called "Gang of Four," including Mao's widow, wanted to continue the Cultural Revolution. In a showcase trial in 1978, they were found guilty and imprisoned.

In December 1978, the Central Committee of the Communist Party convened in Beijing (Peking). The session declared that if China were to develop successfully, it must turn from class struggle to modernization and completely restructure its economy. *The Four Modernizations Program*, originally started by Premier Chou in 1975, was incorporated into a Ten-Year Plan that called for increases in grain output, steel production, and capital construction through the purchase of foreign plants and technology. The Program emphasized the development of four major economic sectors: agriculture, industry, science and technology, and national defense. The centerpiece of the program was to be the creation of the massive Baoshan steel complex that would turn out 6.7 million tons of steel a year with the most advanced technology imported from Japan, West Germany, and the United States. However, Baoshan was an expensive failure, caused in part by China's inability to assimilate foreign technology and in part by an unrealistic emphasis on the role of heavy industry in developing the Chinese economy.[5] A period of retrenchment and reappraisal of Chinese economic goals set in.

1980 to the Present

The 1980s marked a liberalization of the Chinese economy from state control and direction. The ambitious goals of the Four Modernizations Program were scaled down, and the government turned its attention to more immediate objectives such as improving productivity and increasing output. It introduced more competition into the economy, not only by permitting private businesses to exist but also by turning over small, unprofitable state-owned enterprises to private collectives. A measure of private enterprise was introduced into agriculture. Ability to produce rather than ideological purity became the measure of success. In October 1984 a number of reforms were announced by the Central Committee of the Communist Party that are aimed at improving the structure of the Chinese economy. These reforms included:

1. Creation of a national price system. The prices of many products reflected neither their value nor the relation of supply and demand. Prices were restructured away from uniform prices set by the state and toward a floating price system for some products and free prices for others, based on the relation of supply and demand.[6]
2. Separation of government from enterprise functions. The purpose was to give state enterprises more autonomy over their operations. More competition be-

---

[5] Robert F. Dernberger, "The Chinese Search for the Path of Self-Sustained Growth in the 1980's: An Assessment," Vol. 1, U.S. Cong., 2nd Sess., 1983, pp. 27–29. A basic feature of any Communist economic policy, be it Poland or China, is the development of a steel industry.

[6] On May 9, 1985, the government announced that the price of meat, fish, and eggs was raised by an average of more than 50 percent. The higher prices were aimed at eliminating government subsidized food prices and subjecting these products to the forces of supply and demand.

tween state enterprises was encouraged to stimulate improved use of technology and management.

3. Use of reward system based on work. In enterprises, differences in wages between various trades and jobs were widened so as to apply fully the principle of awarding the diligent and punishing the indolent.

4. Promotion of diversified forms of economic organization. During the 1980s there had been an increase in the number of private industrial and commercial enterprises licensed to operate. The reforms stressed the continued need for diversity in forms of production, with some state enterprises leased to individuals or collectives.

5. Expansion of foreign and domestic economic and technical exchange. Using foreign funds and attracting foreign investors for joint ventures or exclusive investments in enterprises is necessary for the modernization of the economy.[7]

6. Training of management personnel for the economy. Measures were to be taken to train engineers who could promote technological progress and accountants who could uphold financial and economic discipline.[8]

THE ECONOMIC SYSTEM

The institutional arrangements in China are basically the same as those for all socialist countries. There is, of course, the Communist Party hierarchy and its all-pervasive influence in economic and political activity. The state prescribes the ultimate objectives to be achieved by all Chinese. Society is controlled for the purpose of accomplishing specific economic and social goals. Although it is true that many changes are taking place in China, including a much greater reliance on private enterprise and the market mechanism, changes occur only with the approval of party leaders. Another swing of the pendulum, even back to a more rigidly controlled society emphasizing political ideology before everything else, however, is always a possibility. The following sections present the institutional arrangements of the Chinese economy as they existed in 1988.

Economic Planning

The Chinese have developed seven formal five-year plans, the latest of which was to run from 1986 to 1990. The goals of each plan have varied, and many of them were not completed.

---

[7] On May 8, 1985, Ingersoll-Rand, an American manufacturer of machine tools, pneumatic drills, and other manufacturing equipment, and the Chinese government announced a joint venture to produce these products in China. Modern Western-style hotels have been built by foreign investors to attract tourists. Many other joint ventures have been included with American and other firms.

[8] The Chinese government has entered into exchange agreements with a number of American universities to train engineers, managers, and accountants. Virginia Tech is one of those universities.

Formulation of Economic Plans. The State Planning Commission has overall responsibility for economic planning, including the drafting of the five-year plans and the annual operating plan. An Economic Commission reviews the fulfillment of the annual economic plans and institutes economic reforms. Both are responsible to the State Council, which is the executive branch of the government. It, in turn, is responsible to the National People's Congress, the highest elected organ of the Communist Party.

The five-year and annual operating plans can be broken down into sectoral plans that indicate what and how much individual enterprises should produce. In agriculture, specific goals are set for consumption within the agricultural sector and for distribution to other sectors. In transportation, the plan covers the construction of facilities, with particular emphasis placed on the development of the railroad system. Then there is a plan that covers capital formation for individual economic sectors and is concerned with resource allocation. There is a labor plan involving the allocation of labor inputs to the various sectors of the economy. Plans for foreign trade, social and cultural development, and regional development are also used. The foreign trade plan covers export and import commodity targets and the use of foreign exchange. Finally, a set of financial plans controls government income and expenditures. The objectives are to regulate resource allocation between consumption and investment and to regulate the flow of credit from the banking system.

Implementation of the Plans. The State Council, through its various ministries, is responsible for implementation of the economic plans. There are 27 ministries, each dealing with different segments of the economy. These ministries also operate at the intermediate levels of Chinese government. The central government prepares its economic plans through the administrative units at the different levels. Directions pass downward through the various administrative levels to the factories and enterprises.

Public Finance

The function of taxes in China is to ensure control through the state budget over a part of the incomes of state enterprises as well as over the financial and economic activities of those engaged in private enterprise. The state budget itself is very important to the national economy because a very large part of all investment is undertaken with funds allocated through it. In addition, normal government expenditures such as national defense and social welfare expenditures are financed through it. Local governments have some autonomy in levying certain taxes, including a profits tax on enterprises directly under their jurisdiction. The economic reforms have changed the tax system of China to some extent.

Government Revenues. Revenue is obtained from both tax and nontax sources. In the tax revenue category, the bulk of tax receipts comprise industrial and commercial taxes. Taxes are collected at various levels of government by a system of collection agencies and are deposited in the People's Bank of China.

The Turnover Tax. This tax, which is common to all socialist countries, is the difference between the producer price and the retail price, excluding the wholesale and retail margins for trading enterprises. These taxes are levied on most consumer goods and some consumer services. The government imposes a turnover tax to separate retail prices from producer prices, and so is in fact redistributing money incomes. Some consumer goods, such as foodstuffs sold by peasants to consumers directly, are free from turnover taxes. Whatever the basis of fixing this tax, the rates are highly differentiated. The size of the turnover tax does not determine the level of prices—on the contrary, the magnitude of these taxes depends on the predetermined price level.

Agricultural Taxes. Agricultural taxes are usually levied in kind rather than in monetary amounts. One reason for this type of levy is that a more important problem than a lack of adequate revenue is the lack of marketable agricultural products. The tax is levied on the most important crop in each region—usually a grain crop such as wheat or rice. There is also a pastoral tax levied on livestock. The agricultural taxes have declined in importance as the economic reforms have emphasized allowing farmers to keep more of their output as an incentive to increase production.

Other Taxes. The economic reforms have had an impact on the Chinese tax system in several ways. First, a corporate income tax went into effect in June 1983. There are now many private enterprises from which the state hopes to derive revenue. Business firms that make more than $100,000 in annual profits must now pay a 40 percent tax to the Ministry of Finance.[9] Smaller businesses are also taxed based on an eight-bracket scale. Second, most state-owned enterprises no longer have to hand their profits directly over to the state. Previously, a certain percentage of profits had to be remitted to the national government by each enterprise. These state enterprises are also taxed at the maximum rate of 40 percent on profits over $100,000. Individuals pay a personal income tax, but are allowed an exemption of $400 a month.[10]

Government Expenditures. Expenditures in the Chinese state budget are categorized according to their role in the creation of national income. In the past, more than one half of total expenditures was devoted to financing material production,

---

[9] There are two tax rates, 30 percent levied by the national government and 10 percent levied by local government.
[10] There is a six-bracket tax rate ranging from 5 to 45 percent.

including allocations to state enterprises for capital investment and financial capital. However, under the economic reforms, enterprises now may retain their earnings for direct reinvestment in capital and use as financial capital. Appropriations from the state budget are also used to finance the construction of transportation facilities, investments in state farms, and housing construction. Social security benefits consisting of old-age and disability pensions, sickness and maternity benefits, and work injury compensation are also financed out of the state budget.

Banking

The banking system in the People's Republic of China represents a financial control mechanism for carrying out economic planning. All state enterprises and cooperatives have accounts with the central bank, and control can be exercised because most transactions are in terms of money through bank transfers. Purchases and sales of goods by each enterprise can be matched against authorized payments and receipts. Government control over income and expenditures is also expedited through the credit and cash plans of the banking system.

The People's Bank of China. The People's Bank of China was formed in 1959 as the central bank of the country. It is under the jurisdiction of the Staff Office for Finance and Trade and is responsible for the supervision of financial transactions that correspond to the physical production plans. All state enterprises have accounts in branch banks under its direct jurisdiction. In this way, the People's Bank can exercise control because all expenditures and transfers made by the enterprises come under its scrutiny.

The People's Bank, as the central bank of China, has the following responsibilities.

1. Issuing Chinese currency.
2. Financing credit to state enterprises. Funds to support credit expansion are obtained from the national budget, from retained profits, and from customer deposits.
3. Supervising expenditures of state enterprises to see that they conform to national planning objectives.
4. Developing the Credit Plan and the Cash Plan, which are financial counterparts of the physical economic plans.
5. Monitoring the performance of state enterprises.

The Credit Plan involves the amount of short- and medium-term credit that is to be provided to state enterprises and agricultural communes by the People's Bank. Funds can be allocated only for purposes that conform to the national plan. The Cash Plan consists of a set of cash inflows and cash outflows essentially in the form of a balance sheet. Cash inflows include retail sales receipts, savings deposit receipts, repayment of agricultural loans, deposits of communes, and public utility receipts. Cash outflows consist of wage payments by state enterprises and communes, government purchases of industrial and agricultural products, government administrative expenses, transfer payments by the state to individuals, management expenditures of state enterprises, new loans to agriculture, and withdrawals of savings deposits.

The Credit and Cash Plans are coordinated with the physical production plans to provide financing for expenditures required by the production plans. This means that the People's Bank can supervise the operations of state enterprises to enforce conformance to production plans because purchase and sales of goods can be matched against authorized payments and receipts.

Other Financial Institutions. There are several specialized financial agencies that also provide money to finance the transactions of enterprises in certain areas of production. These specialized financial institutions, like the People's Bank, do not allocate funds independently of national planning objectives and thus have no influence on resource allocation, as they would in a market economy.

The Agricultural Bank provides agricultural loans. It also controls the allocation of rural savings to rural credit cooperatives that provide credit to communes and to individual members of communes. Loans are also made to individuals for sideline undertakings involving private plots of land. The Agricultural Bank is under the jurisdiction of the State Council and is operated independently of the People's Bank. It has provincial branches and also branches that operate at the municipal level.

There are several specialized banks under the jurisdiction of the Ministry of Finance. One bank, the People's Construction Bank, is responsible for providing investment funds to enterprise. These funds are obtained from the national budget and do not have to be repaid. It is also responsible for providing short-term loans to enterprises for capital construction projects.

Interest has no significant role in resource allocation in the Chinese economic system. Interest rates are charged on all loans by the banks to industrial enterprises, communes, and individuals, but the rates are far below those that would prevail under a free market system. Also, the interest charges are mostly offset by a reduction in the enterprise's profit tax liability. Grants provided by the People's Bank to enterprises for capital investment are interest free.

Organization of Industry

Although agriculture, providing the raw materials for industry and food for a growing population, remains the foundation of the Chinese economy, any meaningful move to a greater-power status must be based on the development of industry. The process of industrialization has been difficult, and the Chinese people have paid a price in terms of resources sacrificed to achieve this end. At present, the Chinese have a long way to go before they can match the industrial potential of the Soviet Union or any of the Western industrial nations. Even within their own sphere of influence, the Chinese do not come close to rivaling the industrial base of Japan; they are behind South Korea in overall economic development. Moreover, undue emphasis has been placed on the development of heavy industry, in particular steel manufacturing.

Economic Reforms in Industry

Sweeping economic reforms have been introduced by the Chinese to improve economy efficiency and increase output in industry. Prior to 1979, factory managers were essentially cogs in a machine controlled from above. A factory would be allotted a certain amount of raw material and told to produce a certain number of units by the appropriate ministry in Beijing. Any profit had to be remitted to the central government. It was then up to the ministry to determine how much profit would be returned to the factory. In 1978 the Central Committee of the Communist Party called for the abandonment of the old Stalinist model of production, which rigidly maintained all planning and decision-making authority in the hands of the central ministries. Since that time, much of this authority has been delegated downward so that state-owned enterprises have become more independent economic units and their managers have become responsible in large measure for planning, use of capital, and distribution of profits.

The Contract System. The contract system is designed to improve enterprise profitability. It involves an arrangement under which state enterprises sign performance contracts with supervisory bureaus specifying minimum output earnings and taxes. Three-fourths of China's large- and medium-scale state industrial enterprises and commercial entities have adopted the contract system. In addition, a majority of China's smaller state and collective enterprises have adopted a contract-leasing system that allows factory managers to retain a share of after-tax profits. Also, there is a bankruptcy law that provides the legal framework for the government to institute bankruptcy procedures against unprofitable state enterprises.[11] Mandatory planning was relaxed for a number of industries to the point that by 1987 only 20 percent of all industrial output was subject to it.[12] Enterprises were given responsibility for finding their own raw materials, setting their own production targets, and hiring and firing their own labor force.

Private Enterprise. Probably the most dramatic aspect of Chinese economic reforms is the rebirth of private enterprise. A private sector has been introduced where market forces are at work. Most private enterprise is small scale, ranging from family-owned restaurants to chicken farms. There are private repair shops for

---

[11] Central Intelligence Agency, Directorate of Intelligence. *China: Economic Policy and Performance in 1988* (Washington, DC: Joint Economic Committee, Congress of the United States, 1988), pp. 21–25.

[12] Jan Prybyla, "China's Economic Experiment: Back from the Market," *Problems of Communism*, Vol. 38 (January–February, 1989), p. 1.

television sets and radios, bicycles, and motorcycles. Private barbers and shoemakers are commonplace, and street vendors sell a wide variety of products. In 1988 the private sector of the Chinese economy included up to 300,000 enterprises and an additional 20 million individual enterprises. Some private enterprises employ several hundred persons. The private sector generally leads the country in growth in productivity and output but employs less than 3 percent of China's industrial labor force and produces less than 1 percent of industrial output.[13]

Enterprise Bankruptcy Laws.   Bankruptcy has long been the domain of capitalism, where inefficient firms fail and go out of business. In the socialist economies, inefficient firms have been propped up by subsidies out of the state budgets, thus promoting continued inefficiency. However, this is changing. In November 1988 the Enterprise Bankruptcy Law went into effect in China, and China joined Hungary as the first socialist countries to establish bankruptcy laws. A major rationale for the passage of the bankruptcy law is to reduce the amount of subsidies that have to be paid to inefficient enterprises. Deficits have been incurred in the state budget, and rising inflation has occurred. The law is also designed to purge the economy of firms that are either technologically obsolete or inefficiently managed.[14]

The law has several features:[15]

1. It defines an enterprise as bankrupt if the cause of a deficit is mismanagement, meaning that it can't pay debts that come due.
2. The government industrial department that is responsible for the overall supervision of a state enterprise can be held liable if its officials, through their actions, cause the enterprise to lose money.
3. It is the responsibility of the governmental industrial department to initiate bankruptcy and reorganization proceedings against a bankrupt enterprise.

Takeovers.   Another way in which inept and inefficient firms can be handled is through the takeover, although the Chinese do not have their own version of a T. Boone Pickens or a Kohlberg, Kravis, Roberts (KKR). An example of a takeover was the absorption of an inefficient electrical equipment factory which had been insolvent for several years by a solvent firm.[16] By the end of 1988, more than 1,800 factories had been merged to form 1,779 new enterprises.[17] A rational for mergers is that there is a gain to the state budget because state investments can flow to more

---

[13] *China: Economic Policy and Performance in 1988*, p. 25.

[14] Dorothy J. Solinger, "Capitalist Measures With Chinese Characteristics," *Problems of Communism*, Vol. 38 (January-February 1989), pp. 19–21.

[15] Ta-kuang Chang, "The Making of the Chinese Bankruptcy Law: A Study in the Legislative Process," *Harvard International Law Journal* (Spring 1987), pp. 333–372.

[16] This was really more of a merger than a takeover in that there was a pooling of assets.

[17] Solinger, "Capitalist Measures," p. 24.

viable enterprises. A merger can allow no enterprise to expand production while reducing costs, thus achieving economies of scale. Profitable mergers can result in money flowing into the state budget to offset subsidies to inefficient enterprises.

Private Collectives. The reforms permit the formation of collectively owned enterprises. A group of citizens can take the initiative to establish a collectively owned enterprise subject to regulation by the government. Collective enterprises can be set up by workers from their own funds. The means of production are neither private property nor state property, but the property of the collective. Many state enterprises that were losing money have been turned into private collectives in the hope that autonomous management and capitalist incentives might revive them. The collective has the exclusive right to own, control, and handle its means of production and products. It keeps its own accounts and is responsible for its own profits or losses.[18] State administrative agencies may apply economic levers to influence and guide the operational activities of collective enterprises, but they cannot interfere with their internal affairs.

Foreign Investments. For many years China was isolated from outside influences. During the time of Mao, ideology was supposed to solve economic problems; Western, particularly United States, influence was regarded as degenerate. The current Chinese leaders have adopted a much more pragmatic approach to the solution of the country's economic problems. During the 1970s, little was invested in modernization, so most of China's factories have machinery 10 to 40 years old. Much of its industry was built with Soviet aid during the 1950s; the technology was already obsolete by the time the Chinese received it. The Chinese entered the 1980s with an industrial base that was 50 years behind the rest of the industrial world. To accomplish industrial modernization, they are willing to accept infusions of foreign capital and foreign technology. These infusions may take several forms.

1. *Joint ventures.* A joint venture is simply an arrangement where a foreign company and a *host* country agree to provide a product or a service jointly.[19] In China, joint ventures between the Chinese and Western corporations have been permitted since 1980. In 1985, Occidental Petroleum signed an agreement with China to develop and jointly operate what could become the world's largest open-pit coal mine. China is responsible for providing the site and construction of railways, highways, and power facilities. Occidental is to provide the equipment and personnel. Profits from the sale of coal are to be divided evenly for five years, after which China is to get 60 percent.

---

[18] Lin Wei and Arnold Chao, eds. *China's Economic Reforms* (Philadelphia: University of Pennsylvania Press, 1982) pp. 160–169.

[19] A joint venture can also involve two companies. An example is the General Motors–Toyota joint venture in California to produce subcompact cars.

2. *Foreign loans.* The Chinese, unlike Mexico and Nigeria, have been rather circumspect when it comes to borrowing from abroad. However, economic modernization is one of the basic goals of the economic reforms. China has signed loan agreements with several capitalist countries, notably Japan. These agreements provided loans to finance projects for the construction of railroads, ports, and a hydroelectric station. Belgium has granted an interest-free 30-year loan to purchase power generating equipment.

3. *Licensing agreements.* A number of American firms are licensed to produce and sell products in China. A prime example is Coca-Cola, which has the exclusive right to produce and sell Coca-Cola in China. Coca-Cola provides the syrup and the authorized use of the trademark, and the drink is bottled in China and sold to foreign tourists.

4. *Direct investment in China.* Foreign investment in China can be channeled to certain priority areas such as hotel construction and operation, which are designed to attract foreign tourists who bring hard currency to spend. A number of hotels have been built with foreign capital, including the Great Wall Hotel, a part of the Hyatt Regency chain.

Reduction in the Number of Administrative Units. Economic planning has been cumbersome, with layer upon layer of administrative units responsible for its implementation. Industrial enterprises have always been the last link, with ultimate authority concentrated in a hierarchy of bureaus and ministries. Bureaus in charge of production had no authority over personnel, finance, and material supplies of state-owned enterprises, while bureaus in charge of the latter functions had no control over production. Thus, enterprises have had to deal with many bureaus, particularly at the provincial and local levels of government.

Many countries and cities have now abandoned their bureaus and have replaced them with economic commissions that have been given authority over all functions of state enterprises.[20] The planning directors go from the national ministry to their regional and local counterparts to the commissions to the enterprises. Managers of the enterprises have been given more control over production, sales, bonuses, hiring and firing of workers, and distribution of profits.

Organization of Agriculture

Agriculture is the foundation of the Chinese economy. At least 80 percent of the people work in agriculture, which furnishes the raw materials necessary for the performance of the planned economy. Unfortunately for the Chinese, most of the land area is not suitable for agricultural production. Much of China is mountainous and dry, and unfavorable soil and climate inhibit agricultural development in other ar-

---

[20] Gregory Chow, *The Chinese Economy* (New York: Harper & Row, 1985)

eas. In addition, the ratio of population to cultivable land is very large. The country has had to operate at a margin that is very close to a minimum subsistence level. It also means that the Communists have to face the problem of a growing population and a technically backward agricultural base while at the same time trying to build up an adequate industrial base in order to become a major world power.

The Collectivization of Agriculture. Agriculture has gone through several distinct phases of collectivization since the Communists came to power in 1949. At that time the farms were privately owned either by landlords or by peasants. To win the support of the masses of the peasants, landless or otherwise, the Communists redistributed millions of acres of land and eliminated landlords as a class. Once the land was redistributed, peasants were allowed to operate the land as private owners.[21]

Producers' Cooperatives. Agricultural producers' cooperatives were established in 1955. Peasants were organized into these cooperatives and had to pool their lands for cultivation. The land, however, was still held privately, the cooperatives paid rent for its use. The cooperatives were run by central committees and were divided into production teams. The agricultural output was distributed by the cooperatives and the peasants were compensated on the basis of labor contributed.

Collective Farms. The next stage in the socialization of agriculture occurred in 1956.[22] The agricultural producers' cooperatives, which had retained many of the elements of private property ownership, were consolidated into collective farms. On these collective farms the peasants were supposed to pool their land, animals, and livestock. Land was no longer privately owned; it was collective property. However, the peasants were permitted to own small plots of land to be used for their own purposes. Similarly, domestic livestock and small farm implements were left in private hands. The peasants were formed into brigades, with brigade leaders given the responsibility for assigning workers their tasks.

Communes. In 1958 communes replaced the collective farms. A commune was a multipurpose unit that would perform administrative as well as economic functions. The transition to the commune system was rapid. The decision to form communes was announced in August 1958. By the end of the year, some 750,000 collective farms representing virtually all of the peasant households had been formed into 26,578 communes.[23] All vestiges of private property ownership were removed.

---

[21] Marion B. Larsen, "China's Agriculture under Communism." In *An Economic Profile of Mainland China*, Vol. 1 (U.S. Congress, Joint Economic Committee, 90th Cong., First sess., 1967), pp. 212–218.

[22] Larson, "China's Agriculture," pp. 218–220.

[23] Larson, "China's Agriculture," p. 213.

The peasants ate in mess halls, and the distribution of food was based in part on the needs of individuals and in part on work performed. Workers had to perform tasks that were by no means limited to agriculture, such as producing steel and mining coal.

By the end of the Great Leap Forward there was a shift in agricultural policies with respect to the communes. The complete collectivization of nearly all production and consumption had not achieved the desired results. Private plots of land were restored to the peasants, and the free market was permitted in which the peasants could sell their produce for income. Pigs were in short supply as a result of mismanagement during the Great Leap Forward, and peasants were given incentives to raise pigs for sale to the government. However, communes remained the highest level of collective organization in China until the end of the 1970s.

Agricultural Reform. Probably the most important aspect of the current economic reforms has been the decollectivization of farmland. The communes have ceased to exist. Although still owned by the state, land has been divided into small plots and contracted out by the production teams to be farmed privately under a program referred to as *baochan dasho*, or "fixing farm-output quotas for individual households." The production team also assigns to each farm family the necessary inputs—including land, cattle, farm equipment, and machinery. A farmer's only binding obligation, besides paying rent and a small agricultural tax, is to deliver a fixed amount of produce to the team as a contribution to the production quota. This is sold to the state at a fixed price. Any amount produced in excess of the fixed amount belongs to the farm family to consume, to sell to the state at a higher price, or to sell in the free market. Both compulsory delivery and land rental are fixed costs that do not affect the willingness of the individual farmer to increase output. The relevant marginal cost calculation of the farm household applies to the extra output after the delivery has been made. As a result of individual incentive, agricultural output has grown significantly.

Agriculture reforms continue to be liberalized. In 1988 purchase prices for grain produced under state contract were raised. The dual-track pricing system was changed by reducing the share of grain produced under state contracts and increasing free-market transactions. Compulsory contract procurement quotas for grains and cotton have been replaced by contract purchases. In 1988 the government raised the price it pays for contract grain and instituted price differences based on grain quality. Peasants were given permission to purchase and transfer land lease rights, which would permit more efficient, larger scale operations. The government also lengthened the land-leasing period for rural land from 15 to 30 years to provide greater incentives for farmers to adopt land use measures.[24] Finally, the govern-

---

[24] *China: Economic Policy and Performance in 1988*, p. 21.

ment increased investment in fertilizer and pesticide production, transportation and distribution networks, and agricultural infrastructure projects such as irrigation.

Private Plots. Private plots serve an important role in the economy by providing most of the poultry, pigs, and vegetables consumed in China. The private plots have been expanded under the reforms and account for larger fractions of total cultivable land. Private plots are often the most productive tracts of land in China, in part because the farmers are strongly motivated to maximize the output in order to increase family income. From the standpoint of the state, while these activities do not have a central place in large-scale agricultural production, they are a practical way of obtaining the intensive use of peasant labor for the production of some highly valued items.

CHINA ENTERS THE 1990s

Change and the impermanence of any particular form of economic and social organization have been the dominant realities of Chinese life since 1949. A good example was the Cultural Revolution of 1966–1969, during which a goal was to destroy the elitism of the bureaucracy and technocrats by, among other things, making them work on the farms. The Four Modernizations Program of 1978 had goals directly opposite to those of the Cultural Revolution. It involved a commitment toward modern economic growth that continued during most of the 1980s. State control over the economy and the people were relaxed. All of this changed when the Chinese students demonstrated for more freedom and participation in political affairs. After the demonstrations were put down, party hard-liners assumed control of the government and, as Table 17-1 indicates, many reforms were cut back or put on hold. Problems have developed in the Chinese economy because of an economic downturn that occurred in 1989.

Economic Growth

The average rate of economic growth in China has been around 6 percent since 1949. For the period 1980–1988 the growth rate increased at an average rate of around 9 percent, but a slump occurred in 1989. Real GNP declined to around 4 percent, and the deficit in the state budget increased by 40 percent to $8 billion. Unemployment increased and living standards declined. Tourism and foreign investment declined as a result of the suppression of prodemocracy student demonstrators. Industrial production declined to a 2 percent increase for the year, the lowest increase for the decade. Table 17-2 presents the rate of real economic growth in China for selected time periods.

Agricultural Production

Agriculture is the mainstay of the Chinese economy and serves many purposes. It is needed to feed the people and to provide raw materials for industry. In addition,

TABLE 17-1

Status of China's Reforms as of 1990

Prices	Reforms remain on hold and controls on the prices of consumer necessities and industrial goods have been tightened.
Banking	Reform has been reversed as decisions based on political objectives are carried out by administrative decree rather than using economic efficiency criteria. Tight used it policy has damaged other reforms.
Enterprises	The contract responsibility system, which gives managers greater autonomy in return for their promises to deliver a specific amount of output, remains in place. However, the government is attempting to exert greater control over industry through increased mandatory planning.
Bankruptcy	The government remains unwilling to enforce bankruptcy law.
Rural enterprises	The government has eased its hard line against rural enterprises because they absorb surplus labor.
Agriculture	The household responsibility system, which gives farmers control over crop choice and earnings in return for contract deliveries to the state, remains in place.
Foreign trade	The state is recentralizing control over trading and foreign exchange.

Source: Central Intelligence Agency, The Chinese Economy in 1989 and 1990: Trying to Revive Growth While Maintaining Social Stability, Report Presented to the Subcommittee on Technology and National Security (Washington, DC: Joint Economic Committee, Congress of the United States, June 1990,), p. 15.

TABLE 17-2

Changes in Growth Rates in Real GNP for China, 1961–1990

Years	Percent Change
1961–1965	−0.2
1966–1970	8.3
1971–1975	5.5
1976–1982	6.2
1983	8.1
1984	12.0
1985	12.0
1986	7.5
1987	8.5
1988	11.0
1989	4.0
1990 (est.)	4.0

Source: Economic Report of the President, 1990 (Washington, DC: USGPO, February 1990), p. 419.

the Chinese agriculture goods used as export commodities are extremely valuable as a source of hard currency, which is needed to buy Western equipment and technology. Improvement of agriculture is the linchpin of economic reform. As Table 17-3 indicates, there was a slump in agricultural production in 1988. Total output increased by 3 percent in 1989. Grain production increased to 407 million metric tons in 1989, but that total was 5 million metric tons short of the target plan. China had to increase its imports of grain to 16 million metric tons. The output of other agricultural products declined in 1989 because low producer prices made farmers reduce acreage for their crops.

Industrial Production

To improve industrial production, the Chinese have made a number of changes. There has been a shift to enterprise management by professional managers. To promote efficiency, more emphasis has been placed on profit and quality of production, and prices have been based on realistic calculations of costs. Table 17-4, which presents industrial production growth, indicates an improved performance for the 1980s. However, industrial growth declined in 1989 to 8 percent and the growth of state-owned industries was less than 4 percent.

Inflation

The rapid rate of economic growth in China during the 1980s has contributed to an overheating of the economy (see Table 17-5). A number of austerity measures were imposed by the government on the economy in 1989. State investment spending was cut by 9 percent and foreign borrowing was reduced. Interest rates were raised and credit ceilings were imposed on banks. These austerity measures caused

TABLE 17-3
Agricultural Production in China, 1970–1988 (metric tons)

Year	Meat (thousands)	Rice (thousands)	Soybeans (thousands)	Wheat (millions)	All Grains (millions)
1970	5,965	109,990	11,645	29.19	239.96
1975	7,970	125,560	12,062	45.31	284.52
1980	12,054	139,910	7,966	55.21	320.56
1983	14,021	168,865	9,769	81.39	387.28
1984	15,406	178,255	9,705	87.82	407.31
1985	17,607	168,569	10,521	85.81	379.11
1986	19,183	172,224	11,010	90.30	391.09
1987	19,210	173,900	12,100	87.70	402.41
1988	21,880	171,800	10,900	87.50	390.00

Source: Central Intelligence Agency, Directorate of Intelligence, Handbook of Economic Statistics, 1989 (Springfield, VA: National Technical Information Service, 1989), pp. 73, 111, 112, 114, 116, 122.

TABLE 17-4

Index of Industrial Production for China, 1960–1988 (1980 = 100 percent)

Year	Percent of 1980
1960	24
1970	42
1975	66
1980	100
1983	124
1984	141
1985	167
1986	182
1987	209
1988	221

Source: Central Intelligence Agency, Directorate of Intelligence, Handbook of Economic Statistics, 1989 *(Springfield, VA: National Technical Information Service, 1989), p. 36*

TABLE 17-5

Rate of Inflation in China as Measured by the Consumer Price Index (1980 = 100 percent)

Year	Percent of 1980
1980	110
1984	110
1985	123
1986	131
1987	143
1988	169
1989	194
1990 (est.)	201

Source: Central Intelligence Agency, Handbook of Economic Statistics *(Springfield, VA: NTIS, 1989), p. 39; Central Intelligence Agency,* The Chinese Economy in 1989 and 1990: Trying to Revive Growth While Maintaining Social Stability, *Report to the Subcommitte on Technology and National Security (Washington, DC: Joint Economic Committee, Congress of the United States, June 1990), p. 8.*

debt defaults among state enterprises and depressed demand, causing an increase in unemployment Urban living standards also declined in 1989 as real wages of workers declined. Nearly two-thirds of urban factories were closed or operated below capacity at the end of 1989. There is concern that the hard-line conservative government will be unable or unwilling to develop programs capable of moving China forward.

SUMMARY

The Chinese economy is in a state of flux. A number of economic reforms have been introduced to improve output and productivity. While the Chinese economy remains basically a planned socialist economy, market mechanisms have been introduced to improve resource allocation and provide incentives. Agricultural reform has been significant. Urban private markets for the sale of agricultural products have been developed and sideline income-earning opportunities encouraged. In addition, there has been a move to increase the amount of land allocated to private plots. Reforms have also been made in industry. Bankruptcy and takeover laws have been introduced to promote efficiency and reduce the waste of resources. Enterprise managers have been given more latitude making management decisions. Emphasis has also been placed on the import of technology and services from Western capitalist countries.

Nevertheless, as the crackdown on student demonstrators in Tiananmen Square has demonstrated, China is a controlled society run by an oligarchy of communist leaders who will brook no challenge to their authority. There is the question of where do the reforms go from here? Also, will foreign firms continue to invest in China to create the goods that the economy needs in order to advance its industries? It is doubtful that there will be a reversion to the Cultural Revolution because China cannot afford this extreme. There is also the matter of world opinion. China is much more exposed to the world today than it was during the days of the Cultural Revolution. Business will return to China, if nothing else, to oversee its investments, but China may have a difficult time attracting new foreign investment.

REVIEW QUESTIONS

1. Discuss agricultural policy during the Great Leap Forward.
2. Chinese economic policy between 1949 and the present has oscillated between economic rationality and idealistic extremism. Discuss.
3. What was the goal of the Cultural Revolution?
4. Evaluate the performance of the Chinese economy in terms of living standards and economic growth.

5. What impact did the demonstrations in Tiananmen Square have on the Chinese Communist Party?
6. What is the current status of economic reforms in China?
7. What are some of the problems faced by China as it enters the 1990s?
8. Will the current hard-line regime in China inhibit foreign investment in China?

RECOMMENDED READINGS

Browning, Graeme. *If Everybody Bought One Shoe: American Capitalism in Communist China*. New York: Hill and Wong, 1989.

Central Intelligence Agency, Directorate of Intelligence. *China: Economic Policy and Performance in 1989*. Joint Economic Committee, Congress of the United States, 1989.

Chow, Gregory. *The Chinese Economy*. New York: Harper and Row, 1985.

Harding, Harry, *China's Second Revolution*. Washington DC: The Brookings Institution, 1987.

Percy, Elizabeth J., and Christine Wong. *The Political Economy of Reform in Post-Mao China*. Cambridge: Harvard University Press, 1987.

Prybyla, Jan S. "China's Economic Experiment: Back from the Market." *Problems of Communism*, Vol. 38 (January-February 1989), pp. 1–18.

Shell, Orville. *To Get Rich is Glorious: China in the Eighties*. New York: Pantheon Press, 1985.

Solinger, Dorothy J. "Capitalist Measures With Chinese Characteristics." *Problems of Communism*, Vol. 38 (January-February 1989), pp. 19–33.

The World Bank. *Finance and Investment in China.* New York: Oxford University Press, 1988.

U.S. Congress, Joint Economic Committee. *China Looks Toward the Year 2000*, Vols. 1 and 2. Washington, DC: USGPO, 1986.

Walder, Andrew G. "Wage Reform and the Web of Factory Interests." *The China Quarterly*, Vol. 109 (March 1987), pp. 22–41.

Winiscki, Jan. "Why Economic Reforms Fail in the Soviet-Type System: A Property Rights-Based Approach," Seminar Paper No. 374 (1986). Stockholm: Institute of International Economic Studies, University of Stockholm, 1986.

Woodruff, John. *China in Search of Its Future*. Seattle: University of Washington Press, 1989.

Worthy, Ford. "What's Next for Business in China?" *Fortune*, July 17, 1989, pp. 110–112.

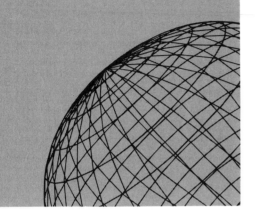

CHAPTER EIGHTEEN

MEXICO

Mexico is one of 20 Latin American countries that occupy over half of the land area of North and South America.[1] These countries possess a number of common sociocultural characteristics. First, with the exception of Brazil, all are former colonies of Spain and achieved their independence from her.[2] Second, with the exception of Brazil, Spanish is the common language. Third, Catholicism is the common religion of all of the countries. Fourth, Latin America is a hierarchical society, which is an inheritance from Spain and Catholicism. Finally, there is the belief that chance dominates a person's life. Most Latin Americans are convinced that outside forces govern their lives. The rich are rich and the poor are poor because God intends it to be that way.[3] This attitude has had a deleterious effect on economic development.

THE ECONOMY OF LATIN AMERICA

Most of the Latin American countries are in either the lower stage or intermediate stage of economic development, and all have per capita incomes of between approximately $600 to $3,200. Two countries, Mexico and Brazil, have an industrial base and, along with South Korea and Taiwan, are considered newly industrialized countries. Nevertheless, in Mexico and Brazil and most of the other Latin American countries, there is economic de-

---

[1] The Caribbean countries are excluded, although many are considered Latin American countries.

[2] Brazil was a colony of Portugal and Portuguese is its language.

[3] This sense of fate is a part of the Hindu and Moslem religions. In the Hindu religion, it is called karma, which holds that a person's lot in life has been predetermined and not even God can change it. Religion has had a considerable impact on economic development in all societies (e.g., the Protestant work ethic and capitalism).

pendence on a single export. For Mexico it is oil, and for Brazil it is coffee. The Latin American countries experienced hard times during the 1980s, with negative growth rates and high rates of inflation.

Per Capita Income

Table 18-1 presents per capita GNP for selected Latin American countries for 1988. The real per capita GNP growth rate for 16 of the 20 Latin American countries showed a decline for the period 1980–1988. There were several reasons for the decline in growth rates. One reason had to do with exports. When oil prices declined in the 1980s, the value of exports declined in such countries as Mexico. Many of the Latin American countries attained relatively high rates of economic growth during the period 1961–1980. Brazil led the way with an average annual rate of growth of 4.7 percent for the period, and Mexico had a rate of growth of 3.6 percent.

Inflation

In addition to stagnant economic growth, inflation has been a problem in the Latin American countries. Argentina, once the dominant economic power in Latin America, is a case in point. It experienced hyperinflation during the 1980s. The political pendulum swung between government populists and market-oriented reformers, with the result that much of the national wealth is held abroad, taxes are being paid by only a few, and the general atmosphere is one of cynicism. As Table 18-2 indicates, the rate of inflation in Argentina was worse than in other major Latin

TABLE 18-1
Per Capita GNP and Real Growth Rates for Latin American Countries

	Per Capita GNP for 1988	Real Per Capita Growth 1980–1988
Argentina	$2,640	− 1.6%
Bolivia	570	− 4.3
Brazil	2,280	1.2
Chile	1,510	− 0.1
Colombia	1,240	1.2
Guatemala	880	− 3.1
Honduras	850	− 1.7
Mexico	1,820	− 1.4
Nicaragua	·830	− 4.7
Peru	1,440	− 1.2
Uruguay	2,470	− 1.4
Venezuela	3,170	− 2.4

Source: The World Bank, World Bank Atlas, 1989 *(New York: Oxford University Press, 1989), pp. 6–9.*

TABLE 18-2
Changes in the Consumer Price Index for Latin American Countries, 1984–1988

	1984	1985	1986	1987	1988
Argentina	626.7	622.2	50.1	131.3	342.5
Bolivia	1,281.6	11,747.8	276.4	161.6	16.0
Brazil	156.8	226.9	145.2	229.7	682.5
Chile	19.9	30.7	19.5	19.9	14.8
Colombia	18.1	24.0	18.8	23.3	28.1
Guatemala	3.4	18.7	37.0	12.3	10.8
Honduras	4.2	4.3	4.4	2.5	4.5
Mexico	65.5	57.5	86.2	131.8	114.2
Nicaragua	35.4	219.5	681.5	911.9	14.295.3
Peru	110.2	163.4	77.9	85.5	667.9
Uruguay	55.5	72.2	76.4	63.6	62.2
Venezuela	12.2	11.4	11.5	28.1	29.5

Source: Inter-American Development Bank, Economic and Social Progress in Latin America, *1989, p. 228.*

American countries from 1984 to 1988, with an inflation rate estimated at around 600 percent for 1989.

Foreign Debt

Foreign debt is the number one problem for most of the Latin American countries. It is the one thing that threatens economic and political stability in Latin America. The foundation of the debt crisis was laid during the 1970s when Latin American governments, including Mexico's, were spurred by optimistic forecasts for the prices of their commodity exports, borrowed heavily from foreign banks, usually at floating interest rates. Foreign banks, including those in the United States, were more than eager to lend. Unfortunately for Mexico and other Latin American countries, the 1980s was a bad decade, particularly for the countries that depended on oil as their main export. When world oil prices declined, revenue from oil exports declined, and a debt crisis occurred. The impact of the debt on Mexico and the other Latin American countries is enormous, with Mexico paying an average of 6.6 percent of its GNP in interest payments alone.[4]

Table 18-3 presents the debt of various Latin American countries compared to GNP and merchandise exports. A frame of reference is the U.S. foreign debt of approximately $535 billion in 1988. Although the United States is the world's largest debtor nation, its debt is around 12 percent of its gross national product. The United States then is far more capable of carrying its foreign debt than Mexico

[4] Carol L. Graham, "The Latin American Quagmire: Beyond Debt and Democracy," *The Brookings Review,* Vol. 7, No. 2 (Spring 1989), pp. 42–47.

TABLE 18-3

Foreign Debt, GNP, and Merchandise Exports for Selected Latin American Countries for 1988 (billions of dollars and percent)

	Debt	GNP	Debt/GNP	Exports	Debt/Exports
Argentina	$ 59.6	$ 79.8	74.6%	$ 11.3	527.2%
Bolivia	5.6	4.1	133.9	.7	776.1
Brazil	115.0	330.4	54.5	35.1	325.3
Chile	19.4	18.7	103.4	7.9	246.0
Colombia	17.1	40.2	42.4	6.9	245.7
Ecuador	10.7	10.2	104.4	2.9	368.8
Honduras	3.4	4.3	79.0	1.1	293.2
Mexico	100.3	94.8	105.9	32.1	312.2
Peru	19.0	33.5	56.6	3.7	507.7
Uruguay	4.3	7.9	54.8	1.8	239.3
Venezuela	35.8	59.2	60.5	12.5	285.3
United States	$535.0	4,900.0	11.8	321.6	169.0

Source: The World Bank, World Debt Tables 1989–1990 (New York: Oxford University Press, 1990).

or Brazil. The latter countries are far more dependent on exports to finance debt repayments than is the United States. Also, capital flight is a major problem. This can be attributed to the considerable degree of political instability that exists in Latin American countries.

Foreign debt has increased social tensions in Latin America because it contributes to inflation. Social programs have had to be reduced in order for the countries to meet interest payments on their debts. For example, debt service on the Mexican foreign debt amounted to 43 percent of Mexico's exports in 1988.[5]

Foreign Trade

Latin American foreign trade is similar to African foreign trade in that the bulk of exports consists of fuels, minerals, and agricultural products and the bulk of imports consists of manufactured products. For example, 55 percent of Brazil's merchandise exports in 1988 consisted of fuels, minerals, and agricultural products while 56 percent of its merchandise imports consisted of manufactured products. Sixty-nine percent of Argentina's merchandise exports in 1988 were fuels, minerals, and farm products while manufacturing imports accounted for 74 percent of Argentina's imports. As Table 18-4 indicates, the terms of trade for the oil-producing countries of Latin America were the worst for the 1980s. The terms of trade for the two major net petroleum exporters, Mexico and Venezuela, were more than 40 percent below the levels obtained in 1980.

---

[5] The World Bank, World Debt Tables, 1988–89 (New York: Oxford University Press, 1989), p. 65.

TABLE 18-4

Latin American Terms of Trade for Selected Years (1980 = 100 percent)

	1980	1985	1986	1987	1988
Argentina	100	81	73	72	79
Brazil	100	84	91	82	86
Chile	100	73	79	83	101
Colombia	100	92	20	92	90
Ecuador	100	97	73	72	67
Guatemala	100	83	108	89	92
Mexico	100	72	52	58	52
Peru	100	90	87	94	108
Uruguay	100	89	103	106	116
Venezuela	100	111	54	68	55

Source: Inter-American Development Bank, Economic and Social Progress in Latin America, *1989, p. 8.*

Population

Most Latin American countries have high birth rates and a short population-doubling time. An example is Brazil with the largest population in Latin America and a population-doubling time of 29 years. This means that Brazil and the United States will have the same population by the year 2017. In 1989 the per capita GNP of Brazil was one-tenth that of the United States. Population growth creates several major problems for the Latin American countries. First, the rate of economic growth is going to have to expand much more than it has in order to provide more jobs for an increasing labor force. Second, the existing infrastructure of the Latin American countries is not adequate to support an expanding population. In most large cities, water supply and educational and health facilities are becoming more inadequate as urbanization continues. Third, an increasing population compounds the problems of unemployment and underemployment in both urban and rural areas. Table 18-5 presents birth and death rates and population-doubling times for the Latin American countries.

Unemployment and Poverty

March 1989 riots in Caracas, Venezuela, over the elimination of food subsidies left hundreds of persons dead and did $400 million in damage.[6] Venezuela had been regarded as one of the more stable countries in Latin America, but rising inflation linked in part to foreign debt problems caused the government to impose austerity measures. Also in 1989, a leftist coup against a military garrison failed. Latin America has a host of economic and social problems. Around 50 percent of

---

[6] *El Universal,* March 9, 1989, p. 1

TABLE 18-5

Birth and Death Rates and Population-Doubling Time for Latin American Countries, 1988

	Birth Rate (per 1,000)	Death Rate (per 1,000)	Doubling Time
Argentina	24	9	45
Bolivia	40	14	27
Brazil	26	8	34
Chile	22	6	45
Colombia	26	7	34
Ecuador	36	8	25
Guatemala	41	9	21
Honduras	39	8	22
Mexico	30	6	29
Nicaragua	43	6	20
Peru	34	9	26
Venezuela	29	5	26
United States	16	9	98
Sweden	12	11	673

Source: Mary M. Kent and Carl Haub, 1988 World Population Data Sheet, (Washington, DC: Population Reference Bureau, 1988).

its population live at the marginal level of subsistence, either unemployed or underemployed, contributing nothing to mainstream economic activity and receiving no benefits. Negative growth rates, which the Latin American countries have had during the 1980s, exacerbate the problem of poverty and increase social unrest. Urban unemployment has increased as thousands of people migrate to the cities. This increases pollution to the point that cities such as Mexico City are among the most polluted in the world.

There is also great inequality in the distribution of income in Latin America. Brazil has one of the more unequal income distributions in the world. The highest 10 percent of households receive 50 percent of household incomes compared to 33 percent for the bottom 80 percent of households.[7] Government attempts to redistribute income through progressive income taxation have generally proved to be ineffectual because the rich can transfer their wealth to safe havens in Europe or the United States. Within the Latin American countries, the rich are more likely to speculate in real estate ventures than putting their money into business enterprises. To a considerable extent, the actions of the rich are based on the fact that political instability is a fact of life in Latin America.

---

[7] The World Bank, *World Development Report 1989* (New York: Oxford University Press, 1989), p. 223.

MEXICO: THE ECONOMIC SYSTEM

Mexico is a land of contrasts. There is extreme wealth and extreme poverty; there are vast natural resources and little arable land. It has many of the advantages necessary to become one of the world's most prosperous nations, yet 40 percent of the labor force is either unemployed or underemployed, and the population continues to grow at a rate of 2.4 percent a year. It is one of the *nearly industrialized countries* that are still struggling with the problems of economic development but that have emerged as important economic powers. Moreover, it has a strategic location next to the world's largest consumer market, the United States. However, prices increased by more than 600 percent during the period 1982–1985, and the peso lost more than 90 percent of its value against the dollar. Mexico's foreign debt is, along with Brazil's, the highest of any developing country in the world, which places a burden on the development of the Mexican economy.

Mexico has a characteristic common to many less developed and developing countries: reliance on one major export product. In Mexico's case it is oil. In 1988 oil exports accounted for 70 percent of the total exports of the Mexican economy. Since its discovery in 1863, oil has been both a blessing and a curse to the Mexican economy. It could be the foundation for the development of the Mexican economy, but, unfortunately for Mexico, wide swings in the world price of oil have also created problems. Oil has come to play an important role in Mexican politics, particularly in its relations with the United States. The oil industry, which is a state-owned monopoly, is the largest expense item in the Mexican budget, but its revenues, particularly from exports, are also the single most important contributor to total government revenues.

The Mexican economic system is a mixed system consisting of both public sector and free market arrangements. Private foreign investment has been important in promoting economic development. Most production in Mexico is conducted by private enterprise. Mexico has one of the fastest growing steel industries in the world. A large part of the agricultural system is organized as private commercial firms. The transactions of most economic units in Mexico are basically motivated by the desire to maximize profits and incomes in response to market forces. Rewards in income and wealth have gone in great measure to those units that act efficiently in response to market opportunities. There has been very little comprehensive central planning by the government.

Table 18-6 presents a percentage breakdown of the main components of Mexico's gross national product for 1988. The most important component is private consumption expenditures on goods and services, which accounted for 60.1 percent of gross national product. In total, the government or public sector generates around 25 percent of the Mexican GNP, and the private sector contributes around 75 percent.

Agriculture

Agriculture has been called the Achilles heel of the Mexican economy with good reason. Mexico is highly unsuited for agriculture. Much of the north is desert; two

TABLE 18-6
Mexican Gross National Product Expenditures
by Sectors, 1988

Government consumption	12.4%
Private consumption	60.1
Fixed capital formation	
Public	12.9
Private	13.4
Exports of goods and services	13.4
Less: Imports of goods and services	− 12.2
	100.0%

Source: Banco de Mexico, Informe Anual 1988, p.
172.

mountain ranges run the length of the country; tropical jungles cover the southern
region; and much of the top soil of the country is so thin that little can grow.
Only 15 percent of the total land area of Mexico is cultivatable. Most of Mexico's
agricultural land depends exclusively on rainfall for moisture, and during the 1980s
rainfall was significantly below the national average. Agriculture employs one-third
of the Mexican labor force, while accounting for less than 9 percent of Mexico's
gross national product.

Of major significance to the Mexican economy is the fact that the real growth
in agricultural output has declined over time while the population has increased.
Agricultural production increased at an average annual rate of 4.5 percent during
the period 1960–1970 and at a rate of 2.9 percent for the period 1970–1987.[8]
During the latter period, the average annual increase in agriculture was a little less
than the average annual increase in population. Mexico has also experienced a
decline in self-sufficiency in agriculture and must import more farm products.

There are several factors that contribute to the problems of agriculture in Mexico. First, there is no adequate transportation network to allow quick and cheap
transportation of agricultural products within Mexico. The major railroad and highway systems follow a north-to-south route from the United States to Mexico City.
There is little east-west rail and highway transportation because mountains provide
a barrier to construction. Many of the larger Mexican cities are served by only
one major highway each. Inadequate transportation facilities have hampered the
efforts of the Mexican government to restrain rises in the cost of food production.
Moreover, the transportation problem is not just internal. Mexico has considerable
problems in maintaining adequate distribution channels for imported foodstuffs as
well. Port and storage facilities are inadequate, and roads leading from the seaports
to the major urban areas are poor.

---

[8] Banco de Mexico, *Informe Anual 1988*, p. 162.

As is true of other developing countries, agriculture has generally been neglected by the government in favor of industrial development. The latter offers more tangible results from both political and economic standpoints. However, neglect of agriculture has encouraged urban migration, which has put more pressure on food production. Some price supports have been initiated to increase farm income and to stem the tide of rural-to-urban migration, or, for that matter, rural-to-the-United-States migration. The Mexican government has also imposed export restrictions on the sale of beef abroad to lower the price of beef to domestic consumers. However, export restrictions lower the price of beef and discourage beef growers from producing more cattle, which then necessitates subsidies from the government.

The organization of agriculture is a third factor that contributes to low agricultural productivity. Mexican agriculture is typified by three different types of land holdings: communal, public, and private. The communal, or *ejido,* land holding is unique to Mexico, dating back to the time of the Aztecs. The land is held by the ejido and farmed by *ejidatarios,* or farm laborers, who share in the proceeds. The ejidos are considered inefficient and are criticized on the grounds that not allowing private property ownership weakens attachment to the soil and separates efforts from rewards. The bulk of Mexican agricultural output comes from the private farms, 4 percent of which produce more than 50 percent of total output and 1 percent of which produce all of the agricultural exports.

Only 12 percent of the land area of Mexico is under cultivation, yet almost one-third of the Mexican labor force is still employed in agriculture. This means that labor productivity is low. There is also an imbalance between cultivatable land, population centers, and water resources. Only 10 percent of the water resources are located in the central plateau around Mexico City, the area that contains half of Mexico's population and the greatest concentration of small farms. The bulk of water resources are in the underpopulated areas, and the larger, more productive farm holdings are also in the same areas.

Government Ownership of Enterprise

The Mexican government has intervened directly and indirectly to promote economic expansion in all sectors of the economy. Since the 1930s when foreign oil properties were nationalized, the state has been involved in the economy to a greater extent than in most Latin American countries.

In 1982 the government nationalized the banking system. It owns most of the electrical power industry and has established government enterprises in direct competition with private ones in the same industry, such as steel production. It exercises considerable control over access to credit through state-owned financial institutions and constructs social overhead facilities, such as ports and roads, with the clear intention of influencing the geographical location and other characteristics of new private investment. The government emphasizes economic nationalism through legislation designed to discourage industrial imports, through exchange controls, and through import licensing.

PEMEX. Oil production is the most important sector in the Mexican economy and is run by a government monopoly, Petroleos Mexicanos (PEMEX). This monopoly is the only entity legally entitled to extract, refine, and distribute oil and oil products. The final distribution of gasoline products is made through a national network of privately owned gasoline stations that must comply with PEMEX regulations. PEMEX regulates the final prices of gasoline products, which cannot be changed by the station owners under any conditions. It also sets the hours for selling gasoline, the amount of gasoline to be sold, the architectural design of the gas stations, and the number of pumps allowed to operate in each station. The importance of PEMEX is demonstrated by the fact that its director has the status of a government minister and is a member of the Mexican cabinet.

Domestic price and oil extraction policies are set by PEMEX and are dictated by government economic development policies. Oil pricing policies for the international market follow those set by Saudi Arabia and other OPEC countries. The Arab oil embargo of the early 1970s and the energy crisis that developed afterward encouraged the management of PEMEX to adopt a faster rate of extraction and a more aggressive exploration policy. By 1984 Mexico was the fourth largest oil producer in the world. The increase in the rate of oil extraction required large investment expenditures, mainly for imported capital goods. As a consequence, PEMEX represents the single largest expenditure in the Mexican national budget, accounting for almost a third of total expenditures in 1988.[9]

Banking. Banking is the second area where the Mexican government plays an important role in the Mexican economy. The Central Bank (Banco de Mexico) is a government entity and is responsible for the implementation of monetary policy through control over interest rates and reserve requirements of Mexican banks. It supervises foreign transactions and is the sole issuer of paper currency. Its monetary policy has been a part of Mexican government economic development strategy. During the 1970s and early 1980s, it pursued an expansionary policy of increasing the money supply to stimulate the Mexican economy.[10]

The Nacional Financiera is the second most important government-owned bank. Its function is to promote industrial development by allocating credit to industries both public and private that are a part of the government's program for economic development. Nacional Financiera holds a controlling interest in the country's largest steel producer, Altos Hornos de Mexico. It also holds substantial financial interests in pulp and paper, fertilizer, electrical equipment, sugar, films, textiles, food, beer, chemicals, cement, glass, and motels. Its main sources of revenue are from the government budget and from interest on loans.

[9] Banco de Mexico, *Informe Anual, 1988,* p. 152.
[10] Francisco Carrada-Bravo, *Oil, Money, and the Mexican Economy* (Boulder, CO: Westview Press, 1982), pp. 37–38.

There are also other specialized government lending institutions, such as agricultural banks, that lend to specific sectors. Finally, government control over the banking system was increased in 1982, when the privately owned commercial banks were nationalized.

Public Finance

There are several points that can be made about the Mexican fiscal system. First, the federal budget is an important part of government economic development policy. The fiscal policy of the Mexican government has been to foster economic expansion by running a deficit in the budget. Although Mexico's financial markets are relatively sophisticated by Latin America standards, they are not developed to the extent that large-scale financing of the budget deficit is possible through government bonds. The Banco de Mexico finances the deficit primarily through increases in the money supply. Also, large amounts have been borrowed from U. S. banks and the International Monetary Fund. Second, on the revenue side of the budget, the income tax has declined in importance as a source of revenue, accounting for only 12 percent of government revenue in 1984. The major sources of revenue in the Mexican budget are borrowing and income from state-owned enterprises. Since 1980, PEMEX has provided about half the national government's revenue. Third, the bulk of government expenditures are on infrastructure and housing investment, which is a large and growing sector of the Mexican economy.

Economic Development

In terms of economic production and diversification, Mexico, by international standards, is at the lower-middle stage of economic development. It is far more developed than either China or Nigeria but not as developed as South Africa or Venezuela. Its economy is less autonomous and more vulnerable to external economic forces than the economies of the more developed countries, but more autonomous and less vulnerable than the economies of subsistence level and single-export countries. Its economy is extractive-oriented in that oil is far and away its most important export. When world oil prices were high during the late 1970s, the oil wealth of Mexico not only generated the foreign exchange necessary to finance internal economic development, but also enhanced the country's attractiveness in foreign capital markets. However, the decline in world oil prices in the early 1980s has had a deleterious impact on the Mexican economy, which by that time had incurred a large foreign debt.

Economic Development Strategies. It is evident that economic development has brought substantial economic and social progress to Mexico and to many other countries that were at one time poor. In general this development has come about through the use of one or more of three different growth policy approaches. The first approach is to rely on the export of a primary product, such as copper or oil, to raise living standards. This approach may not involve an attempt to achieve industrialization. For example, the Arab countries have used revenue from oil exports to achieve higher living standards, but there has been very little attempt to achieve widespread industrial development. Oil revenues have been used to improve the infrastructure of these countries through the construction of education facilities, roads, and hospitals. Venezuela, on the other hand, has used revenue from its oil exports to accomplish more broadly based industrialization.

A second approach to economic development is to achieve inward industrialization through import substitution. This has been the development strategy of Mexico, Brazil, Argentina, and several other Latin American countries. Restrictions on imports increase the demand for local consumption and are supposed to encourage the development of domestic industries. Both Mexico and Brazil have established consumer and capital goods industries that provide for local consumption. This strategy is not without its costs; protection from import competition often raises the prices of local goods and limits selection for consumers.

The third approach has been followed by Japan, Singapore, South Korea, and other Asian countries since the end of World War II. This is outward industrialization and involves the export of manufactured goods ranging from clothing to automobiles. Measures to increase exports are for the most part likely to develop rather slowly; it is a matter of improving production techniques, labor skills, and managerial methods, and introducing new industries. An export surplus also involves sacrifices; it means spending more abroad than one gets in return—using labor and other resources to provide goods and services for foreigners.

Mexico's Development Strategy. In pursuing inward industrialization through import substitution, Mexico relies heavily on state intervention in the economy.[11] Exchange controls,[12] import quotas, and other restrictions designed to limit imports are used by the government to promote the development of home industries by making imports more expensive. This compels Mexican consumers either to pay higher prices for imported goods or to buy domestic products. In effect, consumers have been forced to subsidize the development of Mexican industry through the substitution of domestic products for imported products.

Capital investment is stimulated through tax policies and government subsidies to aid business. The government has intervened directly to promote the development of certain industries. For example, the Automobile Manufacturing Law of 1963 required foreign automobile companies operating in Mexico to increase the share of locally manufactured components to 60 precent of each car produced. This law

---

[11] Robert E. Looney, *Development Alternatives of Mexico* (New York: Praeger Publishers, 1982).

[12] Exchange controls involve the decision of a government agency as to what and how much will be imported from abroad. The government allocates foreign exchange to importers, which in effect controls imports.

was designed to stimulate local manufacturing through import substitution and to make the auto industry a primary source of employment.[13]

The world oil shortage of the 1970s caused a new rebirth of the Mexican oil industry and a change in development strategy away from import substitution to the use of oil for export expansion. New oil discoveries returned Mexico to the status it had enjoyed earlier in the century as a major world oil producer. Two important government development policy decisions were made. The first was to push for increased oil production and the second was to base export policy on the sale of oil to the United States and other oil-importing countries. Earnings from oil exports were used to improve the infrastructure of the Mexican economy and to increase social welfare expenditures to the lower income groups in the population.

Earnings from oil exports were also used to promote the capital goods industry in Mexico. Tariffs and import quotas were placed on imported capital goods to promote substitution of locally produced capital goods for those those that were foreign produced. Import controls on capital goods and the promotion of oil exports were the main instruments of Mexican economic development strategy during the late 1970s and early 1980s.

Economic Planning

Economic planning is relatively new in Mexico and is quite similar to the indicative planning that was made popular by France. The length of the economic plan is linked to the six-year presidential cycle, and thus the economic planning process is aligned closely to the political and economic objectives of the incumbent president. Although succeeding presidents are from the same political party, their economic policies are not the same. The policies of the Lopez Portillo administration (1976–1982) were totally different from the policies of the Miguel de la Madrid administration (1982–1988). Economic planning was initiated during the Portillo administration and set forth objectives to increase oil exports, to create more jobs, to raise living standards of the poorest strata of the population, and to increase the rates of saving and capital formation in both the public and private sectors. However, the collapse of world oil prices has had an adverse effect on the Mexican economy, and the economic planning of the de la Madrid administration of necessity reversed most of the goals of the previous administration.

AN APPRAISAL OF THE MEXICAN ECONOMY

Mexico's prosperity has come rather recently. For many years Mexico was a somnolent country, locked into a circle of poverty caused by a lack of savings and

---

[13] Jorge I. Dominguez, *Mexico's Political Economy* (Beverly Hills, CA: Sage Publications, 1982), pp. 142–144.

social capital and by monopolistic foreign exploitation of local natural resources. The Mexican Revolution of 1910 brought changes in the economy. Between 1917 and World War II, emphasis was placed on agricultural reform. The feudal system of land ownership, with its absentee holdings, was abolished and the land was redistributed in a manner permitting the use of modern agricultural techniques. Investments in social overhead capital include literacy campaigns and technical schools. A national bank for agricultural credit was created in 1926; and an industrial bank, the Nacional Financiera, was created in 1934 to provide loans to business firms. Through these banks, the government became responsible for a large share of the financing of economic development.

The Mexican economy expanded rapidly after World War II. There was a 10-fold increase in gross domestic product between 1949 and 1978 that propelled Mexico from the rank of a poor, less developed country to a developing country.[14] Mexico's real output in constant prices increased at an average rate of 6.2 percent a year, well ahead of the annual population growth rate of 3.3 percent. Most of the gain in real output occurred in the industrial sector, which increased at an average annual rate of 7.8 percent for the period. Manufacturing increased from 19 percent of total output in 1949 to 33 percent in 1978. Mexico began to exhibit many of the key features of a large modern industrial nation, with domestic oil promising to guarantee it abundant energy at least until the end of the century. A middle class developed, particularly in the cities, that provided an element of political stability. Moreover, it expanded over a period of time, as the process of industrialization continued.

However, the 1980s have been an unmitigated disaster for Mexico. The official price index multiplied by 13.8 times during the period 1981–1987, but the price of bread rose by 24 times during the same period, the price of tortillas rose 17.4 times, and kerosene rose 93 times.[15] Most of these changes resulted from decreased government subsidies on key commodities, as the government attempted to divert more revenue to debt repayment. The collapse of oil prices during the 1980s reduced Mexican GNP by 6.6 percent in 1986 alone, which increased the deficit in the federal budget to 16.6 percent. The terms of trade, with 1980 set at 100 percent, fell to 51 percent by 1986.[16]

The 1988 Presidential Election

The Institutional Revolutionary Party (PRI) has been the ruling political party in Mexico since 1929. As a matter of fact, it was the only party until the July 1988 election, when it was challenged from both the left and right, and won by a

[14] Looney, *Development Alternatives,* p. 2.
[15] Luis Rubio, "A Second Revolution Advances on Mexico," *Los Angeles Times,* June 24, 1988, p. 2.
[16] Inter-American Development Bank, *Economic and Social Progression in Latin America, 1989* p. 342.

bare majority of the votes.[17] The PRI was charged with election fraud, but that is par for the course in any Mexican election. Its candidate, Carlos Salinas de Gortari, was elected president against the backdrop of an economy that is beset by economic and social problems. The debt problem is the most important, but inflation runs a close second. Political corruption was a major factor that increased voter support for opposition parties in the 1988 presidential election. There is an industrial structure which is inefficient and uncompetitive by international standards and is too dependent upon the Mexican government for assistance. There is rural discontent over the lack of job opportunities and urban crowding.

Population

Demographers estimate that the population of Mexico will exceed 100 million by the end of the century. The country is already hard-pressed to produce enough jobs to absorb the 800,000 new entrants into the labor force each year. Millions of Mexicans have emigrated or are in the process of emigrating, usually illegally, to the United States, where even the most menial jobs provide more money and a better life than the alternative in Mexico. For most countries, more people not only means more labor and output, but also more consumers to share the output. More people also means there will be less real capital and natural resources per capita, and labor productivity may actually fall.

The population-doubling time for Mexico is 29 years and the current ratio of births to deaths is 5 to 1.[18] Given that ratio, Mexico should have a population of 167 million by the year 2017. Mexico is "bottom heavy," with a rapidly growing working population needing employment opportunities. It has an acute need to return to a pattern of rapid growth in GNP. Population demographics indicate that Mexico must find employment for some 800,000 to 1 million new workers each year to avoid having unemployment rise. To achieve this goal, there is a need for real growth in GNP to increase at a rate of 4 to 6 percent a year simply to stabilize the unemployment rate.[19] This increase is highly unlikely, given that the increase in real GNP has been negative during most of the 1980s. If Mexico cannot improve its growth rate, social instability will increase.

Urbanization. Mexico has an urban problem of the first magnitude. Population growth has increased the problem, as jobless peasants stream into the cities in

---

[17] There has been token opposition in previous elections, but the last real election was in 1944 when an opposition candidate probably had the majority of votes, but most of them were thrown out or lost, a classic example of election fraud.

[18] Carl Haub and Mary M. Kent, *1988 World Population Data Sheet* (Washington: Population Reference Bureau, 1988).

[19] Joint Economic Committee, Congress of the United States, *Economic Reform in Mexico: Implications for the United States,* 100th Cong., 2nd Sess. (Washington: USGPO, 1988), p. 34.

search of a higher standard of living. The migration problem is part of a rural unemployment problem that is linked to a decline in agricultural employment and is exacerbated by a high rural birth rate.[20] Unfortunately, this has created a combustible mixture of urban pollution, poverty, unemployment, disease, crime, and corruption. Mexico City is an environmental disaster. Half of Mexico's industries are located here in an area smaller than the state of Rhode Island. The daily total chemical air pollutants is estimated to be 11,000 tons. Unemployment and underemployment run at an average rate of 50 percent of the adult population, and one-fifth of the population has no running water or sewage facilities in their homes.[21]

Emigration to the United States. It is estimated that some 22 million Mexicans have entered the United States either legally or illegally since 1945. There are a number of reasons for this immigration, the most important of which are the following.

1. There is an enormous difference between the two countries in both money and real wages. The real wages differential between the United States and Mexico is about 10 to 1 for unskilled jobs and 17 to 1 for agricultural jobs.
2. The rate of inflation is much higher in Mexico than in the United States. Inflation further depresses the level of real wages for the average Mexican worker.
3. The Mexican labor force is increasing at a faster rate than the capacity of the Mexican economy to create jobs. Many of those who emigrate to the United States are impoverished rural workers from the poorest agricultural states of Mexico: Oaxaca, Morelos, Guerrero, and Michoacan.

Mexican migration to the United States can be considered a safety valve for Mexico in that it reduces pressures of unemployment. At least two-thirds of the emigrants remit money to Mexico. For most of the Mexican households involved, these remittances are their primary source of income. Because most of the migrants come from northern and central Mexico, the Mexican government would face a severe regionally concentrated income and employment problem if the border with the United States were closed. Although migration may reduce unemployment in Mexico, it may increase unemployment in the United States. There is pressure, particularly from U.S. labor unions, to restrict the flow of migrants from Mexico.

---

[20] Elaine M. Murphy, *World Population: Toward the Next Century* (Washington: Population Reference Bureau, 1986). p. 2.

[21] Problems of urbanization are not limited to just Mexico City. Monterrey, Guadalajara, Juarez, Puebla, and other Mexican cities have seen similar population increases. The increased population puts a burden on the infrastructure of these cities, which is often inadequate to begin with. Moreover, slowing internal migration does not offer a real solution to the rate of Mexican population growth.

Income Inequality

"The thing is, there is no equality here. Everything is disproportionate. The rich are very rich, and the poor are infamously poor. The poor stick to the poor, and the rich, well, they go to the Hilton. The day I dare go to the Hilton Hotel, I'll know there has been another revolution!"[22]

This statement was made by one of the people quoted in Oscar Lewis' book *The Children of Sanchez*, written more than 25 years ago. Nothing has changed. In Mexico's case, the chosen strategy for economic development seems to have worked against social improvement. Not only has the economy been unable to create sufficient jobs—the most effective remedy for the amelioration of social problems—but it also had permitted an inordinate concentration of income and wealth in the hands of a few people. Mexico's very rich live in a style that would put all but a few American millionaires to shame, while the majority of its population lives in degrees of poverty that range from mere survival to outright misery. Mexico and Brazil, the two Latin American countries that have enjoyed the fastest economic growth since the 1950s, display the most skewed distribution of income and wealth in the Americas.

Table 18-7 presents the distribution of income in Mexico for 1977. In that year the top 10 percent of Mexican households in terms of income received 40.6 percent of total household incomes, compared to 42.3 percent for the bottom 80 percent. The average household income of those in the top 10 percent was 31 times that of families in the bottom 20 percent.[23] About 45 percent of Mexican families have an income that is less than half the national average. The Gini coefficient for Mexico is about 0.6 percent, indicating one of the world's most unequal income

TABLE 18-7
Distribution of Household Income in Mexico, 1977

Lowest 20 percent	2.9%
Second quintile	7.0
Third quintile	12.0
Fourth quintile	20.4
Highest 20 percent	57.7
Highest 10 percent	40.6
Highest 5 percent	27.7

Source: The World Bank, World Development Report 1989 *(New York: Oxford University Press, 1989), p. 223.*

---

[22] Oscar Lewis, *The Children of Sanchez* (New York: Random House, 1961), pp. 339–340.

[23] David Felix, "Income Inequality in Mexico," *Current History*, (March, 1977), p. 11.

distributions.[24] Contrary to patterns exhibited by other countries in similar stages of economic development, the income gap between rich and poor has widened.[25]

Moreover, there are geographic disparities in the distribution of income that are far greater than those in developed countries such as the United States. The average per capita income in Mexico City is six times that of the state of Oaxaca, a factor that promotes internal migration and contributes to overcrowding in Mexico City.

There are a number of reasons for income inequality in Mexico, most of which are common to other less developed economies. However, there are several reasons that are the result of conditions particular to Mexico.

1. The economic growth policies of Mexico have benefited the upper and middle classes. Import substitution has kept foreign imports out and stimulated Mexican business. Emphasis was placed on industrialization, which did create jobs but particularly benefited a small number of large Mexican-owned firms that are capital-intensive.
2. The Mexican tax system is probably more regressive than progressive. The personal income tax, though progressive, is evaded by many persons and social welfare benefits are low.
3. Much Mexican wealth is concentrated in real estate.
4. Corruption is a factor. One of the more recent presidents of Mexico is alleged to have pocketed one to three billion dollars while in office. Corruption is not new to Mexico; it goes back to the time of the conquistadores.
5. Income inequality is another carryover from the *latifundio* system of the last century, when a few families controlled much of the land of Mexico. Even though the Revolution of 1910 broke up the latifundio system, most families retained their wealth.

Income inequality can also be translated into inequality in the distribution of wealth. Much of the wealth is concentrated in real estate or is invested in foreign holdings, particularly in the United States. Wealthy Mexicans devise elaborate schemes to put their wealth beyond the reach of Mexican tax collectors and give themselves a safe haven outside of Mexico.[26]

The extreme dichotomy in income and wealth between rich and poor increases the potential for social unrest in Mexico. The Mexican fiscal system includes thou-

---

[24] As was pointed out in Chapter 1, the Gini coefficient is a measure of income inequality. It can range from 0 to 1. The coefficient for the United States is around .36, which indicates that there is less income inequality in the United States than in Mexico. The coefficient decreases as a country develops an industrial base and adopts policies of income transfers and progressive taxation.

[25] Woulter van Ginnekin, *Socioeconomic Groups and Income Distribution in Mexico* (London: Groom Helem, 1980), Chapter 1.

[26] Capital outflows from Mexico amounted to $33 billion during the period 1977–1984. Around $20 billion came to the United States.

sands of subsidies and controls that are supposed to benefit low-income groups but often do not. The income tax, though progressive, does very little to reduce income inequality among groups, for there are many loopholes. A developed welfare state like the one in the United States and Western Europe that has narrowed income differences between rich and poor does not exist in Mexico. Only 35 percent of the population is covered by social security.

Foreign Debt

The external or foreign debt of Mexico was $106 billion at the end of 1988. This debt was incurred at a time when world prices for oil were high. As mentioned previously, Mexican industrial development strategy during the late 1970s was predicated on oil, which represented about 80 percent of total exports. As long as there was a world demand for oil and prices remained high, the Mexican government could afford to mortgage the future by borrowing against the expected revenue from oil exports. These loans went to finance a wide variety of development schemes, including a national system of supports for basic agriculture and a plan to build 20 nuclear reactors. However, the Mexican government ignored the consequences of the global oil glut that began to develop in early 1981 and continued to borrow from foreign banks, using anticipated future oil revenue as collateral.

Falling world prices for oil and rising interest rates in the United States exacerbated the difficulty the Mexican government had in meeting payments on the debt it had contracted with foreign banks. Exports declined as a result of the world oil glut, while the price of imports, particularly those from the United States where the dollar gained in value relative to the peso, increased. To correct a negative balance in Mexico's balance of payments, the government devalued the peso in 1982.[27] This did little to stop the flight of Mexican money out of the country because Mexicans had lost faith in the value of the peso. In September 1982 the government nationalized Mexico's private banks, blaming them for the exodus of Mexican money to the United States. The devaluation of the peso made Mexico's imported goods more expensive, further lowering living standards for many Mexicans. Inflation contributed to a further decline in the value of the peso, which by April 1989 exchanged at 2,362 to the dollar.

High interest rates in the United States increased interest payments on Mexico's foreign debt at the same time that Mexico's earnings from oil exports were declining. In 1988, for example, Mexico's interest payments on its foreign debt amounted to about 28 percent of its total export earnings and 3 percent of its gross

---

[27] Currency devaluation refers to a downward adjustment of a currency's official exchange rate relative to other currencies. It has both external and internal effects on a country's economy. The external effect is to increase exports as a result of lower export prices in terms of foreign currencies. The internal effect is to decrease imports because import prices increase in terms of domestic currency. The export advantages of devaluation presuppose no immediate retaliation on the part of other countries.

national product.[28] This means that Mexico was having a hard enough time meeting its interest payments, much less returning any part of the principal. The situation worsened as oil prices continued to fall. In an effort to improve its foreign debt position, the government introduced austerity measures. Taxes have been raised and government spending has been cut, while domestic interest rates have increased.[29] To further help cut imports and promote exports, foreign exchange controls were imposed, making it more difficult for Mexicans to buy products made in the United States. These austerity measures have had mixed results. In early 1989, with oil prices down to $11 a barrel, Mexico was forced to limit interest payments on its debt.

Corruption

"I don't know about political things. The first time I voted was in the last election, but I don't think there is much hope there. The men in the government always end up rich and the poor are just as badly off."[30]

Corruption is endemic in Mexico.[31] It has long been an article of faith that any politician worth his or her salt will amass at least a minor fortune before leaving office.[32] A new president is elected every six years even though the same party remains in office, and he has 45,000 patronage jobs to fill. Each patronage job involves some sort of a political payoff, and there are benefits to be gained. From ministers and directors of government agencies down to the workers on garbage trucks, civil servants have the opportunity to make money. The average minister or director may amass a small fortune during a term in office. It is reported that some ministers leave office with amounts 30 or more times as much as their original salary.[33] Even garbage collectors can demand bribes from the households they serve, threatening to leave the garbage in the streets. In turn, the garbage collectors have to pay off the head of the garbage collectors' union.

Nepotism is always a fact of life in Mexican politics. For example, one former president of Mexico, Jose Lopez Portillo, appointed his son, his mistress, two cousins, and his sister to ministerial positions. Another sister was given the job of his personal secretary, and his wife was appointed head of cultural affairs. All enjoyed an extravagant lifestyle. Lopez Portillo himself constructed a five-mansion complex, with tennis courts, swimming pools, stables, and a gymnasium.

---

[28] Banco National de Mexico, *Indicadores Economicos* (February, 1989), p. 21

[29] Nominal interest rates on one-month certificates of deposits hit a high of 150 percent in 1989.

[30] Lewis, *Children of Sanchez*, p. 342.

[31] It is necessary to emphasize the fact that Mexico has no monopoly on corruption. Bribery and other forms of corruption are an accepted way of life in many countries.

[32] A classic example involves a former police chief of Mexico City who acquired two mansions, property in Acapulco, twelve Mercedez-Benzes, two helicopters, two airplanes, and $12 million in cash during his term in office.

[33] Alan Riding, *Distant Neighbors* (New York: Alfred A. Knopf, Inc., 1985), pp. 117–119.

He bought a two-million dollar villa in Acapulco for his mistress, and, to show no favoritism, built one equally expensive for his wife. One sister built a 36,000-square-foot mansion on government property. It is estimated that Lopez Portillo and his family enriched themselves to the extent of $11 billion during his term in office.[34]

Corruption simply exacerbates the differences between the haves and the have-nots. It is a result of 60 years of one-party rule in which widely diverse constituents have been allowed easy access to the government. Mexicans have socially and cynically accepted corruption as a part of everyday life. The 1985 earthquake that devastated a part of Mexico City revealed that many buildings collapsed and lives were lost unnecessarily because building contractors had used poor quality materials on government buildings.[35] Corruption, particularly as flagrant as it is in Mexico, has the potential for creating social unrest. A system that never worked smoothly without corruption is no longer working smoothly because of corruption. As an historical note, a major reason for Castro's overthrow of the Batista regime in Cuba was the extent of corruption that existed in the country at that time. Although the current president, Carlos Salinas de Gortari, has vowed to eliminate corruption, it will be impossible to destroy completely, for it is too much a part of the system.

Mexico in the 1990s

The new president of Mexico, Carlos Salinas de Gortari, has inherited a number of economic and social problems that have to be solved. Economic deterioration has led to growing political radicalism. Economic growth has been stagnant, the population has increased, and the massive foreign debt burden has to be reduced.[36] To promote more efficiency in the economy, the previous administration of Miguel de la Madrid privatized many state or parastate enterprises.[37] It inherited more than 1,000 of these enterprises when it took office in 1983, and by 1988 had sold 112 of them, mainly in cement, soft drinks, hotels, and petrochemicals. The de Gortari government is expected to privatize most of the remaining state or parastate enterprises, including the state-owned enterprise PEMEX, which has been a model of inefficiency and corruption for many years. In 1988 the government agreed to sell the state-owned copper mine of Minera Cananea to private investors.

The foreign debt problem remains the paramount challenge to the new administration. The government has introduced a program to swap its foreign debt to foreign direct investors in exchange for direct equity investments in Mexican business firms. This gives foreign investors a competitive advantage with respect to

[34] Riding, p. 128.

[35] "A Nation in Jeopardy, *The Wall Street Journal* (October 15, 1985), p. 1.

[36] Graham, *Latin American Quagmire*, p. 45.

[37] Stephen A. Quick, *Economic Reforms in Mexico: Implications for the United States,* Staff Report Prepared for the Joint Economic Committee, Congress of the United States, October, 1988, p. 32.

the ownership of domestic business enterprises. But the debt problem still remains, and it remains to be seen if the Brady plan, which has been initiated by the Bush administration, will help alleviate the burden of the Mexican foreign debt.

SUMMARY

Mexico is one of the largest countries in the world, both in population and land size. Although it is not nearly as rich as the United States and Canada, it has experienced a rapid growth in economic development and ranks as one of the more successful developing countries in the world.

Its economy is mixed in that both the private and public sectors are important. Agriculture is a problem to Mexico for several reasons: inadequate transportation, neglect by government, low labor productivity, and lack of adequate water. Mexico has relied extensively on government intervention in the economy, intervening both directly with controls on investment and trade and indirectly through taxes, subsidies, and other measures affecting the prices in both factor and product markets. Its internal economic development policy has relied on import substitution. This policy was used to develop Mexican oil and steel industries. When oil increased in importance in world markets, Mexico used the earnings from its oil exports to subsidize the development of its capital goods industries.

Nevertheless, Mexico faces a number of problems, most of which are common to other less developed and developing countries. One is overpopulation. The population of Mexico is growing at a rate faster than the country's capacity to support it. One result is a mass migration of Mexicans to the United States, which has put a strain on the relations between the two countries. The external debt of Mexico is a second problem. It places pressure on government policy to earn more from exports while encouraging austerity at home. Oil exports account for most of Mexico's export earnings, and the world price for oil has declined. A third problem is corruption, which permeates much of Mexican life. Income distribution, which is one of the most unequal in the world, is a fourth problem. The enormous income disparity between rich and poor creates a potential for social unrest. The final problem is low productivity in agriculture.

REVIEW QUESTIONS

1. Discuss the importance of oil to the Mexican economy.
2. Discuss some of the problems of Mexican agriculture.
3. What is an import substitution approach to economic development?
4. What are the three approaches to economic development? Which one has Mexico used?

5. Mexico represents a lower-middle stage of economic development. It is far more developed than either China or Nigeria, but far less developed than the United States. Discuss.
6. Discuss the relationship of population growth to economic development in Mexico.
7. What problems does its foreign debt create for Mexico?
8. Population growth has increased more rapidly in the cities of the less developed and developing countries than in the cities of the developed countries. Why is this so?

RECOMMENDED READINGS

Aspra, Antonio. "Import Substitution in Mexico: Past and Present." *World Development* (January–February, 1977).

Buffie, Edward F. "Mexico 1958–1986: From Stabilizing Development to the Debt Crisis." In Jeffrey D. Sachs, ed., *Developing Country Debt and the World Economy*. Chicago: The University of Chicago Press, 1989, pp. 141–168.

Eckstein, Susan. *The Poverty of Revolution*, Princeton, NJ: Princeton University Press, 1987.

Graham, Carol L. "The Latin American Quagmire: Beyond Debt and Democracy." *The Brookings Review*, Vol. 7, No. 2 (Spring 1989), pp. 42–47.

Inter-American Development Bank, *Economic and Social Progress in Latin America 1989 Report*. Washington, DC: Author, 1989.

Looney, Robert E. *Development Alternatives of Mexico*. New York: Praeger Publishers, 1982.

Riding, Alan. *Distant Neighbors*. New York: Alfred A. Knopf, 1985.

Sachs, Jeffrey D. "The Latin American Debt Problem." Testimony for the Subcommittee on International Finance and Monetary Policy, Senate Banking Committee, 101 Congress 1st. Session; February 18, 1989.

U.S. Congress, Joint Economic Committee. *Economic Reform in Mexico: Implications for the United States*, 100th Congress, 2nd Session, Washington, DC: USGPO, 1988.

– – –. *United States-Mexico Economic Relations*, Hearings Before the Subcommittee on Economic Resources and Competitiveness, 100th Congress, 1st Session, Washington, DC: USGPO, 1988.

Williamson, John. "Reviewing the Third World Debt-Strategy." Statement Before the Subcommittee on International Finance and Monetary Policy-Senate Banking Committee, 101 Congress, 1st Session; February 8, 1989.

Lowenthal, Abraham. *Partners in Conflict: The United States and Latin America*. Baltimore: Johns Hopkins Press, 1987.

Dornbusch, Rudiger. "Mexico, Stabilization, Debt, and Growth." unpublished paper. Cambridge, MA: MIT, 1988.

"The Trials of Democracy Latin Style." *U.S. News and World Report* (April 21, 1989), pp. 36–37.

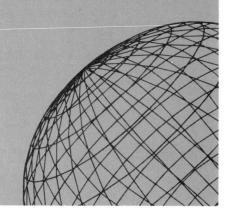

CHAPTER NINETEEN

NIGERIA

Nigeria is one of a number of African countries that have achieved their independence from colonial rule in the last 30 years. However, before Nigeria can be discussed in terms of economic development, the characteristics of Africa, which is the poorest and most diverse of all the continents, must be understood. What is applicable to Africa is applicable to Nigeria as well.

CHARACTERISTICS OF AFRICA

The majority of African countries have three things in common. First, with few exceptions, they were once colonies of a European country; second, they are poor; and third, uncontrolled population growth limits their potential economic development and creates enormous social problems.

Colonialism

For centuries, Africa was called the "dark continent," unknown to all outsiders except a few explorers. All of this changed when European powers decided at the Berlin Conference of 1885 to divide up Africa into enclaves or spheres of influence. Five countries shared in the division of African territory—Belgium, England, France, Germany, and Portugal. Belgium got that area of Africa known as the Congo, which became one of the largest copper-producing areas in the world. England, which was already established in Egypt and the Cape of Africa, acquired the Sudan, southern Africa, and part of southwest Africa. France, which had already conquered Algeria, was given West Africa. Germany was given the right to parts of East Africa and southwest Africa, including the area known as the Tanganyika territory.[1] Portugal,

---

[1] Germany lost its colonies after the end of World War I.

the smallest of the five European countries, was given what was left in southern East and West Africa, including the areas that are now the countries of Angola and Mozambique.

The African colonies served two purposes. First, they provided a source of wealth for their owners in the ruling country. Private companies were given monopoly rights by their governments to operate in the colonies and became the general media of commerce. The South Africa Chartered Company, owned by Cecil Rhodes, was given the right to develop the resources of southern Africa. The discovery of gold in the South African Rand and diamonds at Kimberley made Rhodes one of the richest men in the world.[2] Second, the African colonies served as markets for the products of the ruling countries. Until 1870, British manufactured goods found a market in other European countries. After 1870, Germany, France, Belgium, and other countries were able to satisfy their home markets and began to produce a surplus for sale abroad. With increasing saturation of the European markets, all looked for more markets overseas and for this purpose, Africa served admirably. Thus, the race to acquire colonies began.

The colonies were governed by administrators sent down from London, Paris, Berlin, Brussels, and Lisbon. The colonial civil service and military were run by the ruling countries, and the middle-class merchants were either European nationals, Indians, or Chinese. Native Africans were given little opportunity for self-government and were given no positions of authority in the colonial governments. As a result, when the colonies achieved their independence and became self-governing nations, there was a leadership vacuum. Most of the foreign civil servants, engineers, and merchants who had made up the backbone of government and commerce returned to their home countries. Their positions were filled by persons who had little training in government or who had no technical experience. Animosity toward anything foreign also resulted in the forced departure of Indian and Chinese merchants from some African countries. Unfortunately, the locals did not have the entrepreneurial skills to run the businesses vacated by the Europeans and Asians.

Poverty

Africa is by far the poorest of the world's continents. Its per capita income of around $500 is 3 percent of that of the United States, and it contains 28 of the 50 poorest countries in the world. Mozambique, the poorest country in the world, had a per capita income of $100 in 1988, and the second poorest, Ethiopia, had a per capita income of $120.[3] Only two countries, Algeria and South Africa, would qualify as being in the same stage of economic development as Brazil and Mexico. Libya, which has the highest per capita income of all of the African countries, derives its income from oil exports. Moreover, the average annual rate of growth of the 28 African countries with a 1988 per capita GNP of $500 or less was negative

---

[2] Cecil Rhodes is the man who established the Rhodes scholarships.

[3] The World Bank, *World Development Atlas 1989*, (New York: Oxford University Press, 1989), pp. 6–7.

for the period 1980–1988, with Mozambique having a growth rate of negative 7.5 percent.

Table 19-1 presents per capita GNP and average rate of growth per capita for selected African countries. Most of the countries have per capita incomes of $500 or less and are located in the sub-Sahara region of Africa.[4] With the exception of Ethiopia, all were former colonies of England, France, Germany, or Portugal. It is in these low-income countries that slow economic growth has done the most to perpetuate poverty. The rate of savings for most African countries is low—in some cases it is negative. This reduces capital formation. For example, Nigeria, the largest African country, had an average annual decrease in gross domestic investment of 14.8 percent during the period 1980–1988. Income distribution is far more unequal than it is for the developed countries. In Kenya, for example, the highest 10 percent of households received 45.8 percent of total household income, compared to 39.6 percent for the bottom 80 percent.[5]

TABLE 19-1
Per Capita GNP and Average Annual Growth
Rates for African Countries

	Per Capita GNP, 1988	Average Annual Real GNP Growth Rate 1980–88
Mozambique	$100	−7.5%
Ethiopia	120	−1.4
Zaire	170	−2.1
Nigeria	290	−4.3
Zambia	290	−4.9
Sudan	340	−4.2
Kenya	360	−0.2
Egypt	650	2.8
Zimbabwe	660	−1.0
Ivory Coast	740	−3.7
Tunisia	1,230	0.6
South Africa	2,290	−1.0
Algeria	2,450	0.0
Libya	5,410	−9.9

Source: The World Bank, The World Bank Atlas 1989,
(New York: Oxford University Press, 1989), pp. 6–9.

[4] The sub-Sahara region includes central Africa. Twenty-seven of the 28 countries are in the sub-Sahara region.

[5] The World Bank, *World Development Report 1989* (New York: Oxford University Press, 1989), p. 222.

Population Growth

Africa's population is growing faster than the population of the other continents. In addition, its population is outstripping food production. Famines in Sudan and Ethiopia have been publicized on national television, but other African countries have also had famines. The number of hungry and malnourished Africans had increased to 100 million, which represents almost one-fifth of the continent's population. Moreover, the population increase has put pressure on medical care, housing, and the overall infrastructure of the African countries. Infant mortality rates are much higher than those for other developing and developed countries, but the birth rates are the highest in the world. The average African woman has 6.9 children; the average American woman has 2.2 children; and the average West German woman has 1.9 children. Africa's total population will double in 24 years. Western Europe's will never double.

Their large populations create a burden for most African countries in terms of resource allocation. Most resources must be used for consumption. Incomes are low, so human and physical capital is less developed.[6] The population growth affects both the demand for and the supply of savings. Household savings—usually the largest component of domestic savings—is reduced by the high dependency burdens associated with rapid population growth. At any given level of per capita income, greater numbers of dependents cause consumption to rise, so savings per capita will fall. Governments can, within limits, use fiscal and monetary policies to change a country's rate of savings, irrespective of demographic conditions. However, the effectiveness of fiscal and monetary policies is predicated on the existence of a well developed system of public finance and banking, which most African countries do not have.

Table 19-2 presents population, birth and death rates, and population-doubling time for selected African countries, many of which can be expected to double their population in less than 25 years. The implication is clear, particularly from the standpoint of education. More school-age children require increased spending on education, even if the objective is just to maintain current enrollments and standards. In a world of rapid technological change, these countries need to improve their schools both quantitatively and qualitatively. They will have to generate more national savings, or curtail other investments in, for example, power and transport. But the latter are also an important part of a country's infrastructure and are necessary for economic development. If a country is unwilling or, more likely, unable to make these sacrifices, spending must be spread over a large group of school

---

[6] Human capital represents the skills that people use in combination with their labor effort. These skills are the result of education or training carried out some time in the past and used for future production. A long period of schooling lowers a society's quantity of labor resources, but the lost working time is offset by the greater productivity that results from the knowledge and skill gained from the education. Physical capital, such as factories and machines, makes it possible for countries to produce more efficiently than they can without them.

TABLE 19-2
Population Data for Selected African Countries, 1988

	Population (millions)	Birth Rate (per 1,000)	Death Rate (per 1,000)	Population-Doubling Time at Current Rates (in years)
Chad	4.8	43	23	35
Ethiopia	48.3	46	15	23
Mali	8.7	50	22	24
Zaire	33.3	45	15	23
Burkina Faso	8.5	48	19	24
Uganda	16.4	50	16	20
Tanzania	24.3	50	15	19
Niger	7.2	51	22	24
Madagascar	10.9	44	16	25
Ghana	14.4	42	11	22
Kenya	23.3	54	13	17
Sudan	24.0	45	16	24
Zambia	7.5	50	13	19
Egypt	53.3	38	9	24
Nigeria	111.9	46	17	24
Morocco	25.0	36	10	27
Cameroon	10.5	43	16	26
Ivory Coast	11.2	46	15	22
Algeria	24.2	42	10	22
South Africa	35.1	32	10	31
Africa	623.0	44	15	24
Developed Countries	1,174.0	15	9	120

Source: Mary M. Kent and Carl Haub, 1988 World Population Data Sheet *(Washington: Population Reference Bureau, 1988).*

children to the detriment of the quality of their education; otherwise, a growing number of children have to be excluded.

Political and Social Instability

Political and social instability create economic development problems for many of the African countries. In 1988 the Sudan was wracked by civil war and political discontent over the economic austerity measures of President Gaafar Nimeiri, who was eventually deposed. In South Africa, rioting by blacks over the government's apartheid policies is a daily occurrence. All too frequently, the African countries have become hostage to leaders intent solely on gaining and holding political power.[7] Vast amounts of money and resources are spent for these purposes.

[7] The most infamous leader was Idi Amin, who was dictator of Uganda and who practiced tribal genocide, systematically killing people who were members of tribes other than his own. He patterned himself after Adolph Hitler, whom he greatly admired.

In the past 25 years, more than 70 leaders in the African countries have been deposed by assassinations, purges, or military coups. Most African countries are run either by the military or by one political party that permits only token opposition. Zambia's President Kenneth Kaunda was the sole candidate in his nation's presidential election when he was elected to a fifth four-year term. In Nigeria, a military coup ousted President Alhaji Shehu Shagiri, who had been reelected to office in an election where candidates representing several political parties had participated. Genuine political democracy, with several competing political parties, exists in only a small number of African countries.

There are a number of factors that contribute to the political and social instability of Africa. Poverty is obviously a very important factor, and uncontrolled population growth is another. Corruption is another factor. Politicians and bureaucrats line their pockets at the expense of the public. Even in countries as poor as Chad, ownership of a Mercedes-Benz by government officials is very common.[8] As often as not, large amounts of foreign food, cash, and equipment aid never reach their intended destinations. Tribal conflicts are another major factor inhibiting political stability. In all but a handful of African countries, tribal loyalties still predominate, especially in rural areas where nationalist sentiment has not penetrated.[9] Savage warfare between tribes is common. The bloodiest war in postcolonial Africa was fought in Nigeria from 1967 to 1970, when the predominantly Ibo region of southeastern Nigeria seceded and formed the independent state of Biafra. The civil war cost a million lives before Biafra was brought under control.

The Sudan is a microcosm of the problems of Africa. It is a poor country with few natural resources. Its birth rate is high, and it can be expected to double its population in less than 25 years. In the spring of 1989, it was on the verge of internal collapse. Years of drought had reduced agricultural production below basic subsistence level. Food and other forms of aid have to be obtained from the United States. Its population, enlarged by refugees from Ethiopia, is on the edge of starvation. There was discontent in Khartoum, the capital city, over government austerity measures. Government officials rode around in high-priced limousines, while gas was rationed for ordinary citizens. There are conflicts between Christians and Moslems, and a civil war that is largely based on geographical and racial divisions threatens to pull the country apart.[10]

Foreign Trade

Foreign trade is a factor that works against economic development of many of the poor African countries in that their terms of trade is unfavorable. Nigeria is

---

[8] A Mercedes-Benz costs around $50,000. The per capita GNP of Chad is less than $100.

[9] Zaire has 200 tribes speaking some 75 languages, from the Pygmies to the Baluba. Tribal conflicts may be the reason for the emergence of one-party states in Africa. The ruling tribe simply exterminates other tribes.

[10] The government was overthrown by a military coup in 1989.

a case in point. In 1988, fuels, metals, and minerals accounted for 91 percent of Nigeria's merchandise trade exports. Oil, which is Nigeria's most important export, accounted for 70 percent of its export earnings in 1988. Conversely, machinery and other manufactured goods accounted for 86 percent of Nigeria's imports. Nigeria's terms of trade in 1988 was 54 percent. The price of oil in world markets fluctuates more rapidly than the world prices for machinery and manufactured goods. Table 19-3 presents the major categories of exports and imports and terms of trade for selected African countries expressed in percentages. For example, 79 percent of Sudan's total exports are agricultural products.

THE DEVELOPMENT OF NIGERIA

At the beginning of the twentieth century, Nigeria did not exist as a national entity, and it was notable in world commerce chiefly as a supplier of a few tropical products, such as palm oil and spices. During earlier centuries, its commercial history was very largely dominated by the slave trade. It became a formal British colony in 1860 and was recognized by other European powers as a British enclave at the Berlin Conference of 1885.

British colonial rule provided a mixed blessing for Nigeria. Its main direct contributions were building railroads and developing harbor facilities. Administra-

TABLE 19-3
Structure of Merchandise Exports and Imports and Terms of Trade for African Countries (percent)

	Exports Fuels, Minerals, and Agriculture	Imports Machinery and Manufacturing	Terms of Trade (percent)
Zaire	94	75	74
Burkina Faso	98	76	74
Uganda	96	84	67
Tanzania	82	75	90
Kenya	83	67	80
Sudan	93	58	84
Zambia	97	80	79
Rwanda	99	65	87
Nigeria	99	86	54
Ghana	97	73	83
Japan	2	39	153
United States	22	78	116

Source: The World Bank, World Development Report 1989, (New York: Oxford University Press, 1989), p. 190, p. 192, p. 194.

tive measures were also used to encourage and regulate the production of cotton and other crops for export.[11] Trade and banking were run by companies chartered in England. Barclay's Bank ran the banking system and the Royal Niger Company was responsible for the development of crops for export. Rules, attitudes, and monopolistic practices by the British colonial administration, churches, and firms excluded Nigerians from any participation in government and commerce.

The economic and social orientation of the British colonial government in Nigeria changed dramatically after World War II. It moved from maintaining the existing colonial economy to a new approach that allowed more Nigerian participation in the economy. Priority was placed on the development of industry and trade that would be run by Nigerians. An increasing degree of local self-government was embodied in successive constitutions of 1951, 1954, and 1957; by then, Nigerian control over the government apparatus was substantial. A colonial-nurtured capitalism developed, particularly in the areas of trade and light industry. The British–Nigerian colonial relationship came to mean planned economic development, the spread of industrialization, and better social services for the Nigerian people. England systematically extended the rights of self-government, so when Nigeria achieved its independence in 1960, it had a bureaucracy that had some experience with government and a small but expanding business class. The British had also spent money on developing agriculture and transportation systems and on extending medical and educational services.[12]

The Nigerian Economy

In 1988 Nigeria had a per capital GNP of $290, which was down from a per capita GNP of $380 in 1987 and from a high of $860 in 1981. It is the largest country in Africa, and its fertility rate of 6.4 percent is about average for the African countries.[13] The population-doubling time is 24 years, compared to the same average for all of African taken together. This can be compared to a population-doubling time of 398 years for Western Europe. Despite the fact that Nigeria is more industrialized than most of the African countries, more than two-thirds of the labor force is employed in agriculture. Agriculture accounted for 30 percent of gross domestic production in 1988, compared to 2 percent for the United States and West Germany.[14] In terms of value added by manufacturing, Nigeria ranked third among

---

[11] Gavin Williams, *Nigeria Economy and Society* (London: Rex Collings, 1976), pp. 18–19.

[12] It should be pointed out that the post–World War II England was far different from the England that was the dominant world power of the last century. Imperialism led to the development of the British empire. However, by the end of World War II, the empire was a thing of the past, and the colonies no longer served the purpose of providing markets and raw materials.

[13] Mary M. Kent and Carl Haub, *1988 World Population Data Sheet* (Washington, DC: Population Reference Bureau, 1988).

[14] The World Bank, *World Development Report 1989* (New York: Oxford University Press, 1989), pp. 168–169.

all African countries in 1987 behind Algeria and South Africa. It qualifies as a country in the lower stage of economic development.

Oil

Oil, especially in a developing country, can be a decisive factor in economic growth. It is an easily negotiable source of wealth for the producer, an efficient source of energy for the user, and a good base for industrialization because of the variety of products needed by the petrochemical industry. However, oil can be a mixed blessing. It fueled the prosperity of the Nigerian economy from 1965 to 1980, but it was also responsible for the economic slump during the 1980s. The worldwide oil glut of the 1980s had a disastrous effect on the Nigerian economy. Earnings from exports of Nigerian oil declined from a high of $26 billion in 1980 to $6.2 billion in 1988.[15] The spot price per barrel of Nigerian crude ranged from a high of $18.80 to a low of $13.70 during 1987 and 1988. As oil prices declined, the terms of trade became more unfavorable. Imports increased in price at the same time oil prices were falling. To illustrate the value of oil exports to the Nigerian economy, the GNP fell from $76 billion in 1980 to $31.8 in 1988.[16]

The Role of the Government

Nigeria is a federal republic consisting of 19 states. Although the states have a certain amount of autonomy, they receive most of their money from the federal government, which derives its revenue from taxes and oil exports. The most important taxes are a petroleum profits tax and excise taxes. A personal income tax is used, but the rate of avoidance is high.

There are three ways in which a government can intervene in a mixed economy. First, intervention can occur through fiscal and monetary policies. Second, there can be a more direct intervention through economic planning where government policies are designed to affect resource allocation and business conduct and performance. Third, there can be government ownership and control of the means of production. All are used by the Nigerian government, which plays a dominant role in the economic development of the country. It is the largest single employer, and it is the principal exporter and importer. It is responsible for the development of the national economic plans and the setting of planning priorities. It grants subsidies and makes loans to various sectors of the economy and implements foreign trade policy.

Fiscal and Monetary Policies. The fiscal policy of the Nigerian government is effected in two ways: through the national budget, which is projected to amount to

---

[15] Economic Intelligence Unit, *The Economist*, (Nigeria: Author, 1989–90), p. 26.
[16] The World Bank, *World Bank Atlas 1989* (New York: Oxford University Press, 1989), p. 8.

$16 billion in 1988, and oil revenues, which amounted to $6.2 billion in the same year. The combined oil and tax revenues amounted to approximately one-third of the gross national product of Nigeria for 1988. Essentially, fiscal policy is used by the government to alter the level of aggregate demand either directly by changing the level of its own expenditures or indirectly by changing tax rates.

Fiscal policy is also used to stimulate economic development. Funds from the national budget are channeled into various development funds used to finance capital expenditures. Special tax breaks are used to stimulate the private sector of the economy. The government has also used deficit financing to increase the rate of capital formation. However, the use of deficit financing has proved to be at best a mixed blessing. The proceeds have been spent to finance projects that were often never completed and that have provided little or no value to the Nigerian economy. Deficit spending has also contributed to the rate of inflation.

The state-owned Central Bank of Nigeria is responsible for the implementation of monetary policy. It conducts monetary policy through the traditional techniques available to all central banks—rediscounting, control over legal reserve requirements or bank liquidity ratios, and selective credit controls. The commercial banks of Nigeria are both publicly and privately owned; the Nigerian government owns about 60 percent, and foreign or local banks, the remainder. The majority of the merchant banks that provide wholesale banking and equity investments are owned by the government; there are also state-owned development banks. Through the Central Bank, the government designates preferred sectors for resource allocation.

Monetary policy is set forth once a year as a part of overall government budget policy. The Central Bank of Nigeria implements this policy in several ways. First, it may grant assistance to the government to fulfill economic development goals by making credit available to finance government deficits. It has not only made credit available for financing government deficits, but has promoted a capital market through which funds are made available to finance government debt. Second, through the Nigerian banking system it promotes policies that increase the availability of credit for economic development. Third, the bank has control over the use of foreign exchange. It places a limit on the total amount of foreign exchange each commercial and merchant bank has to allocate among its customers. It also regulates the use of these currencies by mandating a certain percentage to specific functions. For example, in 1988, 60 percent of foreign exchange was allocated for imports of industrial raw materials.

Economic Planning. Economic planning represents an effort to facilitate the process of economic and social development through the creation of national goals and priorities. Financing for projects that have planning priority comes from the federal budget and from credit provided by the banking system. Some projects are financed by various international lending institutions, including the World Bank.

Since it became independent in 1960, Nigeria has formulated several economic plans, the last of which was the Fourth National Development Plan. The purpose of the plan was to provide a general guideline for Nigeria's economic and social priorities. The basic goals of the Fourth Plan were to develop Nigeria's physical and social structure and agricultural and industrial bases, so that the country would become less vulnerable to the fluctuations of the world oil market. Some 8,000 development projects were listed in the Plan, with an estimated investment of $125 billion during its duration. Most of these projects were cancelled in 1984 when the military government that deposed the civilian government of President Shagari in the 1983 military coup imposed austerity measures on the Nigerian economy.

A key policy in Nigerian economic planning has been import substitution. Manufactured goods constitute the main targets of Nigeria's import substitution policy. The policy has been implemented in three ways. First, Nigerian industries, including textiles, furniture, motor vehicles, glass products, and consumer appliances, are heavily protected by tariffs. Successive increases in tariffs have produced a sharp decline in the absolute level and in the rate of increase of imports of such goods. Second, these and other manufacturing industries have been favored by tax policies including accelerated depreciation and special relief from taxes for a period from three to five years depending upon the amount of local capital invested. Third, many businesses are exclusively reserved for Nigerians. This restricts the amount of foreign involvement in local activity.

Much of the growth in Nigerian manufacturing is a result of the planned policy of import substitution. However, the process of import substitution has not helped the foreign debt problem, because it has resulted in an increase in imports of raw materials.[17] To produce at home the goods previously imported, many of the basic raw materials that have not been available locally have had to be imported.

Government Ownership of Industry. Nigeria has basically a mixed economic system, with government ownership in certain areas of economic activity. Public utilities and transportation systems are owned and operated by the government. There is a state-owned National Oil Corporation, and the Nigerian government has joint ventures with American and British oil companies. Coal is produced by a government-run corporation. The banking system is for the most part owned and operated by the government, and foreign banks are required to have at least a 60 percent Nigerian government interest. Seaport facilities are owned by the government, as is the Nigerian National Shipping Lines, which has the carrying rights to at least 40 percent of the freight to and from Nigeria. Communications facilities, including television broadcasting, are owned by the government.[18] The state-owned Federal Radio Corporation is solely responsible for radio broadcasting

---

[17] A. Olaluku, *Structure of the Nigerian Economy* (New York: St. Martin's Press Inc., 1979), pp. 201–220.

[18] Each state government also has its own radio station, but is allowed to broadcast only within state boundaries and only in the local language. State governments also own and operate many forms of enterprises.

to all parts of Nigeria. Sixty percent of the Daily Times Group, the largest publishing house in Nigeria, is owned by the government, which also operates its own daily newspaper.

Private Enterprise

Economic activity in most sectors of the Nigerian economy is primarily the function of private enterprise. To some extent, British colonial rule facilitated the development of a local entrepreneurial class in Nigeria. The British financed the development of railroads and port facilities. They abolished the trading monopolies of coastal tribal kingdoms, internal tolls, and the arbitrary interference of African tribal rulers with the free conduct of commerce.[19] The British pound was introduced as the common medium of exchange. The increase in world demand for export crops in the early years of the twentieth century encouraged British firms to advance credit for the production of cash crops. This credit in turn facilitated the sale of imported goods. The expansion of export production and the increase in the money supply in the form of produce advances increased local opportunities in retailing and in handicraft and food production for the domestic market. The initial expansion of British colonial rule encouraged competition in the distributive trades.

In order to develop new export crops, traders and farmers adapted existing social institutions to regulate land ownership or use, mobilize savings and credit facilities, and recruit labor to clear, weed, plant, and harvest crops. The successful creation of export production by Nigerian traders and planters contrasted with the failure of British government and foreign company plantations. Thus, in Nigeria, colonialism enabled Africans to develop agricultural production and generally stimulated the domestic production of other goods.

British ownership and operation were limited primarily to railroad investments, banking, and mineral resources. A dual economy developed, with the Nigerians controlling farm production, trading, and small business enterprises. Nevertheless, the British controlled the economy, and Nigerian private enterprise was not allowed to compete with British commercial interests. British investments in railways led them to prevent the development of any form of local transportation system that might provide competition.

The economic orientation of British colonial rule changed after World War II from maintaining the dual colonial economy to increasing the extent of Nigerian participation in all sectors.[20] This goal was to be accomplished through government financial support of private enterprise, which the Nigerians themselves would run, but the British would control. However, increasing nationalism sharply increased the Nigerian desire for more participation and control in the development of the

[19] Williams, *Economy and Society*, pp. 13–18.
[20] Sayre P. Schatz, *Nigerian Capitalism* (Berkeley: University of California Press, 1977), pp. 4–7.

economy. Control by Nigerians over private enterprises increased. This participation was limited primarily to the trade and services sectors of the economy. Very few Nigerians possessed the expertise or the capital to own and manage a modern production enterprise. Publicly owned Nigerian corporations began a growing number of enterprises intended to be run as profitable business ventures. At the time of Nigerian independence in 1960, state capitalism existed side-by-side with private capitalism. Political abuses of the public corporations made them largely unsuccessful, and Nigeria relied increasingly on foreign-owned enterprises for the development of a modern economy.

Postcolonial Development. The private sector of Nigerian economy increased in importance during the period following independence. Gross private fixed investment increased from less than half of the total fixed investment in 1960 to 65 percent by 1975.[21] Most of this increase took the form of foreign direct investment. The reliance on private investment in general and foreign direct investment in particular has brought many government approaches and measures to stimulate private investment. The government has encouraged foreign and private domestic investment by offering financial incentives to invest in those sectors that contribute most to economic development.

The oil boom of the 1970s also contributed to the development of both public and private enterprise. Possession of oil reserves gave the government sufficient leverage over foreign oil companies to insist on joint sharing of oil revenues. In 1977, a decree was passed by the government transferring certain economic activities from public to private Nigerian ownership. Also, certain activities, mainly in small-scale industry, services, and retail trade, were reserved exclusively for Nigerian ownership.

Results of Private Enterprise. Nigerian entrepreneurs have established a large variety of very small enterprises. Such undertakings are easy to start, even by men and women with little education, training, or business experience, and barriers to entry are negligible. The technical knowledge is simple and many have acquired it as workers or apprentices in other small firms or through experience with large firms or in government. Capital requirements are usually minimal, and individual entrepreneurs can often operate with virtually no capital of their own, relying instead on advances from their suppliers. Requirements for skilled labor are usually negligible, and there is an abundance of semiskilled and unskilled labor. What all of this means is that there is a very large number of small enterprises in Nigeria producing and distributing in local markets. However, it is difficult for any of these enterprises to acquire the capital and technological know-how to make the transition to large-scale operations.

---

[21] Schatz, *Nigerian Capitalism*, pp. 20–27.

Performance of the Nigerian Economy

The performance of the Nigerian economy can be divided into two time periods—
from 1960 to 1980 and from 1980 to 1988. During the period 1960–1980 real per
capita GNP increased at a rate of 3.3 percent a year, a rate that was well above
average for all of the African countries.[22] There was a decline in the importance
of agriculture relative to other sectors of the economy and an increase in the
importance of manufacturing and trade. Agriculture accounted for 65 percent of
Nigerian GNP in 1960; by 1980 it contributed around 25 percent. Conversely,
manufacturing increased its share of GNP from 4.4 percent in 1960 to 9.0 percent in
1980.[23] However, the country's manufacturing activity, which consists essentially
of light consumer goods, is highly concentrated in a few largely urban centers,
such as Lagos, the nation's capital. The mineral extraction sector increased from
1 percent of GNP in 1960 to almost one-third by 1980, with virtually all of this
increase accounted for by the growth of oil production.

The Nigerian economy deteriorated during the 1980s. Real per capita GNP
declined at an average annual rate of −4.3 percent for the period 1980–1988, and
−3.6 percent for the period 1986–1988.[24] GNP fell from $77 billion in 1980 to
$32 billion in 1988.[25] This decline can be attributed to one factor—the drop in
the world price of oil from $40 a barrel in 1980 to $15 a barrel in 1988. This
drop had an adverse impact on Nigerian foreign trade, for exports of goods and
services declined from $28 billion in 1980 to $12 billion in 1988. Oil accounts
for around 70 percent of Nigerian exports. In spite of its attempts to modernize,
the Nigerian economy is still largely undeveloped and is subject to the vagaries
of the world market price of oil. The problems of Nigeria are similar to those of
Mexico—a large foreign debt, a rapidly increasing population, political corruption,
and inefficient agricultural production.[26]

Foreign Debt

The foreign debt of Nigeria at the end of 1988 was $32 billion, which was about
the size of its GNP and was almost three times the amount of export earnings for
the year. Debt problems are complicated by Nigeria's dependence on oil exports.
Oil revenues accounted for 86 percent of federal government revenues in 1988,
compared to 76 percent in 1987.[27] In 1988 Nigeria spent 60 percent of its foreign
exchange to pay the interest on the debt, and it has had to reschedule payments

[22] The World Bank, *World Bank Atlas 1985* (New York: Oxford University Press, 1985), p. 8.

[23] Central Bank of Nigeria, *Annual Report 1984*, p. 2.

[24] The World Bank, *World Bank Atlas 1989* (New York: Oxford University Press, 1989), p. 8.

[25] The World Bank, *World Debt Tables, 1988–1989* (New York: Oxford University Press, 1989), p. 88.

[26] Mexico has two important advantages over Nigeria—it has a more developed industrial base, and it has a closer proximity to a major world market, the United States.

[27] Economic Intelligence Unit, *The Economist*, p. 36.

on the principal. The debt was incurred on the assumption that oil revenues would continue to rise, thus facilitating its repayment. The loans were supposed to go to improve the infrastructure of the economy; unfortunately, much of the money was wasted on projects of little value or was siphoned off by politicians in the form of graft.

Table 19-4 presents the foreign debt of Nigeria in comparison to GNP and exports. The comparisons illustrate the problem that can occur in borrowing when the economy depends upon revenue based on the export of one major product. When oil prices were high in 1980, Nigerian foreign debt was 32 percent of exports and 9 percent of GNP. The debt itself was $9 billion and international reserves were $11 billion, which was more than the debt.[28] By 1988, international reserves were 5 percent of the debt, and to make matters worse, long-term debt increased from $5 billion in 1980 to $28 billion in 1988. The result of all of this debt was to increase the rate of inflation, decrease the real per capita GNP growth rate to an annual rate of negative 4.7 percent from 1980 to 1988, cause debt repayment problems, and make the government introduce a series of austerity measures in budgetary expenditures.

Population Growth

The economic development of any country depends on the quality and quantity of its human and capital resources. Rapid population growth in Nigeria has put a strain on agricultural resources. There have been reports of starvation in parts of the country. Population growth has caused deforestation, which has contributed to

TABLE 19-4
Nigerian Foreign Debt, Exports, and GNP 1980–1988 (Millions of Dollars)

	Foreign Debt	Exports	Debt/Exports	GNP	Debt/GNP
1980	$ 8.8	$27.7	31.9%	$99.5	8.9
1981	12.0	19.7	61.1	93.0	12.9
1982	12.8	12.9	99.1	91.7	13.9
1983	18.4	10.9	169.1	88.0	20.9
1984	18.4	12.4	148.5	90.9	20.2
1985	19.4	13.0	149.1	88.4	21.9
1986	23.5	7.0	338.4	40.0	50.9
1987	29.8	7.8	382.2	23.0	129.9
1988	31.9	12.5	261.1	32.1	99.9

Source: The World Bank, World Debt Tables, 1988–89 (New York: Oxford University Press, 1989), p. 88, 91.

---

[28] The World Bank, *World Debt Tables, 1988–1989*, pp. 88–92.

water pollution, and urbanization, which has contributed to air pollution, poverty, higher infant mortality, and social and political unrest. Rapid population growth has reduced the potential for saving and capital formation because production must go for consumption.

The population of Nigeria is growing rapidly due to a high fertility rate and a declining mortality rate.[29] The size and composition of the population is affected by several factors. First, given the high birth rate and declining mortality rate, it is young, with 49 percent of the population 15 years of age or younger. A young population tends to have an adverse effect on the size and productivity of the labor force. Also, population growth will increase as the female children reach childbearing age. Second, there is an enormous ethnic diversity. There are more than 250 ethnic groups with different languages and customs. Active tribal rivalries compound the problems of government. Third, the population is unequally distributed geographically. The areas of greatest population density are either the cities, which do not have an adequate infrastructure, or areas that are remote from transportation facilities. Fourth, more than half of the population is illiterate. Only 16 percent of the relevant age group is enrolled in secondary schools, and only 3 percent of the college age group is enrolled in college.

Corruption

Corruption, a fact of life in Nigeria, assumes many forms. There is the standard low-level bribe, called "dash" or "chai," which is payment rendered for services performed or anticipated. It may take the form of a package of razor blades, a case of Scotch, or a digital watch. Higher level bribes include payment of money or an expensive gift such as a car. State-owned corporations are often run by political hacks rather than trained civil servants and management experts. Public projects are often not completed because politicians and contractors have appropriated the funds.[30] The tax system of the country is so inefficient that much of the revenue potential is not realized because tax evasion is widespread and tax officials are often corrupt. Conspicuous consumption by public officials, which takes the form of expensive foreign automobiles or villas in exclusive residential areas, creates resentment on the part of the impoverished and is responsible for the periodic military takeovers of the government.

Corruption carries with it many costs. There are wasteful expenditures on projects that do not get built, or, if built, serve no particular purpose. Economic development is retarded because money is wasted on projects that have little pay-off. Bribery is an impediment to entrepreneurship because it diverts energy from the pursuit of excellence in economic performance into political performance and

---

[29] The population of Nigeria was 112 million in 1988.

[30] Olaluku, *Structure*, pp. 166–167.

cultivation of the right contacts. Citizens will have little incentive to work or save when they see the pay-off to corruption. Educated young people will leave at their first opportunity. When government projects are so mishandled that it is necessary to terminate them, then all or virtually all of the costs of the equipment and structures are expenses of corruption. Even attempts to avoid political corruption may affect the composition of expenditures by causing the government to avoid worthwhile projects that are prone to political abuse.

Political Instability

Nigeria has been ruled by military governments for most of the time since it gained its formal independence from England in 1960. A relatively stable civilian government ruled Nigeria from 1960 to 1966, when it was overthrown by a military coup. A second military coup later in the same year led to an attempted secession by the eastern part of the country under the name of Biafra and resulted in two and a half years of civil war between 1967 and 1970. The civil war also split the population along tribal lines, with the Ibo tribe seceding from the rest of Nigeria. The civil war cost at least one million lives and huge amounts of badly needed resources before Biafra was brought back under Nigerian control.

In 1975 another military coup overthrew the previous military government of General Yakubu Gowan. Nigeria was then organized into 19 states, largely on the basis of tribal lines. After 13 years of military rule, free elections were held in 1979 and Alhaji Shagari was elected president. He was reelected in 1983, but was deposed by another military coup at the end of the year. The military is still in power.

Political instability in Nigeria has been caused by a number of factors, not the least of which is very limited experience with democracy. Nigeria is an amalgam of 250 tribal and religious groups, each of which wants to preserve some degree of autonomy.[31] When free elections are held, political support is usually based on regional and tribal identity. It is difficult to reconcile the differences of competing groups. Corruption is a second factor that contributes to political instability. Fueled by money from the oil boom, corruption became more blatant in the late 1970s and early 1980s and contributed to the overthrow of the Shagari government. Unemployment and high inflation also led to political instability in an impoverished nation. The decline of world oil prices and a rising foreign debt created a period of readjustment in the middle 1980s. Prices and unemployment increased at the same time oil revenues decreased. The decline in oil revenues made it more difficult to import both consumer and industrial goods, and shortages of each caused prices of some goods to rise as much as 200 percent in 1988.

---

[31] Reuters, the British news agency, announced that 100 Nigerians were killed in a conflict between Christians and Moslems in April, 1985.

Agriculture

Despite Nigeria's oil wealth and increasing industrial base, agriculture is still the mainstay of the economy, with more than half of the labor force employed in this sector. There is considerable underutilization of labor, given the seasonal nature of agricultural activity. The performance of the agricultural sector has been poor in part because it has been neglected as emphasis was placed on the development of industry. The land tenure system also inhibits the development of agriculture. Control over land is vested in clans, villages, and communities. Farmers work the land as tenants and pay a portion of what they produce to the village or clan. There is little incentive to invest in land and equipment.

Agricultural output actually declined during most of the 1970s. The decline occurred despite an increase in the population and cultivation of large tracts of land that were in the area previously affected by the civil war. A drought in the early 1980s also had an adverse effect on agricultural production, with famine in several regions of the country. The drought also affected the export of cocoa, Nigeria's leading agricultural export.

Poverty

It must be remembered that Nigeria is an underdeveloped country. Its per capital GNP of $290 in 1988, while about average for Africa, is low when compared to the incomes of the developed countries. Moreover, the per capita GNP has shown a decline of $400 for the period 1983–1988 as income from oil exports has declined. Poverty and unemployment have been exacerbated by the decline in oil earnings and by drought, which has affected food production in part of the country. What Nigeria seems to have achieved, particularly during the period when world oil prices were high, was a rapid rate of economic growth accompanied by little internal economic development. There is a growing pattern of unequal income and wealth distribution between rich and poor, between urban and rural areas, and between the employed and unemployed.[32] The great majority of agricultural workers receive an income that is less than one-eighth of the national average, which has engendered unrest in rural areas. The use of government power by politicians for self-enrichment contrasts with widespread poverty and encourages social unrest.

The Structural Adjustment Program

The Nigerian economy developed serious problems by the middle of the 1980s. The real rate of economic growth was negative and there was a decline in per capita GNP. Oil prices continued to fall, exposing the dependence of the Nigerian economy on oil exports. There was a large deficit in the merchandise trade account,

---

[32] William Zartman, *The Political Economy of Nigeria* (New York: Praeger Publishers, 1983).

and foreign investment in Nigeria declined. The country had a problem in meeting its external debt payments, and internally a fiscal deficit that amounted to 12 percent of GNP increased the rate of inflation, which reached 40 percent in 1984. In 1986 the government announced a development plan that would reduce the country's dependence on oil export revenues, achieve a balance of payments equilibrium, and produce noninflationary growth for the economy.

The Structural Development Program placed reliance on market forces instead of government fiat to determine exchange rates. This resulted in the depreciation of the *naira* by 67 percent.[33] The purpose was to stimulate Nigerian exports. The government also abolished import licensing and exchange controls, and allowed non-oil exporters to retain 100 percent of their foreign exchange earnings.[34] The government also reduced many of the barriers to foreign investment in Nigeria by abolishing import controls and permitting the remission of profit and dividends. Subsidies were reduced for many industries to make them more competitive and to reduce the deficit in the national budget. But the greatest emphasis has been placed on reforming agriculture. Two thirds of Nigeria's population work in agriculture, the production of which has to be increased to support the growing population. Priority is given to improving the rural infrastructure and providing farm extension services.

SUMMARY

Nigeria is the largest country in Africa in terms of population and is also one of its wealthier countries. It was a British possession from 1868 until 1960, when it became an independent country. The economy can be considered underdeveloped, with a majority of Nigerians still employed in agriculture and an industrial base concentrated in a few relatively large urban centers. Manufacturing is a rather small source of employment, accounting for around 10 percent of total employment in the country. The oil sector has been the main source of the rapid growth of the country's economy over the last 10 to 15 years. Revenues from oil exports have been used to finance the economic development of the country. However, dependence on oil exports has put Nigeria into a precarious economic position. As the world price for oil has declined, revenue from oil exports and per capita GNP have also declined. Nigeria is in the same position as Mexico in that it has a large foreign debt and declining earnings from oil exports. However, Nigeria is less developed than Mexico and lacks the internal industrial base that Mexico has developed over time.

Nigeria has a mixed economy, with the private sector providing the bulk of capital formation. Economic activity in the directly productive sectors of the

---

[33] The naira is worth $.20.

[34] Nigeria's approach to improving productivity and economic development is similar to Mexico's. There is more reliance on the free market and privatization.

economy is primarily through private enterprise. Government investment and ownership is concentrated mainly in the infrastructure of the economy. Nevertheless, the role of government in the economy is important and extensive. It provides much of the savings in the economy, which is channeled into various sectors through state-owned lending institutions. Economic planning is also used by the government to establish priorities in resource allocation. The plans have generally stressed the development of industry, while neglecting agriculture. They have been interrupted by periodic military coups, the last of which occurred in December, 1983. The role of the national government in the Nigerian economy is made very complex by the regional factionalism of the country, which is based on tribal and religious loyalties. Corruption is also an inhibiting factor in the development of the economy.

REVIEW QUESTIONS

1. What was the impact of British colonialism on the development of the Nigerian economy?
2. What role does private enterprise play in Nigeria?
3. Discuss the influence of oil on the Nigerian economy.
4. The economic and social problems of Nigeria are common to the great majority of African countries. Discuss.
5. What are some of the problems of economic and social development in Nigeria?
6. Why has democracy failed to take hold in Nigeria and other African countries?
7. Discuss the impact of Nigeria's foreign debt on its economy.
8. Compare the Nigerian economy to the economies of Mexico and China.

RECOMMENDED READINGS

Balakkins, Nicholas. *Indigenization and Economic Development: The Nigerian Experience*. Greenwich, CT: JAI Press, 1982.

Collier, Paul. "Oil Shocks and Food Security in Nigeria." *International Labor Review*, Vol. 127, No. 6 (1988), pp. 761–782.

"Nigeria: A Time of Pride and Pessimism." *The Economist*, January 7, 1989, p. 36.

Okwudibu, Nnoli, ed. *Path to Nigerian Development*. Westport, CT: L. Hall, 1981.

Pinto, Brian. "Nigeria During and After the Oil Boom: A Policy Comparison with Indonesia." *World Bank Economic Review*, Vol. 1 (May 1987), pp. 419–445.

Schatz, Sayre P. *Nigerian Capitalism*. Berkeley: University of California Press, 1977.

The World Bank. *Africa's Adjustment and Growth in the 1980's*. New York: Oxford University Press, 1989.

———. World Development Report 1989. New York: Oxford University Press, 1989.

Zartman, William. *The Political Economy of Nigeria*. New York: Praeger Publishers, 1983.

CONCLUSION AND EVALUATION

20
ECONOMIC SYSTEMS: WHERE TO GO
FROM HERE?

PART SIX

CHAPTER TWENTY

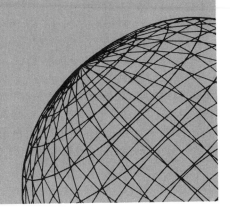

"SEVENTY-TWO YEARS ON THE ROAD TO NOWHERE"[1]

Many dramatic changes have taken place in the world since the fourth edition of this textbook was published in 1987, the most dramatic of which has happened in the Soviet Union and Eastern Europe; free elections were held in Poland in 1989; and for the first time in 40 years, a non-Communist was chosen to lead the government. Hungary formally changed its name to the Republic of Hungary, the Communist Party was dissolved and renamed the Hungarian Socialist Party, and free elections were held in the spring of 1990. In Romania, the dictator Ceausescu was deposed and executed, and free elections were held in June 1990. Bulgaria has also deposed its communist leaders and has scheduled free elections for late summer 1990. The Soviet Union has been experimenting with numerous economic and political reforms in order to improve the efficiency of its economy. It is a country in crisis, where there is a bankruptcy of ideology and a mismatch between visions of what might be and the realities of institutionalized rigidity and societal backwardness.

However, the greatest change has taken place in East Germany and Czechoslovakia, the former showcases for communism. In the summer and fall of 1989, hundreds of thousands of East Germans left East Germany for West Germany, prompting a shakeup in the government. The Berlin Wall, the dividing line between East and West Berlin since 1961, came down and the Brandenburg Gate was reopened. Free elections

---

[1] Sign carried by a counterdemonstrator at ceremonies in Moscow marking the 72nd anniversary of the Bolshevik Revolution of 1917.

were held in April 1990, and a coalition of conservative parties finished first. German reunification will probably be a fait accompli by the end of 1990. The Eastern Europe domino effect also spread to Czechoslovakia, where political repression outweighed the benefits of a relatively high standard of living. Communist Party hard-liners who had ruled Czechoslovakia since the "Prague Spring" of 1968 were ousted, the party itself lost its credibility, and Vaclav Havel, the Czech playwright and political dissident who had spent time in prison for criticizing the state, was named president of Czechoslovakia.[2]

Rapid change has not been limited to just the communist countries. In 1992, 12 Western European countries will form the European Community and will literally become the United States of Europe—with a population, gross national product, and living standards equal to the United States. Its goal is to create a single unified market for its members. With harmonized regulation, there will be free movement of capital, goods, labor, and services across country boundaries. The driving force behind the formation of the European Community is a desire to encourage economic expansion in a region that has been stagnating during the 1980s with low growth, high inflation, and high unemployment. Western Europe has felt that it is being left behind by the United States and Japan, so radical action has to be taken to reverse this trend.

Japan has become a major economic superpower and rival to the United States. However, Japan is only a part of a group of East Asian nations that may well make the 21st century the East Asian century. It is the East Asian countries that are providing the most economic competition for the United States. The United States does more business with East Asia than it does with Western Europe. Almost half of U.S. merchandise imports come from the East Asian countries compared to less than one-fourth for Western Europe.[3] More than half of the U.S. merchandise trade deficit, which was $108 billion in 1989, was with Japan and Taiwan. The growth rates of the East Asian countries are the highest in the world, and Japan is now the wealthiest country in the world.

The world economic system has become increasingly interdependent and increasingly vulnerable; it is also increasingly multipolar and less hegemonic. So instead of comparing "isms" because there may be no "isms" to compare in the future, economic comparisons may be between the United States, the European Community, and East Asia, while the Soviet Union and Eastern Europe hunt for solutions to their economic and political problems. It is the same planet, but an entirely different world from that which existed 20 years ago. Technology has come to transcend the role of state. Particularly important have been technical innovations that drastically reduced cost and increased the mobility of capital, people, and

---

[2] Free elections are scheduled to be held in Czechoslovakia in the late summer or early fall of 1990.

[3] U.S. imports from East Asia amounted to $177.9 billion in 1989. Of that amount, $93.6 billion was from Japan. Imports from Western Europe amounted to $86.2 billion.

information across national borders. Nevertheless, the problem of world poverty looms larger than ever. The poor are still very poor, and because of population growth, there are more of them.

PROBLEMS FACING COMMUNISM

Communism became the most compelling economic and political doctrine of this century. When the century began, there were no communist countries. Democracy was ascendant and the world was prosperous and at peace. Science was regarded as the panacea that would uplift the lives of the masses. World War I brought about the collapse of the existing order, and the Bolshevik Revolution of 1917 introduced the communist state into Russia. The depression of the 1930s convinced many persons that capitalism was collapsing and that communism was the wave of the future. After World War II, Eastern Europe was partitioned off by the Allies and became a part of the Communist bloc dominated by the Soviet Union. In 1949 China fell to the Chinese communists, and for many years the world was split into two competing ideologies, Capitalism and Communism, and, at least for awhile, it appeared that Communism would be ascendant.

In 1958 Nikita Khrushchev boasted in public that the Soviet Union would "bury" America in economic competition. He was to repeat that boast on numerous occasions, even going as far to say that he Soviet Union would surpass the United States in per capita production by 1970 and in total GNP by 1980. He had much to back up his assertions. The economic performance of the Soviet Union was superior to that of the United States during the 1950s. By 1970, the Soviet economy had actually increased to more than half the size of that for the United States. The performance of the Eastern European countries was equally good. The first decade of Communist rule in Eastern Europe was marked by rapid industrial development and social improvement. Economic growth continued during the 1960s and 1970s. Despite periods of ideological turmoil, the Chinese economy also did well in terms of economic growth.

However, economic performance was only a facade for what was really happening in the Soviet Union and Eastern Europe. Industrial goods were often of poor quality and were uncompetitive in world markets. An overemphasis on industrialization did not do consumers much good. Consumer goods were often in short supply and waiting in line was and still is common. Living standards, although increasing, were falling further behind those in the Western countries. New technology, particularly in the areas of computers and industrial robots, exploded in the Western countries during the 1970s and 1980s, leaving the Soviet Union and Eastern Europe technologically far behind. The position of the Soviet Union as the second largest economic power in the world is changing, with Japan catching up to and eventually surpassing it, and the formation of twelve Western European countries into a new Economic Community in 1992 will create an economic bloc far larger than that of the Soviet Union and Eastern Europe.

Economic Change

The 1980s was a decade of dramatic change in the world that has broken down barriers between countries and has made political ideologies seem obsolete. Broadly speaking, two major developments have changed the nature of the world economy. The first is technological: the explosive advances in the speed and effectiveness of international communication and transportation. The second is economic: the reduction or dismantlement of national barriers to the international movement of goods, services, technology, and capital. Consider the following:[4]

1. There has developed a global market for goods and services, which implies a closer integration of the world economy.
2. Technology has been internationalized through technology transfer, the cross-border education of students, including those from communist countries. Modern technology has no distinctive nationality and crosses all boundaries.
3. Production has been internationalized, which has created two important dimensions. The first is direct investment in foreign affiliates by global corporations, and the second is sourcing in other countries for individual processes and components within a chain of production.
4. Globalization of financial markets has changed the world economy. More than $300 billion a day is transferred between financial institutions in various countries. The pool of savings is worldwide today and knows no international boundaries.

In 1947 Winston Churchill spoke of an "iron curtain" that separated communism in Eastern Europe from capitalism in Western Europe, with each side free to develop its own ideology and identity within its own sphere of influence. However, the world has changed dramatically from the past, and ideologies developed in a prior time period can become obsolete in a rapidly changing world. Any country that remains locked in an ideological mindset risks being left behind because of rapid technological change. The Soviet Union and other communist countries are well aware of the fact that they are lagging behind the West in technology and will have to import it from the West in order not to lag further behind. This will lead inevitably to the breaking down of national barriers and the revision of an ideology to make it more consistent with reality.

Decline of Communism as a Development Model

Communism has lost its vogue in most of the world, and many countries are either trying to reform it or abandon it completely. China has tried to postpone

---

[4] William J. Beeman and Isaiah Frank, *New Dynamics in the Global Economy* (New York: Committee for Economic Development, 1988).

inevitable change by massacring student demonstrators who were for democratic change, but by doing so, China has probably set back its economic development for some time. But more than anything else, the spectacle of hundreds of thousands of East Germans swarming across the border to West Germany is proof positive that communism has failed to deliver a better economic society. Even though East Germany had by far and away the highest living standard of all communist countries, the quality and abundance of its goods paled into insignificance when compared to the cornucopia that the East Germans saw for the first time in the shopping centers of West Berlin.[5] Even East Germany is no longer a viable role model for communism.

The twentieth century has witnessed the beginning of communism and may also witness its demise. It was a compelling doctrine based on the reality of a class struggle and the anticipation of a state of social bliss that would be achieved by a communist society. It appealed to intellectuals and to the downtrodden masses of the world. To the former, it had appeal as a philosophy and as a science; to the latter, it provided justification for class hatred. However, no Communist regime ever came to power with the freely expressed will of the people, and communism's historical cost has been high relative to the economic and social gains it is supposed to bestow on the people. Living standards are far behind those of the West and continue to decline. Yet millions of people have sacrificed their lives in the process of communist societal transformation. It has been estimated that some 20 million people were killed in the Soviet Union during Stalin's regime. There has been the destruction of talent and the suppression of creativity, high human costs for the economic gains actually achieved.

The Soviet economy, which has served as the role model for the communist world, is moribund. Perestroika has been plagued by irrational pricing, overcentralized bureaucracy, and antiquated equipment. Its manufacturing exports are not competitive; like many Third World countries, the Soviet Union depends on the export of raw materials to earn income. The deficit in the 1989 budget is estimated at 200 billion rubles, and the growth in real GNP is estimated at less than 1 percent. The government has financed its deficit by printing billions of rubles. In an economy where prices are fixed, too much money chasing too few goods has created shortages. Agriculture is inefficient. Twenty-five percent of the Soviet labor force is in agriculture compared to less than 3 percent in the United States, but the Soviet Union averages a little more than half the per-acre output of the United States. Despite increased investments in agriculture, Soviet farmers cannot produce enough food to feed the nation.

---

[5] Free access to West Berlin by East Germans was permitted on November 11, 1989. Much of the world watched on television the carnival atmosphere created when hundreds of thousands of East Germans converged on West Berlin. West German banks provided each East German with 100 marks ($55) spending money, since the East German mark was inconvertible into West German marks. The East Germans were overwhelmed by the abundance of goods that were available in the West Berlin stores.

ECONOMIC REFORM
IN EASTERN EUROPE

The road toward economic reform in Eastern Europe will not be easy, for there are many problems. Overall economic growth is likely to continue to decline in the immediate future, and performance will be poorest in Hungary and Poland, the two countries that have pushed reforms the hardest. Productivity has declined, heavy industries are obsolete, foreign debt has increased, exports have become more noncompetitive, the infrastructure is decaying, and environmental problems are among the worst in the world. The rate of unemployment is expected to increase as inefficient and obsolete industries are shut down. The unemployment rate in Poland is increasing and is projected to be around 10 percent of the labor force by the end of 1990. The unemployment rate in East Germany is estimated to rise to 15 to 20 percent of the labor force by 1991. Price rises and falling wages could cause considerable social unrest. Also, as the East European countries declare their economic independence from the Soviet Union, they lose the benefits of oil, coal, and raw materials sold at exceedingly low prices.

Table 20-1 presents the performance of the East European countries as measured by the average annual growth of GNP for specific time periods. The record of economic growth during the 1970s was reasonably good and was facilitated by several factors. One was the ability to divert resources for investment in heavy industries without having to worry much about competing consumer demand.[6] A second was increasing supplies of Soviet raw materials at low prices, and a third was a growing and guaranteed Soviet market for industrial and consumer goods. The economies of the Eastern European countries turned sour during the 1980s,

TABLE 20-1

Average Annual Rate of Economic Growth in Eastern Europe (percent)

	1971–1975	1976–1980	1981–1985	1986–1988	1989	1990–1991
Bulgaria	7.5	1.0	0.9	1.6	−0.3	−2.5
Czechoslovakia	4.7	2.2	1.7	1.7	1.0	2.0
East Germany	3.1	2.3	1.9	1.4	1.2	0.4
Hungary	3.3	2.0	0.7	1.6	−1.3	−0.5
Poland	6.5	0.7	0.7	0.8	−1.6	−3.0
Romania	6.8	1.3	1.0	1.5	−1.5	−2.0

Source: Central Intelligence Agency. Eastern Europe: Long Road Ahead to Economic Well-Being, *paper presented to the Subcommittee on Technology and National Security, Joint Economic Committee, Congress of the United States, May 16, 1990, p. 1.*

---

[6] Central Intelligence Agency, *Eastern Europe: Long Road Ahead to Economic Well-Being,* paper presented to the Subcommittee on Technology and National Security, Joint Economic Committee, Congress of the United States, May 16, 1990, pp. 1–5.

with four of the six countries showing a negative growth rate. Hard currency debt to the West increased as consumer shortages developed and imports from the West increased. A further decline in the growth rates of the countries is projected for the period 1990–1991.

Problems of Reform

There is no economic blueprint to tell the Eastern European countries how to go from a centrally planned economy to a market economy. Isolated and inconsistent reforms to attack the vast and interrelated economic problems that affect their economies, where bureaucrats have determined production levels under central economic planning, must give way to learning how to compete in a global market economy. The experiences of the Soviet Union and Eastern Europe suggest that a major threshold of political change is necessary before major economic reforms can occur. Despite real progress in moving the Eastern European economies toward a market economy, there are many obstacles left before they can be viable. They must recover from four decades of economic mismanagement and change deeply rooted patterns of economic behavior, and they must learn the institutions, legal framework, and business practices that support a market system.

Privatization. For 40 years wealth, as represented by land and capital, was owned by the state, supposedly in the interest of the people. Now state farms, collective farms, industrial firms, and real estate are supposed to revert to private ownership. The East German government has agreed to privatize some 10,000 firms that were confiscated by the state during 40 years of communist rule.[7] There is also the problem of what to do with the giant industrial combines that dominate East German industry. In Poland most of the state and collective farms are to broken up and sold. Hungary allows private and foreign ownership rights, permits private firms to hire up to 500 workers, and has established markets for stocks and bonds. However, some concern has been expressed over privatization. East Germans and Poles claim that the main beneficiaries of privatization are members of the old *nomenklatura* system, the party elites who are able to buy state assets cheaply and then convert them into private property.

Income Distribution. Excluding the nomenklatura elite, incomes were more evenly distributed in the communist countries than in the Western capitalist countries. Moreover, deprivation was commonly shared. Most people had to wait years to buy a car or get an apartment, and most people had the experience of queuing up in lines to buy scarce consumer goods. Food and basic necessities were subsidized by the state. With the privatization of property and a commitment to a free market

---

[7] Some 50,000 West Germans have put in claims for their former houses that were appropriated by the communists.

system, inequality in the distribution of income and wealth is bound to increase in Eastern Europe. Income from the use of property will increase. It remains to be seen whether increased income disparity will cause social discontent. Sweden and other Scandinavian countries may serve as role models of capitalism combined with welfare statism.

Pricing. In the Eastern European countries, food and other basic necessities were subsidized by the state at prices well below their costs of production. These subsidies amounted to at least one-fourth of state budget expenditures and were becoming a larger financial burden. There have been many attempts at price reforms, usually with disastrous results. An economic system must be reasonably consistent in order to be effective. In a free market economy, prices are influenced by the market mechanism of supply and demand, not by the arbitrary decisions of state planners. The problem facing the Eastern European countries is how fast to proceed with price reforms. With a conversion to market economy, prices will inevitably rise to reflect supply and demand. Poland has decontrolled prices for most goods and services, and at the same time reduced the level of wage indexation. The result, at least in the spring of 1990, was a marked increase in the supply of consumer goods and a reduction in income to buy them.[8]

Foreign Trade. International trade has become the locomotive for economic development to many countries. Japan and South Korea are cases in point. The Soviet Union and Eastern Europe are falling far behind the developed countries and many of the developing countries in both consumer and industrial technology. There is a need to be more closely integrated into world markets and to earn hard currency in order to reduce foreign debt. There is also a need for Eastern Europe to cast off economic dependency on the Soviet Union. Trade with the Soviet Union usually involved barter swaps of high-value East European manufactured goods for low-value Soviet raw materials priced in artificial transferable rubles. In order to end their isolation from the world economy, the Eastern European countries and the Soviet Union have to reduce mutual trade dependence and reliance on CEMA trade mechanisms to stimulate trade.

Joint Ventures. Joint ventures are regarded by the Eastern European countries as an excellent way to acquire Western goods and technology essential to modernization without having to add to their foreign debts. Joint ventures will help them earn hard currency through exports to Western countries and also acquire Western inputs of marketing and technology. Most joint ventures that have been concluded so far have been with Hungary and Poland, which have liberalized their laws to the extent that they permit majority ownership. The majority of joint ventures are with West Germany and Austria. However, what may very well happen as privatization of

---

[8] It has been the other way around for years.

Eastern European state enterprises occurs is that Western firms will acquire them directly.

Legal System. One thing that has to be done as the Eastern European countries convert into free market economies is that the legal system will have to be changed. One example is contract law. In a centrally planned economy there is no need for contract law because the relationship is between the state and the buyer or seller based on economic planning directives. As the countries move from planned economies to market economies, however, producers are going to obtain inputs and distribute outputs on the basis of contractual agreements with suppliers and customers. A second type of law that will have to be implemented will be anti-monopoly, or antitrust, law that will apply to price fixing and acquisitions. A third area of law is bankruptcy law. State-owned enterprises in a planned economy are immune from bankruptcy laws, but this will change with privatization.

Banking. Banking activities are circumscribed in a planned economy, with all power residing in the state, or central, bank. The central bank is a vital cog in the implementation of economic plans. It is responsible for the cash and credit plans, and it holds the accounts of state enterprises. There are also specialized state banks responsible for financing foreign trade or agriculture. The role of banking will change as the East European countries convert to a market economy. In East Germany, a new central bank that is independent from state control and commercial banks that will provide credit to firms and individuals based on risk and credit rating may have to be created.[9] Western-style banking systems with a central bank and commercial banks have already been introduced in Hungary and Poland.

The Sinatra Doctrine

The American singer, Frank Sinatra, has sung popular songs for many years, but one song that will always be associated with him is "My Way." To paraphrase the words of the song, "he did everything his way and never settled for anything second best." The "Sinatra Doctrine" is a term now being applied to Soviet policy toward Eastern Europe. It supersedes the Brezhnev Doctrine, which held that the Soviet Union would fight to keep its Eastern European satellites within its sphere of influence. This doctrine was enforced when Brezhnev sent tanks into Prague in 1968 to suppress reforms. Now the Soviet Union has turned its former satellites loose to "do it their way," and that is what the East European countries are doing. It won't be easy, for there are many problems: an inadequate infrastructure; an obsolete, uncompetitive, and energy-intensive industrial base; a neglected agricultural sector;

---

[9] The West German central bank, the Bundesbank, will have formal power in synchronizing monetary and fiscal policies when the two countries unite. The East German state bank will be absorbed by the Bundesbank. West German commercial banks will dominate East Germany by establishing subsidiaries.

massive environmental problems; and four decades of economic mismanagement and distorted economic incentives.

Czechoslovakia and East Germany, of the six countries that have broken from communist rule, have the greatest chance of economic success. Czechoslovakia had one of the highest living standards in Europe before World War II as well as an industrial base and an entrepreneurial class. East Germany has been reunited with West Germany, and the short-term transition will be difficult. Poland and Hungary have had free elections, with a new form of government, but face the prospect of a prolonged recession and declining living standards, at least in the short run. Romania has been slow to implement reforms, and free elections were held in May 1990. In Bulgaria, a Communist reform government has tentatively moved toward implementing market reforms. The constitution has been amended to legalize private property.

COMPARISONS WITH THE WEST

By any measure of economic performance, the centrally planned economies are falling further behind the market economies of the West. They have suffered from slow global economic growth, which has contributed to weak demand for their exports. Central planning has provided inadequate incentives for innovation, is accompanied by low levels of productivity, encourages inefficiency, and results in low living standards. Declining competitiveness has resulted in the loss of world market shares to the newly industrialized countries. High levels of defense spending have diverted resources away from investments that could aid economic development. Standards of living, as measured by consumption, per capita income, and life expectancy, have stagnated or fallen. There has been neglect of essential infrastructure investments, especially the development and maintenance of rail transport and other distribution facilities.

Table 20-2 presents a comparison of the economic performance of the major market and centrally planned economies for several time periods. The performance of the United States was better than that for the Soviet Union for all three time periods, but it was significantly better during the period from 1984 through 1989. The comparison does not reflect factors such as environmental pollution, which is worse in the centrally planned economies than it is in the market economies; declining living standards and health problems, which have worsened during the 1980s in the centrally planned economies; or an overall neglect of agriculture in favor of heavy industry.

Table 20-3 presents estimates of total factor productivity growth in agriculture for the time period 1960–1980 for the United States, the Soviet Union, and Eastern Europe. As the table indicates, Soviet agricultural growth and the growth of most of the Eastern European countries has been negative. The evidence shows that they have a tendency to move out along a given production function by adding more and more resources rather than shifting the production function out over time by

TABLE 20-2
Real Per Capita Growth in GNP Average Annual Rate of Growth (percent)

	1976–1980	1981–1985	1984	1985	1986	1987	1988	1989
Market Economies								
United States	2.2	2.0	6.0	2.1	2.0	1.9	3.8	3.0
Canada	2.7	1.7	5.3	3.3	2.0	2.7	4.1	2.8
Japan	4.0	3.2	4.3	3.9	1.9	3.6	5.4	4.8
France	2.8	1.0	0.9	1.3	1.8	1.5	2.8	3.4
Italy	3.5	1.7	3.2	2.5	2.5	2.9	3.1	3.3
United Kingdom	1.6	1.7	1.8	3.6	2.6	3.3	3.5	1.3
West Germany	3.4	1.4	3.2	2.9	2.4	1.7	2.9	4.3
Centrally Planned								
U.S.S.R.	1.4	0.9	0.5	−0.2	2.9	−0.5	2.0	0.9
Bulgaria	0.7	0.5	3.0	−3.6	4.8	0.6	1.9	−0.1
Czechoslovakia	1.5	0.9	2.1	0.5	1.8	1.1	2.3	1.0
East Germany	2.5	2.0	3.6	3.0	1.6	2.3	2.4	1.2
Hungary	1.7	0.8	2.8	−2.4	2.3	1.4	1.1	−1.3
Poland	9.9	−0.3	2.7	0.3	2.1	−3.1	−0.5	−1.6
Romania	3.0	1.4	5.6	0.8	5.3	2.7	3.2	1.5

Sources: Economic Report of the President, 1990 *(Washington: USAPO, 1990), p. 419; Central Intelligence Agency,* Eastern Europe: Long Road Ahead to Economic Well-Being, *paper presented to the Subcommittee on Technology and National Security, Joint Economic Committee, Congress of the United States, May 1990, p. 1, Central Intelligence Agency and the Defense Intelligence Agency,* The Soviet Economy Stumbles Badly in 1989, *paper presented to the Subcommittee on National Security and Technology, Joint Economic Committee, Congress of the United States, April 1990, p. 3.*

TABLE 20-3
Estimates of Factor Productivity in Agriculture
for the United States, Soviet Union, and Eastern
Europe

Country	Rate
United States	+ 1.69
Soviet Union	− 1.69
Hungary	− .19
Poland	− 3.35
Bulgaria	− .90
East Germany	+ .83
Czechoslovakia	+ .17
Romania	− 1.67

Source: Robert B. Koopman, Efficiency and Growth in Agriculture: A Comparative Study of the Soviet Union, United States, Canada, and Finland, *Economic Research Service, U.S. Department of Agriculture, October 1989, p.32.*

changing technology. This is logical for a planned economy, since planning is easier with known technology. The planning process, which is material balance planning, would eliminate the need to plan for innovations or to incorporate innovations not yet known into the plan. Thus, there is a built-in incentive not to innovate.

ONE WORLD OR SEVERAL?

A global economy exists in the world today and the United States is a part of it. There are several factors that have contributed to globalism. The first is that multinational corporations have expanded across national boundaries and have created a borderless world economy. A second factor is that advances in transportation and communications technologies have made information available rapidly and inexpensively worldwide, thus making closed national systems less tenable. Even the poorest countries are aware of what is going on in the world. A third factor is that world economic and financial markets have been increasingly integrated. For example, U.S. trade in goods and services as a percentage of GNP has more than doubled since 1970, and world trade has quadrupled while world output has tripled. Financial markets are even more open, with an estimated $300 billion crossing the world's financial exchanges every day. No one economic power has the luxury of making economic decisions in isolation. A fourth factor is that there has been a major dilution in the central role of a single country's acting as the world's economic leader.

A MULTIPOLAR WORLD ECONOMY

At the same time and as a counter to globalization, regionalism has increased. Three major world economic regions are in the process of developing. The first is the European Community of 1992, which may expand from its original 12 countries to include as many as 25 countries. The EC may include a common market of at least 300 million people and with a GNP comparable to that of the United States. The second is East Asia, with a population of 300 million, which includes Japan, South Korea, Taiwan, Singapore, Thailand, and Malaysia. The East Asian countries have the highest rates of economic growth of any region in the world. The third economic region consists of the United States, Canada, and perhaps Mexico, which would constitute the North American region. It, too, would have a population of around 300 to 400 million people. The three regions would include around one-fifth of the world's population, 90 percent of the world's GNP, and all of the developed countries.

This leaves out countries with four-fifths of the world's population and all of the poor countries of the world, including China and India.[10] Some of the countries are newly industrializing, including Brazil and Mexico, but most are not. There is a

---

[10] The World Bank, *World Bank Atlas 1989* (New York: Oxford University Press), pp. 6–9.

dual-track world economy, with the developed and the developing countries on the fast track and the poor and less developed countries on the slow track. The disparity between rich and poor countries in levels of income has been supplemented by the difference between dynamic and stagnant economies in rates of economic growth. Whether the poor countries, including most of the African countries, are irrevocably on the slow track remains to be seen. One issue facing the world in the 1990s is how to increase capital flows to the poor and less developed countries to expand their export trade. Can economic growth, technological development, and social progress spread from countries on the fast tract to countries on the slow track so that the latter have any chance of catching up?

THE EUROPEAN COMMUNITY

Twelve European nations, among them countries who have been traditional enemies and whose differences with each other dragged the world to war twice in this century, have pledged to complete by 1992 a unified European market place. This is a continued trend toward a unified Europe which began in 1950, when French diplomat Jean Monnet worked out a plan for the war-devastated French and German coal and steel industries to join in a common market. His plan became the precursor of the European Community of Six Nations, which was created in 1955. The European Community of 1992 could prove to be one of the seminal events of the latter part of the 20th century. It is certain to have a dramatic effect on world trade because it would constitute the world's largest single consumer market, with a population a third larger than the United States and a trading volume more than twice that of Japan.

Table 20-4 presents the population and gross domestic product (GDP) for countries that will become members of the Economic Community in 1992. They range from Luxembourg, with a population of 400,000 and a GDP of $400 million to West Germany, with a population of 60.1 million and a GDP of $1.1 trillion. They also range from a developing country, Portugal, with a per capita income of $2,250, to a world industrial power—West Germany—with a per capita income of $12,080.

Organization of the European Community 1992

The European Community will have four main institutions:

1. The European Council. It is to be the main decision-making body, and will be filled by one member from each of the twelve countries.
2. The European Commission. It will draft proposals for the Council's decisions and will carry out the policies established by the Council.
3. The European Parliament. It will consist of 518 directly elected members who will sit in political groups, not national groups. It has the right to draft proposals and make amendments that cannot be overturned by the Council, save by unanimity.

TABLE 20-4

Population and Gross Domestic Product (GDP) of
the Countries in the 1992 European Community

Countries	Population (millions)	GDP ($billions)
Belgium	9.9	138.5
Denmark	5.1	101.4
France	55.6	879.9
Greece	10.0	47.0
Ireland	3.5	29.1
Italy	57.3	751.5
Luxembourg	0.4	6.2
Netherlands	14.7	214.6
Portugal	10.2	26.1
Spain	38.7	288.0
United Kingdom	56.8	662.6
West Germany	60.1	1,118.8
Total	322.3	4,263.7
United States	246.2	4,472.9

*Source: Organization for Economic Cooperation and
Development, Department of Economics and Statistics,
National Accounts, 1960–1987 (Paris: OECD, 1988), pp.
32–36.*

4. The European Court of Justice. It will have the same power as the U.S. Supreme Court.

The European Community is designed to eliminate the following barriers:

1. Border controls. There are currently differences among the countries in terms of tariffs and excise taxes, plant and animal health restrictions, and import restrictions.
2. Limitations on freedom of access. While ordinary citizens have freedom of movement, there are restrictions placed on the movement of professionals.
3. Different rates of value-added taxation. The rates and coverage now vary considerably from country to country.
4. Lack of a common legal framework. To a considerable degree, operations of enterprises are governed by national laws, thus cross-border business is more complicated than in an integrated market.
5. Controls on capital movements. While full freedom of capital movements has been achieved in a few countries, there are restrictions of varying intensity on short-term capital movements.
6. Regulation of services. Currently the service sector is much more regulated by national governments—particularly financial, broadcasting, and transportation.

7. Divergence of regulation and technical standards. Sellers must currently confirm with regulation and standards set in each country, which adds to the cost and complexity of doing business.
8. Public procurement policies. Contracts on public projects are now given to public entities in each country, with some exceptions.

European Community–U.S. Relations

Many Americans perceive the European Community as an attempt to create a "fortress Europe" that will shut the United States out of its markets. This is not likely to happen, but there is no question that the European Community will become one of the power centers of the world. American preeminence in the Western alliance of nations is not in question; as long as global security rests on nuclear deterrents and the American economy maintains some economic superiority over the European Community, it will maintain a leadership role. It is hard to conceive of a more important international event than the unification of Europe, and the potential consequences of that act are critical for U.S. policy, for a newly involved U.S.-European relationship, and for East-West relations.

EAST ASIA

Many people are calling the 21st century the "Pacific Century," and for good reason. Japan is the leading creditor country in the world, and it is also the wealthiest. It is also the leading economic competitor to the United States. But East Asia, or the Pacific Rim, has other countries that are emerging in importance and share an aptitude for combining Western technology with the Oriental virtues of self-discipline, patience, and persistence. South Korea is an example, with a real GDP growth rate which exceeds that of Japan. It has become a major exporter of cars, personal computers, and steel. South Korea, like Taiwan and Singapore, was not a country until after the end of World War II, and then was completely destroyed by the fighting that took place during the Korean War of the early 1950s. It has had little more than 30 years to transform itself into a modern industrial economy.

A historic shift in U.S. trade patterns has developed, with East Asia replacing Western Europe as the most important trading partner of the United States. In 1989 Japan, South Korea, and Taiwan ranked in the top 10 U.S. export countries, and the same countries and Hong Kong ranked in the top 10 import countries. Total imports from Japan in 1989 exceeded the value of all imports from Western Europe. Total trade turnover (exports plus imports) between the United States and Japan and Taiwan exceeded total trade turnover between the United States and Western Europe. The U.S. merchandise trade with East Asia was negative in 1989 and has been negative throughout the 1980s, with the terms of trade generally favoring East Asia. This may be explained by the fact that many U.S. exports to East Asia consist of farm products and natural resources such as coal, while East Asia sells its manufactured products to the United States.

Table 20-5 presents population, real GDP, and real GDP growth rates for the major East Asian countries, including China, whose living standards are far below those of the other countries. However, prospects for an East Asian century may depend upon China because of its natural and human resources. China has to solve its internal problems, including the negative world image that resulted from the Tiananmen Square massacre. Foreign investment is needed to help modernize the Chinese economy, but there is uncertainty. Growth in industrial production has declined and the trade deficit with the rest of the world has increased during 1989. Agricultural shortages have occurred because state purchasing agents pay less than the world market price for grain.

Japan

Although the United States continues to hold a lead in world trade and investment, its relative position has been considerably reduced. The most striking change in its relative position has been in its relation to Japan. During the four decades from 1950 to 1990, the increases in Japan's productivity and gross national product were more than those of any other industrialized country. Starting from scratch in 1950, Japan has accomplished a number of things. Consider the following:

1. Japanese exports account for 30 percent of the world exports.
2. Japan is the largest creditor country in the world.
3. Japan is the wealthiest country in the world: The total value of all its assets amounted to $43 trillion in 1989, compared to $37 trillion for the United States.
4. All of the 10 largest banks in the world are Japanese (see Table 20-6).
5. The Japanese growth rate remains the highest for all industrial nations.
6. Japanese firms lead the world in the number of patents granted.

These and other factors might lead one to conclude that it is inevitable that Japan will eventually overtake the United States and become the world's leading economic power. This may not be the case. For one thing, Japan is heading into a

TABLE 20-5

Comparison of Population, Real GDP, and Real GDP Growth Rates for Major East Asian Countries, 1988

Country	Population (million)	Real GDP (billion)	Per Capita GDP	Real GDP Growth Rate (five-year average)
Japan	123.2	$2,805.5	$22,772	4.5%
South Korea	45.0	154.4	3,436	11.4
China	1,100.0	269.4	245	11.2
Taiwan	19.8	95.8	4,837	9.3
Hong Kong	5.6	45.7	8,158	8.4
Singapore	2.7	23.8	8,817	5.6

Source: "Asia in the 1990's," Fortune (Fall 1989), pp.72–82.

TABLE 20-6
Comparisons of Changes in Distribution of the 100 Largest Industrial Corporations and 50 Largest Banks, 1970–1988

	Total Sales in Billions of Dollars		Percent of Sales	
All Industries	**1970**	**1988**	**1970**	**1988**
European Community	82	768	24	33
United States	236	1,044	69	45
Japan	21	336	6	15
Other	4	169	1	7
Total	$343	$2,317	100	100

	Total Assets in Billions of Dollars		Percent of Assets	
All Banks	**1970**	**1988**	**1970**	**1988**
European Community	156	2,258	31	29
United States	188	484	38	6
Japan	89	4,662	18	59
Other	63	504	13	6
Total	$496	$7,908	100	100

Source: Gary Clyde Hufbauer, "Europe 1992: Opportunities and Challenges," The Brookings Review, *Vol. 8, No. 3 (Summer 1990), p. 21.*

postindustrial society. South Korea and Taiwan, with lower labor costs, have made inroads in industries formerly dominated by the Japanese. The steel industry is a case in point. Japanese society is aging and the number of skilled workers will decrease in the future. The Japanese infrastructure needs rebuilding. They realize that they have paid heavily for their obsession with economic growth. Finally, with dominance comes leadership and the Japanese have not demonstrated any capacity for world leadership or vision for the future.

"The Little Dragons"

South Korea, Taiwan, Singapore, and Hong Kong are called "The Little Dragons" because although much smaller than Japan, their performance, if anything, has been even more spectacular.[11] Three were created after World War II. Singapore was a British crown colony that was occupied by the Japanese during the war, and became an independent country in the 1950s. South Korea was part of Japan as was North Korea before World War II. When the war was over, North Korea became communist and South Korea became a U.S. protectorate. The Korean War completely destroyed the South Korean economy. Taiwan was formerly Formosa, which belonged to Japan before World War II but was given

[11] Hong Kong is a British crown colony which will be ceded to China in 1997.

back to China after the war. When the communists under Mao took over main-land China in 1949, the nationalists led by Chiang Kai-shek fled to Formosa, which eventually became Taiwan. Each country has risen from poverty to prosper-ity in a period of thirty years.

South Korea, Taiwan, and Singapore are examples of state-directed capitalism, with emphasis on state planning. South Korea has relied on an export development strategy based on the Japanese model. Through a series of five-year plans, the idea has been to use labor to make increasingly sophisticated and expensive products for export. A shipbuilding industry was created to build ships to carry exports. Government capital provided development funds. The steps in the Korean devel-opment process moved in a logical progression. The plan was to move from simple goods that required much labor and little machinery such as textiles, and then on to metalwork and steelmaking. The steel would be used to make ships and cars. Technology that was picked up from foreign countries would be used to make increasingly more complicated and higher priced goods such as computers.

THE UNITED STATES
AND THE NEW REALITIES

In 1988 the dominant issue was whether or not the United States was declining as a world power and there was plenty of evidence to suggest that it was. But in 1989, "declinism" has been replaced by "endism," which holds that bad things such as wars are coming to an end and that democratic liberalism as represented by the United States and Western Europe was won out.[12] One manifestation of "endism" is the presumed end of the Cold War, and much happened in 1989 to substantiate this point. The Eastern Bloc countries experienced enormous change with communism being repudiated in East Germany, Czechoslovakia, Hungary, and Poland. Bush and Gorbachev met in Malta in December 1989 to conclude economic and arms control agreements. It would appear that wars, at least among developed nations, have also ended, and the message that is being sent is that the United States as the main representative of Western liberalism has won and history is at an end.

The triumph of one ideology does not preclude the emergence of new ide-ologies. History did not end with the triumph of communism, as Marx predicted, nor is it likely to end with democratic liberalism. The success of communism was predicated on the assumption that human nature could be changed by changing the environment in which human beings functioned. But the self-sacrificing, altruistic

---

[12] "Endism" is associated with an article published by Francis Fukuyama in the *National Interest* in the summer of 1988. The struggles of history, Fukuyama states, will be replaced by economic calculation, the endless solving of technical problems, environmental concerns, and the satisfaction of sophisticated consumer demands. Fukuyama says liberalism is the end of history, but then Marx said communism was the end of history.

"communist man" failed to appear, thus giving the lie to the notion that human beings are perfectable. The struggle that is history is rooted in human nature, and there is one absolute: Human nature does not change. It can be rational and irrational, generous and selfish, and wise and stupid. People will continue to develop belief systems that legitimate what they have and will justify getting more, and new concepts, ideologies, and theories will emerge.

The New Realities

New economic realities will dominate American political life in the 1990s.

1. There is an enormous debt obligation to foreigners. The level of the federal government's total debt is not the problem. The problem is that the United States does not save enough and many creditors are foreign. This debt, or much of it, is in the form of government bonds that require fixed annual debt servicing. Private companies have also borrowed abroad, increasing the nation's debt obligations still more. Coupled to the foreign debt is the deficit in the federal budget, which reduces the level of savings. Much of this deficit is financed by the sale of U.S. Treasury debt obligations to foreigners.
2. There is concern about the patterns of international trade. Protectionism and a demand for access to foreign markets will be based on continued trade deficits. To improve the trade deficit means taking economic and political initiatives against Japan and Taiwan with whom the bulk of the trade deficit exists.
3. There is a need for international cooperation in regulating financial markets. It is easy to avoid indigenous rules by transferring money to other countries. For example, insider trading is illegal and punishable on the New York Stock Exchange but not on the Tokyo Stock Exchange. The United States requires companies to disclose far more information before selling securities in the United States than they must in Europe and Japan.
4. Another major reality will be a large and growing level of foreign ownership of America's productive base. The so-called "buying of America" has become a controversial subject, particularly when it involves increased purchases of American assets by Japan.
5. A final reality is the need on the part of the world economic powers to cooperate in the making of economic policy. This means central bank cooperation and government cooperation on monetary policy and fiscal policy. The fact that different countries have different priorities for how economies function will cause coordination to become a bone of contention.

The United States and the Year 2000

The place of the United States in the world picture has changed dramatically since 1950 when it was the unquestioned leader of the world. The world has become increasingly interdependent; problems are more complex and global in nature and

By permission of Doug Marlette and Creators Syndicate.

require global solutions. Table 20-7 presents some of the changes that have occurred in the United States and the world since the 1950s. Today's world is different across all dimensions. The pace of technology is unlikely to slow. The key constraining factors will be the availability of labor skills and capital. What all of this means is that the United States will have to develop a strategy for the future if it expects to play a viable role in the global economy in the year 2000.

Table 20-8 presents per capita income for the United States and the other top 10 countries in the world for 1988. The United States slipped from the second position in 1987 to the fifth position in 1988, while Japan jumped to the second position. Much of the rise in the Japanese income can be attributed to an increase in the value of the yen in comparison with the dollar, as well as to increased Japanese productivity. Elsewhere, differences could be linked to shifts in the value of the dollar compared to other currencies. Conversely, at the other end of the income scale, China and India, the two largest countries in the world, had per capita incomes of $330 a year, while Mozambique, an African nation, had a per capita income of $100.

THE THIRD WORLD COUNTRIES: ORPHANS AT THE FEAST

The Third World countries suffer from three problems, foreign debt, a low rate of economic development, and political instability. Economic progress has been

TABLE 20-7
The Global Economy in the Year 2000

Characteristics	1950s	1990s
Global economic structure	Independent nations	Global interdependence
Security	Cold war	Thaw
U.S. role	Dominant	First among equals
Global leadership	Super powers	Void
Ideology	Anticommunism	Liberalism
Currencies	U.S. dollar dominant	Yen, DM, Swiss Fr. dominant
Technology	U.S. clear lead	Globalization-shared lead
Communication	National	Global
Energy	Cheap	Expensive
U.S. competitiveness	U.S. no. 1	Still no. 1
European economy	Reconstruction	Regionalism
Japan economy	Postwar reconstruction	Global dominance without global leadership
	Start industrialization	Postindustrialization
Developing countries	Postcolonial birth	Emerging global competitors
Poor countries	Poor	Poor
Environment	Local	Global
	Low concern	Serious problem

Source: Jan V. Dauman, "The Global Economy in the year 2000: Driving Forces, Scenarios, and Implications," in William Brock and Robert Hormats, eds., The Global Economy (New York: W. W. Norton, 1989), pp. 206–207.

TABLE 20-8
Per Capita Income for the Ten Highest Countries
in 1988

Country	Per Capita Income
Switzerland	$27,260
Japan	21,040
Iceland	20,160
Norway	20,020
United States	19,780
Sweden	19,150
Finland	18,610
West Germany	18,530
Denmark	18,470
Canada	16,760

Source: The World Bank, World Bank Atlas 1989 (New York: Oxford University Press, 1989), p. 2.

shared unequally by the Third World countries, with some countries, notably the Pacific Rim and Mexico and Brazil performing somewhat better than others. But any progress that was made came to a halt during the 1980s, and in terms of economic growth, the decade was a debacle for most of the Third World countries. High interest rates, falling commodity prices, heavy debt burdens, and volatile exchange rates plagued most countries. World recession and high debt service payments caused growth rates among the Latin American countries to be negative during most of the 1980s, and per capita income at the end of the decade was lower than it was in 1980. If anything, the performance of most African countries was worse, where real gross national product grew at a negative rate.

Foreign Debt

The foreign debt of the Latin American and African countries creates economic and social problems. It contributes to inflation, which increased by as much as 1,000 percent in Argentina, which had to sacrifice spending on social programs, thus increasing the class division between rich and poor. Table 20-9 presents the foreign debt of various Latin American and African countries and the relationship of the debt to gross domestic product (GDP). Although the United States is the largest debtor country in the world, its foreign debt equals less than 10 percent of its GDP—compared to Mexico, whose foreign debt is equal to 76 percent of its

TABLE 20-9

Foreign Debt for the United States and Third World Countries for 1988 (in billions of dollars and percent of GDP)

Country	Foreign Debt	Percent of GDP
United States	$368	8.0
Brazil	121	37.0
Mexico	106	115.0
Argentina	55	79.0
Nigeria	29	85.0
Venezuela	36	73.0
Chile	21	113.0
Tanzania	4	105.0
Malaysia	22	78.0
Kenya	6	66.0
Honduras	3	98.0
Sudan	11	135.0
Zaire	9	151.0
Zambia	6	433.0

Source: The World Bank. World Debt Tables, September 1989 (New York: Oxford University Press, 1989).

gross national product. These countries rely far more on exports to finance debt repayments than does the United States.

Inflation

Inflation is a second problem that confronts many Third World countries. Argentina provides an excellent case in point. The average annual rate of inflation in Argentina for the period 1980–1988 was 298.7 percent, while Bolivia's was 601.8 percent (see Table 20-10). The countries with the most acute inflation problems are generally those with the most acute foreign debt problems. The financial policies pursued by these countries during the 1970s made their economies vulnerable to world change, such as declining oil prices. Central bank monetary policy was aimed at pumping more money into the economies of these countries to make it easier to finance the foreign debt, while at the same time trying to prevent social unrest at home. As inflation increased, so did interest rates. In Argentina, the average annual increase in interest rates was around 80 percent for the period 1980–1988, encouraging speculation and discouraging capital formation.

Economic Growth

The growth rates of many Third World countries have been negative during the 1980s (see Table 20-11). A case in point is Mexico whose money and real GNP were lower in 1988 than they were in 1980, and Nigeria whose money and real GNP in 1988 was about half of what it was in 1980. But it is the poorest countries

TABLE 20-10

Average Annual Inflation Rates for Selected Third World Countries 1980–1988 (percent)

Country	Inflation Rate
Brazil	166.3
Bolivia	601.8
Argentina	298.7
Mexico	68.9
Peru	101.3
Zambia	28.7
Sudan	31.7
Uganda	95.2
Zaire	53.5
Charro	48.3
Philippines	16.7
Nicaragua	86.6

Source: The World Bank, World Development Report, 1989 *(New York: Oxford University Press, 1989), pp. 164–165.*

TABLE 20-11
Growth Rates in GDP for Selected Third World
Countries 1980–1988 (percent)

Country	Average Annual Increase
Bolivia	− 2.1
Argentina	− 1.5
Mexico	− 0.1
Venezuela	− 0.1
El Salvador	− 0.5
Guatemala	− 0.7
Zambia	− 0.3
Nigeria	− 2.1
Sudan	− 0.9
Mozambique	− 3.2
Uganda	− 0.2
Philippines	− 0.7

Source: The World Bank. The World Bank Atlas, 1989
(New York: Oxford University Press, 1989), p. 2.

of the world that have the lowest rates of economic growth. In sub–Saharan Africa, where two-thirds of the people live in poverty, rapid population growth rates combined with declining economic growth, falling agricultural production, and natural disasters have contributed to widespread malnutrition and decreased social welfare. Economic stagnation has reversed gains made in earlier decades. For example, the growth rate for the poorest countries in the world, those with per capita incomes of $500 or less, averages 1.5 percent for the period 1965–1987, but −0.1 percent for the period 1980–1988.[13]

In the two decades between the early 1950s and the early 1970s, the world economy achieved both high growth and low inflation. The Third World countries shared in that success. They grew at more than 5 percent a year, probably the best record for any group of countries over such a period. But this changed during the late 1970s and particularly the 1980s. Output in the industrial countries fluctuated more than in earlier years, causing variations in demand for the products of the less developed countries. Certain sectors in the industrial countries, especially agriculture, became protected against the exports of developing countries. Exporters of primary products suffered a significant deterioration in their terms of trade during the 1980s, as the world price of these products declined in the world markets. Examples are tin from Bolivia and copper from Zambia.

---

[13] The World Bank, *World Development Report, 1989* (New York: Oxford University Press, 1989), pp. 164–165.

THE FUTURE WORLD ECONOMY

There will be three leaders in the race for world economic supremacy—the United States, Japan, and a unified Germany. Germany's economic rise as the powerhouse of Europe has evoked memories of World Wars I and II, when the Kaiser's soldiers and Hitler's stormtroopers wreaked havoc in Europe. However, the concern in Europe is not that it will hear the *Horst Wessel Lied* again,[14] but that Germany will accomplish economically what it could not accomplish militarily. The West German deutsche mark is the world's strongest currency as of 1990. It is possible that Germany may have the world's fastest growing economy in this decade, the highest per capita GNP, and the dominant world currency. West Germany, by itself, is the world's largest exporter, and the addition of East Germany will increase its position. Moreover, Germany has a strategic location as the pivotal point where East meets West.

Table 20-12 presents an economic comparison of Germany, Japan, and the United States for 1989. Germany includes both East and West Germany. The U.S. GNP is larger than the combined total for Germany and Japan. But countries cannot be compared on the size of GNP alone. The GNP for the Soviet Union is much larger than that for Germany, but Germany has a much higher standard of living.

Why Nations Triumph

Many books have been written on why nations decline, the most recent of which is Paul Kennedy's *The Rise and Fall of the Great Powers*, which ascribes the decline

TABLE 20-12
A Comparison of Japan, Germany, and the United States

	Germany	Japan	United States
GNP (trillions)	$1.5	$3.0	$5.2
Exports (billions)	396.2	280.4	344.2
Trade deficit or surplus (billions)	+89.0	+60.0	−121.0
Per capita income[a]	18,530.0	21,400.0	19,780.0
Rate of economic growth (%)	4.3	4.8	3.0
Population (millions)	77.0	122.0	244.0
Savings rate (% of disposable income)	13.2	16.8	4.0

[a] West Germany only. East Germany's per capita income is around $12,000.
Sources: Economic Reports of the President 1990 *(Washington: USGPO, 1990), pp. 412, 413, 419; Central Intelligence Agency,* Handbook of Economic Statistics, 1989 *(Springfield, VA: National Technical Information Service, 1989), pp. 24, 25, 56.*

---

[14] The *Horst Wessel Lied* was the national anthem of the Nazis.

of great powers to simple economic overextension.[15] However, a book has now been written on why nations win. The book *The Competitive Advantage of Nations* has been written by Michael Porter, a management professor at the Harvard Business School.[16] Porter has proposed a new paradigm to explain the dynamic relationship among a country's industries, institutions, and people that is pivotal in achieving economic advantage over other countries. He contends that classical economic theories of comparative advantage emphasizing only natural resources and other cost factors are obsolete. His paradigm takes the form of a dynamic diamond whose parts push each other forward or backward. It is competition itself—the fiercer the better—that is likely to produce a country's success. As Figure 20-1 shows, Porter's dynamic diamond is divided into four parts, one at each point of the diamond.

1. Company Strategy, Structure, and Rivalry. These are the conditions that determine how a nation's businesses are created, organized, and managed, as

FIGURE 20-1
Porter's
Diamond of
National
Competitive
Advantage.

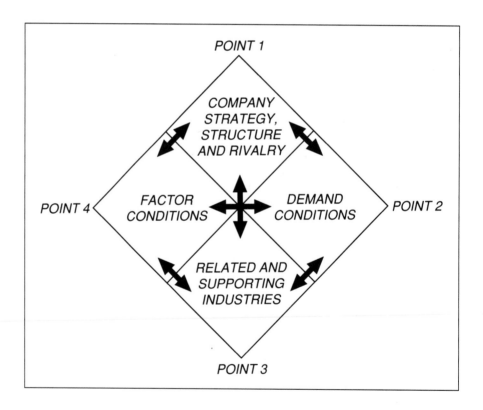

[15] Paul Kennedy, *The Rise and Fall of the Great Powers* (New York: Random House, 1987).
[16] Michael Porter, *The Competitive Advantage of Nations* (New York: Free Press, 1990).

well as the nature of domestic competition. Goals are also vital. Countries and industries committed to achieving long-term advantage are often the ones that get it.

2. Demand Conditions. This includes size of market, sophistication of consumers, and media exposure of product. Consumer demand for convenience, utility, and affordability made the United States the first mass-market, mass-production society and put U.S. industry in a strong position to capitalize on subsequent demand all over the world for goods that have those qualities.

3. Related and Supportive Industries. An industry moving toward the top needs world-class suppliers, and it benefits from competition among companies in fields related to its own that march with it in lockstep. These manufacturers and suppliers form an industrial cluster that accelerates innovation.

4. Factor Conditions. They include natural resources, education, and skill levels, *as well as* wage rates and infrastructure.

Two other factors, chance and government, also have an important role to play. Chance developments outside of the control of companies, such as wars and embargoes, can reshape industry structure in a country's favor or against it. An example is World War II, which benefited American industry by spurring research and development financed by government. Many products were produced during the postwar period long before they would have normally been produced. Government can improve or detract from the national advantage. Japan is an excellent case in point. Government and business in Japan have maintained a close working relationship going back to the last century. Japanese economic policy has utilized tax breaks and a variety of other measures to stimulate saving and capital formation.

·The competitive diamond is a dynamo whose parts push each other forward or backward. Competitive advantage based on only one or two points on the diamond usually proves unsustainable because global competitors can easily circumvent it. For example, a country that depends on lower labor costs for an advantage can be undercut by another country with even lower labor costs. All four points on the diamond must work together. All facets of the diamond favored the United States in the 1950s and 1960s—world demand, mass consumption, mass marketing, mass media (including radio and television), and low-priced consumer goods such as appliances. But times have changed and the United States no longer enjoys its preeminent position in the world. Japan and Germany have come on strong, and it remains to be seen which of the three economic powers will ultimately triumph.

Germany, Japan, and the United States Compared

Germany, Japan, and the United States are in fairly similar positions on the diamond. What advantages the United States had in the 1950s and 1960s have been largely lost, in part as a result of complacency. It is losing its ability to create specialized factors that lead to competitive advantage. An example is education. Both Germany and Japan have a more skilled labor force. The high school dropout rate in the United States is around 30 percent compared to 3 percent in Germany and 2 percent in Japan. Both German and Japanese students score much higher on international math and science achievement tests than do U.S. students. This also holds true for other types of achievement tests. Another example is that American consumers are no longer the most affluent or the most demanding. They tolerate products that no German or Japanese would accept. Rather than fight competitors, U.S. companies prefer to buy them, or, if the competition is foreign, have the government establish quotas or other barriers.

SUMMARY

East-West relations have entered a new phase. Changes in the Soviet Union's domestic and foreign policies have already affected the climate of East-West relations and, in some areas, its substance. Gorbachev's new policies involve new approaches to the future of the Soviet Union's economic system, its foreign policies, and East-West relations. There are those who believe that, until much more has changed in the Soviet Union, the West should either wait and watch or continue the same containment policy they have pursued since World War II. Others argue that the Soviet Union has changed so completely that existing defense and political arrangements can be dramatically altered. This view is reinforced by what has happened in Eastern Europe with Poland, Hungary, Czechoslovakia, Bulgaria, Romania, and East Germany detaching themselves from communism, reflecting a crisis in the whole communist system. The West has a profound stake in what has happened in the Soviet Union and Eastern Europe and cannot afford to be passive.

The United States has its own problems, not the least of which is the deficit in the federal budget. The deficit's greatest long-term damage to the economy is the limitation it places on available savings for private investment. It is the availability of savings, and hence investment, that will ultimately decide the economic fate of the United States. If the budget continues to drain potential savings from the economy, private savings will decline, making the United States less competitive in the future. Coupled with the budget deficit is the trade deficit, most of which is with the East Asian countries. This impacts on U.S. relations with Japan. Fundamental differences divide the two major economic superpowers. Distrust has grown between them, and their relationship is marked by a rivalry for world leadership. The U.S. infrastructure is eroding and its educational system has been called by the *Washington Post,* "The $500 Billion Flop."

Much change will happen in the 1990s. The European Community will be formed in 1992, creating a new global sphere of influence. The Pacific Rim countries will continue their rapid rate of economic growth and will become a second global sphere of influence. The United States and Canada and perhaps Mexico will have their own version of the European Community and will become a third sphere of influence; this leaves out much of the rest of the world. Most of the poor countries of the world are in Africa. As national income has declined and population has increased, the per capita income has declined. In

Asia, China, and India, the two largest countries in the world are held back from economic development by large rural and very poor populations. Most of the Latin American countries showed a negative or minimum growth rate during the 1980s.

REVIEW QUESTIONS

1. Why should the quality of life be used as a measure of comparison of economic systems?
2. What were some of the economic and financial changes that took place during the 1980s?
3. What are some of the economic and social problems that have to be confronted before reforms can be effective in Eastern Europe?
4. How can a free market economy be established?
5. Discuss the European Community of 1992. Why was it created?
6. Discuss the changes that will have happened in the world economy by the year 2000.
7. Will the 21st century become the East Asian Century?
8. What is the difference between "declinism" and "endism"?
9. What are some of the problems that affect the development of the Third World Countries?

RECOMMENDED READINGS

Alton, Thad P. "East European GNP's; Domestic Final Uses of Gross Product: Rates of Growth, and International Comparisons." In *Pressures for Reform in the East European Economics*. Vol. 1, U.S. Congress, Joint Economic Committee, Washington, DC: USGPO, 1989, pp. 77–96.

Aho, C. Michael, and Marc Levenson. *After Reagan: Confronting the Changed World Economy*. New York: Council on Foreign Relations, 1989.

Bosworth, Barry P., and Robert Z. Lawrence. "America in the World Economy." *Brookings Review*, Vol. 7, No. 1 (Winter 1989–1989), pp. 39–51.

Brock, William, and Robert Hormatz, eds. *The Global Economy*. New York: W.W. Norton, 1989.

Brzezinski, Zbigniew. *The Grand Failure*. New York: Charles Scribner's Sons, 1989.

Central Intelligence Agency. *Eastern Europe: Long Road Ahead to Economic Well-Being*. Paper presented to the Subcommittee on Technology and National Security, Joint Economic Committee, Congress of the United States, 1990.

Central Intelligence Agency and the Defense Intelligence Agency. *The Soviet Economy Stumbles Badly in 1989.* Paper presented to the Subcommittee on National Security and Technology, Joint Economic Committee, Congress of United States, 1990.

d'Estaing, Valery, Yasuhiro Nakasone, and Henry A. Kissinger. "East-West Relations." *Foreign Affairs,* Vol. 67, No. 2 (Summer 1989), pp. 1–21.

Drucker, Peter. *The New Realities.* New York: Harper and Row, 1989.

Fukuyama, Francis. "The End of History?" *The National Interest,* No. 16 (Summer 1989), pp. 3–18.

Kelly, Brian, and Mark London. *The Four Little Dragons.* New York: Simon and Schuster, 1989.

Porter, Michael. *The Competitive Advantage of Nations.* New York: Free Press, 1990.

"The Changing Map of Europe." *Harvard Business Review,* Vol. 7, No. 3 (May–June 1989), pp. 77–95.

"The Uncommon Market." *Wall Street Journal,* September 22, 1989.

"Under Construction: A Survey of 1992." *The Economist,* July 8–14, 1989.

APPENDIX

THE CAPITALIST MANIFESTO

In early September 1990 the Soviet Union announced a plan to junk communism in 500 days and convert the economy into a free enterprise market economy. The plan was issued at a time when the economy had gone from bad to worse. There were bread lines but no bread. Despite the best grain harvest in years, less than half of it would get to the consumer and the rest would be lost along the way for several reasons. Much of it rotted in the fields because of inefficient methods of harvesting. Some of it was kept by farmers and fed to livestock, where the profits are greater, or bartered in exchange for building materials. The transportation system was poor because of a nationwide shortage of railroads. Few farms had enough trucks to get the grain to market and there were not enough roads. There were not enough grain elevators for storage and processing.

The 250-page plan indicts 72 years of communism in the Soviet Union for offering the average Soviet citizen little more than despair. Under the plan, the central planning apparatus would be dismantled and the 15 republics would be turned loose to build a free market economy. Most of the capitalist institutions that have been decried by communists going back to Marx and Engels would now be put in place. The privatization of farming, housing, and business enterprises is supposed to occur, and a new banking system and a stock market will be created. Wages are to become more flexible and business firms will be able to make direct hard currency deals abroad instead of going through Moscow. Properties and resources of the state will be sold, and apartment houses and small land plots will be given outright to the people.

INDEX

a

Advertising, 78–79, 93, 321
Advisory, Conciliation, and Arbitration
    Service (ACAS), 206
Afghanistan, 283, 288
Africa
    agriculture in, 359, 367, 437
    colonialism, 420–421
    corruption in, 425, 434–436
    foreign trade, 425–426
    instability of, 424–425, 436
    population of, 359, 423–424
    poverty in, 421–422, 437
    tribal conflict in, 425, 435, 436
    See also names of countries
Agency of Industrial Science and
    Technology (AIST), 187–188
Agricultural Bank, 384
Agriculture
    in centrally planned economies,
        232–233
    government support of, 36, 38, 39, 40
    in less developed countries, 350–352,
        366
    See also names of countries
Agriculture, Forestry, and Fisheries Finance
    Corporation, 184
Air France, 151
Alcoholism, 109, 274, 275, 281, 287, 288,
    317
Algeria, 420, 421, 422, 424, 428
Altos Hornos de Mexico, 406
Aluminum Company of America (Alcoa),
    92n
American Brands, Inc., 89
American Federation of Labor (AFL), 95
Amin, Idi, 424n

Angola, 421
Animal Farm (Orwell), 245
Antitrust laws, 27–28, 91, 101, 174, 187,
    451
Apple Computer Company, 92
Aquinas, Thomas, 44
Argentina
    economic growth in, 354, 398, 408,
        466
    foreign debt, 364, 400, 464
    income, per capita, in, 349
    income distribution in, 353
    inflation in, 68n, 354, 465
    population of, 402
    trade by, 363 , 401
Australia, 13, 65, 76, 136n
Austria, 77, 281, 450
Authoritarianism, political, 291, 373
Automobile Manufacturing Law (1963),
    408

b

BAA, 208
Babeuf, François-Noël, 45
Balance of payments, 69, 122, 130, 172,
    193, 309, 333.
    See also Foreign debt; *names of*
        countries
Banco de Mexico, 406, 407
Bangladesh
    economic growth of, 354, 357, 367
    education in, 360
    foreign debt of, 364
    health-related indicators in, 360
    income of, 347, 349
    labor force of, 351
    natural resources of, 370

Bangladesh, (cont.)
  population of, 349, 350
  women, status of, in, 352
Bank of England, 99, 140, 142, 198,
    202–203
Bank of France, 141, 151, 158, 160
Bank of Japan, 173, 182-183, 185, 188,
    190, 192
Bank rate, 203, 204
Banking, 183, 368–369, 451, 459.
    See also names of banks; names of
    countries
Banking Control and Guarantee Act
    (1947), 203–204
Bankruptcy, 5, 38, 52, 186, 194, 337,
    385, 386, 392, 451
Banque Nationale de Paris, 159
Baochan dasho, 390
Barclays Bank, 203, 427
Bargaining power (of workers), 57
Basic banks, 326
Basing point system, 27n
Batista y Zaldivar, Fulgencio, 417
Belgium
  African colonies of, 420
  economic growth of, 210
  GDP of, 456
  government, role of, 144
  income distribution in, 145
  loan to China, 388
  taxes in, 146, 157
Bell, Daniel, 17n, 37, 112, 124, 147n,
    352n
Berlin Blockade, 220
Berlin Conference (1885), 420, 426
Berlin Wall, 219–220, 222, 229, 241, 443
Biafra, 425
Big push theory of economic development,
    355
Bismarck, Otto von, 143
Bleak House (Dickens), 46–47
Blum, Léon, 152n, 163
Bolivia
  economic growth in, 398, 466
  foreign debt of, 364, 400
  income, per capita, in, 349
  inflation in, 399, 465
  physiography of, 361, 366, 367
  population of, 402
Bonaparte, Napoleon, 158
Bookkeeping, double-entry, 15n
Bourgeoisie, 50, 55, 62

Brady plan, 418
Brazil
  climate of, 367
  as a developing country, 79, 371, 397,
    421
  economic growth of, 354
  exports from, 362, 398, 400, 401
  foreign debt of, 364, 400, 403, 464
  income, per capita, in, 348, 349
  income distribution in, 353, 361, 402,
    413
  industry in, 397, 408, 454
  inflation in, 399, 465
  labor force in, 351
  population of, 66, 350, 401, 402
  trade by, 363
  women, status of, in, 352
  world GNP, percentage of, 66
Brezhnev, Leonid, 244, 272, 274, 286, 451
Brezhnev Doctrine, 451
British Aerospace, 208
British Airways, 208
"British disease." See Work ethic, decline
    of
British Empire, 197, 214
British Gas, 208
British National Oil Company (BNOC),
    206
British Petroleum, 208
British Rail Hotels, 208
British Steel Corporation, 142, 206
British Sugar Corporation, 208
British Telecom, 213
British Trades Union Congress (TUC), 206
Britoil, 208
Broz, Josip. See Tito, Marshal
Brzezinski, Zbigniew, 219, 290
Budget, government, 225, 256, 261,
    382–383. See also names of countries
Bulgaria, 236
  agriculture in, 297, 303, 453
  communism, fall of, in, 470
  economic growth of, 338, 448
  free elections in, 294, 443
  GNP of, 453
  industry in, 298, 337
  inflation in, 299
Bureaucratic collectivism, 43, 63
Burger, Warren, 111
Burkina Faso, 424, 426
Burma, 350
Burstein, Daniel, 108

Bush, George, 272, 274, 418, 460
Business cycle, 37, 58, 69

C

Cable & Wireless, 208
Caisse de Dépots, 160
Caisse National de Crédit Agricole, 159, 166
Call loan basis, 208
Calvin, John, 10
Cameroon, 424
Canada, 197
    economic growth of, 168, 210, 211
    education in, 360
    freedoms in, 76
    GDP of, 119
    GNP of, 114, 453
    government, role of, 153
    health-related indicators for, 360
    imports by United States, 122
    income, per capita, in, 399, 463
    income distribution in, 13, 145
    productivity in, 119
    taxes in, 146
    unemployment in, 125
    women, status of, in, 352
Capital
    charges, 311
    equipment, and Marxism, 50
    as factor of production, 3, 4, 43, 58, 91
    goods, 3, 15, 71
    human, 79, 173, 423
    in less developed countries, 72
    physical, 359, 423
    as requisite to economic development, 346
    social overhead, 359, 360
Capitalism
    capital formation under, 3, 14–15, 35n
    competition in, 7–8
    consumer sovereignty, 9
    consumer welfare under, 78
    and democracy, 24, 75–76
    enterprise, freedom of, 7
    finance, 17–18
    government intervention and, 10–11, 21, 23
    history of, 15–18
    income distribution under, 11–14, 24, 35, 57, 72, 135
    individualism, 8–9, 21, 36

institutions of, 4–11, 20–21
    laissez-faire, 4, 10
    limited government, 10–11
    Marxist criticisms of, 52–53, 60, 290, 460
    modifications of, 18–20
    price system, 5–7
    private property, 4, 21
    pure, 4–11
    saving under, 3, 10, 14–15, 21, 35n
    and socialism, 43–44, 49
    work ethic, 10, 21
Cartels, 20, 24n, 142, 174
Carter, Jimmy, 127
Cash plan, 264, 270, 383–384
Castro, Fidel, 417
Caveat emptor, 9
Ceausescu, Nicolae, 220, 294, 443
Center des Jeunes Patrons, 160
Central Bank of Japan, 192
Central Bank of Nigeria, 429
Central Committee (U.S.S.R.), 244
Centrally planned economies
    agriculture in, 232–233
    banking in, 368–369
    budget in, 225
    comparison with market economies, 71, 72, 452–454
    distribution in, 61
    economic growth in, 72
    income distribution in, 74
    industrial concentration in, 91
    planning in, 61–62
    prices in, 70, 276
    shift to market economies, problems of, 449–451
    See also Socialism; *names of countries*
Ceylon, 197
Chad
    economic growth of, 337, 367
    education in, 79, 80
    health-related indicators for, 81
    labor force in, 351
    population of, 424
Chance, 469
Charro, 465
Chase Manhattan Bank, 177
Chevron Oil Company, 275
Chiang Kai-Shek, 460
Children of Sanchez, The (Lewis), 413
Child-labor laws, 38
Chile, 398, 399, 400, 401, 402, 464

China
    agriculture in, 376, 388–391, 393
    appraisal of the economy of, 65
    banking system of, 383–384, 392
    Communist Party in, 43, 291, 322, 373,
        380
    contract system, 385
    Cultural Revolution, 360, 377–378, 391,
        395, 445
    democratic reforms in, 219, 314, 373,
        394
    economic growth of, 192, 378, 391,
        407, 471
    economic reforms in, 379–380,
        385–388, 392
    economic system of, 380–391, 394
    education in, 80, 360
    food production in, 359
    foreign investment in, 387–388
    Four Modernizations Program, 379,
        391
    GDP of, 458
    GNP of, 391, 392
    government, role of, 379, 381–383
    Great Leap Forward, 375–377, 390
    health-related indicators for, 81, 360
    history of, 358, 374–380
    income, per capita, in, 349, 371, 374,
        463
    industry in, 376, 384–388, 393, 394
    inflation in, 393, 394
    and Japan, 123n, 192, 374, 388
    joint ventures in, 387
    labor force in, 79, 351, 376, 380
    market economy in, 135
    nomenklatura system in, 374
    physiography of, 367, 388
    planning in, 380–381, 388
    population of, 66, 67, 345, 349, 350,
        375, 380
    price system of, 379, 392
    private enterprise in, 380, 385–386
    public finance, 381–383
    socialism in, 43
    standard of living in, 374, 391, 395
    takeovers in, 386–387
    taxes in, 381–382
    Tiananmen Square massacre, 219, 373,
        395, 447, 458
    trade by, 363, 392
    and the United States, 380n
    and the U.S.S.R., 375, 377, 387
    wage system in, 380

    women, status of, in, 352
    world GNP, percentage of, 66
Chou En-lai, 378
Chrysler Corporation, 20, 38, 93n
Churchill, Winston, 220, 446
Citicorp, 183
C. Itoh and Co., 179
City-state
    Greek, 75
    Italian, 15
Class system, 60, 206, 361, 365
Classical economic theory, 28–29
Clayton Antitrust Act (1914), 174
Coca-Cola, 93, 388
Colbert, Jean Baptiste, 151, 167n, 169
Cold War, 460
Collective bargaining, 94, 95, 160, 206
Colombia, 349, 363, 398, 399, 400, 401,
    402
Colonialism, African, 420–421
Combines, 91, 174, 224, 240
Comecon, 316
Coming of Post-Industrial Society, The
    (Bell), 17n, 124, 147n, 352n
Common Market, 316. See also European
    Economic Community
Communes, 322, 324, 389–390
Communism
    bureaucracy in, 315–316
    collapse of, 219–220, 290
    compared to socialism, 63
    decline of, as a development model,
        290, 446–447
    future of, 291
    institutions of, 61–63, 220
    problems facing, 445–447
    pure, 49, 61, 135
    stages of, 43
    theory of, 50–61
Communist Party, 62, 150, 160, 219,
    243–245. See also names of countries
Companie Générale d'Electricité, 153
Competition
    benefits of, 8
    as a component of capitalism, 7–8, 21,
        38
    and externalities, 41
    global, 91, 93
    and industrial concentration, 92–94
    pure, 25, 39n, 89
    restrictions on, 20, 24–28
Confederation Française Democratique du
    Travail, 160

Confederation Générale du Travail (CGT), 160
Conglomerate merger, 88
Congo, 420
Congress of Industrial Organization (CIO), 95
Congress of People's Deputies, 219, 248, 289
Congressional Budget Office (CBO), 128
Conseil National du Patronat Française, 160
Consumer
 goods, 3, 78
 protection, 41, 101
 sovereignty, 9, 79, 138
 welfare, 78–79
Consumer Product Safety Commission, 102
Consumption function, 30
Cooperation, in communist countries, 62–63
Corporations
 multinational, 93, 454
 U.S., 87, 88–94, 104
Council of Ministers (U.S.S.R.), 246, 247, 250
Council for Mutual Economic Assistance (CMEA), 247, 450
Creative destruction (Schumpeter), 108n
Crédit Commercial de France, 159
Crédit Foncier, 166
Crédit National, 159, 166
Credit plan, 263–264, 383–384
Creusot Loire, 168
Crime, 109, 112, 130, 287
Crises, in Marxist theory, 52–53, 58–59
Cuba, 43, 65, 80, 81, 417
Culture, 288, 364
Currency, 68n, 70, 238, 239, 263, 280, 281, 316–317, 415n
Czechoslovakia
 agriculture in, 303, 453
 communism, fall of, in, 220, 294, 295, 444, 460, 470
 economic growth of, 338, 448, 452
 GNP of, 297, 453
 industry in, 298, 337
 inflation in, 299
 productivity in, 339
 and the U.S.S.R., 220, 295, 444, 451

d

Dai Ichi Kangyo Bank, Ltd., 176, 183
Daily Times Group, 431
Darwinism, social, 8, 27, 36, 315
Dassault aviation, 153
de Gaulle, Charles, 137, 141
de Gortari, Carlos Salinas, 411, 417
de La Madrid, Miguel, 409, 417
de Maiziere, Lothar, 239
Decline of the West (Spengler), 197–198
Deficits, government
 and inflation, 69
 Japanese, balance of payments, 172, 193
 in less developed countries, 369
 U.S., balance of payments, 122, 130
 U.S., budget, 121–122, 130
Demand, 5–6, 9, 29, 469
 aggregate, 30, 41, 69, 71, 148, 182
Democracy, and capitalism, 24, 75–76, 81
Demokratizatsiya, 273, 288–289
Deng Xiaoping, 378
Denmark, 145, 146, 210, 456, 463
Dependency theory of economic development, 355
Depression of the 1930s, Great, 20, 24, 28, 67, 101, 104
Deutsche Bundesbank, 99, 451n
Devaluation, currency, 70, 415n
Developed countries, defined, 347n
Dialectic, the, 54
Dickens, Charles, 46, 197
Differentiation, 27
Dirigisme, economic, 141, 152, 163
Discount houses, British, 202, 203
Discount rate, 99n, 185, 192
Disposable income, 30, 36, 71
Distribution, 3, 61, 249, 283n, 332
District Bank, 203
Dr. Zhivago (Pasternak), 288
Drug abuse, 109–110, 130
Dual economy, 175, 431
Dubcek, Alexander, 220, 295
DuPont de Nemours & Co., E. I., 177
Dynamic random access memory (DRAM) products, 117

e

East Asia, 310, 370–371, 444, 454, 457–460. *See also names of countries*
East Germany
 agriculture in, 221, 224–225, 229n, 232–235, 240, 303, 453

East Germany, (*cont.*)
  combines in, 224, 240
  Communist Party in, 222, 295, 460, 470
  consumer goods in, 229, 230–232, 238
  development of, 221–223, 226
  economic growth of, 338, 452
  education in, 80
  enterprises in, 223–224
  free elections in, 220, 238–239, 241,
    294, 443–444
  GNP of, 239, 297, 453
  government, role of, 225–226
  health-related indicators for, 81
  income distribution in, 227–229
  industry in, 298, 337
  inflation in, 299
  infrastructure in, 240
  labor in, 235, 241
  as a model for communism, 221–226,
    240–241, 447
  nomenklatura system in, 449
  planning in, 222–223, 235
  pollution in, 236
  price reforms in, 240
  privatization in, 449
  productivity in, 339
  reunification with West Germany,
    226–236, 241, 447
  standard of living in, 229–232
  unemployment in, 448
  West Germany, compared with,
    226–236, 447
  World War II, effect of, 226, 229
Eastern Europe
  compared with West, 452–454
  dramatic changes in, 294–295, 443–444
  economic reforms in, 448–452
  foreign trade, 310
  industry in, 298
  and the U.S.S.R., 220, 226, 243, 290,
    295, 296, 308, 445, 448, 451–452
  See also names of countries
Eastman Kodak, 275
Economic change, 446
Economic determinism, theory of, 53–55,
  59–60
Economic development
  defined, 346
  of less developed countries, 347–355
  obstacles to, 357–367, 371
  requisites to, 346–347
  solutions for, 367–371

  theories of, 355–357
  See also names of countries
Economic growth
  defined, 346
  as goal, 67, 70–72, 80, 139
  in Third World countries, 465–466
  See also names of countries
Economic insecurity, 24, 36–39, 41, 148
Economic institutions, 4
Economic Planning Agency, 188
Economic security, 67–68
Economic stability, 33, 99, 139
Ecuador, 349, 400, 401, 402
Education, as social goal, 79–80
Egalitarianism, 14, 19, 378
Egypt, 349, 350, 352, 420, 422, 424
El Salvador, 349, 353, 362, 466
Elf-Aquitaine, 153
Employment
  as economic goal, 67, 80
  and economic security, 67–68
  in Keynesian theory, 29–30
  lifetime, 179, 181, 185, 190
  public sector, 102–103
  See also Unemployment; *names of*
    countries
Employment Appeal Tribunal, 206
Employment Protection Act (1975), 206
Endism, 460n
England. *See* United Kingdom
Enterprise, 7, 21
  See also names of countries
Enterprise Bankruptcy Law (1988), 386
Entitlement, 38, 100, 126
Environment, clean, as economic goal,
  77–78
  See also Pollution; names of countries
Environmental Protection Agency (EPA),
  102, 187n
Equal Employment Opportunity
  Commission, 102
Equilibrium price, 5–6
Equity, and income distribution, 34–36
Erhard, Ludwig, 226
Essay on the Principles of Population, An
  (Malthus), 357
Ethiopia
  education in, 360
  famine in, 345, 423
  health-related indicators for, 360
  income, per capita of, 347, 349, 422
  labor force in, 351

population of, 350, 424
women, status of, in, 352
European Community (1992), 444, 445,
    454, 470
  banking in, 459
  in a global economy, 123
  industry in, 459
  organization of, 455–457
  U.S. relations with, 457
European Community of Six Nations
    (1955), 455
European Economic Community, 165, 322
Exchange controls, 408n
Export-Import Bank of Japan, 180, 182,
    184
Exports, from less developed countries,
    362
Externalities, 41

f

Factory system, 17
Fair Labor Standards Act (1938), 96
Family allowances, 68, 143, 156–157,
    201, 260, 325
Farms
  collective, 225, 232–233, 244, 258,
      260, 264, 268–269, 327, 328, 389
  cooperatives, 276, 313, 328–329, 389
  private plots, 269, 391, 395
  state, 224–225, 232–233, 268, 269n,
      313n, 327, 328
Federal Aviation Administration (FAA),
    102
Federal Housing Administration (FHA),
    103
Federal Radio Corporation, 430
Federal Republic of Germany. See West
    Germany
Federal Reserve System, 34n, 99, 127,
    140, 182, 202, 215
Federation of Economic Organizations, 186
Field, Marshall, 18
Finance, public. See names of countries
Finance capitalism, 17–18
Financial Loan and Investment Program,
    181
Financière de Suez, 153n
Finland, 353, 463
Fiscal policy, 181–182, 423
  and economic growth, 71–72, 369
  in Keynesian theory, 33–34

in mixed economic systems, 99,
    139–140, 148
  See also names of countries
Flynn, Errol, 171
Food shortages, 359
Force Ouvrière, 160
Ford, Henry, 78n
Ford Motor Company, 26
Forecasting, 139, 148
Foreign aid, 367–368. See also names of
    countries
Foreign Bank, 266
Foreign debt, 363, 464–465. See also
    names of countries
Formosa, 459, 460. See also Taiwan
Fourier, Charles, 44n, 46
Français de Petroles, 153
France
  African colonies of, 420
  appraisal of the economy of, 168–169
  banking system of, 140, 158–160
    nationalization of, 48, 136n, 137,
        138n, 150, 151, 153
  Communist Party, 150, 160
  decline of, 107
  Depression, effect of, 152
  economic growth of, 205, 210, 211
  education in, 80, 111
  GDP of, 114
  GNP of, 199, 453
  government, role of, 20, 103, 140,
      151, 156–158, 161–162, 165,
      169
  health-related indicators for, 81
  income, per capita of, 349
  income distribution in, 13, 145, 158
  Industrial Revolution and, 151
  industry in, 165, 198
    concentration of, 90
    nationalization of, 48, 136n, 137,
        141, 150, 151–154, 161–162
  inflation in, 139n, 211
  labor in, 160–161, 186
  as mixed economic system, 136, 147,
      169
  planning in, 137, 162–168
    indicative, 137, 138–139, 148, 163
  Popular Front, 150, 152, 163
  private property in, 136n, 150, 169
  productivity in, 119
  public investment, 139
  social welfare in, 156–157, 164

France (*cont.*)
  socialism in, 43, 45–46, 48, 49, 63,
    150, 169
  standard of living in, 116
  taxes in, 154–156, 167, 169
  trade by, 151
  unemployment in, 125, 139n, 152, 168,
    211
  unions in, 161–162
  World War II, effect of, 114, 141, 151,
    152, 161, 169
Freedom
  of choice, 9, 79
  as economic goal, 74–77, 81
  of enterprise, 7, 21
Fuji Bank, Ltd., 183
Fukuyama, Frances, 460n
Fund for Economic and Social
    Development, 166
Fuyo, 176

g

Gallatin, Albert, 138
Gandhi, Indira, 365
Gang of Four, 378n
General Motors Corporation, 26, 78n, 88,
    89, 176, 179
*General Theory of Employment, Interest,
    and Money, The* (Keynes), 30
Genoa, 15
German Democratic Republic. *See* East
    Germany
Germany
  African colonies of, 420
  Depression, effect of, 28
  and Hungary, 308
  inflation in, 68n
  and Poland, 226, 295, 300n
  social welfare in, 143
  and Yugoslavia, 321–322
  See also East Germany; West Germany
Ghana, 424, 426
Gierek, Edward, 304
Gini coefficient, 12, 229n, 413, 414n
Giscard d'Estaing, Valery, 164
Glasnost, 273, 286–288
Globalism, growth of, 463
Globalization, 446
Goals
  economic, 67, 81
  social, 77–80, 82
  See also names of countries

Gompers, Samuel, 95
Gorbachev, Mikhail, 219, 221, 247–248,
    269, 272, 277n, 291, 296, 460, 470.
    See also Glasnost; Perestroika
Gorbachev, Raisa, 288
Gosagroprom, 287
Gosbank, 253, 255, 262, 263–265, 266,
    270
Gosplan, 250, 251, 253, 255, 268
Gospriemka, 278
Gossnab, 251–252
Government
  aid to agriculture, 39
  aid to industry, 38–39
  in capitalist economies, 10–11, 21, 23,
    41
  and economic goals, 67, 81
  and economic growth, 71–72, 81
  and economic insecurity, 37–38
  future role of, 469
  in Keynesian theory, 32–33
  limited, 10–11
  in mixed economic systems, 97, 136,
    143–145
  regulation of market structures,
    24–28
  social regulation by, 39–41
  and socialism, 49
  and unions, 95
  See also names of countries
Gowan, Yakubu, 436
*Grand Failure: The Birth and Death of
    Communism in the Twentieth Century,
    The* (Brzezinski), 219
Great Britain. *See* United Kingdom
Greece
  economic growth of, 354
  GDP of, 456
  income, per capita, of, 349
  socialism in, 48, 49, 63
Gross domestic product (GDP), 119,
    455, 456, 464
Gross national product (GNP),
    347–348
  government expenditures and, 144
  in market economies vs. centrally
    planned economies, 453
  trends in, 73, 93
  world, by country, 65, 66
  See also names of countries
Grosz, Karoly, 314
Growth, economic. *See* Economic
    growth

Guatemala, 367, 398, 399, 401, 402, 466
Gysi, Gregor, 241

h

Haiti, 80, 81, 349, 354
Hamilton, Alexander, 138
Havel, Vaclav, 220, 295, 315, 444
Health, as social goal, 79–80, 81
Health insurance, 68, 80, 143, 157, 201
Hegel, Georg, 54
Henley, William Ernest, 36n
Hero theory of history, 60
Hill, Benny, 197
Hire purchase controls, 204
History, monocausal theories of, 60
Hitler, Adolf, 28, 221, 228, 424n
Hobbes, Thomas, 15n
Holding companies, 20
Honda, 175
Honduras, 398, 399, 400, 402, 464
Honecker, Erich, 219, 220, 240
Honeywell, Inc., 153
Hong Kong, 192, 349, 458
Housing Loan Corporation, 180, 182
Hungary
    agriculture in, 303, 313, 453
    banking, 451
    Communist Party in, 219, 291, 294, 295, 318, 443, 460, 470
    consumer goods in, 308
    economic growth in, 297–298, 308, 309, 338, 448
    economic reforms in, 297, 311–314
    education in, 80, 110, 111
    enterprises in, 311, 312–313
    foreign debt of, 309
    foreign trade by, 310–311
    free elections in, 452
    free market economy in, 315, 316–318
    GNP of, 297, 309, 453
    health-related indicators for, 81
    history of, 307–308
    industry in, 91, 298
    inflation in, 297, 298, 299
    joint ventures in, 314, 317n, 450
    labor in, 310
    New Economic Mechanism in, 311–312
    political reforms, 314
    pollution in, 40n, 77, 297, 317
    productivity in, 309–310, 339
    U.S. aid to, 303, 317

and the U.S.S.R., 220, 308
    West German aid to, 317
Hyatt Regency, 338

i

Icahn, Carl, 93
Iceland, 463
Idea theory of history, 60
Illiteracy, 109, 110–111, 361, 435
Imperial overreach (Kennedy), 107
Import quotas, 38n, 194
Income
    distribution of, 4
        under capitalism, 11–14, 24, 35, 57, 72, 135, 227
        equitable, 34–36, 72–74, 81, 129, 145–147
        and marginal productivity, 14
        Marxist theory of, 50–52, 227
        and Reaganomics, 128–129
        and social welfare, 142–147
        in socialist countries, 14, 74, 145–146, 227
    in Eastern European countries, 449–450
    inequality, measures of, 12–14, 129n
    interaction with wealth, 35, 214–215
    in less developed countries, 353–354
    and Marxism, 50–52
    See also names of countries
India, 197
    economic growth of, 367, 471
    education in, 80, 360
    food production in, 359
    health-related indicators for, 81, 360
    income, per capita, of, 349, 463
    income distribution of, 353
    independence movement in, 356
    labor force in, 346, 351
    population of, 65, 66, 345, 349, 350
    women, status of, in, 352
    world GNP, percentage of, 66
Individual Retirement Accounts (IRAs), 72n
Individualism, 8–9, 17, 21, 36
    decline of, 18–19
    and socialism, 76–77
Indonesia, 350, 351, 360, 363, 364
Industrial Bank of Japan, Ltd., 183
Industrial concentration
    advantages of, 91–92
    and competition, 92–94

Industrial concentration, (*cont.*)
  extent of, 89
  by firm size, 88–89
  issues involving, 89–91
  problems of, 92
Industrial Revolution, 16–17, 18, 50, 74,
  151, 198, 370
  and socialism, 45, 46–47, 63
Industrial society, 352n
Industry
  government support of, 38–39
  state ownership of, 140–142, 148
  See also names of countries
Inflation, 398–399
  and balance of payments, 69, 70
  consequences of, 68, 69–70, 136, 369n
  control of, 99, 185
  See also names of countries
Infrastructure, 359–361
  See also names of countries
Ingersoll-Rand, 380n
Inland Steel, 177
Input-output analysis, 253–254
Insecurity, economic, 24, 36–39, 41, 148
Institutional arrangement, 4
Interdependence, 17, 444
Interest rates
  under capitalism, 14–15, 327
  under socialism, 74, 327
Internal banks, 326
International Business Machines (IBM)
  Corporation, 92, 177
International Monetary Fund (IMF), 308,
  309, 341, 407
International Workers of the World (IWW),
  95
Investment
  by businesses, 15, 180–181
  public, 139–140, 167–168
Investment Bank, 265–266
Investment banking, 17–18
"Invictus" (Henley), 36n
"Invisible hand" (Smith), 9, 23
Iran, 347, 365
Ireland, 349, 456
Iron Curtain (Churchill), 220, 446
Israel, 68, 349
Italy
  communism in, 290
  economic growth of, 168, 205, 210, 211
  education in, 80, 360
  GDP of, 119, 456

GNP of, 239, 453
  government, role of, 144, 153
  health-related indicators for, 81, 360
  income, per capita, in, 349
  income distribution in, 13
  productivity in, 119
  standard of living in, 116
  taxes in, 146, 157
  World War II, effect of, on, 114
ITT Business Communications
  Corporation, 153
Ivory Coast, 422

J

Jackson, Andrew, 19
Jaguar Cars, 208, 213
Japan
  agriculture in, 123
  antimonopoly laws in, 174n
  appraisal of the economy of, 65,
    189–192
  balance of trade in, 193–194
  banking system of, 140, 182–185, 459
  business and government in, 186–188
  and China, 123n, 192, 374, 388
  as a creditor nation, 115, 120, 130, 189,
    195
  Depression, effect of, 28
  economic growth of, 123, 168, 172,
    173–179, 189–192, 194, 210, 211,
    408, 445, 458–459, 467
  education in, 79, 80, 110, 360, 470
  exports by, 467
  family, role of, 366
  freedoms in, 76
  future of, 192–195
  Germany, compared with, 467, 469–470
  GDP of, 119, 120, 457, 458
  GNP of, 114, 123, 189–190, 191, 209,
    239, 453, 467
  government, role of, 141, 144, 153,
    161, 173, 175, 179–182
  health-related indicators for, 81, 360
  income, per capita, in, 349, 463, 467
  income distribution in, 12, 145, 353
  import quotas on, 38n, 194
  imports by United States, 122
  industry in, 90, 172, 175, 187, 190,
    384, 459
  inflation in, 69n, 123, 190, 191, 211
  infrastructure in, 194

labor in, 124, 173, 175, 179, 185–186,
    351
life expectancy in, 123
management practices in, 113
as mixed economic system, 136, 147
natural resources of, 172, 173, 175
planning in, 139, 188–189
pollution in, 78
population of, 66, 123, 194, 467
private enterprise in, 173–174, 175–176
productivity in, 118, 119, 190
public finance, 179–182
savings in, 115, 124n, 180, 190, 467
social welfare in, 179, 181, 186
standard of living in, 116
taxes in, 99, 145, 157, 175, 180–181,
    195
technology in, 108, 109, 130, 173, 188,
    193, 195
trade by, 123, 177, 179, 190, 281, 426,
    450, 457, 467
unemployment in, 123, 125, 179, 190,
    191, 211
urbanization, 194
and U.S., 116–119
    aid to, 175
    compared with, 467, 469–470
    competition with, 39, 93, 107, 108,
        109, 116–118, 130, 171, 444,
        470
women, status of, in, 352
world GNP, percentage of, 66, 189
World War II, effect of, 114, 174,
    189–190, 193
Japan Development Bank, 180, 182, 184,
    189
Japan Monopoly Corporation, 180
Japan National Railways, 180
Japan Telephone and Telegraph Company,
    180
Jaruzelski, Wojciech, 299, 307, 318
Jefferson, Thomas, 19, 138
John Paul II, Pope, 300
Joint ventures, 274–275, 314, 317n, 325,
    333n, 387, 450–451
Junkers, 221n

k

Kadar, Janos, 308
Kapital, Das (Marx), 50–55
Karma, 365, 397n

Kaunda, Kenneth, 425
Keidanran, 186
Keiretsu, 176–177
Kennedy, John F., 138
Kennedy, Paul, 107, 130, 467
Kenya
    education in, 360
    foreign debt of, 364
    health-related indicators for, 360
    income, per capita, of, 349, 422, 464
    income distribution in, 353
    labor force in, 351
    population in, 350, 424
    trade by, 363, 426
    women, status of, in, 352
Keynes, John Maynard, 30
Keynesian economic theory, 29–34, 69
Khozraschet financing, 258
Khrushchev, Nikita, 244, 445
Kipling, Rudyard, 197
Knights of Labor, 95
Kohlberg, Kravis, Roberts (KKR), 93,
    386
Korea. *See* North Korea; South Korea
Korean War, 220, 457
Krenz, Egon, 241

I

Labor
    as factor of production, 4, 43, 58, 91
    management, relations with, 51,
        160–161
    in Marxism, 50–51, 55–58
    as requisite to economic development,
        346
    socially necessary, 50, 56
Labor theory of value, 50–51
    criticisms of, 55–56
Labor-Management Relations Act (1947),
    96
Laissez-faire, 95, 369
    capitalism, 4, 10, 17
        decline of, 16, 19–20, 24
        rejected by Keynesian theory, 32
Lamm, Richard, 109
Land, as factor of production, 4, 43, 58,
    91
Latifundo system, 414
Latin America
    economic growth of, 398
    foreign debt of, 399–400

Latin America, (*cont.*)
  foreign trade and, 400–401
  income distribution in, 397, 402
  inflation in, 398–399
  physiography of, 366, 367
  population of, 349, 401
  poverty in, 401–402
  unemployment in, 402
  See also names of countries
League of Communists of Yugoslavia
    (LCY), 322
Lenin, 60, 61, 219, 242, 243, 286n
Less developed countries, 65
  agriculture in, 350–352
  classes in, 365
  culture in, 364–366
  economic development in,
      347–355
    obstacles to, 357–367
    solutions to, 367–371
    theories of, 355–357
  education in, 360, 361
  exports from, 362
  food shortages in, 359
  foreign aid to, 367–368
  foreign debt of, 363–364
  income, per capita, in, 347–348
  income distribution in, 353–354
  industry in, 351
  infrastructure in, 359–361
  internal policies of, 368–370
  physiography of, 366–367
  population of, 347, 348–350,
      357–358
  poverty in, 347, 350
  religion in, 364–365
  savings in, 72, 361–362
  technological dualism in, 354–355
  terms of trade, 363
  urbanization in, 358
  women, status of, in, 352–353
  See also names of countries
Lewis, Oscar, 413
Libya, 421, 422
Licensing agreements, 388, 438
Liquidity ratio, 204
"Little Dragons," 459–460
Lloyds Bank, 203
Locke, John, 16, 75
London Discount Market Association,
    202
Lopez Portillo, Jose, 409, 416–417

Lorenz curve, 12, 13, 228–229
Luxembourg, 456

m

Madagascar, 424
Malaysia, 349, 350, 353, 454, 464
Mali, 424
Malthus, Thomas, 57, 357–358
Mao Tse-Tung, 61, 377–378
Marginal physical product (MPP), 14
Marginal revenue product (MRP), 14
Market
  demand, 5
    and supply, 5–6
  free, 23
  sharing, 101
Market economy, comparison with centrally
    planned economies, 14, 71, 72
Marketing, 78, 113, 283n
Markets, Say's Law of, 29
Marshall, Alfred, 28n
Marshall Plan, 152, 226
Martins Bank, 203
Marubine Corporation, 179
Marx, Karl, 50–55, 60, 219, 460
Marxism, 43, 290
  basic tenets of, 50–55
  merits of, 60–61
  theory of economic development,
      355–356
  weaknesses of, 55–60
Material balances, 253–255
Materialism, 53–54
  dialectical, 54–55, 59–60
Matra, 153
Mazowiecki, Tadeusz, 299, 307
McDonald's, 242
Medicare, 100
Meiji Restoration (1868), 141, 173–174,
    186
Mercantilism, 11n, 16, 151, 167n
Merchandise trade account, 122, 130, 335,
    437, 444, 457
Merger(s), 93–94, 101
  conglomerate, 88
Meritocracy, just, 19
Merrill Lynch, 120, 183
Mexico
  agriculture in, 403–405, 418
  appraisal of the economy of, 409–418
  banking in, 405, 406–407

corruption in, 411, 414, 416–417, 418
as a developing country, 79, 410, 421
economic development of, 371,
    407–409, 418
economic growth of, 354, 414
education in, 360
emigration from, 411, 412
foreign debt of, 364, 388, 399, 400,
    403, 415–416, 418, 464
GNP of, 398, 403, 404, 410, 411
government, role of, 405–407
health-related indicators for, 360
history of, 410–411, 414
income, per capita, in, 347, 349, 371
income distribution in, 353, 361,
    413–415, 418
industry, 397, 433n, 454
    oil, 362, 363, 398, 403, 406, 407,
        409, 410, 415, 418
inflation in, 68, 399, 410, 412, 465
infrastructure of, 361, 404
labor force in, 351, 412
natural resources of, 403
planning, economic, in, 409
pollution in, 402, 412
population of, 350, 358, 402, 410,
    411–412, 418
private enterprise in, 403
public finance, 407–409
size of, 397, 418
taxes in, 407, 414, 418
trade by, 400, 401, 418
unemployment in, 411, 412
urbanization of, 411–412
women, status of, in, 352
Midland Bank, 203
Mieszko I, Prince, 300
Mill, John Stuart, 28n
Minimum wage laws, 38, 39, 96, 143
Ministry of International Trade and
    Industry (MITI), 187
Ministry of Posts and Communication
    (MPT), 184
Mitchum, Robert, 236
Mitsubishi Bank Ltd., 183
Mitsubishi Corporation, 174, 176, 179
Mitsubishi Trust & Banking Corporation,
    183
Mitsui and Company, 174, 176
Mitsui Bank, Ltd., 183
Mitterand, Francois, 48, 49n, 137, 140,
    150, 152–154

Mixed economic systems, 4, 18, 49, 58,
    136–147.
    See also names of countries
Modrow, Hans, 241
Monetary policy, 69, 70, 99, 185, 204,
    368–369, 423
    in Keynesian theory, 34
    in mixed economic systems, 99, 139,
        140, 148
    See also names of countries
Money supply, 34n, 69
Monnet Plan, 152, 163–164, 455
Monobanks, 270
Monopoly, 24–26, 89, 101, 336
    natural, 101
More, Sir Thomas, 45
Morocco, 349, 364, 424
Mozambique, 421, 422, 462, 466
M3 aggregate, 205
Mutual aid team, 375

n

Nacional Financiera, 406, 410
Nagy, Imre, 295
Nakasone, Yasuhiro, 192
National Army of Liberation, 299
National Bank of Yugoslavia, 325, 326
National Coal Board, 206
National Council of the Resistance,
    163
National Credit Council, 158
National Health Service, 201
National Insurance Funds, 199
National Labor Relations Act (1935),
    95
National Loans Fund, 199
National Oil Corporation, 430
National Party Congress, 244
National Provincial Bank, 203
National Rifle Association (NRA), 112
National Security Council, 219
NATO (North Atlantic Treaty
    Organization), 220
Negative wants, 40–41, 48
Netherlands
    economic growth of, 210
    GDP of, 456
    government, role of, 144
    income distribution in, 145
    taxes in, 145, 146
New Deal, 95, 152

New Economic Mechanism (1968), 311–312
Newly industrialized countries (NICs), 339, 348, 403
New Zealand, 65, 76, 197
New York Stock Exchange, 120
Nicaragua, 398, 399, 402, 465
Niger, 351, 424
Nigeria, 359, 437
  agriculture in, 359, 437, 438
  banking in, 429
  corruption in, 433, 435–436, 439
  economy, performance of, 427–428, 433
  education in, 360, 435
  foreign debt of, 364, 388, 433–434, 438, 464
  GNP of, 428, 429, 433, 434
  government, role of, 428–431, 439
  health-related indicators for, 360
  history of, 426–427, 436, 438
  income, per capita, of, 371, 422
  industry in, 430–431, 438
    oil, 362, 363, 426, 428, 432, 433, 438
  inflation in, 436
  infrastructure in, 435, 438
  labor in, 432
  planning in, 429–430, 439
  political instability of, 425, 436, 439
  pollution in, 435
  population of, 350, 424, 434–435, 438
  poverty in, 437
  private enterprise in, 431–432, 438–439
  Structural Development Program, 437–438
  taxes in, 428, 435
  trade by, 363, 426
  unemployment in, 436, 437
  women, status of, in, 352
Nigerian National Shipping Lines, 430
Nimeiri, Gaafar, 424
Nisso Iwai, 179
Nomenklatura system, 245–246, 266n, 282, 289n, 316, 374, 448
Nomura Securities Company, 120
Norinchuki Bank, 183
North Korea, 43, 220, 459–460
Norway
  economic growth in, 210
  income, per capita, in, 463
  income distribution in, 145, 353
  taxes in, 146

O

Occidental Petroleum, 387
Occupational Safety and Health Administration (OSHA), 102
Oil
  crisis, 406
  from less developed countries, 362
  Libyan, 421
  Mexican, 362, 363, 398, 403, 406, 407, 409, 410, 415, 418
  Nigerian, 362, 363, 426, 428, 432, 438
  price of, 24n, 136, 163, 308, 406, 407, 410, 415, 426
  Soviet, 280, 308, 310
Oligopoly, 24, 26–27, 336
Olsen, Mancur, 107
Olympic Games, 63, 127, 260
Open market operations, 204
Opportunity, equality of, 8
Organization for Economic Cooperation and Development (OECD), 168, 322
Organization of Petroleum Exporting Countries (OPEC), 24n, 136, 406
Orwell, George, 245
Osaka Stock Exchange, 189
Overemployment, 350
Overpopulation, 348–350, 359, 418
Owen, Robert, 44n, 47

P

Pakistan
  education in, 80, 360
  health-related indicators for, 81, 360
  income, per capita, in, 349
  labor force in, 351
  natural resources of, 370
  population of, 349
  religion in, 365
  women, status of, in, 352
Panama, 353
Pareto coefficient, 12
Paribus, 153n
Pasternak, Boris, 288
Pechiney Ugine Kuhlmann, 90, 153
Pensions, old-age, 38, 68, 143, 194, 201, 260, 325
People's Bank of China, 383–384

People's Construction Bank, 384
People's Republic of China. *See* China
PepsiCo, 93
Perestroika, 273, 274–285, 291, 447
Perry, Commodore Matthew C., 172
Peru, 353, 361, 367, 398, 399, 400, 401, 402, 465
Petit bourgeoisie, 151, 221
Petroleos Mexicanos (PEMEX), 406, 407, 417
Peugeot, 48
Phalanxes, 46
Philip Morris, 89
Philippines, 350, 364, 465, 466
Physiography, effect on economic development, 361, 366–367
Pigou, A. C., 28n
Pittsburgh Plate Glass, 177
Planning
   in centrally planned economies, 61–62
   defects in, 139
   imperative, 138, 148
   indicative, 137, 138, 148
   objectives of, 137
   See also names of countries
Plans, types of, 188, 222, 249–251, 323–324
Plato, 44, 49
Pluralism, 291
Poland
   agriculture in, 300, 301–304, 453
   banking system of, 318, 451
   Communist Party in, 291, 294, 299, 300, 460
   consumer goods in, 301, 302
   economic growth of, 296, 297–298, 318, 388, 448
   education in, 80
   food shortages in, 227
   foreign debt of, 301, 304
   free elections in, 219, 299, 443, 452
   free market economy in, 315, 316–318
   freedom in, 67, 77n
   GNP of, 297, 306, 453
   health-related indicators for, 81
   history of, 296, 299
   industry in, 91, 298, 301, 305
   inflation in, 70, 298, 299, 301
   nationalism in, 299
   nomenklatura system in, 448
   pollution in, 77, 297, 301, 317
   prices in, 305
   productivity in, 339
   religion in, 299, 300–301
   Solidarity movement, 297, 299, 305–307, 315, 318
   subsidies in, 227
   U.S. aid to, 303, 317
   and the U.S.S.R., 296, 300, 307
   and the West, 301, 304, 318, 450
   West German aid to, 317
   World War II, effect of, 296, 299
Politburo, 243, 244–245, 273, 289
Political theory of history, 60
Pollution, 40, 41, 77–78, 82, 140, 402, 412, 435.
   See also names of countries
Popular Front (France), 150, 152, 163
Population
   doubling time, 349, 358, 401, 411
   in less developed countries, 65, 66, 348–350, 423–424
   as obstacle to economic development, 357–359
   world, by country, 350
Pornography, 7, 48n
Porter, Michael, 468
Portsmouth, Treaty of, 189
Portugal
   African colonies of, 420–421
   economic development of, 335
   GDP of, 456
   income, per capita, of, 347n, 349
   women, status of, in, 352
Postal Savings, 180, 182
Postindustrial society, 352n
Poverty, 50, 67, 281–282, 291, 317, 345, 347, 421–422, 437, 445
"Prague Spring," 295, 444, 451
Prestowitz, Clyde, V., 107, 108
Price(s)
   in centrally planned economies, 62, 70
   determinants of, 5–6, 70
   in Eastern European countries, 450
   equilibrium, 5–6
   fixing, 28, 101, 142, 451
   function of, 5
   and negative wants, 40
   under socialism, 48
   stability as economic goal, 68–70, 80
   and supply and demand, 5–7
   supports, 39, 40, 41
Privacy, 9, 76

Produced Net Material Product (PNMP), 305, 306
Production, 3, 9, 53
Productivity
  consequences of low, 118
  marginal, 14
  in the public sector, 102–103
Profit(s)
  as a component of capitalism, 5
  payments from, 257–258
  and prices, 5
  in the U.S.S.R., 267
Profit motive, 4–5
Profit sharing, 161, 162
Proletariat, 50, 52, 55, 59, 62, 243
Property
  private, 4, 21, 48, 62
  state ownership, 62
Protectionism, 461
Prussia, 20, 221, 226

q

Quality circles, 113
Quality of life, 59, 71, 81–82

r

RABA, 91
Racial purity, 123n
Reagan, Ronald, 49n, 93–94, 99, 127, 140, 207, 212, 244
  Reaganomics, 126–130
Reformation, Protestant, 10
Reforms, economic
  in Eastern Europe, 448–452
  See also names of countries
Religion, 54–55, 59, 76, 77, 288, 347, 352, 364–365, 397n
Renault Company, 48, 137, 141, 153
Rentier class, 146
Republic (Plato), 49
Resources
  allocation of, 3, 5, 11, 21, 23–24, 25, 61, 144, 248
  human, and Marxism, 50
  natural, 50, 242
  as a requisite to economic development, 346, 370
  scarcity of, 3, 5
Revolution of rising expectations (Bell), 37
Reynolds Industries, 89, 177

Rhodes, Cecil, 421
Rhodesia, 356.
  See also Zimbabwe
Rhone-Poulenc, 153
Ricardo, David, 16, 28n, 50
Rise and Fall of the Great Powers, The (Kennedy), 107, 467
Rise and Fall of Nations, The (Olsen), 107–108
RJR-Nabisco, 93
Rockefeller, John D., 10, 112
Rolls-Royce, 208, 213n
Romania
  agriculture in, 303, 453
  communism in, 291, 294
  economic growth of, 338, 448
  GNP of, 297, 453
  industry in, 298, 337
  inflation in, 299
  productivity in, 339
  revolution in, 220, 294, 443, 470
Roosevelt, Franklin D., 95, 152
Rostow, Walt Whitman, 356–357
Rotary Clubs, in Eastern Europe, 313, 314n
Royal Niger Company, 427
Russia. See Union of Soviet Socialist Republics
Rust Belt, 126
Rwanda, 426

s

SACILOR, 153
Safety laws, 38
Saint Gobain, 153
Saint-Simon, Comte de, 44n, 46
Samurai, 174
Sanwa Bank, Ltd., 176, 183
Saudi Arabia, 406
Saving, 180
  under capitalism, 3, 10, 14–15, 21, 29, 35n
  in less developed countries, 72, 361–362, 422
  as requisite for economic growth, 29, 71, 115
Say, Jean Baptiste, 29
Scarcity, 3, 5, 54, 56
Schumpeter, Joseph, 108n, 146n
Scientific Research Institute of Economics, 251
Semiconductors, 107, 116–117, 161

Senegal, 364
Senior, Nassau, 10
Service sector, growth of, 124, 351–352
Shagari, Alhaji Shehu, 425, 430, 436
Sherman Anti-Trust Act (1890), 101, 174
Shunto, 186
Sinatra, Frank, 451
Sinatra Doctrine, 451–452
Singapore, 192, 349, 370–371, 408, 454,
    458, 459–460
Small Business Finance Corporation, 180,
    182, 184
Smith, Adam, 9, 10, 16, 17, 21, 23, 28n,
    50, 75, 78n
Social Darwinism, 8, 27, 36, 315
Social dualism, 355
Social goals, 77–80
Social regulation, 39–41, 102
Social Security Act (1937), 100
Social welfare, 7, 101–102, 142–147, 148,
    179, 181, 186, 325
Socialism
    and capitalism, 43–44, 49, 152
    vs. communism, 43, 63
    consumer sovereignty under, 79
    decentralized, 321
    history of, 44–47
    income distribution under, 14, 74,
        145–146, 152
    individual freedoms under, 76
    industrial concentration under, 91
    institutions of, 47–49, 140
    modern, 47
    non-Marxist form of, 44, 47
    utopian, 45–46
    See also Centrally planned economies;
        names of countries
Socialist Party. *See names of countries*
Socially necessary labor, 51, 56
Société Générale, 153n, 159
Sociocultural forces, and economic
    development, 347, 364–366
Soga shoshas, 177, 179
South Africa, 197
    freedom in, 67
    income, per capita, of, 421, 422
    manufacturing in, 428
    population of, 424
South Africa Chartered Company, 421
South Korea, 220
    economic development of, 192,
        370–371, 384, 408, 454, 459–460
    GDP of, 457, 458

imports by United States, 122
income, per capita, of, 349, 422
industry in, 198, 339, 397
trade by, 450, 457
Southeast Asia Development Corporation
    Fund, 184
Soviet Union. *See* Union of Soviet
    Socialist Republics
Spain, 107, 349, 369, 397, 456
Spengler, Oswald, 197–198
Stages theory of economic development,
    355–356
Stagflation, 211
Stalin, Joseph, 221, 244, 285, 286, 298,
    377, 447
Standards of living, comparisons of,
    229–232
State Enterprise Law, 275
Stock market crash of 1987, 107, 189
Strikes, 62, 95, 96, 186, 273, 286, 289,
    306, 307
Subsidies, 11, 20, 21, 36, 97
Sudan
    as a colony of England, 420
    economic growth of, 354
    education in, 79, 80
    famine in, 423, 425
    foreign debt of, 364
    health-related indicators for, 81
    income, per capita, of, 422, 464
    inflation in, 465
    labor force in, 351
    political instability of, 424, 425
    population of, 350, 424
    trade by, 426
    women, status of, in, 352
Sumitomo Bank, Ltd., 183
Sumitomo group, 176, 177, 178, 179
Supply, 5–7, 29, 252
    aggregate, 31, 204
Supply-side economics, 126, 204–205,
    212
Supreme Soviet, 246, 247, 250, 289
Surplus value, theory of, 51–52, 58
Sweden
    economic growth of, 210
    education in, 360
    government, role of, 144
    health-related indicators for, 360
    income, per capita, of, 349, 463
    income distribution in, 13, 145, 353
    labor in, 186
    population of, 350, 402

Sweden, *(cont.)*
    taxes in, 146, 157, 199
    as a welfare state, 450
Switzerland, 281, 463
Syria, 351

t

Taft-Hartley Act (1947), 96
Taiwan, 65, 122, 192, 339, 374, 397, 444,
    454, 457, 459–460
Takeoff theory of economic development,
    356–357
Takeovers, corporate, 93–94
Tanganyika, 420
Tanzania, 354, 364, 424, 426, 464
Tariffs, 11, 19, 70
Taxes
    incentives, 167, 169, 175
    in Keynesian theory, 34
    in less developed countries, 369
    as method of allocating resources, 137,
        144–145
    as method of distributing income,
        35–36, 81, 97, 98–99, 145, 158,
        212, 228
    and savings, 15, 72, 99
    types of
        agricultural, 258–259, 382
        corporate income, 154, 155, 167,
            180, 200, 205, 212, 382
        excise, 199, 200
        inheritance, 35, 158
        payroll, 100, 200, 212
        personal income, 155, 180, 199, 200,
            212, 258–259, 325, 369, 428
        progressive personal income, 35–36,
            154, 155, 158, 213
        property, 154
        sales, 145, 154, 156, 325, 369
        social insurance, 258
        turnover, 256–257, 260, 270, 284n,
            382
        value-added, 145, 154–155, 156, 167,
            200, 456
    See also names of countries
Technological dualism, 354–355
Technology
    change in, 24, 37, 70
    competition in, 93, 108, 116–118
    and industrial concentration, 89
    internationalization of, 446

    in Japan, 108, 109, 130, 173, 193, 195
    as requisite to economic development,
        346, 370
    state and, 444
    in the United Kingdom, 198
    in the United States, 116–118, 130
    in the U.S.S.R., 278, 291
Tekhpromfinplan, 267
Tennessee Valley Authority (TVA),
    103–104
Tennyson, Alfred, 197
Thailand, 350, 351, 454
Thatcher, Margaret, 136, 140, 197, 198,
    204–205
Third World, future of, 462, 464–466.
    See also Less developed countries
Thomson-Brandt, 153
Time preference, 15
Tito, Marshal, 322, 333
Tocqueville, Alexis de, 145
Tokai Bank, Ltd., 183
Tokyo Stock Exchange, 120, 189
Totalitarian system, 4, 291
Toyota, 179
Trade
    balance of, 16
    terms of, 363
    See also Foreign debt
Trade Union and Labor Relations Act
    (1974), 206
Trading Places (Prestowitz), 107
Transfer payments, 35, 36, 44, 81, 97,
    100–101, 136, 143, 148, 147, 211,
    228
Transportation, 17, 103, 240, 360, 361,
    367, 404, 454
Transportation Act, 142
Treatise on Political Economy (Say),
    29n
Trinidad, 349
True Grit, 19
Trump, Donald, 93
Trusts, 20, 27
Tunisia, 363, 422
Turkey, 349

u

Uganda, 354, 360, 424, 426, 465, 466
Ulbricht, Walter, 221, 222
Underemployment, 68, 401, 402
Unemployed, reserve army of, 52, 58

Unemployment, 24, 37, 67, 148, 201
  classical economic theory and, 28–29
  compensation, 143, 201, 318
  Keynes' view of, 29–30
  Marx' view of, 52, 58, 60
  rates of, 68, 123, 125, 139n
  See also Employment; *names of
    countries*
Union of Soviet Socialist Republics
    (U.S.S.R.)
  agriculture in, 123, 268–269, 277,
    278–279, 287, 447, 453
  alcoholism in, 274, 275, 281, 287, 288
  appraisal of the economy of, 65
  balance of payments, 280–281
  banking system in, 253, 261–266, 270
  bureaucracy in, 245, 255, 273, 274,
    286, 287
  and China, 375, 377, 387
  Communist Party in, 243–245, 248,
    255, 266n, 269, 282, 289–291,
    322, 445
  consumption in, 262, 295
  cooperatives, 276
  corruption in, 244, 273, 274, 287
  crime in, 287
  culture in, 288
  and Czechoslovakia, 220, 295, 444, 451
  development of, 243–244
  discrimination in, 147n
  and Eastern European countries, 220,
    226, 243, 290, 295, 296, 308, 445,
    448, 451–452
  economic growth in, 123, 205, 244,
    277, 445
  economic reforms in, 262, 267, 272,
    273–285, 286–287, 443
  economic system of, 248–267, 290
  education in, 80, 111, 260, 360
  elections in, 219, 248, 289
  enterprise in, 245, 253, 255, 263,
    266–267, 275, 278
  ethnic nationalism in, 243, 246,
    272–273, 277n, 288, 291
  GNP of, 123, 239, 283, 291, 447, 453
  government
    budget of, 256, 261, 262, 271
    organization of, 246–247
    role of, 11, 256–261, 270
  health-related indicators for, 81, 360
  income distribution of, 260, 282, 283,
    291

  industry in, 205, 274, 275, 278, 291
  inflation in, 123, 205, 242, 277, 283n,
    285
  joint ventures, 274–275, 450–451
  labor unions in, 94–97, 205–206, 286
  life expectancy in, 123
  marketing in, 283n
  military spending in, 242, 259, 261,
    283–284
  nomenklatura system in, 245–246, 266n,
    282, 289n
  planning in, 138, 248–255, 263–264,
    267, 269–270, 283
  and Poland, 296, 300, 307
  political system of, 243–248
  pollution in, 40n, 77, 281, 287
  population of, 66, 123, 243, 287
  price reforms, 276
  problems of, 242–243, 273
  religion in, 77, 288
  social consumption in, 254
  socialism in, 43
  standard of living, 248, 252, 261, 277,
    281–283
  taxes in, 256–257, 270, 284n
  technology, 278, 291
  trade by, 123, 279–281
  unemployment in, 68, 123, 205
  wages in, 255
  and the West, 283
  women, status of, in, 147n, 282n,
    287–288
  world GNP, percentage of, 66
  World War II, effect of, 114, 272n, 296
  and Yugoslavia, 263n, 322, 336, 340
Unions
  in France, 161–162
  labor, 20, 47, 94–97, 104
  Solidarity, 297, 299, 305–307, 315,
    318
  trade, 62, 160, 185
  in the United Kingdom, 206,
  in the United States, 94–97, 104–105
  in the U.S.S.R., 94–97, 286
  See also Labor
United Agricultural Bank, 327
United Kingdom (U.K.)
  African colonies of (England), 197, 356,
    420, 427
  appraisal of the economy of, 209–215
  banking system of, 99, 140, 158,
    202–204

United Kingdom (U.K), (*cont.*)
  economic growth of, 148, 168, 197,
    205, 209–211, 215
  education in, 80, 110–111
  GDP of, 119, 456
  GNP of, 114, 190, 199, 209, 239, 453
  government, role of, 140, 144, 153,
    200–201, 205
    nationalization of industry, 103, 199
    privatization of industry, 201,
      207–208, 215
  health-related indicators for, 81
  income, per capita, of, 349
  income distribution in, 13, 145,
    211–215, 353
  Industrial Revolution in, 17n, 198
  inflation in, 211, 212, 215
  labor-management relations in, 205–206
  as a mixed economic system, 136, 147,
    198
  monetary policy of, 204
  productivity, 119, 211
  public finance, 199–202
  public investment, 139
  socialism in, 150
  taxes in, 146, 157, 199–200, 205, 212
  technology in, 198
  unemployment in, 68, 125, 211, 212,
    215
  welfare state in, 112, 136, 143, 201
  World War II, effect of, 198, 209, 427n
United Nations, 347n
United States (U.S.), 65
  agriculture in, 123, 453
  banking system of, 99, 140, 459
  corporations in, 87, 88–94, 104
  crime in, 109, 112, 130
  as debtor, 120–121, 130, 195, 400, 461,
    464
  decline in industrial competitiveness of,
    108–114, 130
  Depression, effect of, 28, 101, 104
  discrimination in, 87, 147n
  drug abuse in, 109–110, 130
  economic growth of, 98, 123, 127, 168,
    210, 211, 467
  economy
    current state of, 107–126
    problems of, 108–122
  education in, 80, 110–111, 130, 360,
    470
  exports, 467

  foreign aid, 303, 317
  foreign investment in, 461
  freedoms in, 76
  Germany, compared with, 467, 469–470
  in a global economy, 123, 470
  GDP of, 119, 120, 456
  GNP of, 114, 123, 127, 239, 453, 467
  government
    budget, 99
    deficit of, 99, 115, 121–122, 128,
      130, 194, 195, 283n
    role of, 87, 97–104, 105, 144, 151,
      153, 161
    spending by, 98
  health-related indicators for, 81, 360
  and Hungary, 303, 317
  income, per capita, in, 349, 467
  income distribution in, 13, 129–130,
    145, 282n, 353
  illiteracy, 110–111
  industry in, 88–94, 125–126, 459
  inflation in, 69n, 123, 127, 130, 139n
  Japan
    aid to, 175
    compared with, 467, 469–470
    competition with, 39, 93, 107, 108,
      109, 117, 118, 130, 444, 470
  labor force in, 96, 104, 111–112, 124,
    130, 186, 351
  life expectancy in, 123
  management practices in, 113
  and Mexico, 412
  as a modified market economy, 87, 105
  monetary policy of, 99, 105
  nationalism in, 370
  natural resources of, 370
  new economic realities for, 460–462,
    470
  Poland, loans to, 303, 317
  population of, 65, 66, 123, 350, 402,
    467
  productivity in, 112, 114, 118–119
  public finance, 97–101
  public investment, 139
  religion in, 76
  saving and investment in, 115, 467
  social welfare programs in, 100, 105
  standard of living in, 115–116, 127,
    128–129
  taxes in, 97, 98–99, 146, 157, 212n
  technology in, 110, 116–119, 130
  trade by, 123, 426, 461, 467

unemployment in, 68, 123, 125, 127,
    130, 139n
unions in, 94–97, 104–105
women, status of, in, 352
world, GNP, percentage of, 65, 66
United States Steel, 126
Urbanization, and economic development,
    77n, 194, 358, 401, 411–412
URSUS, 91
Uruguay, 298, 299, 400, 401
USINOR, 153
Utilities, public, 97, 101–102
Utility analysis, theory of, 73n
Utopia (More), 45
Utopias, 45–46, 273

V

Value, 50n
Veblen, Thorsten, 15n
Venezuela, 349, 352, 363, 398, 399, 400,
    401, 402, 407, 408, 464, 465
Venice, 15
Versailles, Treaty of, 307
Veterans' Administration (VA), 105
Vietnam, 43
Vietnam War, 220, 283

W

Wage rate, as price of labor, 51
Wages, subsistence theory of, 51, 57–58
Walesa, Lech, 305–307
Wall Street Journal, The, 108, 123n
War theory of history, 60
Warsaw Pact, 220
Watt, James, 17
Wayne, John, 18, 171
Wealth, and income, 35
Wealth of Nations, The (Smith), 78n
Welfare state, 18, 35, 136, 143, 201, 211
West Germany
    agriculture in, 232–235, 303
    banking system of, 99, 451n
    East Germany, compared with, 226–236,
        447
    economic growth of, 168, 205, 211
    education in, 470
    GDP of, 456
    GNP of, 114, 190, 199, 209, 239, 453
    government, role of, 103, 144, 151, 153
    Hungary, loans to, 317

income, per capita, in, 349, 463
income distribution in, 13, 145, 227–229
industry in, 27, 90, 198
inflation in, 211
joint ventures, 317n
labor in, 124, 186, 235, 351
Poland, loans to, 317
pollution in, 78, 236
population of, 66, 350
reunification with East Germany,
    237–238, 240, 444
savings in, 124n
socialism in, 150
standard of living in, 116, 229–232
taxes in, 145, 146
trade by, 281
unemployment in, 125, 211
women, status of, in, 352
world GNP, percentage of, 66
World War II, effect of, 114, 152, 226,
    229
Westminster Bank, 203
Women
    in ancient Greece, 75n
    employment opportunities for, 39
    in less developed countries, 352–353
    in a utopia, 45
    See also names of countries
Work ethic
    decline of, 18, 112, 194
    Japanese, 112, 194, 195
    Protestant, 10, 21, 36
Workers' compensation, 68
Workers' councils, 323, 330, 332
World Bank, 368n, 429
Why Nations Triumph (Porter), 468–469
Wyszynski, Stefan Cardinal, 300

Y

Yalta Conference, 295, 299, 300
Yeltsin, Boris, 245n, 289
*Yen! Japan's New Financial Empire and Its
    Threat to America* (Burstein), 108
Yugoslav Bank for International Economic
    Cooperation, 327
Yugoslav Foreign Trade Bank, 327
Yugoslavia
    agriculture in, 327–329, 339–340
    appraisal of the economy of, 321, 323,
        333–340
    banking system of, 325–327, 337

Yugoslavia, (*cont.*)
  budget, government, in, 324–325
  Communist Party in, 291, 322, 332, 337, 340
  economic growth of, 334, 335, 338, 354
  economic problems of, 333–336, 340
  economic reforms in, 336–337
  enterprises in, 323, 329–333
  foreign debt of, 335, 336, 340–341
  GNP of, 338
  history of, 321–322
  income, per capita, of, 337–338, 349
  income distribution in, 333, 336–337
  inflation in, 333, 334–355
  labor in, 334, 338, 339, 351
  planning in, 321, 323–324, 329, 334
  prices in, 329, 330, 334–335, 336
  private enterprise in, 325n, 337
  productivity in, 339
  public finance, 324–325
  regional differences, 333, 335–336
  socialist economies, compared to, 321, 337–340
  taxes in, 325
  unemployment in, 325, 340
  and the U.S.S.R., 263n, 322, 336, 340
  wages in, 330, 332
  and the West, 322
  workers' councils in, 323, 330, 332

Z

Zaibatsu combines, 174, 187, 193
Zaire, 349, 354, 363, 364, 422, 424, 425, 464, 465
Zambia, 354, 363, 364, 422, 424, 426, 464, 465, 466
Zeiss firm, 229n
Zimbabwe, 356, 422
Zusammenbruch, 221